THE LOS
IS KNOWN A

"An adventurer cuts
—T

"One long tale of quest ↳
inevitable partings, meals relished and hotels endured, camel caravans
caught and buses missed–spun through with his
ecclectic gleanings from obscure works of archaeology,
history and explorers' diaries. Also woven throughout the books,
in a crazy-quilt jumble of innocent awe and hard bitten savvy,
are reflections on the people and places he encountered...
...There is a disarming casualness and a kind of festive,
footloose fancy to his tales that are utterly beguiling."
–The San Francisco Chronicle

"...a tonic...experiences in exotic places the rest of us think
only Indiana Jones visits...it will whet your appetite
and leave you chomping at the bit."
—The Missoulian

"...an offbeat travel guide that is fun to read even if you
don't have plans to duplicate author David Hatcher Childress'
remarkable journey. A thoughtful young man, Childress tells
a good story and his book is lively and interesting."
—The Washington Post

"Explore for lost treasure, stone monuments
forgotten in jungles...and hair-raising terrain
from the safety of your armchair."
—Bookwatch

"A fascinating series of books, written with humour,
insight, depth and an astonishing knowledge
of the ancient past."
—Richard Noone, author of 5/5/2000

Other books in the **Lost Cities Series**:

Lost Cities of China, Central Asia & India
Lost Cities & Ancient Mysteries of Africa & Arabia
Lost Cities of Ancient Lemuria & the Pacific
Lost Cities & Ancient Mysteries of South America
Lost Cities of Europe and the Mediterranean

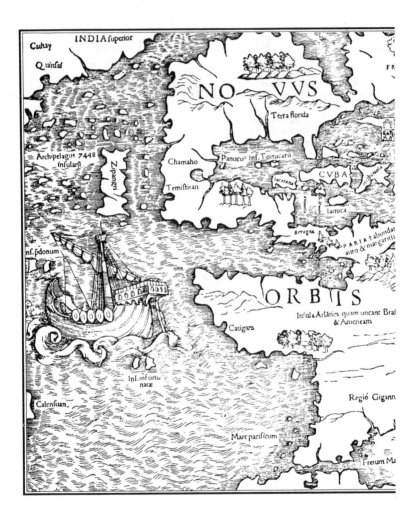

LOST CITIES OF
NORTH &
CENTRAL AMERICA

To John —
Keep searching for
lost cities
Dick
Childress
Phoenix
3/3/2013

ADVENTURES UNLIMITED PRESS
STELLE, ILLINOIS

I dedicate this book to the great American explorers and to the indigenous peoples of America and their wide ethnic backgrounds. The many races of mankind are indeed the "lost tribes."

Lost Cities of North & Central America
©Copyright 1992
David Hatcher Childress

Cover photograph by G. Irving.
© 1992 by G. Irving

Printed in the United States of America

This Printing May 1998

ISBN 0-932813-09-7

Published by
Adventures Unlimited Press
One Adventure Place
Kempton, ILLINOIS 60946 USA

The **Lost Cities Series:**
Lost Cities of China, Central Asia & India
Lost Cities & Ancient Mysteries of Africa & Arabia
Lost Cities of Ancient Lemuria & the Pacific
Lost Cities & Ancient Mysteries of South America
Lost Cities of North & Central America
Lost Cities of Atlantis, Ancient Europe and the Mediterranean

TABLE OF CONTENTS

THANKS to Mom, Dad, Linda, Richard, Carl, Frank, Carole Gerardo, Robert Stanley, Richard Dannelley, Dr. Oscar Padilla, Norman Baldwin, Terry Glavin, Richard Noone, Carolyn Jacobson, Tim Wilhelm, Dr. Gabriel Abreu, Bob Stone, Jim Brandon, Greg Deyermenjian, Albert Sindlinger, Trickster from Madison, Kingsley Craig, Mark Segal Photography, Therese O'Halloran & her Art Studio, George & Morrey at Blackman Ceramic Studios; and many more people too numerous to mention.

Acknowledgements: Many thanks to Barry Fell and the Epigraphic Society, John H. Tierney, Donald Cyr at Stonehenge Viewpoint, plus Dr. Scherz at the Wisconsin Mound Society, Joseph Mahan, and the many others who gave me information for this book.

Every mystery solved brings us to the threshold of a greater one.
—Rachel Carson

The Mystic Traveller Series:
•IN SECRET TIBET by Theodore Illion (1937)
•DARKNESS OVER TIBET by Theodore Illion (1938)
•TENTS IN MONGOLIA by Henning Haslund (1934)
•MEN AND GODS IN MONGOLIA by Henning Haslund (1935)
•MYSTERY CITIES by Thomas Gann (1925)
•IN QUEST OF LOST WORLDS by Byron de Prorok (1937)

The Lost Science Series:
•THE ANTI-GRAVITY HANDBOOK
•ANTI-GRAVITY & THE WORLD GRID
•ANTI-GRAVITY & THE UNIFIED FIELD
•VIMANA AIRCRAFT OF ANCIENT INDIA & ATLANTIS
•THE MANUAL OF FREE ENERGY DEVICES & SYSTEMS
•TAPPING THE ZERO POINT ENERGY
•THE BRIDGE TO INFINITY
•THE ENERGY GRID
•ETHER TECHNOLOGY
•THE DEATH OF ROCKETRY

The famous Mayan frieze from Tikal showing the destruction of Atlantis. Housed in the Berlin Museum until 1945, it was destroyed during the bombing of Germany.

Chapter 1

Costa Rica & Nicaragua:

Marbles of the Gods

Writing, like life itself, is a voyage of discovery.
—Henry Miller

There was a loud shooosh in my ears as I walked down the long hallway of the modern San José airport toward Immigration. I looked out the window to see the clear blue skies and a jet pulling out onto the runway for takeoff.

Standing in line at Immigration, a sudden realization came over me. It was a strange feeling: it was a feeling that everything I knew was wrong. Maybe not everything, but a lot of things. It was also a feeling of discovery, of adventure, of a quest for something missing and valuable!

Part of this feeling was that I was seeing the United States, Mexico, Canada, the Central American states quite differently than I had before. North America fascinated me as it had never before. It had everything that I was searching for: ancient cities and pyramids; vast complexes of tunnels and spectacular gold treasure beyond one's wildest imagination; sunken ruins; anachronistic and geographically impossible artifacts which defy rational explanation; and colorful legends that make the most outrageous science-fiction sound like docile children's stories.

I was no newcomer to adventure and danger. As a maverick archaeologist and writer I had been travelling the world for the last ten years: exploring for mysteries, hiking ancient trails and investigating the cities of antiquity.

I love to travel, and the more remote or inaccessible the place, the more I like it. I love people and I love knowledge. I had grown up around books and maps. I can remember my father getting out maps and pointing out places to me where I had been as a small child. Maps had always fascinated me, and as I kid I dreamed of exploring the Amazon or journeying to hidden monasteries in Tibet in search of arcane knowledge.

Sometimes it seemed as if my life were like a beer commercial: grabbing for all the gusto I could! Whether crossing a snowy pass in the Himalayas or Andes, hitchhiking through a remote desert in Africa, or trying to keep alive in a war-torn, third-world country, I continually wore my perpetual foolish grin of delight, eagerly lapping up the last few drops of excitement. That is not to say that I was not frightened from time to time, or miserable on many occasions—the beer commercials always end long before the going gets bad.

But, once back home comfortable, again at some friend's house, or restlessly working a job, I would look back at even the most uncomfortable times with a certain amount of yearning and wistful remembrance. Perhaps you know the feeling.

My quest for lost cities began at 19 when I left Montana to travel and study in the Far East. I lived and worked in India and the Middle East for a few years, then went on to Africa. There, I worked and traveled my way for two-and-a-half years around the continent before hitching my way on yachts back across the Indian Ocean. I lived, worked and studied on the Indian sub-continent for another year or two before going on to China, where by sheer luck I became one of the first shoestring travellers ever to vagabond around China.

When I returned to the United States at the age of 25, I had been gone for almost six years. I realized that I wanted to continue travelling, but I would have to earn a living doing it. So I began my somewhat questionable career as a writer.

I returned for some months to Egypt, Israel, Turkey and Europe and began a long sojourn in South America. For years, off and on, I began roaming the Andes, from Argentina to Ecuador and into the jungles of Peru and Brazil. Now after so many years of world travel my search for lost cities would all eventually lead me to North America—the land in which I had been raised.

Over the years I have developed a travelling pack, my trusty "bag of tricks"—which I felt was adequate for survival in most parts of the world. I list the contents here in case anyone wants to start trekking on his or her own:

1 down-filled sleeping bag (warm enough for chilly nights high in the Rockies, also good for the North American deserts, or anywhere in Canada. In Central American jungles, I either slept on top of the bag, beneath mosquito netting, or inside the sleeping bag with the side zipped all the way down.

1 wool sweater

1 nylon/cotton parka with hood (When worn with the wool sweater and a couple of shirts, this parka is sufficient to keep me warm on even the most freezing night.

1 ground sheet/poncho (This can be used underneath the sleeping bag for sleeping outside, or rigged into a makeshift tent.

The combination of this sheet with my sleeping bag and other gear enabled me to spend the night outdoors in almost any weather.)

1 backpack (Mine is an internal frame type with one large main compartment, which can also be used as a "bivouac sack.")

1 large plastic water bottle

1 bottle of water purification tablets

1 Swiss-Army knife (with can opener, scissors, and plenty of other gadgets. My knife has a key ring, which allows it to be attached to my belt with a length of nylon cord.)

2 pairs of long pants (one a pair of jeans for rough travelling, plus one pair of respectable-looking tan khakis for dining at a nice restaurant or getting a permit at a government office.)

1 leather belt with a secret zipper pocket (inside, folded American bills of various denominations can be stashed.)

1 nylon valuables packet (large enough for a passport, travellers cheques and documents, worn inside the clothes.)

2 cotton T-shirts

1 permanent-press shirt (for looking sharp when dealing with officials or border guards, or for going out in the evening.)

1 khaki safari shirt with many pockets

1 pair of walking shorts

2 pairs of shoes (one pair of comfortable sports shoes, another pair of leather walking shoes or hiking boots.

4 pairs of socks, some cotton, some wool

1 pair of rubber thongs, "flip-flops" (wearable in the shower or on the street.)

1 small first-aid kit and toiletries (Carry disinfectant, band-aids, aspirin, gauze, needle and thread, plus other medicaments).

1 flashlight, compass, and a length of nylon cord

5 boxes of matches and a butane lighter

2 candles

1 small deck of cards and a pocket chess set

5 or 6 assorted books (including a blank journal)

1 map of North America

1 camera with 10 rolls of color slide film

1 pair of sunglasses

A large assortment of souvenirs, knick knacks, postcards, snacks, etc. (It is important to carry food with you in certain areas, especially when you are on an unfamiliar road with an unknown distance to the next town.)

Travelling light is a key to real adventure travel. Be sure that you can fit everything compactly into your backpack. Make sure also that you can carry your backpack comfortably, as well. You may be walking down a road for quite some time before a truck or bus comes along, therefore never carry more than you can handle.

🐾🐾🐾

"Passport?" asked the uniformed man in the small booth.

I handed him my passport and greeted him in Spanish. He nodded, opened my passport, hardly even looking at my photograph, and than began flipping through the pages to find a blank page where he could press the entry stamp. This was not too easy because my passport was quite full, and the only pages that did not have four or five stamps on them already were toward the back.

I politely found a mostly blank page for him, and he gave it a firm punch with his ink stamp and handed it back to me. "Enjoy Costa Rica," he said.

I changed some money and shortly, with my pack over my shoulder, I was waved through customs and was out on the street. The usual gaggle of airport taxi drivers assaulted me, grabbing at my pack and herding me into one of the old Toyotas with a taxi sign on top.

I bargained weakly for the taxi ride, got some small discount which at least made me feel better—I didn't want to get ripped off on my very first transaction on the trip, and within seconds we were zooming off through the early evening streets to a hotel I had picked out from a guide book: the *Hotel Cacts* just of the Paseo Colón in downtown San José.

Leaning back in my seat, I let myself relax from the flight and thought about the mysteries that I was here to seek. According to many of the so-called experts, mankind came to North America via a land bridge across the Bering Sea into Alaska and Canada a few thousand years ago. Conservative "experts" place this crossing at about 12,000 B.C. Other more radical "experts" date it to about 28,000 B.C.[1] And yet, human bones found in California, Arizona, Alberta, and Ecuador have shown by carbon-dating techniques that man was present in the Western Hemisphere by about 30,000 years B.C.[2] A skull found at the Otavalo archeological site in Ecuador was radiocarbon dated at 30,000+ B.C.

In the early seventies, a new method of dating bones was developed at the San Diego Museum. Known as Aspartic Acid Racemization (AAR) dating, this technique tagged skeletal remains found in the Americas at 38,000+, 40,000+, 45,000+, 50,000+ B.C. Incredibly, one human bone found in Sunnyvale, California, was pinpointed at 70,000 years and possibly older! It was so old, no radio-carbon was left in the skeleton![2]

However, it was discovered in 1985 that these figures were erroneous, having been based on calibration skeletons which had been erroneously dated by radioactive methods. AAR dating requires an accurately dated reference skeleton, and once these had been recalibrated, the skeleton which had originally been dated at 38,000 B.C. was redated to 5,100 B.C. Dr. Jeffrey Bada, a leading proponent of AAR, announced the mistakes in *American Antiquity* magazine in 1985.

This does not necessarily destroy those theories that would place original occupation of the Americas before 30,000 B.C. Artifacts that cannot be carbon—or AAR-dated have been found in geological strata that date thousands of years earlier. Some artifacts, isolated at 70,000 B.C., have been found at El Bosque, Nicaragua; Old Crow, Yukon; Crown Point and Texas Street, San Diego; and Santa Barbara, California. A Mission Valley, California artifact was dated at 100,000 B.C., and artifacts found at a famous Flagstaff, Arizona dig have been dated at 100,000 to 170,000 years old. To raise eyebrows even higher, dates of 250,000 B.C. have been assigned to El Horno and Hueyatlaco, two sites in Mexico, while excavations at Calico Hills, California have been given dates of 500,000 B.C.![2]

Frankly, dating arrowheads and stone tools is quite tricky. One must guess the age by dating the geological strata where the tool is found. Given the possibility that our whole understanding of geological change could be totally erroneous, our current usage of geological dating may be far from accurate. If this is true, things are probably younger. However, radio carbon dating is still a fairly accurate method for tagging organic objects. Yet, when dating bones older than about 30,000 years old, radio-carbon dating becomes grossly inaccurate.

As Dr. Goodman points out in his book, *American Genesis*, dates for human bones and artifacts found in North and South America are generally twice the age of those found in Europe. For instance, the oldest human skulls in Europe carry dates of 35,000 years, compared with 70,000 years in America. However, Goodman is referring to AAR dates, now known to be inaccurate, ironically, because of inaccurate carbon dating. Artifacts such as projectile points and bone tools have been dated at 20,000 years in Europe, but 40,000 years, if not more, in the Americas.

Yet, these startling finds point to a conclusion that humans lived in South America long before crossing a Bering Straits land bridge during the last ice-age. There is little doubt that such a land bridge existed between Alaska and Siberia, but it may have been unnecessary. In the winter of 1985 a young American wandered across the frozen Bering Strait to the Soviet Union, where he was arrested, detained, then flown back to Alaska by helicopter. In fact, rather than ask if it were possible to cross the strait at all, maybe we should ask which way early man crossed it! To quote the archaeologist, C. W. Ceram: "Instead of assuming that the Indians came from the Old World, he (a European freethinker) could have decided that they represented the primitive human race from which he himself was descended."[3] Ceram, at least, felt it possible that the migration across the Bering Strait may have proceeded from the Americas to Asia.

But why do we limit our understanding of the past, by insisting that our ancestors crossed oceans only by means of land bridges? Vast oceans have not proven a serious barrier to people over the last several thousand years. The Polynesians and Micronesians navigated vast expanses of oceans in outrigger canoes, sailing more than three times the distance between Africa and South America. Malaysians in prehistoric times crossed the Indian Ocean and colonized Madagascar. If "stone-age" Polynesians and other cultures could sail vast oceanic distances thousands of years ago, then why could not more advanced cultures sailing larger ships in the Mediterranean have done the same thing at the same time?

Most people have heard speculation that the Vikings sailed their long ships to Greenland and Labrador about a thousand years ago. But can we take seriously more radical proposals of Irish monks sailing up and down North America, as well as Portuguese and Basque fishermen, Roman, Greek and Phoenician explorers, Hebrew gold miners, and Egyptian traders?

Impossible? Why? Is the Atlantic so impassable? Hardly. People have crossed the Atlantic in rowboats, kayaks, and simple rafts. The ancient sailors of the Mediterranean sailed ships far superior to those in which Columbus sailed across the Atlantic. In fact, on Columbus' second voyage to the New World, he wrote about finding the wreckage of a European ship on the Island of Guadalupe in the French West Indies.[4]

Many historians find the evidence of visitation to the Americas by ancient explorers and traders to be overwhelming. In 1976, a Brazilian diver named Jose Roberto Teixeira was spearfishing around a rock off Ilha de Gobernador in the Baia de Guananbara near Rio de Janeiro, when he found three intact Roman *amphorae* (clay vessels used to hold wine), in an area with several shipwrecks, some dating from the sixteenth century A.D. He reported that the area of his find is littered with pottery shards and large pieces of other amphorae.

The Brazilian Institute of Archaeology was extremely interested in these amphorae and sent photos to the Smithsonian Institute, which identified them as Roman. Later, Dr. Elizabeth Lyding Will of the Department of Classics at the University of Massachusetts, Amherst, identified the amphorae as Second to First Century B.C., "...apparently manufactured at Kouass, the ancient port of Zilis (Dchar Jedid) on the Atlantic coast of Morocco, southwest of Tangiers." Dr. Michel Ponsich, the archaeologist who had conducted excavations at Kouass, agrees with Dr. Will on the place of manufacture, and gives the amphorae a date of Second Century B.C.[4]

An American archaeologist who specializes in underwater digs, Robert Marx, investigating the site near Rio de Janeiro where the amphorae were found, located a wooden structure in the muddy bottom of the bay. Using sonar, Marx discovered that there were actually two wrecks at the site, one a sixteenth century ship, and another which was presumably a more ancient ship, the source of the amphorae.

But before Marx could dive to the site, trouble started. Brazilian authorities did not savor the idea of a Roman ship-wreck off their coast, and Spain and Portugal are still disputing who first discovered Brazil. Marx was even accused of being an Italian agent sent out to drum up publicity for Rome. Under pressure, the Brazilian authorities refused to grant permission for Marx to keep diving; and later permanently banned him from entering Brazil. Marx felt that the ship might have been blown off course in a storm. Wrecks thought to be Roman have been found off the Azores. Indeed, many modern sailing ships make the Atlantic crossings in only 18 days. In the last century alone, over 600 forced crossings of the Atlantic have occurred as ships and rafts were blown to the Americas by storms. But, I do not personally believe that the Roman sailors were accidentally blown across the Atlantic, only to while away their remaining years sun-bathing in Rio. More than likely, they were deliberately sailing to the New World.

Many other Roman artifacts have been found in Latin America. A large hoard of Roman jewelry was found in some graves near Mexico City by Dr. Garcia Payón of the University of Jalapa in 1961. Roman *fibula* (a clip used to hold together a Roman toga), as well as Roman coins have frequently been found. In fact, a ceramic jar containing several hundred Roman coins, bearing dates ranging from the reign of Augustus (31 B.C. to A.D.14) down to 350 A.D., was found on a beach in Venezuela. This cache is now in the Smithsonian Institution. Experts there have stated that the coins are not a misplaced collection belonging to an ancient numismatist, but probably a Roman sailor's ready cash, either concealed in the sand or washed ashore from a shipwreck.[4]

The Romans are not as often associated with world travel as another great ancient power: their deadly rivals, the Carthaginians. In the first century B.C., Greek geographer, Strabo wrote, "...far famed are the voyages of the Phoenicians (who were also known as Carthaginians, from their two main colonies, Phoenicia and Carthage), who, a short time after the Trojan War (circa 1200 B.C.), explored the regions beyond the Pillars of Hercules, founding cities there and in the central Libyan (African) seaboard. Once, while exploring the coast along the shore of Libya, they were driven by strong winds for a great distance out into the ocean. After being tossed for many days, they were carried ashore on an island of considerable size, situated at a great distance to the west of Libya."[4]

In 1872, near Paraiba, Brazil, a stone bearing a Phoenician inscription was discovered. It was thought to be a forgery for almost a century, when in 1968, Dr. Cyrus Gordon, Chairman of the Department of Mediterranean Studies at Brandeis University, announced that the inscription was genuine. Copies of the Paraiba inscription speak of a Phoenician ship circumnavigating Africa until it was blown to the shores of Brazil.[5,6] Indeed, the discoverer of Brazil, Portuguese explorer Pedro Alvares Cabral, was attempting to round Africa in A.D. 1500 when he was blown off course and landed in Brazil. It is believed that he named Brazil after after the legendary Irish Island of Hy-Brazil.

A Carthaginian shipwreck containing a cargo of amphorae was discovered in 1972 off the coast of Honduras, according to Dr. Elizabeth Will.[4] Some scholars believe that the Toltec Indians were in fact Carthaginians, who, after being defeated by Rome in the

15

Punic Wars, left the Mediterranean for West Africa. From there they migrated to the Yucatan Peninsula of Mexico, where they re-established their civilization. The Aztecs later destroyed them, and Carthaginian gold bars fell into the hands of the Aztecs, later surfacing in the United States as part of Montezuma's gold and the "Seven Gold Cities of Cibola."

The point is that crossing oceans is not very difficult—not now, not in ancient times. Not only could the Portuguese and Christopher Columbus have crossed the Atlantic in the Middle-Ages, but just about anyone in an earlier time with a seaworthy ship could have done so as well.

The subject of ancient voyagers to the Americas could easily take up an entire book, and has many times. Knowledge of ancient seafaring is important because there is a strong connection between these ancient voyagers and the lost cities of North Central America.

🐾🐾🐾

I dumped my luggage at the hotel. Like much of San José, it was modern, airy and friendly. I was on a strict budget, but this hotel wouldn't break my pocketbook for a night or two.

After stashing my passport and travellers cheques in a secret place in my backpack, I decided to go out and walk around the city for awhile. I was excited about the trip, and needed to burn off some energy. I walked down the brightly lit streets past restaurants and movie theaters, gazing at the various signs and advertisements. I ended up at the Key Largo, an old fashioned bar with nautical motifs, Tiffany lamps, a casino and live music.

A charming young woman, well dressed to show her shapely figure asked me if I would buy her a drink at one point. Suspecting that she worked for the establishment, and knowing that Costa Rica has quite liberal laws concerning ladies of the evening, I declined, and after finishing my drink, returned to my room.

I was up early the next morning, and after a leisurely breakfast, I took a walking tour of the city. The street was busy as I walked toward the Parque Central in downtown San José. A steady stream of traffic, horns beeping, ran down the wide Avenida 2, the capital's main street. Office buildings and billboards towered overhead and shopkeepers stood outside of their stores.

In the middle of this hustle and bustle, as San José is a thriving city, is the pleasant Parque Central, an oasis of calm and quietness in this modern city. Sadly, almost nothing of the old colonial San José exists today. Instead there was the familiar concrete and glass. Where were the lost cities and ancient mysteries I had come to see?

Lying between Panama in the south and Nicaragua in the north, Costa Rica is a small country that just slightly exceeds the size of New Hampshire and Vermont combined. Most of Costa Rica is a tableland, covered with jungle, and with some spectacular active

16

volcanoes strewn about the countryside.

Columbus on his fourth voyage stopped briefly along the Caribbean coast of Costa Rica in September of 1502. The Spaniards noted that the local natives wore golden discs and other jewelry. The early conquistadors believed that the interior of the area was rich in precious metals and so named the area the "Rich Coast" or Costa Rica.

However, it was found that Costa Rica wasn't so rich after all. No mines were found, and the Atlantic coast area was virtually uninhabitable because of the swamps. Eventually the Pacific coastal area and central valley were colonized, though it remained a remote backwater even after its independence from Spain in 1821.

🌺🌺🌺

Costa Rica is believed by many historians to have always been well off the beaten path of the main cultures of Central and South America. The Mayas, Toltecs and Aztecs of the area to the north must have had some contact, but not much. Similarly, some small trade with the Incas or Moche culture of Peru and Columbia acknowledged, though it would not have been much. Apparently, however, none of these great cultures ever succeeded in dominating the region. Who then were these ancient peoples at the very end of the narrow funnel of Central America? What great civilization had they created which still eluded modern archaeologists?

My next stop from the park was to visit the excellent Jade Museum at the Institute Nacional de Seguros. The name of the museum is misleading, because the collection is much more than jade, being a collection of gold, native clothing and weapons, as well as stone artifacts like *metates* (grinding stones).

Pausing for a moment at a glass case with several ancient jade pendants and necklaces, I reflected on how this jade alone was proof of continued contact between such important centers as Copán in Honduras and Quirigua in Guatemala. The mystery of jade distribution, and the source of the many objects that are found throughout Central America and Mexico is something that I wanted to pursue on my journey.

My next stop was San José's other archaeological museum, the *Museo Nacional,* which had a very complete selection of ceramics from each of the various cultural groups known to live in Costa Rica. There were five known cultural groups in Costa Rica when the Spanish arrived: Carib Indians who inhabited many of the off shore islands, hence the name of the sea, the Caribbean; Borucas Indians, related to tribes in Columbia; the Corobicis Indians who lived in the north, thought to be the oldest tribe in Costa Rica; the Chorotegas Indians of the Nicoya Peninsula; and a few Nahautl (Aztec) speaking tribes who had recently immigrated into the extreme southern region of the North American continent.

In all, at least 25,000 people probably inhabited Costa Rica at the

17

time of the conquest, though they spoke different languages and lived in relative isolation from each other, separated by volcanoes, rivers and jungle. At the time of the conquest, they were a primitive bunch, warring among themselves and practicing both human sacrifice and cannibalism.

❀❀❀

For a long period it was believed that Central America, with the exception of the Mayan city of Copán, had no ruins to speak of, nor lost cities. Says the French archaeologist Claude Baudez, "In general, with one or two exceptions, scholars tended until about 1950 to deny the existence in Central America of any historical dimension: their writings implicitly assumed that all the archaeological remains belonged to the tribes found in the area at the time of the Conquest.

"The pottery and sculpture of southern Nicaragua were labeled Nicarao or Chorotega, the corresponding material found in the Central Valley of Costa Rica was inevitably known as Huetar, and so on. This kind of assimilation is dangerous, for it implies that the cultures of these areas have remained unchanged since a remote period, or that the areas were first settled in relatively recent times.

"These two hypotheses, which seem unlikely enough on the face of it, have been finally put out of court by later work. In a short article published in 1927, S.K. Lothrop drew attention to the existence at Cerro Zapote (El Salvador) of two archaeological levels separated by a layer of volcanic ash; the upper level was rich in polychrome shards, while the lower level had none but yielded instead fragments of figurines showing striking affinity with the Pre-Classic figurines of the Valley of Mexico.

"The two kinds of pottery clearly belonged to different periods, and the site thus provided convincing evidence that El Salvador at least had an archaeological history. The tombs at Playa de los Muertos (Honduras), excavated by D. Popenoe in 1934, yielded pottery which was shown by Vaillant to have analogies with the Pre-Classic pottery of the Valley of Mexico: here again at least two different periods were represented on the same site."[78]

Here we see the debate between modern archaeologists—does Central America have a prehistory going back thousands of years? Even though it is recognized that man has been in both of the American continents for 30,000 years, and must have reached Costa Rica by at least that time, they argue whether this area ever had advanced civilizations in antiquity or contact with other cultures.

Fortunately, Costa Rica does give evidence of a great megalithic culture that once built great monuments in remote parts of the country. The forest floor of Costa Rica is littered with one the world's enduring ancient mysteries. When the Diquis Delta was being cleared for plantations by the United Fruit Company in the 1930s, the workers found their task hindered by hundreds of stones that

18

appeared to have been artificially smoothed and scattered over the jungle floor. The largest were about eight feet (2.5 meters) in diameter, and were nearly perfect spheres.

The American archaeologist Dr. Samuel Lothrop and his wife were brought in to explain the spheres. He suggested that the stones were probably roughly shaped as they were hewn from natural blocks and then polished with smaller stones, with wet sand as an abrasive medium. Their shape must have been frequently checked with accurate cut-out templates. The whole process must have required the patient labor of huge numbers of people over a long period.

The the stones, some weighing as much as 16 tons, had to be dragged (or rolled) from where they were quarried, possibly at the mouth of the Diquis River, to their final resting places, perhaps 30 miles (48 kilometers) distant. They were often placed in groups, or in straight or curved lines.

Some are to be found over human graves. But the purpose of this enormous effort is quite unknown. Some people speculate that these giant "marbles of the gods" stones represent the Sun and Moon (and other heavenly bodies as well); others think they are intended as a physical embodiment of perfection. The two ideas may not be distinct if the makers of the stones viewed the heavenly bodies as perfect, as some ancient Greek philosophers did.

There is no technique for determining the date at which the stones were shaped. Remains associated with some particular ball occasionally give clues, but on the whole these conflict. So we do not know who the makers of the strange spheres were, nor what the aim of the activity was.[81]

Just what the actual purpose of the stones may be is anyone's guess. What is curious to me is the absence of large ruins or lost cities in the area. Were the stones scattered about the Costa Rican jungle in some cataclysmic tidal wave during a pole shift?

Similar round stones may be found in such various and mysterious places as Easter Island, Peru and Mexico.

The round sphere on Easter Island is at the northern coastal area of the island, just north of the statue quarry at the volcanic crater of Rano Raraku. This single round stone is said to have been used by "Masters" on the island to focus their mental powers through as a sort of lens to levitate the statues and make them "walk" around the island in a clockwise vortex pattern.[59]

This would hardly seem like an adequate explanation for such a large group of spheres. Some have suggested a moving, gigantic map of the heavens. Sort of like a rolling astronomical chart.

☜☜☜

After several days of tourism and business, I left San José one morning, and took a bus north in my effort to get out of the city. I was headed for the Arenal Volcano, a huge, steep cone that is still active. At 1633 meters high, I could see it from quite a distance on packed with locals on their way home from business the capital.

I got off the bus at Fortuna and checked into the Central Hotel for a few dollars a night. I looked into hiking up the volcano, having climbed a number of active volcanoes in Africa, including Mount Kilimanjaro. However, it was just too dangerous. The Arenal Volcano not only looks like a typical volcano, steep and conical, but it acts like one too, spewing ash into the air and bubbling from various vents along the side. Several tourists have attempted to climb it in the past few years, some of the them have been killed as well, and the government generally discourages such attempts.

The glow of the active crater was the main evening attraction in town with the occasional blast of fireworks into the sky. The last spectacular eruption was in 1968, so the volcano is gathering steam for a future eruption.

From Fortuna I made an excursion to the east to the ancient city of Cutris. I hitchhiked along the highway, getting a ride in a delivery van driven by a young man in a gray uniform. We went up hill and down dale, past small houses with red tin roofs until he let me off at the small town of Venecia. The pre-Columbian ruins of Cutris can be found five kilometers to the north of the city. I got a lift up a road toward the ruins and then walked the two kilometers to the site.

There was not much there, some mounds overgrown by the jungle, and the remains of walls, streets and some small pyramids. It was unexcavated nor were there any visitor facilities. The place bespoke an advance culture however: the streets were wide and well-ordered, running at right angles and showing evidence that this was a planned city, perhaps the capital of an ancient empire. Now it was the silent ruins of a city lost to the jungle, forbidden to tell its secrets. No one seemed to care anymore, not even the Costa Rican government.

I left Fortuna the next morning, a huge plume of cloud and smoke coming off the summit of the volcano. I decided to head for Liberia, a town near the Nicaraguan border but the local bus wouldn't be coming by for several hours. I decided to hitchhike.

I said goodbye to the charming young gal who gazed glassy-eyed from the reception desk, fingering her long black hair with one hand. With my pack on my back I strode down main street for the few blocks to the end of town and then prepare to hitch a ride. I had hitchhiked for years across Africa, Asia and South America and knew what it was all about. Often you had to pay for lifts, especially in Africa, and in many places trucks were the only transport in an area devoid of buses or passenger cars.

After waiting for twenty minutes, a small red Japanese pick-up truck started coming down the road toward me. Using my best technique, I swept my whole arm down toward the road and in the direction that I wanted to go. I then motioned downward that wanted the vehicle to stop. I then waved at the approaching truck which was occupied by a middle-aged man and his wife.

I jumped up and down again, waving down the road. All this time I was smiling, and occasionally glancing at the active volcano above the road. Not surprisingly, the truck came to stop nearby me, and the driver asked me where I was going.

"Liberia," I said and he nodded to me. His wife, graying a bit on wavy black hair smiled and pointed toward the back of the pick-up. I grabbed my pack and threw it into the box. There were a few cartons of cooking oil and some sacks of corn meal against one side. I settled in near the cab as the truck lurched into gear and headed down into the dark green jungle.

"This is the life," I sighed as I leaned on my pack and looked up at the towering shape of the Arenal Volcano. I was on the road again and it felt good to be alive!

A few hours later they dropped me off in Liberia, a major city in the northwest section of the country and the capital of Guanacaste province. It is from Guanacaste that the marimba, a xylophone-type instrument used by the ancient natives of the area originated.

Guanacaste is largely Mestizo, or mixed Indian and Spanish. Chorotega Indians of this area had strong ties to the Toltec and Aztec kingdoms of Mexico. Guanacaste today is a sparsely populated area of cattle ranches and brown Costa Rican cowboys mounted on their horses with elaborately carved saddles.

After a quick chicken and rice lunch, I caught a bus up to La Cruz, only 20 kilometers from the Nicaraguan border and there after a bus on up to the border. Costa Rica and its mysteries were now behind me.

✿✿✿

Revolutionary posters still hung on the wall of the Immigration Office as I handed the tall, thin and handsome man my passport. He smiled at me in greeting and then glanced at my passport.

He looked at the photograph and then at my face. Satisfied that I was the person in the photo, he flipped through looking for the visa that I had gotten at the embassy in San José. He then took an entry stamp and gave my passport a good whack.

With that, I entered Nicaragua and was now standing on the street of the border town of Peñas Blancas. I hung on to a bit of strap as my pack lay at my feet.

"Auto-bus por Managua, señor?" asked a young kid with a burnished brown face and a grease stained shirt. He then pointed down the street to an old school bus that was loading cargo onto the rack fixed to the roof. This was the bus to Managua...

"Gracias, amigo," I said to the boy. He helped me grab my pack, his eyes full of wonder at this gringo with a backpack newly arrived to see his country. Nicaragua hadn't gotten many tourists of late, I surmised.

"Via con Dios," (Go with God) he called after me as I headed for the bus. With my pack secured on the top of the bus, several hours later I arrived in downtown Managua.

21

I was dropped off in the area of the bus station where I checked into the Royal Hotel. It was a nice, clean, family run place, and I could pay in the local currency, córdobas, rather than in U.S. dollars. Nicaragua is slightly larger than New York state and is the largest, though least densely populated of all Central American states. Nicaragua is mountainous in the west with a plateau sloping to the Caribbean coast. The two large lakes in the west, Lake Nicaragua (about 100 miles long) and Lake Managua (about 38 miles long) are the most important features of Nicaragua and as we shall see, were major civilization centers in ancient times.

Conquistadors first came to the country in 1522, though Columbus had landed in nearby Honduras on his last voyage in 1502. The chief of the country's leading Indian tribe at the time of Spanish exploration was named Nicaragua, and so the country got its name. Nicaragua, like neighboring Honduras and El Salvador declared itself independent from Spain in 1821 and was part of the Federation of Central American states until 1838. In that year the Federation broke up and the independent states of today were created.

It is a little known bit of Central American history (to Americans, at least) that Nicaragua was once ruled by an American adventurer named William Walker who took over the entire country with an army of only 56 men, repeating the incredible exploits of Cortez and Pizzaro before him.

William Walker (1824-1860) was born in Nashville, Tennessee, graduated from the University in 1838, studied medicine at Edinburgh and Heidelberg, was granted his M.D. in 1843, and then studied law. He apparently had a yearning to have his own country, and on October 5, 1853, he sailed with a force to conquer Mexican territory, declaring Lower California and Sonora an independent republic. This first incursion in taking over Latin American countries was a failure and he was driven out by Mexican forces.

Then in May of 1855, with 56 followers armed with a new type of repeating rifle, he sailed for Nicaragua, where a belligerent faction had invited him to come to its aid. In October he seized a steamer on Lake Nicaragua belonging to the Accessory Transit Company, an American corporation controlled by Cornelius Vanderbilt.

He was then able to surprise and capture Granada and make himself master of Nicaragua. Walker installed a puppet presidenté while he retained real control as Commander of the Forces. Two officials decided to use him to get control of the Accessory Transit Company so it was seized and handed over to his friends.

A new government was formed and in June 1856 Walker was elected President. On September 22, to gain support from the southern states in America he suspended the Nicaraguan laws against slavery. His government was formally recognized by the U.S. that year. A coalition of Central American states, backed by Cornelius Vanderbilt, fought against him, but he was able to hold his own until May of 1857, when he surrendered to the U.S. Navy to avoid capture.

In November 1857, he sailed from Mobile with another expedition, but soon after landing near Greytown, Nicaragua, he was arrested and returned to the U.S. In 1860 he sailed again from Mobile and landed in Honduras. There he was taken prisoner by Captain Salmon, of the British Navy, and handed over to the Honduran authorities, who tried and executed him on September 12, 1860. Walker was to author a book before his death entitled *The War in Nicaragua*, a fascinating document, no doubt.

🐟🐟🐟

That night I went out to dinner with a Canadian traveler, an art student from Toronto named Cary that I had met at the hotel. We walked along the shores of Lake Managua and then stopped by the Sorbeterías Restaurant for a beer.

"You known that the U.S. invaded this country once, don't you?" asked Cary sipping from his *Cuba libré* or rum and cola.

"Really?" I grunted. "It seems like I might have heard that, but I don't think we get that story told to us in much detail in our schools."

"Well," said Cary, taking another sip, "because of their desire for control of Atlantic-Pacific potential trade routes, the United States invaded Nicaragua in 1909 and U.S. Marines were kept in the country between 1912 and 1933. During this occupation period the Bryan-Chamorro Treaty of 1916 (terminated in 1970) gave the U.S. an option on a canal route through the country plus the use of several military bases. The Bryan-Chamorro Treaty was only terminated in 1970.

"A guerrilla leader, General César Augusto Sandino, began fighting the occupation force in 1927. He fought the U.S. troops successfully until their withdrawal in 1933. The U.S. meanwhile had trained General Anastasio Somoza García to head a National Guard. In 1934, Somoza assassinated Sandino and overthrew the Liberal President Juan Batista Sacassa, establishing a military dictatorship with himself as president.

"Somoza spurred economic development of the country while at the same time enriching his family through large estates in the country. On his assassination in 1956, Nicaragua was firmly controlled by the dynastic Somoza family and was succeeded by his son, Luis, who alternated with trusted family friends in the presidency until his death in 1967. Another son, Major General Anastasio Somoza Debayle, became president in 1967.

"It was May of 1979 that a civil war was launched by revolutionaries who called themselves Sandinistas, taking their name from the assassinated General Sandino. Only one year later the Sandinistas were in control of the country."

Cary took a drink and glanced at a waitress behind the bar. "During the entire 1980s," he continued, "the leftist government of Nicaragua was the target of economic embargoes and espionage from the United States. Only with the election of Señora Pedro Chamorro, widow of an assassinated newspaper editor, did the U.S. re-establish normal relations with Nicaragua. Cary leaned back in his chair and finished his drink. "You see, the U.S. has interfered with Nicaragua's politics and economy for more than a hundred years."

"That's an interesting story," I admitted. "It is sad when we Americans, who prize our own revolution against tyranny so much, are the ones most responsible for aiding the suppression of other revolutions for liberty and democratic government."

"Maybe the U.S. is earning some bad karma for its efforts. And what is it that you are doing here in Nicaragua?" he asked.

I took a last swig of my beer. "I'm here looking for lost cities," I said. "I'm just looking for something out of time."

❀❀❀

Near to Managua on Zapatera Island in the middle of Lake Nicaragua were once an astounding collection of ancient statues. These were a collection of ten to fifteen foot statues and rock-cut temples that are largely ignored by modern day Mesoamerican scholars.

Most of the gigantic statues from Zapatera Island are now at a museum in Juigalpa, a town situated on the Atlantic Highway along the east side of Lake Nicaragua. Zapatera Island being in the lake opposite the city.

Zapatera Island is toward the northwest shore of the large lake, close to the mountain range that separates the lake from the Pacific Ocean, only 30 kilometers away. The gigantic statues and other colossal heads were found on the north edge of the island at a spot called Punta de las Figuras. To the east is Punta del Zapote.

The Swedish explorer Carl Bovallius visited the massive ruins in 1882-83, though most had been destroyed in earthquakes, and portions were now underwater in the lake.[121] This is a highly active earthquake zone and many huge earthquakes must have occurred over the past three or four thousand years.

Underwater ruins are believed to be near small islands to the west of Zapatera Island such as Punta Arenosa, Pedrarias, Guanacaste and Estero de La Cruz. This area is generally known as the Charco Muerte, or so shown on Bovallius' map.[121]

Zapatera Island seems to have been a major governmental and probably religious center for the trade across Nicaragua. Gold, jade, furs, exotic feathers, exotic herbs and hallucinogenic mushrooms, plus other metals and precious stones such as obsidian were moved from coast to coast and further south to Columbia or north to Guatemala. A wealthy society may have developed where Egyptian merchants, Phoenician traders, Hindus and Chinese met. Nicaragua, like all of Central America was a meeting ground of east meets west, and it developed its own special culture, traditions and art styles.

The evidence suggests that a great deal more ruins should be found in Nicaragua. Lt. Lawrence Frego, a satellite photo expert for the World Explorers Club, has been searching recent satellite scans for traces of the ancient civilization that once covered all of Nicaragua. He has discovered that Nicaragua was once apparently the ancient Panama canal route which used the natural river and lake system to trade from the Atlantic coast to the Pacific.

In as much as Central America was the easiest way for the Atlantic to connect the Pacific, it would make sense to think of Nicaragua and its river systems as a major crossroads of the ancient world. Ancient Phoenicians, Egyptians, Jews, Romans and Celtic sailors could well have sailed up the Rio San Juan to Lake Nicaragua and from there taken the short trail over the mountains down to ports on the Pacific coast.

Nicaragua was long thought of as an alternative to Panama as a site for a canal linking the Caribbean and the Pacific oceans. In 1850 the United States sent the well known American historian E.G. Squire to survey Nicaragua for potential locations of a canal. He proposed no less than five different spots for canals to be built over the narrow western mountains that would link the lakes of Nicaragua with the Pacific.

Zapatera Island was obviously an important ancient center, and the major megalithic finds have been in this area. Curiously, the statues at Zapatera appear to be in a Sumerian style!

As part of the Atlantean League, Indus Valley and Sumerian sailors could have sailed reed boats through the Maldive equatorial channel and then out through Indonesia into the Pacific. Bali and many archaeological ruins on Java are all that remain of the great Dravidian, Indus, Sumerian League of sailors, sailing reed ships around the world and even mapping Antarctica! (For more information on transpacific travel see my book *Lost Cities of Ancient Lemuria & the Pacific* [59])

The main Caribbean port was San Juan de Nicaragua on the mouth of the Rio San Juan. The rivers original name is now lost, but a significant clue is that the next river north is called the Indian River and the natives who formerly inhabited this area, including the Bay of San Juan, were the *Rama Indians.* On Squire's 1851 Map of Nicaragua, the Rama Indian territory is marked as being just north of the river. Other smaller tribes in the vicinity are named the Melchora Indians and the Woolwa Indians.

Was it then the Rama River that originally drained Lake Nicaragua? Again we have links to the ancient Rama Empire of India and Persian Gulf, a time described in the great Indian Epics of the Ramayana and the Mahabharata. Scholars agree that these amazing stories of heroic adventure and far flung conflict between several nations were written at least 3000 years ago and are speaking of a time which the epics state is many thousands of years before that.

❦❦❦

The distribution of certain plants on both sides of Pacific is an interesting way to search for evidence of ancient explorers. The anthropologist George Carter gives a good account of how difficult it is to battle the traditional academics and their dogma as well as fascinating information on the distribution of plants in his article *Megalithic Man In America:* [113]

"Because of my long interest in transoceanic influences in America , I was recently asked to visit Vermont to look at some of the interesting stone structures there. This followed on my visiting Mystery Hill where I met for the first time Barry Fell, who has been upsetting the scholarly world by interpreting inscriptions in America as Libyan records, and others as Ogam from Spain, and others as Arabic, and so forth. I take a modicum of pride in having started Barry Fell on his meteoric career in American epigraphy.

"For years, I had carried around a small collection of obviously alphabetical inscriptions that I had found in the literature. No one would pay the slightest attention to them until I sent some of them to Barry Fell. He found some of them obvious and easy to read; the most exciting set being records of the arrival of a Libyan fleet that was sailing for Egypt and that had crossed the Pacific to reach the west coast of South America. The navigator of this fleet was Maui, the name of the legendary progenitor of the rulers of Polynesia.

"I was surprised to find Libyans from North Africa in the Pacific, but not surprised at all at the evidence for successful crossings of the Pacific. For decades, I had been trying to get scholars to take seriously the evidence from plants and animals that said in absolute terms that men had crossed the Pacific carrying useful plants and animals both ways. A bit of humility can be entered here. I was properly raised in anthropology and knew with great certainty that no one crossed the great oceans to pollute the American Indian cultural growths and developments. This is the anthropological Monroe Doctrine. Zeros, arches, calendars, agriculture, metallurgy, weaving, pottery—the American Indians invented them all, all on their own. To say otherwise is to expose yourself to the formidable charge of being a racist. 'What do you mean the Indians didn't invent all those things? What do you think they are? Some kind of inferior men?' The first time that this was thrown at me, I recoiled in horror. What kind of idiots must I contend with? I have argued for years, humorously, that the British were exceedingly stupid people. Everything they had was borrowed; mostly from learned Mediterraneans, especially the little swarthy ones at the eastern end. This is the reverse of the doctrine of the superiority of the Big Blonde race thesis. Both are nonsense, of course.

"Any rational survey of mankind will show that all peoples everywhere were great learners, and the more access to ideas and the greater willingness to borrow ideas, the better people have done in the climb towards civilization. This is absolutely not bound to race and if the American Indians borrowed ideas they were just being normal humans. If they did it all by themselves, in a short space of time, then they were super humans. I think that they are just good old normal Homo Sapiens.

"My disillusionment with the Anthropologists' Monroe Doctrine began with my work in plant geography. I had used the kinds of corn, beans and squash that the people in our Southwest possessed as evidence of their origins. Plants are useful tracers for amongst other things, they are relatively fixed in their natures, not like art styles for instance, that are relatively changeable. When claims were made that plants had been carried across the Pacific, I was incredulous; but I decided to look. The first checks were negative, but then I found the sweet potato. It is American botanically, but it was outside American before 1500 A.D.—widespread in the Pacific. Even more startling, its name was the same on the north Pacific coast of South America as in Polynesia: kumar. Worse, in the 1890s, it has been noted that this is a Sanskrit word. Now sweet potatoes are reproduced vegetatively–from vines or tubers. They don't fly with the winds, nor can they float in salt water. If they crossed the Pacific, man surely carried them. But if one plant, wouldn't there be more evidence? In fact, the sweet potato is quite a mouthful all by itself.

"Anyone coming to America would have to have been here long enough to get to like sweet potatoes. They would then have to learn to grow them, harvest them, store them (a tricky business), cook them, and carry the name along too. The name suggests that people with a Sanskrit background reached America, put their name on this American plant in one area of America, and sent examples of the plant westward into the Pacific.

"We have an interesting parallel. This is corn, Zea maize. To an Englishman, corn means any or all small grains. In America, faced with a new grain they put their name on the new plant. But this only occurred in British North America where the impact of colonization removed the native population. In Latin America, native names were used, most often a name picked up in the Caribbean: mahiz, or maize. Does the word kumara on the northwest coast of South America point to a colonization by Sanskrit speakers there? I simply don't know, but I don't consider it at all impossible. Few parts of the Americas have more complex and persistent folklore dealing with the arrival on their shores of strange people from overseas than does that part of America. Maybe we should be looking.

"If people carried the sweet potato out of America, what if anything did they bring to America? Well, coconuts for one thing. While the coconut can float, and probably sprout on beaches, though there is some argument about that, virtually no one argues that coconuts can float across the large spaces in the Pacific. Elaborate computer simulations of drift show that man had to carry coconuts to America. They were on the southwest coast of Mexico

27

when the Spanish arrived there. So, what else?

"Peanuts of a type known archaeologically but not modernly on the coast of Peru are grown modernly in China where they are known archaeologically as early as Lungshanoid times—perhaps as early as 2000 B.C. Corn also appears in southeast Asia under peculiar circumstances. The Chinese were growing it in quantity in the southwest corner of their country within 50 years of the discovery of America. The hill tribes of Assam state that they had corn long before they had rice, and it is corn that they use in their ceremonies and not rice. Vishnu-Mittre in India has found corn pollen in levels that he considers to date a few centuries before 1500 A. D. Stephen Jett has published a frieze in India showing the figure of a woman with an ear of corn. From the shape of the ear (remember, I did a PhD thesis on corn, beans and squash) I would say that corn came either from the Valley of Mexico (Mexican pyramidal) or is some form of Cuzco flour, from Peru. The time is 1200 A.D.

"The list tends to grow. For some years, I have pursued *Hibiscus rosasinensis.* This is the showy flower that every Polynesian girl wears behind her ear. As the name says, the botanists considered it to be an ancient endemic of China. As a Dutch ornithologist noted however, it is not suited for pollinization by anything but a humming bird. Careful now: humming birds are strictly American. The Chinese accounts state that they got the flower from the little black folk of Namviet (northern Vietnam and southern China). They, the little black folk , stated that they got it from the great land below the eastern horizon. The only great land below the eastern horizon (out in the ocean) from Namviet is America, the home of this kind of hibiscus and its companion the hummingbird. The Chinese had already exported the flower to Persia before the time of Christ.

"Perhaps the most interesting item in this list is the chicken whose homeland is southeast Asia. Chickens have races as striking as those of mankind. Any chicken fancier can look at a collection of chickens and say: That is a Malay. That is a Chinese chicken. That is a Mediterranean chicken, etc. It is easy. Only Mediterranean chickens lay eggs with white shells. They are also small, nervous, flighty, tight feathered, high combed, etc. Chinese chickens are the opposite on all counts. Malays include giant chickens with few feathers, necks especially as naked as a turkey buzzard. Oddly the chickens in the hands of the American Indians are still clearly Asiatic in origin. Worse, many Indians will not eat chickens or chicken eggs today. 'So, why keep chickens.' I asked when travelling in Mexico. 'Oh, señor, you have to have chickens for divination, for prayers, and sacrifices.' Now that is not something that you would learn from a 16th century Spaniard. They eyed chickens hungrily. A survey of the uses of chickens in Asia shows that the ceremonial usages are all there.

"So, a whole trait list: the animal, the attitudes toward it, and the specific ceremonies were transferred. Whoever did it could travel the oceans so readily that he could carry small live stock with him: feed and water beyond human needs. The Pacific list could be lengthened, but the point should be clear. There was a fairly extensive exchange going on in plants and animals. No one can invent a plant or a chicken, so the argument of independent invention is totally wiped out. Simultaneously, one can not start admitting the exchange of plants and animals, complete with attached names and ceremonial complexes, and deny the probability that more things were carried: calendars, architecture, art styles, and hosts of other kinds of evidence that people like Gordon Ekholm and Robert von Heine Gelern, and others have been pointing to for years."

❦❦❦

History in Nicaragua may go back much further than even Sumerian times if current geological dating is correct. An article written for the *American Antiquarian* in 1889 (Vol.11, pages 306-311) by Earl Flint a geologist working for the Peabody Museum and Harvard University stated that he had found fossilized human tracks in a rock quarry near Managua on the shores of Lake Gilva. The human footprints were in a layer of rock 16 to 24 feet below the surface. Said Flint in the *American Antiquarian* article, "The footprints are from one-half to three inches in depth... (and) none exceeded 18 inches. Some of the impressions are nearly closed, the soft surface falling back into the impression, and a crevice about two inches in width is all one sees, and my first glance at some parallel to one less deep, gave me an idea that the owner of the latter was using a stave to assist him in walking. In some the substance flowed outward, leaving a ridge around it—seen in one secured for the museum; the stride is variable, owing to the size of person, and the changing nature of surface passed over. the longest one uncovered was seventeen inches, length of foot ten inches, and width four inches, feet arched, steps in a right line, measured from center of heel to center of great toe over three steps. The people making them were going both ways in a direction consonant to that of the present lake shore east and west, more or less."

Among these, and other nearby sites, Flint found examples of both barefoot, and sandaled-foot impressions. All were dated geologically as being over 200,000 years of age!

Lake Nicaragua, just south of Lake Managua is the home of the world's only freshwater sharks. It is assumed that at some time in the distant past (200,000 years ago?) Lake Nicaragua was connected with the Pacific Ocean and sharks freely swam from the ocean into what was then a bay. An immense earthquake then sealed the lake off from the Pacific and the sharks were trapped inside the now isolated lake. Over thousands of years the saline water changed to fresh and the sharks adapted to the change.

Could the cataclysmic forces that created the fossilized human

29

footprints have been the same destructive force that cut off Lake Nicaragua? It is worth noting here that all fossils are created by some sort of cataclysm, whether it be an earthquake, a volcanic eruption or a tidal wave (or possibly a combination of all three, as in a pole-shift scenario). Animals do not normally die and become fossils. Rather, under normal conditions, an animal will simply decay and disappear.

For instance, during the 1800s literally thousands, even hundreds of thousands of bison were slaughtered on the great plains of the United States and left to rot after their tongues had been cut out. Not one of them became a fossil! The creation of a fossil or of fossil footprints requires that the article be suddenly preserved moments after its creation. In the case of a fossil footprint, after the footprint is made, volcanic ash or something similar must cover the footprint and preserve it. Other strange, out-of-place fossils and articles play a large part in the mysteries of North America, as we shall see later in this book.

The Managua area is undoubtedly one of geological change. The city was completely destroyed in an earthquake in March of 1931, and then totally rebuilt. Then in December of 1972 it was destroyed again in another earthquake. With two major earthquakes in 41 years, one can only wonder at the occasional devastation that has shaken the area over the past ten or twenty thousand years, not to mention two-hundred thousand.

I took a bus one day down to the lake shore at the end of the South Highway to the site of the strange footprints. The spot is near the center of town and is called the Huellas de Acahualinca. I bought a ticket for the small museum exhibiting a variety of prehistoric artifacts, including the human footprints alleged to be 200,000 years old. There were animal footprints there as well, all nicely preserved in volcanic tufa. At least Flint hadn't made up the story about the footprints. They definitely exist and according to my guide book were the "only site of archaeological interest" in all of Nicaragua!

I left the next day for Tegucigalpa in Honduras by express bus. It was was only 214 kilometers from Managua to Tegucigalpa, and the road, the Pan American Highway, passed along the scenic southern shores of Lake Managua, the active volcano of Momotombo smoking in the distance. Gazing out the window of the bus, I couldn't help but think that there was a lot more to Nicaragua than the history books tell us. But then, since it was a history of which there was no record, what was there to say?

MAP
of
NICARAGUA
and
COSTA RICA
to illustrate the journey
of
CARL BOVALLIUS
1882 – 1883.

An 1883 map of Nicaragua &
Costa Rica by the Swedish
Explorer Car Bovallius. Note
the Rama River in center of
the map, the territory of the
Rama Indians. Rama was the
great Hindu hero of the
Ramayana, an epic story of
3000 B.C.

Dr. & Mrs. Samuel Lothrop with one of the huge stone spheres they found in the jungles of Costa Rica in the 1940s. Many of the stones were as much as 8 feet (2.4 meters) in diameter.

This stone ball with a 7 foot diameter stands outside a commercial building in San José as an ancient monument.

Top left: A jade birdman figure from Guanacaste, Costa Rica. The man with wings and an elongated head is an "Olmec" or "Proto-Mayan." Right: A plumbate ceramic vessel from El Salvador. Note the hook-nose and full beard. Below left: Cave paintings from the Oxtotitlán Cave, Mexico. The dragon is highly realistic and modern looking. The man is an "Olmec," wearing a mask. No date has been given to any of these objects, but circa 1000 B.C. may be correct.

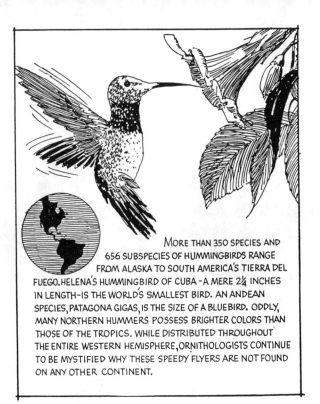

MORE THAN 350 SPECIES AND 656 SUBSPECIES OF HUMMINGBIRDS RANGE FROM ALASKA TO SOUTH AMERICA'S TIERRA DEL FUEGO. HELENA'S HUMMINGBIRD OF CUBA - A MERE 2¼ INCHES IN LENGTH - IS THE WORLD'S SMALLEST BIRD. AN ANDEAN SPECIES, PATAGONA GIGAS, IS THE SIZE OF A BLUEBIRD. ODDLY, MANY NORTHERN HUMMERS POSSESS BRIGHTER COLORS THAN THOSE OF THE TROPICS. WHILE DISTRIBUTED THROUGHOUT THE ENTIRE WESTERN HEMISPHERE, ORNITHOLOGISTS CONTINUE TO BE MYSTIFIED WHY THESE SPEEDY FLYERS ARE NOT FOUND ON ANY OTHER CONTINENT.

THE ONLY KNOWN FRESH WATER SHARKS ARE FOUND IN LAKE NICARAGUA, IN CENTRAL AMERICA'S REPUBLIC OF NICARAGUA. THIS INLAND BODY OF WATER, 110 FEET ABOVE SEA LEVEL AND COVERING 3,089 SQUARE MILES, IS THE LARGEST BETWEEN THE GREAT LAKES AND PERU. THE SHARKS EXCEED 10 FEET IN LENGTH AND ARE RATED AMONG THE MOST FEROCIOUS. GREAT EARTH-QUAKES PROBABLY ELEVATED AND CUT OFF THE LAKE FROM THE PACIFIC. IT HAS NEVER BEEN DETERMINED HOW LONG THE SHARKS HAVE BEEN THERE.

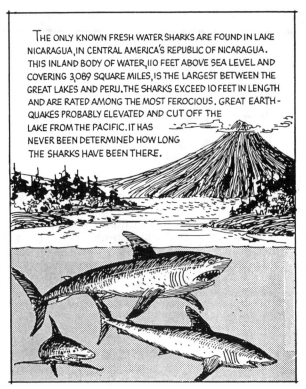

Gigantic rock-hewn statues from Zapatera Island.

One of the gigantic statues from Zapatera Island, Nicaragua.
This man is kneeling beneath a gigantic eagle's head.

One of the gigantic statues from Zapatera Island, Nicaragua. Note the long, Middle-Eastern-style beard and the dot in the middle of the forehead. Hindus and Buddhists use a dot in the forehead like this today to symbolize the pineal gland, or chakra.

Basalt statues from Nicaragua, both about 15 feet high. Date unknown. The statue on the left seems similar to the huge statues at St. Augustine in Colombia. The one on the right holds a sword and seems rather Celtic in style. From the Juigalpa Museum, Chontales, Nicaragua.

Basalt columns from Zapatera Island, Lake Managua. The man on the left wears a bird mask, looking similar to the Egyptian god Horus. 2.25 meters high. The man on the right holds a round sheild and is wearing a dinosaur (?) mask. 1.75 meters high.

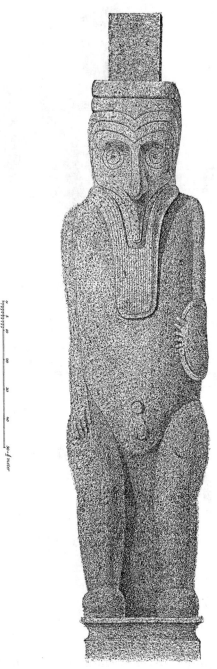

One of the gigantic statues from Zapatera Island, Nicaragua. Note the long, Middle-Eastern-style beard. He seems to be holding a round shield in one hand. 2.5 meters tall.

Chapter 2

Honduras:

Chinese Taoists & the International Jade Trade

The *Uinal* [twenty-day cycle] was created,
the earth was created;
sky, earth, trees and rocks were set in order;
all things were created by our Lord, God the Father.
Thus he was there in his divinity,
in the clouds, alone and by his own effort,
when he created the entire world,
when he moved in the heavens in his divinity.
Thus he ruled in his great power.
Every day is set in order according to the count,
beginning in the east,
as it is arranged...
— *Chilam Balam of Chumayel*

Honduras was a country that I had never thought about very much. Now, with a fresh stamp in my passport and a handful of Lempiras, the local currency, I was heading up into the mountains to the capital.

The coast of Honduras was first sited by Columbus on his last voyage in 1502. Honduras, with four other countries in Central America had declared its independence from Spain in 1821 and was part of the federation of Central American states until 1838. In that year it seceded from the federation and became a completely independent country.

Typical of U.S. intervention in the region, U.S. Marines intervened in 1903 and 1923. In 1931, 1932, and 1937, major revolutions were crushed by force.

In July of 1969 El Salvador invaded Honduras after Honduran landowners had deported thousands of El Salvadorans. The fighting left 1,000 dead and tens of thousands homeless. By threatening economic sanctions and military intervention, the Organization of American States induced El Salvador to withdraw.

In 1971, Ramon Ernesto Cruz, a lawyer, diplomat, and teacher, became Honduras's first freely elected president since 1949, but was soon ousted by the military citing "chaos and weakness." Various forms of the military have been in control of Honduras since.

I was still gazing at the steep hills of Tegucigalpa when the bus pulled into the central bus station. With my pack over my shoulder, I grabbed a taxi and paid a dollar to be driven to the Hotel Excelsior, a hotel that had been recommended to me by a Peace Corp volunteer I had met in Managua.

Tossing my pack in the corner, I unzipped it, flipped a few items onto my bed, hid my passport and travelers cheques, and decided to hit the town.

Tegucigalpa is a city of 800,000 inhabitants and stands on the slopes of the *Montañas de Comayagua*. It was founded as a mining camp in 1578, the miners having found silver and some gold and the name, Tegucigalpa, means "silver hill" in the native Nahuatl tongue of Honduras. On three sides it is surrounded by sharp, high peaks. Being off the main earthquake fault line, Tegucigalpa has never been destroyed by earthquakes.

I stopped in at a restaurant for some fried chicken and a *Port Royal* "Export" beer, which tasted especially good after the bus ride. The next day I walked around the city. It had a pleasant, colonial atmosphere, with tiled roofs, narrow winding streets and an old world atmosphere. It didn't take me long to figure out that Tegucigalpa was a small city, easily seen in a day, and after stopping in at the Parque La Concordia which contained small size replicas of Altar Q and Stela C from the fabulous Mayan city of Copan, I was taken by the desire to get north, and begin seeing some of the Mayan sites.

I took a bus out of Tegucigalpa, passing Comayagua, once the capital of Honduras, and then on to Lake Yojoa, a famous tourist spot in central Honduras. Indeed, the jungle covered mountain of Mount Maroncho was quite beautiful. Pumas, bears and jaguars roam the slopes. The whole mountain has an ecosystem all of its own, though it is dangerous to try and ascend the mountain without a guide and a machete, as the the dense jungle has virtually no trails, and the forest floor can be a meter thick with moss, branches and leaves.

I checked into the Hotel Maranta in Peña Blanca, a small town on the west side of the lake. It was basic and clean, and I paid about three dollars for a single room with a table, chair, lamp and bed. The bathroom was outside in a courtyard.

Eleven kilometers north of Peña Blanca is the Pulhapanzak Falls, a popular swimming spot for tourists. There are several lost cities in the vicinity—Mayan ruins that are so overgrown with jungle that it is difficult to spot them through the jungle. Often, in the jungles of Central America, a small hill covered with forest growth is in fact an ancient pyramid! Farmers around the lake have discovered numerous Mayan artifacts, though little official archaeological work has taken place here.

The next day I was off by bus to San Pedro Sula, the second largest city in Honduras. As the bus ground along the paved, but narrow highway, I noticed that my guide book said that to the north lay the ruins of the once impregnable mountain-top fortress of Lempira at Cerquin. Lempira was the native chief who had led the great Indian revolt of 1537-38 against the Spanish. The conquistador Montejo, thrice governor of Honduras finally put down the revolt by luring Lempira out of his fortress under the guise of a truce. He was then ambushed and killed. Today, the Honduran currency is named after him and features the likeness of Lempira.

✪✪✪

I arrived in San Pedro Sula late in the afternoon and checked into the Hotel Brisas del Occidental, a cheap hotel with rather spartan rooms, though at least it seemed fairly modern, toilets that flushed and a ceiling fan that worked.

Quickly I headed the four blocks down to the main square to change money. Money changers found me quickly, wavy blond hair, jeans and gold-frame glasses and screamed "turista" a block away. I fought several moneychangers off, and then changed with an older lady in a Disney World t-shirt and a pocket calculator in her hand.

Once I had changed money, the other hustlers departed, and I was left counting the Lempiras while a heard of homeless street urchins began to move in my direction. One young boy without shoes began to dance to Boy George and the song *Karma Chameleon* being played through loudspeakers into the square.

I laughed and gave him some change, hoping he would spend it on something more nutritious than a donut at the nearby Duncan Donut shop.

I walked around the square for a bit and then, as the sun was setting over the buildings in the west, I popped into a local restaurant for dinner. In an adventurous mood, I decided to throw all caution to the wind and ordered a horse steak, something I had never had in all my travels around the world.

While sipping a *Salva Vida* beer and chewing slowly on the horse, I couldn't help notice the young and beautiful lady sitting at the table to my left. I watched her casually. She seemed to be waiting for a date, drinking a Pepsi cola very slowly.

As I ordered a second beer and decided that it might be wise not to finish my horse steak, I got up the courage to ask her if she was waiting for someone. She replied that she was, but her date was late.

We chatted pleasantly for a bit. Her name was Cecilia and she was from a small town near Puerto Cortez, but was staying in San Pedro de Sula with her aunt. I offered to buy her a drink or something, and she graciously accepted, ordering a dish of ice cream.

43

After we had both finished eating, we left the restaurant together. We sat in the park for an hour and talked. She wanted to travel, and was hoping to go to Florida some day. We walked down the street toward my hotel, and we arranged to meet in the central square the next morning. When we came to my hotel, I invited her up for a moment to show her a map of Honduras that I had, so she could show me where she was from.

Shyly, she came to my room, but refused to sit down. We stood while I unfolded my map and she pointed out the small town to me. We talked for a few minutes and then I escorted her downstairs. At the desk the clerk demanded that I now pay for a double room since I had had a woman up to my room.

Cecilia turned red and I argued with the clerk, an older woman who spent her time doing crossword puzzles, that she was the sister of a friend and had only been to my room for a few minutes. I indignantly refused to pay for a double, and after a few minutes of arguing won my case.

Cecilia, however, was quite embarrassed, and I was not to see her again, even though I went to the Central Square the next morning to meet her.

I didn't let this small thing depress me, and cheerfully packed up and grabbed a bus to the coastal port of La Ceiba. This is the busiest port in Honduras, exporting bananas and pineapples to the US and Europe.

It was a short trip to the port, and in the early afternoon I was checking into the Hotel Principal for two and half dollars a night. I headed down to the port past the many bars along the main street and came to the long pier. It was all a rather run down and sleepy jungle port, something out of a Graham Greene novel. Seedy dock workers loitering around the bars. Women of questionable virtue drinking at sidewalk tables in the afternoon. Unlike the interior of Honduras, along the coast here were many blacks, imported in the 1700s from Caribbean islands to work the plantations.

I walked down the largely deserted pier. It didn't seem like a very busy port to me, there was only one ship at the pier and it was being loaded with black Caribes for deck passage to go down the shore to the Mosquito Coast near Nicaragua.

🌸🌸🌸

Over a beer at sunset along the pier, I thought about the strange tales of lost cities in this part of Honduras. There is a curious legend of a lost city on the Mosquito Coast named the *Ciudad Blanca*. Honduran legends tell of an ancient empire, now lost, that flourished in the unexplored jungles of the southeast coast. Beginning in the sixteenth century, the Spanish invaders of Honduras were told of a mysterious white city lost in the rain forests of the interior. Since that time, hunters and explorers have often claimed to have seen a white-walled city in the largely unexplored

Mosquito area (16,000 square miles) of northeastern Honduras.

By 1856 the persistent legend of the white city had led to the Honduran publication of a romantic engraving of the mysterious city. A 1954 government map located La Ciudad Blanca (with a red question mark) near the Wampu and Platano Rivers.[115]

The main archaeological exploration of the Mosquito area was done in 1933 when in February the archaeologist William Duncan Strong and others departed from Puerto Castilla for Brus Lagoon and five months on the Patuca River and its headwaters. This survey was a joint Johns Hopkins and Smithsonian project launched to track down reports of great stone cities with carved monuments in the interior. The expedition had sought to learn if the Maya culture extended beyond Copan on the western border of Honduras. No light was shed on either of these questions. The expedition did discover a rectangular stone ruin whose front was measured one hundred feet in length; this was on the Bonito River. Large mounds were also discovered on the Patuca River at Wankybila, as well as Chorotega-type pottery on the Patuca River. The Chorotega are one of the Central American tribes found at the time of the conquest.[115]

The area of the Mosquito Coast, as popularized in the book and film with Harrison Ford, is one of the last regions of Central America to be explored. It is a dense tropical rain forest that starts with swampy lagoons and beaches along the coast of Honduras and Nicaragua and quickly gives way inland to a thick jungle teaming jaguars, howler monkeys, frenetic army ants and 19 of the world's 26 highly poisonous snakes, including the much feared fer-de-lance.

In 1976, Dr. David Zink, who had done a large amount on the underwater ruins at Bimini, journeyed to Honduras with the distinguished Mayan expert Dr. Edwin Shook and a television crew from the ABC network to search for the lost city. They flew by charted plane from La Ceiba to the small community of Brus Lagoon, on the coast near to the Rio Patuca. The next day they flew again, in a smaller chartered plane to Palacios, a short distance back to the North from Brus Lagoon on the Laguna Bacalar.

The next day they taken by helicopter to a small site nearby called Aguacate. The helicopter hovered over a swampy field below some thirty-foot high mounds upon which three thatched huts stood. The team jumped off and into the mud several feet below and then struggled up the pyramidical mounds to the huts where they met the local patron, Panfilo. He had built his huts on mounds originally built for houses some 800 years or more earlier.

Making Panfilo's small settlement of Aguacate their base, they then were shown by Panfilo nearby basalt cylinders more than a meter long as well an enormous monolith that lay partially uncovered in a pit where treasure hunters had left it twenty-five years earlier. At that time a stone sculpture of a jaguar-headed man about six feet tall was taken—likely lost now in some private collection.

The monolith they saw was described as 2.7 meters tall and averaged about 75 cm in width. As Dr. David Zink was later to say, "Quarrying and moving such stone was certainly not likely the work of any of the known Circum-Caribbean cultures, such as the Paya or Sumos."[115]

The next day, after cutting a trail through the dense jungle, Panfilo showed them a large altar-stone partly submerged in a pool of water. He told the expedition that he had found it looking for gold a year earlier. The stone measured 2.03 meters in length, and .94 meters wide, except that both front corners had been broken away. Nearby was a 1.29 meter column or phallic stone.

The team began clearing the area with their machetes and Dr. Edwin Shook suddenly came across a sophisticated megalithic stone sculpture, partly submerged in the swamp, of an owl. It was of basalt and stood about a meter high and "seemed related to stone carvings in Nicaragua and Costa Rica, yet was superior craftsmanship. On its back were carvings suggestive of petroglyphs in Panama."[115]

The next day they began a march through the jungle to the site known as Búkara. Búkara was just to the north, located on the Rio Klaura. At Búkara the team found four houses built on mounds thirty to fifty feet high. There were two rows of ten mounds running parallel for about 500 meters.

During two days of explorations around Búkara they were told of a stone with writings in an unknown language deep in the mountains of the interior. Exploring the area they discovered a large granite slab with hole drilled in it and some pottery fragments. Then at length they made their exciting discovery: fragments of beautifully carved metates of megalithic proportions. A metate is a stone bench with a trough in it for grinding grain. Most likely maize in this case. Unlike many grinding stones, which can be a small stone slab only a few feet square, these metates were two meters long with large megalithic legs to support it, and weighed, they estimated, about twenty tons!

Said Dr. Zink about the exciting discovery, "Half buried in the jungle, these graceful objects spoke of a sophisticated culture able to carve metates with legs nearly two meters long from a block of hard metamorphic rock probably weighing at least twenty tons! If the indigenous peoples had had anything to do with these artifacts, many centuries must have elapsed to reduce them to the present cultural level."[115]

One thing that seems clear from these reports, is that a megalithic civilization once existed in Central America, in an area that is now swamp and jungle. Megalithic remains stick out of swamps and matted forest like the scattered building blocks of some child—helter skelter and broken as if in some cataclysmic change that buried the great cities and apparently changed the climate of the area. As Zink notes in his book, it is curious that they did not find any cities at all, but merely superficial traces of them.

And what of the Ciudad Blanca, the mysterious white washed city in the interior? It would be curious indeed if this city was still inhabited, or was at the time shortly after the conquest!

🐉🐉🐉

Just opposite the port of La Ceiba are the Bay Islands of Roatan, Utila, Barbareta and Guanaja (called Bonacca by the English). While only a few years ago these were sleepy, isolated islands, they are now becoming popular scuba diving resorts. In the early colonial history they were major pirate bases for raiding the rich Spanish ports and fleets.

The famous discover of the Crystal Skull from the lost city of Lubaantun, F.A. (Mike) Mitchell-Hedges, spent a great deal of time in the Bay Islands in the 1930s and discovered ruins on the island of Guanaja (Bonacca) which he believed to be the ruins of part of Atlantis.

In a series of articles written in 1935 for the *New York American* newspaper, as well as in his biography, *Danger My Ally*,[116] Mitchell-Hedges described the archaeological discoveries he made in the Bay Islands, now largely forgotten. One article published on March 10, 1935 in the *New York American* was headlined, "Atlantis Was No Myth but the Cradle of the American Races, Declares Hedges." Another headline read, "Explorer Hedges Finds Pre-Mayan City Buried Beneath Caribbean Sea."

Said the *New York American* article "Off the Bay Islands, Mitchell-Hedges pulled many pre-Flood remnants and excavated twenty-one sites in the five tiny islands. Mitchell-Hedges was careful to note that in some cases the stone faces were anthropologically similar to the Central American Indian while others were crafted with the high cheekbone and aquiline nose of the North American Indian.

"Upon the island of Bonaca[sic] he discovered an eight-hundred-yard mound wall enclosure, the top of which was paved with flat stones. In this place of worship he discovered two immense monoliths which, he noted, were similar to stone formations at Stonehenge. The stones measured almost seven feet in height and two and half feet through the base.

"He also unearthed well-proportioned vases, objects of copper and bronze, and found upon a hilltop a huge hewn stone with strange markings upon it. There was no known mechanism that could have moved it to this remote pinnacle.

"In hastily abandoned chambers, among the awe-inspiring evidence of nature's upheaval, he discovered oddly carved stones and weird figurines of grotesque animals and reptiles, which, he surmised, might once have roamed the earth. But out of all these artifacts not one had any relation to the culture of the Maya, Aztec, Toltec or to other cultures of the area.

"On the slope that was once terraced downward to the sea he

found a specimen in the form of an animal. It was about four inches long and pierced with round holes. Another similar object was also found in the form of a man. It appeared at first to be a solid piece of stone but upon closer examination he found it packed with dirt. Subsequent cleaning proved it to be a simple wind instrument—perhaps the original ocarina.

"It must have been an eerie experience to experiment with those instruments—unplayed for centuries.

"The authenticity of the Mitchell-Hedges finds received wide endorsement. George C. Heye, Director of the Heye Foundation at the Museum of the American Indian in New York, wrote, "Your own observations, and the United States Government surveys in Nicaragua, prove conclusively that at some remote period a tremendous earth movement of cataclysmic force must have taken place in that part of the world...and that your excavations have actually unearthed the cultural artifacts of a prehistoric people that existed prior to the great earth movement...your discoveries open up an entirely new vista in regard to the ancient civilizations of the American continent." (*New York American,* February 10, 1935).

Among the interesting artifacts shown in the articles and Mitchell-Hedges' book is a petrified stone head that was once the wooden top of chief's staff and an assortment of greenish pottery vases and figurines.[116,117]

Mitchell-Hedges presented the statues to the Museum of the American Indian where they can be seen today. It is definitely an interesting find, though hardly proof of Atlantis, I thought, as I sipped a Port Royal *cerveza* near the La Ceiba pier that evening. The vases looked rather Mayan to me, and it is no mystery that the Mayas are an ancient civilization with the undoubted capability of sailing large canoes to the Bay Islands and other Caribbean destinations. Most interesting of the discoveries of Mitchell-Hedges in the Bay Islands are the large standing stones, literal menhirs, and the photos in his book reminded me of compass stones that were used on remote islands in Polynesia and Micronesia in the Pacific, though this was on the other side of the world.

Mitchell-Hedges was an exciting and highly interesting person, and some people believe that he was the model for Indiana Jones. His exploits were of the same time frame at least. We will hear more about Mitchell-Hedges and his discoveries in the chapter on Belize.

꧁꧁꧁

I had been eager to see the Caribbean before I headed inland again into the Mayan jungles of Honduras and Guatemala, and so I had come to La Ceiba. But after a day in this sleepy port, I was already to leave again. Perhaps if Cecilia had come with me, I would have felt more like staying on the beach for a longer time. But lost cities in the interior beckoned, so I paid my meager hotel bill and headed for the bus station to get a bus back to San Pedro de Sula.

Passing a sleeping street urchin on the sidewalk at seven-thirty in the morning, I left him an old pair of tennis shoes that I had been wearing, hoping they would somehow fit his bare feet. He was sleeping on a torn card board box on the side walk with a mongrel dog standing guard next to him.

I placed the worn shoes next to him on the cardboard. He didn't stir, but the dog suddenly jumped up and starting barking at me. I hastened down the street with the scurvy dog nipping at my heels, barking loudly. Holding the straps of my pack so it was tight against my pack, I picked up pace so as not to get bitten, and felt that I had had enough of La Ceiba!

It was a short bus ride back to San Pedro de Sula and after buying some popcorn snacks and a lemonade, I grabbed another bus west toward the fabulous Mayan city of Copán. We were going along fine for several hours when suddenly the old bus, a decrepit Bluebird bus made in Iowa, got a flat tire and skidded to a stop by the side of the road.

There was a great deal of commotion, and everyone piled out of the bus. I followed after everybody else had gotten off and stood around with the crowd for a few minutes while the driver and his mechanic looked things over. They talked among themselves and then there was a general sigh among the crowd.

I asked a young man standing next to me "what was happening?"

He replied in Spanish that they did not have a spare tire. So it seemed as if we would be there for awhile until another bus from the same company came along or something like that.

Since it was obvious that it would be awhile before the bus was going again, I went back in the bus and got my pack. Slipping a strap over my shoulder and waved goodbye to the driver and started walking down the road.

Rather than being frustrated and impatient at my journey, I was delighted. I loved that moment of being on the road, not knowing what was going to happen next. Some vehicle would come along, no doubt. In the meantime, I would enjoy walking the road with sun on the horizon, moving slowly through the blue sky.

After awhile, I could see coming down the road a large four-wheel drive wagon of some sort. Maybe a Toyota Landcruiser or Wagoneer. I stopped and looked at them down the road. With my pack still on my back and waved at them with both arms. Then with one arm and motioned for them to stop. This was the technique of hitchhiking that I had developed so successfully in Africa some years before.

The Landcruiser slowed down and came to a stop just near me. I stepped up to the passenger door as it was opened for me by a young woman with shoulder length brown hair and a big smile.

I climbed in back, pulling my pack in behind me. At the wheel was a civil engineer named Eduard, who was checking out the progress of paving the road. The young lady was Libby, a photographer for the newspaper in Tegucigalpa.

We had a good time talking and telling each other about our lives.

At the crossroads of La Entrada, they told me they were going on to Nueva Ocotepeque, on the border with El Salvador. It was getting late in the day, and I decided just to go with the flow.

Eduard made every effort to miss all of the potholes that continuously dotted the pavement—a feat which took him all over the road! We swerved to the far left and then back into our lane just in time to make another sharp jerk to avoid some other hole in the road. I held onto the back of Libby's seat and watched the road.

We moved down the narrow, but paved highway and into the mountains that separate El Salvador with Honduras and Guatemala. Just as the last rays of the setting sun were lighting up the sky, we pulled into Nueva Ocotepeque.

Eduard and Libby let me off at a street corner in the center of town, a downtown of only four blocks long. I shouldered my pack as they drove off, out toward the far edge of town. With the bewilderment of being in any new town, I looked around. Was there a hotel somewhere around here?

Up one street I saw a sign for a hotel. Passing a rather noisy bar, I strode up the dirt road toward the sign. A large garage-door type security gate was already pulled down over the entrance to the hotel, but there was a small door built into the wide steel gate.

I ducked in the gate and into the central courtyard of the hotel. A small group of people were watching television in the lounge room, and a young man stood up when he saw me enter the courtyard.

"Do you have a single room?" I asked him in Spanish.

"Si," he replied and led me to a room on the opposite side of the courtyard. After dropping off my pack I headed down to find a restaurant. The downtown seemed strangely deserted, and the only place that I could find open was the noisy bar I had passed earlier.

That was OK with me, and I stepped in, having a good look around before I walked up to the bar. It was like something out of a Dodge City skit, with wooden walls, tables, chairs and and swinging doors. A few beer posters and calendars on the otherwise bare walls.

Four Hondurans in cowboy hats were drinking at the bar and a number of other people were sitting at the tables against the wall. At a table near the door was a young man literally dressed in rags. His dress was so unusual, I had to stop for a moment and look at him.

He was apparently a beggar, with short patchy hair. He seemed unusually young, I thought instantly. Only in his twenties. Perhaps he was a refugee from the war in El Salvador.

His clothes, which had originally caught my attention, were a carefully sewn together patchwork quilt of small squares of different fabric, each the same size. It was clothing that was at the same time carefully made and of rags. It was a coat and pair of paints that could have sold for hundreds of dollars in a New York chic boutique, yet here in Honduras, they were the clothes of beggar.

Shocked by his strange appearance and downtrodden sadness, I handed him a large coin. Graciously he thanked me.

50

I stepped up to the bar and ordered a beer.

"What kind of cerveza do you want?" asked the waitress, a tall, shapely young woman with long brown hair.

I looked at the four men around the corner of the bar from me. They were drinking *National* cerveza. As they looked me up and down, I wisely ordered a bottle of *National.*

The waitress popped a cap off a bottle and gave me an alluring look. Knowing that the four men across from the bar were watching my every movement, I nodded to her as I took my beer, but otherwise ignored her.

The men naturally wanted to know who I was and where I was from. I told them, in my best Spanish, more or less who I was, and toasted them, afterwards taking a big gulp from the bottle. It had been a long dust day all the way from La Ceiba. The cold foamy liquid tasted good going down.

Soon, as I stood drinking at the bar, they bought me a beer. Several in fact, which was a good trick, because since there was four of them, and only one of me, when it came my turn to buy a round, it would be four beers, and not one, that I would be buying.

Pulling out a wad of dough, I bought them each a beer and ordered a full meal from the kitchen for the strange country boy in rags in the back. I questioned her as to who he was.

The barmaid told me that he was sick. He was wandering about the mountains of this area. She didn't know who he was.

I felt especially sympathetic for this lost, sick kid. His clothes were quaint; an admirable patchwork made with great care. By his mother, I wondered? Or perhaps made by himself?

She served him the typical evening meal: a fried banana, some chicken, rice and beans. After ordering dinner myself, I couldn't help glancing at the poor boy occasionally to see that he was being properly served and not harassed by the other rowdy customers.

Others came and went in this remote mountain bar. There were handless types who had been in the notorious machete fights of Honduras. It was customary to fight with machetes until one person is wounded, either with a hand cut off, an eye put out, or the tendon on either foot severed, making the victim limp for the rest of his life.

It was a macho world where if one took out his machete in anger, he could not put it back without blood on the blade. Several people limped into the bar, and I saw at least one man with his hand cut off at the wrist. It was at this same bar that I learned of the Honduran law that you cannot have more than three drinks in any bar or restaurant!

That night in Nueva Ocotepeque, I realized why Honduras had that law as it was indeed a wild west type of place. I finished the simple, but tasty, meal, and as I stood looking around, a fight suddenly broke out in the back room where a couple of pool tables were being used by a bunch of rowdy locals who obviously had had more than the officially allotted three beers.

I heard the crack of a pool cue being smashed against the table

and suddenly a tall, thin man came flying into the restaurant area
and landed sprawling on the floor. He cursed and pulled himself to
his feet. A machete hung from his belt and he pulled it out in a long,
smooth stroke. I knew this meant trouble, and eased back toward
the wall, taking what was left of my *National* cerveza with me.

With bloodshot eyes and a confused daze he looked in my
direction, perhaps wondering if I was up for a fight. I looked at the
barmaid and then at the open door in the front. I knew I could make
it to the door if I ran. I felt in my pocket for my tear gas clip, but I had
left it in my room. If I had to I would break the bottle on the bar and
use it to defend myself—but that would have been a desperate move.

In an effort to defuse the situation, the barmaid began shouting
some obscenities at the machete waving drunk, and he sheathed his
machete and tried to order another beer. The barmaid continued to
yell at him, making it obvious that he wouldn't be served. He had had
enough, and his third beer according to Honduran law had obviously
occurred some hours before.

I finished my last *National* and then asked the poor country boy
dressed in rags if he was full, or if he wanted more.

He was full, he replied, and thanked me again for the meal. I
nodded to the many patrons as I left the bar. They watched me
carefully as I left. And I, with a similar awareness, watched that I
wasn't being followed out of the bar.

Curiously, the next morning, as I looked about town for breakfast,
several beggars came up to me asking me for money. I refused,
naturally, and was confused at first, until I remembered the boy in
rags the night before. Apparently word had already gotten around
town that I was a soft touch.

I turned down the main street, a dirt road five blocks long, I
suddenly met another American. He was an ex-Marine in his forties
with short blonde hair and a khaki shirt and shorts. He seemed a
strange site out here on the remote border of Honduras and El
Salvador.

"Do you know a good place around here for breakfast?" I asked
him, speaking English for the first time in a week.

"Yea, follow me," he said, and we headed down the street. "That's El
Salvador, over that mountain," he said pointing. I nodded.

At breakfast, he explained that he had been a Warrant Officer in
the Marine Corp and was now an insurance investigator working out
of his own office in Miami. He prowled the ports of Honduras,
Guatemala and Honduras checking out thievery, claims of damaged
or missing cargo and other insurance claims.

He hated blacks, Black Caribes especially, and called the
travellers from Germany, England and France that were coming to
Central America "Eurotrash" whom he was trying to get the port
authorities in these various countries to refuse admittance to the
countries.

"I hate this Eurotrash that is coming to Guatemala, Belize and
Honduras," he confessed. "I'm trying to get to get the port authority

in Puerto Barrios to stop letting them in, or make them get a hair cut. I hate these long haired hippy travelers!"

Fortunately I had just had a haircut and my hair was rather short. I was suspicious of this guy, though. There was something strange about him. What was this right-wing militant doing hanging out in this nowhere village in the remote mountains of Honduras? It didn't make sense. I asked him, in different words, "what was he doing in Nueva Ocotepeque?"

"Oh, I like coming out here, getting away from the coast. The air is crisp and cool. It is so hot and humid on the coast. Besides, you never know what will happen on the El Salvador border."

I surmised that he was probably a C.I.A. operative of some sort, and maybe an insurance investigator as well. Fortunately he did most of the talking, and I gladly kept asking him questions about himself. In some ways he was a riot, and I struggled hard not to laugh outright at many of things he said. Sadly though, I realized that the attitude that he held, one of intolerance and hatred to other cultures, was an attitude that was gaining popularity around the world.

I checked out of the hotel, and throwing my pack over my shoulder, I headed back down the road toward Santa Rosa de Copán. The call of the road kept me moving. It seemed like I hardly stayed in one place for more than a day or two. The call of the highway and the lure of new places kept me going. Where was I off to next? The lost Mayan city of Copán beckoned. With a little luck I would be there before dusk.

🐲🐲🐲

I caught a ride in the back of a pickup, a ride I always enjoy, because I can stand in the back and have the wind in my hair. The drivers, a father and son, took me into Santa Rosa de Copán and on to La Entrada, the crossroads for the small side road that would take me to the famous Mayan city of Copán.

I stood by a small roadside store and asked the elderly woman who ran it if there was a bus to Copán. She replied that a bus would stopping at any moment. Suddenly, a rusty old Japanese mini-bus pulled up. "Copán?" asked the driver.

I jumped on board, my pack being tossed onto a rack on the top of the bus. I grabbed a seat among the half dozen or so passengers, and we were off down the bumpy dirt road to the lost Mayan city of Copán.

I looked at the woman sitting next to me on the bus. She was small, with long, brown, hair, and quite beautiful. She turned and smiled broadly at me, but remained silent.

"Are you going to Copán ?" I asked her in Spanish. She explained that she was going to help her sister run a juice stand at the bus station. She went on to tell me that her husband had abandoned her and the four kids. Two of them were with her, Garcia Lopez and Luis.

53

Suddenly, there was a hand on my shoulder. I turned and saw the smiling young face of Garcia Lopez, her oldest son, ten years old. "My name is Aida Blanca. What is yours?" she asked me. "David," I told her. We chatted for a while. She was very sweet and quite beautiful. Towards the late afternoon, we arrived at Copán Ruinas, the small town a mile away from the archaeological site. I thanked Aida Blanca for her company. She blushed. She invited me to visit her at the juice stand of her sister near the center of town. Picking up my pack I told her that I would enjoy that. A hotel sign for the Brisas de Copán caught my eye, and soon I was in my own room, tossing my pack on the floor and flopping onto the bed to rest after the dusty, jolting ride.

Early the next morning I began walking the kilometer out of town that was the distance to the ancient Mayan city.

Copán is situated in a valley among the hills of the mountainous border area of Honduras and Guatemala. It is closely connected by the Rio Copán and Rio Motagua to Quirigua, the site of the highest steles in the world.

Copán is known today as one of the great Mayan observatories for astronomy and calculations for the elaborate Mayan calendar, the most accurate calendar ever devised. The Egyptians were similarly occupied with astronomy and observatories. Copán is situated in the mountains between the Rio Motagua and the Rio Ulua. By heading down the Copán river one reaches the important Rio Motagua valley in which the source of jade in the Americas was found. Jade was of mystical importance to both the Chinese and the ancient Mayas.

Copán was a temple city, perhaps a mining city, and an observatory. The area is famous even today for its clear nights in which to view the stars. Copán has often been described as the Athens of the New World, and even though Mayan cities to the north are larger with grander pyramids and plazas, Copán has more carved monuments than any other city.

Copán may have been settled as early as 2000 B.C., however the classic years of Copán are given by archaeologists as being from 465 A.D. to 800 A.D. There is a certain air of mystery surrounding Copán, though some of the rulers are known: Smoking Rabbit lived to the ripe age 82 and was succeeded by 18 Rabbit, who broke the tradition of destroying monuments with each change in rulers and using the rubble to fill in new structures. 18 Rabbit's successor, Squirrel, commemorated rulers of old whose monuments had been destroyed, and rebuilt the ball court.

This Mayan custom of destroying the monuments of previous rulers is certainly one reason why no hieroglyphic dates earlier than 465 A.D. have been found at Copán—they have all been destroyed!

The city grew to perhaps 15,000 inhabitants and then suddenly, about 800 A.D., the city was abandoned and soon the great plazas and pyramids were covered with jungle growth. There is no archaeological evidence of any attack or violence, no hasty burials, lost weapons or valuables, no demolished houses or forgotten household goods. The ancient Maya seem simply to have moved away, leaving the city to the ravages of the jungle. For a thousand years the once magnificent city was lost to the world.

The city was brought to the attention of the archaeological world in 1835 when Colonel Jan Galindo, an officer of the Guatemalan army, published his *Description of the Ruins of Copán,* which contained many drawings of the site and its architecture. Intrigued by Galindo's account, the American diplomat John Lloyd Stevens and the English artist Frederick Catherwood visited the ruins and spent several weeks there sketching the steles and buildings. Stevens like the ruins so much that he bought them for fifty dollars!

Stevens and Catherwood produced the classic archaeology volume, *Incidents of Travel in Central America, Chiapas and Yucatan* [84] which was published in 1839. Said Stevens in the book when they came to Copán, "The sight of this unexpected sculpture once and for all dispelled from our minds all doubt on the character of American antiquities and confirmed us in our conviction that the objects we were looking for were worthy of interest not only as relics of an unknown people but also as works of art proving, as a newly discovered historical text might have done, that the peoples who once occupied the American continent were no savages."

Because of Steven's book, the British archaeologist Alfred P. Maudslay arrived in 1881 and began the excavation of the city. Excavation continues to this day with the Government of Honduras and the University of Pennsylvania directing the work.

I paid the small entrance fee at a booth with a gate just in front of the central plaza of the ancient city. A colorful macaw sat by the gate, a captive parrot which was apparently there for the purposes of tourist photographs. He squawked loudly as I went through the turnstile and I gave him a respectful nod.

Walking around the Great Plaza or Ceremonial Court as it is sometimes called, I marveled at the magnificent statues. Steles and other stones, some as high as four meters (12-13 feet). They are some of the most beautiful statues carved by the Maya, and have a controversial archaeological history. Stela B commemorates the accession of the ruler 18 Rabbit and above his head on either side of the top of the stela are the heads of elephants, each with a turbaned mahout or elephant driver leaning on the head of the elephant. Yin-Yang symbols literally cover the stela and are especially prominent on the belt. Curiously, since Stevens and Catherwood visited and drew the stele, the top portion has been destroyed, so that the man, who had previously been above the head "elephant" of "macaw," was no longer there. It is known that such a small figure was originally on the stele from Catherwood's early drawings, and others. Some European archaeologists have even accused American archaeologists of purposely defacing the stele.

Since elephants were no longer present in Central America in the year 800 A.D., many archaeologists used this stela as evidence of contact between Southeast Asians and the Mayas. Since traditional archaeology does not accept this interpretation of cultural contact between Asia and the Americas, it was decided that these sculptures could not be elephant heads, but had to be something else.

Generally they are said to be stylized representations of the head of a macaw, with the beak curved backward in an exaggerated way. Why miniature turbaned men should be leaning on the stylized heads of these bizarre macaws has never been explained. But then, there are lots of things about the Mayas that remain unexplained, even to the traditionalists.

Personally, I was amazed at the oriental look to all the statues. Having lived and travelled in China for several years, I was immediately struck at how Chinese looking everything was. Many of the men had thin mustaches and thin wispy beards that are the exact caricature of the Fu Manchu-type of Chinese. Had I not been completely aware that I was standing in the jungles of Central America, I would have thought that I was viewing a selection of Tang Dynasty statues from China!

Yin-Yang symbols were everywhere, and there was even a large stone ball, about three feet in diameter and weighing several tons, which was carved a perfect yin-yang pattern on it. Around the edge was a braided rope effect and the whole stone was an oval-oyster shape, rather being perfectly round.

Curiously as well, I noticed that light green geodes were embedded in some of the steles, and incorporated into certain glyphs. Later I asked an archaeologist about this, and informed me that since the stone that was used to carve the steles had these geodes in them, the Mayas would just incorporate them into the carvings as best as they could.

I wandered around the plaza toward the pyramids, stopping at each one and taking notes. Stela H showed an unusual figure wearing a skirt. Underneath this stela was found a statue made of solid gold which is believed to have come from Panama or Columbia. Stela J is completely covered with hieroglyphs and the only known other stela so carved is at Quirigua.

I then came to the ball court with a narrow paved area and three sloped sides. There is still a debate today whether the losers of these ball games were executed, or whether it was only prisoners who were executed, or sometimes ceremoniously tied into balls themselves and used as victims in the games. One bizarre off-shoot of the execution after the game theory is that the winners were executed! It being an honor to be sacrificed, the promoters of this theory propose.

Copán's most spectacular treasure is found just south of the ball court, the magnificent hieroglyphic stairway. More than a thousand glyphs set in the 63 steps make this the longest known Mayan inscription. It apparently relates the history of Copán's rulers up to the date 755 A.D. when the structure was dedicated under ruler Smoke Shell. Unfortunately, the text cannot really be read because the stairway was rebuilt with stones set in random sequence, sort of like a scrabble game all jumbled up.

In 1989, archaeologists excavating behind the hieroglyphic stairway stumbled upon a noble tomb. There are other tunnels and tombs inside the main structure behind the hieroglyphic stairway, and I noticed that some excavation was taking place inside.

I had hopes that I might be able to gain entrance to the inside of the tunnel system inside the pyramid, and hung out by an opening where workmen were bringing out wheelbarrows of dirt.

There I met an American woman from the University of Pennsylvania and a Honduran archaeologist educated at the University of Texas. I asked them what they had found inside, and they said that there were some tombs of Mayan nobles.

When I commented that I thought that the statues looked very Chinese, the young archaeologist from the University of Pennsylvania raised her eyebrows. "How do they look Chinese?" She had long blond hair tied in pony tail and wore a khaki shirt and pants.

"They have the thin wispy mustaches and beards, worn just like the ancient Chinese. Why, you could take one of these statues and put it in China and no one would bat an eye." I pointed to a huge dragon that came down the side of the pyramid. "Look at this dragon, it is identical to oriental dragons. Don't you think there might be some connection?"

"There is no connection between the Chinese and the Mayas," she said. "These statues don't look even remotely Chinese to me."

"Really?" I replied. "Have you spent some time in China studying their art and motifs?"

"No, never, I know very little about ancient China," she replied. "I don't need to know much, I am a specialist in Mayan studies. That has nothing to do with China."

I thought to myself that it seemed rather difficult for her to make judgments about similarities between Mayan and Chinese sculpture if she knew nothing about Chinese art. She was typical of today's archaeological "experts," they are highly specialized in one field, but know absolutely nothing about the art, archaeology or history of other areas. How can anyone see similarities in other cultures when one is ignorant of other cultures? Perhaps this was an advantage that I had over these "specialists."

"What about all the yin-yang symbols around Copán and the huge yin-yang ball in the courtyard, surely you've seen that?" I asked.

The Honduran archaeologist responded to that question when the University of Pennsylvania archaeologist hesitated. "That stone ball in the central courtyard represents the ball used in the ball games. It is not a yin-yang symbol. It just looks like one. The yin-yang type curve is just how the leather ball is sewn together, like a baseball."

I didn't buy that one, because the balls used in the games were not leather at all, but made out of solid pieces of rubber. I could see that my conversation was starting to irritate the two, especially the woman. "Do you think that it is impossible for the ancient Chinese to have come to Central America?" I asked.

"Pretty much," she replied. "How would they have gotten here?"

"In boats," I said. "They had very large ships, even in ancient China. Bigger ships than Columbus had."

"Why would Chinese come to Central America?" she asked.

"Why would the Spanish come here? Or anyone? One special product that the Chinese may have been looking for was jade. You know it was sacred to them, as it was to the Mayas."

"You know," she said, standing, and obviously tired of our discussion, "it is a racist argument to say that the Mayas did not develop their civilization on their own. You should think about that." And with these final words, I was left standing outside the tunnel to the pyramid by myself. Any hopes of charming these two into letting me inside was totally quashed. A guard with a machete stood at the entrance, glowering at me. I figured it was time to move on.

🌸🌸🌸

Another fascinating aspect of the Mayas is the importance of colors to the directions of the compass. The Mayas believed that the sky was held up by four gods. Each god had a color associated with him. Red is for the east, white is for the north, black is for the west, and yellow is for the south. The earth was believed to rest on the back of a great crocodile which itself rested in a pool filled with water lilies.

Similarly, the ancient Chinese had a directional color scheme. Near Xian, central China is the largest pyramid known to exist in the world. It is sometimes known as the Great Pyramid of China. Traces of the original coloring have been found on the Great Pyramid of China: it was black on the north, blue-gray on the east, red on the south, and white on the west. The apex was painted yellow.[16]

The significance of the colors apparently has to do with the Taoist (and pre-Taoist) system of five phases or five elements and everything may be catagorized under five elements (fire, water, earth, metal and wood). The directions of the compass, emotions and colors are included in this system. Black is for the north (water); green is for the east (wood); red to the south (fire); white to the west (metal); and yellow to the center (earth). (For more information on pyramids in China see my book *Lost Cities of China, Central Asia & India*[16])

Is there some connection between the Mayan directional color scheme and that of ancient China? I think so. The colors seem to have switched around, perhaps this is because the Maya lands need a different color scheme, or so the priests may have believed. Just the concept of ascribing colors to various directions seems to be a rather unique Chinese/Mayan concept. Similarly, it was the popular belief in both India and China that the earth sat on the back of a great turtle, much like the Mayan concept of it resting on an alligator's back. Just a coincidence?

As the archaeologist from the University of Pennsylvania pointed out to me, there is some danger in speculating about transoceanic contact and its ramifications. Today, the label given to those who champion diffusionism and contacts in pre-Columbian times from across the Atlantic and the Pacific is that of a "racist."

Anthropologist George Carter had this to say about the racist accusations leveled toward Diffusionists:

"If man was voyaging back and forth across the vast Pacific—it spans 1/3 the world—how about man crossing the puny Atlantic? Well, let's be racists. Who? Those dumb Europeans who were primarily still rowing their galleys around into the 18th century, and who were amongst the last to take up such nautical advancements as stern rudders, and fore and aft rigged sails? Well, fortunately, the Atlantic is so small and the winds and currents flow so strongly and persistently from the mouth of the Mediterranean to the Caribbean that there is no escape. Even a ship wreck will make it in short time. In modern times men have crossed it on a hay stack (Heyerdahl) and a Scandinavian did it on a canvas craft. Even if the Europeans didn't want to, they would arrive in America now and then. The evidence now accumulating is that they wanted to, and did get here, and probably messed up American Indian culture history considerably, though we still can't see, because we haven't tried to see, just when, and where, and how much.

"To toss in a few straws to indicate the wind direction: The Spaniards were given European coins when they reached Mexico. One of the Mexican idols had a helmet just like an old helmet worn by one of Cortés soldiers. A pottery head found in Mexican archeology has been identified as made in Rome in the second century A.D., and I have written a little article pointing out that Mexican cylinder seals and many stamps carry alphabetical inscriptions. Well, if all this, one is looking at considerable contact. Did anyone go home? Was this possibly a two-way trade? My answer is: Yes, trade and deliberate voyages, and possibly even colonization.

"At Pompeii are portrayals of pineapples. Pineapples are strictly American in origin. So, a pottery head from Pompeii (Rome) and an American pineapple to Pompeii—and the dates match. There is another curious one. The Jews that died at the time of the great revolt against Rome (end of the first century A.D.) in part had fled to the desert. In caves their clothing was preserved so well that even the colors lasted. A study of these dyes showed that one of them was cochineal, and cochineal is produced by an aphid like insect that grows on cactus. Cactus is strictly American. This like so many of these items needs some further work, but that is the probable answer as of this moment. Was there then a trade in dyes? Well the Phoenicians (the name means purple) traded in purple dyes that they made from a shell fish. In America, the natives made the same purple from the related shell fish. This was once fluffed off as: The

Spanish taught them. But we have C-14 dates for such dyes as early as 200 B.C. Is this a reasonable trade item? It certainly is. Distant trade must rest on light weight, low bulk, high value materials. Dyes fit this perfectly. What else?

"Well, a final bit, to take this back to Vermont where we began. In the bronze age, men began going to the ends of the earth for metals: copper, tin, gold, silver. Southern New England is, or was, rich in copper. In southern New England there is a wealth of evidence of inscriptions, standing stones, huge stones set up on lesser stone, large stone chambers. All of this would fit a bronze age, or megalithic European pattern, and it probably does.

"The trend of the data is to show that man was crossing the great oceans far earlier that we have thought. I was chastised twenty years ago for suggesting that this could have begun as early as 2500 or even 3000 B.C. Now we have an African plant being grown in America around 7000 B.C. (*Lagenaria siceraria,* the dipper gourd) and one of my friends is casually mentioning the possibility that men were crossing the Atlantic as early as perhaps 15,000 years ago. THAT is a high date even for me, but give me a month or so to digest it and I may begin to toy cautiously with the possibility.

"And that is where we stand. We know with considerable certainty that voyages and meaningful exchanges of plants and animals occurred, and that trade is very probable, and that colonization is quite possible. We have lots to learn and a lot of stubborn people doing their best to block serious inquiry. In too many cases, this leaves the field to what is known as 'the lunatic fringe' and since there are incautious souls out there they often give the professionals the very ammunition they need to smear everyone. If the whole thing weren't so exciting, and so important for the understanding of the origins of civilization and the nature of man, one would be tempted to give it up and just let the Phuddies, to borrow Harold Gladwin's phrase, *own the field.* But, it is all too important for that."[101]

Carter, in his last sentence, was referring to the book *Men Out of Asia,*[113] written in 1947 by Dr. Harold Gladwin. Gladwin's book is the classic attack on the academic dogma of isolationism and it was in his book that the term "Phuddy Duddy" was coined for smug experts with Ph.D.'s who sit in their high academic chairs pronouncing what is correct as far as history is concerned.

While Gladwin's book made some inroads at the time and the term Phuddy Duddy has been popularized, the dogma of isolationism remains, and, as George Carter points out, it has now taken on the repugnant slant of calling those who favor a diffusion of ideas through various migrations and explorations by sea in antiquity as "racist" talk. The racist point is that those who believe that so-called Native Americans may not have invented everything themselves independently of the rest of the world are "racists." This is not a label that any researcher, archaeologist or historian would want to accept, and it therefore makes the entire subject rather volatile and tricky.

We could turn the argument around and say that it is racist to suggest that Chinese, Burmese, Libyans and Jews were too simple minded to have crossed the ocean. History and truth are matters of scientific investigation and evidence and are not dependent of what is politically correct today.

❦❦❦

As I sat by the dragon and a strange three foot high stone statue of a winged bat-man figure with a breastplate and unusually large genitals (a strange figure by any stretch of the imagination), I wondered if I was truly some racist nut. Was it really so insane to think that somehow Chinese Taoists had made some contact with Central America and influenced their culture? I didn't think so.

Anthropologist Gunnar Thompson makes a good case for a Taoist influence in Central America in his book *Nu Sun, Asian-American Voyages 500 B.C.*[119] Thompson starts his case by describing the ancient Shang dynasty culture of China, showing its symbols and motifs (the yin-yang is the most famous, but there are many more) and then relating them to known Mayan art and sculpture.

Jade was of particular importance to the Shang Chinese. Says Thompson, "Sometime during the Late Neolithic, the concepts of *yin* (darkness) and *yang* (light) became apparent in the religious practices of the more sophisticated astrologers. The relationship of *yin* and *yang* was conceived of as the passage of a shadow from one side of a mountain to the other as the sun moves across the sky. Presumably, all of life's experiences, including death, could be explained as continuously repeating processes that were regarded as keys to the understanding of these processes and predicting the future. It was an important advancement over the previous reliance on superstition, and it marked the beginning of the end for shamanistic religion in urban areas.

"The importance of beliefs concerning cosmic forces in Chinese religion is apparent from stone carvings attributed to the Late Neolithic. The square-shaped objects, or *tsung*, represent the earth, while the jade *pi* disks represent the sun, or heaven. They are usually manufactured from jade—a stone which the Chinese have traditionally valued above gold as a magical substance of natural purity. It is a material that does not occur naturally in China. The closest known source lies two thousand miles to the west—requiring an elaborate trade network to bring raw materials to the Hwang Ho Valley. The surface of *pi* disks is frequently embellished with a pattern of raised whorls or hemispheres in a uniform pattern. These designs are often referred to as a 'grain pattern,' or a 'tadpole pattern.' Both tadpoles and germinating grain have a scroll shape that Asian mystics identified as symbolic of life force emerging into the physical realm. Therefore, these motifs actually represent the matrix of cosmic power that was believed to encompass the heavens.

61

It was a transformational matrix of creative energy that could assume the shape of germinating plants, rain clouds, or dragons."

According to Thompson, jade was probably imported into China from Baikalia along the Amur Valley to An-Yang in China. Because there were no jade sources in China, the Chinese were intensely interested in finding jade deposits. One of the few known jade deposits in the world is in the Motagua Valley, near to Copán. The so-called Olmecs also used jade a great deal, starting about 2,000 B.C. or earlier. That jade could be found in Central America would have been known to ancient travelers who might have journeyed in the area. Jade can also be found in Nevada and New Zealand.

Thompson's theory is that Chinese explorers circa 500 B.C. sailed down the coast of Central America in search of new lands and exotic products to take back to China. Because the Pacific coast of Mexico and Guatemala was controlled by the war-like, cannibalistic Olmecs, who at that time who would rather attack and eat strangers rather than trade with them, the early Chinese explorers were forced to continue via ship well to the south of the Olmec heartland.

Thompson theorizes that the Chinese eventually used the Gulf of Fonseca as their base, founding a small trading colony. Here they were far enough away from the Olmec heartland to protect it from any sudden attack. It was also "located in a strategic position to dominate the coastal trade routes between Mexico and Panama; and it was at the center of abundant sources of trade goods that were suitable for Asian markets. These included exotic feathers, jadeite, gold, and hallucinogenic mushrooms."[119]

Thompson points out that so far, the source of Chinese jade has not been pinpointed. Much of it may have come from Central America. Even the source of Central American jade is a mystery; many ancient jade mines are believed to be still undiscovered.

Thompson also quotes the anthropologist Jennings who suggests that Chinese voyages to Mexico, between 500-300 B.C., may have been related to Taoist trade in magic mushrooms or "drugs of longevity."

Certainly, Chinese explorers would have been delighted to find their most precious of all stones, jade, as a commodity to trade for in Central American. Thompson suggests that the Chinese established a permanent outpost which later expanded and was to eventually flower into the Mayan empire. Taoism, like the wave of religions that has continually swept our planet from time to time, became the popular religion of Central America, at least for awhile, along with its many symbols and motifs.

🐾🐾🐾

I still had time that afternoon to visit the small museum at Copán, so I popped in for a look. It was nicely done, and I took my time going from display to display. There was an ultra sharp obsidian blade with a monomolecular edge, the sharpest blades known, used today in special surgical operations.

I marveled at a skull whose teeth had been replaced with jade. There were more "Chinese" looking statue heads and a dragon urn that was three feet high with a dragon lid.

One display had a burial pot beneath an altar discovered at the Hieroglyphic staircase and inside it were jade objects, knives, a clam shell and other items.

A map with some photos showed the early Olmec site of Piedra Canteada, near to Copán, that is currently dated at 900 B.C. I read with interest the explanation that said the skeletons of people were just lying in the streets when the city was excavated. I was suddenly reminded of Mohenjo Daro in Pakistan that also had dead people lying in the streets after some great doom had obliterated the city.[16]

I walked on back to the town and had a meal of rice, chicken and fried bananas at the Mini-Hotel Paty which has a small restaurant by the road. Afterwards, I walked down to the plaza of the town to look for Aida Blanca. She was serving juices at her sister's concession just as she said.

She smiled broadly as I approached her. She was quite beautiful and had a simple country girl charm about her. I sat and talked with her for a bit, drinking an orange juice. Suddenly I felt someone holding my hand. It was Garcia Lopez, one of her young sons. I put my arm around him and gave him a hug.

I laughed to myself and looked at Aida Blanca who gave me a loving look. Here I had been in Copán Ruinas for one full day, and already I had a family! This, I knew, was a sign that it was time to move on.

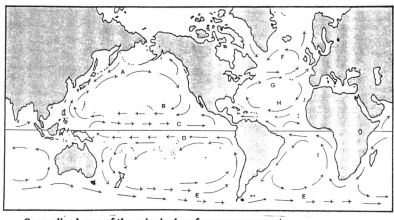

Generalized map of the principal surface ocean currents.
A. Japan-North Pacific Current   E. Antarctic Drift
B. California-North Equatorial Current   F. Irminger Current
C. Equatorial Countercurrent   G. Gulf Stream-North Atlantic Current
D. Peru-South Equatorial Current   I. Benguela-South Equatorial Current

Above: Small leg from a megalithic metate, or corn grinder, found at Búkara in the remote jungles of eastern Honduras. It is 84 cm long of hard granite. Right: Another fine-cut granite leg from a megalithic metate discovered in the wild jungles of Honduas by Dr. David Zink while searching for the ancient city known as the *Ciudad Blanca*.

One of Catherwood's drawings of a stele and "monster" at Copan.

Step temples on both sides of the Atlantic. **Top**: Reconstruction of the *Marduk* temple in Babylon (about 600 BC) with the Temple of the Convocation (*Esagila*) on the left and the stage tower (*Etemenanki*) in the walled temple courtyard. **Bottom**: Reconstruction of the temple comples of Copan in Honduras, about 100 BC. The similarity between the ancient Central American temples and those in ancient Mesopotamia, India and Angor-Wat is striking.

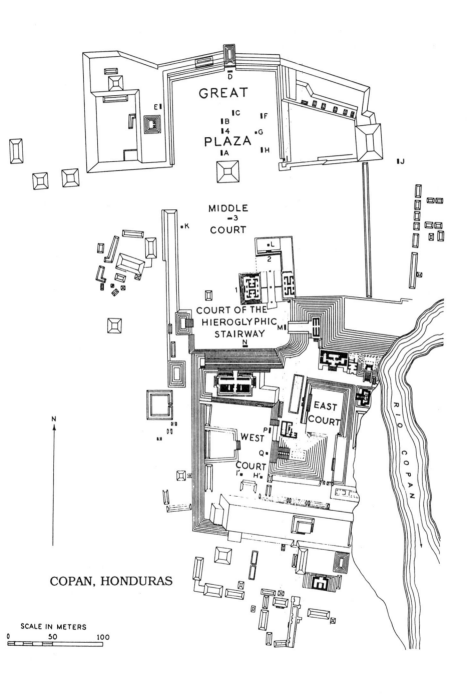

GREAT

PLAZA

E

IC
IB
I4
IA

IF
IG
IH

D

IJ

MIDDLE
=3
COURT

K

L
2

1

COURT OF THE
HIEROGLYPHIC
STAIRWAY
N

M

EAST
COURT

WEST

COURT

P
Q

H'

F'

D'

N

RIO COPAN

COPAN, HONDURAS

SCALE IN METERS

0   50   100

Jade plaque from Copan, 4 inches, and a jade disc from Pomona, Belize, 7 inches in diameter with four undeciphered glyphs. To the ancient Chinese such jade discs were the symbol of Heavenly Authority. Jade was the most valuable of all substances to them.

The controversial Stela B at Copan. It is alleged that elephants, complete with a "mahout" or driver, are on either side of the figure. Others claim that they are stylized representations of macaws.

The Sun God at Copan. By Catherwood.

Chapter 3

Guatemala South:

Lost Megaliths
of the Pacific Coast

The use of traveling is to regulate imagination by reality,
and instead of thinking how things may be,
to see them as they as are.
— Samuel Johnson

Crossing over the border from Honduras into Guatemala, I looked around at the ramshackle border post. I tucked my freshly stamped passport into my pouch, and headed toward a rusty Japanese mini-bus. The teenage co-pilot and ticket-taker looked at me eagerly. Where did I go from here?

"Chuquimula?" asked the oil stained Indian kid as he grabbed my pack and attempted to pull it toward the bus. I held fast to the strap of my pack while he pulled.

"Chuquimula?" I muttered. Was that where I was going? In the bright sun and confusing dialects of Central America, I was somewhat dazed and confused. Realizing that there was really only one way to go, and it was really only a question of how far this mini-bus would be going, I released my hold on my pack. Seconds later it was secure on the top of the minibus, and I was in a torn seat next to the driver.

After a few more passengers boarded, he started the mini-bus and we were bouncing down the dirt road toward Chuquimula. Like any bus in some Latin or Asian country, it had its protecting deities glued to the front windshield and dash. I was amused to note that rather than the typical Jesus, Mother Mary, Buddha or Krishna protecting the passengers, this bus' protecting deities were Snoopy, Bambi and Thumper. As the driver shifted up or down (it was hard to tell) and swerved to avoid a large hole in the road, I leaned back and enjoyed the view.

My quest for answers to the riddles of lost civilizations in North America had been drawing me to Guatemala for a long time. As the bus bounced and rolled over the dirt road, I thought of the photo of the gigantic carved head which had brought me to this ancient land of Quiche Mayans, the *Popul Vuh* and ancient cities. I dug down into my pocket and held it up in front of me.

It was a photo given to me by Dr. Oscar Padilla, a lawyer in Guatemala City, and it showed a huge stone statue of a man's face. The photo amazed not only me, but everyone I showed it to. It was many things to many people. It was an ancient Proto-Mayan figure to some, an Atlantean King to others or kin to the famous "Face On Mars" that looks into space surrounded by *Martian pyramids*.

The photo had first been printed in the newsletter of the *Ancient Astronaut Society*. I had since contacted Dr. Padilla and my search for one of the wonders of the world was to commence. I gazed at the face; at least thirty feet high with three people sitting on top of it. The nose was sharp and long, the lips thin. Eyelashes could be seen on the eyes. Perhaps that was just jungle growth...

I looked at the man standing next to the auto. What model was that? His face was covered in shadow. I assumed that he was the owner of the homestead that this statue was on.

Who was this ancient man in stone? It was as beautiful a statue as I had ever seen. I was certain that it was pre-Mayan. Were there more of these statues and possible ruins in the same area? I was determined to find out and my quest for the lost megaliths of Guatemala had begun.

After changing buses in Chuquimula, I caught another bus for Zacapa, where I stopped briefly at the Estanzuela Paleontology Museum, a small museum noted for its fossils of a megatherum (giant ground sloth), glyptodon (giant armadillo) and a mastodon skeleton. The nearby valley of Motagua is rich in fossil finds, and the reason for the rather remote location of the museum. I was interested to see the jaw of a full sized prehistoric horse, reminding me that horses are said to have originated in the Americas, yet curiously, did not exist in the Americas until the European invasion (at least so we are told, though some authors debate this). It is also interesting to note that both giant ground sloths and glyptodons are said to have become extinct circa 10,000 B.C. though there have been a number of reports of their still living in South America (see my book *Lost Cities & Ancient Mysteries of South America* 57).

After my brief visit to the museum I caught a bus for Los Amates in southeastern Guatemala, near Lago de Izabal and the Sierra del Espiritu Santo. Here, down a side road, was the ancient Mayan site of Quirigua.

Quirigua is famous because it has the largest steles in the Mayan world. Giant steles over 20 feet high were certainly of interest to me, and I gladly walked the few miles down a banana plantation road owned by the United Fruit Company of America to get a look at them. After paying one quetzal (about twenty five cents) admission to the site, I found myself in a large grassy plaza with a pyramid at one end and a number of gigantic and ornately carved steles at the other.

I stood in awe and wonder for a few moments, truly amazed at the height of the tall, thin moments and then began to examine the closest one to me. It was Stele D, about 20 feet tall with an oriental-looking man sporting a thin Chinese-type beard carved into the backside. Stele F, nearby, was even taller, and it too was carved with a bearded, Chinese-looking figure. According to a plaque at the base, the Mayan date, via the so-called long count system (the Mayan calendar and dating system is controversial with different schools of thought, although the long count is generally accepted) was 15 March 761 A.D.

Further along the grassy plaza was Stele E, which at 28 feet high, is the tallest Mayan stele known to exist. The long count date of the stele is said to be January 22, 771 A.D. Like the other steles, it is made of sandstone and weighs between 10 and 20 tons (twenty to forty thousand pounds). The steles were believed to have been brought from sandstone quarries more than ten miles away. Since the Mayans, like other early American cultures, allegedly did not use the wheel, the method for bringing the huge stones to the site is unknown. Ancient roads converging at Quirigua are thirty feet wide.

Lizards ran about the ruins and the occasional butterfly swept over the grass as I walked toward the crumbling pyramids at the southern end of the plaza. Quirigua, like Copan, is essentially a river city. In fact, the Honduran ruins of Copan are farther up river from Quirigua. That the steles might have arrived at the city by boat seemed a possible solution to their transportation.

Near the pyramids are the strange and gigantic "zoomorphic glyphs" that Quirigua is also famous for. These "zoomorphic glyphs" are gigantic stones four feet high and eight to ten feet long, roundish, and carved in a bizarre way that makes them appear to be monsters, often dinosaur and dragon-like animals, sometimes with a man coming out of the mouth. They literally appeared to be stylized extinct monsters, though more conservative guesses claim that they are jaguars or lizards.

Zoomorph B was a massive stone, weighing 20 tons or more, I guessed, with a man coming out of a monster's mouth. It was given a date of Nov. 30, 780 A.D. (long count). I wondered if they had been carved in place, as if they had had nothing more to do with a couple of gigantic boulders in the middle of their new city than carve them up into weird zoomorphic shapes.

My muse was instantly proven wrong by the fact that this massive stone was placed on top of three large cut slabs. Looking up, I gazed at the crumbling pyramids. Nicely fitted and dressed stones approximately two by three feet in size were fitted along the base without mortar. There were also small notch stones to fill in small gaps, much like the construction in the high Andes at Cuzco or Machu Picchu, or similarly at the ancient Phoenician city of Lixus in Morocco. Just as interestingly, the pyramid had once been faced with marble. A highly sophisticated plumbing and drainage system was also in place.

Quirigua was an unusual and fascinating place, quite reminiscent of Copán, an obvious sister city. The strong oriental flavor of the bearded men and weird dragon megaliths could not escape my notice. After climbing the crumbling pyramids and walking around the ball court, I returned through the plaza to the entrance. As I stepped back onto the road, there was one thing that seemed to be missing at Quirigua, that was the typical house platforms of northern Guatemala cities. Here, there were none. Was Quirigua merely a ceremonial center, and not an actual population center?

🐾🐾🐾

The next morning, after spending the night at a small guest house, I began to walk back toward the main road that would take me into Guatemala City. The sun shone brightly on my backpack. The endless banana fields were a wavy green. A young boy stood by the road; I tipped my hat to him, shouting "*Buenos dias!*"

He suddenly ran up to me and handed me a banana. I thanked him, and while hardly missing a step, began peeling it for my breakfast. Shortly thereafter I heard a banana truck rumbling down the road in my direction and waved them down, asking in international sign language for them to stop and give me a ride. They obliged, and I dumped my pack in the back and sat in the cab.

Two plantation workers gave me a ride to the main road, where I jumped off and began walking in the direction of Guatemala City. I flagged down a rusty mini bus going my way and climbed on board. I had barely taken a seat next to the driver when the van lurched into gear and was off down the road. I could not understand why it was so breezy in the van until I noticed that there was no windshield in front!

"Naturally air conditioned," said the driver, and we all laughed!

At the Rio Hondo crossroads I changed to a larger bus, which was, in fact, a converted Bluebird school bus made in Iowa, just like I used to ride to Junior High in. I leaned back in my seat and was soon being sucked into Guatemala City. It was late when I arrived, and I took a taxi to a hotel recommended to me, the Chalet Suizo on 14th street.

The next day, after looking around town a bit, I called Dr. Padilla to arrange a meeting concerning the photo of the giant statue and went out to the airport to meet a Swiss-American friend, George, who was flying in that afternoon.

"George!" I called as he came through immigration.

"David, good to see you," he said.

George was an experienced adventurer in his fifties, an engineer from Switzerland, who had traveled a great deal in Asia and Africa in the 1960s, had gotten married, had three daughters, divorced after twenty years of marriage and now lived near Chicago. Because we were both members of the World Explorers Club, George and I had arranged to meet in Guatemala many months before.

George sat his backpack down on the pavement outside of the airport. "Well, what's happening?" he said.

"We are having dinner tonight with Dr. Padilla, who sent me the photo of the giant statue," I told him. With that, we headed for the hotel, and then had a dinner meeting with Dr. Padilla, a lawyer by

74

profession and a keen explorer into the unknown.

Dr. Padilla was a middle-aged man with two children and a wife who lived in Venezuela. He apparently divided his time between them and his work in Guatemala. When it came to the mysterious megaliths of Guatemala, he was an expert.

After a few formalities, he took a drink of his *Gallo cerveza* and sadly informed us, "Unfortunately, the statue you seek has been destroyed."

"What?" demanded George.

"How could that be?" I asked. "It's so huge. How could it be destroyed?"

"It was destroyed by revolutionaries along the Pacific coast about ten years ago. We have located the statue too late. It was used as target practice by anti-government rebels. They totally disfigured it, sort of like, the way the Sphinx in Egypt had its nose shot off by the Turks, only worse!"

"That's terrible!" cried George.

"When did this happen?" I asked.

"About 1981," said Dr. Padilla. "I have been searching for fifteen years for this statue. Only a year ago I learned the location. But it was too late."

We were all silent for a moment, saddened by this news that one of the worlds great archaeological and artistic treasures had been destroyed.

I pulled out a map of Guatemala, and Dr. Padilla then began pointing out to us where the monument, what was left of it, could be found. "Other gigantic, pre-Mayan monuments can be found nearby in this area," he said, pointing to the town of the La Democracia near the Pacific coast. "And here," he said, pointing to to a small dot on the map, you will find strange and unusual statues and heads."

George and I invited Dr. Padilla to accompany us, but he had to stay behind and help monitor the upcoming national election being held that weekend.

The next day, George and I rented a car, and with George behind the wheel of the Toyota Corolla, we were racing out of Guatemala City, past Lago de Amatitlan toward the town of Escuintla. From there we turned west and then south to the small town of La Democracia.

We pulled into the main square of La Democracia and parked. It was a small, sleepy town, and ours was the only car on the square. Even before I managed to get out, I was amazed: gigantic "Olmec" statues were situated in a ring around the plaza. I immediately got my camera and began to wander the park and take photographs. These were some of the strangest statues I had ever seen!

Typical of the famous "Olmec heads" (I have been informed by archaeologists that the term "Olmec" is no longer popular, and the term "proto-Mayan" is now preferred) of Tabasco state in Mexico, these gigantic basalt heads and full bodies were often Negroid in appearance. Quite a number of them were large, fat men with wide noses, thick lips and their arms wrapped around their stomachs. They had huge, goggle eyes, similar to statues at Tiahuanaco in

Bolivia. The stone was of the hardest kind, basalt or granite.

Some of these fat figures may have been women, Mother-Goddess figures who were pregnant, though they seemed like men. Others were bizarre Asian type heads, one had ram horns curling down on his head and strange signs on his cheeks. I had the impression of a tattooed Sumo wrestler from Japan.

After walking around the park, George and I entered the museum, paying 25 centavos (about seven cents) to enter. Inside were more giant heads, these with large patches of lichen on them. There were carved mushroom stones that measured one to one-and-a-half feet tall. I conjectured that they probably referred to psychedelic mushrooms, the divine Soma of the ancient near East and India. There were solar discs in stone, a Jade Mask (probably the museum's most important piece) some very large stone pots and stone maces.

There were also stone "yokes" (U-shaped stones of granite about a two feet long). According to a sign in the museum these were for "holding a victim's neck while his living heart was torn out"!

One sign in the museum said that "Mexican influence in 1000 A.D.—Kulkulkan surfaced in the Mayan Pantheon and Mexican rule encompassed the entire Mayan territory. With this integration the best of Mayan civilization was exported into the Mexican culture and the Mexicans imposed their bloody worship on the Mayas."

Another sign in the museum claimed that the Mayan homeland was a land called Tulan to the north. The current Tulan is in Hidalgo state in Mexico, though I was fascinated to note the similarity to the word Thule. Thule was allegedly a land in the present day arctic, which existed in the time of Atlantis, and is now covered with ice. Adolf Hitler and many high ranking Nazis were members of a secret society called the the Thule Society. Today, an American Air Force base located on the north west coast of Greenland is named Thule. Was there any connection between the Mayan homeland Tulan and the ancient, mystical land of the Thule? It was a bizarre thought.

Perhaps the most interesting items of all in the museum were quite tiny. They were in a glass case near the door, and they were stone seals about two inches high. Having lived in Taiwan, Hong Kong and China back in the mid-1970s, I was quite familiar with Chinese seals, and had several of them myself. The owner's name in an artistic motif is carved into the base and it is used with lacquer or ink to authenticate documents, letters, etc. In China they are called "chops." What these "proto-Mayan" versions were called, we have no idea, yet they were obviously seals.

❀❀❀

I tipped the curator of the museum several Quetzals (eight times the admission price) as I left and walked back out into the bright sunlight of La Democracia. George and I then walked around the park again and left. As we drove out of town, we discussed the strange museum and statues in the park.

"Pretty weird stuff, eh?" said George, swinging around a truck and accelerating into the open road. Sugar cane fields were on either side of us, and volcanoes could be seen in the distance.

"I'll say," I replied. "This is old stuff, older than any Mayan artifacts."

"Olmec stuff from northern Mexico, right?" asked George.

"Well, that is one of the debates among archaeologists," I replied. "It is admitted that this stuff, like that found at La Venta in Tabasco state of Mexico, came before the Mayans. They use the term 'Olmec,' which means 'Rubber People,' but there is a hot debate as to where these people originated. Traditionally they are said to have originated in the Gulf Coast region of Tabasco, though others claim that they originated on the Pacific coast of Guatemala because of all of these strange statues."

"Probably they are all wrong," commented George dryly, hitting the main east — west road. We headed west, searching for a remote and little-known farm that Dr. Padilla had told us about, *Finca el Baul.*

When I saw two American-looking young men in pressed white shirts, black ties and black slacks, walking along the road, I told George to stop.

"Why?" he asked.

"Because those are Mormon missionaries," I replied, "and they probably know where this Finca el Baul is." I was absolutely correct, and they did know where the farm was.

"Up this road for about five miles and then to the left," one said helpfully after I had asked him directions. "Why do you want to go there?"

I told him about the strange, ancient statues that were supposed to be there, and suggested that he may want to visit them himself sometime, though I had yet to visit the site. "Yes, it sounds interesting, I think I would!" he replied. We thanked him for the directions, and headed up the narrow paved road to the north.

After a few miles, we stopped and asked a road crew where the "finca" (farm) was. They pointed up a small road, and within a minute we had arrived at what was essentially a cooperative sugar cane processing station. As we parked our car at the main office, I asked a man standing by the porch if this was the Finca el Baul.

Yes, it was, he replied. What did we want there?

"We are looking for a giant statue," I told him Spanish. "We were told that we might find it here."

Just then George called to me, "David, look at this!"

Around to the other side of the house was an open building with a corrugated tin roof. Inside it was one of the most bizarre collections of statues I had ever seen! The worker went inside and got a key to the gate and allowed us to enter this fascinating, private museum. The delight on my face pleased the caretaker, and he stood by watching George and I as we walked in awe around the gigantic granite figures and steles, all pre-Mayan.

There were at least twenty or thirty megalithic figures, many of bearded men and others of monsters, dragons and jaguar-men. Other blocks of stone were rectangular ornamental blocks or smaller skulls with wide eyes and a toothy grin. There was a huge ancient stele, with a large glyph said to be the ancient Mayan glyph for jade, the only recognizable glyph, except for some Mayan numerals of dots and dashes.

I was particularly fascinated by a large stele with man in a jaguar mask. It was eight-and-a-half feet high with an Egyptian-like collar (I am referring to a collar that is wide, and was typically made out of gold or copper plates, the Mayans wore similar collars). He was conquering a bearded prisoner and there were three round glyphs in the upper portion of the stele. One of the glyphs was of a man coming out of a cloud (?) in the upper left corner. At the bottom of the stele were six cross-legged men with their arms folded across their chest.

Another statue was a massive stone head, three feet high of a bearded man with an Egyptian-type headdress and collar. Many statues had their arms crossed, and one was headless, though it had a stone pin to fit into the socket of a head, now gone. Another was of a dragon head with crab claws. A skull sculpture had a snake coming out of it's head. Another large statue had a huge, five-feet-tall, solid granite jaguar sitting up like a dog begging. It too had a large, Egyptian-like wide collar around it's neck. It had fangs and its tongue was sticking out.

There was also a six-foot high head without a body that had an elaborate headdress on and no beard. There was a hole through the top of his head, possibly to suspend the statue from ropes. Perhaps the most curious of all was a rectangular stone pillar about three feet high with a perfectly round ball on top. The whole thing was carved out a solid piece of granite and two Maltese crosses were carved onto each side. It sort of reminded me of a small street light-globe that one might find in the garden of a hotel or something, though made out of granite, I couldn't imagine what its function might have been.

All of these things had just bccn found lying around in the fields by workers when they began clearing them for sugar cane planting. Yet, the best was yet to come. I asked about a gigantic head that Dr. Padilla had told me could be found in the vicinity and the caretaker went and brought a hunchbacked teenaged boy, to guide us to the site.

Our guide's name was Fredrico, and he was a handsome, and obviously intelligent young man who had been born on the plantation. Because of his deformity, he was sort of the house boy of the plantation headquarters, and did not work in the fields like the others.

Fredrico guided us back to the main road and then up several dirt roads to a small, little used track through the sugar cane fields. Then we arrived a small mound and parked the car. Walking around a portion of the mound, we were suddenly shocked to see what I call the Giant Head of El Baul. It was a massive, 8 ton head, partially buried, with a hook nose, headdress, ear rings and big eyes.

Just as astonishing, there were two men there worshiping the ancient statue! Fredrico explained that people will come to this remote site and pray to the "ancients" for good luck, wealth, happiness or a special favor. They burn incense, a traditional Mayan (also Hindu) custom, light five candles around the base of the statue, and make offerings of food, liquor and jade.

I examined the statue closely, as the two worshippers backed away for a few moments. It was made out of extremely hard basalt and was covered with soot and wax from candles and incense. From the lower lip it was still buried in the earth, and the portion above ground stood five feet high. Behind it there were grooves that were seemingly for attaching it to a building or some other stone structure, perhaps a massive body.

A second megalith was nearby, a six-foot stele entirely above ground and beneath a tree. A man with a headdress, clean shaven, stood facing to the right. Around his head were nine circles. There were six circles on the left and three on the right. The third circle on the right had an animal, with a collar in it, facing the man. I looked at the animal trying to figure out what kind of animal it might be. My own conclusion surprised even me!

"George," I called, "what kind of animal do you think that this is?"

George looked at it and concluded, "I think that must be a bull. Look at the ears and snout. It is just like a bull. I can't think of any other animal it could be."

That was my conclusion as well. I then noticed that the man in the stele was wearing a skirt (like the ancient Egyptians wore, or like the Scots and their kilts) and that there was another circle on the skirt which had a ram inside it. Neither of these animals were supposed to be in the new world before the Spanish invasion!

Could the bull represent the Age of Taurus and the Ram the Age of Aries? The main avenue leading into the famous Karnak Temple at Thebes (modern Luxor) was lined with statues of Rams on either side, symbolizing the Age of Aries.

If the symbols represent the passing of the age of Taurus into the Age of Aries, that would place the date of the stele at approximately 2500 B.C. As a proto-Mayan "Olmec" date, that would fit well, though more stuffy academics might feel that this was a bit old. Certainly, they would find it hard to admit that a bull and ram were featured on an ancient American stele.

I asked Fredrico what the name of this place was.

"*El Castillo* (the castle)," he told me. When I asked him if the gigantic head, currently being worshipped by the two men, had a name, he replied, that it had no special name.

Looking around, I realized, just like the gigantic statues at La Democracia, there had to be more. Where were the buildings? Most of this stuff was buried or half buried. The gigantic statues at the finca had just been lying around in fields, also buried, when discovered. It seemed obvious to me that at one point this whole Pacific area of Guatemala had been a thriving, sophisticated, megalithic culture. As I am wont to often ask, "where are the lost cities?"

"Buried," I said under my breath, looking at the mounds around me. This "castle," if excavated, would no doubt reveal more structures. Indeed, there were a number of large, squared blocks lying around, once part of whatever structure that had once contained the statues.

Many of the massive statues found in the park in La Democracia came from a nearby pyramid site named Monte Alto. Today, and even in classical Mayan times, apparently, this area was a wilderness backwater. Most of the statues were probably buried even then. What cataclysmic change had wiped out this bizarre and fascinating civilization? Could it have been the same alleged cataclysm of the Bible, Sumerian texts, Hopi and Chinese legends? It seemed plausible to me. The varied racial nature of the different statues, everything from Negroid heads, Asiatic types and bearded Mediterraneans seemed to be in evidence here. At the very least, even the stuffy, conservative academics touting the isolationist view of world history had to admit that this stuff was old, very old. As far as I know, there is no conclusive dating on any of these strange artifacts.

We left the Giant Head of El Baul to be worshipped by the two men, who were obviously relieved to be able to continue their ceremonies without the disruptive gaze of a couple of gringos. Fredrico guided us back to the plantation headquarters. George and I gave him a big tip as we let him out, and he thanked us graciously. He was a nice kid, and obviously intelligent. I wished him the best, hoping that perhaps he would have a chance to continue his education at a university, and would not spend the rest of his life sweeping up the plantation offices.

🐗🐗🐗

George and I pointed the rented car west and headed for Retalhuleu, a major commercial center along the western Pacific coast. We passed no less than three bridges that had been bombed by the recently active revolutionary army of Guatemala. The large steel girder bridges were twisted and broken by the sabotage. The roads were diverted to make-shift bridges down by the river banks. We stopped by the ancient Mayan site of Abaj Takalik near El Asintal, where I showed my photo of the giant head to a young female Guatemalan archaeologist named Liwy.

It seemed familiar to her and she asked several other workers at the site if they had seen this statue. Several believed it to be the same statue that we had just seen at El Baul, but I informed them that it was different.

Liwy showed us the Abaj Takalik site. It had been named by an American archaeologist named Susan Miles who had discovered the site in 1965. The name was Quiché Mayan for "stones standing up." A dated Mayan stele at the site gave the date (in long count) as 126 A.D. although so-called Olmec statues have been found at the site, pushing the date back hundreds or even thousands of years. A 1902 volcanic eruption had covered the entire site in volcanic ash. There is a pyramid at the site, a number of steles, all of which have been purposely destroyed and pushed over. A carved stone by the river was said by some archaeologists to be Olmec and dated at about 600 B.C. Others are more conservative.

"The most important thing about Abaj Takalik," said Liwy, "is that excavation proves that the Mayas were also on the south Pacific coast, this had always been a controversial issue before. There is also a strong debate as to whether the Olmecs originated in this area, or on the gulf coast of Mexico. Anyway, we archaeologists in Guatemala and Mexico (Liwy had gotten her Ph.D. at the University of Mexico in Mexico City) do not like to use the term 'Olmec' anymore, as it is devoid of meaning. These days, we prefer to call these statues 'proto-Mayan'. "

George and I were just getting ready to leave, when Liwy came running up and gave me an article. "Here, I found an article on your stone head! But I am afraid it is not so ancient as you think. It was only made in 1936! Here, read it!"

I was amazed at her last statement, and as George and I headed for our hotel in Retahuleu at dusk, I read aloud the strange article on the giant head.

Written by an American archaeologist named Lee A. Parsons in 1973, the brief article was entitled, "A Pseudo Pre-Columbian Colossal Stone Head On The Pacific Coast of Guatemala." (Sorry, I do not know what publication this article is from). In the report Parsons states, "Since A. Ledyard Smith appeared in some of the photographs (of the head), I then asked him for the story of this sculpture. He and Richardson (the Massachusetts archaeologist Francis B. Richardson) had found it during Pacific coastal reconnaissance for the Carnegie Institution of Washington in the 1941-42 season. Smith recalled that the carving was situated on a finca called Las Victorias in the department of Retalhuleu, Guatemala. He also pointed out the commemorative plaque in the photos which was inscribed with the date of dedication. The plaque read, 'E.G.M. 16 Abril 1936'. They were told that this enormous monu-ment was created by the administrator of the farm as a memorial to his deceased wife. Apparently the initials pertain to that person.

"When we relocated the sculture in 1970 it already was laced with tropical vines and creepers and was considerably eroded. Moreover, the identifying inscribed plaque had disappeared. The present administrator of the finca knew absolutely nothing about the history of the carving. It was just there, like so many other stone sculptures of the Pacific coast....The colossal stone head stands in an uncultivated narrow ravine only a few hundred meters north of the road and about the same distance west of the toll road. Because of the lush vegetation it now cannot be seen until one is immediately in front of it—when it looms like Neptune rising from the sea. The total height is between twenty and twenty-five feet. It was carved in situ from the face of a consolidated pumice cliff. The base of the monument presumably is still attached to the matrix of the volcanic outcrop, though the back is cut free. The sandy, porous nature of the rock would have permitted relatively easy carving, but the effort nevertheless must have been considerable. The elongated face is tilted slightly upward and rests solidly on a thick neck. The eyes are closed, the nose is long and sharp and the mouth is straight.

"One wonders what model was used for this ambitious monument. Possibly it was the famous Easter Island heads or, more likely, the Mount Rushmore heads of United States' presidents. Whatever the inspiration, its very existence could confound future archaeologists and lead to unwarranted explanations of transpacific contacts or even of mysterious Pre-Columbian megalithic complexes. Anticipating such interpretations, I have titled this paper a 'pseudo' Pre-Columbian colossal stone head. actually there was no intention whatsoever to defraud, but through the years the sculpture has become increasingly difficult to identify. Therefore, it is here recorded that the Las Victorias stone head is recent, having been carved in 1936. Further, it has no meaningful relationship to any American Indian, living or dead. I regret that I am unable to supply the name of the Guatemalan for whom the monument is a true modern memorial."

Later at the hotel I read the article again and mused over it. Was this head *really* constructed in 1936? Well, it was certainly possible, but elements of the story just didn't add up, I thought. Apparently, the plaque 'E.G.M. 16 Abril 1936' did indeed exist at one time on the statue. Yet the identity of the carver and his wife, whom the statue was allegedly dedicated to, remained a mystery. They were told that this enormous monument was created by the administrator of the farm as a memorial to his deceased wife and apparently the initials pertain to that person. Yet, the statue was obviously not of anyone's dead wife, and was apparently a man. Could it be that the plaque did not commemorate the carving of the statue but rather the discovery of it? Was E.G.M. the explorer (and possible land-owner or local) rather than a deceased spouse?

Furthermore, it is curious that no less than five years after the alleged carving of the admittedly colossal statue, no one could remember who made it? I find that more incredible than the possibility that it may be a genuine ancient artifact. Parsons' statement about "unwarranted explanations of transpacific con-tacts or even of mysterious Pre-Columbian megalithic complexes," is curious because mysterious Pre-Columbian megalithic complexes do indeed exist in this area as evidenced by the gigantic statues at El Baul and Monte Alto. They are exactly that, and no one doubts that they are both Pre-Columbian and pre-Mayan!

Personally, I would call a bunch of gigantic, magnificently carved basalt and granite statues lying helter-skelter and buried along the Pacific coast of Guatemala rather mysterious. Though many of the so-called experts apparently find nothing particularly interesting in this fact. Nor, curiously, do they find it strange that these bizarre statues feature just about every race of mankind and wear some pretty curious clothing and ornaments.

Later I was told that the builder of the statue was not the farmer on whose land it exists, but, actually carved by the engineer of the highway being built in 1925 from Quetzaltenango to Retalhuleu. This man was apparently the sculpter of the giant stone, though his exact name escapes history. It is said that he used George Washington as his model. Unlike Mount Rushmore, the stone in this head was quite soft, making it easy to carve, and easy to destroy, as well.

"Do you think that statue was really carved in 1925?" asked George over dinner at the Hotel Don José in Retalhuleu.

"I don't know," I answered honestly. "It doesn't quite all add up, although I can accept that the statue is of modern manufacture. It is curious, though, that such a massive monument, carved so recently, would have just faded into obscurity within five or six years? Even the Carnegie Institution expedition in 1941-42 could not find the alleged originator of the statue, only the plaque. Well, it does kind of look like George Washington, though."

"Could be," said George, sipping his *Cabro cerveza.* "Could be."

๑๑๑

The next day George and I drove back over the mountains into the central highlands of Guatemala. We stopped for lunch at Quetzaltenango, the second largest city in Guatemala and then headed on down to Chichicastenango, an Indian town with a famous handicraft market. We continued on to Santa Cruz del Quiché, the capital of El Quiché department, and three kilometers further west to the ruined city of Utatlán, or Cumarcaj, as the inhabitants called it, the pre-Conquest capital of the Quiché Mayans.

Surrounded by deep canyons and approachable only by steep steps and a narrow causeway, Utatlán was the center for the royal court and priests. The common people lived outside the fortress.

In 1524, Tecún Umán, one of the Quiché rulers, was killed in single combat by Pedro de Alvarado near the present site of Quetzaltenango. the Quiché lords invited the Spanish to their capital, planning to trap them inside and burn them alive. Alvarado discovered the plot and had the Quiché nobility burned and destroyed the city. Some of the stones were removed and used to construct the city of Santa Cruz del Quiché.

George parked the car and we got out to walk around the pleasant, grassy hilltop, now a state park and archaeological site. Because of the intentional destruction of the fortress, not much remained of the city, though the remains of two sloped pyramids were quite evident. The buildings of the city were once covered with plaster, but little remains of them.

A herd of sheep moved lazily through the ruins as George and I strolled casually through. We then met a local man who offered to guide us to a tunnel which he told us all tourists must see. Both George and I eagerly agreed, and the man led us down a hill to the north of the city to the beginning a tunnel system that went beneath the city.

With flashlights and a torch, we cautiously entered the tunnel,

83

following our   guide. It had a high ceiling, twelve feet or more
followed it in for a hundred yards. Side tunnels branched off the
main tunnel and our guide told us that they went to the main plaza
and pyramid temple. At the end of one tunnel, it was obvious that
someone had been burning incense in a prayer or to ask a favor of
the ancient gods.

To the right, on one side tunnel, was a deep shaft that dropped
down for twenty feet or so. Using my flashlight, I attempted to
illuminate the pit. A tunnel seemed to extend from the south side of
the pit. I asked our guide what this was.

He explained that it was a tunnel going south which was believed
to go for several miles, under a river, and to the nearby fortress town
of Paismachi.

I asked him if it might be possible to follow this tunnel all the way
to Paismachi, a town eight kilometers or more away. He replied that
it was not possible to go the entire way as the tunnel had collapsed
at some point. George and looked at each other with expressions of
wonder. This was indeed a strange find, the first of many mysterious
tunnel systems in North America I was to come in contact with.

🌸🌸🌸

George and I drove back to Chichicastenango and explored the
market for the rest of the afternoon. On a hill above the city is a
small stone idol, only a few few tall called Pascual Abaj. It is an
ancient statue, now partly destroyed because orthodox Catholics
had resented the continued worshipping of the stone and had
attempted to destroy it in the 1950s.

We hiked the kilometer up a hill above the city and visited the
statue. It was small and unimpressive compared to the massive
statues found at El Baul and La Democracia. A headless duck and
some flowers had been placed before it by worshipers a few days
before. George and I took a few obligatory photos and left.

From Chichicastenango we drove to Panajachel, on the popular
lake of Atitlan. Panajachel is something of the main tourist hangout
in Guatemala, and suddenly we were attacked by curio hawkers and
typical tourist souvenir shops. Despite the obvious feeling of over-
developed tourism, Panajachel was a pleasant and refreshing break.

One night at a local restaurant, George and I met two other
tourists, an Aussie gal named Sharon and an American named
Leslie. They were both here in Guatemala as part of their clothing
export business. When George informed Leslie that he was driving
back to Guatemala City the next day, she asked him if she could
have a ride. Since I was staying for a few more days at the lake,
George was happy to give her a ride and they arranged to meet the
next day at the home of a local artist where she was staying.

We arrived the next day in the early afternoon, and Leslie
introduced us to her hostess, Paloma, in whose small but
comfortable house she had been staying in. Paloma looked more

84

Italian or Spanish than Guatemalan with platinum blonde hair that formed a large Veronica Lake wave down over one eye. She also had a strong limp. It took Leslie about thirty minutes to get her things together, and during that time Paloma, George and I had a nice conversation about Guatemala and Lake Atitlan. I was curious about Paloma's limp, wondering if she perhaps had an artificial leg.

As I helped Leslie get her luggage into George's rented car, I asked her if Paloma had an artificial leg.

"Oh, no," said Leslie, her voice low. "She hurt her toe. Her big toenail came off and her toe hurts terribly!"

I waved goodbye to George as he and Leslie took off out of the driveway. When I turned, Paloma was standing there by the door, her platinum blonde hair curled down over one eye and her glossy red lips forming slowly the words, "Come inside, I'll make you some tea."

While a cup of tea brewed she asked me about my expeditions and books. In return I asked her about her art and jewelry business. In the end it seemed natural to go out to dinner, to which I invited her.

We enjoyed a nice meal and then I invited her for a drink at the nearby club, which she had recommended earlier. Once there, she drank several quick *cuba libres* (rum and cola) and then started to dance. I learned, bit by bit throughout the evening, that she was the daughter of a career military officer and diplomat and was divorced with two teenage sons. She was an artist in ceramics and had lived in Spain when her father had been the Guatemalan ambassador. She had narrowly escaped being gunned down as a little girl in Guatemala City during a military coup in the 50s. She had followed the general, her father's friend, after he had kissed her and said goodbye. Suddenly, her mother and nursemaid grabbed her and held her from running down the estate's driveway after the general.

"Moments later," she recalled, taking a gulp of her *cuba libre,* and ordering another, "I heard the machine gunfire. The military had assassinated him. I might have been with him..."

Suddenly a snappy tune was pulsating through the dance floor. She grabbed me and we danced. Her bleached blonde hair flowed down over one eye and she eyed me seductively with the other. The two *cuba libres* had taken their effect, and I was quickly moving to the sensual Latin beat.

I sat down for a moment and talked with a young traveler from Vancouver, Canada, who was sitting near to me. Suddenly, a fight broke out between Paloma and another girl, apparently a Guatemalan. Friends broke up the fight, and Paloma came and sat next to me, her face flushed.

"Did you see her push me?" she asked. I admitted that I hadn't. "She just pushed me for no reason."

"Maybe it was just an accident," I suggested. "Do you know her?"

"I've never seen her before in my life," said Paloma. "I'm sure she is from Guatemala City. She is lucky, I could really hurt her."

Paloma starting a bar room brawl at Lake Atitlan that night was not part of my schedule, so I suggested that we leave. I had already promised to walk her home. Suddenly, a German in a black leather jacket and a shaved head began to bother her. Apparently they knew each other.

She cursed at him and then turned to me and said, "Let's go!"

She was in a foul mood when we left the bar. She still limped, but feeling no pain from the alcohol she had consumed. She was ready to let some one have it, especially the Guatemalan tourist back at the bar. "I'd better not see her tomorrow..." she threatened. Suddenly she drew a pistol out of her purse and held it up to the moon. "I'll show her how I defend myself!"

She was like some Betty Davis underworld chick from a detective movie of the 40s. Plus she was raised in a violent military atmosphere and ready to pull the trigger on anyone who crossed her. I wondered if her limp was from nicking her toe with a bullet. She was definitely intoxicated, and the gun in her hand gave me a momentary shock.

"I've got my pistol. Let them come after me!" And she suddenly laughed. I steadied her as she limped over a sewage drain. She then confessed to me that some years before a thief had broken into her house, hit her over the head and raped her. Since then she keeps two dogs in the house and carries a gun. Now that Leslie was gone she was in the house alone.

We came to her house, and after quieting her dogs, she let me in.

"Will you stay the night, as a gentleman?" she asked me. "The bed is big enough for two." I could see that with her friend Leslie gone, she was still a bit afraid to stay in her house alone. I said that I would stay.

"Will you change my dressing?" she asked, reclining back on the bed.

With scissors, I cut away the tape, and then dressed her toe with antibiotic powder. As I finished winding her foot with gauze and surgical tape, I looked back and saw that her eyes were closed. She was asleep.

After pulling the covers over her, I picked up the pistol, a small Brazilian revolver, and looked at it. She was a wild, unpredictable woman. And not one to mess with, I decided. Carefully I unloaded each chamber of the revolver and placed it on the dresser next to me.

I pulled back the woven Quiché Mayan bedspread and slid beneath the sheets. My quest for the ancient megaliths of Guatemala had yielded many surprises. As my head hit the pillow, my thoughts were muddled by the rum of the evening. Before the wave of sleep came over me, I smiled at the strange evening that had just happened and the thought that lay on my mind as I fell into the deep: Guatemala was like the woman next to me—wild and unpredictable.

The photo of the mysterious statue which sparked our hunt in Guatemala.

One of the smaller stelae found at Quirigua.
Photo by Maudsley, 1890.

Cylinder Seal from Tlatilco (Mexico) with stylized writing. (Milwaukee Public Museum photo.) This writing has not yet been identified.

Cylindrical and Stamp Seals from the Pacific coast, now in the Guatemala City Museum. Seals like this, for officially sealing documents or letters, is a common Asian practice. They are nearly identical to Chinese seals, still in use today.

Colossal head from Monte Alto (Monument 3) and now in the city park of La Democracia, Guatemala. Five and half feet tall with ram's horns, pug nose, slanted eyes and designs on cheeks.

Monument 1 from Monte Alto. A gigantic head nearly
five feet high. Now at the city park of La Democracia.

Left: Monument 4 from Monte Alto. 5 feet high. These giant statues were mostly buried until discovered while clearing sugar cane fields in the 1950s. Right: Monument 5 from Cerro de las Mesas near Vera Cruz, Jalapa, Mexico. It is very similar to megalithic statues found on the Pacific slopes of Guatemala. Note the strange, Egyptian-type "fake" beard.

Left: The Great Tiger of El Baul. 7 feet tall. Middle: "Olmec" Monument 47 from Bilbao, Mexico. 3 feet 8 inches tall. Right: 5 foot tall statue found at Finca Arévalo in Guatemala. While plenty of giant heads and other statues have been found, where is the rest of this ancient civilization?

Monument 3, in a cane field outside of El Baul. This gigantic head is five feet high and half buried in the ground. It is still worshipped by locals as a god.

Chapter 4

Guatemala's Northern Jungles:

Lost Cities of the Maya

*There are some secrets which
do not permit themselves to be told.*
—Edgar Allan Poe, *The Man of the Crowd*

I woke up late the next morning and staring about the room, I wondered where I was. Then I remembered the night before. Paloma was gone, and I was still wearing my clothes, though I had taken off my shoes and socks. The pistol that I had placed on the dresser was now gone, back to the safety of Paloma's purse, I surmised.

Hearing some activity in the kitchen, I carefully peered out the bedroom door to be sure some jealous boyfriend or ex-husband wasn't in the house. It was only Paloma and her maid. After the obligatory cup of coffee for breakfast, I said goodbye to Paloma and her dogs, and left for my hotel. There was much to do, and I wanted to get up to the northern Petén jungle area of Guatemala as soon as I could.

As the bus was winding along the mountain roads by Lake Amatitlán, I recalled the curious tale of underwater archaeological discoveries reported by Stephan Borhegyi. In an article entitled "Underwater Archaeology in Guatemala," published at the Thirty Third International Congress of Americanists in 1959, and reprinted in Leo Duel's classic book *Conquistadors Without Swords*,[120] Borhegyi describes his underwater discoveries of 1957-58: "Beautiful Lake Amatitlán, known by its Maya name meaning 'under (or near) the Amatle tree,' is a popular resort area only 17 miles south of Guatemala City....The lake is seven and one-half miles long, three and a quarter miles wide, and its depth varies from 30 to 131 feet. Lava hills surround the lake, which owes its origin to a volcanic dam, subsequently breached by the Rio Michatoya working headward up the Pacific slope. The major inlet, the Rio Lobos, has built a large delta into the lake on the north side, and the river has shifted its course so that it now has its outlet close to the extreme right edge of the delta....

"Meanwhile we also proceeded with the mapping of the archaeological sites located on the southern shore of the lake. *Contreras* (Site B on Borhegyi's map), the oldest, shows continuous occupation from the beginning to the end of the Maya Formative period (approximately 1000 B.C. to 200 B.C.). None of the five mounds of the site have been examined more than cursorily except for a burial in Mound 2 that was exposed by treasure hunters. *Contreras* lies at or a little above the level of the modern lake, which suggests that this level has not been higher than today for the last two thousand years or more, but more excavation is needed to establish this important point. The Early Classic (300 to 600 A.D.) site of *Mejicanos* (Site C) consisting of four mounds is also at or a little above the lake level while the large (about 25 mounds including 2 ballcourts) late Classic (600 to 900 A.D.) site of *Amatitlán* (Site A) is on higher ground. Movement to higher, more easily defensible positions, however, was characteristic Maya behavior during periods of disturbance, and does not necessarily imply that the lake level rose. Two additional archaeological sites were located during the summer of 1958. Contreras Alto (Site D1) and Los Jicaques (Site D2) were discovered on the slopes some 500 feet higher than the previously known site Contreras (Site B). Both sites must have been quite extensive with large mounds and excellently cut cyclopean masonry...."

Borhegyi and his divers discovered hundreds of pieces of ceramics underwater during their many dives. Continues Borhegyi: "Another important discovery was made by Mr. James Kitchen, a local petroleum geologist. We were test diving at Lavaderos (Site 1A) when Mr. Kitchen surfaced with a rather ordinary looking face-neck jar. This brown-black ware jar with a modeled Tlaloc face on the neck was found 30 feet from the shore at a depth of 20 feet. It was unusually heavy and upon investigation turned out to contain liquid mercury. After further cleaning we also found in the jar fragments of cinnabar, graphite, and nearly 400 of what appeared to be ceremonially smashed fragments of jade ear spools. This is the fourth instance that a vessel, containing liquid mercury, has been found under archaeological conditions in the New World. In all three previous instances...offerings also contained, in addition to shell and pearls, jade and cinnabar and were of Early Classic date. The Tlaloc jar with its unusual contents suggests that some of the specimens found under the waters of Lake Amatitlán must have been special offerings to the lake gods and were ceremonially cast into the lake waters."[120]

Borhegyi mentions the presence of geysers and natural hot springs, which he feels may have inspired awe in the locals, causing them to throw offerings into the lake. Yet some discoveries could not be explained that way. Says Borhegyi, "On the southern shore many of the offering bowls were found stacked in piles and in some cases the incense burners were found in groups of four or five, standing erect and occasionally embedded in lava on the lake floor. This may indicate that to placate the angry volcano many of the objects were placed along the shore within the lava flow and were carried by the flow into the lake. Other artifacts, haphazardly strewn over the lake floor, were found so distant from shore and at such a great depth that they must have been thrown deliberately into the lake as ceremonial offerings."[120]

Borhegyi seems to avoid any discussion of the possibility that there may actually be sunken ruins in the lake, a point that seems obvious. Although literally hundreds of ceramic vessels, including some stacked vessels which could not have possibly been thrown in the lake were found, the possibility of the lake's having risen or some other earth change was not a popular theory among archaeologists of the fifties. He prefers to believe that the pots were carried into the lake by a lava flow, which could possibly explain those pots being embedded in lava (still, this seems a bit far fetched) but could hardly explain stacked and nested pots that are not embedded in lava.

Two other things in Borhegyi's paper bear repeating: the mention of "excellently cut cyclopean masonry" and the fascinating discovery of a vessel containing mercury and cinnabar (also jade). Mercury is a rare and important metal, especially to alchemists. Cinnabar is a mineral from which mercury is obtained through smelting. Cinnabar/Mercury mines are extremely rare, and their location in Central America is not known. Today, Mercury is used in a large variety of electrical devices, vacuum pumps, liquid seals, fluorescent lamps, and thermometers. Mercury was used by hat makers in Europe, but the exact uses of Mercury to the Mayas, besides offerings to the gods, is today unknown. Where the Mayas got their Mercury, how they refined it, and what it was used for, remains a mystery to archaeologists.

Curiously, Mercury was also the important element in the power source of ancient Indian-Hindu *Vimanas*, a type of ancient aircraft described in the Ramayana and the Mahabharata and allegedly in use during the Rama Empire.[138]

Is there a sunken city in Lake Amatitlán? Perhaps it is covered by a lava flow. Embedded in parts of that lava flow are ancient Mayan ceramics. Other lakes in North America, such as Lake Texcoco, where Mexico City stands today contains sunken cities and several lakes in the U.S., including Rock Lake in Wisconsin, have underwater ruins in them. Why not Lake Amatitlán in Guatemala?

🜨🜨🜨

The bus arrived back to Guatemala City, and after spending the night, I caught a flight up to Flores on Lake Petén the next morning. The flight was early in the morning, and only an hour north into the dense, unpopulated Petén area of Guatemala—an area that houses some of the most astonishing architecture in the world. It was abandoned about a thousand years ago and the disappearance of this civilization is still one of the great mysteries of history.

I took a taxi from the airport into the town of Santa Elena, and then over the causeway to the island city of Flores. At the Hotel Casona de la Isla, I met a traveller from California named Albert.

"Are you going to Tikal?" asked Albert. We were standing at the dock in the back yard of the small hotel. The lake stretched out blue and calm in front of us. Jungle covered hills and some boats could be seen in the distance.

"Yes, I wouldn't miss it for anything. How long have you been here?"

"Just two days. I flew right up here from Guatemala City and I've been here for a day. Its a nice town. Tomorrow I am heading for Tikal," he said. "The mini-bus leaves at six in the morning."

"I'll go with you," I said, throwing a stone into the water, "Flores will be my base for the next few weeks."

The beautiful island city of Flores was founded in 1700, and is the successor to the last stronghold of the Mayans. Centuries after Tikal and other cities in the Petén had been abandoned, some of the inhabitants of Chichén Itzá in the Yucatán migrated southward and founded the city of Tayasal on an island in the lake they called Petén Itzá. The Spaniards were aware of the existence of Tayasal. Cortez spent three days there in 1525 while on a march from Mexico to Honduras, and a statue of one of Cortez's wounded horses became one of the principal idols of the town. But for almost 200 years, the Spaniards were occupied with conquering and administering a continent, and paid little attention to the city in the jungle. Some friars visited Tayasal in about 1618, but they only managed to earn the hatred of the people by destroying their equine idol. A military expedition led by Martin de Usúa finally managed to subjugate Tayasal in 1697.

By the time the Spaniards moved into the area, the old Mayan causeways had long been covered with jungle growth. The building of a road through the Petén linking Flores with Guatemala City in the south and Belize in the east was only a dream for hundreds of years, though now it is complete.

With flights to the airport and trucks coming overland, the area around Flores has boomed, especially the towns of San Benito and Santa Elena opposite Flores on the mainland. Flores itself sits on a small island and cannot expand, therefore it remains a charming place of obvious antiquity, and vehicles are only found on the dusty road along the edge of the island near the causeway to the mainland.

Albert and I had breakfast in the hotel restaurant and then took a hired boat around the lake that afternoon. We first went to San Andres across the lake to investigate trucks or buses that were going north up to the road to Carmelita, from where we would be able to hike to El Mirador, the site of the hightest Mayan pyramids in Central America.

Our boat guide Carlos helped us translate and told us, via conversation with locals, that even the road was impassable after 24 kilometers and it was 60 kilometers to Carmelita alone, and then another 40 to El Mirador. El Mirador seemed too difficult to reach on this trip. For now it would have to remain only the home of jaguars.

We were told that two tourists had bought horses and went riding to El Mirador. After five days they had not returned, and it was believed that they may have been mired down by the miles of mud.

Near to El Mirador is another city, that of Nakbe. The University of California at Los Angeles has been excavating the ancient city, and report that the city is built over a much older city. While Nakbe itself is a city dating back to at least 200 B.C., the ancient city that it is built on may have been built by 1000 B.C. or before.

Recently, UCLA announced that an astonishing discovery had been made, a gigantic stone head of a bird, 34 feet wide and 16 feet high was found at the base of a pyramid. The carving is dated before 300 B.C. It is thought to be the bird-like deity or god called Itzam-Ye or also spelled Itzama. Itzam-Ye was an important god to the Mayas, who is associated in Mayan cosmology with the creation of the universe and with Big Dipper constellation. The Mayans were known to sacrifice victims to the god.

The statue found at Nakbe is huge, weighing many tons. It has been suggested that Itzam-Ye may be the representative of pterodactyls that were possibly worshiped by the Mayans. They perceived Itzam-Ye as a huge, terrifying bird which ate people. As we shall see, such birds, similar to pterodactyls, are a common belief among ancient Native Americans. Is the Nakbe megalith an early representation of a Thunderbird? At the time of Cortez's visit to lake Petén, the Itza were still sacrificing victims to their god, Itzama (Itzam-Ye).

Nakbe is pushing back the dates of occupation in the Petén, and pushing back the dates of the Mayan civilization. Until excavations at Nakbe, no Mayan artifacts were believed to be older than 150 B.C. Now the dates are 300 to 1000 B.C. The Mayans may be just as old as the Olmecs. Nakbe is a city of pyramids, towering temples, tombs, limestone murals and the source of tens of thousands of artifacts. Unfortunately, Nakbe is as remote as El Mirador. They would have to wait for another trip.

Albert and I then crossed the lake with Carlos with intermittent showers dumping on the boat. Carlos told us that the lake had risen four and a half meters in eleven years. This rising of the lake had submerged quite a few buildings, including several hotels on some of the nearby islands of Flores. Even much of Flores, as one sees it from the lake, is submerged, windows half sunken on the bottom floor of buildings along the lake shore. Flores may one day be a sunken city I thought!

The last Mayan city of Tayasal is not on the island of Flores but on an isthmus into the lake. When Cortez came to the lake in 1525, all of the cities in the Petén were inexplicably deserted and Tayasal was the only one with any inhabitants.

We got off the boat by a small house and Carlos showed us a look-out tower built for tourists to get a good view of the lake and the town of Flores on the island nearby. All around us were jungle covered hills which were the earthen ruins of Tayasal, a relatively primitive city when compared to Copán or Tikal—certain evidence of the gradual decline of the Mayas. Like many civilizations, their earlier ruins were more advanced than their later constructions.

We stopped at the ruins of a hotel started 12 years ago by the owner of the famed Jungle Lodge in Tikal. The hotel was never completed, and was quickly becoming an ancient ruin itself. It suddenly began to rain and we took shelter in the concrete shell of the hotel.

Staring down into a gaping pit about 20 feet long and fifteen feet deep, Carlos told us that it was the beginning of a swimming pool. He said that during the excavation of the pool for the hotel a cavern system was discovered that went deep into the artificial hills behind us, now jungle ruins. Not wanting to have the local archaeological authorities close them down or confiscate the site, they walled the tunnel up.

Later, the work crew discovered some Mayan ceramic ware and a large jade turtle! The workmen promptly quit work, left the site and never returned. Presumably they went to Guatemala City or Belize and sold the artifacts. The hotel has stood unfinished ever since.

When it stopped raining, we returned to the boat and headed back to the island city of Flores. It was dusk, and the city was nicely silhouetted against the orange sky. Just as we reached the docks on the east side of the island, it began to pour again. We paid Carlos, thanked him for being our guide, and ran for the hotel.

🐗🐗🐗

We left the next morning by mini-bus for Tikal. It was only an hour drive or so, and we arrived at the ruins by 8:30. After checking out a few of the local lodges, we checked into the Tikal Inn, dumped our packs on the beds, and headed into the the National Park to explore the sprawling city.

Tikal is said to be the greatest of all the Classic Mayan cities and is certainly the largest and most important of the lowland Mayan sites. Tikal is a place for wondering, not only at the engineering accomplishments of the Maya, but at the jungle splendors of the Petén . The site is a national park, one of the few accessible areas of the Petén that has not been taken over by agriculture, and where the native flora and fauna still flourish relatively undisturbed.

The park is dense with mahogany, cedar, ceiba and palm trees, all intertwined with vines. Howler and Spider monkeys swing in the treetops, snakes prowl in the undergrowth and coatimundis, foxes, jaguars and wild turkeys roam the ground. Within the park can be found hundreds of bird species including toucans and macaws, easily visible for their size and bright colors plus curassows, egrets, vultures, road runners, harpy eagles, motmots, Montezuma's oropendolas, tinamous and more. Many tourists come here just to watch the birds.

Albert and I wandered down the groomed trails through the jungle until we suddenly came down the Maler causeway to the Great Plaza. Here we were caught by the stunning view of Tikal's most famous pyramids known as Temple I and Temple II.

The Maler causeway is named after the German archaeologist Teobert Maler (1842-1917) who did much of the early documen-

100

tation and excavation at Tikal. Maler found a frieze at the North Acropolis at the Great Plaza of a Mayan in a boat rowing to escape from a land being destroyed in volcanic cataclysm. The entire top of the North Acropolis was a continuous frieze in very good condition, and Maler removed every section and sent it back to Germany. The astonishing frieze was taken to the Berlin Museum where it was on display for more than 30 years but was tragically destroyed in 1945 at the end of World War II by the bombing of Berlin.

The frieze is a startling and controversial piece of Mayan art. Does it depict an escape from Atlantis? The ancient Mesoamericans called this land Atlan. Certainly it depicts earth changes of a cataclysmic sort that would fit into the legend of Atlantis, an island kingdom that sank beneath the Atlantic in a volcanic upheaval. Some evidence suggests that at least parts of Atlantis may have been in the present day Caribbean.

Albert and I explored the North Acropolis area and discovered a tunnel going inside the lower part of the structure. I had my flashlight with me and we entered a dark tunnel going parallel to the stairs. There were some giant faces carved into the walls, covered by later construction on the building. There was even a giant, living spider with his equally large web stretched across one far corner. He looked big enough to eat small birds!

We climbed to the top of a temple and then heard a great roar.

"What was that?" asked a woman standing near us. The roar suddenly occurred again. It was deep and resonant.

"It sounds like a jaguar," said Albert calmly.

"Maybe it is a jaguar!" said the woman, alarmed. The roaring continued, it was loud and obviously coming from some animal. I saw someone walking on the trail below, it was a local worker.

"What is that noise?" I asked him in Spanish.

"Monos," was his reply—howler monkeys.

"Don't worry, its only some Howler monkeys," I said.

We spent the day climbing each pyramid in succession, and having a great time. Tikal is a city that amazes and is awesomely beautiful at the same time. All the buildings at Tikal were painted red at one time, and the red still shows on a few of the structures.

At the small museum at the site in the late afternoon, I marveled at the jade on display. One piece was a solid jade head about four inches high with a thick beard, like an Egyptian false beard worn by the Pharaoh as a symbol of authority. The face struck me as something from the cliff face of Abu Simbel in the lower Nile.

Other interesting items at the museum included a fascinating set of carved bones, one rather Chinese in the way a delicate hand held a paint brush for calligraphy while another bone depicted the famous boat scene of a Mayan ruler being paddled down the subterranean river into the underworld with four animal-men, an alligator, a monkey, a parrot, and a furry animal. This Noah's ark type scene is actually reminiscent to the Egyptian mythos of the Pharaoh descending down the River Stix into the underworld. This same mythos was found in ancient dynastic China. The tomb at

Palenque, in Mexico, shows a similar descent into the underworld. Other interesting displays were a set of tiny bone tweezers, incense burners and food pots with lids. One lidded food storage bowl had a man with a blue head and large fangs coming down from his mouth. This is in fact a common Indonesian motif. Also present were some interesting painted bowls, with Mayan comic book type art depicting bizarre costumes, rituals and battles. These Mayan murals are more colorful and far-out than a Batman comic!

We had a couple of beers at the museum cafe in the late afternoon, and then watched the sunset from a treehouse a short walk from the Tikal Inn.

We decided the next morning to spend a few days hiking through the jungle north of Tikal to the ruins of Uaxactún, another Mayan city 25 kilometers to the north of Tikal.

El Mirador had been the powerful capital of the Early Classic period of Mayan culture, but about 300 A.D. Tikal and Uaxactún became the successors.

Uaxactún is one of the oldest Mayan cities known. It is older but smaller than Tikal, with the highest pyramid rising only 27 feet (8 meters). It retains a certain air of antiquity, much of it still unexcavated and the area around the city abounds in undiscovered mounds, cities and pyramids. It has been estimated that there are more than 10,000 undiscovered pyramids in the Petén region of Guatemala, many of them in the vicinity of Uaxactún.

Shouldering our packs, Albert and I stepped onto the narrow jeep road between Tikal and Uaxactún. Because it had rained the night before, the road was quite muddy in spots. We hadn't walked far before we came to a small Suzuki four-wheel-drive pickup truck that was stuck in the mud. Two men were attempting to free it with some branches they had cut from the forest while a girl of about thirteen sat in the cab watching the proceedings anxiously.

Albert and I offered to help but there was little we could do. We would have gotten completely muddy in the process of pushing the truck from behind, standing in several feet of mud while the spinning back tires flung more of the wet matter on our clothes.

Fortunately, they refused our polite offer and we continued our hike through the jungle to Uaxactún. Along the 26 kilometers of jungle, I reflected on those who had walked this road before: Mayan warriors, traders and priests.

According to most students of the Maya, this civilization had taken mankind's favorite sport to a pinnacle, but then Tikal in the end cheated on the rules, and the game, as it were, was over. What is mankind's favorite sport? Warfare, of course!

From the beginning of time, it seems, mankind has waged war against his neighbor. The Romans brought the sport of warfare to the Colosseum where all could watch it in comfort. Not only did gladiators in their armor fight it out to the cheers of the spectators, but the Romans would actually flood the Colosseum in Rome with water and have mock naval battles!

Mankind's favorite sport of warfare is also the logical reason why men have been getting shorter throughout history, rather than taller, as our high school history teachers may have wrongly told us. The reason that people have been getting shorter throughout history (there were giants in those days...says the first book of Genesis) is that when one has a ritual battle (or any battle, for that matter) one will naturally place the larger men at the front, much the same as in a football game. However, since battles with deadly weapons tend to permanently eliminate a large number of the participants, especially those that are at the front, the big guys were typically killed. Leaving only the smaller men to breed, we see how warfare makes people shorter over a period of time. The Napoleonic wars reduced the average height of Frenchmen by several inches and today the French are not well known for their stature.

The Mayans took the sport of warfare to new heights of ritual sport. Each city state within the Mayan civilization waged war on its neighbor. It was as if instead of Chicago and Milwaukee having a football game and cheering each others team, they sent an army each to meet half way between the cities and fought until a certain number were killed and captured, and then the referee would blow his whistle and the two teams would return to their respective cities.

Say the archaeologists Schele and Freidel in their book, *A Forest of Kings,* "Warfare was not new to the Maya. Raiding for captives from one kingdom to another had been going on for centuries, for allusions to decapitation are present in even the earliest architectural decorations celebrating kingship. The hunt for sacrificial gifts to give to the gods and the testing of personal prowess in battle was part of the accepted social order, and captive sacrifice was something expected of nobles and kings in the performance of their ritual duties. Just as the gods were sustained by the bloodletting ceremonies of kings, so they were nourished as well by the blood of noble captives. Sacrificial victims like these had been buried as offerings in building terminations and dedications from Late Preclassic times on, and possibly even earlier. Furthermore, the portrayal of living captives is prominent not only at Uaxactún and Tikal, but also at Rio Azul, Xultún and other Early Classic sites."[122]

According to Schele and Freidel, what happened on September 13, 379 A.D. was totally against all the agreed rules for ritual warfare. The combatants were supposed to fight for awhile, take captives for sacrifices, and then withdraw to their respective cities, however, the Tikal forces, under the leadership of Smoking-Frog, attacked and defeated the forces of the neighboring kingdom of Uaxactún and then did the unthinkable, they did not retreat to their own city, but continued on to Uaxactún and claimed it at as their own, placing Smoking-Frog on the throne of the city.

Monuments commemorating the event were erected in both Uaxactún and Tikal, and a new phase in the history of the Mayas began. This was a phase in a civilization already in a serious decline. From a glorious past of great science, philosophy and achievements, the Maya had now degenerated into human sacrifice and conquest of their of their own brothers.

Schele and Freidel suggest that one of the prizes in the conquest of Uaxactún was the control of trade with Teotihuacán, the magnificent city of the Toltecs in the Valley of Mexico. They even suggest that Tikal's inspiration for this new fighting tactic came from Teotihuacán. "From the Teotihuacanos the Maya gained a sacrificial ritual and a new kind of warfare that would remain central to their religion at least until the ninth century. We know less about what Teotihuacán gained from the interchange. The end result, however, was the establishment of an international network of trade along which moved material goods and ideas. This interaction between the peoples of Mesoamerica resulted in a fluorescence of civilized life, a cultural brilliance and intensity that exceeded even the accomplishments of the Olmec, the first great civilization to arise in Mesoamerica."[122]

Schele and Freidel, therefore, see this new facet of Mayan warfare as beneficial, one that brought on a flowering of culture, and among the "isolated" Mesoamerican kingdoms (who are incredibly only a few hundred miles apart) a new era of cultural interchange now takes place.

On the walk to Uaxactún, I reflected that more probably the truth is just the opposite. Mayan and Mesoamerican civilization had been on the decline for centuries. It was only with the arrival of the Toltecs and later the ministry of Quetzalcoatl (see chapter 8) that a renaissance of any kind in Mesoamerica occured, and even then, only for a very short time, as all the civilizations reverted back to warfare and human sacrifice shortly after Quetzalcoatl left via boat for the east.

The Mayans were no doubt in contact via ship with all sorts of coastal areas up and down the Caribbean and Gulf of Mexico. Tulum in Quintana Roo was a major port city. Schele and Freidel's reasoning is based on the logic of isolationism, that somehow the Mayas had existed for hundreds of years in the Petén and Yucatan without contact with their neighbors, a scenario that is highly unlikely, but fits well with general isolationist theories of Mesoamerica. When archaeologists will only begrudgingly admit contact between neighbor cultures in Mesoamerica, how could they possibly admit to contact with more distant civilizations across the oceans?

🐉🐉🐉

Albert and I had nearly reached Uaxactún when we heard the sound of a motor behind us. We stopped and saw the Suzuki pickup coming toward us. We waved to them, indicating to the driver that we wanted a ride, and he bounced to a stop in front of us. We dumped our packs in the back and climbed on top of them. With a jolt, we were on our way.

The truck was loaded with sacks of rice and cartons of foodstuffs for a general store at Uaxactún. As we rounded one corner we

104

suddenly saw a spotted cerval cat, sort of a miniature jaguar, cross the road.

"*Gato monte!*" cried our driver, which was Spanish for mountain cat.

The truck arrived shortly at the small town of Uaxactún, located in the middle of the Mayan ruins. Uaxactún means "Eight Stones" in the Mayan language. The main street, I observed, was an airstrip for small planes. Because of the small groups of cattle grazing in the center, it did not seem like it was much in use.

Albert and I inquired as to where there might be a hotel in town, and we were directed to the home of Doña Juana, which consisted of a few thatch-roofed huts in a compound with a kitchen in back. Doña Juana herself was in the back. A cigarette smoking older lady from Cuba, she had been raised in Mexico and came to the Petén because of the chicle-gum boom. Now she ran Uaxactún's only flophouse and café.

The room she gave us was nothing more than a shack with a dirt floor. "You can string your hammocks up here," she told us.

We didn't have hammocks, but I set up my tent inside the room, and we threw our sleeping bags inside.

We had a quick lunch of tortillas and beans in Doña Juana's quaint kitchen with a wood stove made of adobe clay and chairs around a wooden table made from sawed logs. Afterwards we explored the ruins of Uaxactún which are on either side of the town.

The ruins to the south contained some pyramids and other structures, including a pyramid which had been dug up to expose a huge stone snake running down the side of the pyramid. Unfortunately, this stone snake has been reburied because the government is afraid the snake would be broken and stolen.

The ruins to the north of the airstrip have a more substantial complex of buildings including a quarry where massive slabs three feet thick were being cut in the bedrock. For unknown reasons these gigantic blocks were never removed from the bedrock, although the work had been started.

Back at the main street of Uaxactún (the wide, grassy airstrip) Albert and I stopped for a cold beer at one of the few stores in town. To our surprise it was run by the same man who had been driving the Suzuki truck. The beers were cold and tasted good on the hot afternoon.

The man, Daniel, began telling us of lost cities in the jungles around Uaxactún. He told us of one large city that was three days away, while others were only a few hours from Uaxactún.

"Do you want to visit a lost city?" asked Daniel in Spanish.

Albert put down his beer. "Of course!" he said. "When can we go?"

"Tomorrow," said Daniel. "We can leave tomorrow morning. I will make arrangements." Then he suddenly got quiet. "But do not tell anyone. We must go in secret!"

We promised not to talk about our trip to the lost city and then returned to Doña Juana's kitchen for dinner. The next day we met with Daniel and went with him to explore the lost city.

Daniel blazed a trail through the thick jungle with a machete held firmly in his hand. Albert and I followed behind.

"Watch out for snakes," he said, turning suddenly. "They are deadly poisonous!"

Albert and I looked at each other and nodded. "Watch out for snakes," we both said under our breath.

After an hour or two of moving through narrow, virtually invisible jungle trails we came to a jungle covered hill. "La ciudad (the city)," said Daniel.

The city? I looked around. I didn't see any city. Then Daniel took us around to one side of the hill. A trench had been dug from the base going towards the center of the hill. It was a pyramid, completely overgrown, and it had been looted!

There were more pyramids in the vicinity, and I decided to name the lost city the City of the Robbers. Most of the small pyramids had already been trenched, and artifacts found in the center of the pyramids had been taken: ceramics and possibly jade or gold. A famous jade mask, once on the cover of National Geographic magazine was taken from the city of Rio Azul, 100 kilometers to the north.

We climbed up the jungle covered pyramids, keeping our eye on the ground for snakes, and found five pyramids in all. One had a cavern inside it, and I crawled up to the entrance and used my flashlight to illuminate the inside. Most of it had caved in, but Daniel assured us that artifacts had been found inside the pyramid. These small pyramids were house platforms that were also used as tombs and, apparently, secret escape chambers and tunnels.

He then showed us a small hole near a pyramid that he said was an escape tunnel from the pyramid in case of warfare. The whole area was terribly overgrown and was populated by thick hordes of mosquitoes and the occasional jaguar or fer-de-lance.

Back at Doña Juana's kitchen that evening, Albert and I sat at the ancient, stained table, drinking the matron's soup and waiting for a plate of rice, beans and chicken.

Doña Juana's asked us how long we would be staying in Uaxactún and whether we were married.

She leaned on the table, puffing slowly on her cigarette and looking at us each very carefully. Albert was about the same age as I was and he was single like me. Doña Juana seemed to think we were both prime candidates for some of the single women around Uaxactún, and offered us her services as a matchmaker.

"There are some beautiful women here in Uaxactún. And they know how to cook. They would make great wives!"

An attractive young woman with long black hair and oriental eyes gave me a sudden glance from the adobe stove. I hadn't seen her before. Perhaps she had come to help our host cook on this evening to meet the new gringos in town. I was shy, and looked away.

"There is a truck going to a chiclero ranchero near Rio Azul, tomorrow," said Doña Juana. "You can stay there and go on to the lost city."

Rio Azul was a newly discovered Mayan city 104 kilometers to the north of Uaxactún and very close to the Mexican border. There was rumored to be a road there, passable only one month a year, that went north out of Uaxactún. It was only passable to four-wheel drive vehicles during the one month that it was open. She was referring to a ranch in which the chicleros, those who harvested the sap of the chiclé tree, came to sell their bricks of chiclé. Chiclé is a natural type of rubber used in chewing gum, and is where the name "Chiclets" for a brand of chewing gum came from. Chiclé is harvested by slashing the outer bark of the tree and allowing the the sap to be collected in a bucket, much as maple syrup is collected, except chiclé hardens into a rubbery solid. It was chiclé that formed the first rubber balls of the Mayan, Toltec and Aztec game players.

"The very first truck to get the chiclé will be going tomorrow," Doña Juana repeated. She saw my interest and then said, "I will inform you when it comes into town."

We met another traveller from Canada at Doña Juana's cantina that night, a Canadian traveller named Ziggy. Ziggy came from a Polish Canadian family that had moved to Ontario and his real name was Zbigniew, everyone called him Ziggy for short, or so he claimed. A burly autoworker from Oshawa, he was now on a two week trip through Guatemala.

That night we camped at the ruins to the south of town. Ziggy slept on top of one of the pyramids, while Albert and I slept inside my tent at the base. In the morning we asked Ziggy how the night had been at the summit of the stepped pyramid. We had expected him to describe a mystic experience, but instead he scratched at his neck and said, "Lots of mosquitoes."

It was almost noon the next morning when the blue, Toyota four-wheel-drive pick-up arrived at the nearby store and prepared to go on to the ranch that was farther into the Petén jungles. It was full of cargo and gasoline. The gasoline was one full drum and eight large plastic containers. A steel cage with a bar running the length of the bed was welded and bolted to the truck.

We piled in the back, though the driver invited me to ride in front. His name was Manuel and he was young with a wife and child back in Flores. This was his job, driving one of the trucks for the ranch.

I asked him how many times he had made this trip through the muddy backroads of the Petén jungles. He blew out of his lips like a trumpet, indicating that it was a good many trips. He didn't know.

Meanwhile we bounced and slid down this muddy, wet, terrible road. There were deep sets of tracks through the mud which he would sometimes drive in and sometimes avoid. Occasionally he would stop the truck and put it in first gear and then drive slowly through a sea of mud. Thick jungle was all around with cedar, chiclé trees, coconut palms and ceiba trees.

I looked in the glove compartment; inside were some faded playing cards, only four or five. Each card had a photograph of a nude, or partially nude, woman on it. They were old cards, and the worn photographs and coy poses of the women were from the fifties and early sixties.

Manuel suddenly braked and then drove off into the jungle to the right. A gigantic mud lake, with several deep ruts disappearing into the water were just before us and had to be avoided. Instead we drove off to the left, and the truck crashed through the trees, following the deep ruts of the trucks before it. Then we crashed through the brush and back onto the main road.

With a touch of irony Manuel griped the steering wheel tightly and said in Spanish, "This is a bad road."

"This road is not bad," I said. "This road is horrible."

Suddenly we lurched and bounced into the Ranch Antonio D'alcoa, the local chiclé baron. He was a large man, a Ladrino from Guatemala City now carving out his mini-empire in the remote hinterlands of Guatemala. Don Antonio graciously allowed us to camp for the night and eat at his ranch kitchen.

The ranch was essentially two walled buildings, one a kitchen and the other his office with store room full of blocks of chiclé. There were several other buildings that were thatched but without walls on the compound. In these were a dozen or so chiclé gatherers lazing around in hammocks.

Scores of chickens, ducks, roosters and guinea hens wandered about the ranch and they had their own building to roost in. Curiously, there were no turkeys. I was amused when a flock of guinea hens would occasionally parade across the main yard, squeaking and squealing in their peculiar high pitched manner. Ducks from the nearby pond would waddle by as well.

Several lean, yellow, short-haired dogs roamed the grounds. They were friendly and came by to be petted now and then. Apparently, they were virtually pure bred dogs from ancient Mayan times.

After a meal of tortillas and beans at the kitchen, I sat in one of Don Antonio's chairs outside of his storeroom. The sun had set and a sliver of a moon hung in the sky. Don Antonio came over and told us that we were lucky that it hadn't rained for two weeks and the first of the trucks would be leaving at four in the morning for Rio Azul to pick up bricks of chiclé that had been accumulating for the past three or four months.

I thanked him for his hospitality and said we would be ready to go at four. I looked up at the moon and at the several coconut palms that grew around the ranch. I thought that it was curious that coconuts, a plant I had always associated with tropical islands, would be found out here in the middle of this jungle, a thousand miles away from any ocean.

The coconut palm is a cultivated plant and was cultivated in all the Mayan lands, even far inland. The distribution of coconuts is by man throughout the world. Curiously, typically, where one finds coconuts, one will also find bananas, the world's most amazing and nutritious fruit. Every banana is like an ancient seedless plant. Bananas give a fruit but it has no seed. Bananas are the world's

108

tallest grass and reproduce via shoots from their root system. Like coconuts, they must be taken by man from one location to another. Bananas are found in all tropical areas of the world, even remote islands. They are like the prehistoric version of seedless grapes.

The Mayas and other ancient cultures never ceased to amaze me. What had happened to these once great cultures to cause their decline? Who were these strange people anyway? Out in the jungle lay forgotten cities of the Maya. Tens of thousands of pyramids were scattered through the now uninhabited forest.

Now the jungle was silent except for the birds, insects and howler monkeys. The lives of those millions of Maya with their intensive agriculture were now like those worn girlie cards in the glove compartment of the Toyota: just a faded memory of the past.

❧❧❧

The next morning we were up at four and dismantled the tent via the light of our flashlights. The truck was warming up as we had a cup of coffee and ate a corn tortilla. Then, in the predawn darkness, we started the grueling five hour trip to Rio Azul.

Naturally, the road was as bad as we could possibly have imagined. We slid and bounced through 80 kilometers of mud and forest while Albert, Ziggy and I sat or stood in the back, holding desperately on to the side of the truck and ducking the branches that were continually coming at us.

It was late morning when we arrived at Rio Azul. We crossed the river and came to a group of thatched buildings. This was the chiclé camp and the camp of the *vigilantés* who watch over the known archaeological sites in Guatemala.

We had a breakfast of the usual tortillas and beans (no need for menus at these places) at the small kitchen run by the family of one of the chicléros. Then we took off down the wide trail and sometime road toward the ruins. We soon realized, however, that we could not find the ruins without a guide and returned to the camp to get one.

With our new guide, a young man named Rolando, we were on our way to the city. He was a handsome fellow with a thin black mustache and a large machete. I carried my own machete as well.

It was a one hour walk or so, and in the trees above us howler monkeys screamed and jumped about the jungle canopy. We encountered ancient tombs and walls—these monkeys were the only denizens of the ancient ruins.

Suddenly we came to over grown pyramids with tunnels dug by artifacts merchants into the center of the monuments, searching for a tomb. We explored some of the trenches and tunnels into the main pyramid and examined some steles that had been carved and later buried in the rebuilding of the pyramid, something the Mayans did as often as every fifty-two years.

A jade mask taken from one of the tombs was later sold to a collector in France and is offered for sale in an antiquity catalog published in Europe. This mask was even featured on the cover of

109

National Geographic a few years ago, a stolen art treasure now owned by a private collector.

We climbed the highest pyramid. A temple with hieroglyphs was on one side of the steep, forest covered structure. The walls were 50 feet high and a stone face was fixed to the outer wall. A true archway, in the sense of it curving to the top and having a keystone, much like a Roman wine cellar, was also part of the temple. The Mayas, curiously, are said to not have known the principle of the keystone arch.

From the top we could see another large pyramid to the north and a circle of mountains. Were they the border with Mexico? Exploring the summit of the pyramid, there was the remains of a temple with several large rooms and a few arches.

Back at camp, we sat in the small kitchen and had a dinner of tortillas, beans and a wild game bird, something like a pheasant or a wild turkey. The wife of one of the chicléros ran the kitchen, cooking meals with her two daughters, Daisy Lopez and Judy. Judy was a cute eight-year-old with brown hair in a pony tail. She wore a worn, but pretty dress.

Her older sister, Daisy Lopez, was 18 and absolutely gorgeous. She was well figured, with long brown hair and bangs on her forehead. She wore a fashionable Batman t-shirt and a skirt, and looked like she knew how to flop tortillas as good as any woman. She was definitely the object of a great deal of jungle-love, and was no doubt the sweet dream of many a napping *chicléro.*

Meanwhile, while I chewed on my food and imagined a date with Daisy Lopez, her young eight-year-old sister, Judy, stared up at me with loving eyes and a deep smile. My blond hair and gringo ways were something she had never seen before and she was mesmerized by the sight of me. She couldn't keep her eyes off me as I reached for another tortilla and grabbed some mashed beans.

The girls, mom included, were wonderful, and Albert, Ziggy and I asked them lots of questions about their life here. They lived in Melchor de Mencos, the Guatemalan bordertown with English-speaking Belize, and therefore spoke a bit of English. However, we spoke to them in Spanish. They found Rio Azul boring, but they had no choice. They had not seen a gringo here in the nine months they had been camped at Rio Azul.

The next morning I went down to the river, the so-called Rio Azul, or *Blue River.* It was a small and dirty waterway. After gazing upon it for a moment, I realized that it wasn't a river at all. It was a canal!

Indeed, Rio Azul, and the other waterways in this whole area were artificial canals that were dug many hundreds, if not thousands, of years ago by the Maya. One of the astounding realizations of the Mayan civilization is that the entire landscape of the Petén was engineered with canals, pyramids, elevated roads and mounds.

Canals beneath the Petén jungle were discovered using new techniques of radar photography. In 1977 and 78, NASA tested a new kind of radar from aircraft over the jungles of Guatemala and

Belize. The system was built by the Jet Propulsion Laboratory for NASA and then flown over jungles to photograph what might be found beneath the green canopy.

The new radar, called Synthetic Aperture Radar, or SAR, can penetrate clouds and provide higher resolution for comparable antenna size than other radars. The radar photos of the Petén jungles showed an extensive ancient canal system hidden for more than 1,000 years and built between 2000 B.C. and 900 A.D.

This extensive canal system extends from the Caribbean coast well into the central jungle of Guatemala, a considerable distance, and one that covers a vast area that is mostly unexplored jungle today. Indeed, the ancient Maya, or even another earlier culture, must have created an agricultural wonderland with their vast canal system. The canals would have been well used for a river highway system, utilizing the natural river and lake system of the Petén with the sophisticated network of artificial canals.

Suddenly, the trucks were back to pick up more chiclé. We grabbed our packs and jumped on the truck after it was loaded. It was another five hours in the back of the truck to the ranch where we spent another night.

The next morning we asked if there were any trucks going to Uaxactún. Don Antonio shook his head. All his trucks were going back to Rio Azul, but it was only 24 kilometers back to Uaxactún.

"Its not too far," he said. With that we shouldered our packs and began walking down the road. It would get hot in the middle of the day, and we wanted do the distance in the morning.

We stopped to rest a few times along the trail. Howler monkeys occasionally screamed overhead while colorful butterflies fluttered along the road. There were plenty of diversions a long the trail, and at one break a small ocelot, a wild cat came by to see who we were.

When we finally stumbled into Uaxactún, I set my pack down and found the first household shop with cold drinks. The lady handed me a cold beer from the propane refrigerator (Uaxactún has no electricity). I finished it in three big gulps, ordered another and collapsed into a chair. It was now blazing hot in the middle of the afternoon and I had just finished walking 24 kilometers. I drank the second beer more slowly, relishing the coldness of it.

Later that day we were back at Doña Juana's kitchen and shack where we had a hammock and a dirt floor to stretch our sleeping bags. Albert, Ziggy and I sat once again at the stained and ancient table drinking the matron's soup and waiting for a plate of rice, beans and the specialty of the day.

Doña Juana asked us again how long we would be staying in Uaxactún and whether we were were interested in getting married.

She sat in her chair, puffing slowly on her cigarette and looking at us each very carefully.

"I know just the right woman here in Uaxactún. She knows how to cook. You will be very happy!"

The attractive young woman with long black hair and oriental eyes

111

was once again cooking at the adobe stove. I had noticed her when I came in. I smiled at her and took a big scoop of rice with my spoon and shoved it in my mouth.

Uaxactún was a fascinating place; charming and mysterious. Here we were in a jungle town that was situated smack dab in the middle of a Mayan city! It wouldn't be such a bad place to live. One would need a four-wheel drive vehicle, then maybe open a hotel...

The town reminded me of the 30s pulp fiction hero Doc Savage. According to the popular novels, Doc Savage had a secret base in the Guatemalan jungles that was a lost Mayan city. On occasion, Doc Savage would leave his New York headquarters and fly down to this lost Mayan city where he had his secret headquarters. Maybe that place was Uaxactún! After all, it had an airstrip and was situated in a Mayan city.

Though in my fantasies it was fun to imagine myself as Doc Savage in my own lost world, it didn't seem realistic to move into Uaxactún at this time. Maybe in the future. I told Doña Juana that we appreciated the offer for her matchmaking talents, but Albert and I would have to leave tomorrow.

"I may be back someday, though," I told her, glancing at her young kitchen maid.

The next day Albert, Ziggy and I headed back to Tikal, getting a ride on the back of a large Toyota truck. A second truck began following us, and we all bounced along the rough road, weaving in and out of the muddy patches that threatened to halt our voyage.

Occasionally the driver would suddenly careen off the road into the the jungle, avoiding some sea of mud and water that was impassable. At one point, we watched in horror and then great laughter as one of the passengers in the truck behind us was bounced right out of the back of the truck and onto the road! He wasn't hurt, and after the truck stopped he climbed back in, grinning sheepishly at the comical scene.

We arrived at Tikal in the early afternoon, and returned to our earlier hotel. It was good to have a shower again, as Doña Juana's place had neither running water or a sink.

Albert and I then headed back to the Great Plaza at Tikal to watch the afternoon go by from the top of one of the pyramids. As I sat there looking out over the vast, seemingly endless jungle, I couldn't help but think that this whole area had once been very densely inhabited with much of the forest cleared away. No doubt there had been intense agriculture and an abundance of food.

It was like an old world culture from 3,000 B.C. with its pyramid temples, and priesthood dominated agrarian lifestyle. Yet what had caused this area to become entirely deserted?

This is the great mystery of the Mayas. What caused them to just abandon their cities? Where did they go? It is believed that around 800 A.D. the Mayas of the central Petén area migrated elsewhere, leaving their cities intact. What was the reason? Mayan culture, on a diminished scale continued in the drier Yucatan area to the north and in the Guatemalan highlands around Lake Atitlán. But what had happened to the great cities of the Petén?

Theories abound, but no one pretends to know the answers. One theory is that there was a climate change that altered the ecology of the area. A similar theory proposes that over population depleted the resources, yet why would *everyone* be gone?

Diseases or a plague might have wiped everyone out. Another theory is that there was a prophesy based on the carefully calculated and cyclical Mayan calendar that predicted an end to the Mayan civilization or some cataclysmic collapse, and therefore the entire population left *en masse*. But where did they go? Did they all they all go north to Chichén Itza and Uxmal?

A popular theory among some Mayanists now is that there was a popular revolution against the priests and rulers who controlled every aspect of life among the people. The civilization, without rulers, then collapsed. But would it have left no one at all? This is indeed the great mystery, that this vast area was absolutely uninhabited for hundreds of years, and even today has a very sparse population. The riddle of the disappearance of the Maya is one of the great archaeological mysteries of North America!

Albert, Ziggy and I returned to Flores the next day and then went on to Sayaxché, a river town to the west of Lake Petén Itza. We checked into the Hotel Guayacán, the local hotel right on the waterfront of this important river town.

The hotel was straight out of a 30's movie with ceiling fans, cargo traffic on the river outside and complete with a strange old character who spoke English, was from Guatemala City and could have been Sydney Greenstreet's older brother.

We dumped our packs in the room and then chartered a boat up the Rio de la Passión to the Mayan site of El Ciebal. It was one and a half hours by motorized launch up the river. We saw turtles basking in the sun and herons along the shore.

Then it was a half hour walk from the river up to the temple area known as El Ceibal, named after a tree. Like many Mayan cities, we have no idea what the original name was, nor what the glyph for the city might have been. El Ceibal was only discovered in 1963.

The site at El Ceibal includes a number of interesting steles, many which are deeply and clearly cut, unlike many steles at Tikal, for instance. They are all quite old, some with large lichen patches of on them. Some of the steles depict Toltec warriors, men with beards, mustaches and weapons. They look distinctly Mediterranean, possibly Phoenician.

One warrior had an Olmec type head on his belt, a souvenir of the wars that consumed Central America for many thousands of years.

Several other steles have bearded warriors, sometimes holding long scepters and other symbols or authority.

Another cut stele was allegedly of a king of the city. He wore a jaguar coat, had no beard and held a weird staff that seemed to have an electric cord coming out the bottom. Was it some sort of electrical device or merely an ornate scepter of authority? Maybe both?

Ziggy looked at it and decided that it was an electric device. "This guy's holding some sort of laser rock cutter," said Ziggy.

"Are you sure?" I asked.

"That's what it looks like," he replied. "And look at this weird stuff on his face, its like he has headphones over his ears with a microphone coming to his mouth. There is even a small cylinder under the nose, a breathing apparatus?"

The face did have all this strange apparatus on it. The man looked just like a telephone operator with a small microphone coming from an earphone down to his mouth.

"It may just be his helmet and armor, they wore some strange outfits, usually as protection in wars," I suggested.

We walked among the central pyramid-temple and looked at other steles. One, our guide, the local vigilanté, told us was a visiting Toltec warrior. He had a feathered crown, a large mustache and held a war club. He also had a sun shield on his chest and an Egyptian-type wide metal collar that came around his shoulders and chest.

I asked if he was Quetzalcoatl, because of the feathers. Our guide said he was probably a Toltec who worshiped Quetzalcoatl.

After climbing up one of the pyramids we found a stele with a jaguar altar, probably for sacrifices at the base. Like the rest of the world, occasional cults and various religions would sweep through an area, becoming popular for a few hundred years or even a millennia. In this case, the jaguar or puma cult, one of sacrifice and death, succeeded in eclipsing the more human philosophy of Quetzalcoatl, called Kukulkan by the Maya.

As we headed back toward the river, I wondered a bit about these bearded and mustachioed men. They were unusual, and did not fit with prevailing history. Anthropologists tell us that American Indians have no facial hair. Zechariah Sitchin makes an interesting suggestion in his book *The Lost Realms*,[128] that North and South America, especially Mesoamerica, were what is known in the Bible as the lost realm of Cain.

According to the Biblical tale, Cain, because he had killed his brother Abel, (in many ways the Biblical story is an allegory for the supremacy of agriculturists over those who herded animals) was banished by the Lord from the settled lands and decreed that he become a wanderer in the east. Cain, however, was concerned about vengeance seekers, so the Lord, to indicate that Cain was wandering with the Lord's protection, "set a sign unto Cain, that any one finding him should not smite him."

Although no one knows what this distinguishing "sign" had been, it has been generally assumed that it was some kind of a tattoo or "birthmark" on Cain's forehead. But from the ensuing Biblical narrative it appears that the matter of vengeance and the protection against it continued into the seventh generation and beyond. A tattoo on the forehead would not be passed down from generation to generation, as such a sign would have to be a genetic trait. What therefore is the sign?

Says Sitchin, "In view of the particular genetic trait of the Amerindians—the absence of facial hair—one wonders whether it was this genetic change that was the 'Mark of Cain' and his descendants. If our guess is right, then Mesoamerica, as the focal point from which Amerindians spread north and south in the New World, was indeed the Lost Realm of Cain."[128]

Clearly, however, these bearded warriors are of a different strain, and do not bear the "mark of Cain" as Sitchin would put it. The many statues and other art of Toltecs makes them appear as Semitic or Mediterranean in nature. Phoenicians perhaps?

As we walked back to the river, we passed two more steles. One was of a monkey god who stood at least 15 feet high. I was reminded of the monkey-man demigods of ancient China and India, such as the hero Hanuman who had helped the Hindu prince Rama save his beloved wife Sita in the Ramayana.

According to our guide, the monkey was the totem or mascot of El Ceibal, sort of like the team symbol. When the ritual warfare would take place and the two teams would meet, it was sort of like the Chicago Bears meeting with the Cincinnati Bengal Tigers, with each displaying their totem on their helmets and uniforms.

The last thing to see at El Ceibal was a curious circular platform by itself off to the side of the trail. It was well built in three tiers, about 20 feet high and 60 feet in diameter. It was perfectly flat on top and had a spiral staircase that went completely around the circular structure. Apparently this round building is rather unique in the known Mayan world.

We looked at it carefully, and then Ziggy said, "Looks like a flying saucer landing pad doesn't it?"

We all looked at him and back at the structure. "Well, I guess you could land a discoid craft here," I admitted.

"I suppose that it is possible," said Albert, but maybe some other building sat on top of the platform."

"Who knows," I said, as we started back to the canoe, "out here in these strange jungles, I guess anything is possible!"

🐾🐾🐾

After a night at the hotel in Sayaxché, we left again via motorized canoe for the Mayan City of Aguateca. It was several hours down the river and then into a small lake. At the far side of the lake we entered a small, winding river, possibly an artificial canal, and then docked below a cliff on top of which was the city of Aguateca.

The local vigilanté, a man named Benito, who was soft spoken and carried a large machete in a well worn leather sheath, showed us around the ruins.

115

The city was largely ruins, but there were several interesting steles. According to Benito the actual Mayan name of the city was Monoc-Ha. According to him it had been conquered by the Toltecs about 350 A.D. and used as the main Toltec base in the area to war with the Mayas. He showed us several steles of Toltecs, some with masks and others with beards and mustaches.

Aquateca was a Toltec city, at least for a while, but was eventually conquered by the Mayan king of Dos Pilas to the west. One of the curious elements of the city was a huge chasm, apparently created by an earthquake, that made a natural tunnel and fortification in front of the city. The builders had created a bridge over this deep, vertical slash in the earth. It went straight down for about 75 meters.

"Don't get too close to the edge," warned Benedicto.

The central pyramid at Aguateca was built over natural limestone caves that were linked, artificially or naturally, to the chasm and tunnels beneath the city. Because of the caverns beneath the pyramid, the pyramid had collapsed into itself. Benedicto then showed us the glyph for the god of the subterranean world, known in Mayan as Hobun-Huitz-Na. According to Benedicto, this glyph was here because of the underground tunnels. These tunnels were used as protection and as an escape route during war.

Albert, Benedicto and I then entered one of the tunnels, going down steeply into the earth for a hundred feet or more. We used our flashlights, and stopped at an area deep underground where the tunnel leveled off and then was blocked by a large cave-in.

"Be careful down there!" called Ziggy from up above. Exploring tunnels was always good fun, but it wasn't for everyone.

Benedicto then showed us the ball court. According to him, the winner of the ball game was executed, however, this is a controversial point.

As we were leaving I asked Benedicto about the "river" coming up to Aguateca, was it artificial?"

Benedicto looked at me. "Yes," was his answer. "This is an artificial canal." Like at Rio Azul, the artificial canal system ran many hundreds of miles throughout the Petén region.

We returned once again to Sayaxche for the night, and the next day tried to make arrangements to visit Yaxchilán, Altar de los Sacrificios and Piedras Negras farther north up the Usumacinta River. This would require a trip of at least five days and many hundreds of dollars.

Instead we took a long day trip to the Mayan site of Dos Pilas, "Two Wells," that required a boat trip and then a 24 kilometer walking trip (12 kilometers each way).

It was a three hour walk to Dos Pilas, a site of two wells, or springs, coming out of the ground. The site, even though remote, had several huge modern buildings for housing the yearly army of archaeologists who descended on the site.

We walked among giant steles, 6 meters tall and broken. There were several giant Mayan steles, all broken, that were once nearly 20 feet tall. One was of a huge Mayan Jaguar warrior standing on a conquered enemy. This was 10 meters tall, nearly 30 feet!

There were several large, unexcavated pyramids among the forest canopy, and these also had the remains of hieroglyphic stairways, partially preserved. I marveled at the extent of the city and size of the broken and destroyed steles. Some, because they had been buried, were well preserved. Even some of the original paint that had once covered the stone could be seen; red, green and white.

At a ball court with two steles, our local guide pointed out to us that the warriors were wearing Olmec style head protection, which was the large round disc over the ears for protection with football helmet like face guards coming down in front of the face.

Albert pointed out how if Phoenicians had come to Mesoamerica, they would have already have found a thriving armor industry, one that dated back several thousand years. Carthaginians, fresh from the Punic wars with Rome, would have used the various helmets, costumes and weapons that were already in use by the Mayas, Olmecs, Mixtecs and others. Perhaps this is why both Toltecs and Mayas often dressed in what was already the older "Olmec" style.

"Isn't there a cave system or something around here?" asked Albert suddenly as we stood around one of the broken steles that lay on the ground.

"Yes," said our guide, a young man in his early twenties. He led us down one of the jungle paths and in five minutes from the central plaza we came to the collapsed entrance to a cave.

Albert and I followed our guide down for more than a hundred feet through the wide opening in the cave. From here we continued through low ceilings another several hundred feet inside the tunnel system. Ziggy waited on top for us.

Our guide told us that the tunnel continued underground past burial vaults to another site about a fifteen minute walk away. With flashlights we scanned the muddy tunnel floor as we crouched in the low ceiling of this subterranean world.

Our guide pulled out some bones from beneath a dark overhang. "Here is part of a burial," he said. "Much jade and gold found here."

We marveled again at the amazing system of underground tunnels that seemed to be found at many Mayan sites. Their purpose, it was generally agreed, was as a special escape route in times of war.

An article on Dos Pilas was published in the May 15, 1991, issue of *The New York Times*. The article was about the discovery of a tomb inside one of the pyramids at the city. The discovery was announced by Dr. Arthur Demarest, from Vanderbilt University in Nashville, who said that the tomb was of an 8th-century ruler who they believe began the policies of militarism and conquest that eventually led to the collapse of the classical Mayan civilization.

Demarest's belief is that Dos Pilas was once the capital of the Petexbatun region and that the tomb is of a ruler whose glyph is still undeciphered, and therefore his name still unknown. Naming the king "Ruler 2," Demarest believes that he "was a pivotal figure in the initiation of the catastrophic events in which the polity broke up into a dozen warring states that militarized the landscape within a period of 50 years and may have destroyed the ecology of the region."

This ruler reigned between 698 and 725 over the Petexbatun region. The kingdom controlled by Dos Pilas, disintegrated in 760 A.D. and the area was abandoned in 830, according to Demarest.

Was this ruler then the cause of the decline and mysterious disappearance of the Maya, simply because of continued warfare? Other Mayan scholars disagree, including Dr. Jeremy Sabloff of the University of Pittsburgh who is quoted in the article as saying that he doubted that a single factor, like destructive warfare, accounted for the fall of the Maya civilization. He also noted that "contrary to some accounts, the entire Maya civilization did not collapse at the end of the classic period. The cities in the southern lowlands of present-day Guatemala declined, but in the north the major ceremonial centers of the Yucatan in Mexico were built."

Not mentioned in the article are the curious wars with the Toltecs, such as the ruler of Dos Pilas conquering the Toltec stronghold of Aguateca nearby. It is a fact that the central Petén area was absolutely deserted by about 900 A.D. Surely warfare would not have wiped out everyone? Apparently some other cause, perhaps the fulfillment or nonfulfillment of some prophesy was responsible. Certainly a general decline of the Mayas had been occurring over hundreds of years, and this decline plus warfare among the city states of the Petén must have had a negative impact, to say the least.

We walked on through the vast, overgrown city. We skirted along a flat topped pyramid with several large steles about half way up the north side. One stele was over 15 feet long with a warrior standing on a vanquished enemy. Curiously, a dwarf stands next to him.

Another stele was of a warrior with a strange mask on. The mask had a long nose, something like an elephant's trunk.

I asked our guide what the mask was supposed to represent. He had no idea.

"It looks like an elephant to me," said Albert. Ziggy nodded his approval.

It was a long trip back to the river, taking us three more hours to walk the the 12 kilometers. We had arranged for our boat to pick us up at three in the afternoon, and he arrived exactly on time. Jumping into the canoe, we began the long trip back up river to the jungle port of Sayaxché.

The next day we were back in Flores and staying at the Hotel Casona de la Isla. Ziggy left for the airport to fly back to Guatemala City. Albert and I would be heading for Belize the next day.

Pedro, the owner of the hotel, knew of our interest in the mysteries of the Petén. "You should go to Topoxté, near to Nakum," he said to us that afternoon as he leaned on the reception desk of the hotel.

"Where is Nakum?" asked Albert.

"Nakum is near to Tikal, a bit to the east," said Pedro.

"And why should we go there?" I asked.

"Well," he said, "it is a very strange, miniature city with miniature temples, buildings, pyramids, staircases and everything. But everything is small—miniaturized."

Albert and I looked at each other. This was a strange story. "Is it a city for elves or something?" I asked.

Pedro looked at us with a curious expression. "Well, maybe so. It is like a city for little people. Maybe it is just a small scale model of another city. I do not know."

The American author and researcher Loren Coleman has an entire chapter about the little people of the Maya, called the *Alux,* in his book *Curious Encounters.*[171] Says Coleman, "Tales and rumors of these little people extend far back into the Yucatan's prehistory. At some Mayan temples there exist bas-reliefs of pairs of naked little men who are shown smaller than both the truly large priests and the five-foot tall Mayan Indian peasants represented in the carvings. The Mayas of today are still short people by Western standards, but these little people of the ancient petroglyphs were not Mayas and not children. They were full grown peoples, shown amongst the legs of warriors and the like, carrying on adult activities. They were the Alux, a race of pygmies."

Continues Coleman, "Travel writer Bill Mack and others have pointed out that at almost every Mayan archaeological site, one startling feature stands out. In front of the main temple usually are 'either singly or in clusters... tiny houses with doorways less than three feet high. Archaeologist write them off as "votary shrines" but present-day Mayas say they were the homes of the favored Alux,' according to Mack who has been on five major expeditions to the area. Rolf Schell, author of *A Yank in Yucatan,* photographed a group of these tiny huts at a secluded coastal site in the late 1950s. Asking his guide what they were, he was told 'unequivocally' that the cluster was an Alux settlement."

Coleman gives a few examples of encounters with the Alux, mentioning a 1944 Belize newspaper account that tells of a government timberman's encounter with two small people deep in the British Honduras hardwood jungles. Coleman then describes an interesting encounter with an Alux: "From 1977, we have the sterling report of a young Mayan named Xuc (pronounced 'Chuck'). Xuc was at the time the caretaker of the archaeological site of Mayapan, an ancient walled Mayan city that became the capital after the fall of Chichen Itzá. Bill Mack, in his excellent article, *Mexico's Little People,* in the August 1984 issue *Fate,* tells of Xuc's meeting with an Alux:

"Mayapan is closed to visitors after 5:00 P.M. and therefore ...Xuc was puzzled late one night in 1977 to hear the sound of a machete chopping wood. Unlocking the entry gate, he started in the direction of the sound. As he rounded the corner of the dilapidated Temple of the Birds, a small clay pellet whizzed perilously close to his head. He ducked behind a pile of fallen masonry and heard pellet after pellet strike the ancient stones around him.

"During a pause in this strange barrage, Xuc raised his head and peered out cautiously. What he saw shook him to the very foundations of his traditional Indian stoicism. Outlined in the wavering moonlight wazs a tiny man. His head was disproportionately large, his beard was jet-black and he was clad in a white *hupile,* a Mayan dress-like garment or tunic. Slung over his shoulder was a standard-sized machete almost as long as the man was tall.

"What Xuc saw was living proof—for him at least—that the Alux exist." [171]

Coleman says that when Bill Mack interviewed Xuc late in the 1970, he found the young man to be bright, personable, and well-educated. Still, Mack had problems with the disturbing story the man had to tell. Xuc, sensing disbelief in the American's questions, left his hut and returned soon with a small cloth sack. In it were about eight clay pellets the size of walnuts. Mack felt that they had been carefully made and baked to "bullet-like" hardness. These pellets were the ones Xuc had found the day after his encounter with the Alux. [171]

Was Topoxté, the miniature city near Nakum, built for or by the Alux? Did this legendary race of little people still live in an undiscovered city in the jungle? Like many of the mysteries of the Maya, there were many things that we did not know.

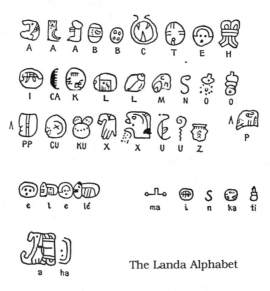

The Landa Alphabet

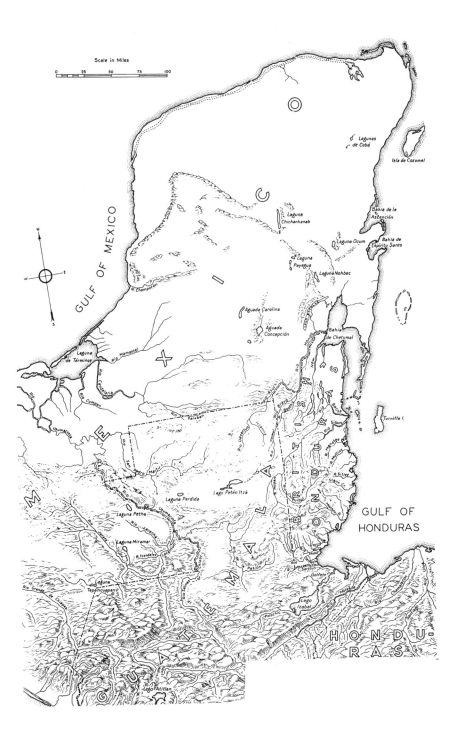

Scale in Miles

0   25   50   75   100

GULF OF MEXICO

N
W — E
S

Lagunas
de Cobá

Isla de Cozumel

Bahia de la
Ascención

Laguna
Chichankanab

Laguna Ocum

Bahia de
Espiritu Santo

Laguna
Payegua

Laguna Nohbec

Aguada Carolina

Aguada
Concepción

Bahía
de Chetumal

R. Champotón

Laguna
de Términos

Rio Mamantel

Rio Candelaria

Rio Cumpan

R. Usumacinta

Rio Palizada

Turniffe I.

Laguna Perdida

Lago Petén Itzá

Laguna Petha

GULF OF
HONDURAS

Laguna Miramar

R. Tzendales

R. Pasión

Golfete

Laguna
Tepancuapan

Rio Grande
de Chiapas

Lago
Izabal

Polochic

HOND-
U-
RAS

GUATEMALA

Lago Atitlán

Divers at Lake Amatitlán, Guatemala, a rich source of Maya artifacts. *Courtesy Milwaukee Public Museum, Milwaukee*

Maya clay vessels recovered from bottom of Lake Amatitlán. *Courtesy Milwaukee Public Museum, Milwaukee*

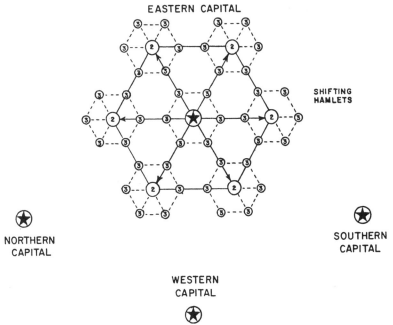

EASTERN CAPITAL

SHIFTING HAMLETS

NORTHERN CAPITAL

SOUTHERN CAPITAL

WESTERN CAPITAL

Above: A drawing the gigantic stone head, 34 feet long and 16 feet wide, discovered at the ancient Mayan city of Nakbe. Excavations at Nakbe have pushed back dates of Mayan civilization to at least 1000 B.C. Below: An idealized diagram of the territorial organization of lowland Maya from regional capitals (signified by the numeral 2) to secondary centers. From the Archaeologist Joyce Marcus' article in *Science*, No. 180, 1973.

Stela 10 from El Seibal in the Petén. This ruler with a thick mustache wears a jaguar skin decorated with pineapples. He holds some bizarre scepter, either a jade symbol of his authority, or possibly even some electric device or weapon.

Comparison of radar imagery and regular aerial photograph taken over Guatemalan jungle. The lines in the radar imagery photograph prove to be irrigation canals dug by the ancient Maya. *NASA*

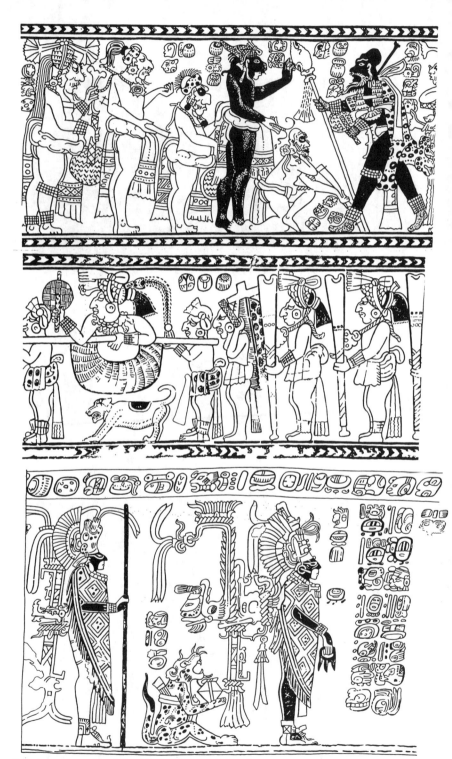

The strange world of the Maya. Many of the their murals were as fantastic as any Batman comic book.

Part of a wooden door lintel from Temple IV, Tikal, Petén. Now in the British Museum.

General view of a restored Piedras Negras along the Usumacinta River.

A reconstruction of Temples II, III, and IV, at Tikal in the Petén.

Chapter 5

Belize:

Alien Gods &
the Crystal Skull

A hard time we had of it,
with an alien people
clutching their gods.
—T.S. Eliot, *Journey of the Magi*

After the two and a half hour trip over the rutted dirt road from Flores, crossing the frontier into the Belize was like stepping onto a modern freeway. Roads were paved, uniforms were ironed, and all manner of business was found along the highways. In the Petén area of Guatemala, it seemed that everything was uninhabited jungle.

With the black immigration and customs officers, I could have sworn I was stepping into an African country, or a Caribbean nation, like Jamaica.

"Tourist?," asked the trim immigration officer in the neatly pressed British style shorts, cotton shirt and hat. "How long will you be staying in Belize?"

"Oh, two weeks or so, I suppose," I told him. "Is there any charge for the entry visa?"

"None at all," he said, stamping my passport and handing it to me. "None at all."

"Any fruits or vegetables?" was the familiar English phrase from the customs officer. I shook my head and he waved me on through, turning his attention to a young German woman and her backpack.

With that, I stepped outside through a torn screen door into the back parking lot of the border post. The bright sunshine of Belize was shining down on me as I hoisted my pack to my back and braced myself for the onslaught of money changers and taxi drivers.

"Bus to Belize city?" asked one.

"Change money?" asked another.

I gazed around, signs were English, the road was paved, cars were large American cars like Buicks and Cadillacs. Later I learned that because of the heavy taxes on vehicles, new or used, only used cars that are at least six years old are imported to Belize, usually from the United States.

Albert and I shared a taxi with some German travellers into San Ignacio, that largest town in western Belize and only fifteen miles or so away from the border. It was a clean and pleasant city, nestled into the green hills and jungle that are everywhere in Belize.

The downtown is several blocks long and in the center of the city is the famous traveller's restaurant and hotel called Eve's. Eve's is the hub of the "Greater Cayo Jungle Telegraph" as my guide book put it. Indeed, I hadn't seen so many young travellers with their backpacks and sunburns all together in one place since the last time I was in Cuzco.

We had lunch while taxi drivers expounded on their guide skills to local scenic spots and travellers swilled down their Belikin beer and watched each other, trying to guess each other's nationality.

Scores of postcards from past patrons were tacked to the walls. Hand-lettered posters announced tours, goods for sale, new cottage industries and even notes left by travellers for each other. A small gift shop with postcards, books, and handicrafts from Guatemala rounds out the atmosphere of Eve's.

I finished my lunch and we checked into the Jaguar Hotel across the street from Eve's. It had a bar downstairs and some rooms upstairs. It was primitive, but cheap for Belize, which was a great deal more expensive than Guatemala had been. The room was a couple of beds, a table and a naked bulb hanging from the ceiling.

I noticed that the lock on the door, a strap that was bolted to the door and with which one used a padlock, had been shifted around and repositioned many times. It appeared as if it had been kicked in several times and had to be replaced. Was someone going to kick our door in during the middle of the night?

I asked the manager about this, a Belgian in his 40s who had lived for a while in South Africa (what he was doing in Belize I had no idea), and he assured me that no one would kick in my door and that the locks were constantly changed because clients kept leaving with the keys.

San Ignacio is a good base for visiting the nearby Mayan ruins of Xunantunich. Xunantunich is only about ten kilometers from San Ignacio and is the largest archaeological site in the Belize River Valley. Albert and I took a taxi to the village of Succotz where a hand-operated cable ferry runs across the river.

We crossed the river on the raft, and was surprised that there was no charge. Xunantunich was just up the hill from the other side, and there was a small entrance fee to see the ruins.

Xunantunich means Stone Woman in Mayan, but this is not the original name of the city. Like most Mayan sites, the real name of the city is unknown. The early investigation of Xunantunich was conducted in 1894 and 1895 by Dr. Thomas Gann, a British medical officer, who later published his discoveries from the site in his book *Mystery Cities,*[132] published in London in 1925. Gann, who was also a close friend of F. A. "Mike" Mitchell-Hedges, famed discoverer of the

"Crystal Skull of Doom," uncovered and removed large quantities of burial goods, as well as some carved hieroglyphs which encircled Alter 1 at the site. Presently, the whereabouts of these glyphs and much of the burial goods remains unknown.[131]

In his book, Gann records the discovery of some jade or greenstone artifacts that are apparently much older than Xunantunich itself. Commenting on the 590 A.D. date given to the city, Gann says, "The neighborhood of Xunantunich was, however, probably occupied many centuries before this date, as in constructing a path from Succots to Benque Viejo along the western branch of the Mopan river, two very crude fineness of greenstone were discovered buried in the sand and gravel along what had originally been the bed of the river. Both these were typical specimens of archaic figurines, the prominent eyes surrounded by a ridge, and the crude outlining in incised lines of the upper and lower limbs and fingers and toes on the greenstone of which the figurines were composed, being characteristically archaic. But the archaic was a highland civilization which flourished from Mexico to the Andes some 2000 years B.C.; how then do these specimens come to be embedded in the river-drift near Xunantunich? this is one of those many mysteries of Central America which nothing but intensive work in this field can solve."[132]

Gann is basically saying that Mayan civilization in the Xunantunich area is to be dated to 2000 B.C. or more, a date far in excess of the dates given to the Maya at the time (100 AD. to 850 A.D.) Gann has been proven correct by the recent discoveries at Nakbe, as mentioned in the last chapter.

My attention at Xunantunich was immediately drawn to the tall pyramid to the south. This pyramid rises to 130 feet (40 meters) above the plaza, and a staircase for tourists allows access to the summit. I stood on top and admired the fine view.

To the south, in the northern part of the Maya Mountains, lies the recently discovered city of Caracol. In A.D. 562, Caracol defeated Tikal in a war and then dominated the region. Thus we see that in the degenerating city-state battles of the Maya, Tikal eventually conquered Uaxactún, but was in turn conquered by Caracol.

Caracol was only discovered in 1936 by *chicleros* and is still only accessible by foot, a journey which takes several days, though a road is being built to the site. Caracol is the largest known ancient Maya site in Belize and is a Classic Period urban center comprising a central ceremonial area converged on by causeways which linked the center to its outliers—to the areas whose production supported the nucleus. Its tallest pyramid, standing 137 feet (42 meters) has ousted the pyramid at Xunantunich as the tallest Maya structure in Belize.[131]

Caracol contains an ancient astronomical observatory and is particularly mysterious because this obviously important site is totally devoid of any running water. Indeed, if visiting the site, one must be sure to take plenty of water. Says the British archaeologist Byron Foster in *Warlords and Maizemen, A Guide to the Maya Sites of Belize*, "Why such a powerful site as Caracol should have been located in an area bereft of running water is one of the site's mysteries. Yet in a sense, the Maya created their own fertility: the main reservoir at Caracol is an engineering masterpiece providing water to this day."131

Eight miles south of Caracol are the vast Chiquibul Caves, the longest cave system in Central America with the largest cave room in the Western Hemisphere and the fourth largest cave room in the world. Only a lucky few have ever entered these remote and virtually inaccessible caves. Were these caves part of the reason that Caracol was built where it is, even without running water?

Considering that the Maya often built their pyramids and other structures directly over such caves, it seems highly likely that Caracol is connected via a tunnel system (partly natural and partly artificial) to the Chiquibul Caves.

That night Albert and I drank *Belikin* beer at Eve's and talked to other travellers. I was planning on heading into southern Belize in order to visit the mysterious site of Lubaantun. Albert had very little time left, so he was going to go to Belize City for a day and then return to Guatemala.

At breakfast the next day, Albert having already left by bus for Belize City, I was enjoying some fried eggs, mashed beans and tortillas when a older American couple at the next table suddenly said to me, "Are you a tourist down here too?" They had a southern accent and seemed like a typical middle-America couple. The man, about 60, wore a visored hat that said "Jackson Wrecking Co." on it, while the woman, about 55 and a bit heavy set, had short curly hair and cat-woman type glasses. They seemed more appropriate for a *Far Side* cartoon than to be here at a traveller's restaurant in Central America.

I told them that I was a tourist here in Central America as well. "And what are you folks doing here?" I asked politely.

"Oh, we drove down from Missouri," said the woman. "I'm Betty Jackson from Cape Girardo. This here's my husband, Orley."

I raised an eyebrow and took a bit of mashed red beans. "You drove down here from Missouri?" I asked. That seemed like quite an adventure for this elderly couple.

"You bet," said Orley, digging into his wallet. "I'm in the *Guinness Book of World Records!*"

"You're in the *Guinness Book of World Records* for driving to Belize from Missouri?" I asked in astonishment.

"Heck no," replied Orley. "I'm in there because I own the world's largest tow truck! Yessir, I built it myself. It's the largest wrecker in the world."

"Orley built it himself," repeated Betty.

Orley than showed me his business card. On it was a color photo of a huge tow-truck with the words *Guinness Book of World Records* underneath it. "My wrecker weighs 22 tons and is 36 feet long. It'll pick up a railway locomotive. Yessir. I've been in the *Guinness Book of World Records* since 1987!" He was obviously proud of his tow-truck, and I could tell that this was no ordinary Midwest couple.

"So what all are you doing down here in Belize?" asked Betty.

I told them, more or less, what I was doing. Then, seizing a possible opportunity for a free lift, I asked them if they were going toward Belize City and passing by the new capital Belmopan.

"Sure," said Orley, "we're leaving right after breakfast. You want a ride?"

I sure did, I told them, and then went to get my luggage. I checked out of the Jaguar Hotel and left the key at the desk so they wouldn't have to kick in the door and change the lock. Orley and Betty were waiting for me with their Buick station wagon outside of Eve's. Orley put my pack in the back, and I sat in the back seat.

With that, we were off down the Western Highway, heading east toward the coast. Looking out the window, I marveled at the bizarre adventures and chance encounters that made up my life. Just as Orley and Betty were not exactly as they seemed, neither is the history of the rise and fall of empires in Central America.

�����

Orley and Betty let me off at a bus station in Belmopan, the newly constructed capital of Belize, and a new city that was just getting going. Except for the museum, which wasn't even open when I was there, there is little in Belmopan for the traveler.

I waited for half an hour and then caught a bus for Dangriga, known until recently as Stann Creek. Dangriga is one of the principal settlements of the Black Caribs (also known as Garifunas) who are people of mixed African and Carib Indian descent. The Black Caribs trace their arrival in Dangriga to 1823, when their ancestors fled Honduras in the wake of a failed rebellion.

Because of the local citrus industry, Dangriga is a bustling commerce center of 8,000 people with nice sea views. Excursions to some of Cays offshore can be arranged. Anxious to get down south to Punta Gorda and the lost city of Lubaantun, I caught another bus in the early afternoon that made the long run through the dirt highway that connects southern Belize with the population centers of Dangriga and Belize City.

It was a bumpy, rutted road and a four hour trip, that made me feel like I was back in Guatemala. A few German travellers were on the bus, two attractive women who were going to the Cockscomb Jaguar Reserve an hour or two down the southern highway. I had seen plenty of animals in Guatemala, and it was well known that tourists would not see a jaguar at the reserve, but if lucky, maybe a few Howler Monkeys. I waved goodbye to them as they departed the bus at the small town of Maya Center to walk the seven miles with their packs to the reserve.

It was just dusk when the bus arrived at Punta Gorda, the last town of any size in southern Belize and the end of the Southern Highway. With a population of about 3000, it is mostly Black Caribs with a large selection of creoles, mestizos, Mopan Maya Indians and even a few Chinese and Lebanese merchants. From Punta Gorda it is possible to take a boat to Livingston in Guatemala, another Black

133

Carib settlement.

The town was only a few blocks long, but strangely, many of the hotels were closed. A couple of Black Carib kids helped me find a hotel that was open, and I settled into Foster's Hotel, a small two story building with a dozen rooms on Main Street.

I was unpacking and preparing for a shower when I heard them arguing over the commission that they had earned for bringing me to the hotel. When one knocked on my door and requested several dollars in commission from me because his friend would not share the commission he had gotten from the hotel, I politely told him that I wasn't in the habit of paying kids on the street for directing me to a hotel that was one block away and had already passed on the bus.

"Tell your friend to share his commission," I suggested.

I walked around town a bit and then had dinner in the only restaurant I could find, a popular but simple place on the northern edge of the town square. After some chicken, rice, beans and tortillas, I nursed a beer for a while, and then went to bed. I had discovered that the only bus out of town in the morning left at 5 a.m. and I would have to take that bus to get into the vicinity of Lubaantun.

With the help of a dozen mosquitoes, I got up in time for the 5 a.m. bus and sat behind the driver as he headed back out of town in the darkness. An hour later I got off the bus at the crossroads of the Coastal Highway and began walking down the road in the pre-darkness toward the Kekchi Indian town of San Pedro Columbia.

The sun rose in the east as I walked down that dusty road to the legendary lost city of Belize. For me, Lubaantun was a lost city that had intrigued me for many years, largely because the famous Crystal Skull was found in the ruins. Lubaantun means "place of fallen stones" in the local Mayan dialect, and the actual name of the city remains unknown. Lubaantun was first reported to the British colonial government late in the last century by the inhabitants of the Toledo settlement near Punta Gorda and in 1903 the Governor of the colony commissioned Thomas Gann to investigate it. Gann explored and excavated the main structures around the central plaza and concluded that the site's population must have been large. His report was published in England in 1904.

In 1915 R.E. Merwin of Harvard University investigated the site, locating many more structures, recognizing a ball court and drawing the first plan. His excavation of the ball court revealed three carved stone markers, each depicting two men playing the ball game. Curiously these are the only carved stones found at Lubaantun.

It wasn't until 1924 when F.A. "Mike" Mitchell-Hedges arrived at Lubaantun to help Thomas Gann with the excavations of the city. In 1927, while digging in a collapsed altar and adjoining wall, Mitchell-Hedges' adopted daughter, Anna, discovered the life size crystal skull on her seventeenth birthday. Three months later a matching jawbone was discovered 25 feet from the altar. And thus, one of the world's strangest ancient objects came to the attention of the world.

The age of the skull is unknown. Rock crystal cannot be dated by conventional means. Hewlett-Packard laboratories, which studied the skull, estimated that its completion would have require a minimum of 300 years' work by a series of extremely gifted artisans. On the hardness scale, rock crystal ranks only slightly below diamonds.

The mystery of the skull deepened when it was discovered that the jaw bone was carved from the same piece of crystal and that when the two pieces were attached the cranium rocked on the jawbone base, giving the impression that the skull was talking by opening and closing its mouth. In this manner, the skull could have been manipulated as a temple oracle by priests.

Even more incredible properties are ascribed to the skull. The frontal lobe is said to cloud over sometimes, turning milky white. At other times the skull is said to emit an aura of light, "strong with a faint trace of the color of hay, similar to a ring around the moon."[117]

According to Frank Dorland, a crystalographer for Hewlett-Packard who studied the skull for years, the skull's eyes would sometimes flicker as if they were alive and observers have reported strange sounds, odors, and various light effects emanating from the skull. Bizarre photographs have been taken of "pictures" which sometimes form within the skull. An example of such "pictures" forming within the skull are images of flying discs (UFO-flying saucers) and of what appears to be the Caracol observatory at the Toltec-Mayan site of Chichen Itza. In the past few years the skull has become quite famous because it has been displayed at Psychic Fairs in the U.S.A. and Canada. The skull now resides with Anna "Sammy" Mitchell-Hedges in Kitchener, Ontario.

Suddenly, I heard the sound of the car coming down the road. I turned and saw a beat-up old van heading for me. I stood my ground and waved at the driver. I then pointed to the Maya Mountains in the distance to indicate that this was where I was going.

The vehicle, an ancient delivery van, slowed to a stop and the driver opened the passenger door for me. He was a young man, apparently of Lebanese or Latin descent.

"Are you going to San Pedro Columbia?" I asked him.

"Yes," he replied. "Get in." With that, we were bouncing up the dirt road into the Indian village a few miles up into the green hills. Soon we were passing through the colorful village of farmers. Men and women were just starting their day as we drove through town.

The Kekchi Indian's forbearers had come to this area of Belize more than a century ago to escape forced labor on coffee plantations in the Verapaz region of Guatemala. Now a road had actually reached their small village, and I gathered that this was a relatively recent modernization.

The driver let me off a kilometer or so past the village to where a narrow dirt road branched off to the ruins another kilometer away.

I thanked the driver for my lift and shouldered my pack for the walk to the city. I reached the ruins after a ten minute walk, they were situated on top of a ridge that dominates the countryside. Though it is 25 miles from the coast, one can see to the ocean on a

135

clear day.

I was sweating and breathing hard as I reached the first pyramid on the top of the ridge. I dumped my pack and sat on one of the cut-stones of the side of the structure.

I was immediately impressed by what I saw. The construction at Lubaantun was quite unlike anything else I had seen in all of Central America so far. I then learned that Lubaantun is unique in the Mayan world for being a city built out precision cut stones and fitted without mortar. It is the only Mayan city built in this way. The pyramids at Lubaantun have rounded corners, a characteristic that is also highly unusual and is only seen at some sites along the Usumacinta River to the north. Clearly, Lubaantun is an unusual site.

A series of plazas, each surrounded by stone temples and palaces, ascends from south to north, conforming with the rising ridge line. The major structure is a pyramid 40 feet high and 100 feet in length. Because of the city's being built on a ridgetop, the impression is that the pyramid is taller.

Walking around the city, it was the precision cut stones that impressed me the most. Having spent quite a bit of time in Peru, the similarity in the construction technique of Lubaantun and the amazing cities of the high Andes around Cuzco, Machu Picchu for example, was quite striking. Lubaantun reminded me not of Tikal or Copán in Honduras, but of cities in South America.

Furthermore, hieroglyphs, steles or any other typically Mayan features are entirely missing from Lubaantun. The only carved monuments discovered were the three carved ball court markers.

Yet, molded figurines, jade figures, clay whistles, obsidian, flint and of course, the crystal skull, have been found in the ruins. There is a spring at Lubaantun, but there are no palaces or buildings used for family dwellings. These may have been nearby, though, built out of wood.

Because of the similarity with such megalithic ruins as Machu Picchu, where perfectly cut stones are fitted without mortar, I wondered if any of the stones at Lubaantun were megalithic in nature. The rock was sandstone and limestone, not particularly difficult stone to work with, yet if I could find blocks of stone that weighed tons rather than just a few hundred pounds, as most of the blocks that I saw weighed, than maybe I could prove to my own satisfaction that there was some relationship.

As I explored the ruins in the mid-morning sun, I suddenly found what I was looking for. There, at the base of a second pyramid to the south of the main structure, down in a gully, were massive blocks of squared stone. Unlike the blocks making up the bulk of the pyramid which were about three feet long and two feet wide and deep, these stones were five or six feet long and three or four feet wide, weighing several tons. Were these the megalithic blocks I was looking for?

The ruins were originally known as the Rio Grande ruins (because of the nearby river of that name) and introduced to the world in an article in the *Illustrated London News* (July 26, 1924). In the article,

Dr. Gann says, "On a second pyramid we found a cave-in, stone-lined chambers, from one of which we endeavored to clear out the debris of stone and rubbish with which it was filled, but soon had to desist, as the great weight of the stones took the combined exertions of all our laborers to recover through the narrow aperture at the top, and we soon realized that, if we were to do any other work at all in the limited time at our disposal, we must leave these vaults within the pyramids till later." These vaults have never been excavated, and in fact, most of Lubaantun is just as it was found by Gann, though cleared of the surrounding jungle.

Gann believed the city was older than any other Mayan city yet discovered. In the *Illustrated London News* article Gann concludes, "Before leaving, we christened the city 'Lubaantun'—literally 'the place of fallen stones' in the Mayan language. This city differs from all other known Maya cities, in that there are no stone palaces and temples standing upon the great pyramidical substructures, and in the entire absence of stone sculptures and of the great monoliths upon which were inscribed the days of their erection, put up at twenty-year intervals, and later at five-year intervals by the Maya throughout Central America and Yucatan.

"It would appear from the absence of stone sculptures, temples and palaces that these ruins antedate Copan, Quirigua, Uaxactun and other cities of the Old Empire, the earliest recorded dates at which go back to about the beginning of the Christian Era, for it is almost certain that prior to this Maya dates were recorded on wood, and the earliest temples and palaces constructed of the same material."

Gann believed that Lubaantun had been built circa 2000 B.C. and the absence of any hieroglyphs, steles or dates of any kind were evidence to him that the city had been built before any of the classical sites that are now so famous.

He makes a good point, but Gann is overlooking a very important idea that comes with his evidence. This is that Lubaantun *is not a Mayan city at all.*

Sitting on the stone steps of the city, I recalled other cities that I had seen that had a similar appearance to that of Lubaantun. One was the city of Lixus on the Atlantic coast of Morocco. Lixus is a Phoenician city that was later taken over by the Romans after the Punic Wars. Could it be that Lubaantun was a Phoenician city. Both cities were built out of precision cut stones fitted without mortar. Was there a connection?

Curiously, Lubaantun is generally dated as being a fairly late city in the Mayan empire. When the Cambridge archaeologist Norman Hammond excavated at the city in 1970, he ascribed the occupation as being from 730 to 890 A.D., the typical dates of cities at the final decline of the Mayan civilization. Hammond theorized that the main economy of Lubaantun was the cultivation of cacao beans, which were used as a form of currency throughout the Mayan realm.

So on one hand we have Dr. Thomas Gann and Mike Mitchell-Hedges believing that Lubaantun is the oldest Mayan city ever found, having been built three or four thousand years ago, while the traditional archaeologists are ascribing a date of 730 A.D. to the structure. The fact that hieroglyphs, steles or even typical construction techniques of the Mayas are totally absent at Lubaantun does not seem to enter into their calculations of the city to any degree at all. They simply find it "odd."

While certain figurines, cacoa beans or whatever might be found in the city that can be dated from 800 A.D., they may be there because Mayans from the nearby site of Nim Li Punit, which is less than ten miles away, had put them there. Most certainly Mayans visited the site of Lubaantun in the eighth century A.D., though they did not necessarily build the city. Kekchi Maya currently live within two kilometers of Lubaantun and it is an undisputable fact that they did not build the city, but moved to the vicinity from Guatemala within the last two centuries.

Nim Li Punit is unquestionably a Mayan city, it has steles, is built with limestone cement, has Mayan hieroglyphs giving dates between 700 and 800 A.D. In fact, one stele, 31 feet high, is the tallest stele in Belize. Nim Li Punit was only discovered in 1974 during exploration for oil, and as often happens, was soon looted. The unexcavated site includes a number residential buildings set on plazas and a ball court.

Lubaantun also has a ball court, but this is not necessarily a Mayan invention. Ball courts are found in Toltec cities, in northern Arizona (more on this in a later chapter), and among the earlier Olmecs, whose name means "rubber people" referring to the rubber ball used in the games. Certainly it would not be said that these ball courts were Mayan in origin.

Therefore, we have two cities within the same area, one has Mayan hieroglyphs, steles and typical Mayan architecture. The other has none of the above and was apparently destroyed in an earthquake. Nim Li Punit was also destroyed by an earthquake, one which fractured most of the steles at the site.

The lines of stones at Lubaantun are in rows that are alternately in and out. In 1926 the British Museum sent an expedition to Lubaantun under the directorship of T. A. Joyce. Joyce concluded that Lubaantun had been built in an "in and out" style because of the unusual alternating of the stones, every other row being pushed out. The famous British archaeologist J. Eric Thompson then arrived in 1927 to contradict Joyce's conclusion, showing that alternating courses of protruding and recessed stones were due to root action and probably earth movements.[131]

🐉🐉🐉

"And what of the famous crystal skull?" I thought, standing on top of the central pyramid and looking out toward the coast. Where did it fit in regards to this strange city?

While the skull was found in the ruins by Mitchell-Hedges adopted daughter on her seventeenth birthday, there are many who believe that Mitchell-Hedges put it there for her to find. If this is the case,

138

where did Mitchell-Hedges get the skull?

F.A. Mitchell-Hedges was a fascinating person, and in some ways, his life was very much a model for an Indiana Jones sort of character. Born in 1882, "Mike" Mitchell-Hedges was destined for life of adventure. He chronicles many of his adventures in his book *Danger My Ally*,[116] which was published in 1954. Mitchell-Hedges came to Canada and the United States in 1899, met with J.P. Morgan, won a fortune in a card game, and took off for Mexico. He was then captured and held prisoner by Pancho Villa, and then later rode with Villa in Northern Mexico.

He eventually ended up in Central America. With his girl friend, the wealthy Lady Richmond Brown (who was married at the time), he cruised the Caribbean, exploring the Bay Islands off Honduras, the San Blas Islands off Panama and the area around Jamaica.

He believed that artifacts which he had found in the Bay Islands pointed to a high civilization that was now beneath the water, and equated it with Atlantis. Mitchell-Hedges had a penchant for mystical sciences and secret societies, and championed the cause of lost civilizations and Atlantis. Eventually, he ended up in Lubaantun and the crystal was "discovered" in 1927.

Curiously, he devotes only three paragraphs to the famous crystal skull in his book, and these few paragraphs were even removed from the American edition of his book, which was published later.

Says Mitchell-Hedges, referring to a trip to South Africa in 1947, "We took with us also the sinister Skull of Doom of which much has been written. How it came into my possession I have reason for not revealing.

"The Skull of Doom is made of pure rock crystal and according to scientists it must have taken over 150 years, generation after generation working all the days of their lives, patiently rubbing down with sand an immense block of rock crystal until finally the perfect Skull emerged.

"It is at least 3,600 years old and according to legend was used by the High Priest of the Maya when performing esoteric rites. It is said that when he willed death with the help of the skull, death invariably followed. It has been described as the embodiment of all evil. I do not wish to try and explain this phenomena."[116]

A photograph of the skull is reproduced in the book with the caption, "The Skull of Doom, dating back at least 3,600 years, and taking about 150 years to rub down with sand from a block of pure rock crystal, nearly as hard as diamond. It is stated in legend that it was used by a high priest of the Maya to concentrate on will death. It is said to be the embodiment of all evil; several people who have cynically laughed at it have died, others have been stricken and become seriously ill."

That some curse may come with this skull is an interesting theory, though it does not seem that there is a fatal curse for the owner of the relic such as with the Hope diamond. Mitchell-Hedges had himself rarely let the skull from his sight for 30 years, during which time he survived three knife attacks and eight bullet wounds. At his death on June 12, 1959, aged seventy-seven, he bequeathed the crystal skull to his adopted daughter. Belizean authorities however want the skull returned to Belize.

Revealing is Mitchell-Hedges' cryptic remark, "How it came into possession I have reason for not revealing." When the much repeated story is that his adopted daughter Anna found the skull on her seventeenth birthday in the lost city, why should Mitchell-Hedges say he has reason for not revealing how he got the skull?

Because of this cryptic statement, some researchers into the skull have suggested that Mitchell-Hedges was already in possession of the skull in 1927 and that he placed the skull in the ruins for eighteen year old Anna to find on her birthday.

If he was already in possession of the skull, where did it come from and where did he get it? One theory was that the skull was a 12,000 year old relic from Atlantis that had been handed down through Knights Templar and ultimately came into possession of the inner circle of the Mason Lodge. Mitchell-Hedges was an inner Mason and may have somehow acquired the skull either through the secret society or as part of a gambling debt. He then introduced it to the world through the ingenious device of the lost city.

Another possibility is that the skull came from another Central American ancient city, possibly, Mexico, and was looted from some pyramid. Mitchell-Hedges then bought the skull as a stolen artifact. He was sworn not to reveal the origin of the skull, thereby his statement that he had reasons for not revealing how he acquired it.

An even more interesting scenario is that the Knights Templar were in possession of the skull and later moved the skull to Central America at about the time of demise and eradication by the Catholic Church in 1314 A.D. In this theory, Knights Templar were aware of the sea routes across the Atlantic and sent the skull to some remote spot across the Atlantic (Lubaantun) where it could be kept in safety, keeping it from falling into the hands of the Vatican.

Later, Mitchell-Hedges was sent by the Masons to Lubaantun to retrieve the skull.

At any rate, Lubaantun is a good place to have stashed the skull, whether it had been done hundreds of years before or by Mitchell-Hedges.

The Crystal Skull of Mitchell-Hedges has become a popular subject in recent years, with a number of books being written about them (there are a number of known crystal skulls, coming from various sources, including Tibet and Mexico. The Mitchell-Hedges skull is the most advanced, it has a movable jawbone). In one book, *Mystery of the Crystal Skulls Revealed,*[130] crystal researcher Nick Nocerino relates that he believes that the crystal skulls (especially the Mitchell-Hedges skull), "record vibrations in the form of images of the events that have occurred around them. In this way, they seem to work as video cameras of sorts, recording holographic scenes."

In *Mystery of the Crystal Skulls Revealed,*[130] the general consensus is that the various skulls are extraterrestrial in nature. Most of their material is channeled through trance mediums, and is therefore highly suspect. The authors believe through their channeling that "many of the Crystal Skulls were brought or projected here from other parts of our galaxy. ...some of the Crystal Skulls we are currently familiar with were created on the Earth, but they were copied from the Thirteen Original Skulls, some of which may still be in Tibet. Others have been moved to an underground city near Salt Lake City in Utah."[130]

The authors contend that thirteen crystal skulls exist in a set and were once kept (or still are—this point is unclear) beneath the Potala Palace in Tibet. However, they were originally created in Atlantis and were used in the "Thirteen Healing Temples of Atlantis." Generally, it is believed by these researchers that the Crystal Skull is from 10,000 to 30,000 years old. One date given for the skull is 17,000 years old.

According to the researchers, many crystal skulls have been used for human sacrifices, and therefore "perverted." However, the authors of *Mystery of the Crystal Skulls Revealed* believe that the Mitchell-Hedges skull was never used for such terrible purposes.

𝄞𝄞𝄞

I stopped in the small village of San Pedro Columbia on my way out back from the ruins and found a small shop with some soft drinks, oranges and a bag of corn chips. I sat by the dusty road for a bit hoping that a car would come along, but after a bit, it seemed unlikely.

So, shouldering my pack, I began the four mile walk back to the crossroads of the Southern Highway where I could catch a bus or truck back north to Dangriga and eventually on to Belize City. It was a bright sunny day, and rather hot for walking with a full pack, but I was used to such things.

It took me an hour and half to hike the distance, and just as I came to the Shell station on the crossroads, the last bus from Punta Gorda pulled up and let off passengers. I ran to the bus, and climbed aboard. It was a typical old American school bus, still painted that familiar school bus yellow. Small aluminum signs with messages about how important the safety of school children was were still riveted to the front of the bus. To my amazement the bus was not full, and I easily found a seat.

Happily settled in behind the driver, I gazed out the window and thought back on the strange city of Lubaantun.

Was I correct in my theory that Lubaantun was a Phoenician city in the new world? Perhaps their main trading base along the eastern Yucatan coast? Did Phoenician ships coming from Carthage, Tarshish (modern day Cadiz) or Lixus on the the west coast Morocco arrive at Lubaantun to trade circa 1000 B.C.?

It was a fascinating thought, I mused. If the Mayas were already well established along this coast and the northern Yucatan, perhaps the Phoenicians were able to get a trading concession, much as the British and Portuguese were able to do with the

141

Emperors of China in setting up their trade cities of Hong Kong and Macao.

One clue to support this theory was use of special dyes by both the Mayas and the Phoenicians. The Phoenicians were named by the Greeks, giving them the name the "Purple People." This is the name Phoenician, a Greek name, and we do not know what name the Phoenicians actually called themselves. They were called the Purple People because they wore beautiful purple robes which they dyed with a rare and special dye derived from a sea snail.

In an article on Mayan dyes by Laura de los Heros that was published in the Aeorcaribe magazine *Kukulcán* (year III, No. 11, February 1991), it is shown that the Maya used the exact same dye. "In the course of the trading, the Mayas also received plants and animals that produced coloring substances. Perhaps the most valuable dyes were the scarlet extracted from the cochineal bug that lives as a parasite in the nopal cactus, and the purple derived from the inky secretions of seasnails along the Pacific coast."

Where did the Mayas learn this purple dye secret? Perhaps from the Phoenicians, or, on the other hand, perhaps it was the Phoenicians who learned this secret from the Mayas!

The bus got a flat tire about half the way back to Dangriga. I got out and walked around while about half the males on the bus fussed and argued about how the tire should be changed. Butterflies were everywhere in the jungle, delighting in the rare open space created by the Southern Highway through the thick hardwood forest. I occupied the half hour by wandering amongst these clouds of colorful fluttering wings that swept down the dirt road.

Eventually, we made it back to Dangriga, picked up more passengers, and the bus continued on to Belmopan and then to Belize city. That evening I was walking the streets of Belize City, and my first stop was the Seaside Guest House, a budget hotel popular with travellers run by an American couple.

The proprietor, an expatriate who had been living in Belize for eight years or so, showed me the dormitory room and took a deposit on a key. I swung my pack down on the floor and flopped down on my bunk bed.

Suddenly I heard a familiar voice say, "Well, it's about time you made it!"

I looked up to a top bunk to my left and there was Albert lying on a bed. "Albert," I cried, "Are you still here?"

"Sure," he said, "I'm thinking about going out to one of the Cays off the coast. Maybe Cay Caulker. How was the lost city of Lubaantun?"

"I'm dying for a cold drink," I said, "Come with me and I'll tell you over a beer."

🌟🌟🌟

We popped around the corner to the Bellevue Hotel where we sat at the port-side, upstairs bar having a cold Belikin Export beer. I told Albert about my trip to Lubaantun and how unique the city was and my theory of it being a Phoenician city. We also discussed the Crystal Skull, something which Albert was somewhat familiar with.

Albert took a gulp from his beer and said, "Not only is the Crystal Skull an unusual relic, said by some to be from an alien civilization, but the Mayas themselves are said by some 'Maya scholars' to be extraterrestrials as well."

"Really?" I said. "That seems like a rather far-out notion. Why do they think that?"

Albert pulled a book out of his day pack and put it on the table. It was *The Mayan Factor*,[67] by José Argüelles. Said Albert, "Argüelles is a Mexican anthropologist and a University of Colorado art historian. He says in his book *The Mayan Factor*, that the Maya were interdimensional travellers who settled in Mexico around 600 B.C. They had come from another planet to place earth and its solar system in alignment with the universe."

"Really?" I said. "But there were cities in this area before 600 B.C. If the Maya did not arrive until then, I wonder who built them?"

Albert ignored me, saying, "Argüelles claims that he met a Mayan holy man who told him our solar system is the seventh one the Maya navigated. The leaders departed in the ninth century A.D., their mission completed, and they left behind their sacred calendar as a system of prophesy. Argüelles claims that when the Mayan calendar ends in 2012, mankind will shift to a decentralized, nonindustrial culture in which contact with alien beings is commonplace."

Albert then opened the book to show me some relevant passages. In *The Mayan Factor*,[67] Argüelles states, "The Mayan Great Cycle is actually the description of a galactic beam measuring 5,200 tuns, or 5,125 earth years in diameter. The earth entered such a beam August 13, 3113 B.C., and will leave it in the year 2012 A.D. The purpose of the electromagnetically charged beam is to accelerate the evolved DNA into a technology-extruding organism that creates in effect a planetary exo-nervous system. When the exo-nervous system is in place, acceleration becomes exponential and phases into synchronization.

"Acceleration is measured by the collapse in the time it takes one human to communicate to another from halfway around the globe. Once maximum acceleration is achieved, when communication is electronic and virtually instantaneous, then it becomes synchronization: the equally exponential rate of linking up every single human organism with each other through utilization of the planetary exo-nervous system, thus creating a sensitive aggregate operating as a unified, planetary consciousness. Once maximum synchronization is attained, the exo-nervous system will fall away, being replaced by the more efficient medium of telepathic synchronicity. The planet will then be initiated into the Galactic Federation.

"August 16-18, 1987 marks the point at which the galactic beam phases from acceleration to synchronization, while December 21, 2012 is the date of galactic synchronization.

"The purpose of the classic Maya was to synchronize the terrestrial calendar cycle with the galactic acceleration beam. Once done, they left, leaving the precise calendar and the knowledge transmitted by seers and symbols cloaked in the garb of myth, the prophecy of the return of Quetzalcoatl. The return is set for August 16, 1987."[67]

"That is a fascinating theory," I had to admit.

"Because of the Harmonic Convergence," said Albert, "It has gained a great deal of popularity. What do you think of this?"

I took a sip of Belikin and thought for a moment. "Certainly traditional Maya scholars would hold the idea that the Maya were extraterrestrials as totally ridiculous. While the strange, elongated heads of the Maya elite did make them look, to our eyes at least, like aliens, this isn't a genetic trait at all, but a skull deformation that resulted from the compression of the skull as an infant with a board.

"It is not something that just the Mayans did, Egyptian royalty in the Amarna period also did this (witness frescoes of the Pharaoh Akhenaton), plus skulls of this type have been found in South America. More mundanely, the Flathead Indians of western Montana also deformed their crania in this way, hence their name and the name of Flathead Lake. I know, this is the area where I went to high school."

Albert nodded. "It is difficult to imagine that interdimensional, space travelling 'time keepers' dressing in jaguar furs, took part in ritual city-state warfare, played ball games in which some of the players were executed after the game, took captives and slaves, sacrificing them to various blood thirsty gods, and ran around with such primitive weapons as spears and clubs. Frankly, this theory that the Mayans were extraterrestrials is about as valid as the belief that Columbus was the first European to discover America.

"Yet, Argüelles is a genius," Albert continued. "His comparison of the I-Ching and the Gate at Tiahuanaco to the 64 character genetic code is brilliant. There is no doubt that the Mayan calendar is a fascinating and exact bit of time keeping, basically based on 52 year cycles. That the Maya were obsessed by time, there seems to be no doubt, and one theory on the demise of the Maya has to do with a prophesy, such as the return of Quetzalcoatl, which failed to come true. Considering that Quetzalcoatl was a real person, not just some 'convergence,' it does not seem that there is any evidence that he 'returned' on August 18, 1987. The Aztecs, for instance believed that Quetzalcoatl would arrive on a 'One Reed Year.' This year comes up every 52 years. Cortez, incredibly, arrived not just on a One Reed year, but on the personal name day of Quetzalcoatl, a 9 Wind day. This was April 21st, 1519."

I finished my beer with a big gulp. I could certainly see Albert's point, from what we know of the Maya, they were no doubt a fascinating and weird bunch with a calendar that was extraordinarily exact, but if they were extraterrestrials, they were rather cruel and primitive, at least in the later years.

In all fairness to Argüelles' Galactic Beam theory, such a beam does apparently exist, and is known to scientists as the "Photon

Belt." In an article first published in Australia in 1981, and reprinted in the Feb-March 1991 issue of *Nexus* Magazine (Australia, Vol.2, No.2), it is stated that Dr. Paul Otto Hesse made a special study of the Pleiades star system and discovered, at absolute right angles to the movements of the suns, a *Photon Belt* or *Manasic Ring*, of light particles. According to the article, it takes 24,000 years for our solar system to complete an orbit of this system, and during this time, our solar system would enter the Photon Belt twice.

Supposedly, there is a period of 10,000 years of "darkness" (which we are in right now) followed by 2,000 years of "light" while we are in the Photon Belt. As earth enters this Photon Belt, according to the article, all molecules will become excited, all atoms will change, things will become luminescent, and there will be constant light. Even the deepest cave underground will be illuminated by the Photons. This 2,000 years of the Photon Belt would be a good time to explore the many tunnels and caves in the earth, as they would be continually lit, and flashlights would be unnessesary. Allegedly, during the day, things will seem normal, but at night, an eerie light will pervade everything. This Photon Belt of the 1981 article seems analagous to Argüelles' Galactic Acceleration Beam. According to the article, we will enter the Photon Belt about the year 1999.

While Argüelles gives the date for the galactic synchronization as December 21, 2012, using the Mayan calendar, what one needs to ask is why do extraterrestrials need to come here to synchronize our calendar with this Photon Belt? Apparently, it just happens whether our calendars are adjusted to it or not. Does a team of experts have to travel to some remote part of the earth to make sure that the equinox or solstice happens on the right day? Such cosmic occurances happen no matter what one's calendar says, and while watching the movements of heavenly bodies may be important to any calendar, the calendar itself does not have to be "synchronized." The Mayan calendar is fascinating, and without a doubt, the world's most unusual and accurate. Its study could easily last several lifetimes.

"Where do you suppose the Mayans got their sophisticated calendar and where do you suppose they came from?" I asked Albert.

"The Mayans probably inherited their calendar from older civilizations," said Albert, "just as much of the knowledge that the ancient Egyptians, Chinese, Hindus and others did. These ancient civilizations even stated that they derived their knowledge from such semi-mythical cultures as Atlantis and Mu. These ancients were highly advanced and had knowledge of all things. Though I believe that extraterrestrials do indeed exist, there is no need to derive technology or calendrical knowledge from them, all of these things have existed in the past. Dark ages of 'anti-science' have attempted to wipe out such knowledge however."

"Sort of like King Solomon of the Bible saying that there is nothing new under the sun," I suggested.

"Exactly. Probably the ancient Maya derived much of their

science, including the calendar, from the ancient Chinese. The ancient Chinese claim that their ancient knowledge was derived from a now sunken continent in the Pacific Ocean (see *Lost Cities of China, Central Asia & India*,[16] for more information on this)."

"To me," said Albert, "Argüelles is more correct when he relates the Chinese *I Ching* to the Mayan numerical and calendrical system. The *I Ching* is probably something from the ancient civilization of Mu."

"Perhaps the Chinese got their system from extraterrestrials," I commented with a smile.

Albert smiled back and laughed. "Well, I guess anything is possible," he said. "Anything."

���

The next day Albert was off to Cay Caulker, and I took a day trip to Altun Ha, probably the most visited archaeological site in Belize, mainly because of its close proximity to Belize City.

Altun Ha is interesting for several reasons. The largest piece of jade ever found in Mesoamerica was discovered at the Sun God Temple (structure B-4), which is also the tallest structure at Altun Ha, rising a rather unimpressive 59 feet above the main plaza.

This huge piece of jade, now at the so-called museum in Belmopan, is apparently a jade statue of Kinich Ahau, the Sun God to which Altun Ha was dedicated. The round piece of jade is 14.9 cm high and weighs 4.42 kg or 9.75 pounds.

Burned fragments of jade suggest that some sort of ceremony involving the throwing of sacred objects into a fire occurred at Altun Ha at regular intervals. That Altun Ha was a religious city dedicated to the Sun God draws certain parallels to other sun worshiping centers in Egypt, Peru, Polynesia, India and China.

Altun Ha also provides evidence that the Maya did not simply vanish in some mysterious "rapture" or UFO exodus. At approximately 900 A.D. the city was sacked and much of it destroyed. Said David Pendergast, the archaeologist responsible for most of the excavation at the site, "Of the seven tombs encountered in (structure) B-4, one had been largely destroyed by collaps of the surrounding construction, and three, including the last two built atop the structure showed unmistakable signs of having suffered desecration, involving destruction of contents, burning of some portions thereof, filling of the crypt with soil, and tossing of the roof slabs back into the pile. Such activity, clearly not the work of looters, very probably took place at the time of the final collapse of the Maya civilization at Altun Ha, and may well be an indicator that the collapse was ...attended by some violence, perhaps taking the form of a peasant revolt."[131]

One theory for such a peasant revolt was the failure of an important prophesy to occur, such as possibly the return of Quetzalcoatl (called Kukulcán by the Maya).

I spent another night at the Seaside Guesthouse, wandering

around Belize City for the afternoon. It was a pleasant city, though small, with the air of a Caribbean port.

Belize City has a bad reputation among travellers, mainly because of a few street hustlers who tend to bother people who are obviously tourists, offering them illegal drugs, prostitutes, blackmarket money-changing or what not. Though I ran into a few of these guys, I did not find them to be particularly annoying, at least not any worse than any other hustlers I had ever run into.

Certain areas of the city, mainly the neighborhoods west of the Albert Street in downtown Belize City, are relatively dangerous to walk around in at night if you are tourist, but apparently the hysteria and bad publicity that Belize City has gotten are rather overblown in proportion to the actual problem. Maybe I was just in a good mood while I was in Belize City, but I felt safer walking around there than I do in New York.

Certainly Belize City does not have a great deal to offer the traveller or tourist, and most people merely transit the city for a day, or even a few hours, on their way to the cays offshore or on to Guatemala or north to the Mexican state of Quintana Roo.

North to Quintana Roo was the direction I was going, as I was't that interested in the small, nearly deserted island cays, that dot the barrier reef of Belize. The scuba diving is good, but the resorts are expensive. And anyway, I was in Central America to search for lost cities and ancient mysteries, not get a sunburn on the beach.

I left Belize City early one morning and headed out on the Northern Highway for Orange Walk, the major city in the northern section of the country. A bus took me up to the town, a place of largely mestizo population with a smattering of Mennonites from Germany (by way of Canada) who farm the land in traditional old European ways.

In Orange Walk I met a British traveller named Brian who worked for a large tour company out of London. He was in Belize to reconnoiter the country for a forthcoming tour that his company was running in the months to come. He invited me to share a boat he had chartered to the Mayan site of Lamanai.

We climbed into small motorized boat on the west bank of the New River Lagoon and began the one hour trip by river to the site. Each bend of the river held new surprises for us: herons and other birds stalking fish in the shallows, Mennonite farms along the shore, even an alligator was basking in the shallows. Palm fronds were mirrored in the water while water lilies bloomed along the shore.

We saw turtles sunning themselves on logs that lay in the rushes. The aluminum speedboat leaned into the curves of the river, and different channels split off from the main river. Thick jungle was to the west, and kingfishers, ospreys and grebes flew overhead.

Lamanai, whose name means "submerged crocodile" is interesting because it has one of the longest continuous occupations in the Mayan world. Lamanai was probably first inhabited 3500 years ago, or 1500 B.C. It was still inhabited by Mopan Maya to 1800. The tall pyramid at the site was probably completed around 100 B.C. and has a height of 112 feet, making it possibly the tallest Mayan structure of its day.

We alighted from the boat on the shores of the New River, and then began our walk through the site. Our guide, a jolly, rotund man named Homer, who was working with Brian's British tour company, gave us his tour guide lecture as we walked around the extensive site.

"Lamanai was burned and attacked in the tenth century," said Homer as we walked down a jungle trail. "Now, over here, this is where the bones of children were discovered. It is believed that they were human sacrifices to the gods in a last attempt to save the dying Mayan civilization."

Brian kept asking him questions and taking notes for use back at the London office.

"There was no more construction at Lamanai after the 12th century," Homer went on. "They made an interesting discovery near the ball court over here, ritual objects of beads, jade, and flint in a bowl of mercury."

"Really?" I said, suddenly taking notice to what he was saying. "They found these objects in a bowl of mercury?" To me this was unusual, and I thought of the bowl of mercury found submerged at Lake Amatitlan in Guatemala.

"Oh, yes indeed," said Homer, though for him this was just one of those facts that tour guides are told and have to repeat to tourists. "Probably they were offerings to the ball players."

I asked Homer about the controversial question of whether it was the winners or the losers that were executed after the game. His reply was that the winners were executed and were happy to be sacrificed to the gods.

"Maybe they should install that practice with the World Cup," Brian commented dryly.

I laughed but Homer looked on humorlessly. "Oh, the Queen of Belize wouldn't allow that," he said.

"The Queen of Belize?" I asked. It was then explained to me that under Belize's constitutions, Queen Elizabeth was the Queen of Belize, not just the Queen of England. We then climbed the pyramid, which had a commanding view of the countryside. We could even see the tallest pyramid of Altun Ha in the distance.

We continued on to the older section of the city where Homer told us that the small pyramid had been built over a period from 400 B.C. to 200 A.D. and contained an "Olmec influence." There was a huge head on one wall which had been covered up during one of the periodic reconstructions of the pyramid (every 52 years claim archaeologists). I was particularly interested in a beautiful cut stone chair at the base of the western side of the pyramid that had an exquisite yin-yang stone below it.

I marveled at the round stone and deeply cut curving line of the yin-yang symbol. All tourists were shown this chair, though apparently any reference to the Chinese aspect of the yin-yang motif was left out. That seemed typical.

Lamanai is in a good position to move via river to important cities on the coast. The New River flows to the Mayan city of Cerros, a major coastal city where the trade in vanilla, chocolate, allspice, jade, copper, gold and other products (such as bird feathers) took place. Just to the west of Lamanai was the Rio Hondo which went north to the Yucatan and then to the coast. This made Lamanai an important crossroads town located between two major transportation rivers.

An hour or so later we were back in Orange Walk and I thanked Brian and Homer for the river trip to Lamanai. It had been a very interesting trip, and I had found Lamanai an even more interesting city than Altun Ha.

There was still some time left in the afternoon, and so I caught a bus north to Corozal and later a minibus to the Mexican border. It had been an interesting trip to Belize; a strange, English speaking country in Latin America. I had enjoyed meeting Homer, a nice fellow with his quaint expressions concerning the Queen of Belize.

As I reached the border post, I thought about the people of Belize. To me they seemed like the Maya, an alien people, clutching their alien gods.

"Mike" Mitchell-Hedges, Lady Richmond Brown, and Dr. Thomas Gann at the ruins of Lubaantun, about 1924. Note the well-formed blocks of stone behind them, that were once perfectly fitted together without mortar. Now they have been jumbled by an earthquake.

149

Explorer Hedges Finds Pre-Mayan City Buried Beneath Caribbean Sea

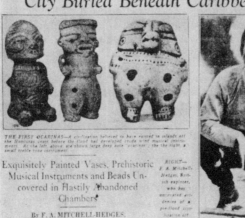

THE FIRST OCARINAS—A civilization believed to have existed in islands off the Honduras coast before the flood had developed crude wind musical instruments. At the left, above, are shown large deep note "ocarinas"; the the right, a small treble tone instrument.

Exquisitely Painted Vases, Prehistoric Musical Instruments and Beads Uncovered in Hastily Abandoned Chambers

By F. A. MITCHELL-HEDGES,
Famous Explorer, F. Z. S., F. L. S., F. F. G. S.,
F. F. A. I., F. R. S., Member of the Maya
Committee of the British Museum.

RIGHT—F. A. Mitchell-Hedges, British explorer, who has uncovered evidences of a pre-flood civilization off the Honduras coast.

THE VESTIGES OF a luxurious civilization which have

'WILL SHED'

Atlantis Was No Myth but the Cradle Of American Races, Declares Hedges

AMAZING—Explorer Hedges (right) examining some astounding discoveries in the "Cradle of Civilization" has max beads reduced to fist size. Left, petrified stone head, once the wooden top of Cheltstick with skull showing same formation as that of the American Indian.

Excavations of Twenty-one Sites on Five Caribbean Islands Confirm His Theory of Pre-Flood Cataclysm, Says Noted Explorer

By F. A. MITCHELL-HEDGES,
Famous Explorer F. Z. S., F. L. S., F. F. G. S.,
F. R. A. I., F. R. S., Member of the Maya
Committee of the British Museum.

MANY weirdly strange mysteries are explained by discovery of evidences of the world's oldest known culture —a pre-Flood civilization—in the Bay Islands, off the coast of Honduras.

The most isolated primitive Indian tribes —I have lived among twenty—retain ancient rituals from some d'or past.

A "Feast to the God of Fertility"! it is the Old World "Harvest Festival"! A "wailing ceremony" for the dead; here we

American Races Born in Atlantis

Two articles about Mitchell-Hedges from the *New York American* in the 1930s. Mitchell-Hedges believed that evidence for Atlantis could be found in the Bay Islands of Honduras.

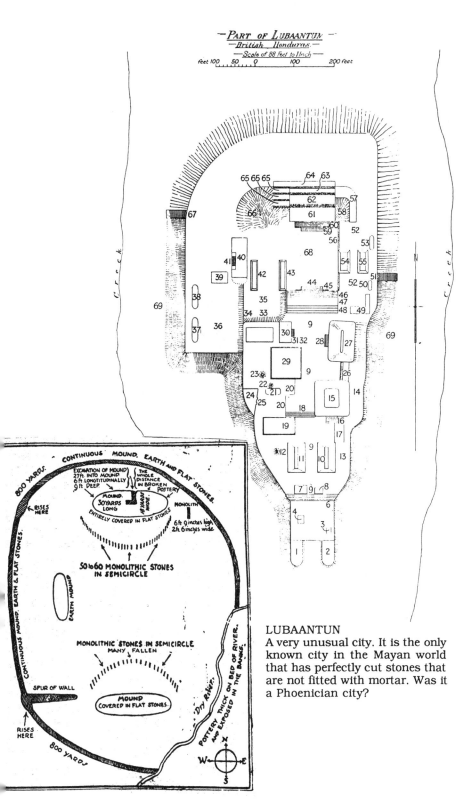

LUBAANTUN

A very unusual city. It is the only known city in the Mayan world that has perfectly cut stones that are not fitted with mortar. Was it a Phoenician city?

A reconstruction of Lubaantun by A. Forestier of the *Illustrated London News*. Lubaantun stood on the summit of high hill, and included several pyramids.

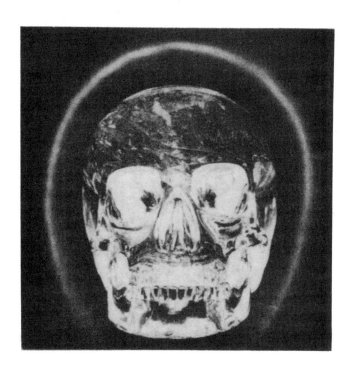

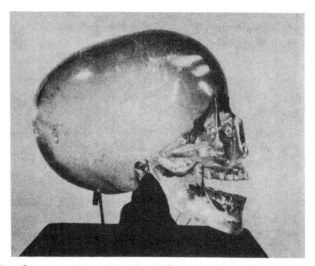

The famous Crystal Skull from Lubaantun, Belize. Above: a simulated halo around the skull, as is often perceived. Below: The skull supported on a stand for which it was created. Ancient priests could manipulate the skull with rods or wires and make the jaw move up and down to simulate speaking.

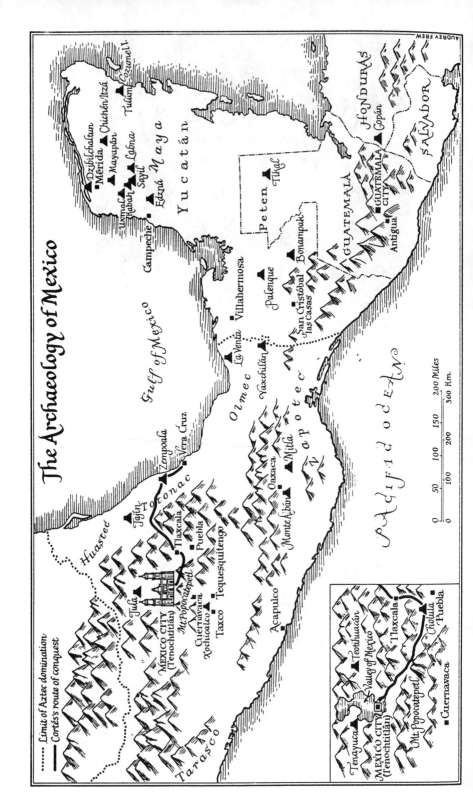

The Archaeology of Mexico

AUDREY FREW

Limit of Aztec domination
Cortés's route of conquest

Gulf of Mexico

Yucatán

Dzibilchaltún
Mérida ▲ Chichén Itzá
Mayapán
Uxmal ▲ Labná ▲ Tulum ▲ Cozumel
Kabah Sayil
Edzná ▲ Campeche

Peten
Tikal ▲

Palenque ▲
Villahermosa
San Cristóbal
las Casas
Bonampak ▲

HONDURAS
Copán ▲
GUATEMALA
GUATEMALA
CITY ▲
Antigua ▲
SALVADOR

La Venta ▲
Olmec
Yaxchilán ▲

Z a p o t e c

Huastec
Tajín ▲
Totonac
Zempoala ▲
Vera Cruz
Tula ▲
Tlaxcala ▲
MEXICO CITY
(Tenochtitlán)
Mt. Popocatepetl ▲
Cuernavaca ▲
Xochicalco ▲
Puebla
Tequesquitengo
Taxco
Acapulco
Oaxaca
Monte Albán ▲ Mitla ▲

Tarasco

PACIFIC OCEAN

0   50   100   150   200 Miles
0   100   200   300 Km.

Tenayuca ▲
Teotihuacán ▲
Valley of Mexico
MEXICO CITY
(Tenochtitlán)
Tlaxcala ▲
Mt. Popocatepetl ▲
Cholula ▲
Puebla
Cuernavaca

Chapter 6

Quintana Roo & the Yucatán:

Pyramids of the Gods

*The problem in archaeology
is when to stop laughing.*
— Dr. Glyn Daniel
Antiquity, December 1961

Hotel, amigo?" asked the taxi driver, leaning against his 60s vintage Chevy Impala. It was pale blue with a festering rust along the edges.

He seemed unconcerned about the odd tourists crossing the border from Belize. Unlike Belize, Quintana Roo, and Mexico in general, were more easy going, without the typical hustle of the tourists. Life had a slower pace here in Quintana Roo, but there was still work to be done, and tourist dollars to be won.

I stood at the border post in the late afternoon sun and looked around. I did need a taxi; Chetumal, the capital of Quintana Roo was still ten miles a way. Maybe the bus would be cheaper.

"No bus for half an hour," said the taxi driver, reading my mind. He was large, fat and brown. His greasy shirt almost covered his entire belly, but not quite. "Come on," he said, "I'll take you for only a few dollars, just a little bit more than the bus."

It was getting late, and I agreed. He opened the rusty trunk and I tossed my pack inside. I then sat up front next to him.

"What hotel are you staying in? I know a good one, the *Hotel Presidente,* only sixty dollars a single. You want that?"

"Sixty dollars a single?" I choked. "That must be the most expensive hotel in Quintana Roo!"

"Oh, no, that is the typical price. Mexico is not so cheap for the gringos anymore. Our prices are the same as yours."

That was not encouraging to a budget traveler like me. "There must be some cheaper hotels in Chetumal," I said.

Indeed there were, and I was left off at the *Hotel Jacaranda* where rooms were cheaper but appropriately rundown. Once settled into the clean, but relatively bare room, I went for a walk along the port looking for a good restaurant.

Quintana Roo was once a backwater territory with Chetumal its sleepy capital port town. But now Quintana Roo is a state of Mexico and the development over the past 20 years has been constant. Mexican cement homes are everywhere, though none of them seemed like they were finished. Steel reinforcing bars stuck out of poured cement longing to be completed.

Because of Chetumal's dutyfree status, the city seemed more like a miniature Mexican Singapore or Hong Kong with Korean electronics and Taiwanese toys in all the shops. Fortunately, Chetumal is not a popular beach resort town, so the hoards of sunbathing tourists are not to be found in Chetumal.

I did find a small restaurant where I could get some chicken, rice and a beer. Sitting at another table was another American who was working on his third or fourth beer.

Before long we were talking about Mexico. He was from South Carolina and was a contractor. Having just gotten divorced, he was down in the Yucatán for a holiday. "Walter's the name," he said, moving over to my table just as my chicken came.

I told him about my trip so far, and that I was researching the ancient mysteries of Central America.

"Where are you going from here?" he asked.

"Oh, north up to Tulúm, Chichén Itzá, Mérida and those places," I said.

"I'll give you a ride if you want," he said, ordering another beer. "I rented a car in Cancún, but can't stand the place. I'm driving back to Mérida on then on to some other places. You can ride with me for free, you just buy the beer."

"Well, sounds like a good deal," I said, hoping that Walter didn't drink more than a case or so a day.

🜃🜃🜃

We left in Walter's rented Japanese sedan, and headed north along Mexican Highway 307 for the Mayan port city of Tulúm. Walter stopped at a roadway liquor store and informed me that there would not be any towns for a 100 miles or so, until we reached Tulúm. I took the hint and ran into the store, purchased some cold beers, and got back in the car.

"With a full tank of gas and a stash of cold beer, we're ready to go!" yelled Walter, throwing the car in gear and lurching out onto the paved two lane highway.

Walter was in his late 40s and had been married three times. His last marriage had just come to an end. His sunburned face highlighted a red nose with a thin black mustache, starting to turn gray, beneath it. He was a contractor back in South Carolina, but liked to get out on an adventure now and then. His recent divorce

156

had sent him south.

When the French explorer Michel Peissel wrote his famous book, *The Lost World of Quintana Roo* [88] in 1963, Quintana Roo was still a remote backwater with hardly any roads in it. Peissel had come to Mexico in 1958 to explore and travel, something other Frenchmen were to do in the 60s and 70s with equal vigor, and the French still today find Mexico and Central America a popular destination.

Peissel was later stranded on the coast of Quintana Roo by boatmen that he had hired to take him to Belize. He then travelled by foot with the occasional help of native Indian guides along deserted beaches and through dense jungle, discovering many ruined sites, cities with pyramids, canals, and temples.

On this journey, Peissel discovered a number of hitherto unknown ruins (except locals and chiclé gatherers) such as Puha, Puerto Chile, Ak, Tupak and the largest, Chunyaxche.

The discovery of the lost city of Chunyaxche became Peissel's claim to fame, and it got him into the New York Explorers Club, at 22 the youngest member ever admitted. Chunyaxche had a number of temples and pyramids, and Peissel was to return again in 1961 to photograph the site. Chunyaxche is now known as Muyil and is located just off the main highway a bit south from Tulúm.

As Walter stepped on the gas and raced through the bush, I mused that 30 years ago, Quintana Roo was an unexplored wilderness full of lost cities. Today it is a major tourist destination.

I cracked open a beer for Walter, who insisted that there were no laws in Mexico against drinking a beer while driving. The road was deserted, and we saw no traffic coming or going, not even trucks carrying supplies to Chetumal. Later I learned that the trucks generally drive at night because of the heat.

We passed the small town of Chan Santa Cruz, the seat of the 1851-1901 Mayan rebellion. It was from here that the Santa Cruz Indians of Belize derive their name, having to flee Mexico when the rebellion was crushed. The town has been renamed Felipe Carillo Puerto. With Walter at the wheel and the windows rolled down, we continued north past Peissel's Chunyaxche (Muyil) and on to Tulúm.

Just to the east of Chunyaxche-Muyil is an artificial canal, one of the many the Maya built throughout the Yucatán and Petén. This one actually links up with the ocean. As I opened another beer for Walter, and had one myself before they got warm, I noticed that the country was no longer tropical jungle as it typically was in Belize, but now a flat, relatively arid area of dry brush, yucca and trees. The sun shown down mercilessly, reflecting hard off the pavement.

We arrived in the early afternoon at Tulúm, the beautiful walled city on cliffs above the sea. Tulúm commands a grand view of white sand beaches and a blue-green sea splashing against large rocks that have tumbled from the cliff into the water.

157

Tulúm is a walled city, a solitary buttress against the sea, and obviously an important port city to the classic Maya.

On Columbus' fourth voyage in 1502, he encountered a large canoe off the coast of Honduras. It was eight feet wide, was apparently trading along the coast and was possibly on its way to Tulúm. The crew and passengers—a number of merchants, their wives and children—were better dressed than any other natives he had seen, and the cargo, arranged under a canopy of woven mats, included an impressive array of copper plates, hatchets, and bells, flint-edged wooden swords, cotton woven in many designs and colors, shirts and cloaks, a fermented drink made of maize, and a quantity of the general Mayan medium of exchange: cacao beans.

The two boats drew along side each other, the natives were brought aboard Columbus' ship and Columbus attempted to communicate with the captain of the canoe—probably unsatisfactorily. This was to be Columbus' last voyage and he recorded his impressions of the seagoing Maya. What the impressions the Maya had of Columbus and his ship, we do not know.[31]

Later, in 1518, a Spanish expedition led by Juan de Grijalva sailed along the coast. They first sailed to the island of Cozumel. Here the Indians hid from the Spaniards and would not come out, and Grijalva took possession of the island for the Spanish crown. Sailing along the coast again, the Spaniards saw a walled city that from a distance seemed comparable to their city of Seville, all white and grand, towering high above them on cliffs. This city was apparently Tulúm.[31]

There are five entrances to the walled city of Tulúm. It covers an area of sixteen acres and is unique as a Mayan site because the streets run parallel to each other and cross each other at right angles. Tulúm was no doubt a planned city that was well thought out before it was built. No other Mayan site is known to have been built like this.

Another unusual aspect of Tulúm is the shocking miniaturization of everything. Says C. Bruce Hunter in his book, *A Guide to Ancient Maya Ruins:*[134] "The buildings, especially the doorways, look as though they had been planned and built for miniature beings from another planet. The buildings resemble dollhouses clustered to form a town. The scale is even more astonishing after one has seen the great towering pyramids and palaces at Uxmal and Chichén Itzá."

Tulúm is said to have been a city in which the *Alux,* or little people, lived. Another unusual aspect of Tulúm is that almost every building has its own figure of a "diving god," set in a niche or on a lintel near the top of the building. The "god" wears boots and a helmet, and is apparently descending from above to Tulúm. Ancient astronaut theorists would probably assert that this man was a "god from outer space." What ever the case, Tulúm was apparently dedicated to this "god." One wonders if this god, like the denizens of ancient Tulúm, was a midget, or dwarf.

Walter and I walked about the city for several hours. The views from the cliffs above the ocean were spectacular, and I couldn't help wonder what ships may have docked at this ancient port. The beaches below were ideal for ships, whether it be a Mayan ocean-going canoe or a Phoenician trading vessel. Was Tulúm once a Phoenician port, like Lubaantun? According to well respected British archaeologist, J. Eric S. Thompson, Tulúm was an important trade center where merchants could route goods from the Caribbean inland to the Petén and Usumacinta regions. The town was no doubt important to the intercoastal trade. Why should't inter-ocean vessels have docked here as well. It seems unlikely that Grijalva's ship was the first European vessel to see the white walls of Tulúm.

Mayanists say that most of Tulúm is late postclassic, making it a city that was occupied in the period after 900 A.D. However, there is evidence that Tulúm was inhabited in the classic period as well, extending the dates to 300 A.D. or so. Curiously, in a temple of Tulúm a broken stele was found with a long date corresponding to 564 A.D. It is believed that the building housing this stele was constructed long after this date, and therefore believed that the stele was moved to Tulúm from another location, possibly Cobá, the huge city nearby. This stele is now at the British Museum in London.

🐉🐉🐉

Walter and I decided to share a cabana at the *El Paraiso Hotel,* one of the small beach resorts just south of Tulúm. After a shower, I strolled down to one of the small restaurants on the beach to find Walter with the inevitable beer in his hand.

"I like it here," he said. "Cancún was like Disneyland, all new and modern with neon signs staring you in the face everywhere. Hell, if I'd wanted that, I'd have gone to Miami or Key West."

As the waves splashed on the beach and the fishing boats were silhouetted in the moonlight, I thought about the rapid development of Quintana Roo and the Yucatán. In ten years the area had gone from being a huge wilderness of lost cities to a major tourist destination for Americans and Europeans. What would be the fate of other similar areas?

The next morning we left in Walter's rented car and drove to Cobá, the largest ancient city so far discovered in Quintana Roo. Cobá is interesting not only because it has the highest pyramid in the Yucatán (80 feet high) but also because of the system of ancient roads, known as *sacbes,* that radiate out from the city.

One sacbe radiates 100 kilometers (60 miles) to Yaxuná, near to Chichén Itzá, and is the longest Mayan causeway known. This one runs perfectly straight, as do all the more than 50 others shown to radiate out from the city center.

One major sacbe extends to the village of Ixil to the southwest. No

159

doubt it continues on through the bush. All the sacbe are very straight and well constructed, often passing through swamps, lakes and other varied terrain. Constructed of inner and outer retaining walls with an inner core filled with stone, these roadways were solidified with lime and then plastered to provide a smooth surface. The width varied from approximately nine feet to sixty feet (where there were plazas), and the height from one to three feet. A portion of one sacbe was actually raised more than twenty-one feet above ground level. The sacbe system was a gigantic engineering project that linked the various cities of the Yucatán, as well as more far-flung areas such as the Valley of Mexico and Nicaragua.

Ramps were sometimes used at large intersections or important civic complexes. Other ramps were designed to accommodate the irregularities in the terrain. Culverts were used in wet areas and defensive walls occurred in other areas. On the sides of these road-ways can be seen the open quarries mined for their construction. Other quarries were in closed mines reached by tunnels.

The Maya were involved in extensive tunneling, according to the book, *Cobá, A Classic Maya Metropolis.*[135] They discovered that one tunnel had 31 hourglass-shaped supports inside a major chamber.

As I stood on top of one of the pyramids at Cobá, I gazed at the road leading into the distance. The sacbe system is evidence that Mesoamerica was linked by a huge road system that facilitated a great deal of traffic. Similar gigantic road systems exist in South America. Some roads in northern Peru were 100 feet wide and went for hundreds of miles. Peru even has its own Great Wall of very similar in construction and purpose as the Great Wall of China.[57]

As in South America, what massive armies must have marched over these ancient roads of the Yucatán? Where were they going and what was it that the made the cities worth conquering?

Sadly, much of the history of Mesoamerica seems to be of warfare, with army after army marching this way and that, much like the armies of the old world. Back in the millennia immediately before Christ, all sorts of Hittite, Greek, Babylonian, Egyptian, Persian and other armies were continually marching somewhere on a mission of conquest. Alexander the Great's army conquered the virtual known world of the time, being stopped from conquering India by a mysterious episode at the Indus river where his legions of war elephants were stampeded by strange fiery shields that were flying in the air. His generals refused to continue on to India, and they turned back to Persia.

Such was the case in Central America—it was the cities and trade routes that these armies fought over, and Cobá was one of the great centers of trade in the Yucatán. What was so important of this dry, scrub-brush country that huge roads were built from Cobá to other cities? The Yucatán has no mineral or animal wealth. Its agricultural wealth would be poor, but at least existent.

The obvious answer is that the Yucatán was a major port area and trading center for distribution to the rest of Mesoamerica. The southern and western realms of the Maya were rich with gold, crystal, cacao, salt, allspice, exotic feathers and furs, psychedelic mushrooms and most important: jade.

Yet, it was the ports of the Yucatán, for commerce going both ways, that made it rich. It was well suited for the transatlantic trade, being one of the first areas on the mainland of Central America that a boat would reach, especially into the all important center of trade at Teotihuacan in the Valley of Mexico. Just as important was the local coastal trade that would include ships from Venezuela and Colombia in the south and from Florida, the Mississippi or the far north.

Contrary to the Isolationist view of anthropologists, the Maya were well set up to communicate with the rest of the world. They had huge roads, their own interstate system, a sophisticated canal network, much like modern Holland of today, and port cities strategically located along the coast.

The Maya no doubt had their own fleet, ocean-going ships that were either large double canoes, similar to Polynesian vessels, or reed ships as used on Lake Titicaca in the Andes and at Chan Chan in northern Peru. By the time Columbus had met the coastal traders in 1502, the Mayan civilization had been in decline for at least a thousand years.

The road system constructed by the Maya was only equaled by their canal system, which stretched deep into the Petén and apparently linked Caribbean coastal cities such as Tulúm and Cobá with the Usumacinta River. A clever engineering feat, to say the least.

🐾🐾🐾

"Hey, David, let's get a beer."

I looked over at Walter. He was in his Banana Republic vest and wearing his Tilley's hat. His nose was as sunburned as ever. The sun was shining down on us with a vengeance. A cold beer did sound pretty good.

"Ok, lets go," I said, starting to get up.

Cobá was a fascinating place. A road was said to go to Tulúm that was still open. A canopy of trees sheltered the road, making it quite cool to walk, even on a hot day. Cobá is largely unexcavated. Much of its secrets are still to be told.

In esoteric literature, it is often said that a secret "Hall of Records" is to be found somewhere in the Yucatán. Frequently it is said to be at Chichén Itzá, though this secret cache of technology and wisdom may well be stored at Cobá.

As the ruins of the great center disappeared into the rear view mirror, I wondered whether Cobá would be in the news in the near future, perhaps tunnels and chambers beneath the pyramids would reveal some startling finds.

161

🐃🐃🐃

The car hood swallowed up the concrete ahead of us. We were on the road, two crazy travelers, headed for somewhere out there. This road went some place. We'd get there and find a bar, or at least that was Walter's plan.

It sounded good enough to me, and I popped open a beer for Walter. We were cruising down the highway of life. Our road was burning tar and hot cement. Yucca plants, thorny and green, were on all sides of us. We rolled the windows down and leaned back in the seats. Hey, Jack Kerouac, you've got nothing on us!

"I love this fucking bush," said Walter, taking a deep gulp of his beer and grinning wildly.

"The old explorers took days...weeks to cross this country. We do it now in hours." I stared out the window and wondered at my own comment.

"You've never been to Cancún?" Walter looked out the window at a distant pyramid covered with jungle growth. "I've got to show you Cancún." Soon we were passing by the island of Cozumel on our way to Cancún, the major tourist center of the Yucatán.

Cozumel, an island about 20 miles off the coast of Quintana Roo, was an important trading center and religious pilgrimage destination. It had a strategic trade location, approximately midway between seaports along the Bay of Honduras and Gulf area of Tabasco.

Cozumel was also important as the site of a shrine at which one could make offerings to the "Lady of the Rainbow." The shrine is believed to have stood on the north side of the island at the site of San Gervasio. It was there the the important deity Ix Chel, wife or consort of the all-embracing Maya god Itzamná, was worshipped.

Ix Chel was the goddess of medicine, and pilgrims, especially prospective mothers, flocked to her shrine from near and far. Cozumel is some sort of power spot where infertile women would come to have themselves activated. Priests, hidden behind the shrine, answered the petitions to the large pottery image of the goddess. Yet the original temple must have been built because of some natural healing spring or vortex area.

"Cozumel is where Quetzalcoatl left Mesoamerica for the east," said Walter. The road sped by outside. Now we had a good view of the coast.

"You knew that, didn't you?" said Walter. "He taught a chant to his followers, the song of Quetzalcoatl. They were supposed to use this chant to call him if they needed him. He left by ship to go east, probably back to Europe or North Africa. Interesting, eh?"

I looked out the window. Indeed, the legend of Quetzalcoatl, or Kulkulcán, is a very interesting story.

Unfortunately for Cozumel, most of the Maya temples were torn down by the Spaniards, who used the stones for their own buildings for roads. Sadly, today ther e is little indication that Cozumel wa; once occupied by the ancient Maya. Instead, modern resorts take their place. Cozumel is a fantastic spot for scuba diving and other sports. It was a pilgrimage in ancient times for young women seeking to have children. As I gazed out out the window, I wondered if their was a high percentage of honeymooners who had children in their first year of marriage because of their vacation in Cancún?

Soon, we were driving around the beach loop of Cancún. Large concrete hotels were packed one right next to the other. It could have been Las Vegas.

"Lets get out of here," said Walter, heading back out out of town towards Chichén Itzá and the yucca desert ahead of us. Once we got out of town, I opened a cold beer for Walter. He took a big gulp.

"How's your divorce going?" I asked him.

"With all these lost cities around," he said, "its not going so bad."

๑๑๑

We arrived after dark at a motel on the main road from Cancún to Chichén Itzá and secured a room. All night, because the motel is right on the highway, I could hear trucks approaching from a distance. They were very noisy, barreling down the highway at high speed. As they got closer, the rumble of their tires and motor became deafening, and then, after passing the motel in a clatter of noise, the drone of the trucks receded quickly into the distance.

After a few hours of this, I expected to hear sirens eventually chasing these racing truck drivers down the road to bring them to Mexican justice, but they never came. Apparently the police only came out during the day and the truck drivers only at night.

Our first stop the next day was the Balankanche Caves near the motel. The caves were first explored in 1959, and a system of tunnels and caves were discovered that contained hundreds of incense burners and miniature *metates*, or corn grinders.

The cave had an interesting sound and light show that progressed as we walked through the caves to a central stalagmite-pillar with ceramic offerings to the gods of the underworld. It was quite hot deep down in the cave, and awesomely beautiful in places, especially at the end of the cave where a shallow subterranean lake ended the tour.

Interestingly, the narrator on the sound and light show made the point that the Maya believed that there were 13 levels of the underworld and nine levels of the upperworld. This is the common belief in both oriental religions and western religions that the world consists of different planes or levels of reality, there being variously seven, nine or thirteen levels of existence.

Our next stop was a full afternoon visit to the famous ruins of Chichén Itzá. Walking into the ruins, our first stop was the well known central pyramid of the city, the Pyramid of Kukulkán. This is

163

the pyramid famous for the unusual equinox phenomena of a shadow moving down the dragon-serpents along the stairs.

Chichén Itzá is a mysterious city, and one that was inhabited by successive waves of civilizations. The earliest date found at the site is equivalent to A.D. 618, though scholars admit that the city must be older than this date.

It is generally believed that the Toltecs invaded Chichén Itzá and the Yucatán in about the year 1000 A.D., conquering the Maya and installing new gods into the local religion and completely rebuilt the city. Archaeologists make many references to the similarity of styles at Chichén Itzá and the Toltec capital of Tollan. While it is assumed that the Toltecs came from Tollan to Chichén Itzá, there is also the theory that Chichén Itzá was built first and that the Toltecs then moved on to Tollan in the Valley of Mexico.

Around 1200 A.D., Toltec power in Mexico waned, and Chichén Itzá was suddenly abandoned by the Toltecs. In the second quarter of the thirteenth century, a group of Maya from Campeche, who called themselves Itzá, wandered into the Yucatán and took over the deserted capital. They gave the city its present name, Chichén Itzá, which means "the mouth of the well of the Itzá, a reference to the sacred well, or cenoté at the north end of the city. These Maya later founded another city not far away which was called Mayapán.

Mayapán was taken over in 1283 by an Itzá family, the Cocom, who then ruled the whole of Yucatán. The second half of the fifteenth century saw the rise of the Xiu tribe. They destroyed the city of Mayapán, massacring the Cocom, and succeeded in driving the Itzá out of Chichén, and tried to conquer the entire country. This attempt failed, and the Yucatán became an area of small, squabbling chiefdoms. The Itzá trekked into the deserted Petén area and set up the last known Mayan kingdom on lake Petén Itzá in Guatemala.[87]

With the departure of the Itzá to the Petén, the city became unoccupied until the current tourist hotels and museum were built in modern times. The Itzá, though they lived for several hundred years in Chichén, made no appreciable change in the city. They are a good example of how wandering tribes often find deserted cities and then move into them, adopting them as their own. It is sad that the original name is now lost, like many of these ancient cities.

Undoubtedly, the Castillo, or Pyramid of Kukulkán, is the main structure of the city, and the center of attraction to visitors. It is 78 feet high and rises in nine platforms that are symbolic of the nine levels of heaven in the mythic Mexican cosmology. On each side a flight of 91 steps leads up to the platform at the top, so that the total number of steps adds up to 364. Counting the platform as one step, the total is 365, equal to the current number of days in a year.

At the top is the *Temple of Kukulkán* (the Mayan name for Quetzal-coatl). Its doorway is divided by a pair of serpent columns. When archaeologists began to reconstruct the pyramid, they discovered a

164

perfectly preserved temple right at the heart of the structure, standing at the summit of a smaller pyramid inside the current structure.

There was an entrance to the inside of the Castillo at the base on the north side. Walter and I entered the pyramid and moved upward through a tunnel system. At the summit of the inner pyramid, we were thrilled to see a marvelous red jaguar throne, studded with jade encrustations as well as a fine Chacmool statue; a statue of a reclining figure with a basin for offerings on his stomach.

Both inside and outside the pyramid I noticed that the stone had been drilled with loop holes for massive stone doors that were now gone. This same unusual technique was used at massive ruins in Peru such as Machu Picchu and the buildings around Cuzco. Was there some connection to the Atlantean League, the ancient seafarers who were to become the Phoenicians? Indeed, it is a popular belief (though not by present day academics) that the Toltecs were Phoenicians who had escaped the Punic wars. The story of collapse of the Phoenician Empire in the Mediterranean and the rise of the Toltec Empire in Mesoamerica is a fascinating tale!

The first Punic War between Rome and Carthage lasted from 264 to 241 B.C. It began when the Sicilian port of Messina (or Messana) called on both Rome and Carthage for help in a quarrel with Syracuse. The Carthaginians arrived first and arranged a peace, but the Romans ejected them and took eastern Sicily. The Roman fleet won at Mylae (260 B.C.) and off Cape Ecnomus (256 B.C.), but a Roman expedition to Africa failed. The Carthaginian general Hamilcar Barca kept the Romans from taking Lilybaeum, but a new Roman victory at sea off the Aegadian Isles (241 B.C.) caused Carthage to ask for peace. Contrary to the treaty, Rome, now in the possession of Sicily, set out to conquer Sardinia and Corsica.

When the Carthaginians, led by Hannibal, took Saguntum (Sagunto) in Spain (219 B.C.), Rome declared war. The Second Punic War (218-201 B.C.) marked the invasion of Italy. The invasion ultimately failed because of lack of supplies, and the Carthaginians ultimately lost their Spanish provinces and much of their war fleet.

Finally, the defeat of Carthage was complete during the Third Punic War (149 to 146 B.C.) when Rome charged Carthage with technical breach of the treaty by resisting the aggression of Rome's ally Masinissa. Carthage was blockaded by the Roman fleet but did not surrender. The Roman general Scipio Africanus Minor then conquered the city and razed it to the ground, even salting the earth so that the Carthaginians could not return to their ancient capital.

However, other Carthaginian ports in Africa, especially at Lixus and other ports on the Atlantic coast of Morocco, were able to escape the destruction by Rome. According to some historians, the remnants of the now destroyed Carthaginian-Phoenician empire made their way across the Atlantic, a trading route that they had maintained for a thousand years off and on, to the port cities along the Gulf of Mexico. With them they took as much gold as they could carry.

This, according to some historians of a diffusionist bent, is the origin of the Toltecs, a people portrayed as having thick beards and being warlike. Was Chichén Itzá one of the last cities conquered by the Toltecs as their new empire rose in Mexico and the Yucatán? The most common theme portrayed throughout Chichén Itzá is that of Toltec warriors conquering the Maya. Gold pieces found in the cenoté, imported from Panama or Costa Rica, also generally depict Toltec warriors in combat or defeating Mayan warriors. A large amount of copper objects, frequently bells, were also found in the cenoté, and these are believed to have come from the Oaxaca area south of Mexico City.

Legend has it that virgins and children were sacrificed in the well. It is true that the bones of women, men and children have been found in the cenoté. Excavations began circa 1900 by the American Edward Thompson, who had bought a hacienda, that included the ruins of Chichén Itzá, for five hundred dollars. He dredged the well and discovered a wealth in gold and jade.

Thompson apparently believed that some of the jade found in the well was of Chinese origin. The jade controversy and the mysterious source of the profusion of jade artifacts in Mesoamerica has stemmed many Chinese-origin theorists ahead on their quest for the origin of the Mayas. Curiously, it is believed the Maya also supplied the Chinese with jade as well, and it was the jade trade that made the Maya fabulously wealthy in the early millennium B.C.

Aside from the cenoté, other interesting features at Chichén Itzá are the huge ball court, the Temple of Warriors and the astronomical observatory. The ball court is the largest ball court in the Americas (545 feet long) and also has very high vertical walls.

On the two sloping walls, called benches, running the length of either side of the court, are six sculptured reliefs, each 40 feet long, placed in panels at three intervals. Virtually the same scene is depicted on all the panels: a victorious ball team holding the severed head of a member of the losing team. Just as in ancient Rome, the preferred spectator sports of the time included the death of one or more players. The Roman's spectator sports included gladitorial combat, the unleashing of hungry lions into the arena on unarmed captives or criminals, and the occasional flooding of the Colosseum for mock naval battles.

The Temple of Warriors, near the Pyramid of Kukulkán, rises in four platforms and is flanked on the west and south sides by approximately two hundred round and square columns. The square columns are in carved low relief, repeating a warrior theme.

The Temple of Warriors is approached by a broad stairway with a ramp on either side. These ramps are surmounted with figures of standard-bearers designed to hold flags. As far as is known, sculptured standard-bearers were not used by the Classic Maya, but they were used by both the Toltecs and the Aztecs at their respective capitals. One belief is that Chichén Itzá was a breakaway kingdom of the Toltec Empire at Tollan (Tula).[134]

Interestingly, a large altar-type platform at the rear of the temple is supported by 19 "Atlantean" figures. Atlantean figures were gigantic statues of men that were used to hold up a roof, and are called "Atlantean" in deference to the common Mediterranean motif of Atlas holding up the world in a similar manner. Certainly, the Atlantean figure is one that spans the Old World and the New.

The observatory, in the southern, older section of the city, has a circular stairway leading to a room at the top of a circular tower. From here sightlines can be obtained for the equinoxes, the summer solstice, and the cardinal directions.

Walter and I walked along and listened to one of the local guides lecturing in English to a tour group of elderly Americans. According to the guide, the observatory was built by the Toltecs circa 900 A.D. and was not only for the purpose of observing the sun, but also Venus, the morning star. According to him, Venus was a god and was associated with Kukulkán (Quetzalcoatl).

"Kukulkán was most probably a Viking explorer," said the guide rather nonchalantly to his tour group.

"Really?" asked one tourist. "I didn't read that in my guide book."

"Oh, yes," replied the guide, "here in Mexico, our archaeologists now believe this." The group shuffled off toward the observatory, the guide telling them about this and that.

I looked at Walter as we started to head back to the entrance gate of the city. It was getting late, and the afternoon sun was hanging low in the sky.

"What do you think about this Viking stuff?" I asked Walter.

"Well, at least it is a step in the right direction," he replied. "It's highly probable that Vikings did eventually come to the Yucatán. But it's not necessarily the case that Quetzalcoatl or Kukulkán was a Viking. His occurrence was more like around 100 A.D. rather than 1000 A.D. Besides, there were several Quetzalcoatls. Many Toltec kings also took the name of Quetzalcoatl."

Recently, a Swedish-born chemistry professor in Cuernavaca, Mexico named Gustavo Nelin wrote a book entitled *The Saga of Votan*. In his book, Nelin claims that Quetzalcoatl was a Viking named Ari Marson. According to Viking legend, claims Nelin, Ari Marson joined Eric the Red on a mission to Greenland circa 985 A.D. According to Viking lore, 11 of Eric's 25 ships were lost en route. Nelin contends that Ari Marson was on one of these lost ships.

Nelin claims the Marson eventually came to Mexico. Says Nelin, "Mexican legend states that Quetzalcoatl came to a place called Tula. Coincidentally—or perhaps not—the old name for Scandinavia is Tule. Just as the Norse called their boats dragons or serpents, the world Quetzalcoatl meant serpent to the Mexicans."

The only problem with the Viking solution to the mystery of Quetzalcoatl is that these theorists are ignorant of the many other foreign visitors and constant trading between the Maya realms and both the Mediterranean and the Far East.

"Hey, look at these boomerangs!" said Walter.

We had stopped at the museum on our way out of the site, and Walter showed me a most interesting mural that is a replica of one that was formerly at the Temple of Warriors. The mural shows men hunting and fighting with boomerangs! While we typically associate the use of boomerangs with Australian aboriginals, it is true that the ancient Egyptians hunted with boomerangs, as did American Indians. At Chichén Itzá the boomerang is also shown as a weapon.

It has been often said that the boomerang is a sophisticated piece of throwing equipment, and it seems unlikely that such a device would be invented separately by various cultures around the world. When king Tutankhamen's tomb was opened in the 1920s, an entire trunk of boomerangs was discovered. They are now on display at the Egyptian Museum in Cairo. Did the use of boomerangs begin in ancient Egypt, and was it then disseminated to Mesoamerica and Australia? Perhaps it was learned from the Australian aboriginals first and then disseminated from there? The unusual use of boomerangs is not a subject that has ever been addressed by the traditional scholars, at least to my knowledge.

❊❊❊

That the Maya used boomerangs wouldn't have surprised Dr. Augustus LePlongeon very much. He believed that the use of these devices had started in a lost continent and that Atlantis and Freemasonry were all part of the legacy of Chichén Itzá. Much of the early archaeological work done at Chichén Itzá was by LePlongeon. However, he is not mentioned in any of the guide books to the site, though a photograph of him and the famous *Chacmool* statue he discovered can be found in the museum.

Dr. Augustus LePlongeon was born the Count de Coquerville on the channel island of Jersey in 1826. He obtained a medical degree in England after completion of his primary education in France. LePlongeon was a mystic by nature and a master Mason, steeped in much of its arcane lore.

LePlongeon published several books on his archaeological excavations and theories. *Sacred Mysteries Among the Mayas & the Quiches* [65] was published in 1886 and his highly controversial *Queen Moo & the Egyptian Sphinx* [66] was published in 1900. In both of these books LePlongeon produced evidence that the Maya were a highly advanced civilization whose origin was many thousands of years ago in Atlantis and pre-dynastic Egypt..

The archaeologist Dr. Daniel G. Brinton wrote in the *American Antiquarian* of Nov. 1885: "I have recently spent an evening with Dr. and Mrs. LePlongeon, who, after spending 12 years exploring the ruined cities of the Yucatán... no one can doubt the magnitude of his discoveries and the new light they throw on Maya civilization."

However, his orthodox contemporaries rejected his metaphysical explanations, his Masonic symbolism in Mayan art, his diffusionist ideas of contact with the ancient world, and his rather wild date of 11,500 years in age for many Mayan ruins. LePlongeon believed that the Mayan civilization had predated ancient Egypt, and that it was from the Maya that the old world cultures were derived. Essentially, he believed that the Yucatán was Atlantis of Greek mythology.

It is estimated that LePlongeon spent half-a-million-dollars on excavations and restorations in Yucatán. His most famous discovery was probably that of the Chacmool statue found at Chichén Itzá. LePlongeon became a naturalized American, wrote numerous articles, and lectured before scientific bodies at Lowell Institute in Boston for many years before dying in 1908 at the age of 83.

LePlongeon was a brilliant man with a great deal of knowledge of the ancient mystery schools. He felt intuitively that the Mayan realms had some connection with all this. Responding to laughter and ridicule, LePlongeon once said, "But who are these pretended authorities? Certainly not the doctors and professors at the heads of the universities and colleges in the United States; for not only do they know absolutely nothing of the ancient American Civilization, but, judging from letters in my possession, the majority of them refuse to learn anything concerning it. Can they interpret one single sentence in the books in which the learning of the Maya sages, their cosmogonic, geographical, religious and scientific attainments are recorded? From what source have they derived their pretended knowledge? Not from the writings of the Spanish chroniclers, surely. These only wrote of the natives as they found them at the time, and long after the conquest of America by their countrymen. The so-called learned men of our days are the first to oppose new ideas and the bearers of these."

LePlongeon would probably not have been surprised to hear that Chichén Itzá is often to be said to be one of the repositories of ancient wisdom, typically known as a Hall of Records. The famous American trance-medium Edgar Cayce once said that a huge storehouse of ancient wisdom, apparently in the form of charged crystals, lies in secret vaults beneath the city.

A similar Hall of Records is said to be in a subterranean network beneath the Great Pyramid. Both are said to have been left by Atlanteans who sealed them in underground vaults and built structures over them. Inside these subterranean time-capsules one would theoretically find books on gold tablets and high tech machinery from the past. Just as we use magnetic tape and laser discs as recording and playback devices, so they allegedly used quartz crystals as a device for storing information.

Banks of such crystals may well be lying still beneath Chichén Itzá. Perhaps the greatest discovery of all at the site is still to come.

169

Quintana Roo & the Yucatán   Pyramids of the Gods

After watching the sound and light show at the ruins that evening, we spent another night at the motel listening to the trucks driving at high speed down the highway to Mérida.

We were off to Mérida ourselves the next day, arriving at the city about noon. Our journey into the "White City" was one that included a cold beer, which I opened with my Swiss Army knife, and handed to Walter.

"Thanks," said Walter, taking a draught.

The glare of the sun was almost blinding, and we kept the windows down to let the wind rush in our faces. We passed carts with bananas piled high, and vendors with tomatoes and chilies.

Walter suddenly pulled into a narrow garage. It was a motel in the middle of the city with a courtyard where we could park the car. Moments later we had a room and Walter was searching for a beer. We found our way to the central plaza and took a table on the street.

Mérida seemed like a nice town It is called the White City because of the white-washed buildings. The central plaza was picturesque, with a park, restaurants, and a white church with big steps in front of it. Young men in straw cowboy hats walked with sweethearts in white dresses. Shoeshine teenagers hung around by the white columns. Old Mayan women, barely four feet tall with gray hair tied behind their back, were heading back from the market, tomatoes, onions, and chillies in their baskets.

The full moon shown on the square and lit the walls of the church. Out in the moonlight were the silent cities of the gods. The gods who had built the cities. The gods who created a great civilization. The gods who knew the many secrets of the calendar. The gods who remembered the previous gods from before...

🌸🌸🌸

The next morning we left for Uxmal, the city of the Magicians. Uxmal is probably the oldest city in the Yucatán⁵⁷ and is probably the most mysterious of many ancient cities throughout the region.

Uxmal reached its last peak in many thousands of years of history in the Late Classic period of Mayan history when the ruling Xiu family occupied it in the 10th century. Sometime toward the end of this century the Xiu abandoned Uxmal and moved their capital to Maní. The original name of the city may have been Oxmal, or "thrice built." However, the city could hardly have been so named when it was first built, and, like Chichén Itzá, its ancient name is unknown. Like most cities in the Yucatán, there is known to be Toltec influence, and some of the motifs are similar to Mitla in Oaxaca.[136]

Over the centuries there was a great deal of rebuilding and alteration and the central structure, a massive pyramid called the Pyramid of the Magician, was rebuilt, getting larger each time, at least five times. Though it is known the Uxmal was first settled thousands of years ago, no systematic excavations have taken place to shed light on the early history of the city.

To illustrate how old the city is and that there has been some sort of serious interruption of the continuous history, there is a Maya legend concerning the building of the main pyramid. The legend tells of an elderly witch who hatched a child from an egg. After a year the child had developed into a dwarf with supernatural powers. Challenged by the Lord of Uxmal to build a temple in one night or face death, the dwarf succeeded in this task, as well as others put to him. Ultimately the magician himself became Lord of Uxmal. And so the great pyramid in the center of the city was allegedly built in a single day by a magician.

Since it seems that this story is probably not true, the story indicates that the post-classic Mayas had no idea who had built the city they were now occupying. The ruling Xiu family may have lived in Uxmal, but they had not built the city nor knew who had.

It would be curious if five centuries from now, the ruins of the Lincoln and Jefferson Memorials were still standing in the rubble of Washington D.C. and local residents, not knowing who these men were and when the monuments were built, then created a legend about two magicians who built monuments to themselves overnight. If this were the case, we would probably surmise that some sort of total history erasing collapse of the civilization had occurred at some earlier point.

As I came through the modern ticket gate with the small museum to one side, I was immediately attracted to the huge pyramid in the center of the plaza. It was steep and had unusual rounded corners. The pyramid is 93 feet high, and I was breathing hard as I climbed the steep steps. It was beautiful construction—cut stone blocks fitted together in a style that reminded me of the Phoenician cities of North Africa, and of Lubaantun in Belize.

According to Mayan scholars, the architects of Uxmal were revolutionary in their design. Buildings were constructed on extremely large platforms, well spaced from one another. The plazas covered extensive areas of the ceremonial center. The typical cut stone decorated with stucco was abandoned in favor of a new method of construction: instead of solid-core walls, the builders used a rubble core faced with clean-cut mosaic stone. Mitla in Oaxaca is built in this same way, as were cities in the Andes of South America.

The main difference with Uxmal and Mitla, or Monté Alban in the mountains south of Mexico City, is that no megalithic architecture is found in the Yucatán (lack of stone may be one reason) while megalithic walls can be found at both Mitla and Monté Alban.

Still, Uxmal is an impressive site. I marveled at the many symbols and decorative motifs that the many buildings were faced with. There were Hindu or Buddhist looking swastikas, as well as yin-yang symbols. I also noticed vortex circles, or spiral patterns in the

171

stone. There are few hieroglyphs, though Uxmal is the only other city in the Yucatán besides Cobá to have had stelae. The remains of fifteen eroded stelae were found on a platform west of the Nunnery. Unlike Mayan cities in the Petén, there are no dated monuments nor even the evidence of the use of the glyphs. The Phoenicians, naturally, had their own writing system, though they rarely left inscriptions on buildings or monuments.

A three-foot iguana suddenly ran across a rock wall while I was walking between buildings. I approached him and he disappeared into the agave cactus that spread around the city. I entered one building and a bat flew out, darting past my face. Around a corner I came to the House of the Turtles, decorated with stone turtles along the roof. As the city was a ceremonial center, apparently this building was dedicated to some sort of turtle cult.

The turtle is a popular motif in India and the Far East. It was believed that the world sat on the back of a great turtle. Similarly, on the island of Pohnpei, a remote Micronesian Island north of New Guinea, a special temple in the megalithic city of Nan Madol was dedicated to the turtle. A sacred turtle was kept in a special pool.

Strolling around the city, I noticed that some of the walls had been shifted by earthquakes. The corners of the so-called Nunnery building curled up at the end, reminding me of Oriental pagoda style. Uxmal had a curious oriental flare, but also blended the unique Mesoamerican culture with the Phoenician building style.

At the museum were several of the stelae that had been discovered at Uxmal. There are two large stelae, ten feet in height, interestingly devoid of hieroglyphs. There were however a few stones with well worn glyphs, along with some numeral-date glyphs.

A large stone turtle altar caught my eye, as did several dragon heads. There were also some curious stone plugs with faces carved on them. This is the same sort of technique of inlaying a stone wall with stone heads that is used at the ancient ruins of Tiahuanaco in Bolivia.

"Come on David, let's go," said Walter. We now had with us another traveler who was hitching a ride with us back to Mérida. His name was Max and he was a young pilot for the Chilean navy. Max was travelling around Mexico for a bit on holiday and was going to write a story for a Chilean magazine called *Adventura.*

At a restaurant, Walter, Max and I ate lunch. Max talked about his five years as a pilot for the Chilean Navy, flying jet fighters along the southern coast of Chile, and even a training exercise in Saudi Arabia with Americans.

"You know, the Chilean government even has its own flying saucers," he said between a mouth full of rice.

"You're joking!" I said.

"Well the American government has their own flying saucers," said Walter. "Maybe the Chilean got them from the Nazis. They were building flying saucers towards the end of the war. They're all Nazis in Chile aren't they?"

Max ignored Walter's comment and continued his story. "The government uses the flying discs to fly over Argentina, Bolivia and Peru. Maybe Brazil as well. It's their secret, and I am not supposed to know. I am a jet fighter pilot, not a flying saucer pilot."

"Is that so?" said Walter. "Aren't you a Nazi? Is that why you don't fly the saucers?"

Max suddenly snapped to attention. "Long life to Pinochet!" he cried above the marimba music.

We laughed, and I asked Max more about the Chilean flying saucers.

"Once, when I was pilot with the navy, the air force told me that there was a crashed plane at a lake in southern Chile. I had been on a navy ship in that same area and was aware that a special team from the air force had been sent to retrieve the craft from the crash site.

"But when I was at the lake, I talked with some local fishermen who told me that they had seen the crash, but that the craft did not have wings, but was a flying saucer that flew differently from an airplane and had four holes in its bottom. I guess they were the engines.

"Other people saw it too, and told me the same. I think the Chilean military has a secret base in the south of Chile where they keep this special craft. Other military officers have told me that these are special spy craft. In Chile we have a lot of special technology that is our own. This is partly because of the arms embargo. Our government cooperates with South Africa and Israel to share some of this special technology." Max concluded his story by taking a deep gulp of his beer.

Walter and I looked at each other. Then Walter said, "The American government's probably helping the Chileans. They're Nazis too."

Max snapped to attention again, "Long life to Pinochet!" he cried.

🎊🎊🎊

We stopped at the nearby Loltun Caves, a huge cavern system that has been occupied for at least ten thousand years. A mammoth bone, cut by humans, has been found inside, as well as many carvings, glyphs, and bizarre statues cut into the solid rock of the caves. Many of these statues are so ancient as to be barely recognizable. Flint and obsidian objects have been discovered and cave is well known for its Mayan art.

We began the drive back to Mérida. Walter insisted on a cool beer, so we stopped at a liquor store and bought some. Walter informed us that it was perfectly legal to drive with a beer in your hand in Mexico, you just couldn't be drunk.

Getting back into the White City of Mérida was a bit tricky, especially with its numerous one way streets. Taking a wrong turn and then suddenly squealing his tires around the corner unfortunately caused some local police to take a sudden interest in Walter and our car.

"Walter please stop the car," I asked. Behind us a Mexican officer pulled up his motor cycle and parked it. He had a mean glint in his eye, sort of like in spaghetti westerns, as he approached the car.

He swaggered up to Walter and peered at him through Ray Ban sun glasses. In Spanish he asked if Walter knew he had just turned down a one way street. Walter did not speak Spanish, and remained silent.

The officer looked at Walter, his sunburned red nose highlighted by the several beers he had just consumed. "Have you been drinking, señor?" he asked in Spanish. "Are you drunk?"

I felt that Walter was in trouble, and in my best Spanish I told the officer that he wasn't drunk, and that we were looking for our hotel, and maybe the officer could give us directions. This was the stupid tourist ploy, and it worked. The officer gave us the directions, gave one more look at Walter and then walked away.

"What did you tell that guy?" asked Walter.

"I told him that you were a stupid American tourist on holiday in Mexico," I said.

"Stupid cops," muttered Walter.

Max and I looked at each other. "Walter," I said, "we have only one thing to say to you..."

And Max and I said in unison, "Long life to Pinochet!"

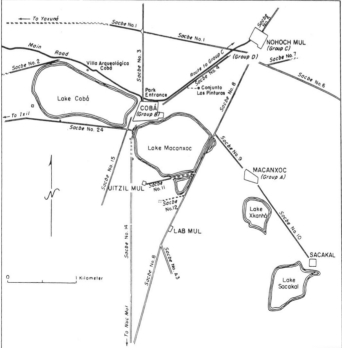

The sacbé system of roads radiating out from Cobá in the Quintana Roo of Yucatán. Though the jungle has covered them up, outlines of the roads can still be seen from the air.

"El Castillo" of Chichén Itzá, the central pyramid, with the Temple of the Warriors in the background.

Las Monjas, Chichen Itzá.

From an engraving of Frederick Catherwood

The Circular Observatory, Chichen Itzá.

From an engraving of Frederick Catherwood

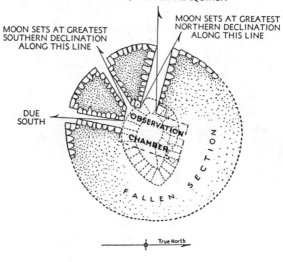

DUE WEST
SUN SETS ALONG THIS LINE ON
MARCH 21, THE VERNAL EQUINOX

MOON SETS AT GREATEST
SOUTHERN DECLINATION
ALONG THIS LINE

MOON SETS AT GREATEST
NORTHERN DECLINATION
ALONG THIS LINE

DUE
SOUTH

OBSERVATION
CHAMBER

FALLEN SECTION

True North

The Caracol Observatory at Chichén Itzá. Its main axis is aligned to the rising and
setting of Venus. In 1895 Augustus LePlongeon asserted that the circular building was
an observatory but was laughed at by his contemporaries.

The Ball Court at Chichen Itzá.

From an engraving of Frederick Catherwood

Dr. Samuel Cabot hunting a wounded jaguar *under the full-lipped god once on the side of a pyramid at Izamal. Now destroyed, this is its only illustration.*

From a lithograph by Frederick Catherwood

Augustus LePlongeon. A Masonic mystic, he believed that the Mayas were just as sophisticated as the Egyptians. His wild theories on Atlantis and dating of the Mayas as 11,000 years old tended to separate him from other scholars of the time.

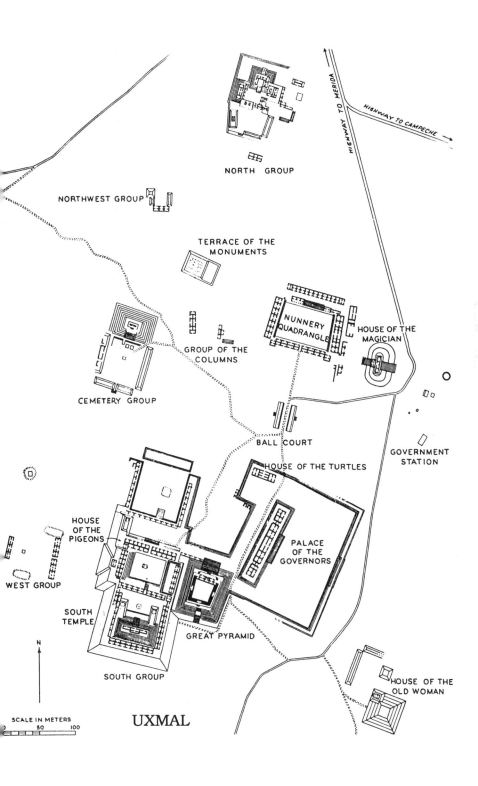

NORTH GROUP

HIGHWAY TO MERIDA

HIGHWAY TO CAMPECHE

NORTHWEST GROUP

TERRACE OF THE
MONUMENTS

NUNNERY
QUADRANGLE

HOUSE OF THE
MAGICIAN

GROUP OF THE
COLUMNS

CEMETERY GROUP

GOVERNMENT
STATION

BALL COURT

HOUSE OF THE TURTLES

HOUSE
OF THE
PIGEONS

PALACE
OF THE
GOVERNORS

WEST GROUP

SOUTH
TEMPLE

GREAT PYRAMID

N

SOUTH GROUP

HOUSE OF THE
OLD WOMAN

SCALE IN METERS

50   100

UXMAL

Head of Nefertiti, wife of Akhenaton, and Queen of Egypt in the 14th century B.C. Nefertiti was not Egyptian, but came from another country. Some scholars have identified her country as Mitanni, a Hindu state near to Persia. Others claim that she was Mayan. Her children also had elongated heads.

A Totonac statue thought to be a goddess of fertility. From Veracruz, Mexico. Note the similarity of the headdress and ankh symbol on the crown to the headdress and ankh worn by Nefertiti.

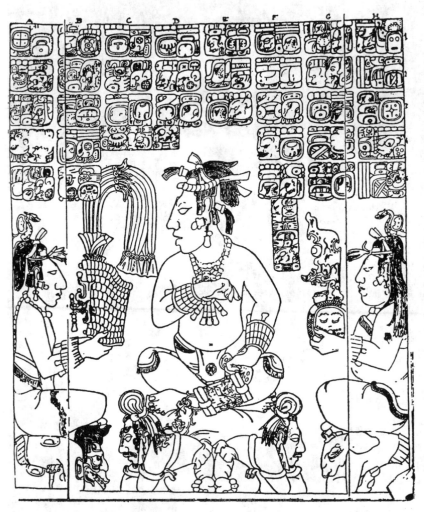

The sculptured panel of the slaves at Palenque. The lord here is sitting on two dwarves or Alux. Note the elongated foreheads. Hieroglyphs undeciphered.

Chapter 7

Southern Mexico:

Lost Golden Books of the Maya

These people also used certain characters or letters,
with which they wrote in their books
about the antiquities and their sciences.
...We found a great number of books in these letters,
and since they contained nothing but superstitions
and falsehoods of the devil we burned them all,
which they took most grievously,
and which gave them great pain.
—Friar Diego de Landa
Relación de las Cosas de Yucatan, 1566

Today only four pre-Conquest Mayan codices are known to exist. The largest of these folding-screen books is twenty-four feet long. Both sides of the screen-fold sheet were used, each fold forming a page, each of which was eight or nine inches high and three to five inches wide. The pages were read from left to right to the end of the sheet, and then back again from left to right on the other side. the Dresden Codex was found in Vienna in 1739; it is now in the State Library at Dresden, from which it takes its name. It is essentially a treatise on astronomy and divination, with tables of eclipse dates and revolutions of the planet Venus, divinatory almanacs, and information on ceremonies. The Codex Tro-Cortesianus, or Madrid Codex, was found in two pieces; one section belonged to a Spaniard named Tro, and the other section was called the Codex Cortesianus because it was said to have been brought across the Atlantic by Cortéz. The halves, now united in Madrid, form a book of horoscopes, which the priests used in making their divinations. The Paris, or Perez, Codex, was found in 1860 in the Bibliothéque Nationale in Paris, where it remains, in fragmentary form. It involves deities and ceremonies on one side and divination on the other. The fourth codex, an 11-page fragment with Venus tables, was found recently and is still questioned by some scholars. Known as the Grolier Codex because it was first exhibited in the Grolier Club, it is now in the National Museum of Anthropology in Mexico.

Friar Diego de Landa has taken a dual role in the history of Central America—one as the infamous destroyer of Mayan Codices in July of 1562 and the other role as the author of the *Relación de las cosas de Yucatan*, from which it has been said comes almost all of our knowledge of the early Mayas.

The infamous cultural *auto-da-fé* occurred at Maní in the Yucatan in July of 1562. De Landa tells us that he burned 27 hieroglyphic rolls along with 5,000 'idols' as "works of the devil." Although he could not read them, de Landa was certain that they were designed by the evil one to delude the Indians and to prevent them from accepting Christianity.

As the noted Mayan scholar William Yates says about de Landa in the first English translation of *Relación de las cosas de Yucatan*, published by the Maya Society of Baltimore in 1937: "Both acts were monumental, one to the ideas of his time, and the other as the basis and fountain of our knowledge of a great civilization that had passed. It is perhaps not too strong a statement to make, that 99 percent of what we today know of the Mayas, we know as the result either of what de Landa has told us in the (*Relación de las cosas de Yucatan*), or have learned in the use and study of what he told....if ninety-nine hundredths of our present knowledge is base derived from what he told us, it is an equally safe statement that at that auto-da-fé of '62, he burned ninety-nine times as much knowledge of Maya history and sciences as he has given us in his book."

It is interesting to note that de Landa's book would never have been written if his superior, Bishop Toral, a man of wholly different character, had not arrived closely on the heels of de Landa and the events at Maní. The bishop released the prisoners and forced de Landa to return to Spain for trial before the Council of the Indies. *Relación de las cosas de Yucatan* was written by de Landa in Spain as his defense for his atrocities, and it can be reasonably said that had de Landa not been forced to defend his actions, the important book would probably not have been written.

As has been the case throughout history, a great library and much ancient knowledge has been purposely destroyed by the dark forces that have periodically taken control of civilizations throughout known history. Writing was banned in the Inca Empire. The Emperor Chih Huang-ti who built the Great Wall of China ordered all books in his realm destroyed. The great libraries housed in Alexandria, Egypt, were burnt by successive waves of fanatical Christians and Moslems. In more modern times the Nazis burnt books in the 1930s and the United States had all the works of the psychoanalyst Wilhelm Reich destroyed in 1957.

The dark forces of history have always considered knowledge to be "works of the devil." It is for this very reason that secret libraries and secret societies have sprung up at various places and times throughout history.

It is interesting to note that de Landa destroyed only 27 codices, and Mayan scholars will readily admit that many more must have existed that were not destroyed. Four can presently be found in museums around the world and others no doubt never survived the rain forest or other possible destruction. Yet, it seems likely that some Mayan texts must still be extant today.

🐾🐾🐾

Max the Chilean pilot was off to Cancún, and I decided to drive to Palenque with Walter. On a bright, hot morning, we left the White City of Mérida, and headed south on the coastal highway to Campeche, with our final destination Palenqué, in the southern Mexican state of Chiapas.

We drove through the flat, dry tableland of the Yucatán, a land without rivers, only wells for water. Occasionally large mounds, sites of ancient ruins, broke the horizon.

On our way to Campeche the road passed near to Jaina Island, where a wealth of clay figurines were found. These remarkable clay figurines were discovered in Late Classic burials (9th-10th century), and some show bearded warriors and other "non-Mayan" types. Some of the statues have the look of Bodhisatvas from Asia: Buddhist saints in meditation and comtemplation, occasionally emerging from a flower or lotus, a common Oriental motif.

As I looked out the window of the car at the agave cactus plantations, I wondered at the secret library of the Mayas that was still said to exist.

Legends have continued for centuries that secret cities housing libraries, including the various Golden Books of the Mayas still exist in the jungles of Guatemala and Mexico. One story of the fabled Golden Books of the Maya and their discovery is told in the rare book, *They Found Gold*,[25] by A. Hyatt Verrill published in 1936.

Verrill was a well-known Yale scholar and lost treasure buff during the 1920s and 30s. He came from a wealthy family and had traveled widely in South America and the Caribbean, as well as Central America and Mexico. *They Found Gold* is an exciting combination of pirate treasure stories and first-hand accounts of treasure hunting. In Chapter IV Verrill relates the strange story of the *Golden Books of the Maya* and his own adventures in an attempt to snatch the treasure.

The story begins in northern Mexico in 1920 with the Escobar Revolution when the rebels ordered six airplanes from a firm in the United States. Under the contract, the planes were to be flown across the border by American pilots and delivered to the Escobar forces. The eventual discoverer of the Golden Books of the Maya was to be one of these aviators.

When the planes and pilots had landed at the rebel headquarters, the Mexicans were two pilots short and General Escobar offered 75 dollars in gold per day for the services of American pilots. The aviator of our story and his friend accepted the offer.

Things went well for a while, the planes were employed solely for scouting and observing, and the promised salary was paid on time. But gradually payments fell off, and when several weeks had passed with no money forthcoming, and when all demands had been met with profuse apologies and excuses, the two Americans decided it was time to quit. That, however, was easier said than done. Being unfamiliar with the Spanish language, they had unwittingly signed papers binding themselves to serve the rebel forces for the duration of the revolution, and to attempt to desert and fly across the border was hopeless—they would never be permitted to take off unless accompanied by a Mexican officer.

Finally, the two men devised a scheme to escape. One morning when they were ordered to make a flight the motors missed and sputtered, and after tinkering with them for some time without improving matters, the two men informed the commandant that the machines required a complete overhauling. When this wholly unnecessary work had been completed, they declared that a "tuning-up flight" would be essential and that to test the planes with an extra man on board would be dangerous. Shrugging his shoulders at the seemingly inevitable, the officer gave his consent and, elated at the success of their ruse and with thoughts of soon seeing the last of Mexico, the two men took off with fuel and oil tanks filled to capacity.

Once in the air they separated. Where his friend went or what became of him, our aviator would never know, but as he himself had heard that there was need of an American pilot in El Salvador, he headed southward.

Thousands of feet beneath him the terrain of Mexico was spread like a vast map. Deserts and plains, jungles and haciendas, ranches and cities, mountains and valleys, unrolled like a gigantic panorama, until to the east appeared the coastline and the sea.

Unfamiliar with the country and fearful of being seized as a rebel if he should be compelled to land, the fugitive followed the shore, hoping to reach the borders of Guatemala or British Honduras before his fuel was exhausted.

He passed Carmen Island off the coast of Campeche, and turning westward high above the lagoon, he set a course for the border. All was going well and it seemed certain he would reach his goal, when his engine began to miss.

It was no temporary or minor trouble, but a broken oil line. He realized that a landing was inevitable. Below him stretched the primeval jungle. To crash among the giant, vine-entangled trees meant certain death or worse. Far off, on either side, he could see the silvery gleam of rivers, but he had lost too much of his altitude and was too low to glide to either stream.

With tensed nerves and set face he stared at the endless sea of forest, searching for some spot where there would be one chance in ten thousand of coming down without being killed or crippled. Each second that he dropped his peril increased; the engine was coughing and spitting, and at any instant it might go dead. Then, when, as he expressed it to Verrill, he had "kissed the world goodbye," he saw a clearing in the heart of the jungle. It was not an open field by any means, but a large rectangular area where there were no big trees, a space that might have been an old clearing grown up to low brush and rank weeds.

There was no time to consider the chances; all he could do was to "pancake" the plane and hope for the best. But luck was with him; the plane tore through the brush for a few yards, swung sharply to one side, ripped off a wing, and then slowly turned turtle.

Shaken but not injured, the aviator crawled from under the wrecked plane. But as he glanced about, he realized that he might almost as well have crashed in the jungle and finished everything. He was miles—he had no idea how many miles—from the nearest settlements. He had no food other than his emergency rations, which would serve for a day; he had no weapons, not even an axe or a machete, and on every side stretched unbroken, uninhabited forest.

From the wreckage of the plane, he managed to retrieve his flashlight, his emergency ration, and his compass. He examined his surroundings seeking the most open spot at which to enter the jungle. A few yards from where he stood was a low hillock or mound, and thinking the slight elevation might provide a better survey, he pushed through the brush towards it. It was covered with a tangle of weeds and vines, and he shuddered involuntarily as he thought what an ideal spot it afforded for snakes. But in the face of his greater and more concrete peril, his inordinate dread of reptiles did not prevent him from forcing his way recklessly up the slope.

Suddenly the ground seemed to open beneath his feet. He shot downward and, amid a shower of earth, stones and leaves, came to an abrupt and jarring stop. Dazed and shaken, he gazed about and found that he was in an underground chamber or vault. Behind him was a flight of stone steps which led up to the aperture through which he had fallen. Above his head arched a stone roof, and on the farther side of the room, dimly outlined in the semi-darkness, he could see an immense sculptured idol and a square stone table.

Rising, he stepped toward the great stone god, and, as he passed close to the table, he noticed that it was hollowed into a deep trough from which hung curious-looking objects resembling gigantic fish-hooks with discs in place of eyes.

Wondering what they were, he examined them closely and discovered that, threaded on to the ends resting in the trough, were numbers of square leaf-like plates of metal. Scraping away the bat guano that covered them, he was amazed to find the plates covered with incised glyphs and figures. And as he raised the uppermost and exposed the surface of the plate below, he could scarcely believe his eyes. The surface gleamed dull yellow—it was solid gold!

Abruptly he burst into peals of wild laughter. He was standing beside a fortune, millions of dollars' worth of gold at least, yet of as little value to him as the great stone idol in the shadows. At that moment he would gladly have traded all that precious metal for a square meal...or a gun. Cursing his luck, he dropped the metal back into the trough, and climbing the stairs, he plunged into the forest.

Realizing that if he went north he must eventually reach a stream which would lead him to the coast, he headed in that direction. But could he survive long enough to make the nearest river? Torn by thorns, beset by swarms of the terrible rodederos or "biting gnats" of the Yucatan, he tramped doggedly on. Without a machete to hew a pathway, he was compelled to make long detours around dense tangles and swampy spots. Conserving meager rations until he was faint with hunger and never stopping to rest, he stumbled forward.

For 17 hours—all through the night—he pushed onward, keeping as nearly as possible to a compass-course until, almost at the end of his strength, he burst from the forest into a small clearing surrounding a chiclé camp (chiclé is the sap of a tree and is used for chewing gum, hence the brand name *Chiclets*). The chiclé gatherers fed the weary aviator who then rested from his incredible adventure. The next day he mounted a mule and was guided to the nearest village, whence by small boat down river, he reached the Gulf of Mexico and then returned to the United States by steamship.

🌸🌸🌸

Back in the States the aviator naturally tried to interest someone in financing an expedition to return with him to the scene of his discovery and secure the treasure. Among others, he approached a fellow aviator—a wealthy young man whom he had met at an aviation school who was willing to finance an expedition. But neither he nor his friends knew anything about the tropics or the jungles, none of them spoke Spanish, and none of them possessed any archaeological knowledge.

Therefore, the well-known adventurer and treasure hunter Hyatt Verrill was asked to take charge of the expedition to return to the Golden Books of the Maya for a share in whatever they might find.

Verrill was skeptical about the aviator's claims. Says Verrill, "Yet as I weighed and measured his statements my doubts began to dissolve. The fellow was absolutely ignorant of archaeology or the ancient Mayan civilization, yet he had correctly described the appearance of the almost legendary Maya 'books.' And he could not have imagined anything of the sort nor could he have read of them, for no book, pamphlet or magazine article describing similar objects had ever been published as far as I could ascertain.

Only in rare, almost unknown writings of the old Spanish priests and and conquerors was there any reference to the traditional, supposedly fabulous, golden books containing the secret history of the Maya race and civilization. Nevertheless, it seemed far too remarkable a coincidence that an aviator, crashing haphazardly in the Yucatan jungles, should have happened to fall in the exact spot where the most valuable of Mayan treasures had been concealed.

190

Still, truth at times is far stranger than fiction. I knew by experience that amazing coincidences do occur far more often than is generally believed, and I decided to secure the opinion of a friend, who is perhaps the best known authority on Mayan objects, before coming to a final decision."

Expecting his archaeologist friend (not named in the book) to scoff at the whole story, he was surprised when he was told: "I am convinced of the sincerity of the aviator, and I believe that he has found something there, probably of great interest. ...Of course, we could not take part in the expedition officially, as it would spoil our cordial relations with the Mexican Government. As far as the objects described are concerned, they are unique. Whether gold or not, they would be of extraordinary archaeological value, and I am extremely interested in the proposition. I hope you will be able to help unravel this intriguing problem."

This decided, Verrill and his group of eight found in Havana a ship with a Norwegian captain, and after outfitting it with supplies, medical stores, camping outfits, arms, and ammunition, they were ready for their search for the Golden Books of the Maya .

When they reached the Yucatan, they stopped first in Progresso, the main port near Merida, and continued on to Campeche and the Laguna de Términos. From this lagoon, they then headed up the Rio Candelaria, which the aviator had assured them was the river he had seen from the air.

Says Verrill: "Our aviator treasure-finder had assured us that the Candelaria was the stream he had noted just before he had crashed and that he could easily identify the proper place to search because of the conspicuous sharp 'S' bend of the stream due south of the spot where he had crashed. But as we chugged up the great river between interminable mangroves and impenetrable jungles, we were unwittingly traveling not nearer but farther from the treasure that we sought. And very soon it became obvious to all that we were on the wrong river.

"The aviator insisted that he had not sighted a house, village or even a clearing other than the deserted spot where he had come to earth. Yet along the Candelaria there were clearings galore, houses and settlements, and even two good-sized villages!"

After doing some obligatory exploration for several days near some rapids where the boat could continue no more, the party returned to the Laguna de Términos. They then headed across the lagoon to the Rio Chumpum, which they then determined was the correct river to ascend to the Golden Books of the Maya .

They ascended the river, sure that they were finally on the right track. "There were no houses, no settlements. Everywhere was jungle containing countless forms of bird-life. Alligators and crocodiles basked on logs beside the banks. There were deer, peccary, jaguars, pumas, ocelot, tapir, and wild turkeys in the forests. Throughout the day we explored the river, cruising for miles upstream, searching for the aviator's peculiar S-shaped bend by which we hoped to locate the treasure. Time after time we would come to a bend which he declared must be the right one. Landing, we would take compass bearings and hew our way into the jungle with machetes. And such jungles! Never in my forty years' experience in the West Indies, and Central and South America, have I seen anything to equal them. It was impossible to move five feet in any direction without cutting a path. Palms with trunks covered with great black spines, wiry bushes armed with crooked thorns, twisted, tangled briars, razor-edged saw-grass, prickly agaves, acacias and cacti, along with fallen limbs and leaves, knee-deep vegetable debris and slimy trunks of wild plantains—all formed an almost solid wall, while underfoot the ground was a sea of sticky black ooze in which we sank to our ankles. It was obvious that the aviator, with no machete, could never have forced his way at night through such a barrier... the aviator was forced to admit that he had made a mistake somewhere, that he was totally at a loss. The river, he argued, when viewed from a boat upon its surface did not look the same as when seen from the air, and also, he pointed out, although he had spotted only one S bend there were scores which, in all probability, had been hidden from his view by the forest. All our hopes were dashed. The one man who knew, or claimed to know, the secret of the Maya's treasure had failed us. And at last, bitterly disappointed and utterly discouraged, we abandoned the search and returned downstream."

Perhaps it was fortunate for Verrill and his companions that they did not find the Golden Books of the Maya because when they returned to the small port of Carmen, they were arrested and the boat thoroughly searched. Finding nothing, they were released, and on the last day before they set off back to Florida they were told that the reason they had been searched was that during the last ill-starred revolution (the Escobar Revolution) an airplane bearing a fleeing rebel leader and laden with gold coin and incriminating documents, had crashed somewhere within the jungle, and that, so the officials surmised, was what Verrill and his group had been seeking.

To Verrill, this was an entirely new angle. By some strange and almost incredible coincidence had two rebel airplanes crashed in the same jungle-covered area? Was the aviator the pilot of the ill-fated plane loaded with revolutionary documents, revolutionist funds and a revolutionary leader? If so, had the aviator really stumbled upon the underground hiding place of the Golden Books of the Maya , or had he invented the tale in hopes of luring an expedition in search of a mythical treasure in order that he might locate the plane and secure the papers for which the Mexican Government would pay a small fortune?

Says Verrill: "Unquestionably, somewhere in the jungle, rests the wreckage of an airplane containing the skeleton of a rebel leader, thousands of dollars in minted gold and paper which, if in the possession of the Mexican Government, would result in many a man facing a firing squad. And possibly, not far distant, the Golden Books of the Maya still lie hidden in their subterranean chamber, a treasure whose value is beyond all estimate."[3]

🐝🐝🐝

Perhaps the story of the Golden Books of the Maya is but a fantasy, concocted by an aviator to regain the lost treasure that he was flying out of rebel-held Mexican territory. But the Golden Books of the Maya are not a legend that will easily die. The Richmond, Virginia, *Wide World News* of February 22, 1942, reported a fascinating tale about a lost city, a forgotten tribe of Indians, and the Golden Books of the Maya from a story that originated from Santa Ana, California.

The news story was about Dana and Ginger Lamb and their adventures with a lost tribe of Lacandon Indians in the jungles of Chiapas, Mexico. Later the Lambs were to write a book about their amazing exploits called *Quest For the Lost City*.[82]

Having set out from Tucson, Arizona, in 1937 with $10.16 in their pockets in the general direction of the distant, unexplored jungles of Chiapas and Guatemala, and traveling by foot, horseback, canoe, and burro-powered Model-T Ford, the Lambs trekked down the west coast of Mexico, traversing the Sonora Desert and thousands of miles of mountains, rivers, and jungle. With sponsorship from the Mexican government, they eventually made contact with a lost tribe of Lacandon Indians in the remote jungles of Chiapas by leaving presents every day for three days.

On the fourth day it was raining more heavily than usual, and they lit a fire beneath a tree. Suddenly Kentin, a small, long-haired Lacandon man carrying a bow climbed down the tree to greet them, jabbering and laughing. He placed the knuckles of his left hand against their hearts in a gesture of friendship and indicated that he wanted to meet them again the next day.

On that next day Kentin brought with him "the fiercest visaged savage" the Lambs had ever seen. He was Chan-Kin, chief of the tribe. His hair was longer than Kentin's He had a narrow, firm mouth, a sharp nose and quick eyes. He wore a feather in his nose. The Lambs gave them more gifts and taught them how to make deer traps.

The next day they set off with the Mayas to visit their village. They crossed the mountain range, descended into a great valley and entered a village spread out over several miles. Each family lived about a mile away from its nearest neighbor. The Lambs made a camp in a clearing near Chan-Kin's house and settled down to win the friendship of their hosts. Dana taught them new ways to make fish traps and tan hides while Ginger began to teach the women first aid, sanitation, weaving, and even how to knit.

In turn, the Mayas cared for the Lambs when they fell ill of malaria. From their vast knowledge of native medicaments, they treated the explorers for insect bites.

193

The Lambs then learned of a lost city where the Mayas went on certain days of the year to worship. Only those who possessed three of the figurine gods bestowed from time to time on members of the tribe were permitted to go. Somewhere nearby the lost city was a great waterfall.

They also learned of a library of sheets of gold, as the Friar Diego de Landa had mentioned in his *Relación de las cosas de Yucatan.*

To quote the Richmond, Virginia newspaper article of February 22, 1942, "They learned that the Maya religion was remarkably like Christianity, encompassing teachings of 'the great flood and the Son of God.'"

Eventually, Dana and Ginger were made members of the tribe and were told that the Golden Books of the Maya had said that, "the people in civilization were very bad and would destroy themselves, that water would come and wash clean the land, that people would die because they chose the wrong chiefs, that men's hearts were so full of bad there was no room for good."

"But," added Chan-Kin, "the writings told that after great suffering people would become humble and the great true writings would be shown to the world."

The newspaper article of February 22, 1942, hinted that the Lacandon Maya of Chiapas knew in advance that World War II was coming. Paragraphs two and three of the article say, "For hundreds of years they have lived in the jungles of the 'Forbidden Land' of virtually unexplored Chiapas, Mexico. There, where it rains everyday and the sweat trees drip water continuously, live the last of the Mayas who fled the conquest of the Cortéz.

"That was the last war of which they knew. But carefully guarded in their 'lost city' is the golden library which told them of a great war to come."

According to their book, *Quest For the Lost City,*[82] the Lambs were aware of Verrill's book, *They Found Gold,* and had even corresponded with Verrill about the Golden Books of the Maya and their supposed location. While they lived with a lost tribe in the junglcs of Chiapas, Dana asked his Mayan "brother" about the Golden Library, as he called it.

"As well as I could I also tried to ask about the Golden Library, describing the subterranean chamber into which the American flyer had stumbled, the great stone trough, and the plaques of gold.

"Chan nodded. He called them the Sacred Books. That's as near as I can come to translating his words. And certainly the word 'book' is my own, for these people apparently had lost the art of writing a long time ago."

Dana attempted to get Chan to take him to the lost city they had been searching for, and to show him the Golden Library. One night while out in the jungle away from the village, Dana made his move. "Close to sleep, but eager for tomorrow, I said, with gestures and the few words I knew, 'Tomorrow, we will go to the east. We will look upon the Golden Books.'

"Chan swung upright in his hammock, talking fast. 'No, no, not now. Now is not the time! No, no!'"

The Lambs eventually returned to the United States at the outset of World War II. They met with President Franklin Roosevelt, and told him of the lost cities in Central America, of the Golden Books of the Maya, and the forgotten tribes of Lacandon Indians.

After the war, they returned to Mexico to find their lost city and the Golden Books of the Maya. They had corresponded with Verrill who had given them advice on where to find the hidden library. In their book, the Lambs name the aviator who had crashed and discovered the gold books as Wallace Hope. In Verrill's book the aviator is never named.

They chartered an aircraft at the island of Carmen and then flew down the Rio Candelaria in search of the S bend where they would find a small mound: the ruin covered with jungle which had inside it the Golden Books.

After flying upriver for a quarter of an hour or more. "Finally, a clearly defined S bend appeared under our wing....I swung the plane around. Ginger's voice cracked with excitement, 'Dan there it is! There's a little flat-topped hill beside the S bend!'

"I looked out on my side. Beside the hillock was a flat place where a plane might attempt a landing. 'This must be it!' I shouted. 'It checks with everything Hope told Verrill. We'll go up the river a ways, but I think we've found it.'

"We flew on up the river and in about ten minutes came to another S bend. Circling this, we found a second flat-topped hill and a clearing where a plane could land. 'Double take,' I called to Ginger, who was busy photographing the place.

"Again we swung along the winding course of the river, and passed over the railroad which ran between Campeche and Tenosique. Below us, beside the bridge spanning the water, was the little settlement of Candelaria.

"Five minutes later we came to another S bend, and believe it or not, another small hill with a clearing near by.

"I shouted to Ginger, 'This is getting monotonous.'

"'How many Golden Libraries are there anyway?' she demanded.

"No wonder Hope (the aviator, with Verrill) had not succeeded in his quest. He had hunted for an S bend in the river, combined with a small hill and a clearing in the swampland. In less then an hour we had found three.

"On our return to the airfield we determined that some day we would find the time to take a canoe up the Candelaria and further investigate Hope's story."

Yet, the Lamb's never did return, but they did eventually find a lost city. "It was a pyramid and temple somewhere to the west of the Usumacinta River. The three main rooms of the temple were clean, and there were fresh clay statuettes of gods placed in the rooms. Obviously someone had been going to the city in recent years. The Lambs felt that they may have found the city with the Golden Books

195

of the Maya, but they were reluctant to tear up the floor of the temple.

While the Lambs were in their "lost city," it was hit by a hurricane. A giant tree which was part of the jungle growth covering the temple was ripped out by the strong winds and the weakened roof collapsed inward. The couple had to find a way to escape the storm-damaged area. They used their machetes to fashion a canoe out of one of the fallen trees and followed a flooded arroyo back to the Usumacinta.

With their Mexican companion back at basecamp, they finally made their way back to civilization, still wondering what the truth was concerning a lost city and a golden library somewhere in the jungles of Central America. Did the Lambs discover the city of the legendary golden books or is it in some other repository? Perhaps it still waits today for an intrepid explorer with determination and luck.

🐾🐾🐾

*Civilized people talk a lot and think they've
done something. We Kaispo just act.*
—Chief Paiskon, an Indian from the Amazon rainforest.

"Bananas?" asked the young brown girl with a basket on her head. "Do you want bananas, gringo?" she asked again in her tourist lingo.

"Cuanto cuestan?" I asked, smiling at her.

"Only five hundred pesos por uno," she said earnestly. I bought three and wandered toward the ticket booth.

"So this is Palenque..." I wondered as I gazed around. A distance away I could see a pyramid rising out of the green jungle in the distance. Walter and I had just arrived, and parked the car in the parking lot next to the many souvenir sellers.

Moments later, with a ticket to the site in one hand and a banana in the other, I was heading down the walk way to the verdant jungles of Palenque.

Located on a tributary of the important Usumacinta River, Palenque is thought of as a Classic Mayan city that was particularly active in the A.D. 600-900 period. It is magnificently situated in the foothills of the Chiapas Mountains overlooking the Tabasco plain that stretches to the gulf of Mexico.

Important structures like the Temple of the Cross and the Temple of the Sun distinguish the archaeological site, but it is the Pyramid of the Inscriptions with its fabulous tomb that Palenque is most famous.

In 1948, the Mexican archaeologist Alberto Ruz Lhuillier discovered a secret passage beneath a floorstone at the summit of the pyramid. The secret passage was completely filled in with stone rubble, but over a period of four years of excavation, he succeeded in clearing out the passage. It was a stairway that descended deep inside the pyramid to the royal tomb of Lord Pacal.

Descending into the tomb with my flashlight, because the power had gone out in the ruins, as it frequently does, I imagined the thrill of entering such a tomb for the first time and discovering the sarcophagus of Lord Pacal with its massive five-ton, carved lid.

The monolithic sarcophagus is 5 feet 5 inches high, 6 feet 10 inches wide and 9 feet 9 inches long. The massive, 5 ton cover slab is 12¹/₂ feet long by 7 feet 2 inches wide and 8 inches thick.

The contents of the sarcophagus, now at the Museum of Anthropology in Mexico City, were the remains of the ruler, apparently a very tall man. He was covered with jade ornaments: earplugs, pendants, beads, rings for each finger of both hands, and a mask consisting of two hundred pieces of brilliant green jade. Also in the tomb were a smaller jade mask representing an old man and two life-size stucco heads.

Says Bruce Hunter in *A Guide to Ancient Maya Ruins,* [134] "Pieces of jade were placed in the mouth of the dead ruler and in each hand, a burial custom similar to that of the ancient Chinese...Before the tomb was closed, the whole chamber was sprinkled with powdered red cinnabar, widely used in burials throughout Mesoamerica. The red color symbolizes the east, the rising sun, and resurrection."[134]

That the Chinese used identical burial customs concerning jade doesn't seem to make a dent in the typical Mayan dogma of limited cultural contact within the Americas, and none with cultures overseas. The use of a red ochre on the burial is reminiscent of the Red Paint people who covered burials in the arctic regions with a red powder, often cinnabar. Red Paint people burials have been found in Labrador, Newfoundland, Norway, Finland and Siberia. The rare liquid metal mercury is derived from cinnabar.

The sarcophagus is a large one, and Pacal Votan has been said to have been nine feet tall. The lid of the sarcophagus was nearly 13 feet long. The Maya were small people, however. Men were usually only about five feet tall.

The sarcophagus lid has attracted a great deal of attention because of its fascinating detail of a rather odd scene. A man, apparently Lord Pacal, is in a seated position and has an intricate, decorated scene around him.

Erich von Däniken popularized the notion in the late 1960s that this sarcophagus lid showed the portrait of an ancient astronaut taking off or landing in his spaceship, a stylized rocket. Von Däniken is worth quoting, "Altogether the tombstone forms a frame in the middle of which a being is sitting and leaning forwards (like an astronaut in his command module). This strange being wears a helmet from which twin tubes run backwards. In front of his nose is an oxygen apparatus. The figure is manipulating some kind of controls with both hands. The fingers of the upper hand are arranged as if the being was making a delicate adjustment to a knob in front of him. We can see four fingers of the lower had, which has its back to us. The little finger is crooked. Doesn't it look as if the being were working a control such as the hand-throttle of a motorbike? The heel of the left foot rests on a pedal with several steps."

Von Däniken goes on to say, "In my view, the apparatus in which the space traveler crouches so tensely, presents the following technical characteristics: The central oxygen machine lies in front of the straped-in astronaut, as do the energy supply and communications system, not to mention the manual controls and equipment for observations outside the spacecraft. In the bow of the ship, i.e. ahead of the central unit, large magnets are recognizable. Presumably their purpose was to create a magnetic field around the ship's hull that would prevent it from being struck by particles when traveling at high speeds in outer space. Behind the astronaut we can see a nuclear fusion unit. Two atomic nuclei, probably hydrogen and helium, which finally merge, are schematically depicted."

I stared at the sarcophagus lid for a while, it was indeed fascinating. It was a bizarre scene, though von Däniken's explanation didn't quite make sense to me. The man was barefoot and wore no shirt, a typical dress for the Maya, but is this how one dresses when one is one's space ship? Maybe tomorrow's astronauts will wear surfer shorts and rubber flip-flops.

Similarly, a bird stands at the top of the "spaceship," sun-god symbols appear on either side of him. Was this the typical prow of a Mayan ship, sort of like a mermaid head on Medieval ships or a dragon's head on Viking long boats?

Lastly, it is unlikely that any sort of rocket power was ever used in the past or will ever be used in the future, by visiting astronauts, whether extraterrestrials or ancients returning to earth. That other civilizations (of other planets or from earth) would have ever traveled via rocket power is unlikely considering the nature of flying saucers, cylindrical airships and the science of anti-gravity, gravity control and electro-magnetic space craft.

When von Däniken wrote his books, in the late 60s and early 70s, NASA had placed the first men on the moon, and rocket power was the method that was used. Rocket power may have seemed like a nifty way of getting around the solar system and galaxy back then, but with the advent of anti-matter reactors, gravitational pulse and jumps to hyperspace, the idea of extraterrestrials using rocket powered vehicles to arrive on our planet is about as outmoded as extraterrestrials arriving here fired from a great cannon on another planet as Jules Verne had the first visitors to the moon traveling through space in the 1800s. It all made sense back then.

The ancient epics of India, the Mahabharata and the Ramayana, speak of *Vimanas,* a type of airship similar to discoid aircraft or tubular airships of the turn of the century, such as the Hindenberg. The famous Hindu king Rama, according to the epics, flew his Vimana from Ayodha in northern India to the island of Lanka where his beloved wife Sita had been kidnapped. Ancient Indian texts, as well as texts from China and the Middle East (including the Bible) mention these ancient aerial vehicles.[138]

That a Vimanas might have landed in the realms, or used by them in their early history is a fascinating thought. One as incredible as the Mayans being extraterrestrials themselves. I couldn't help think of the circular platform at El Ciebal in the Petén. It was perfect for the landing of a discoid craft. Not a rocket, however. I also thought of the Rama Indians that formerly inhabited the east coast of Nicaragua.

A more credible, and in fact, as interesting an explanation for the sarcophagus lid of Lord Pacal is that the engraved relief represents a division of the universe in three layers: the Upper World, the Middle World, and Under World. Underlying the engraving is the theme of interworld penetration with various devices, such as animals, birds, the sun, the cosmic tree of life. A silk painting from the Han Dynasty tomb at *Ma-wang-tuei* is highly similar to the sarcophagus cover at Palenque. It too has birds, the sun and moon at the top, with the deceased ruler, standing near two Taoist priests in the center of the scroll (the Middle World) and the dragons of the Underworld beneath them all.

While Mayanists claim that the relief shows Lord Pacal, sometimes called Pacal Votan, descending into the Under World (he may be ascending, actually, this is the direction he faces), they fail to observe the Chinese symbolism (even the jade discs in the mouth).

Curiously, the pyramid and tomb was constructed after the sarcophagus was placed inside it, as the lid is too large to be removed through the door to the chamber. Megalithic stones have been placed up against the sarcophagus so that it cannot be moved either. Outside the tomb wall were found the skeletons of several youths who may have been left to guard the tomb.

The sacrificing of warriors and servants to guard important tombs was both a Chinese and an Egyptian custom, and, apparently, a Mayan custom as well. Was it necessary to execute innocent people for a space traveler? The rite seems oddly primitive for one from a space-traveling nation.

Was this a visitor, some important personage who came from afar? While the possibility that he may have come from outer space cannot be entirely ruled out, the explanation that he was some tall Viking explorer or Irish Christian priest of the fourth century A.D. is more probable. The bird at the very top of the sarcophagus is most probably a quetzal bird,[77] his long feathers can be seen behind him. In this case, Pacal Votan may have been one of the special Quetzalcoatl priests. It is known that the sarcophagus was put in place before the pyramid was built, and therefore, this was an especially important burial.

Walter suddenly came up behind me while I stood at the tomb. "Ah, it Pacal Votan, the Navigator." he said.

"The navigator?" I asked.

"That's right, that's what they called him, the Navigator. The Navigator is also what the leader of the Knights Templar were called in Medieval Europe. Jacques DeMolay was the Navigator. Do you suppose that Pacal Votan was a Knights Templar?"

I laughed. There were more theories about this guy than you could shake a stick at.

🐃🐃🐃

The amazing scene of the stealing of a gold idol from a lost temple that began the first Indiana Jones film, *Raiders of the Lost Ark*, was actually based on real occurrence. The time frame is the 1940s and the young explorer was a German-American named Charles Frey.

The idea of a lost temple, often containing the lost golden books of the Maya, as well as other treasures such as gold statues and jade, has been suggested in the literature of Central America since the American diplomat, John Lloyd Stevens traveled through Chiapas in 1838-39. He chronicles his various adventures in two large volumes illustrated by the British artist Frederick Catherwood: *Incidents of Travel in Central America, Chiapas, and Yucatán,* (1841)[84] and *Incidents of Travel in Yucatán* (1843).[139]

The British writer Harold T. Wilkins, in his rare book, *Mysteries of Ancient South America,*[140] quotes Stevens from newspapers published in New York and London in 1839 and 1840: "The padre of the little village near the ruins of Santa Cruz del Quiché, had heard of this unknown city when he was in the village of Chajul (Chajul lies in the mountains, in Western Guatemala, close to the headwaters of the Rio Usumacinta). the priest was then a young man, and with much labour, climbed to the naked summit of the topmost ridge of the sierra of the Cordillera. When arrived at the height of ten or twelve thousand feet, he looked over an immense plain extending to Yucatan and the Gulf of Mexico. At a great distance, he saw a large city spread over a great space, and with turrets white and glistening in the sun. Tradition says that no white man has ever reached the city; that the inhabitants speak the Maya language, know that strangers conquered their whole land, and murder any white man who attempts to enter their territory.... They have no coin; no horses; no cattle; mules; or other domestic animals, except fowls; and the cocks they keep underground to prevent their crowing being heard."[140]

Wilkins quotes Madame Blavatsky, one of the founders of the Theosophical Society as telling the same story. She traveled through South America and Central America by ship between 1851 and 1853. Wilkins speaks about how she met the an old Peruvian, a Quechua Indian, who had lived in Guatemala with the Quiché Indians (James Churchward believed that the Quiché and Quechua were related as well) and told Blavatsky, "I keep friends with them, these *banditos* (the Spanish colonials) and their Catholic missioners, for the sake of my own people. But I am as much a worshiper of the sun as if I had lived in the days of our murdered emperor, the Inca Atahualpa. Now, as a converted native and missionary, I once took a journey to Santa Cruz del Quiché, and when there, I went to see some of my people by a subterranean

200

passage leading into a mysterious city behind the cordilleras. Herein, it is death for any white man to trespass!"[140]

Wilkins was a pirate treasure expert who, starting in the 1930s, wrote a number of popular books. He believed that ancient tunnels and lost cities that were to be found in South America and Guatemala and Chiapas as well. Says Wilkins, "Fuentes, who lived about A.D. 1689, and wrote an unpublished manuscript on the history of Guatemala, speaks of the amazingly large and ancient towns found there by the conquistadors.

"Fuentes says: 'The marvelous structure of the tunnels (subterranea) of the pueblo of Puchuta, being of the most firm and solid cement, runs and continues through the interior of the land for the prolonged distance of nine leagues to the pueblo to Tecpan, Guatemala. It is a proof of the power of these ancient kings and their vassals.'" Wilkins points out that these tunnels are more than thirty miles long, by the old Castillian league.[140]

Subterranean tunnels to lost cities of living Mayans, complete with the lost books of gold, is a story with a great deal of substance. Tunnels between cities in Guatemala absolutely exist (see chapters 3 and 4). There seems to be little doubt that some Mayan codices must still exist (especially if made of gold), and that some Mayans were still living undiscovered (especially in the late 1800s). That all these things should be wrapped into one lost city makes the plot of as popular an Indiana Jones film as one could make.

Charles, "Carlos" Frey, was to step into just such an incredible scene when he decided to leave the United States in 1942, rather than have to go into the American Army and fight in World War II.

For years, with very little money, Frey walked all over southern Mexico, starting in the Yucatán. He visited Tulúm, then reachable only by foot or by boat, and, occasionally traveling by third class train, reached the area around Palenque. From Palenque, Frey continued deep in the Usumacinta River area with chicléros.

In this area, he married an Indian girl, and began to live as a farmer in the El Real valley. However, he learned that the Maya would go away occasionally to an unknown city in the forest. Finally, he persuaded a Lacandon Indian friend named Chan-Bor to take him to the secret city. The year was 1945.

Apparently, there was a gold statue in the city that was still worshiped as a god, though only on special days, being kept in this temple. The city had been abandoned only a hundred years or so before. This city is the now famous archaeological site of Bonampak, about a hundred miles south of Palenque in the Lacandon mountains.

Apparently, according to my source, the esteemed Brazilian archaeologist Dr. G. Abreu of the University of Sao Paulo, Charles Frey stole the gold statue, which was either one or two feet high, and probably a representation of either Tlac, the Rain God, or of the Corn God or Sun God. He took it with him to Mexico City, where he sold it. According to Dr. Abreu, there were various newspaper

201

reports in Mexico City at the time about a mysterious gold statue being sold privately. Frey was known to be in the capital at this time.

Frey soon ran out of money, and desired more publicity. He met a photographer named John Bourne, whom he took to Bonampak in February of 1946. Four months later he took the British photographer Giles Healey. Healey discovered the magnificent murals and took photos of Bonampak which were published in *Life* magazine and made quite a sensation.

Apparently, the Lacandon tolerated Frey's having stolen the gold statue at first. They allowed him to bring a friend who photographed the ruins. Then Healey and Frey returned in another year with Dr. J. Eric Thompson, the most eminent British Mayanist of his time.

This expedition was sponsored by the Carnegie Institution in Washington, which ten years later produced a richly illustrated and exhaustive work on Bonampak.

In early 1949, Frey returned one last time from Mexico City, this time with a large expedition from the Mexican government, complete with a small detachment of soldiers. Frey had stolen the gold statue, and now he was bringing the Mexican government into the Sierra Lacandon. Charles Frey had finally stepped across the line as far as the Lacandon were now concerned.

On returning from Bonampak, Charles Frey was killed by the Lacandon. Wolfgang Cordan, who helped raise Charles Frey's son, and knew Chan-Bor personally, gives this account of the death in his book, *Secret of the Forest*,[33]: Frey, with two of the members of the expedition, a mestizo guide and a draughtsman named Gomez, were returning via a short-cut. Instead of the long route through the swamps, they walked to a dug-out canoe, which Frey was commandeering for their return to the main camp. "None of the three ever reached Campo Cedro. The upturned boat was found downstream by some Lacandon, and, a little later, Chan-Bor recovered the body of his friend, Carlos Frey, from under a fallen tree in the river. Gomez was also found at the same spot. The guide turned up two days later."[33]

The Mexican expedition dispersed almost immediately, and the Lacandon were then left in peace. Just how three men were somehow unable to swim ten feet or so to the banks of a river has never been explained by any of the archaeological books that briefly mention the Charles Frey episode of Bonampak. In fact, Charles Frey is typically not credited for the discovery of the city. Giles Healey is generally named as the discoverer of Bonampak, though it is true that he is the discoverer of the famous murals.

The *Illustrated London News* ran two stories on Bonampak on June 28 and August 9 of 1947. Both fail to give any credit to Frey. Said the *News* on August 9, "Mr. Healey has located forty-eight building sites, and a number of carved stelae or recording stones." A photo is included in the story showing a Lacandon standing next to a broken stele. Even the broken portion of the stele is huge, compared the Lacandon, who probably stands only five feet tall. Yet the complete stele was obviously megalithic in proportions, being perhaps as tall as 25 or 30 feet high, similar to stelae at Quirigua.

The murals themselves are considered one of the great artistic masterpieces of all time. Though the Maya must have painted thousands of murals, most of them have eroded away or been destroyed. The Bonampak murals were partially preserved by a coating of calcium bicarbonate produced by moisture reacting chemically with the limestone. These murals are now over a 1,000 years old.

J. Eric Thompson interpreted the murals as the first being a scene of important personages preparing for a raid on some nearby village. The scene is a realistic one clearly depicting the action, the manner, the social classes, the dress, and the ceremonial regalia of the 8th-century Maya. Wars were an activity of the elite class, commanding great prestige for its members. The lower section of the mural represents musicians and masked participants in a processional. The next scene is of the actual raid, showing warriors and their enemies engaged in battle. The next scene is a judgment scene where the captives are being arraigned before the great lords of Bonampak. A following scene depicts the execution of a prisoner and the pleading for mercy from the other captives. The final scene is of a celebration and dance by the finest nobles and entertainers in their jaguar skins, jades, and feathers.

But perhaps the greatest treasure of Bonampak was sold in Mexico City, and now resides in a private collection. Do the lost books of the Maya still reside in another city? Even Dana and Ginger Lamb wrote about Charles Frey in their book *Quest For the Lost City*.[82] But they knew that Bonampak was not the site of the golden tablets. Perhaps they can only be reached by a subterranean tunnel!

❀❀❀

A few days later in Villahermosa, Walter and I talked about various theories concerning lost cities, vanished civilizations and ancient mysteries. We had been looking at the gigantic Negroid heads that were found at the Olmec site of La Venta, and were now in the park at Villahermosa.

"Do you suppose that these guys are explorers from Africa?" I asked Walter.

Walter thought for a moment and replied, "The world as we know it has been destroyed many times over. Civilizations have risen from the dust and then declined. According to some people, the greatest of all civilizations was on a now-submerged continent in the Pacific."

Walter continued, "According to that theory, Negroes are really not from Africa. Negroes, like all people, are originally from the vast continent in the Pacific, where all the races of man originated. In the later days of that great civilization, the different tribes of Mu, as the continent is sometimes called, began to migrate around the world.

Negroes, one of the twelve tribes of Mu, settled largely in Central America. That is why we can find these huge Negroid heads, many thousands of years old, here in the jungle. Other Negroes managed to survive in the New Guinea area of South East Asia after Mu was destroyed in a cataclysmic pole shift some twenty four thousand years ago.

"Africa was largely depopulated after the last poleshift about 10,000 years ago. Seven to eight thousand years ago, Negroes from Central America migrated into the area around Nigeria, and began to populate that area of Africa. Meanwhile, Dravidians had settled in Abyssinia and Southern Arabia, while Asians began settling Madagascar and East Africa. The Bushmen and Hottentots are the remnants of these people. The world is one long history of migrations, invasions and, unfortunately, of war and cruelty. Central America, like Asia, apparently had just about every race in the world living here at one time or another."

"I've read the James Churchward books on Mu," I said. I then Walter that on the traditional academic level are the books edited by Ivan Van Sertima of Rutgers University in New Jersey. His books, *African Presence in Early America* [150] and *African Presence in Early Asia*, are filled with articles and photos that show without a doubt that Negroes have lived, literally, all over the world, including the ancient Americas. While Van Sertima does not bring in such unorthodox theories as a lost continent in the Pacific, he is clearly of the belief that Negroes in ancient times developed many advanced civilizations and lived all over the world.

We glanced at one of the massive heads in the park. On it's head was a strange leather helmet, making the man appear like a football or rugby player.

Walter was reading *The Ancient Kingdoms of Mexico*,[22] by the British historian Nigel Davies, a well-known critic of theories of ancient seafaring. Davies flatly rejects any theories of Phoenicians, Egyptians, Chinese, Vikings, African sailors or anyone else ever reaching Mexico by boat. Yet, unlike some historians, he readily admits that Olmecs are Negroes. His explanations of Negroid Olmecs in Mexico is interesting.

Walter pulled out a well worn paperback and began to read from *The Ancient Kingdoms of Mexico* [22]: (page 26-27) "Insofar as Negroid features are depicted in pre-Columbian art, a more logical explanation surely exists that does not depend upon flights of fancy involving African seafarers. Negroid peoples of many kinds are to be found in Asia as well as Africa, and there is no reason why at least a few of them should not have joined those migrant bands who came across the Bering land bridge that joined north-east Asia and north-west America for so many millennia.

"Small men with Negroid features were the aboriginal inhabitants of many lands facing the Indian Ocean, including India itself, the Malay Peninsula and also the Philippines, where they still exist today. One need go no further than Manila International Airport to find proof of their existence. Nearby stands the Museum of Philippine Traditional Cultures; facing the entrance is a wall covered with photographs of 'unfamiliar faces'. In marked contrast to the typical Mongoloid Filipinos of today, many of these are dark-skinned aboriginals, known as 'Negritos', who now live scattered along the east side of the main island of Luzon; they mostly have thick lips and black skins. The Weddas of Ceylon are another of these Negroid aboriginal groups. It is therefore not in the least surprising that such elements should have joined the ranks of those early migrants who crossed the Bering bridge before it sank beneath the waves; their presence offers a more logical explanation of Negroid features than any other.

"Therefore, even if one accepts the uncertain premise that Olmec art is based on the portrayal of true Negroids, this does not warrant the conclusion that such people were Africans. It is perfectly possible to find individuals in Tabasco today who have faces not unlike those of the colossal heads, whose features also somewhat recall the large stone carvings of the Cham culture of Cambodia, another country that still has a Negroid aboriginal population."[22]

"The logic of these 'experts' is curious," I remarked. "While it seems impossible to them that ancient people would have traveled anywhere by boat, how does Davies suppose that Negroes got to the Philippine Islands? Did they walk across an ancient land bridge at the same time that the Bering Strait was walked across?

"Does Davies suppose that the myriad islands of the Pacific were populated by people walking across ancient land-bridges? Hardly! While these 'experts' are forced to admit that Polynesians and Micronesians colonized remote islands in Pacific, many of them tiny dots of land thousands of miles from anywhere, they cannot admit that seafarers in ancient times could similarly find such huge continents as North and South America! In the same vein, Madagascar was colonized by Malaysians traveling the entire length of the Indian Ocean to a remote corner of south-east Africa, yet ancient seafarers with sophisticated navies such as the Phoenicians could never have duplicated such a feat!

"The bizarre logic defies the imagination, yet it is the dogmatic 'truth' of today's universities. Essentially the argument is that primitive seafarers with a double canoe, some fishing line, chickens and bananas can explore and settle remote oceanic islands, but not more civilized nations with bigger ships and larger navies. That ancient peoples may have come by boat to the Americas (or from the Americas, for that matter), rather than walking through Siberia, Alaska and the entire North American continent, is a totally untenable theory proposed by unscientific 'nuts'."

"Indeed," said Walter, "who are the nuts? The isolationists or the diffusionists? It seems that our halls of higher learning have taken a strange turn down the road to ancient history."

The origin of the Olmecs is a mystery, even if we discontinue the line of thought of how Negroids arrived in Central America. Says Davies[22]: "Discounting the more romantic notions of an Olmec seaborne migration, doubts persisted as to which part of Mexico was their place of origin, since they were later present in almost every region. The problem has been hotly debated; Miguel Covarrubias became convinced that Olmec civilization first flourished in the state of Guerrero, bordering on the Pacific Ocean, but won little support for this view. Others have insisted with equal force that they originally came from highland Mexico. However, a fairly broad consensus now maintains that their heartland or home territory lay in the rubber land of southern Veracruz and Tabasco."

Davies is essentially saying that the Olmecs may have originated at Monte Alban in the Oaxaca highlands, Oxtotitlan or Juxtlahuaca near Acapulco on the Pacific or, most likely at Tres Zapotes and La Venta in the swamps along the Gulf of Mexico. All of these areas have known Olmec sites. He is missing one theory on the original homeland for the Olmecs, and that is that the Olmecs are originally from the Pacific coast of Guatemala and Chiapas, Mexico. Here we have such sites as El Baul, San Isidro, El Alto and Izapa (see Chapter 3). Here too are gigantic Negroid heads, as well as other ancient peoples. Yet, where are the cities of these people—buried beneath tons of rock or at the bottom of Lake Atitlan or the Pacific?

There are two kinds of statistics;
the kind you look up and the kind you make up.
—Rex Todhunter Stout

🦬🦬🦬

Walter offered me one last ride in his rented car, this time from Villahermosa to the city of Oaxaca in the state of the same name. We left Villahermosa early in the morning and began the drive to Oaxaca.

Along the way we passed by one of the more mysterious Mayan sites, the ancient Mayan city of Comalcalco, the western-most Mayan site known in Mexico. Comalcalco lies near the coast of the Gulf of Mexico, only a few west of the delta of the Usumacinta River, the important river that leads into the Mayan cities deep in the Petén area of Guatemala.

Comalcalco was a major Mayan port city which flourished between 700 and 900 A.D. Like most Mayan sites, it is no doubt much older than this Classic Mayan period, and with the recent discoveries at Nakbe in the Petén, it may go back to 1000 B.C. or more. Comalcalco was still a flourishing Mayan port at the time of the Spanish conquest, but fell into decay soon afterward.

Comalcalco is unusual for two reasons. The first is that since there are no stones in the area for building, Comalcalco is built out of mud bricks. The Maya raised huge structures of brick at the city, unique in the Mayan world.

The other aspect of Comalcalco that makes it rather unique is that many of these bricks have inscriptions on them. In 1977 and 1978, the National Institute of Anthropology and History excavated the site and found that it was entirely made of baked bricks. Of the bricks which make up the site it was discovered that approximately three percent of them were found to have inscriptions on them.

In a study done by the Mexican archaeologist Neil Steede for the National Institute of Anthropology and History[137] it was discovered that 3671 bricks had inscriptions on them. Of these bricks, 2129 or 58 percent had Maya hieroglyphs on them. 499 of the bricks (or 13.6 percent) had old world inscriptions on them in Arabic, Phoenician, Libyan, Egyptian, Ogam, Tifinag, Chinese, Burmese and Paliburmese (actually 640 bricks or 17.3 percent had Old World inscriptions on them, but if any brick had Mayan hieroglyphs on them with notes in Old World inscriptions, they were placed in the Mayan brick category). Other bricks had drawings on them (735 bricks or 20 percent) and 308 bricks were mixed or unknown (8.4 percent).

According to Steede, a complete set of the photographs of the bricks was taken to the Epigraphic Society in San Diego, California where they were examined by linguists. It was here that the above mentioned languages were identified. Some of the bricks even had inscriptions of elephants on them. Several bricks had Mayan inscriptions mixed with other languages, typically translations.

Dr. Barry Fell of the Epigraphic Society felt that the bricks were part of a language school at Comalcalco where students, studying various languages, drew on wet bricks. Afterwards the bricks were used for the construction of buildings. The bricks with inscriptions were discovered by Mexican archaeologists as simple construction bricks and the inscriptions or drawings were not placed in such a way as to be visible. They were only discovered in the dismantling of structures during the government's archaeological excavations.

Steele makes a good point when he says that there is a problem with the dating as the languages present in the bricks are from a period of approximately A.D. 0 to 400 while Comalcalco is generally ascribed to dates of A.D.700 to 900. Steele points out the possibility that these bricks might have been taken from an earlier structure and used in the construction of the present structure.

Steele suggests that since only one half of one percent of the bricks have been looked at so far, there is the possibility of there being more than one million inscribed bricks still waiting excavation at Comalcalco. Steele has something very interesting to say about the currently accepted Mayan dating correlation: "...the dates seem to be clustered around the accepted classic Maya period (that is from A.D. 700-900). This would strongly suggest that our correlation of the Maya calendar is off by some 300-400 years. Correlation for the present correlation was done basically

Thompson. The Goodman-Martinez-Thompson (GMT) correlation used three basic factors as signs of the entrance of the classic period. These factors were the arch, polychrome pottery and Carbon 14 dates. All three have been pushed back by some 300 years since the establishment of the present correlation, but we have not changed the correlation itself. We have very strong indications at Comalcalco to do so. It would tentatively seem as though the Spinden correlation, which sets all dates some 260 years earlier, would be more meaningful."[137]

Steele goes on to say that so far linguists are in agreement that the bricks at Comalcalco show a variety of foreign languages, while archaeologists are in disagreement, simply because what the linguists say "just cannot be correct." This, I dare say, is not a very scientific argument on the archaeologist's part.

I would also like to remind the reader that the ruins of Comalcalco and the discovery of the inscribed bricks has been done by a highly respected group: The National Institute of Anthropology and History of Mexico. However, the entrenched dogma of the current isolationists does not change easily. Most likely, the discoveries at Comalcalco will be suppressed as much as possible by the academics, and it will be the rare student of archaeology at any university who even hears about the controversy over the Comalcalco bricks.

❀❀❀

In 1944 an accidental discovery of an even more controversial nature in Acámbaro, Mexico, yielded over 33,500 objects of ceramic, stone, including jade, and knives of obsidian (sharper than steel and still used today in heart surgery). In addition, statues from less than an inch to four feet high or six feet long were discovered of great reptiles, some of them in active association with humans, generally eating them, but in some bizarre statuettes, an erotic nature was indicated. To observers many of these creatures resembled dinosaurs!

Startling representations of Negros, Orientals, and bearded Caucasians were included as were motifs of Egyptian, Sumerian and other ancient non-hemispheric civilizations, as well as portrayals of Bigfoot and aquatic monster type creatures, weird human-animal mixtures, and a host of other inexplicable creations. This fantastic collection drew the attention of a number of investigators and believers in lost continents, including Erle Stanely Gardner, creator of the Perry Mason series.

The ancient people who produced these objects lived on the beach of a lake in a woodland surrounding. Today, Acámbaro is an arid valley with eroded and dessicated surrounding highlands. Geologists have found that the valley itself was filled by a huge lake until sometime after the end of the Ice Age.

Radio-carbon dating performed by Dr. Froelich Rainey in the

208

laboratories of the University of Pennsylvania indicated the age of the samples. Additional tests using the thermoluminescence method method of dating pottery were performed to determine the age of the objects. The objects are today dated as having been made about 6,000 years ago, about 4000 B.C.

After two expeditions to the site, in 1955 and 1968, Professor Charles Hapgood, a professor of history and anthropology at Keene State College of the University of New Hampshire recorded the results of his eighteen year investigation of Acámbaro in a privately printed book entitled *Mystery In Acámbaro*.[154]

The extremely controversial discovery at the town of Acámbaro in Guanajuato state, 175 miles northwest of Mexico City began in 1944 when Waldemar Julsrud, a prominent German local merchant, then 69 years old, made the first discoveries at the edge of the town. These culminated in a collection of more than 33,500 objects made of clay and stone, which were then crammed into twelve rooms of his expanded home.

Julsrud was the co-discoverer of the Chupícuaro site in 1923, an important Western Mexico archaeological find of pre-classic bowls and figurines, that was eight miles away from Acámbaro. This early find was considerably more mundane than the discovery that was to be made some twenty-one years later.

The archaeological investigator John H. Tierney, says that Julsrud was discredited from the important 1923 discovery by a rival Acámbaro collector who also fed an American archaeologist named Charles C. DiPeso the story that an unlocatable family of peons had hoaxed Julsrud with the controversial artifacts. In 1952, in an effort to debunk the bizarre collection that was gaining a certain amount of fame, DiPeso claimed to have minutely examined the then 32,000 pieces within not more than four hours spent at the home of Julsrud. In a forthcoming book, long delayed by continuing developments in his investigation, Tierney, who has lectured on the case for decades, points out that to have done that DiPeso would have had to inspect 133 pieces per minute steadily for four hours, whereas in actuality, it would have required weeks merely to have separated the massive jumble of exhibits and arranged them properly for a valid evaluation.

Tierney, who collaborated with the late Professor Hapgood, the late William N. Russell and others in the investigation, charges that the Smithsonian Institution and other archaeological authorities conducted a campaign of disinformation against the discoveries. The Smithsonian had early in the controversy dismissed the entire Acámbaro collection as an elaborate hoax. Utilizing Freedom of Information Act approaches, Tierney discovered that practically the entirety of the Smithsonian's Julsrud case files are missing.

Arthur M. Young, the inventor of the Bell Helicopter, who had sponsored Hapgood's investigation, submitted Julsrud artifact samples to the University of Pennsylvania for thermoluminescence dateing. They produced produced dates of up to 2500 B.C. which upset the professional archaeologists and set off within the scientific and museum world a controversy over the accuracy of thermoluminescence dating. Retesting was done and it was announced that because of anomalous factors in the clays that it was impossible to determine an accurate date. However the techicians then cotrived what Tierney, who monitored and documented the tests, calls a phony one-of-a-kind method of slap a modern date on the samples by claiming that they could estimate the age from regenerated light signals. Tierney submitted two of his own samples to an independent expert who both disproved the earlier debunking attempt and determined that those particular samples were up to 2000 years old, although the exact age could not be determined. A team of experts at another university who were unaware of their origin ruled out the possibility that a half dozen of his different samples could have been a modern reproduction but fell silent when told they were artifacts from the Julsrud collection.

Teeth from an extinct ice age horse, the skeleton of a mammoth, and a number of human skulls, were found at the same site as the ceramic artifacts.

Hapgood decided to try to reopen this pit where the skull had been found. he noticed that the ground therein was still powdery, as though it had been refilled four or five years previously. The flat stone was not found, but rather something even stranger, a flight of stairs leading downward! The Colonel remembered that the previous dig had found suggestions of a tunnel going back into the hill. The stairway was filled with what appeared to be hard-packed volcanic material, but unfortunately neither time nor money allowed it to be excavated further. Where might this stairway have led—to some huge underground vault or buried city? Later, Hapgood decided that it had been a natural formation and not a staircase.

Hapgood, who was initially an open-minded skeptic concerning the collection became a believer after his first visit in 1955, at which time he witnessed some of the figures being excavated, and even dictated to the diggers where he wanted them to dig.

Hapgood introduced two very credible people to the Acámbaro mystery, Erle Stanley Gardner, the creator of the Perry Mason mystery novels (Gardner later mentioned his adventures with Hapgood at Acámbaro in his last published work, an autobiographical book on Mexico entitled *Host With the Big Hat*[55]) and Ivan T. Sanderson, a well known zoologist and frequent guest on Johnny Carson's *Tonight Show* in the 1960s. Both of these well known figures both wrote that the Acámbaro collection was bizarre, but authentic.

When Teledynes Isotopes laboratories performed dating tests on the carbon depostited during firing on ceramic samples submitted by Hapgood, and financed by Young and Gardner, dates of up to 4530 B.C. optained.

Adding to the mind-boggling aspects of this controversy is the fact that the Instituto Nacional de Antropologia e Historia through the late Director of Prehispanic Monuments, Dr. Eduardo Noguera, (who as head of an official investigating team at the site issued a report which Tierney will be publishing) admitted "the apparent scientific legality with which these objects were found." Despite evidence of their own eyes, however, officials declared that because of the objects "fantastic" nature, they had to have been a hoax played on Julsrud!

A disappointed but ever-hopeful Jalsrud died. His house was sold and the collection put in storage. The collection is not currently open to the public.

Erle Stanley Gardner, the best selling author of the century, related the entire story of Acámbaro in his autobiographical book, *Host With The Big Hat.*[155] Gardner gave the entire history of the case, including photos, and related that Peter Hurkos, a well-known psychic, had visited Acámbaro and the exact hill where the figurines had been unearthed and had announced "that his extrasensory perceptions told him that within Bull Hill (the site of the discoveries) was a cave, the entrance had been closed, but that this cave was filled with relics of a vanished civilization."

Looking out the window of the rented car as we headed for Oaxaca, I thought about the lost city that could possibly lie beneath Acámbaro. Had weird reptiles, literal dinosaurs, actually roamed Mexico with humans some six to ten thousand years ago? It seemed incredible. Scientists tell us that dinosaurs became extinct 65 million years ago. Yet, this was only a theory!

Fossil dating is still controversial, and, just because fossils are discovered of animals, this does not necessarily mean that they are extinct. The famous coelacanth of Southern African waters is a good example of this. It was thought extinct for 70 million years, yet several have been captured since 1938. The Acámbaro collection is about as controversial a set of artifacts as you can find. Most "respectable" archaeologists wouldn't touch them with a ten-foot pole. Their very existence threatens the ivory tower of the current paradigm of history.

🐟🐟🐟

It was early in the evening when we arrived in Oaxaca, the capital of Oaxaca state. Walter drove around the main plaza once, and noticing all the sidewalk cafes around the pleasant square in the middle of town instantly proclaimed, "What a great town. I love this place."

We were shortly checked into a small, family run hotel called *Los Golondrinas*, "The Swallows," with a nice colonial atmosphere. "Come on," said Walter, getting impatient, "lets go down to the plaza, I'll buy you a beer."

With that, we sauntered the few blocks down to the plaza and found ourselves a table on the side walk. In the cool evening air, it was great fun to sit and eat tacos, burritos, drink Corona beer and watch the many locals and tourists walk by. There were Japanese girls strolling by, always in pairs, German tourists in their locally bought costumes, Canadians in jeans and T-shirts who had managed to escape the arctic winter, and Oaxacan musicians who strolled from table to table singing songs and asking for money or beers.

Walter, the gregarious and sometimes obnoxious American talked with everyone, especially women, inviting them to our table. Soon we had several people sitting at our table and Walter invited them all to a shot of tequila. I reluctantly agreed, and that led to a wild evening of Coronas, tequila, jalapeño peppers, nachos and a lot of laughter.

Sitting next to me was a Mexican American named Mario who was down from Sacramento, California. He was tall, wearing a white shirt, blue jeans and cowboy boots. After another shot of tequila, I asked him what he was doing in Oaxaca.

"I'm down here researching my new book," he told me.

"What is your book about?" I asked him.

He suddenly got more serious, putting down his beer and looking me in the eye. "I'm glad you asked that question," he replied. "My book is called 'The UFO Exodus'."

"That sounds interesting," I said, raising an eyebrow. Walter, too, suddenly took interest and turned his attention away from a Japanese girl who was sitting at our table with a friend. "Do you mean an exodus like in the Bible?"

"Exactly," said Mario, switching into some automatic explanation mode. He had obviously explained his book many times to people. "The book is about how our Lord Jesus Christ is coming back in a flying saucer to take the faithful. That is what happened to the Mayas, you know. They left in UFOs. They are all coming back in their space craft to get the good Christians. The time is coming soon. Are you ready? You are a Christian aren't you?"

I nodded to Mario in vague agreement. This was a fascinating conversation, though I was afraid that Walter might stir up a can of worms with our new friend.

"I'm no UFO Christian," said Walter, slamming his empty shot glass of tequila down on the table. "I'm a Mason."

Mario looked at him in horror. "A Mason? You're damned for sure. That's as bad as being a Catholic. Repent, or you will miss the UFO Exodus."

Walter was busy ordering more beer and tequila, but took a moment to exclaim, "Who cares? I don't care. I'm not ready for space travel yet. I still haven't seen all of this planet."

I politely asked Mario more about his book. He had been raised a Catholic in Oakland where his parents had owned a Spanish language movie theater. He had married a young lady from Mexico, and after an industrial accident that had crushed one of his legs, he had gotten a huge insurance settlement and had become a born-again Christian. Though his faith had a strange twist, he believed that Jesus was coming back in a UFO and that the rapture, as fundamentalist Christians believe, would be in spacecraft.

"Of course, the Baptist church I go to in Sacramento think I'm crazy. I can't talk to them about my book. They think its the work of the devil. I wish I could convince them," said Mario.

"It is a rather unusual combination of beliefs," I said. That was OK with me though, I had heard plenty of strange beliefs in my travels all over the world. It seemed that everybody had his own reality structure that made sense to him. I was no different.

"Yes, people just don't understand what I am trying to say," lamented Mario. "But once my book comes out, then they'll understand that metaphysics is the correct notion of science of the contemporary philosophy of the UFO exodus."

Walter nearly fell off his chair laughing, but, in a refreshing change of the conversation, several street musicians came to our table and Mario borrowed one of their guitars. He was quite a good guitar player, and with the tequila starting to kick in, he played several songs. We sang along with him—everything from the traditional Mexican folk song *La Bamba* to the Gypsy Kings and John Lennon's *Imagine*. It was one o'clock when we finally staggered back to the hotel to sleep off the evening's socializing.

The next day we drove to the top of a hill outside of town that was the ancient city known today as Monte Albán. Monte Albán is an enigmatic ruin that had been occupied and built onto for thousands of years. It is built on a flattened mountain top 2000 feet above the modern city of Oaxaca in the valley below and is officially said to go back to at least 700 B.C., though neither the earliest phases nor the original inhabitants have been identified.

The earliest inhabitants of Monte Albán are generally said to be the mysterious Olmecs, though the Zapotecs were the later inheritors of the huge city.

The origins of the Zapotec civilization, which flourished in southwest Mexico from 200 B.C. until the Spanish invasion in 1519, are shrouded in uncertainty, for even its earliest known remains are those of a culture already at a high level of urban and agricultural development. In art and architecture, mathematics and calendrical science, the Zapotecs have clear affinities with the earlier Olmec and Mayan civilizations to the south, but their history contains no record of migration from those or any other parts. Instead, and to the contrary, the Zapotecs believed themselves to be descended from trees, rocks, and jaguars.

The Zapotec capital was at Monte Albán, seven miles from Oaxaca. It lies at the top of an artificially leveled mountain promontory and is centered on a huge plaza, roughly 1,000 feet long and 650 feet wide, flanked on all sides by terraced steps, sunken courtyards, and low, handsome buildings. The first systematic excavation of the site began in 1931, and treasures of gold, jade, rock crystal, and turquoise were soon found in several of the tombs.

But the most remarkable discovery was of something more mysterious than fine artwork and rich materials; it was a complex network of stone-lined tunnels, far too small to used by adults or children of average stature.

The first of these tunnels, discovered in 1932 but not explored until 1933, was 20 inches high and 25 inches wide—so small that the excavators could make their way along it only on their backs. After they had inched through it in this way for 195 feet, they came to a skeleton, an incense burner, and funeral urns; there were also ornaments of jade, turquoise, and stone, and a few pearls. Some yards beyond this the tunnel was blocked, and to enter it again the explorers had to dig a 25-foot shaft from the surface beyond the blockage.

As they wormed along this next stretch, they found even smaller passages, no more than a foot high, branching off the main tunnel. Leading down into one of these was a tiny flight of steps. At a distance of 320 feet from the main entrance, the archaeologists found another skeleton, and a few yards beyond this, at the edge of the northern terrace of the great plaza, the tunnel came to an end.

Further excavations revealed two similar tunnels, both packed with clay. Finally, to the east of tomb number seven, where the richest treasures had been found, a complex network of miniature tunnels was discovered, all lined with stone and some of them less than a foot high. Smoke was blown into these in an effort to trace their course and "revealed a number of unexpected exits."

The excavators initial guess that they had discovered an abandoned drainage system. Also ruled out was the idea that the tunnels had been a network of emergency escape routes (or had been of any other service to humans of ordinary size), and official speculation about their purpose ceased. Since then, the pygmy tunnels of Monte Albán have remained on of the major mysteries of the unexplained.

As Walter and I walked through the city, I marveled at the megalithic architecture. I have always had a fascination for massive stone building, and here at Monte Albán, there were plenty of megalithic walls, arches and stones. Much of it had obviously been rebuilt from earlier, ruined walls. As is typical with such cities, the earliest faze of construction is megalithic, while later walls of of smaller, cruder stones used to fill gaps in the deteriorating megalithic walls.

Walter and I stood by as a group of tourists crawled through one of the tunnels, this one large enough for an adult to barely crawl though. Afterwards Walter and I also crawled through the narrow, claustrophobic passage. I wormed my way along the stone passage on my stomach, occasionally hitting my head on the domed roof. It was indeed a true arch. I was hoping that there would not be an earthquake during the fifteen minutes that it took me to slowly inch my way through the passages until I could exit out of a narrow square hole back into the plaza.

"Tight squeeze?" asked a man, the head of the tour group we had seen. I agreed, and it turned out that they were a group of psychics

from New Jersey who had come to Mexico to explore its mysteries.
"What do you think of Monte Albán?" I asked them.
"It's an Atlantean city," they replied.
"Really?" I asked. "Why do you think that?"
"The megalithic architecture, look at the massive stone blocks around you. It has obviously been reconstructed in later periods, but its earliest phase is from Atlantis, about 10,000 years ago."
I looked around at some of the gigantic blocks of stone. It certainly was construction on a megalithic scale.
One of the women in the group, a middle-aged woman about 45 said, "Let me share a past life experience with you—after Atlantis I lived in a dark tunnel place." She pointed to a tunnel in one of the pyramids. "That is the place where I lived. I felt it when I was inside."
I walked with the group around the main plaza. We came to a small, central pyramid that was honeycombed with passageways and staircases. Weird Olmec drawings and some hieroglyphs were on gigantic slabs that were placed along the outside of the pyramid. I pointed out to the group proof of the reconstruction by showing them that the megalithic slabs were embedded in walls with smaller stones and some of portions of the reliefs came to an abrupt end where they must have originally continued with an another slab.
We climbed the various pyramids where great views of the Oaxaca valley could be had. Men who were loitering around the ruins—workmen or villagers of some kind—came up to us and offered to sell us jade and other artifacts.
Tombs at the far northern end had megalithic slabs in them and sun symbols and corn gods in ceramic on the walls. At tomb number 7, a fantastic treasure was discovered, which included gold masks, sort of a Oaxacan Tutankhamum's tomb. After a look through the on sight museum, I noticed a huge megalithic doorway, with two upright rectangular slabs and a third slab across the two, just outside the main entrance, where the road made a sharp curve on its downward path into the valley.
I walked down to the massive doorway. Like much of Monte Albán, it was inconsistent in that the gigantic megalithic doorway had much smaller, cruder walls around it. Obviously, these were two different construction phases, and the older phase was the far superior of the two. As in South America, it was evident that a huge megalithic city of astonishing engineering skill had once existed here, but had been destroyed. Later, it had been rebuilt, but by considerably less sophisticated builders.
What was it that had destroyed the earlier megalithic construction? Was it some devastating earthquake or war? Maybe this city was from Atlantis, and its destruction had something to with whatever it was that had destroyed that legendary continent.
The next day we visited the ruins of Mitla, another megalithic site 25 miles southwest of Oaxaca city.. The name is derived from the Nahuatl *Mictlan*, or "Place of the Dead" though the Zapotecs called the city *Lyobaa*, "Place of Rest." As the British archaeologist Michael

215

Coe says, "Not much is known of the archaeology of Mitla, but it is thought to have been constructed in the Monte Albán V period, corresponding to the Toltec and Aztec eras; it was still in use when the Spaniards arrived."[85]

Mitla is considered one of the most beautiful cities in ancient Mexico because of its architecture. At Mitla are long panels and entire walls covered with geometric stonework mosaics, the intricate arabesques of which are almost entirely based on the step-and-fret motif, each piece of veneer being set into a red stucco background. Pierre Honoré in his book *In Quest of the White God* [76] finds Mitla to be highly similar architecturally to the Minoan palace of Knossus on Crete, thereby lending evidence to his theory that ancient Minoan sailors were partly responsible for many Mesoamerican civilizations.

In the 17th century a Spanish priest named Burgoa visited Mitla while it was still a living city. Burgoa claims that gruesome sacrifices took place there continuously: numberless captives had their hearts torn out and offered to the High Priest and the Zapotec gods. Somewhere beneath Mitla was supposed to be a great secret chamber where the Zapotec kings and nobles, as well as heroes killed in battle, were interred, hence the name for the city, "Place of the Dead." This secret chamber has never been found, but according to Burgoa the passage leading to it was found in his day and entered by some Spanish priests, who were so horrified by what they saw that they quickly left and sealed the off the underground chambers as an abomination against God.[85]

Mitla was a city of the Mixtecs, who were a branch family of the Zapotecs, and they claimed descent from Quetzalcoatl. Like the Zapotecs, they also claimed that their ancestors were born from trees (a rather odd progeny). By the beginning of the Post-Classic period, says Coe, the leading power among the Mixtecs was a town called "Mountain that Opens," a curious name, perhaps signifying some underground realm as yet undiscovered.

Eight pre-conquest codices of Mixtec origin were discovered at Mitla, and one tells the strange tale of a ruler named 8 Deer. Apparently born in A.D. 1011, his eventful life continued until 1063, during which time the Mixtecs were clearly under powerful Toltec influence. In 1045, 8 Deer made a journey to the Toltec capital of Tula (there were apparently several Tulas, each a Toltec capital in succession as other cities were abandoned) and was crowned king of the Mixtecs, the ruler of the Toltecs fulfilling the same function as the Pope crowning the Holy Roman Emperor.

Coe has an interesting thing to say about 8 Deer, "The most mysterious event in his life is the record of his visit to the king of a place called "Hill of the Sun," believed by some to be in southern Puebla near Teotitlan del Camino; not only 8 Deer, but the lord of Tula paid homage to this man. Who was he? Was there some empire more powerful than the Toltec about which we know nothing? This is one of the great unsolved puzzles of Mexican archaeology."[85]

Mitla is a city that was planned in one phase, not built in stages over time. Megalithic pillars and doors abound, and there are even huge megalithic tombs cut out of solid rock in the form of crosses. Undoubtedly, the mysterious Quetzalcoatl had much to do, in some way, with Mitla.

In the northern group of the ruins, most of the city was dismantled by the Spanish to build a church, yet, because of the massive, megalithic construction, the Spanish were unable to move many of the gigantic slabs of rock. Therefore they just built around it, constructing primitive walls of adobe and rock and combining it as best they could would the finely cut megalithic stones.

On the way back to Oaxaca we stopped at El Tule, an ancient tree. It is the largest tree in the Americas, and perhaps the world. It is also, perhaps, the world's oldest tree. It is at least 2000 years old. It is 40 meters high and 42 meters around the base. It takes 26 men holding hands to encircle it.

Walter and I paid a small entrance fee and were then shown various natural figures in the wood as we walked around the gigantic plant. Legend associates the tree with Quetzalcoatl, and it is truly an astounding sight.

Back at the plaza in Oaxaca we relaxed for the evening at a sidewalk cafe having dinner and a cold beer. Colorfully dressed Indians moved gracefully with the tourists. The night sky was full of stars. The cathedral bells rang. For Walter, it was the end of his trip.

"I'm flying back to Mexico City and the North Carolina tomorrow," he told me.

"Thanks for the lift," I told him. "It's been a fun trip. You're a crazy driver though. You know that, don't you?"

Walter looked at me with a wild grin. "I know," he said. "That's why I came to Mexico. Where else could I drive like a maniac and be just another ordinary driver on the roads?"

Clay figurines from the Island of Jaina, off Campeche, Mexico. Note the many bearded men, and the figures emerging from a lotus flower. American Indians do not have beards, and the lotus figure is typically Hindu-Buddhist.

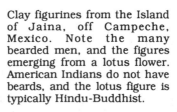
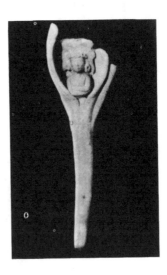

The sarcophagus lid on the interior of the secret crypt deep inside the main pyramid at Palenque.

The lid of the controversial sarcophagus inside the secret crypt beneath the pyramid at Palenque. In the highly stylized drawing, Lord Pacal is descending into the underworld. The sacred bird, sun and moon motifs at the top signify the upper world, while the monster below signifies the under world. The ancient Chinese had the exact same belief in three interlocking worlds.

In the mid-1800s, the Austrian artist and Masonic mystic, Baron de Waldeck made these illustrations at Palenque. Waldeck believed that there was a great deal of Masonic symbolism in Mayan art that was found at Palenque. In the above left illustration, two priests are passing a coded scepter-cross object. The above right illustration, is of the "Lion Throne," which was removed from the ruins by a Mexican official in the early 1800s. It is reminescent of the Lion Thrones of South East Asia. Below is the relief inside the famous Temple of the Cross, still to be seen at Palenque.

A gigantic Olmec-Proto-Mayan Head from La Venta, Mexico. These basalt statues are at least 3.000 years old and similar to both African art and South East Asian art, such as at Angor Wat, Cambodia.

The Tuxtla statue, now at the Smithsonian Institution in Washington D.C. It is covered in hieroglyphs from the Olmec-Proto-Mayan culture that existed 1,000-3,000 B.C.

Lacandón Maya standing next to a gigantic, but broken, stele, at Bonampak. Photo by Giles Healey.

Monument 13 from La Venta. The man is certainly uncharacteristic of the gigantic Negroid heads. He has a beard and wears a turban. Three early hieroglypyhs appear on the right. The bottom glyph seems to be an elephant.

Left: Charles Frey, the American who was first shown Bonampak. **Right:** A stele from Bonampak showing a Mayan warrior emerging from the mouth of a dragon. The hieroglyphs remain undeciphered.

Harold Wilkins 1945 map to the secret Mayan city that he believed still existed.
One year later, Bonampak was discovered. Do more secret Mayan cities still exist?

Detail from the Bonampak stela, Kuná-Akaché. Note the Chinese looking man with wispy mustache and beard. His hair is knotted in front. He holds a dragon stick, something like the combination of an electrical device-flame thrower and a jade authority scepter.

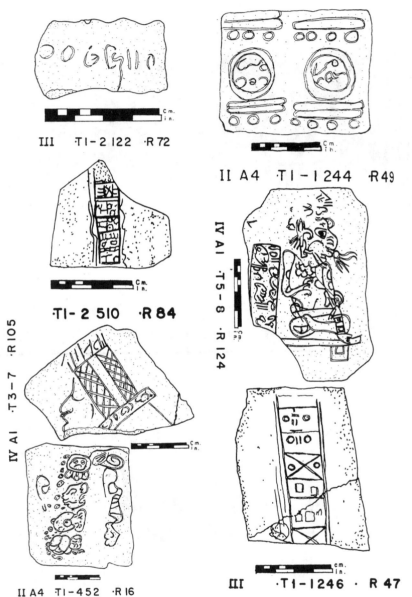

III　　Tl-2 122　·R 72

II A4　　Tl-1 244　　·R 49

·Tl-2 510　·R 84

IV AI　·T5-8 ·R 124

IV AI　·T3-7 ·R 105

II A4　Tl-452　·R 16

III　　·Tl-1 246 ·　R 47

A few of the Comalcalco bricks. Many of these bricks have not only Mayan glyphs on them, but inscriptions from other languages as well. Clockwise from upper left: A Libyan inscription; Mayan written in Arabic; unknown hieroglyphic inscription, possibly Egyptian; unknown signs; a bilingual Mayan inscription with Manding, a script of Upper Nubia (Egypt); Phoenician; unknown hieroglyphs.

Chapter 8

Northern Mexico:

Quetzalcoatl and the Pyramids of Sun

Throw yourself out into the
convolutions of the world...
Take chances, make your own work,
take pride in it. Seize the moment.
— Joan Didion

My next move was to take a bus north to Cholula, where it is said that the largest pyramid in the world is located. This is the massive pyramid of Cholula de Rivadahia, Mexico. It is 181 feet tall and covers 40 acres. The location of the largest pyramid in the world has long been a topic of heated discussion, and this was a new one to me.

When the famous German naturalist Alexander von Humboldt arrived in Mexico in 1803, the pyramid at Cholula amazed him. Humboldt found the pyramid to be a truncated structure with four terraces. It was 367 feet from east to west, and 348 feet from north to south. He described it as "a mountain of unbaked bricks" dedicated to Quetzalcoatl.[141]

The gigantic pyramid could be entered through a small opening in the east side. Inside were miles of tunnels in a bewildering maze. Murals and frescoes can be found throughout the strange tunnel system. According to Humboldt, the pyramid had been topped with a jade image of Quetzalcoatl. Today, a Catholic church can be found at the summit.[141]

The Great Pyramid of Cholulu may be the largest pyramid in North America, but is it really the largest pyramid in the world? It is believed by a number of authors that the largest pyramid in the world is in China, forty miles southwest of Xian, known generally as the Great Pyramid of China. It is part of a group of 16 ancient pyramids built by unknown engineers at an unknown time. Unfortunately they are in a "forbidden zone" and tourists are not allowed to visit them. There may be a military base nearby and, as a consequence, very little information about the pyramids has been released. American aviators before World War II photographed the largest and believe it to be at least twice as high as the Great Pyramid of Egypt (450 feet) and have suggested a figure of 1,000 feet. It seems to date from the Hsia Dynasty, about 4,000 years ago, though other dates given are that it is at least 1,000 years older than that.[16]

Another large pyramid is the Cahokia Pyramid in Illinois, which allegedly has a base even larger than that at Cholula.

According to Peter Tompkins, one of the world's pyramid experts and author of *Secrets of the Great Pyramid* and *Mysteries of the Mexican Pyramids*,[141] "The Cholulu Pyramid is the largest known structure in the world in terms of cubic content. Two hundred and ten feet high, it covers forty-five acres. The pre-Conquest Mexican legend about Cholula is very similar to the Biblical account of the Tower of Babel. According to the legend, after the deluge which destroyed the primeval world, seven giants survived, one of whom built the great pyramid of Cholula in order to reach heaven, but the Gods destroyed the pyramid with fire and confounded the language of the builders."

According to *Facts and Artifacts of Ancient Middle America,* Cholula was the "seat of the Olmeca-Xicalanca (Historic Olmecs), who were finally driven out by Toltec-Chichimecs in A.D. 1292."[136]

That the pyramid of Cholula is dedicated to the "white god" Quetzalcoatl, the mysterious figure whose legend and prophesy was the cause of the downfall of the Aztec empire at the onslaught of a handful of conquistadors.

The fascinating story of Quetzalcoatl is one that has inspired many people, and like the life of great philosophical and religious leaders such as Krishna, Gautama Buddha, Confucius, Lao Tzu, Zoroaster and Jesus of Nazareth; the native American Messiah, Quetzalcoatl, has changed lives.

There is much confusion concerning Quetzalcoatl, and many scholars argue about the identity or even the existence of such a figure. The modern Mayan esotericist, Hunbatz Men, in his book, *Secrets of Mayan Science/Religion*,[133] has some useful information on the similarities of esoteric Mayan Science with the sciences of ancient India. He points out that the Mayas used the same chakra system as the Hindus, and even many of the words are the same. He also points out that the *Naga Maya* held many of the priestly secrets of the Maya. James Churchward of the popular "Mu" books likewise considered the *Nagas* as the source of Hindu wisdom.

Hunbatz Men also shows that Mayan glyphs, words and concepts had different levels of meaning, much as ancient Egyptian and Hebrew had different levels of meaning in their inscriptions and books, and the level of initiation of the reader determined the knowledge that was gained from any text.

Thus, Hunbatz Men maintains that Quetzalcoatl, or Kukulcán in

Mayan, is not meant to be a real person, but essentially the embodiment of a perfected man, a yogi, adept, or Master in eastern terminology, or a saint or Master in western terminology.

Hunbatz Men maintains that "Self-appointed 'official' historians have created the great colonial lie of the 'white, bearded, and blue-eyed' Quetzalcoatl—a deception still perpetrated in histories of our beloved Mexican people. The true nature of Quetzalcoatl/Kukulcan [sic] remains a mystery that is accessible only through Nahua/Mayan science/religion."

This true nature, according to Hunbatz Men, is that we are all Quetzalcoatl, and that the perfect being inside each of us can be reached through the correct use of yoga, etc. While Hunbatz Men may be correct in that we all have the capability of perfecting ourselves and becoming as Quetzalcoatl, a sort of god on earth, he is most definitely incorrect when he says that the notion of a bearded man walking throughout Mesoamerica is a fabrication of Spanish historians.

Hunbatz Men seems to forget that the very conquest of Mexico itself would never have happened if Cortez had not been believed by the Aztecs to be this mysterious bearded stranger returning to them.

When, in 1519, Cortez and his 600 companions landed in Mexico they were astonished at being hailed as the realization of an ancient native tradition, which was generally told as follows: Many centuries previously a white man had come to Mexico from across the sea in a boat with wings (sails) like those of the Spanish vessels. He stayed many years, traveled all over North America and taught the people a system of religion, instructed them in principles of government, and imparted to them a knowledge of many industrial arts. He won their esteem and veneration by his piety, his many virtues, his great wisdom and his knowledge of divine things.

His stay was a kind of golden age for Mexico. The seasons were uniformly favorable and the earth gave forth its produce almost spontaneously and in miraculous abundance and variety. In those days a single ear of maize was a load for a man, the cotton trees produced quantities of cotton already tinted in many brilliant hues; flowers filled the air with delicious perfumes; birds of magnificent plumage incessantly poured forth the most exquisite melody. Under the auspices of this good white man, or god, peace, plenty and happiness prevailed throughout the land.

The Mexicans knew him as Quetzalcoatl, or the feathered serpent. The quetzal is a rare bird in the forests of Central America whose long feathers were more valuable than gold to the ancient Mesoamericans. After some twenty years of visiting the various civilizations of North America, Quetzalcoatl eventually left the country. On his way to the coast he stayed for a time at the city of Cholula, where subsequently a great pyramid surmounted by a temple was erected in his honor. On the shores of the gulf of Mexico (the island of Cozumel it is often said) he took leave of his followers, soothing their sorrow at his departure with the assurance that he

231

would not forget them, and that he himself, or some one sent by him, would return at some future time to visit them. He had made for himself a vessel of serpents' skins, and in this strange contrivance he sailed away in the northeasterly direction for his own country, the holy island of *Hapallan*, lying beyond the great ocean.[142]

Such was the strange tradition which Cortez found prevalent in Mexico on his arrival there, and powerfully influencing every inhabitant of the country from the great Montezuma, who ruled as king paramount in the city of Mexico, to the humblest serf who tilled the fields of his lord. Equally to their surprise and advantage the Spaniards found that their advent was hailed as the fulfillment of the promise of Quetzalcoatl to return.

The natives saw that they were white men and bearded like him, they had come in sailing vessels such as the one he had used across the sea; they had clearly come from the mysterious Hapallan; they were undoubtedly Quetzalcoatl and his brethren come, in fulfillment of ancient prophecy, to restore and permanently re-establish in Mexico the reign of peace and happiness of which the country had had a brief experience many centuries before.

Furthermore, it was predicted that Quetzalcoatl would return on a one reed (Ce-actl) year. The one reed year reoccurred every 52 years, and 1519 was such a year. Furthermore, Cortez arrived on the very day associated with Quetzalcoatl, as he is the ninth of the 13 lords of the day. By a fascinating coincidence (though prophesied by Quetzalcoatl), the priests had predicted from the ancient records that Quetzalcoatl would return in the year one reed on the day "nine wind." This day was the arrival of Cortez on the coast, April 22, 1519.

Montezuma and his priests had been anxiously awaiting the arrival of Quetzalcoatl since early in 1519. In the beginning of that year there were many portents in the sky that showed that the tribulation of the Aztec empire was at hand: For a time the night sky was lit by a northern light; a volcanic disturbance caused the water in the Mexico lake to boil up and flood the city streets; the temple of the sun god went on fire; a spirit speaking a woman's voice wailed at night: 'My children, my children, ruin is at hand.' Magicians were called to interpret these signs. They could not pretend that their meaning was good. Montezuma had these magicians then strangled, "for in magic it is some remedy to destroy the bearer of bad news."[143]

Montezuma and his priests had reason to dread the return of Quetzalcoatl. Quetzalcoatl had preached against human sacrifice, yet in their worship of him, they used human sacrifice (though sparingly). That Quetzalcoatl would be angry with them, and naturally wish to reclaim the kingdom that was rightfully his, was something they did not doubt for a moment.

Cortez was presented by messengers from Montezuma with the feathered crown of Quetzalcoatl. He immediately sent it back to Spain, and it is now in the Vienna Ethnology Museum, its most important piece. Cortez was a tall, handsome, intelligent and bearded man. He was an adventurer, perhaps cruel, but the least that one can say of him was that he had a great deal of courage. He burnt his ships upon arriving at Veracruz from Cuba so that his men would have no choice but to march on with him to their destiny—A destiny foretold by Quetzalcoatl more than a thousand years before.

🐟🐟🐟

One early article on Quetzalcoatl appeared in the November 14 issue of American Antiquarian of 1889 and was reprinted in William Corliss' compendium *The Unexplained*.[142] The article was by Dominick Daly and it was appropriately entitled *The Mexican Messiah*. Daly had some interesting insights into Quetzalcoatl, and his article was well researched.

Says Daly, "The Mexicans had preserved a minute and apparently an accurate description of the personal appearance and habits of Quetzalcoatl. He was a white man, advanced in years and tall in stature. His forehead was broad; he had a large beard and black hair. He is described as dressing in a long garment, over which there was a mantle marked with crosses...This is a description which was preserved for centuries in the traditions of a people who had no intercourse with or knowledge of Europe, who had never seen a white man, and who were themselves dark skinned with but few scanty hairs on the skin to represent a beard.

"It is therefore difficult to suppose that this curiously accurate portraiture of Quetzalcoatl as an early European ecclesiastic was a mere invention in all its parts—a mere fable which happened to hit on every particular and characteristic of such an individual. Nor is it easier to understand why the early Mexicans should have been at pains to invent a messiah so different from themselves, and with such peculiar attributes. Yet in spite of destructive wars, revolutions and invasions—in spite of the breaking up and dispersal of tribes and nations once settled in the vast region now passing under the name of Mexico—the tradition of Quetzalcoatl and the account of his personal peculiarities survived among the people to the days of the Spanish invasion. Everything therefore tends to show that Quetzalcoatl was an European who by some strange adventure was thrown amongst the Mexican people and left with them recollections of his beneficent influence which time and change did not obliterate. But time and change must have done much in the course of centuries to confuse the teachings of Quetzalcoatl. These would naturally be more susceptible of mutation than the few striking items of his personal appearance which (if only on account of their singularity) must have deeply impressed the Mexicans, generation after generation.

"Not-withstanding such mutation, enough remained of the teachings of Quetzalcoatl to impress the Spaniards of the sixteenth century with the belief that he must have been an early Christian missionary as well as a native of Europe. They found that many of the religious beliefs of the Mexicans bore an unaccountable

233

resemblance to those of Christians. The Spanish ecclesiastics, in particular, were astounded at what they saw and knew not what to make of it. Some of them supposed that St. Thomas, "the apostle of India," had been in the country and imparted a knowledge of Christianity to the people; others with pious horror and in mental bewilderment declared that the Evil One himself had set up a travesty of the religion of Christ for the more effectual damning of the souls of the pagan Mexicans.

"The religion of the Mexicans as the Spaniards found it was in truth an amazing and most unnatural combination of what appeared to be Christian beliefs and Christian virtues and morality with the bloody rites and idolatrous practices of pagan barbarians. The mystery was soon explained to the Spaniards by the Mexicans themselves. The milder part of the Mexican religion was that which Quetzalcoatl had taught them. He had taught it to the Toltecs, a people who had ruled in Mexico some centuries before the arrival of the Spaniards. The Aztecs were in possession of power when the Spaniards came and it was they who had introduced that part of the Mexican religion which was in such strong contrast to the religion established by Quetzalcoatl. It appeared further that the Toltec rule in the land had ceased about the middle of the eleventh century.

"...After the lapse of a century or more from the era of the great Toltec migration the first bands of Aztecs began to appear. They were wanderers from the Northwest, the Pacific slopes of North America, and were a fierce and warlike people, possessing little capacity for the mental and moral refinement and high civilization of their Toltec predecessors. It was not until the middle of the fourteenth century that the Aztecs acquired sufficient settled habits to enable them to found states and cities, and by that time they seem to have adopted so much of what had been left of Toltec civilization and Toltec religion as they were capable of absorbing, without, however, abandoning their own ruder ideas and propensities. Hence the incongruous mixture of civilization and barbarism, mildness and ferocity, gentleness and cruelty, refinement and brutality, presented by Mexican civilization and religion to the astonished contemplation of the Spaniards when they entered the city two centuries later. "Aztec civilization was made up" (as Prescott, the author of the *History of Mexico*, says), "of incongruities apparently irreconcilable. It blended into one the marked peculiarities of different nations, not only of the same phase of civilization, but as far removed from each other as the extremes of barbarism and refinement."

"All that was savage and barbarous in the religious rites of the Mexicans was attributed by the Mexicans themselves to the Aztecs; all that was gentle and humanizing to the Toltecs, and probably with substantial justice in each instance. To a Toltec origin was assigned those doctrines and practices which struck the Spaniards as remnants of an early knowledge of Christianity. The Aztecs only came into the inheritance of those doctrines and practices at second hand—that is from the remnants of the Toltec people. The new-comers were probably little disposed to submit wholly to the influence of alien religious ideas essentially different from their own gloomy and sanguinary notions of divine things. Some they adopted, while still retaining their own national observances, and hence the extraordinary mixture of brutality and gentleness presented to the wondering contemplation of the Spaniards by the Mexican cult as they saw it in the early part of the sixteenth century. The better, that is the Toltec side of this mixed belief included amongst its chief features a recognition of a supreme God, vested with all the attributes of the Jehovah of the Jews. He was the creator and the ruler of the universe, and the fountain of all good. Subordinate to him were a number of minor deities, and opposed to him a father of all evil.

"The Mexicans believed in a universal deluge, from which only one family (that of Coxcox) escaped. Nevertheless, and inconsistently enough with this, they spoke of a race of wicked giants, who had survived the flood and built a pyramid in order to reach the clouds; but the gods frustrated their design by raining fire upon it. Tradition associated the great pyramid at Cholula with this event. This was the pyramid which had been erected to Quetzalcoatl, and which had a temple on the summit dedicated to the worship of him as the god of air. The Mexicans regarded Cholula as the one holy city—the Jerusalem or Mecca of their country—from having been the place of abode of Quetzalcoatl. The pyramid in a dilapidated condition still remains, and is surmounted by a chapel for Christian worship. It is scarcely necessary to suggest that the traditions of Cicacoatl, Coxcox, the giants and the pyramid at Cholula, are extremely like a confused acquaintance with biblical narratives.

"The foregoing are merely specimens of the more remarkable features of Mexican belief, and they are so special and peculiar in character as to leave no reasonable alternative to the supposition that the Mexicans must have had imparted to them at one time a knowledge of the bible. This has induced in some quarters the opinions that the Mexicans are descendants of the lost tribes of Israel; but whatever may be the arguments for or against this theory, the still more abundant knowledge of a Christian-like character possessed by the ancient Mexicans is strongly suggestive of Christian teachings, which would sufficiently account for familiarity with narratives contained in the Old Testament.

"Whether due to such teaching or to accidental coincidence, it is certain that the Mexicans held many points of belief in common with Christians. They believed in the Trinity, the Incarnation, and apparently the Redemption. One of the first things which struck the Spaniards on their arrival in Mexico was the spectacle of large stone crosses on the coast and in the interior of the country. These were objects of veneration and worship. One cross or marble near one of the places the Spaniards named Vera Cruz was surmounted by a golden crown, and in answer to the curious inquiries of the Spanish ecclesiastics the natives said that "one more glorious than the sun had died upon a cross." In other places the Spaniards were informed that the cross was symbol of the god of rain. At any rate it was an object of divine association and consequently adoration. In the magnificent pictorial reproduction of Mexican antiquities published by Lord Kingsborough there is a remarkable sketch of a monument representing a group of ancient Mexicans in attitudes of adoration around a cross of the Latin form. The leading figure is that of a king or a priest holding in his outstretched hands a young infant, which he appears to be presenting to the cross."[142]

Concerning such accusations as Hunbatz Men's that the story of a white, bearded Christian missionary was merely fabricated by the conquistadors and their priests, Daly makes a good point when he says, "There is no reason to doubt the concurrent testimony of their writers and historians, lay and clerical, as to what they did find. There could be no adequate motive for a general conspiracy amongst them to manufacture evidence and invent fables for the purpose of making it appear that the people whom they were about to plunder, enslave and slaughter were a sort of Christian. On the contrary, their expressions of surprise and horror at finding Christian doctrines and Christian practices, intermingles with the grossest idolatry and most barbarous and bloody rites, are too natural and genuine to be mistaken. They—the direct observers with the best opportunities for judging—had no doubt that what they saw was a debased form of Christianity. The points of resemblance with real Christianity were too numerous and too peculiar to permit the supposition that the similarity was accidental and unreal. With them the only difficulty was to account for the possession of Christian knowledge by a people so remote and outlandish—or rather to trace the identity of Quetzalcoatl, the undoubted teacher of the Mexicans. Their choice lay between the devil and St. Thomas. However respectable the claims of the former, it is clear enough that St. Thomas was not Quetzalcoatl and had never been in Mexico. That he was dragged in at all was because the Spaniards long clung to the idea that America was a part of India, and St. Thomas was styled 'the Apostle of India,' on the authority of an ancient and pious but very doubtful tradition. The weakness of the case for St. Thomas secured a preference for the claims of the devil, and the consensus of Spanish opinion favored the idea that *Quetzacock* (sic) was indeed the devil himself, who, aroused by the losses which Christ had inflicted upon him in the old world, had sought compensation in the new, and had beguiled the Mexicans into the acceptance of a blasphemous mockery of the religion of Christ infinitely more wicked and damnatory than the worst form of paganism."

Daly continues, "Another theory as to the identity of Quetzalcoatl may here be noticed. Lord Kingsborough makes the startling suggestion that Quetzalcoatl was no other than Christ himself, and in support of this maintains that the phonetic rendering, in the Mexican language, of the two words "Jesus Christ" would be as nearly as possible "Quetzat Coatl."

"...But whoever Quetzalcoatl may have been, and whatever might be the right designation of the religion which he taught, it is clear beyond question that he was the medium through which the Mexicans obtained their curious Christian-like knowledge. Of him there is no rival. The Aztecs claimed the honor of being the importers of the terrible Huitzilopochtli and all the unholy rites connected with his worship. They, and all other Mexicans, agreed in assigning the milder features of Mexican worship to the teachings of Quetzalcoatl. To him also they attributed the foundation of the monastic institutions and clerical systems, and the introduction of baptism, confession, communion, and all the beliefs, ceremonies, and practices, having a greater or less resemblance to those of the Christian religion.

"It is therefore, hard to understand what it was that Quetzalcoatl taught if it was not Christianity, and equally hard to conceive what he could have been if he were not a Christian missionary. His personality and attributes are altogether, and without a single exception or the slightest qualification, those of an early Christian missionary."[142]

🐉🐉🐉

Certainly, a good case has been made for Quetzalcoatl having been a very real person. One of the things that is a bit confusing is that there was apparently more than one Quetzalcoatl, including a number of Toltec rulers who assumed the title of Quetzalcoatl.

Also, as far as a man walking about Mexico and preaching brotherly love, harmless living, and above all, the abolition of warfare, is concerned, there are other legends that place a similar figure walking throughout South America, certain Caribbean Islands, and most of North America, including areas of Canada, the central Plains and Mississippi Valley.

Hubert Howe Bancroft, the historian of *The Native Races of the Pacific States* says this about the many identities of Quetzalcoatl: "All the myths relative to the founders of the different American civilizations make reference to persons who have the same characters. All are white, bearded, generally covered with long vestments; they appear suddenly and mysteriously, give laws, instruct and introduce religions ... Such have been *Quetzalcoatl*, who appeared in Cholula, *Votan* in Chiapas, *Wixepecocha* in Oaxaca, *Zamna* and *Kukulcan* in Yucatan, *Gucumatz* in Guatemala, *Viracocha* in Peru, *Bochica* in Colombia, and *Sume* and *Paye-Tome* in Brazil."[113]

In his diary of Peru, begun in 1541, Pedro de Cieza de Leon wrote: "... a white man of great stature, who, by his aspect and presence, called forth great veneration and obedience....They say this man went on towards the north working these marvels along the way of the mountains; and that he never more returned so as to be seen. In many places he gave orders to men how they should live and spoke lovingly to them, and with much intelligence, admonishing them that they should do good and no evil or injury to one another and the they should be loving and charitable to all."[113]

Another man, Sarmiento, describes this teacher as "...white and dressed in a white robe like an alb, secured around the waist, and that he carried a staff and a book in his hands."[113]

E.B. Taylor, the father of British anthropology and the author of the book *Early History of Mankind* quotes the following tale, "Quetzalcoatl appeared at Panuco, up a river on the eastern coast. He had landed there from his ship, coming no man knew from whence. He was tall, of white complexion, pleasant to look upon, with fair hair and bushy beard, dressed in long, flowing robes. Received everywhere as a messenger from heaven, he travelled inland across the hot countries of the coast to the temperate regions of the interior, and there he became a priest, a law-giver, and a king. The beautiful land of the Toltecs teemed with fruit and flowers, and his reign was their Golden Age. Poverty was unknown, and the people reveled in every joy of riches and well-being. The Toltecs themselves were not like the small, dark Aztecs of later times; they were large of stature and fair almost as Europeans, and (sun-like) they could run unresting all the long day. Quetzalcoatl brought with him builders, painters, astronomers, and artists in many other crafts. He made roads for travel, and favored the wayfaring merchants from distant lands. He was the founder of history, the law-giver, the inventor of the calendar of days and years, the composer of the *Tonalamatl*, the 'Sun-Book,' where the Tonalpouhqui, 'he who counts by the sun,' reads the destinies of men in astrological predictions, and he regulated the times of the solemn ceremonies, the festival of the new year and the fifty-two years' cycle."[113]

🌀🌀🌀

Who was this mysterious Quetzalcoatl? Daly in his 1889 article makes a judgment that was to be resurrected a century later. Says Daly, "Three points in relation to Quetzalcoatl seem well established: (1) He was a white man from across the Atlantic; (2) He taught religion to the Mexicans; (3) the religion he taught retained to after ages many strong and striking resemblances to Christianity. The conclusion seems unavoidable—that Quetzalcoatl was a Christian missionary from Europe who taught Christianity to the Mexicans or Toltecs."

Daly tries to pinpoint a date for the time period of Quetzalcoatl, relating it to the period of Toltec domination of Mexico, from about A.D. 400 to A.D. 1050. Says Daly, "The Toltecs must have been well established in the country before Quetzalcoatl appeared amongst them, and he must have left some considerable time before their migration from Mexico. The references to Quetzalcoatl's visits to the

Toltec cities prove the former, and the time which would have been required to arrange for and complete the great pyramid built at Cholula in his honor, and after his departure, proves the latter. From a century to two centuries may be allowed at each end of the period between A.D. 400 and A.D.1050, and it may be assumed with some degree of probability that Quetzalcoatl's visit to Mexico took place some time between A.D. 500 and A.D. 900." However, Daly is unaware that Teotihuacan has a Quetzalcoatl temple in it, and this city was begun circa 100 B.C. Therefore at circa 50-150 A.D. the temple of Quetzalcoatl could have been built, which would place the period of the first Quetzalcoatl as before 400 A.D.

However, Daly goes on to make the first known historical conjecture that Quetzalcoatl might have been an Irish missionary: "If attention is directed to the condition of Europe during that time it will be found that the period from about A.D. 500 to A.D. 800 was one of great missionary activity. Before the former date the church was doing little more than feeling its way and asserting itself against the pagan supremacy in the basin of the Mediterranean and elsewhere. After the latter date the incursions and devastations of the northern barbarians paralyzed European missionary efforts. But from the beginning of the fifth century to the beginning of the eighth there was no limit to missionary enterprise, and if even a Christian missionary had appeared in Mexico all probability favors the theory that he must have gone there during those centuries. The era of Quetzalcoatl may therefore be narrowed to those three hundred years, and the task of tracing his identity thus simplified to some slight extent.

"It may now be asked: Is it reasonable to expect that there are, or ever were, any European records of the period from A.D. 500 to A.D. 800 referring to any missionary who might have been Quetzalcoatl? It is a long time since Quetzalcoatl, whoever he was, sailed from the shores of Europe to carry the truths of Christianity into the unknown regions beyond the Atlantic, but the literary records of his assumed period are numerous and minute and might possibly have embraced some notice of his undertaking. It seems unlikely that his enterprise would have escaped attention altogether, especially from the ecclesiastical chroniclers, who were not given to ignoring the good works of their fellow religionists. Moreover, the mission of Quetzalcoatl was not one which could have been launched quietly or obscurely, nor was there any reason why it should be. The contemplated voyage must have been a matter of public knowledge and comment in some locality; it could not have been attempted without preparations on some scale of magnitude; and such preparations for such a purpose must have attracted at least local attention and excited local interest.

"It is thus reasonable to suppose that the importance and singularity of a project to cross the Atlantic for missionary purpose would have insured some record being made of the enterprise. A *fortiori* if the venturesome missionary ever succeeded in returning—if he ever came back to tell of his wonderful adventures—the fact would have been chronicled by his religions confreres and made the most of, then and for the benefit of future ages. It comes therefore to this—accepting Quetzalcoatl as a Christian missionary from Europe we have right and reason to expect that his singular and pious expedition would have been put upon record somewhere.

"The next step in the inquiry is to search for the most likely part of Europe to have been the scene of the going forth and possible return of this missionary. The island of *Hapallan*, say the Mexican tradition, was the home from whence he came and whither he sought to return. The name of the country afforded us assistance, and it might not be safe to attach importance to its insular designation. But in looking for a country in Western Europe— possibly an island—which, from A.D. 500 to A.D. 800, might have sent out a missionary on a wild trans-Atlantic expedition, one is soon struck with the possibility of Ireland being such a country. To the question, *Could Ireland have been the Hapallan, or Holy Island, of the Mexican tradition?* An affirmative answer may readily be given, especially by any one who knows even a little of the ecclesiastical history of the country from A.D. 500 to A.D. 800.

"In that period no country was more forward in missionary enterprise. The Irish ecclesiastics shrank from no adventures of land or sea, however desperate and dangerous, when the eternal salvation of heathen peoples was in question. On land they penetrated to all parts of the continent, preaching the gospel of Christ and founding churches and religious establishments. On sea they made voyages for like purposes to the remotest known lands of the northern and western seas. They went as missionaries to all parts of the coast of Northern Britain, and visited the Hebrides, the Orkneys, and the Shetland and Faroe Islands. Even remote Iceland received their pious attention, and Christianity was established by them in that island long before it was taken possession of by the Norwegians in the eighth century.

"Prima facie, then, Ireland has not only a good claim, but really the best claim to be the Hapallan of the Mexicans. It is the most western part of Europe; it is insular, and in the earlier centuries of the Christian era was known as the "Holy Island;" between A.D. 500 and 800 it was the most active center of missionary enterprise in Europe, and its missionaries were conspicuous above all others for their daring maritime adventures. It is natural therefore to suspect that Ireland may have been the home of Quetzalcoatl, and, if that were so, to expect that early Irish records would certainly contain some references to him and his extraordinary voyage. Upon this the inquiry suggests itself: Do the early Irish chronicles, which are voluminous and minute, contain anything relating to a missionary voyage across the Atlantic at all corresponding to that which Quetzalcoatl must have taken from some part of Western Europe?

"To one who, step by step, had arrived at this stage of the present

240

inquiry, it was not a little startling to come across an obscure and almost forgotten record which is, in all its main features, in most striking conformity with the Mexican legend of Quetzalcoatl. This is the curious account of the trans-Atlantic voyage of a certain Irish ecclesiastic named St. Brendan in the middle of the sixth century—about A.D. 550. The narrative appears to have attracted little or no attention in modern times, but it was widely diffused during the Middle Ages. In the Bibliotheque at Paris there are said to be no less than eleven MSS. of the original Latin narrative, the dates of which range from the eleventh to the fourteenth centuries. It is also stated that versions of it, in old French and Romance, exist in most of the public libraries of France; and in many other parts of Europe there are copies of it in Irish, Dutch, German, Italian, Spanish and Portuguese. It is reproduced in Irsher's "Antiquities," and is to be found in the Cottonian collection of MSS.

"This curious account of St. Brendan's voyage may be altogether a romance, as it has long been held to be, but the remarkable thing about it is the singularity of its general concurrence with the Mexican tradition of Quetzalcoatl.

"St. Brendan—called *The Navigator,* from his many voyages was an Irish bishop who in his time founded a great monastery at Cloufert, on the shores of Kerry, and was the head of a confraternity or order of 3,000 monks. The story of his trans-Atlantic voyage is as follows: From the eminence now called after him, Brendan Mountain, the saint had long gazed upon the Atlantic at his feet and speculated on the perilous condition of the souls of the unconverted peoples who possibly inhabited unknown countries on the other side. At length, in the cause of Christianity and for the glory of God, he resolved upon a missionary expedition across the ocean, although he was then well advanced in years. With this purpose he caused a stout bark to be constructed and provisioned for a long voyage, a portion of his supplies consisting of five swine. Taking with him some trusty companions he sailed from Tralee Bay, at the foot of Brendan Mountain, in a southwesterly direction.

"The voyage lasted many weeks, during several of which the vessel was carried along by a strong current without need of help from oars or sail. In the land which he ultimately reached the saint spent seven years in instructing the people in the truths of Christianity. He then left them, promising to return at some future time. He arrived safely in Ireland, and, in after years (mindful of the promise he had made to his trans-Atlantic converts) he embarked on a second voyage. This, however, was frustrated by contrary winds and currents, and he returned to Ireland, where he died in 575 at the ripe age of 94 and "in the adorn of sanctity."

Daly believes that the evidence is clearly there for ancient Irish voyages to North America. He continues, "The story of St. Brendan's voyage was written long before Mexico was heard of, and if forged it could not have been with a view to offering a plausible explanation of a singular Mexican tradition. And yet the explanation which it

241

offers of that tradition is so complete and apropos on all material points as almost to preclude the idea of accidental coincidence. In respect to epoch, personal characteristics, race, religion, direction of coming and going—the Mexican Quetzalcoatl might well have been the Irish saint. Both were white men, both were advanced in years, both crossed the Atlantic from the direction of Europe, both preached Christianity and Christian practices, both returned across the Atlantic to an insular home or Hold Island, both promised to come back and failed in doing so. These are at least remarkable coincidences, if accidental.

"The date of St. Brendan's voyage—the middle of the sixth century—is conveniently within the limits which probability would assign to the period of Quetzalcoatl's sojourn in Mexico, namely from about the fifth to the eighth centuries. The possibility of making a voyage in such an age from the Western shores of Europe to Mexico is proved by the fact that the voyage was made by others at about the same time. The probability of St. Brendan designing such a voyage is supported alike by the renown of the saint as a "navigator," and by the known maritime enterprises and enthusiastic missionary spirit of the Irish of his time; the supposition that he succeeded in his design is countenanced by the ample preparations he is said to have made for the voyage.

"There is a disagreement between the Mexican tradition and the Irish narrative in respect to the stay of the white man in Mexico. Quetzalcoatl is said to have remained twenty years in the country, but only seven years—seven Easters—are assigned to the absence of St. Brendan from his monastery. Either period would probably suffice for laying the foundations of the Christianity the remnants of which the Spaniards found in the beginning of the sixteenth century. On this point the Irish record is more likely to be correct. The Mexican tradition was already very ancient when the Spaniards became acquainted with it—as ancient as the sway the vanished Toltecs. For centuries it had been handed down from generation to generation, and not always through generations of the same people. It is therefore conceivable that it may have undergone variations in some minor particulars, and that a stay of seven years became exaggerated into one of twenty years. The discrepancy is not a serious one, and is in no sense a touch-stone of the soundness of the theory that Quetzalcoatl and St. Brendan may have been one and the same person.

"A curious feature in the Mexican tradition is its apparently needless insistency upon the point that Quetzalcoatl sailed away from Mexico in a vessel made of a serpent's skins. There seems no special reason for attributing this extraordinary mode of navigation to him. If the design were to enhance his supernatural attributes some more strikingly miraculous mode of exit could easily have been invented. The first impulse accordingly is to reject this part of the tradition as hopelessly inexplicable—as possibly allegorical in some obscure way, or as originating in a misnomer, or in the mistranslation of an ancient term. But further consideration suggests the possibility of there being more truth in the "serpents' skins" than appears at first sight. In the absence of large quadrupeds in their country the ancient Mexicans made use of serpents's skins as a substitute for hides. The great drums on the top of their temple-crowned pyramids were, Cortez states, made of the skins of a large species of serpent, and when beaten for alarm could be heard for miles around. It may therefore be that Quetzalcoatl in preparing for his return voyage across the Atlantic made use of the skins of serpents or crocodiles to cover the hull of his vessel and render it water-tight. The Mexicans were not boat-builders and were unacquainted with the use of tar or pitch, employing only canoes dug out of the solid timber. When Cortez was building the brigantines with which he attacked the City of Mexico from the lake, he had to manufacture the tar he required from such available trees as he could find. Quetzalcoatl may have used serpents' skins for a similar purpose, and such use would imply that the vessel in which he sailed away was not a mere canoe, but a built-up boat. If he was really St. Brendan nothing is more likely than that he would seek for a substitute for tar or pitch in skins of some sort. Coming from the west coast of Ireland, he would be familiar with the native currahs, couracles, or hide-covered boats then in common use (and not yet wholly discarded) for coasting purposes, and sometimes for voyages to the coasts of Britain and continent of Europe. Some of these were of large size and capable of carrying a small mast, the body being a stout frame work of ash ribs covered with hides of oxen, sometimes of threefold thickness. It may have been a vessel of this kind which Quetzalcoatl constructed for his return voyage, or it may be that he employed the serpents' skins for protecting the seams of his built-up boat in lieu of tar or pitch. In any case the tradition makes him out a navigator and boat-builder of some experience, and if he were really St. Brendan he would have had a knowledge of the Irish mode of constructing and navigating sea-going crafts and would probably have employed serpents' skins, the best Mexican substitute for ox-hides, at either of the ways suggested.

"It would be presumptuous to claim that the identity of Quetzalcoatl and St. Brendan has been completely established in this essay, but it may reasonably be submitted that there is no violent inconsistency involved in the theory herein advanced, and an examination of the evidence upon which it is based discloses many remarkable coincidences in favor of the opinion that the Mexican Messiah may have been the Irish saint. Beyond that it would not be safe to go, and it is not probable that future discoveries will enable the identity of Quetzalcoatl to be more clearly traced. It is a part of the Mexican tradition that Quetzalcoatl, before leaving Mexico, concealed a collection of silver and shell objects, and other precious things, by burial. The discovery of such a treasure would no doubt show that he was a Christian missionary, and would probably settle the question of his nationality and identity. But the deposit may have been discovered and destroyed or dispersed long ago, and if not there is little probability now that it will ever see the light of day. It would be equally hopeless to expect that Mexican records may yet be discovered containing references to Quetzalcoatl. A thousand years may have elapsed from the time of that personage to the days of Cortez, and since then nearly another four hundred years have contributed to the further destruction of Mexican monuments and records. In the earlier days of the Spanish Conquest, all the memorials of the subjugated races were ruthlessly and system- atically destroyed, and so effectually that but comparatively few scraps and fragments remain of native historical materials which formerly existed in great abundance. Even these remnants are for the most part useless, for in a single generation or two of Spanish fanaticism and Spanish egotism destroyed all use and knowledge of the native Mexican languages and literature. It may, therefore, be concluded that we know all we are ever likely to know of the history and personality of the Mexican Messiah, and what we do know is this—that he was a Christian missionary from Europe, and is more likely to have been St. Brendan than any other European of whom we have knowledge."[142]

🏵🏵🏵

Others have suggested other identities for Quetzalcoatl. The Franco-German archaeologist Pierre Honoré in his book, *In Quest of the White God*,[76] makes a case for a Greek-Minoan traveler from Crete as having been a possible candidate for the "White God." He makes the very interesting point that feathered headdresses or crowns were the customary adornment of the Minoan civilization of ancient Greece.

He admits, however, that his dates are closer to 500 B.C. for the arrival of his white god, and he theorizes that Viracocha in Peru and Bolivia must have arrived about 1500 B.C.

An even wilder date and identity is given by Harold T. Wilkins in his *Mysteries of Ancient South America*,[140] when he surmises that Quetzalcoatl was from Atlantis, arriving about 8000 B.C. or more. Wilkins, like many Atlantis theorists, thought that evidence for European or other transoceanic contact was really evidence for Atlantis. Their twisted logic is much like today's historians, if early man from the classical times of Rome, Greece, Persia, etc. were incapable of crossing the Atlantic, then obviously the answer for bearded men and obvious similarities between old and new world cultures was a lost continent in the Atlantic that lay between the two and was the originator of both. While Atlantis may well have existed 10,000 years ago, the identity of Quetzalcoatl obviously has nothing to do with this lost civilization.

Actually, it seems that the idea of Saint Brendan as Quetzalcoatl makes a great deal of sense, but there is much more to the story than an Irish monk spending seven years in Mexico, which seems quite likely. Saint Brendan may well have been the identity of one Quetzalcoatl, but the original Quetzalcoatl, or "White God," does indeed have a more fantastic, though on closer examination, credible, explanation.

First of all, as L. Taylor Hansen chronicles in her excellent book, *He Walked the Americas*,[24] the route taken by the "Prophet," as she calls him, first took him across the Pacific to New Zealand, Tahiti and then to the west coast of America. She maintains that the prophet landed near Acapulco, Mexico and identified himself to the Toltecs, who immediately acknowledged him as the Prophet.

From Mexico he went by ship to the west coast of South America and spent years in Peru, the Andes and the Amazon jungle. He then traveled from the north coast of South America through the Caribbean to the Mississippi River. Using the river system, he journeyed far inland to the Mound Builder civilizations of Illinois, Ohio, Michigan and on to the east coast.

Returning to the Mississippi River system, he continued northward into Canada and west to the Olympic peninsula. He then journeyed down the west coast of to the Baja Peninsula and back north to the Cibola civilization of Arizona. At this time Arizona was a vast fertile land irrigated by a sophisticated canal system that made the desert bloom.

The Prophet then returned to Tula, the capital of the Toltecs. From there he travelled through the Mayan realm and departed from Cozumel to return to the Mediterranean by following the Gulf Stream across the Atlantic. She places this incredible journey as occurring during the first century of the Christian era, and taking about 20 years to complete.

Who then is this mysterious person? He worked miracles, healed the sick, spoke out against war, human sacrifice and corrupt priesthoods. He allegedly *walked on water*... According to Honoré, he even preached vegetarianism. "He forbade human sacrifice and preached peace. Men were no longer to kill animals, even for their food; they were to live on fruit and vegetables."[76]

Could it actually be that this person was indeed Jesus of the Bible? Though it seems impossible to most people, especially since Jesus was supposedly crucified circa 33 A.D. How could someone who was dead (or at least had risen to heaven, and was therefore gone) have journeyed throughout the Americas for twenty years at a later date?

Indeed, there is a way! First of all, the historical Jesus was quite a traveler. According to the *Lost Books of the Bible*, ancient Indian texts, *The Aquarian Gospel of Jesus the Christ*, Gnostic writings, and countless other esoteric metaphysical doctrines passed down through "secret societies" such as the Essenes, Rosicrucians, Hermetics and Masons; Jesus traveled through India and Central Asia for many years, basically during those 'missing years' between the ages of twelve and twenty-five, prior to his ministry.

According to most records, he left on a caravan out of Jerusalem with Prince Ravanna from Orissa (Bay of Bengal, India). Jesus studied for four years in the Jaganath Temple in what is present-day Puri in Orissa state. He was taught by a secret group of Great Sages but found the doctrines of castes and transmigration of souls (humans incarnating as animals) which were taught by the local Brahmin priests offensive to his understanding of life, and would often preach his word of love and universal brotherhood to the oppressed lower classes.

At 17 he left Orissa and journeyed to Benares on the Ganges, literally escaping with his life, as the priests in Orissa had him hunted as a seditionary. Jesus was not safe in Benares either, and finally made it to the birth place of Buddha, Kapilavastu in Nepal (now Lumbini) where he was eagerly greeted and protected by the Buddhist priests there. Jesus studied at Kapilavastu for some months and arrangements were made for him to travel on to Lhasa in Tibet. He passed through Katmandu, and on into Tibet where he could study at the vast archives secreted near there by a mysterious group called the "Great White Brotherhood."

Tradition relates that he met the Chinese sage Meng-tse, usually known in the West as Mencius, and famous for his classic commentary on the Analects of Confucius, *The Book of Mencius.* After studying in Tibet for five years, Jesus turned homeward, traveling across Tibet, Kashmir, Persia, Assyria and eventually to Athens. After studying and teaching in Greece for some time, he sailed to Egypt and visited his cousin, John (the Baptist) in Zoan, today a suburb of Cairo. Jesus was twenty-five years old at the time. He then studied in Heliopolis for five more years, before beginning his ministry. The rest is history, according to the New Testament.

The crucifixion of Jesus was a curious event. When in some ways it seems evident that it had been planned hundreds of years beforehand by Jesus himself or the "Masters" for whom in was in supposed contact with, a case can be made that he was not meant to die on the cross. It was customary in Roman times to break the legs and arms of persons who had died on the cross (usually by starvation or by suffocation, from the rib cage pressing down on the lungs). It was also customary for all criminals to be taken down from their crosses just prior to the Sabbath, which starts on Friday at dusk. Jesus was nailed to his cross in the early afternoon of a Friday, and taken down just before dusk, having been crucified for as little as four or five hours, during which time he "gave up the ghost."

It is rather remarkable that a person with the vitality and yogic powers as Jesus would die within a matter of a few hours on a cross, when most criminals took several days to die. Persons are crucified every year on Easter in such diverse places as the Philippines and Mexico in commemoration of the event, all of them coming through it quite safely. Crucifixion does not kill a person in four hours.

It seems more possible that Jesus, who had undoubtedly studied certain forms of yoga, was able to go into an altered state of consciousness: a deep mental state, where he would appear dead to any person, including a doctor.

Such states are not uncommon, and are known generally as catalepsy. Even today, yogis in the Himalayas and elsewhere are still performing such feats.

The crucifixion of Jesus is a remarkable event fraught with interesting contradictions and interpretations. It is worth noting that when Jesus said on the cross, "My God, my God, why hast thou forsaken me?" he was drawing attention to the 22nd Psalm. At that time, it was common for scholars to refer to a whole verse by quoting the first line, as everyone knew the Old Testament by heart. The 22nd Psalm, written by King David, goes on to say, in the 16th verse, " ...a company of evildoers encircles me; they have pierced my hands and feet—I can count all my bones—they stare and gloat over me; they divide my garments among them, and for my raiment they cast lots. But thou, Lord, be not far off!..."

Therefore, it would appear that Jesus was not in despair, but was instead drawing attention to the 22nd Psalm as a prophesy of the terrible wrong that was being committed against him. Taken down from the cross at dusk, Jesus appeared to be dead. His mother, Mary, and Joseph of Arimathea, a tin merchant who spent a lot of time in Britain, stood by to claim the body, which was not "pulverized" (i.e., had its bones broken) as was the Roman tradition. Instead, they wrapped the body in a shroud after they had covered it with aloe sap, known for its natural healing qualities. Jesus had been pierced in the side by a spear, and was bleeding, which is rather suspicious, since a dead person does not normally bleed after his heart has stopped.

The possibility that Jesus survived the crucifixion seems a *credible* one. In fact, what is *incredible* is that someone with the vitality and personal power of Jesus would have died on the cross in such a short time. More likely, he could have lasted many days, probably outliving the common criminals. But what happened to Jesus after his crucifixion?

The New Testament claims that he emerged from the tomb after three days, spoke with his apostles and then rose into Heaven in a shower of light. The same ancient records that speak of his journeys to India, the so-called "lost" books of the New Testament, say that when he last appeared to his disciples, they simply saw his astral body, a mental projection. Jesus asked them not to touch this body (which, although real, was a physical illusion) and then he appeared to float into the sky, dissolving the projection in an explosion of light, which greatly impressed the Apostles.

What to do now? According to the records, Jesus journeyed to England and Europe with his uncle, Joseph of Arimathea, the tin trader. This was only the beginning of his post-crucifixion travels and other legends say that he traveled back to India and Tibet. It is at this point that Jesus, working with the Essenes as both his parents had, that Jesus began his world-wide trek, which included crossing the Pacific to North and South America. He allegedly traveled for nearly 100 years around the world. The Islamic title for Jesus is "the Great Traveler."

It is an incredible story, but those who are familiar with early Christian history will recognize some truth here. Until the 5th century A.D. the Christian church taught reincarnation, karma, different planes of existence, the loving devotion of angels and archangels who were dedicated to the upliftment of mankind and the value of harmless living and brotherly love. Furthermore, Christ according to many early Christians, was the Archangel Melchizedek. They further believed that Melchizedek is the Archangelic regent of our solar system who had used Jesus of Nazareth's body for the all important three year ministry that is chronicled in the Bible. In 431 A.D., a series of councils culminated in the severe editing of the various texts that make up our Bible, and the Nicene Creed was forced on the many Christian Bishops at the time. The Catholic Church was created and all who did not agree to the new, unified church and its revised doctrine of instant salvation and a unified priestly body under control of the newly created Catholic church hierarchy, were banished from the Byzantine Empire.

The former patriarch of Constantinople, Saint Nestorus, was himself banished to the Libyan desert, while his followers were forced to move farther east to Baghdad. Others such as the Coptics moved into Southern Egypt (hence the famous Nag-Hammadi Library) and Ethiopia while the Gnostics went underground within the Byzantine Empire itself. It was also during this period that the greatest library of the ancient world, that at Alexandria, was destroyed by fanatical pro-Catholic Christians. This destruction of ancient knowledge began with the mob death of the Nestorian Christian mathematician and historian, Hypatia, who was dragged from her chariot in the streets of Alexandria and torn to pieces. The hysterical mob then marched on the library and began to destroy the books. Such was the end of the original Christian Church in 431 A.D. Saint Nestorus was spared a mob execution, was sent into the desolate Libyan Desert to the west of Egypt, and was never heard from again. He may have gone to Ethiopia or perhaps to Ireland via North African trade-ships.

Curiously, Ireland was one of the early bastions of "Nestorian Christianity" as the original creed is now called. When Saint Brendan made his journeys to America, the Christianity that he taught was that of the original church. Later, he was excommunicated by the church in Rome for his heretical claims of contact with a transatlantic world.

As far as Saint Brendan and other Irish monks are concerned, it would seem that they were the originators of the Inca dynasty, having arrived at Lake Titicaca circa 500 A.D. and proclaimed themselves to have been sent by God, and the leader calling himself Manco Capac, or in other words, Monko Catholic. See my book *Lost Cities & Ancient Mysteries of South America* [57] for more information on this fascinating episode of Irish monks in Peru. See *Lost Cities of China, Central Asia & India*[16] for information on Jesus in India, *Lost Cities of Ancient Lemuria & the Pacific*[59] for information on Jesus in New Zealand and Tahiti and *Lost Cities & Ancient Mysteries of Africa & Arabia*[58] for more information on the Nicene Creed, the destruction of the library at Alexandria, and the banishment of St. Nestorus to the Libyan desert.

If Jesus did indeed travel around the world after his crucifixion in 33 A.D., whom did he travel with? Unlike Saint Brendan, it seems unlikely that Jesus would have built himself a leather boat and sailed all over the world by himself. No, he arrived across the Pacific and was later taken across the Atlantic in large ships with sails. Did large ships with sails capable of navigating the oceans of the world exist at that time? Of course! The remnants of the Phoenician empire still existed at the time, and other seagoing trading empires had been built by the Romans, Celts, Arabs and Hindus. It seems likely that some Essene group with their ships, probably remnants of the Phoenicians...

The Phoenician empire had only been destroyed in 146 B.C. at the end of the Punic Wars by the Romans. Some of their ships no doubt still remained, though travel by them in the Mediterranean would have been dangerous. It was the Phoenicians who had previously controlled the tin trade in Britain, which Joseph of Arimathea was a merchant in.

It is likely that some Phoenician remnant still existed either in the Celtic lands of Ireland and Britain, as well as in the Red Sea and the Indian Ocean. Perhaps Jesus voyaged to Britain first and then returned to India or the Middle East, where he then continued on across the Pacific. Phoenician and East Indian presence in the Pacific is well addressed in Thor Heyerdahl's 1986 book, *The Maldive Mystery*.[144]

✺✺✺

It would seem that the Phoenicians are an important key in the effort to unravel the many mysteries of North America," I thought as I glanced at the girl next to me and then at the sunset.

The next day I rolled into Mexico City on the bus from Cholula. I had received a postcard from an old friend sent to me in Mérida informing me that he would be in Mexico City for a few days and that I should join him.

From the bus terminal, I took a subway into downtown Mexico City. I had my backpack on my back, and was informed that if it had been rush hour, guards would have stopped me from entering, since no luggage of any kind is allowed. The price of the subway was incredibly cheap—only a few cents. A bargain even for Mexico.

My friend, Peter, a biofeedback expert from San Francisco was staying at the Hotel Doral, a relatively cheap hotel in downtown Mexico City. I tossed my pack down on the lobby floor and asked the receptionist if he had checked in yet.

"Yes, señor," said the young man in a suit behind the counter. He looked at the room list and then back at me. "He is in room 708. Shall I call him for you?"

"David, you made it!" said Peter. "I'm glad you're here. This damn city is so big, I can't find my way around it at all. My Spanish is terrible too. I know the taxi drivers are going to rip me off."

Peter was a clean shaven California kid from the bay. He had grown up in Marin County, and worked variously in pizzerias, folk cafes and biofeedback programs. A typical California way to make a living, I guess. We had met in Peru a year or two before, and it was good to see him again. We reminisced for a while and then went out for a meal.

I told Peter about the pyramid at Cholula and we talked about the mysteries of Quetzalcoatl.

Suddenly Peter said, "Hey, what about James Churchward and those Mu books. A lot of his material came from the valley of Mexico, didn't it?"

"That's right," I agreed. "Much of Churchward's information was collaborated by a Scotsman named William Niven. There is supposed to be a museum here in Mexico City with much of his material."

"Really?" asked Peter, "Let's find it!"

Yet, what was there to find, and who was William Niven? Niven had worked as a mining engineer for a Mexican corporation and between 1910 and 1930 made several discoveries that were so controversial that the established archaeologists completely ignored them.

Niven had been exploring in Mexico since 1899 and while exploring in some ruined cities to the southwest of Mexico City he discovered that the locals had terra cotta figurines for sale. He bribed one Indian to show him the location and then discovered that between Texcoco and Haluepantla, hamlets just north of Mexico City, there are hundreds, if not thousands, of pits dug into the sand and clay used as material for the builders of Mexico City for more than 300 years. While exploring these pits, which Niven says covered an area of about ten or twenty miles in the northwest corner of the Valley of Mexico, he came across vast layers of what appeared to be very ancient ruins, whole prehistoric cities lying as deep as thirty feet below the plain, which appeared to have been overwhelmed by a series of cataclysmic tidal waves, perhaps at several-thousand-year intervals which had left telltale strata of boulders, sand and pebbles. By the depth of the remains beneath the surface, Niven estimated the oldest of these remains might go back fifty thousand years or more.

Four to six feet below the first pavement, Niven says he encountered a second "concrete floor" but could find no pottery or other evidence of habitation in the layers between the floors. Beneath the second pavement, he describes coming upon a layer of ashes from two to three feet thick. Beneath this well-defined layer of ashes was the traces of a large city which appeared uniformly at the same level throughout more than a hundred clay pits. Most of the houses were crushed and destroyed, but in one he found an arched wooden door which had petrified and turned to stone. The walls of this house were bound together with white cement, harder than the stone itself. In one uncrushed room, about 30 feet square, full of volcanic ash, with a flat roof of concrete and and stone, Niven says he came across many artifacts and human bones, which "crumbled to the touch like slaked lime." He also claimed to have found a complete goldsmith's outfit sill on the floor with some two hundred models of figures and idols molded in clay turned to stone, each model thickly coated with iron, bright and yellow, presumably there to prevent the molten metals from adhering to the patterns while in the casting pot.

Niven says that there were frescoes on the walls that were preserved with some sort of natural wax and they were as fine as any Etruscan, Greek or Egyptian works that he had seen. Beneath the floor Niven found a tomb three feet deep, lined with cement, in which were seventy-five pieces of bone, all that was left of the skeleton. A large fragment of the skull contained the blade of a hammered copper axe, which appeared to have been the cause of death, for it had not been removed. Niven found in the tomb 125 small terra-cotta figurines, idols, dishes and other objects, some with bearded features that were strongly suggestive of Phoenician or Semitic.

Less than three miles from this site Niven found an ancient river bed in the sands and gravel of which he says were thousands of terra-cotta figures with faces representing "all the races of southern Asia."

It was in 1921 that Niven made his most famous find. In the course of excavations at Santiago Ahuizoctla, a hamlet contiguous to Amantla, about five miles northwest of Mexico City, Niven came across a discovery so startling he says it opened up for him a whole new field of archaeological research. At a depth of 12 feet Niven came across the first of a series of stone tablets with very unusual pictographs. Systematically exploring other clay pits and *tepetate* quarries with an area of 20 square miles, he claimed he was able to unearth during the course of the next two years 975 more tablets. In the end he claimed that he found more than 2600. Niven, in his estimate of their age, deduced from the depth at which they were buried and the accumulation of debris on top of them that they were over 12,000 years old and more likely closer to 50,000.

Niven carefully numbered each tablet in the order in which he found them. Some were large, while others small and rounded and appeared to have been water-worn stones that were carved at a later period, often following the natural shape of the stone.

Niven showed tracings of the tablets to the top Mayanist of his time, Sylvanus G. Morley, who told him that the symbols were like nothing he had ever seen before. Niven then made tracings of each and every one of the tablets and sent them to his friend, and fellow Mason, James Churchward, the British Colonel who had lived in

India, traveled throughout the Pacific and South America, and had was soon to write the popular books on the lost continent of Mu.

Churchward wasn't surprised that none of the archaeologists that Niven had shown the tablets to could read them. He, on the other hand, recognized symbols and designs that he had seen on another set of tablets that he had seen many years before in a secret library in a monastery in the Himalayas. Churchward said that these were known as the Naacal tablets that had the sacred writings of Mu on them. Churchward was very excited about Niven's tablets, and he felt that they filled in many of the missing gaps in his knowledge of Mu.

Churchward concluded that the tablets were the work of a colony of Mu that had existed tens of thousands of years ago. Unfortunately for Niven, his association with Churchward, which at least saved him from total oblivion in an archaeological sense, did not help him gain any recognition in the academic archaeological field, and he was totally ignored.

In the late 1960s, the Paperback Library of New York reissued all of Churchward's books again in mass market paperbacks. With the re-release of these books, new interest in Niven's work began, and in 1970 the publishers released a thin paperback called *Mu Revealed* by Tony Earll.[145] In this rare book, the author described how excavations had begun again at Niven's site by a professor Reesdon Hurdlop, who reported the discovery of a stone sarcophagus under the floor of a small temple found by Niven. Inside the sarcophagus were sixty-nine scrolls of papyrus bearing strange writings.

Earll said that by 1964 the scrolls had been deciphered to reveal the story of a young priest named Kland, and the content of the book was then the lifestyle, and other details of life in Mu, or Muror, as Earll claimed the scrolls had related.

The book *Mu Revealed* turned out to be a hoax, and Tony Earll was an anagram for "Not Really," Professor Reesdon Hurdlop was an anagram for "Rednose Rudolph the reindeer. Muror was an anagram for "Rumor" and the real author was a Canadian named Raymond Buckland who was then living in New Hampshire.[141]

Unlike this spurious book, Niven's work was no hoax. Yet, he could not get published, nor even recognized for his work. Niven died in Austin, Texas in 1937 and the New York Times obituary for him described him as having been a distinguished mineralogist and archeologist who had discovered buried prehistoric cities beneath the Valley of Mexico. He was also noted as the discoverer of four new minerals including cytrialite, thorogon, and nivenite. According to the obituary, Niven donated the best of his relics to the Mexican Government, kept some for himself to finance more archaeological expeditions. With the left over pieces, a private museum was established in Mexico City that held over 30,000 pieces.

"Where is the museum now?" asked Peter, finishing a bean and cheese taco. "Let's go visit it."

"No one knows where it is," I replied. "Nor does anyone know where any of Niven's pieces are. According to Peter Tompkins, in the

1920s the American Museum of Natural History in New York was given a collection of artifacts by a man who informed the curator that many of them had been bought from Niven. In the 1976 the curator of Mexican archeology, Gordon F. Ekholm, said the museum still possessed a collection of objects from Guerrero, sold to them by Niven, but that he did not know what had become of the famous Niven tablets."[141]

"That is the fate of the most fascinating artifacts of history," commented Peter, "they always end up hidden at the bottom of some trunk in the back room of a museum."

"Sort of like the last scene in *Raiders of the Lost Ark*, when they put the Ark of the Covenant away in a big warehouse full of other boxes?" I asked.

"Exactly," said Peter, taking a last swig of his Corona beer. "God knows what kind of archaeological time-bombs are hidden away in the Vatican or the Smithsonian Institution. Do you suppose any of Niven's artifacts will ever come to light again?"

"It's possible," I admitted, "that some of them are to be found in Austin or Houston, where Niven spent his last few years."

"There's a quest for you," said Peter, "You said you were heading for Texas."

I laughed. "When I'm at a loss for a good quest, I'll remember that one." And we both laughed.

🌑🌑🌑

"Taxi?" asked the man in the rusty car. He was leaning against his car and looking at us eagerly. These two gringos could be a good days fare.

I looked at Peter. Peter looked at me.

"Taxi?" he asked again. "I take you to Teotihuacan. Cheap. Special price for you. C'mon man, jump in!"

I figured that we'd get a better price if I talked to him in Spanish and asked him what he would charge us for a full day of running around. We wanted to go to Tula and then to Teotihuacan. After a bit of bartering, we struck a deal with the driver and grabbed our cameras and guide books and jumped in the back of the taxi.

It was a 50 mile drive north to Tula, a modern town and an archaeological site. We drove up out of the valley and into the dry desert hills surrounding the city. We passed a number of small towns and then came to the modern town of Tula, a prosperous city by the looks of it, guarded by two gigantic statues standing along the highway. Breezing by the Tula monoliths, we continued on to archaeological site of the same name.

The ancient city itself is on a hill above the city, and is a popular tourist spot. Tula, or Tollan, was long associated with Quetzalcoatl. It was at Tula that Quetzalcoatl lingered and was presented with the "bow string of power."[24] It was of Tula, "the glorious" that the *Song of Quetzalcoatl* was sung about by the Yaqui Indians. It was Tula that was the great Toltec capital.

As the respected British archaeologist Michael Coe points out in his book, Mexico,[85] "It has been the misfortune of modern scholarship that there are not one, but many places named Tula in Mexico—a quite natural circumstance from the meaning of the name. Thus the term was indiscriminately applied to great centers like Teotihuacan and Cholula."

Yet, the site for Tula was for a long time, thought to be a mythical place, much like Atlantis or Shangri-La. It was the French explorer and historian Claude Joseph Désiré Charnay who first began to suspect that Tula-Tollan was a real place. He developed an unpopular theory that there had once been a vast Toltec empire in central Mexico which had spread its dominion from a legendary capital called Tollan as far as Teotihuacan, Toluca, Xochicalco, Cholula, and even Chichén Itzá far away in the Yucatán. Charnay eventually became convinced that the small village of Tula, 50 miles north of Mexico City in the province of Hidalgo, was the remains of the legendary Toltec capital.

The small village had only a few overgrown mounds, but with the help of local laborers, Charnay soon came across huge basalt blocks more than seven feet long that appeared to him to be the giant feet of statues. Indeed they were, the incredible "Atlanteans," as they are known today, huge figures designed as columns to hold up a gigantic temple.[141]

Charnay recognized similarities with the objects he found with those he had seen previously at Chichén Itzá. Charnay was certain that he had found ancient Tula, the legendary city of Mesoamerican myth. The prevailing scholars, high in their ivory towers of academia, firmly denied that he had discovered ancient Tula. However, in the 1930s the archaeologist George Vaillant reexamined the site, and discovered that Charnay was at least correct in his notion that the ruins adjacent to the small village of Tula were Toltec in nature, and indeed, this may well have been the ancient city of Tollan.

Peter and I walked around the site, and were most impressed by the gigantic Atlantean figures that had been erected on the top of one of the pyramids. They were indeed huge, more than 30 feet high in four sections with stone plugs neatly fitting into corresponding contacts. Each holds a strange weapon on his side. Zechariah Sitchin in The Lost Realms[151] claims that these devices are plasma guns, used for melting rock in the mining operations that were the main reason for the construction of many of the early cities in North and South America.

There were three reconstructed pyramids at the site and a ball court. Cement was used in the construction of the city, and there were even a few chacmool statues, such as found at Chichén Itzá or Tulum in the Yucatán. Tula was a fascinating place, well worth a visit, though little is actually known about the site, and the pyramids in them selves are not particularly impressive.

Today, the site is generally recognized as the ancient Tollan-Tula of the Yaqui sagas. But was it?

We continued on in our taxi, heading back toward Mexico City, but swinging east to visit the fantastic site of Teotihuacan. Without a doubt, the site of the vast Pyramid of the Sun and the corresponding Pyramid of the Moon are two of the greatest sights in Mexico, if not the world.

"That pyramid is huge!" cried Peter, heading for the structure. Dodging some souvenir sellers, I followed him. Huffing and puffing later, we found ourselves at the summit of the Pyramid of the Sun, 215 feet above the "Avenue of the Dead" in the plaza below us.

Teotihuacan is not only the most important site in Mexico, it may well be one of the oldest. It is generally acknowledged that the city was in existence in at least 100 B.C. It may well go back many hundreds, probably thousands of years beyond that.

According to Nahuatl myths, still preserved in Aztec times:

> Even though it was night,
> even though it was not day,
> even though there was no light
> they gathered,
> the gods convened
> there in Teotihuacan.[85]

According to the Aztec Nahautl mythology, Teotihuacan was built before a cataclysmic change turned the day to night, and the sun did not rise. The men, or "gods" of Teotihuacan had to save the world and make the sun return to sky. Says Michael Coe, "The most humble of them all, Nanhuatzin, the 'Purulent One', cast himself into the flames and became the sun. But the heavenly bodies did not move, so *all* the gods, sacrificed themselves for mankind. Finally, government was established there; the lords of Teotihuacan were 'wise men, knowers of occult things, possessors of the traditions.' When they died, pyramids were built above them. The largest of the pyramids, those of the Sun and Moon, were said by tradition to have been built by the giants which existed in those days."[85]

Not only do we see a Biblical parallel here in his myth, that of a cataclysmic change in which the sun did not come forth, but also that "there were giants in the earth in those days." (Genesis 6:4)

The controversial Sumerian scholar Zechariah Sitchin, author of the book *The 12th Planet,*[152] points out in his book *The Lost Realms,*[151] that the legend of a cataclysm and period of darkness at Teotihuacan is the same date as the day that the sun stood still in the Middle East as described in chapter 10 of the Book of Joshua:

> Then Joshua spoke unto Yahweh,
> on the day when Yahweh delivered the Amorites
> unto the Children of Israel, saying:
> "In the sight of the Israelites,

255

let the sun stand still in Gibeon
and the Moon in the valley of Ajalon."

And the Sun stood still, and Moon stayed,
until the people had avenged themselves of the enemies.
Indeed it is all written in the Book of Jashar:
The Sun stood still in the midst of the skies
and it hastened not to go down
about a whole day.

Sitchin places the date of this occurrence at about 1433 B.C. Apparently, both ancient chronicles are describing what is known in geological theory as a "pole shift" or crustal slippage of the earth. During such an event, the thin crust of the earth slips on the molten mantel of the earth, much like the thin shell of an egg around the yolk. The earth's crust, in such a theoretical event, is attempting to find equilibrium by shifting ten to twenty degrees of latitude, often shaking off one or two ice caps that have been accumulating since the last such pole shift four to eight thousand years before.

Sitchin's theory that such a pole shift occurred three and half thousand years ago has a great deal of merit, but is Teotihuacan as old as this cataclysmic event? Sitchin gives proof in his book: "Archaeologists had assumed at first that Teotihuacan was established in the first centuries of the Christian era; but the date keeps slipping back. On-site work indicates that the city's ceremonial center had already occupied 4.5 square miles by 200 B.C. In the 1950s a leading archaeologist, M. Covarrubias, incredulously admitted that radiocarbon dating gave the place 'the almost impossible date of 900 B.C.' (*Indian Art of Mexico and Central America*). In fact, further radiocarbon tests gave a date of 1474 B.C. (with a possible small error either way). A date of circa 1400 B.C. is now widely accepted; that is when the Olmecs, who may have been the people to actually toil in the building of Teotihuacan Teotihuacan's monumental structures, were establishing great 'ceremonial centers' elsewhere in Mexico.

"Teotihuacan had clearly undergone several phases of development and its pyramids reveal evidence of earlier inner structures. Some scholars read in the ruins a tale that may have begun 6,000 years ago—in the fourth millennium B.C. This would certainly conform to the Aztec legends that spoke of this Place of the Gods as existing in the Fourth Sun. Then, when the Day of darkness happened circa 1400 B.C., the two great pyramids were raised to their monumental sizes."[151]

One clue to the reason that the Pyramid of the Sun was built where it currently stands was the discovery by accident in 1971 of an extraordinary cave underneath the pyramid. There is a natural lava tube enlarged and elaborated in ancient times, running 100 meters in an easterly direction six meters beneath the pyramid, in from the stairway on its main axis, reaching a multi-chambered terminus shaped something like a four-leaf clover.

Says Michael Coe, "It will be recalled that Aztec tradition placed the creation of the Sun and Moon, and even the present universe, at Teotihuacan. The ancient use of the cave predates the pyramid, and it remained as cult center after its construction. Unfortunately, official excavations carried out in it were never published, but scholars such as Doris Heyden and Professor Millon note that in pre-Conquest Mexico such caverns were symbolic wombs from which gods like the Sun and the Moon, and the ancestors of mankind, emerged in the mythological past. While there is no spring within the cave, there were channels of U-shaped drains (recalling Olmec prototypes), so that water was probably brought into the to flow through them. This immensely holy spot was eventually looted of its contents and sealed off, but the memory of its location may have persisted into Aztec times."[85]

One wonders what was found inside this underground that would make the discovery so important that it had to be suppressed? Important finds such as an ancient cave system beneath Mexico's most important pyramid are not the sort of discoveries that archaeologists find uninteresting. Something of such an unusual nature, a discovery that would rock the then accepted archaeological notions of ancient Mexico, must have been discovered in this tunnel. It might be something as trivial as a carbon date on organic material that goes back tens of thousands of years, or something more significant such as clearly identifiable objects from the Middle East or some other distant area.

It is also interesting to note that many of the pyramids in Mesoamerica are built over natural cave systems. There may be many more such natural caves under known pyramids in North America that have yet to be discovered, and probably never will.

Zechariah Sitchin mentions this unusual underground passage as well. Sitchin makes the fascinating comment that apparently this tunnel system and other tunnels within the pyramid, were used as a sort of waterworks. Says Sitchin, "That the original cave was converted to some purpose intentionally is evidenced by the ceiling being made of heavy stone blocks and that the tunnel's walls are smoothed with plaster... using a variety of materials; the floors, laid in segments, were man-made; drainage pipes were provided for now unknown purposes (perhaps connected to an underground watercourse now extinct). Finally, the tunnel ends below the fourth stage of the pyramid in a hollowed-out area that resembles a cloverleaf, supported by adobe columns and basalt slabs."

Speaking of the long "Avenue of the Dead" between the two pyramids Sitchin says, "The Avenue's cavity is further lined with walls and low structures, resulting in six semi-subterranean compartments open to the sky. The perpendicular walls are fitted with sluices at their floor level. The impression is that the whole complex served to channel water that flowed down the Avenue. The flow may have begun at the Pyramid of the Moon (where a subterranean tunnel was found encircling it), and been linked in some manner to the subterranean tunnel of the Pyramid of the Sun. The series of compartments then retained and eventually let out the water from one to the other, until ultimately the water reached the diverting channel of the San Juan river.

"Could these artificially flowing and cascading waters have been the reason for decorating the facade of the Quetzalcoatl Pyramid with wavy waters—at an inland site, hundreds of miles away from the sea?"

Sitchin concludes with this analysis of the vast complex: "Was Teotihuacan laid out and constructed as some kind of a waterworks, employing water for some technological processes? Before we answer the question, let us mention another puzzling discovery there.

"Alongside the third segment down from the Pyramid of the Sun, excavations of a series of interconnected subterranean chambers revealed that some of the floors were covered with layers of thick sheets of mica. This is a silicone whose special properties make it resistant to water, heat, and electrical currents. It has therefore been used as an insulator in various chemical processes and electrical and electronic applications, and in recent times in nuclear and space technologies.

"The particular properties of mica depend to some extent on its content of other trace minerals, and thus on its geographic source. According to expert opinions the mica found at Teotihuacan is of a type that is found only in faraway Brazil. Traces of this mica were also found on remains removed from the Pyramid of the Sun's stages when it was being uncovered early in this century. What was the use to which this insulating material was put at Teotihuacan?

"Our own impression is that the presence of...the sloping avenue; the series of structures, subterranean chambers, tunnels; the diverted river; the semi-subterranean sections with their sluices; and the underground compartments lined with mica—were all components of a scientifically conceived plant for the separation, refining or purification of mineral substances."[151]

This is Sitchin's fascinating detective work as to the possible true purpose of the Teotihuacan complex: evidence suggests that it may have been a huge refinery for gold or other metals. In his book, Sitchin also maintains that the ruins of Tiahuanaco in Bolivia were built for a similar purpose. It is interesting to note the similarity in the names between the two ancient and massive structures. That the mica used at Teotihuacan allegedly came from Brazil is a point in itself that would change our entire notion of trade between ancient North and South America.

🐃🐃🐃

As Peter and I walked down the Avenue of Dead, I gazed in awe at the majestic power of the ancient city in awe. During Teotihuacan's off and on history, probably one of occupation by a number of different civilizations, it is estimated that the city had a population of 200,000 people by the sixth century A.D. This would have made it the sixth largest city in the world at the time, according to Michael Coe.

At this time, Teotihuacan was a Toltec city. Sitchin believes that the Toltecs began to occupy Teotihuacan at about 200 B.C. He also identifies the Toltecs as probably the descendants of Phoenicians. They are typically depicted as bearded men with light colored skin.

For centuries Teotihuacan was the major city of all of Mesoamerica, trading at least as far as Costa Rica in the south and Arizona in the north. It was renowned for its tools, weapons, artifacts made of obsidian and its cultural and religious influence extended widely. Toltec wars spread deep into the Petén area and the Yucatán. Then, suddenly, Teotihuacan was abandoned and it became a ghost city of the gods.

It is generally believed that the abandonment of Teotihuacan coincided with the rise of Tollan-Tula fifty miles to the north as the new Toltec capital. About 700 A.D. the Toltecs apparently built Tollan-Tula as a mini-version of Teotihuacan.

However, it has been suggested by some authors, notably L. Taylor Hansen, that the real Tula of legend is not the city now located near to the modern town of Tula. The Tula of legend, the Tula of Quetzalcoatl, is in fact Teotihuacan.

Hansen maintains that the current ancient city now called Tula by archaeologists is not extensive enough to have been the Tula of ancient legend. Hansen points out that since the current "Tula" was only built circa 700 A.D. it is far too recent to have been the city at which Quetzalcoatl made his triumphant arrival circa 50 A.D.

Furthermore, the third major structure at Teotihuacan is none other than the Temple of Quetzalcoatl, a vast court over 600 feet wide by 1,900 feet long surrounded by a massive wall 260 feet thick at the base and 32 feet wide, crowned by 15 major temples rising from all four sides. Such was the esteem which the Toltecs showed for Quetzalcoatl.

Hansen claims that she was sure that Teotihuacan was the ancient Tula of legend when she was told that the word for the city had the meaning of "Teo"—"God" in Nahuatl and "Ti"—meaning "city". Therefore the name, Teotihuacan means "The city of the god Wahcan."[24] Wahcan, or Wakea, was one of the many names for Quetzalcoatl. Undoubtedly, when the city was originally built in 1400 B.C. (?) it had some other name now lost to us.

🐃🐃🐃

The next day Peter and I went to the famous Anthropology Museum in Mexico City, one of the greatest museums in the world. It was a fine day as we walked down the wide streets of Mexico City.

259

The city is not only the largest in the Americas, but will soon be the largest in the world. According to the *Guinness Book of World Records* the Tokyo-Yokohama area is currently the largest with approximately 19.5 million, while Mexico City is the second largest with approximately 17 million. However, it is estimated that by the year 2000 Mexico City will be the largest city in the world with 24 million people.

It should be noted, though, that both of these cities are in high earthquake zones, and it is quite possible that neither of them will even exist in their present states by the turn of the century.

Walking down the wide avenues of the city, I was quite aware of not only was there plenty of traffic (rush hours in Mexico City are something to be absolutely avoided) but that the city is extremely polluted. My eyes were already red and burning within an hour of walking through the city.

"I guess I'm just not used to these cities after having spent so much time out in the jungles," I said to Peter, rubbing my eyes.

"I was reading the other day in San Francisco," replied Peter, "about how some Mexico City businessman had this idea of putting special telephone-size booths around the city which would dispense oxygen for a fee of twenty-five cents a minute."

I laughed in astonishment of the concept and then commented, "That's incredible, but I almost feel that I could use such a service right now." Mexico City would soon not only be the world's largest, but also the world's most polluted.

At the museum, Peter and I wandered about the vast complex for hours, marveling at the many wonderful exhibits. There were many interesting curiosities from all over North America, including an exhibit of Hopi Indians in Arizona using a boomerang, may-pole dancing by the Aztecs and illustrations of primitive natives in loin cloths building the incredible pyramids at Tula and Teotihuacan.

A map of the world showed the "probable" crossing of the Bering Strait in the last Ice Age by the Asian settlers who allegedly were the sole populators of the Americas. It was an interesting map, and I lingered there for a bit, noting the curious geological facts such as the map showing how the St. Elias Range on the border of Alaska and the Yukon was totally glaciated, completely cutting off any land route from Alaska into Canada.

Similarly, while the glaciers came quite far south into present-day Wisconsin and Illinois, huge areas in central Alaska and the Baffin Island area of northern Canada were ice-free. In fact, it is known that a gigantic forest covered the Baffin Island area, now arctic tundra, at this time. Similarly, while glaciers were carving out Wisconsin, huge herds of woolly mammoths and rhinos were roaming north central Alaska.

Peter came up to stand next to me while I looked at the theoretical map of the populating of the Americas. "How is it that glaciers of this ice age are deep into the mid-west of America, while the Canadian arctic north of it is ice-free?" asked Peter. "It sure seems

260

like a rather strange to have ice-free areas north of glaciers in Wisconsin."

I looked at him and laughed. Sometimes there is no good explanation for the dogmatic history taught to us by the current pundits of knowledge. "The explanation," I said, "would appear to be that the true answer is that the north pole was in a different place than it is today." Peter nodded and we moved on.

In the Aztec section was a huge feathered headdress of gold and green feathers, macaw and quetzal, that was apparently a Quetzalcoatl-style crown. In many ways it was a prototype of the common chief headdress of the Plains Indians so familiar from western films made in Hollywood.

A huge map of Tenochtitlan, the ancient capital of the Aztecs was quite interesting. It showed how the various causeways came from the shores of the lake to the Aztec capital which was built on an island in the middle of the lake. It could only be reached by one of several cause-ways or by boat. In his final assault on the city, Cortez had built several sailing ships to attack the city.

"They were quite brave to build a city in the middle of a volcanic lake," commented Peter. I nodded in agreement.

The vast lake is now virtually gone, covered by the sprawling metropolis of Mexico City.

Walking through the various exhibits I saw more and more fascinating bits of prehistoric Americana. One of the first items that caught my eye was a ceramic stringed instrument similar to a banjo.

In the Olmec room a badly corroded stone statue of a man who seemed to have an elephant trunk for a nose. Having lived in India for two years, I found it highly similar to the Hindu deity of Ganesh, an elephant-man-god.

There were jade ink wells, jade men with helmets, ceramic whistle and pan flutes, jade jaguar masks and ceramic wheeled toys. There were some jade figures, one with a tattooed face, reminding me of similar tattooed faces from Japan, China and Polynesia.

There were many jade figurines, many with quite an oriental appearance, slanted eyes, and one of a woman with hair tied in a bun on top of her head. One exhibit was of sixteen jade men, about eight inches high standing around six jade steles. The men had elongated heads and slanted eyes. Strange inscriptions, different from the common hieroglyphs and more like ancient Chinese writing, were carved into the small stelae.

In another room was the Huaxteca Stele, eleven feet high with the figure of a man. On his belt was a yin-yang figure exactly as used by the Chinese. The accompanying plaque said that it had been found at the Castillo de Teayo in Veracruz. No date was given. The plaque also said that it was a representation of Quetzalcoatl, with a yin-yang symbol on his belt no less. To the great traveler, an incredible man who traveled the entire world, a yin-yang symbol on his belt seemed quite appropriate.

The Teotihuacan room was quite interesting. There were lots of ceramics, with quite a few yin-yang symbols on the pottery. There were plumb-bobs for use in constructions, carved conch shells and a three-legged type vase, a style well known in ancient China.

A gigantic statue weighing 50 tons, perhaps of Quetzalcoatl, stood in the middle of the floor. It was massive by any standards.

After lunch at the museum cafeteria, we ended up at the Maya room where a collection of eccentric flints (large, ornate flint or obsidian knives), were to be found. There were some nice Mayan murals, with many of the men wearing turbans. A popular exhibit was from the tomb at Palenque, including the priceless jade mask that had formerly rested on the occupant of the tomb. Other jade artifacts from the tomb were included, including some jade wands with tassels that reminded me of Chinese wands.

There was a replica of Bonampak with each of its colorful murals reproduced exactly as they are at the site.

"Look at those turbans that they are wearing," said Peter. "Are these guys Mayas or Turks?"

I laughed and as we left the museum, our feet aching from walking all day through the museum, I suggested that we go to out to the Olympic Village on the far outskirts of Mexico City to investigate the strange circular pyramid known as the Cuicuilco site.

It was mid-afternoon, and the crazy rush hour in the subway system hadn't started yet, so we went via the modern underground tunnels beneath the city out to the last stop, the Olympic Village that had been built for the 1968 Olympics. From the station, we inquired as to how close the Cuicuilco Pyramid was, and were told that we had better take a taxi.

Fifteen minutes later we were at the gates of Cuicuilco site. I went up to the gate and discovered that it was locked. It was only a few minutes past four, and it turned out that the site had just closed.

"Well, that's too bad," said Peter. "Lets go back to the hotel, I'm getting rather tired."

I am not so easily discouraged, and told Peter that I just had to see this pyramid. "Follow me, I'm going to climb over the fence," I said. Peter looked around nervously and then followed me over the 12 foot iron fence and onto the lava fields that cover much of the site.

We discovered a few paved trails working their way over an eerie landscape of broken lava slabs. Suddenly, over a rise of broken black lava was the circular structure known as the Cuicuilco Pyramid. It is 17 meters high and 100 meters in diameter. Most of the site of Cuicuilco is covered by the lava flow from the Xitla volcano nearby.

Cuicuilco was first excavated by the Mexican archaeologist Manuel Gamio in 1917 when he found an overgrown hill off the main road south from the city. It turned out to be a truncated "pyramid" or cone. It has four galleries and a central staircase to the summit. Cuicuilco is said to be one of the oldest structures in the Valley of Mexico, and traditional archaeologists, with their conservative ways, usual say that Cuicuilco is the forerunner of Teotihuacan.

The amazing thing about the Cuicuilco pyramid is the dating that it is given. The site is dated at being built in the in the first century of the Christian era.[22] Yet, incredibly, the lava flow, which covers a portion of the structure, is dated *as being 8,000 years old.* While it may seem quite incongruous to many people that a pyramid that is covered by a 8,000 year old lava flow must have been built sometime before this lava flowed over the structure, this fact is apparently lost on traditional archaeologists who continue to maintain that Cuicuilco is about 2,000 years old.

It was none other than the prestigious publication *National Geographic* which discussed the incredible age of Cuicuilco in issue no. 44 published in 1923 (pages 202-220). In 1922, the author of the article, an archaeologist named Byron Cummings, became interested in the site when he learned that a geologist named George E. Hyde had estimated the age of the flow that covered the pyramid, called the Pedregal lava flow, as being 7,000 years old. Curiously Cummings mentions a strange blue light that appeared at the top of the pyramid when they began to excavate it. The workers were encouraged, believing that it signaled that an Aztec treasure must lie in the mound.[17]

During the excavations, Cummings found 18 feet of sediment and ashes between the bottom of the Pedregal layer and the pavement surrounding the temple pyramid. He tried to estimate as well as he could how long it would have taken to accrete all these layers, and came up with the remarkable figure of 6,500 years. This added to the 2,000 year age of the Pedregal, means the pyramid would have existed 8,500 years ago, or more. Though Cummings' discoveries and assertions created something of a stir at the time, archaeologists have conveniently ignored the fantastically ancient date. Later, carbon 14 tests came up with dates of organic material on the pavement surrounding the pyramid of 4161 before present, making even these mild dates 2,000 years older than the pyramid is currently given credit for being.[17] Scientific tests have therefore shown that a reasonable minimum age for the structure is not 2,000 years ago, but over 4,000, and probably much older. However, the "experts" do not like to be confused by the facts.

I was busy taking a photograph of the structure when one of the guards came running up to me. "Señor, excuse me," he said hurriedly in Spanish, "but the park is closed. You must come back tomorrow."

I replied with a bit of surprise that I didn't know that the park was closed. I told him that I was an archaeology student and was very interested in the Cuicuilco site. He warmed up after that, and allowed me to examine the lava flow and take a quick look in the museum. Peter followed, taking a few photos.

Indeed, lava was covering the southeast portion of the pyramid.

"How old is this lava flow?" I asked the caretaker.

"The geologists say that this lava flow is from 6,000 B.C.," he replied.

"And how old is the pyramid?" I asked him.

"The archaeologists say that it is only 2,000 years old," he answered.

I looked at him with an expression of curious disbelief. The logic was twisted by any standard. He shrugged his shoulders. "I am not a scientist, " he finally said, "I am only the caretaker."

With that, Peter and I headed back for the subway station to return to the center of the city. Cuicuilco is perhaps a good example of how the current dating of ruins in Mexico and over much of the world is spurious, at best. Arbitrary dates, usually conforming to preconceived opinions on the age of structures, are given to stone structures, and these dates are final. Even when it is discovered that a lava flow over a structure is 6,000 years older than the accepted date of that structure, science has spoken, and history books need not be rewritten.

My Mexican odyssey was coming to an end. Peter was off to the airport to fly back to California and I was on a bus heading north to Monterey. It had been some trip, I thought, as I leaned back in the bus. There was a great deal more of Mexico to see, especially in the northwest, but my money was running out.

Some of the things that I would miss on my trip north were the famous Copper Canyon in the state of Chihuahua. Copper Canyon is four times the size of the Grand Canyon in Arizona and 280 feet deeper. Populated by Mexico's largest surviving Indian tribe, the Tarhumaras, some of them still live today in cliff dwellings.

Nearby are the Casas Grandes cliff dwellings, and the Las Cuarenta Casas cliff dwellings in western Chihuahua state. These cliff dwellings are virtually identical to the cliff dwellings that exist in Arizona, New Mexico, Utah and Colorado, and were probably built the same mysterious people, the Anasazi people, who mysteriously vanished about 900 A.D. One theory regarding these people was that because of a climatic change, they moved farther south in central Mexico, becoming none other than the Aztecs themselves.

In the same state, 125 miles from Chihuahua City, is the strange "Zone of Silence." This bizarre, virtually uninhabited desert area, is a twilight zone of bizarre animals, strange magnetic and vortex phenomena, mysterious lights and man-made hills. According to author Gerry Hunt in his book *The Zone of Silence,*[153] the area has seen gigantic UFOs, is bombarded nightly by meteorites and has been the target of government investigations by both the U.S. and Mexico. The area is known as the Zone of Silence because normal radios do not work within the 1,500 square mile area. Some sort of interference generated within the zone is jamming the signals.

According to Hunt, a U.S. Air Force *Athena* rocket was fired in 1970 from Green River, Utah and was programed to land in White Sands, New Mexico but instead was drawn off course 900 miles and plunged into the Zone of Silence. The missile carried a deadly radioactive cobalt warhead, and the U.S. Military then launched a massive recovery operation, building a special railroad spur into the zone and scooping up hundreds of tons of magnetic earth as well as the remains of the rocket.

Curiously, says Hunt, rocket pioneer Werner von Braun made a mysterious visit to the zone just two months before the *Athena* rocket went off-course. This raises speculation that the U.S. military purposely fired the rocket into the zone so as to be able to conduct special experiments there under the guise of recovering the rocket.

Says Hunt, the largest meteorite ever recorded exploded over the zone in 1969 in an earsplitting fireworks that made hundreds of petrified witnesses think that the end of the world was at hand. The meteorite, known as the Allende Meteorite, showered the desert with tons of fragments, portions of which were later recovered by scientists from around the world.

In September, 1976, a gigantic rectangular UFO with lights on its side passed over the small town of Ceballos on the edge of the Zone of Silence. It was witnessed by the entire town who came out into the streets as the craft passed over them.

In exploring the zone, Hunt claims that there are six mile-long rectangular platforms of earth that are apparently man-made, as well as a man-made hill in the shape of a crumbling pyramid. Small carved stone statues have been discovered in the zone, some of the statues are of pumas, while one is of a man wearing a turban.

That this area of the Sonora desert is some sort of vortex area has been known for the past hundred years. According to an old *Ripley's Believe It or Not* cartoon "huge columns of sand appear suddenly in the Sonora Desert, in Mexico, and mysteriously whirl violently—although there is not the slightest breeze in the area." Ripley is speaking of the Zone of Silence.

Hunt says that creatures living inside the zone are often bizarre mutants, including tortoises and insects that grow three times the normal size. Centipedes are sometimes a foot long with purple heads, tortoises have strange markings on their backs and no tails, and it is the only known place where cactus grows in shades of red and purple. There is even said to be a Bigfoot type creature living in the area.

One of Hunt's theories is that the strange magnetism that is part of the zone attracts visitors from outer space who travel to the zone to recharge their silent engines that run on magnetic energy. Hunt likens the zone to the Bermuda Triangle, and says that the instruments of airplanes go crazy when flying over the area.

I leaned back my seat behind the driver of the bus. Outside the window the sun was going down over northern Mexico. The Zone of Silence and its weird critters was out there somewhere. Behind me were the massive pyramid cities built by the followers of Quetzalcoatl. They were now ghost cities trod by sunburned tourists. I had only scratched the surface of the mysteries of Mexico. One day I would have to return.

265

Above: An 18th century drawing of the Great Pyramid at Cholula, dedicated to Quetzalcoatl. **Below:** An aerial photo of the Pyramid of the Sun at Teotihuacan.

Head of Quetzalcoatl found in Mexico.

Mexican stone engraving from the Yucatán. The man's earring has a six pointed Jewish Star of David in the center. Proof of Jewish arrivals to Mesoamerica or mere coincidence?

Megalithic columns at Mitla.

Rectangular Masonry

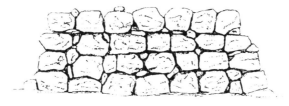

Cyclopean Masonry

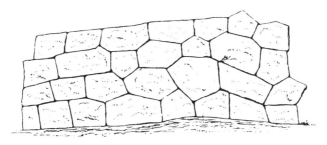

Polygonal Masonry

Different types of megalithic building styles.
Polygonal masonry is the most sophisticated building
style in the world, being virtually earthquake proof.

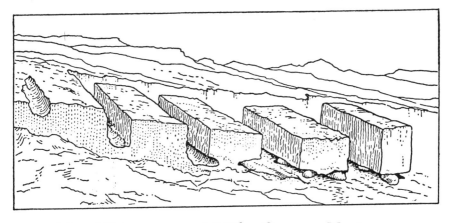

Megalithic quarry at Mitla, Oaxaca, Mexico.

Only a small portion of the thousands of ceramic and stone artifacts from the Acámbaro collection. Photo courtesy of John H. Tierney.

Two photos of the bizarre Acámbaro collection. Top: Some of the figures, including priests in headgear and aprons, plus the ever present "prehistoric animals." Bottom: A strange reptile-anteater-type animal is greeted by a goggle-eyed woman.

Some of the stone tablets from Niven's controversial collection from Mexico. The top symbol was chosen by Churchward to represent what he called the "Cosmic Forces of Mu."

Some of the tablets in Niven's collection.

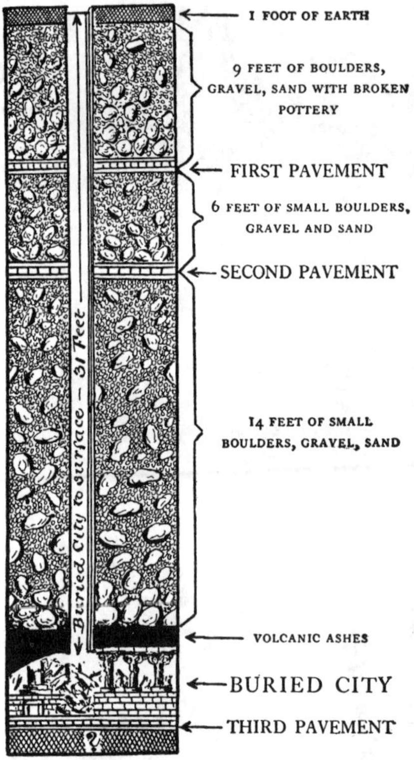
1 FOOT OF EARTH
9 FEET OF BOULDERS, GRAVEL, SAND WITH BROKEN POTTERY
FIRST PAVEMENT
6 FEET OF SMALL BOULDERS, GRAVEL AND SAND
SECOND PAVEMENT
14 FEET OF SMALL BOULDERS, GRAVEL, SAND
Buried City to surface — 31 Feet
VOLCANIC ASHES
BURIED CITY
THIRD PAVEMENT

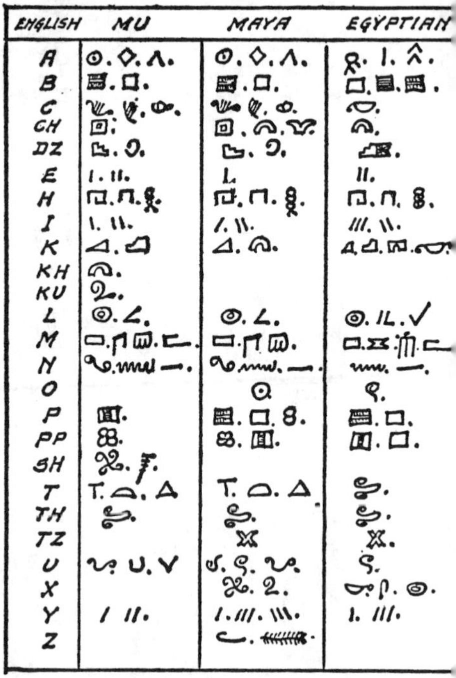
ENGLISH
MU
MAYA
EGYPTIAN
A
B
C
CH
DZ
E
H
I
K
KH
KU
L
M
N
O
P
PP
SH
T
TH
TZ
U
X
Y
Z

Left: Niven's buried Mexican cities. **Right:** Churchward's comparison of the alphabets of the Maya, Egyptians, and "Mu."

Above: A reconstruction of the circular pyramid of Cuicuilco, in the Valley of Mexico. The Xitla volcano is smoking in the background. **Below:** An aerial view of the pyramid. It is partially covered by a 7,000 year-old lava flow.

Fragment of a column found at Tula.

Broken column showing tenon, Tula.

Chapter 9

Texas, Arizona &
New Mexico:

Pterodactyls,
Tunnels
& the
Seven Gold Cities of Cibola

*"...is it that these people cannot face
rewriting all the text books?"*
—Ivan T. Sanderson

"Pterodactyls?" asked the man in the rusty car. "I'll show you the pterodactyl pens nearby if you want."

The sun was beating down mercilessly. It was as hot in Texas as it was in Mexico. I had crossed the border into Texas at Brownsville a few days before and had stayed at a trailer court that my mother and stepfather owned, though they lived in Arizona.

I had promised them that I would look at the trailer court and make sure that the couple they had hired to manage it were keeping it in good condition.

After resting for a few days, I was fortunate that my old pickup truck was sitting in the parking lot. After looking under the hood, and few trips down to the local auto parts store, I had the truck running and was now on my way across Texas, heading for Arizona. My first main stop was Big Bend National Park in the southwest portion of the state.

Texas had its share of mysteries, lost treasure and ancient civilizations. A number of stone heads and pottery figures have been found in Texas, including a ceramic figure found near Cisco, Texas that was identified in 1946 by three professors from the University of Mexico as the figure of the Aztec god of agriculture, Xipe-Totec. They surmised that the head had been made between the 10th and 12th centuries. Larger, stone heads have been discovered at Cross Plains, Texas, that wore conical hats are were "very old." Myself, I was after pterodactyls.

"Pterodactyl pens? How far are they?" I asked. I shielded the sun from my eyes, and looked at the man with a cowboy hat and blue cotton shirt.

"Just nearby, across the creek," said the sun weathered rancher. He had on a brown cowboy hat and a red checkered shirt. I followed him across a bridge that crossed the small creek in front of us and then noticed some rock walls along a cliff.

"These here are the pterodactyl pens," said the man pointing to the ancient, crumbling structures.

"Why do they call them pterodactyl pens?" I asked.

"Well, they have these legends around here about pterodactyls," he said. "I've never seen one around here myself, though. Just in a museum."

I stopped and looked at the walls. They were like pens, and since they were against cliffs, they could have been made into cages. Still, they were maybe just the ruins of a small settlement. Though pterodactyl pens was an intriguing notion, it was less likely an explanation than others.

The subject of living pterodactyls is, however, a fascinating subject, and one that is not to be shrugged off lightly. Strange and persistent legends abound in the South West of giant winged creatures. These stories have been told since before the Spanish arrived and continue to this day. Some radical theorists have gone so far as to say that these legends and sightings can be attributed to still-living flying dinosaurs—to pterodactyls or more precisely, pterodons.

There are literally hundreds of reports of giant birds and flying lizards showing up around the world. And it is a fact that the remains of pterodons have been discovered at Big Bend National Park. The park was the site of the discovery of the skeleton of a giant pteranodon in 1975. It had a wingspan of 51 feet and is the largest such fossil of a flying reptile so far discovered. Other pterodactyls were much smaller and had wingspans from 8 to 20 feet.

Though pterodons are believed to have become extinct about 65 million years ago, this may not necessarily be the case. Many creatures which lived at that time are still alive, such as crocodiles, turtles, and the famous coelacanth. Even the date of the fossil of the giant pterodon recently found at Big Bend is in question. Since fossils cannot be dated by any known technical method, their age is guessed at from the geological strata around it, and since the current dating of geological strata is based on the prevailing Uniformitarian theory of slow geological change, the date of many fossils may be radically closer to our own than 65 million years.

Almost every Indian tribe from Alaska to Tierro del Fuego has legends of a gigantic flying monster so large that, "...it darkened the sun." The Haida natives of the Queen Charlotte Islands of British Columbia believe that some Thunderbirds were so large that they could literally pick up small whales from the sea. Much of their art and woodcarving depicts exactly such a capture by a Thunderbird.

Some South American Indians believed that the bird was constantly at war with the powers living beneath the sea, particularly a horned serpent, and that it tore up large trees in search of giant grubs which were its favorite food.

The clapping of these giants' wings created thunder, so they were known as "Thunderbirds." The Navajo Indians still perform their Thunderbird dance, and tell the legends of the "cliff monster" which lived in a high craggy roost, descending to carry people off to feed to its young. Carvings of what appear to be pterodons can be found in Mayan ruins at Tajin, northeastern Vera Cruz state in Mexico and on a bluff facing the Mississippi River near Alton, Illinois.[20,45]

One amazing story that appeared in the Tombstone, Arizona *Epitaph* on April 26, 1890 related:

"A winged monster, resembling a huge alligator with an extremely elongated tail and an immense pair of wings, was found on the desert between Whetstone and Huachuca mountains last Sunday by two ranchers who were returning home from the Huachucas. The creature was evidently greatly exhausted by a long flight and when discovered was able to fly but a short distance at a time. After the first shock of amazement had passed, the two men, who were on horseback and armed with Winchester rifles, regained sufficient courage to pursue the monster and after an exciting chase of several miles, succeeded in getting near enough to open fire with their rifles and wound it.

"The creature then turned on the men but owing to is exhausted condition they were able to keep out of its way and after a few well directed shots the monster partly rolled over and remained motionless. The men cautiously approached with their horses snorting in terror and found that the creature was dead.

"They then proceeded to make an examination and found that it measured about 92 feet in length and the greatest diameter was about 50 inches. The monster had only two feet, these being situated a short distance in front of where the wings were joined to the body. The head, as near as they could judge, was about 8 feet long, the jaws being thickly set with strong sharp teeth. Its eyes were as large as dinner plate and protruding about half way from the head. They had some difficulty in measuring the wings as they were partly folded under the body, but finally got one straightened out sufficiently to get a measurement of 78 feet, making the total length from tip to tip about 160 feet.

"The wings were composed of a thick and nearly transparent membrane and were devoid of feathers and hair, as was the entire body. The skin of the body was comparatively smooth and easily penetrated by a bullet. The men cut off a portion of the tip of one wing and took it home with them. Late last night one of them arrived in this city for supplies and to make the necessary preparations to skin the creature, when the hide will be sent east for examination by the eminent scientists of the day. The finder returned early this morning accompanied by several prominent men who will endeavor to bring the strange creature to this city before it is mutilated."

Since no mention of this creature is made in any following issues of the *Epitaph*, it would seem to be a hoax, possibly created to boost the circulation of the paper or enliven a boring week in Tombstone. Especially considering the incredible size of this creature, it would seem that there was at least some exaggeration involved. Still, one wonders if these two cowboys encountered one of the last of the Thunderbirds.[46]

There is another variation of this story that says that a photo was taken of a pterodactyl in 1886 when a creature was shot by two cowboys and then nailed to the Tombstone *Epitaph* wall. According to the Fortean investigator John Keel, more than 20 people have written to him claiming to have seen this photo of a dead pterodactyl nailed to the side of a building in Tombstone. Keel claims that he has seen this photo too, but no one can remember where!

In his column *Beyond the Known* in the March 1991 issue of *Fate* magazine, Keel discusses this intriguing photograph at length. He also quotes from a letter from the son of a Pennsylvania man named Robert Lyman who had written numerous articles and books about the weird and the unknown. Lyman wrote about Thunderbirds in one his books entitled *Amazing Indeed:* "About 1900, two prospectors shot and carried into Tombstone, Arizona, one of these birds. When nailed against the wall of the Tombstone Epitaph building its wingspread measured 36 feet. A photograph showed six men standing under the bird with outstretched arms touching. One of them said: 'Shucks, there is no such bird, never was and never will be.' I saw that picture in a daily paper. many other persons remember seeing it. No one has been able to find it in recent years. Two copies were at Hammersley Fork only a few years ago. One burned in a home. The other was taken away by strangers."

Keel goes on to mention briefly his own investigations into a pterodactyl "flap" (pardon the pun) that occurred in 1966-68 where over 100 people in and around Point Pleasant, West Virginia reported seeing a giant, winged creature. The terrifying creature was dubbed "Mothman" by the press because the television series "Batman" was popular at the time. Many of the area's citizens, including a banker, the wife of a police officer and a minister, reported essentially the same thing—this flying thing was taller than a large man, had a wingspan of about ten feet and blazing red eyes. Except for the small wingspan, the Mothman of West Virginia could well have been a pterodactyl. Keel even wrote an entire book on this bizarre episode entitled *The Mothman Prophesies*.[159]

Of the two stories concerning cowboys capturing a pterodactyl, I definitely like the second story with the beast nailed to a barn and six prospectors standing beneath it rather than the first. A wingspan of 36 feet is far more believable than a wingspan of 160 feet or even 78! But where is this photo that everyone claims to have seen? Is it really lost or suppressed? Did it ever exist in the first place?

Most of the people who wrote to Keel about having seen the photo said they had seen it sometime between 1940 and 1960. Robert Lyman believed that the photo had appeared in *True Western* magazine sometime in the 1950s.

It seems likely to me that the so-called photo seen by people was rather an illustration for one of the various "True West" magazines in which these pterodactyl stories have been circulating for the last 60 years. Probably both stories are fabrications. Yet, where there is smoke, there is fire. At the very least, maybe a pterodactyl fossil was discovered that certain tales stemmed from, while other tales were part of a folklore from real but brief encounters with these frightening creatures.

That there were sightings of pterodactyls in the 1800s, I have no doubt. In fact, the sightings in the Sonora Desert continue to this day. In the early months of 1976, a rash of "flying reptile" sightings was seen in the Rio Grande river valley along the Mexican-American border.

One of the first encounters was on the early hours of December 26, 1975 when a rancher named Joe Suárez discovered that a goat he had tied up in a coral in Raymondville, Texas (about 30 miles north of the Rio Grande in south-eastern Texas), had been ripped to pieces and partially eaten by some unknown assailant. Local police examined the remains, could find no footprints and could not explain how the goat had been killed.

Then, in the same town, on January 14, 1976 at about 10:30 in the evening on the north side of Raymondville, a young man named Armando Grimaldo was sitting in the backyard of his mother-in-law's house on a cool Texas winter evening when he was attacked by a strange winged creature.

"As I was turning to go look over on the other side of the house," said Armando to the Raymondville press, "I felt something grab me, something with big claws. I looked back and saw it and started running. I've never been scared of nothing before but this time I really was. That was the most scared I've ever been in my whole life."

This strange flying attacker had dived out of the sky—and it was something Grimaldo described as being about six feet tall with a wingspread he estimated as being from ten to twelve feet. Its skin was blackish-brown, leathery and featherless. It had huge red eyes.

Grimaldo was terrified. He screamed and tried to run but tripped and fell face first into the dirt. As he struggled up to continue running for his mother-in-law's house, the beast's claws continued to attempt to grasp him securely, tearing his clothes, which were now virtually ripped to shreds. He managed to dive under a bush and the attacking animal, now breathing heavily, flew away into the sky.

He then crashed into the house, collapsing on the floor, muttering "*pájaro*" (Spanish for *bird*) over and over again. He was taken to the hospital, treated for shock and minor wounds, and released.

A short time later, in nearby Brownsville, on the Rio Grande, a similar creature slammed into the mobile home of Alverico Guajardo on the outskirts of town. Alverico went outside his trailer to investigate the crash into his house. When he noticed some large animal next to the crash site, he got in his station wagon and turned the lights on to see the creature, which he later described as "something from another planet."

As soon as the lights hit it, the thing rose up and glared at him with blazing red eyes. Alverico, paralyzed with fear, could only stare back at the creature whose long, batlike wings were wrapped around its shoulders. All the while it was making a "horrible-sounding noise" in its throat." Finally, after two or three minutes of staring into the headlights of the station wagon, it backed away to a dirt road a few feet behind it and disappeared in the darkness.

These were just the first of a number of bizarre encounters with seemingly prehistoric "birds." Also in January of 1976, two sisters, Libby and Deany Ford, spotted a huge and strange "big black bird" by a pond near Brownsville, Texas. The creature was as tall as they were and had a "face like a bat." They later identified it out of a book of prehistoric animals as a pteranodon.

The San Antonio *Light* newspaper reported on February 26, 1976, that three local school teachers were driving to work on an isolated road to the south of the city on February 24 when they they saw an enormous bird sweeping low over cars on the road. It had a wingspan of 15-20 feet and leathery wings. It did not so much fly, as glide. They said that it was flying so low that when it swooped over the cars its shadow covered the entire road.

As the three watched this huge flying creature, they saw another flying creature off in the distance circling a herd of cattle. It looked, they thought, like an "oversized seagull." They later scanned encyclopedias at their school, and identified the creature as a pteranodon.[48]

The sightings of flying reptiles subsided for a while, but then on September 14, 1982, James Thompson, an ambulance technician from Harlingen, saw a "birdlike object" pass over Highway 100 at a distance of 150 feet or more above the pavement. The time was 3:55 in the morning, and this huge flying creature was obviously a night hunter.

"I expected him to land like a model airplane" Thompson told the *Valley Morning Star*, the local Rio Grande newspaper. "That's what I thought he was, but he flapped his wings enough to get above the grass. It had a black or grayish rough texture. It wasn't feathers. I'm quite sure it was a hide-type covering. I just watched him fly away." It was as the others had described the same flying creature: a "pterodactyl-like bird."

Pterodons have also been allegedly sighted in remote areas of the Andes. Said the academic journal *The Zoologist* in July, 1868. "Copiapo, Chile, April 1868. Yesterday, at about five o'clock in the afternoon when the daily labors in this mine were over, and all the workmen were together awaiting their supper, we saw coming through the air, from the side of the *ternera* a gigantic bird, which at first sight we took for one clouds then partially darkening the atmosphere, supposing it to have been separated from the rest by the wind. Its course was from north-west to south-east; its flight was rapid and in a straight line. As it was passing a short distance above our heads we could mark the strange formation of its body. Its immense wings were clothed with something resembling the thick and stout bristles of a boar, while on its body, elongated like that of serpent, we could only see brilliant scales which clashed together with metallic sound as the strange animal turned its body in its flight."[45]

❀❀❀

I headed the old pickup out onto the road just after lunch, and began the drive into El Paso. My goal was Tucson, where some friends were operating an art co-op. They had small guest room to stay in, and if I got there in time, I could attend their New Years Eve party in downtown Tucson the next evening.

I got to Silver City, New Mexico a few hours after sunset, and decided to stop there for dinner. Forty-four miles north of Silver City are the Gila Cliff Dwellings, a National Park, and one that interested me quite a bit.

I had dinner at a local restaurant in town and then noticed that one of the several bars downtown was quite lively. I decided to pop in and have a beer to kill the time.

The bar was packed. Folks were lined up against the bar, while others played pool on one of the tables, or were lined up against the far wall. I walked completely along the bar, finding a spot near the far end. I had stood there for a few moments when the bartender, a woman with dark hair in her 30s, asked me what I wanted to drink.

I noticed that others around me had large quart bottles of Coors beer. "Is there some sort of special tonight?" I asked.

"Yeah. Quart bottle of Coors for a dollar eighty-five. You want one?" she said quickly, wiping the bar.

I nodded, and suddenly a young girl with long blonde hair turned to me and said, "Hey, buy us beer? Huh? How 'bout it?"

Next to her, another girl with dark hair looked up from her quart bottle, "Yeah, buy us a beer! Wha' da ya say?"

Well, I wanted to make friends, and I'd only just walked in the bar. It looked like they had some beer already, and in fact, both these girls looked rather inebriated. I was on a budget, yet, I should be generous...

283

"Come on mister," the blonde said, looking at me hopefully. She gave me a friendly smile. "A beer won't kill ya."

"OK, I'll buy you a beer," I said, breaking down. The bartender nodded in acknowledgement of the order.

"You from around here?" asked the blonde.

"No, I'm just passing though," I admitted. "Are you from around here?"

"Yeah, I grew up in this town," she said. The bartender brought our beers. She grabbed hers and took a big gulp. "You'd better watch this bar," she said suddenly, "it can be kind of rough!" With that, she took her beer which I had bought her, and walked away.

I looked up and down the bar and poured some beer into my glass. It was a lively place, that was sure. The music was loud and a few people danced between the pool tables. I watched the activity for a bit and drank my beer. On a whim, I got up and played a video game for a moment and when I came back to my place at the bar, my nearly full bottle of beer was gone!

I looked around and asked the girl with the dark hair what had happened to my beer. "Oh, was this your beer?" she exclaimed, handing me a bottle. I laughed, and took my bottle back.

I had just poured myself another glass, when suddenly a fight began at the pool table next to me, and one of the players was shoved up onto the bar while a pool cue was held in the air, ready to strike him.

Prudently, I grabbed my beer and moved away, taking a good swig, and dodged around a bar stool.

The man holding the pool cue growled at the other who was pressed against the bar and held by the collar, "If you want to start a fight, you just try that again!"

Others had gathered around as I headed for the door. The girls nodded to me as I left. It was a friendly bar, in its own weird way.

I drove on out through the mountains to the north of Silver City that night, and camped in the National Forest. It snowed that night, and I awoke the next morning with an inch of snow on my sleeping bag.

Unfortunately, my truck wouldn't start that morning, even though I tried to roll it downhill and throw it into gear to start it. It was just too cold, and somehow, my battery was now weak. I was wondering what I would do, when a large pickup came along. It was a ranger in her official Ford pickup. She cheerfully gave me a jump start from her own battery, and I got my truck going.

It was still an hour out to the Gila Cliff Dwellings, but the sun was shining and the day was warming up when I got there. I parked the truck at the ranger station and after a brief chat with the ranger and the purchase of a trail guide, I started up the trail to the ruins.

The first time the cliff dwellings had been visited in recorded history was in 1884 when the archaeologist-historian Adolph Bandelier was guided to the ruins by local settlers. While this area of New Mexico was controlled by Apache Indians at the time of the

European invasion, the Apaches themselves had been invaders, and the cliff dwellings had been built by an early culture.

It was a 20 minute hike up a narrow canyon on a trail before I suddenly saw the cliff dwellings. They were quite beautiful: seven natural caves in the cliffs 175 ft. (53 m) above me contained two dozen or so buildings.

The walls of the cliffs were sheer, and the immediate impression was that of an impregnable fortress hidden away up a narrow canyon. I continued to hike up the trail, which went to the far side of the cliffs and then up into the farthest of the caves. Being a winter's morning, there were no other tourists except me.

I walked from room to room through the caves, marveling at the view and wonder of living in a cave so high up on a cliff. Why did they build up here? Wooden beams that had been used for roof supports had been tree-ring dated as having been cut in 1276 A.D., a mere seven-hundred years ago.

Curiously, according to the guide book, the cliff dwellings were abandoned in the early 1300s. They had been inhabited for only about 40 years, hardly for two generations!

As the guide book asked, why did the natives, called the Mogollon culture, named after the high "Mogollon Rim" that sweeps through northern Arizona into western New Mexico, abandon this site after putting so much effort into it? Why did they build here in the first place? Where did they go after they abandoned the site?

No one knows the answer to these questions. Back at the ranger station I asked the ranger if there had been any signs of a battle being fought here. She told me that there weren't. I remarked that it seemed odd that the occupation was for only 40 years. One thinks of these Indian dwellings as having been occupied for hundreds of years by extended families, rather than built hastily and then abandoned a few years later. What was going on?

I drove back to Silver City and then continued on my way to Tucson. The mystery of the Gila Cliff Dwellings intrigued me. This wasn't some ancient megalithic ruin, by any means, but rather a piece in the mystery of the strange vanishing of many of the original natives of the South West. What had happened to them?

For one thing, it was obvious that these cliff dwellings were built up a secret canyon in order to hide from an enemy. This enemy must have been nearby, as the cliff dwellings, though only a hundred yards or so from the Gila River, cannot be seen from this very important river. Who were these invaders that were so feared by the people had to live in cliffs? The invaders were probably the Apache Indians.

Where did these people come from that built a cliff city and abandoned it 40 years later? Since the ruins are at the headwaters of the Gila River, and river systems were the main transportation highways of the ancient world, it makes sense that they came up from the lower reaches of the Gila River. That was an area around Phoenix.

Would I find a lost civilization in the Phoenix area? It seemed a bit far-fetched to me at the time, yet it seemed like a likely probability. Indeed, I was to discover a very sophisticated ancient culture had once lived in central Arizona: the lost civilization of Cibola.

🐗🐗🐗

People call them Pterodactyles: but that is only because they are ashamed to call them flying dragons, after denying so long that flying dragons could exist.
–Charles Kingsley, *The Water Babies.*

I wanted to get to Tucson in time for the party, so I got onto Interstate 10 and headed west. As the sun set over the desert, my mind drifted from lost cities to pterodactyls. Could pterodactyls actually still be living in the remote deserts of the Southwest? In this age of four-lane highways, border checks and gas stations along the highway with brightly lit signs, how could flying reptiles still exist without being seen?

In the glow of failing light, I looked out at the vast desert around me. Mountain ranges that weren't even mentioned on my map shot up in the distance out of the dusty desert floor. Who or what lived out there, I wondered? Apparently there was no road in that direction.

Then it occurred to me that all around me there is an uneasy coexistence between the modern world of glittery shopping malls and the prehistoric world where ancient denizens still carried on their lives as nature intended.

Rattlesnakes and gila monsters still moved through the underbrush and coyotes rummaged through the garbage bins at night. Yet, where were the Thunderbirds? Were they just mythological creations used to explain the sound of distant thunder before a storm, or had they been genuine creatures that the locals natives had witnessed?

It seems likely that if Thunderbirds lived in this day and age, they must be nesting in some pretty remote and probably mountainous area. The most likely area for any concentration of flying lizards to be still surviving would have to be in the Sonora Desert in Mexico, just south of Arizona and New Mexico. From this area it would be quite possible for pterodactyls to still live largely undisturbed and unseen by civilization.

Mexico's Sierra Madre Oriental, only 200 miles east of the Rio Grande sightings, is one of the least explored regions of North America. Flying reptiles or huge birds could still live in such a region, especially if they were mainly nocturnal.

Actually, the thought of these creatures surviving into modern times is not so surprising. In the last few hundred years pterodactyls have been reported all over the world, including many parts of Africa (see my book *Lost Cities of Africa & Arabia*[58] for more information), as well as in Sumatra, South America and even New Zealand.

In 1923 a book entitled *In Witch-Bound Africa* [124] was written by a very respectable British explorer and anthropologist named Frank H. Mellard who was the magistrate for the Kasempa District of Northern Rhodesia from 1911 to 1922. In his book he discussed the *kongamato*, a flying animal like a giant bat, or, indeed, a pterodactyl.

When Mellard asked the Kaonde natives of the Jiundu Swamps in north-west Zambia what a *kongamato* ("overwhelmer of boats") was, they told him, "...it isn't a bird really: it is more like a lizard with membranous wings like a bat...the wing-spread was from 4 to 7 feet across...the general color was red...no feathers but only skin on its body." [124]

Mellard goes on to say that the natives believed that the *kongamato* had teeth in its beak, though no native had seen the animal close up and lived to tell the tale. Mellard sent for two books which had pictures of pterodactyls, "and every native present immediately and unhesitatingly picked it out and identified it as a *kongamato.* " [124]

In 1928 a book was published in London called *A Game Warden on Safari* by A. Blayney Percival. The author states, on page 241, "...the Kitui Wakamba tell of a huge flying beast which comes down from Mount Kenya by night; they only see it against the sky, but they have seen its tracks; more, they have shown these to a white man, who told me about them, saying, he could make nothing of the spoor, which betrayed two feet, and an, apparently, heavy tail." [58]

Could a small pterodactyl (seven-foot wing-span, according to Mellard) survive in remote regions of the globe? A number of reputable scientists and explorers believe so. The famous Swiss zoologist Bernard Heuvelmans suggests that if the creature is not a pterodactyl, it may be a giant bat. Indeed, the late zoologist Ivan T. Sanderson claims to have been attacked by what he believed to be a giant bat or pterodactyl in a river in the Cameroons in 1933. Sanderson also claimed to have seen the photo of the pterodactyl nailed on the Tombstone barn.

Roy Mackal reports in his book, *Searching For Hidden Animals,* [125] that Dr. Courtenay-Latimer, one of the South African zoologists responsible for examining the coelacanth, investigated a strange sighting of a large "flying lizard" in Namibia.

She verified the story of a boy sitting under a shade tree when he heard a great roaring noise—like a strong current of wind. Looking up, he observed what appeared to be a huge snake hurling itself down from a mountain ridge. As the creature approached the sound was terrific, combined now with that of sheep scattering in all directions out of the creature's path. The creature landed, raising a cloud of dust and a smell he described as being like burned brass.

At that point he apparently lost consciousness from shock and fright. The incident was investigated by police and farmers, some of whom actually saw the creature disappear into a crevice in the

287

mountain. Sticks of dynamite were fused and hurled into the crevice. After the detonations, a low moaning sound was heard for a short while and then silence.[125, 58]

Similar cases have happened in Arizona. On my way up to Tucson I stopped in Tombstone, a former wild west town that was now full of tourists because it was the sight of the shoot-out of the OK Coral. I parked the truck and burst in on the local newspaper, just as they were closing.

"Can I help you?" asked the calm lady behind the desk. She was the only person in the office.

"I'm looking for an old issue of the *Tombstone Epitaph*. The one with the article about a giant pterodactyl."

She looked at me with a slight smile and nodded. "Yes, I've heard of that story. However, we do not have those old newspapers. Perhaps I should introduce you to the town historian across the street."

With that she took me across the street from the newspaper office, knocked on the door, and then ushered me inside what was probably the mayor's office.

"This gentleman," she said to the two men sitting casually around a desk and several tables, "is here to investigate Tombstone." With that she returned across the street.

I greeted the two older men and then sat down on a chair. I told them that I was writing a book about mysteries of the southwest and inquired if they knew anything about the *Tombstone Epitaph* story from 1890 about the shooting of a pterodactyl.

The men both laughed. "Oh, that story!" one of them said. "I wrote about that story for *True West* magazine back in the early 60s. But I don't think its a true story. In fact, I once tried to find the original article in the newspaper, and could never find it. It was probably all fabricated back at the turn of the century. I'm not sure where people get these crazy ideas!"

"Then I guess you haven't seen a photo with a giant bird or something nailed to a wall?" I asked.

"Ha, ha!" he laughed. "No sir. I've never even heard of such a thing!"

"Well, have you ever heard any stories of flying lizards out here in the southern Arizona deserts?" I asked politely.

"Well, yes, there are some stories," said the other man, straightening up in his chair. "There's a popular book on lost mines and buried treasure written by Thomas Penfield called *Dig Here*.[126] It was published in 1962. Chapter 50 of that book is about the "Treasure of the Mountain of Noise." Have you ever hear of the lost Treasure of the Mountain of Noise?"

I confessed that I was unfamiliar with the tale, and with that admission, I was given the details of a very interesting story. It seems to the southwest of Tombstone near Cerro Ruido Mountain in the Pajarito Range (now called the Oro Blanco or "White Gold" Mountains) in the area of Arizona-Mexican border around Nogales is a lost mine with at least 30 tons of high grade silver ore in sacks.

Yet, it has never been recovered because the Mexicans who live in that area have a deathly fear of the Pajarito Range. Why? I'll tell you why—because there's some kind of flying lizard out there, that's why!"

"Really?" I exclaimed!

The other man straightened up in his chair. "Are you making this story up?" he asked skeptically.

"Hell, no," said the other. "It's in the book! Besides, I have my own information on this story. One of the people concerned with the story appeared on a television show in 1958. I saw it!

"Listen to me, this Cerro Ruido place is a spooky mountain range. The Mexicans down there won't go near it! However, there is evidence that the early mission padres, in traveling from their station in Sonora to those in southern Arizona, frequently took a shorter, but much rougher trail that took them through the Cerro Ruido. It was long believed a lost silver mine and mission was in this area, and the Jesuits had used this remote area to hide some of their wealth from the Spanish crown.

"Shortly after World War I, two army veterans came down from Tucson and started prospecting in the area. They found a place where a large amount of dirt and rock at the base of a ledge which aroused their curiosity. It appeared to have been put there by man. One man went to Nogales for more supplies while the other investigated.

"When the partner returned from Nogales, he found his companion asleep at the base of an oak tree. His clothing was torn, and his face and arms were badly scratched. He then told his partner of how he had labored all day with a pick and shovel, exposing a small opening into solid rock. On the following morning he had enlarged the opening enough to permit his body to slip through. The opening led to a dark, dry, dusty tunnel. He had used his carbide light to progress further into the tunnel, finally coming to a pile of shapeless sacks stacked along one side. He kicked one of the sacks and it broke open, revealing pieces of glittering ore. He counted the crude rawhide sacks, lifted several pieces of the heavy ore and estimated that the pile contained about 30 tons.

"Exploring further, he had judged the tunnel to be about 400 feet long, with several shafts running off to either side. The following day, he made his way up the canyon, climbed its wall and crossed over into another canyon. He followed up this canyon until he came to a small opening covered with shrubs and dried yellow grass. It was surrounded with trees and his eyes were taking in the beautiful sight when he spotted the remains of an ancient church. Its walls were crumbled and broken, but it was clear and distinct in outline. He had found the lost mission, which also explained the hidden mine.

"Night was approaching, so the prospector made camp. Before he had fallen asleep, a strange feeling of unexplained fear had gripped him. He had the feeling of impending danger. Suddenly, the silence of the ancient mission was pierced by a horrifying scream. The man then saw a strange flying creature that was like a giant bat, perched on the walls of the ancient mission!

"Terrified, he ran down the canyon, tearing through the thorny brush and stumbling over boulders in the darkness. Upon reaching the camp at the mine, he collapsed, exhausted. It was the next day when his companion then discovered him on the ground.

"Together, they explored the mine again and decided that it could still be worked. The man who had returned from Nogales convinced his partner that he had only been the victim of a nightmare, and that samples of the ore should be assayed in Tucson. Although Nogales was closer, Tucson would be better for the assay because the secret of the mine could be better kept.

"So they split up again, with the same partner (presumably the one with money to buy supplies with) left the mountains again and headed for Tucson. As he departed, he noticed a large storm heading for the mountains. Later, he learned that the storm had swept the entire border region, creating flash floods and torrents of rain. On his return to the camp, his partner could not be found. For two days he searched for his partner and then went to Nogales and returned with horses and help.

"No trace of his partner, the mine or the lost mission were ever found again. The rain had hidden the entrance to the mine and only the now vanished partner had ever seen the ruins of the mission. To this day the mystery of the lost mine and the the the unearthly creature have never been solved."

"What happened to the other prospector?" I asked.

"Well, maybe he was eventually a meal for a pterodactyl!" exclaimed the man.

"That's a strange story!" said the other man. Then turning to me he said, "Well, son, I guess you got your pterodactyl story. Haven't seen any around Tombstone myself, though!"

I thanked the gentlemen for their time, and headed out onto the main street of Tombstone. I wandered down the wooden sidewalks, into the saloons and back out again. Tourists walked the streets, and I passed gift shop after bar, and eventually came across a bookstore called the Territorial Book Trader. Being a book lover, I immediately flung myself through the door and began browsing. Eventually, I found a copy of Penfield's *Dig Here* and bought it.

A short time later, I was back on the highway heading for the New Year's Eve Party in Tucson. With my headlights on the tall, human like cactus along the road, it seemed like Arizona was another planet: a planet of pterodactyls, lost cities, gold treasure, weird music and armadillos. Maybe it was all just a fantasy movie from the 50s with old cars, cowboy boots, lost continents, living dinosaurs, unfathomable gold treasure and strange cults. Arizona was all that and more, and the black ribbon of pavement in front of me was like a door through time.

When the going gets weird,
the weird turn pro.
—Hunter S. Thompson

It was only a few hours later that I was pulling off the interstate into downtown Tucson. Minutes later I was knocking on the door of the Artstone Collective, the cooperative venture run by several of my friends.

"David!" exclaimed Harry as I knocked and then entered the door. My old friend Harry was sitting by his computer with several of his friends. A bottle of tequila was on the table and their New Year's Eve party was in full swing.

There were still several hours before the New Year would be ushered in, and I enjoyed a beer with the small crowd in the office. I was introduced to everyone and soon we were all spinning our various tales of adventure and mystery.

"David, you've got to hear this story that Paul and Curt were just telling me. Tell him your story, guys."

I listened intently while Paul, who had grown up in Tucson and Curt, who lived in Phoenix, told me the strange tale of a "gargoyle" that was seen at the Pima Mine to the south of Tucson.

"I know some folks who work at the Pima mine, and they told me of a nightwatchman who was staying at the dumpsite for the mine who suddenly radioed for help from his supervisor. When the supervisor arrived at the mine, the watchman was so frightened that he was shaking. However, he would not say what it was that he had seen that so frightened him. He only insisted that he be driven away from the mine. He refused to stay there any longer and immediately quit his job.

"Then, sometime later another watchman who had taken his place reported that one night he heard the sound of flapping wings and something flying overhead. When he investigated the noise, what he saw raised the hair on the back of his neck!

"He claimed that it was like a gargoyle. It had scaly skin and a beak and, as it perched on a rock in the moonlight, it had bat-like wings that folded up and arched above the shoulders. It was like some flying monster! This is what the earlier watchman had seen that had so frightened him!"

"Wow, that's a pretty wild story," I said, taking a gulp of beer.

"What do you think. Doesn't this sound like those gray aliens that we've been hearing about. They're everywhere!" said Harry.

"Gray aliens?" I asked, somewhat confused. "What does this story have to do with extraterrestrials?"

"Isn't is obvious?" said Paul. "What else could this thing be? They described the creature as like a gargoyle. It was probably some extraterrestrial. What else could it have been?"

I was silent for a moment. It was a popular belief among many of

291

my friends that small gray aliens were somehow involved with the U.S. government concerning certain UFO mysteries, and somehow they were relating this weird gargoyle story with extraterrestrial visits.

"I don't think that this creature was a small gray extraterrestrial," I told them. "But I think that I do know what it probably was."

"What?" exclaimed everyone in unison. They all seemed amazed that I had a different answer than they to this mystery.

"What the nightwatchman at the Pima mine saw was a pterodactyl," I stated. "Pterodactyls are reported all the time, especially in southern Arizona and along the Mexican border. Such an animal fits the description you gave me very well." I then told them the story of the lost mine near Nogales.

"But what about the beak, the scaly skin, the wings above the shoulders?" asked Paul.

"Well, pterodactyls have scaly skin, a beak and large, leathery wings that fold up above the shoulder, similar to a bat. It seems like a gargoyle would be a good description of a modern pterosaur. I'm sure it would be an astonishing sight! Besides, I thought these gray aliens flew around in spacecraft, rather than on leathery wings!"

"Well, maybe your right," said Paul. "A pterodactyl does sort of fit."

Curt suddenly sat up and took a shot of tequila. "Yeah, maybe that's the answer! My dad told me a story about when he was younger and he and a friend went out looking for an old Spanish mine in the desert south of Tucson. They had an old map to the mine and they hauled a dune buggy on a trailer behind their camper-truck.

"They were camped for the night out in the desert near this lost mine when suddenly they woke up because the front windshield of their truck was smashed in. They were sleeping in the back, but couldn't see nothing out there. It was late at night, and there wasn't much they could do, so they went back to sleep.

"Then, a short time later, they woke up again and heard the sound of the flapping of large wings. Whatever that thing was, it was standing on the dune buggy in back, flapping its wings and trying to pick up the dune buggy! This thing was bouncing up and down on the dune buggy making a terrible racket!

"My dad told me that they were scared shitless! It seemed like the thing was trying to get them to come out of the truck, but they weren't moving an inch. There was no way they were going outside. Finally this thing just flew away. In the morning, they drove back to Tucson."

"That's an amazing tale," I said. "I never imagined that there would be this many flying reptile stories here in southern Arizona. They all are similar in many ways."

"Maybe you're right," admitted Paul. "Maybe there are pterodactyls still out in the desert. Perhaps they nest in these old mines and crags in the mountains. Its an unknown desert out there!"

"Maybe these things are interdimensional," said Harry.

"Maybe," I said finishing my beer. "Arizona is kind of an inter-dimensional place!"

As I drifted off to sleep in the Artstone Collective's guest room I thought of Sir Arthur Conan Doyle' description of a living pterodactyl in his 1912 book entitled *Lost World* about the intrepid explorer Professor Challenger:

> *"The face of the creature was like the wildest gargoyle that the imagination of a mad mediæval builder could have conceived. It was malicious, horrible, with two small red eyes as bright as points of burning coal..."*

🦋🦋🦋

It was late the next day that I was driving up to Phoenix from Tucson. Once I was a few miles out of Tucson I was able to relax. My mind drifted to the strange discussion that we had had the night before. There was something real going on here, I genuinely felt. In fact, I had to admit that I was coming to the conclusion that pterodactyls were not extinct at all, but survived to this day!

That Arizona was some sort of Lost World of prehistoric animals two thousand years ago is further evidenced by Roman artifacts that have been uncovered near Tucson. One of the artifacts, a sword held a image of an extinct animal! On September 13, 1924, Charles Manier found something on Silverbell Road northwest of Tucson that was to change the notion of Arizona history for good. The find included an array of ancient Roman artifacts, mostly made of lead. The trove, discovered in a lime kiln, included more than 30 objects, including a 62-pound cross, spear, daggers, batons and swords. The objects were encrusted in caliche—a sheet of hard, crusty material that "grows" due to a reaction of chemicals and water in desert soils over many years. This encrustation was proof to the excavators that the objects were quite old.[155]

In 1925, University of Tucson archaeologists working in the lime kiln outside of Tucson unearthed a short, heavy broadsword of apparent Roman manufacture. Other artifacts found at the site bore both Hebrew lettering and a form of Latin used between A.D. 560 and 900. Even though many of the Tucson artifacts were unearthed by professionals, controversy rages over their authenticity.

Dr. Cyclone Covey, a history professor at Wake Forest University in North Carolina, writes about a Roman Jewish colony in Arizona *Calalus*.[109] Various Jews had sailed from the Portuguese port of Porto Cale and founded a city in Florida, naming it Cale. This city is now modern day Ocala in north-central Florida.

Covey believes that other Jews escaped Rome and also left Porto Cale, Portugal for the New World. The Latin form of Porto Cale was Calalus, which became a Jewish-Roman outpost in 775 A.D. The city, situated where modern Tucson lies today was then named

Rhoda. One of the leaders, or captain of one of the ships, Covey believes, was born on the island of Rhodes.[109]

Covey's fascinating thesis is that the Toltec Empire existed in Northern Arizona about 700-900 A.D. Covey believes that 100 years after the Toltecs had finally defeated the Jews at Calalus and Rhoda, they migrated to Mexico to found the late Toltec capital of Tula. They brought Jewish captives with them on their journey to Mexico, and continued south, defeating the Maya and capturing Chichén Itza. There they built the so-called Temple of Warriors. Covey claims that they had a white king with a beard.

This scenario, quite possible, considering the various evidence, can also be viewed as a continuation of the various wars in Europe, Asia and Mesoamerica. The Toltecs, by many accounts, are the descendants of the Phoenician Empire after the Punic Wars, when all Carthaginians and Phoenicians were either killed or had to flee across the Atlantic. Later, further wars would occur in the Americas, including new invasions of now Toltec-Phoenician areas such as Arizona, Northern Mexico and areas near the Rio Grande. The hated Romans, plus Jews and other Roman subjects arrived to explore and colonize the New Lands. Furthermore, wars continued with the constant migration of various North American tribes and occasional invasion of one area to another. The Toltecs, however, dominated Mesoamerica from Arizona to Yucatán for hundreds of years, and then their empire mysteriously collapsed.

The most startling of the Roman discoveries was a short, heavy broadsword with the clear depiction of a brontosaurus carved into it! Common sense tells us that someone wanting to hoax a Roman-Jewish outpost in Arizona and wanting to be taken seriously, would not have inscribed a brontosaurus on a sword.[155, 141]

What the hell is a brontosaurus doing inscribed on a broadsword? Too bad it wasn't a pterodactyl, I thought as I passed a big truck on the highway. Finding a Roman sword in Tucson is bad enough, but a dinosaur...

Can it be that the theory that dinosaurs became extinct 65 million years ago is incorrect? Many fossils are probably much more recent than is generally believed. Yet, it strains credulity to believe that their were brontosaurus' in Arizona in the year 560 A.D. The climate hardly seems conducive to harbor such animals. The swampy jungles of Central Africa, New Guinea or the Amazon, yes, but the deserts of southern Arizona, no. Was Arizona a swamp 1,500 years ago? Are pterodactyls the last denizens of this prehistoric world to still survive? It cannot be discounted that the Romans of Arizona may have discovered an intact brontosaurus skeleton as a fossil. It is also interesting to think about the Acámbaro figurines of Mexico. They too showed extinct creatures.

Curiously, in 1920 ranch hands were digging on the property of William M. Chalmers near Granby, Colorado, when they discovered a granite statuette weighing 66 pounds and standing 14 inches high. The stone, found at a depth of six feet, portrays a stylized human with what purports to be a Chinese inscription dating approximately 1000 B.C. More intriguing are two inscribed animals on the sides and back that appear to be a brontosaurus and a mammoth. Although clear pictures were made of the object from several angles, the Granby Stone itself has long since vanished. Even the site where it was found has vanished, submerged by the waters of the Granby Reservoir.[141]

🐾🐾🐾

On the way I stopped at Casa Grande, the large ruins near the interstate between Tucson and Phoenix. The main portion of the ancient city is a huge, square ruin that was once an astronomical observatory, archaeologists now believe.

I parked the car and then stared at the impressive four-story structure which gives the site its name (*Casa Grande* means *Big House* in Spanish). According to the tourist literature, the site, like much of the Phoenix area, was built and occupied by the Hohokam culture. Archaeologist's conservative estimates place the building the of large structure at about A.D. 1350 and it was probably used for a hundred years until about A.D. 1450.

Says *America's Ancient Treasures*,[160] about Casa Grande: "It may have been a ceremonial center or fortress or both. Its massive walls, made from a special kind of clay, are not typical of Hohokam. The building is much more like those seen farther south, in Mexico. The usual Hohokam dwellings were separate, single-room houses, made of brush and mud.

"Throughout the semiarid Gila River Valley, the Hohokam managed to raise crops by irrigation. They built more than 250 miles of canals, which were between two and four feet wide and about two feet deep. Some can still be seen today."

The special kind of clay that they are referring to is a cement-like material called caliche. The builders shaped the mud by hand in a layer about two feet thick, let it dry and then added another layer. The site was named by a Spanish explorer-priest named Father Kino in 1694, who was quite impressed by the gigantic ruins.

What is not mentioned by most authors is that the Hohokam not only built a canal system, but it too was lined with caliche, a form of cement. This huge, ingenious canal system was used to irrigate the entire Gila River and Salt River drainage basin. The central desert, where Phoenix stands today, was once the center of great civilization that turned the desert into an agricultural paradise in which the desert literally bloomed with corn, beans, flowers and other plants. Naturally, fish, water fowl and other animals would be attracted to such an artificial paradise.

The early settlers in Arizona believed it to be desert land that had never been occupied by anyone except Apache Indians and a few Pueblo Indians in the north. Zuni Indians lived in seven pueblos to the east in New Mexico. Then, in the late 1800s, the ancient canal system was discovered. A fascinating map of the canals was published by the Phoenix Free Museum in June of 1903, and this map has been expanded on since.

Hohokam civilization is fascinating, though little is actually known about it. The heartland of this ancient culture is the very Phoenix area, where the Gila and Salt rivers meet. The large area of their culture stretched as far south as the Tucson area, as far north as Prescott and probably as far to the east as the headwaters of the rivers, the White River and Black Rivers flowing from the Mogollon Rim.

Like many ancient cultures, a map of the river systems gives a pretty good map of the civilization itself. In this case, the river flows into the Colorado delta and out into the Sea of Cortez, or Baja California sea. While it is never discussed in archaeological literature of this area, it can be assumed that some sort of naval traffic occurred at times along the west coast of Mexico up into the Hohokam area. Present day anthropologists generally considered the natives of the American Southwest as so primitive however, that they did not use large boats. Thus, we are left with the contrary evidence of a sophisticated canal building culture who were ignorant of sophisticated boat-building.

Contrary to Folsom's statement, the Hohokam did not live in mud and stick houses, but in large pueblo buildings, probably the forerunners to the Zuni and Hopi pueblos. At the time of the American colonization of Arizona, the Pima Indians who lived around Phoenix did in fact live in small mud and stick huts. This culture should not be confused with the Hohokam, however. Here it is easy to see how a grand civilization which had collapsed hundreds of years earlier was to be later confused with various wandering tribes who settled in the same area after the collapse.

Other evidence of the high state of civilization and intercity trade of the Hohokam is the various artifacts found in the area. The people did not dress in a buckskin loin cloth as the typical museum display in the west has most natives dressing, but in colorful cotton clothes and ponchos. They made beautiful pottery and artifacts out of sea shells (evidencing contact with the Pacific Ocean) and most importantly, they played the same ball game as was played by the Toltecs, Mayas, Zapotecs and other cultures much farther south in Central Mexico, Yucatan and Central America.

Many scholars argued there could have been no contact with other civilizations further south and therefore, the Hohokam could not have ball courts. They claimed the ball courts were ceremonial dancing platforms.[162] American Indians never went anywhere, they believe. When the "experts" cannot even see inter-American contact among cultures, it is easy to see why they like-wise take a dim view of inter-continental contacts.

Then a rubber ball, obviously coming from southern Mexico, was found at the Hohokam site near Toltec, Arizona. The ball was dated as having been manufactured between A.D. 900 and 1200. The rubber game ball is now at the Arizona State Museum in Phoenix. More than 100 Hohokam Ball Courts have now been identified. So here again we have a sophisticated culture with long links of trade emerging in the Southwest. These people irrigated the desert with cement lined canals, but the archaeologists still want them to live in primitive mud and stick huts, living off prickly pear cactus fruits. How unfortunate for present-day historians that the past refuses to cooperate with their theories!

The rubber ball that proves the relationship between Arizona and the Valley of Mexico and the jungles of Central America was discovered in a town named Toltec. Indeed, as these early settlers guessed, there was evidence to suggest that the Toltecs, or some off-shoot of their civilization had lived in Arizona. As Professor Covey suggests, the Hohokam Indians are really the Toltecs, or perhaps we should call them the Northern Toltecs.

One of the reasons in support of Cibola's having been located in the Four Corners area of Arizona and New Mexico is that this is also the region where rivers from the Gulf of Mexico meet rivers from the Sea of Cortez, or Baja Sea. Therefore, this area was navigable by traders through the river systems of the Rio Grande and the Colorado. This made the Cibola region something of a Panama Canal trading zone of the ancient world.

It is interesting to note is that some of these ancient canals were incorporated into the present-day canal system in use around Phoenix. Phoenix is named after the mythological bird that dies and then rises from its own ashes to another life, an ancient symbol of the cycle of life, death and reincarnation.

Modern-day Phoenix is aptly named, as it is indeed a city which has risen from the ashes of an earlier metropolis, a city of which we do not know its name. The name may have been Cibola.

An hour later, I pulled into Phoenix and called my old high school girlfriend. I hadn't seen Sarah in years. In the twelve years or more since we had been in school together, she had become a lawyer, had lived in various states in the west, and had now settled in Phoenix with some law firm. She invited me to spend the night at her townhouse.

We went out for dinner, and I told her about my visit to Casa Grande. "You know," I said, "the whole Phoenix area was once a great civilization. Sophisticated canals once intersected the entire Phoenix area, and huge buildings were situated throughout the Gila and Salt River valleys."

"Really?" she said. "What was the name of this ancient civilization? I thought that a bunch of primitive Indians named the Hohokam lived in central Arizona in prehistoric times."

"They did," I told her. "Have you ever heard of the legend of the Seven Cities of Cibola?"

"You mean the Seven Gold Cities of Cibola? Isn't that some legend about cities made of gold or something like that?" She lifted a lime flavored mineral water to lips, and ate some of the vegetarian spaghetti on her plate. She was as beautiful as ever, with long brown hair, dark eyebrows and an expression of intense interest whenever I talked.

"Well, the legends of Cibola got rather confusing," I said, "including the story of their being made of gold. In fact, the myth of the Seven Cities of Cibola was prevalent in Spain four hundred years before Columbus' voyages. The story was that in the eighth century seven Spanish bishops, fleeing the approach of invading Moors, fled from Oporto in Portugal westward across the ocean, where they founded seven cities. One Portuguese sailor insisted that he had seen this paradise, where even the sands were made of gold."

I told Sarah that with the conquest of Mexico, the Spanish discovered that the Aztecs had a legend of 'seven caves' to the north, where they and certain other tribes had their origin. This myth was reinforced, according to an account written in 1584 by Balthazar Obregon, when Cortez discovered among the possessions of Montezuma some codices, chronicles, and drawings that revealed that the origin of the Aztecs had been somewhere to the north of Mexico.[29]

Then, in 1530, Nuno de Guzman, President of New Spain, owned an Indian slave, his name was Tejo, and possibly he was a Teja Indian—the same tribe for which Texas is named. This Indian boy told Guzman that as a boy he had travelled with his father on trading ventures. He said that he had seen towns so large that he could compare them in size to Mexico City and its suburbs. There were seven of these towns, and together they were called the kingdom of Cibola. In these towns were whole rows of streets inhabited by gold and silver workers. The buildings were said to be encrusted with jewels. In order to reach these seven towns it was necessary to cross a desert for 40 days, where there was no vegetation except short grass about five inches in height. The direction to this kingdom was north.[29]

"What happened then, did the Spanish send out an expedition?" Sarah asked.

I told her how in 1536 four survivors of an expedition to conquer Florida, the ill-fated Narváez expedition that had begun eight years before, straggled into Mexico after having walked entirely from the Gulf of Mexico to the Baja Peninsula. They had been alternately slaves and guests of various tribes all over the southwest, mostly in Texas and Northern Mexico. In the end they were treated by various tribes as great healers, and they crossed the Rio Grande, arriving in Spanish territory with several hundred Indians following them like wandering prophets (here is an interesting parallel to the Quetzalcoatl myths). They were called 'Children of the Sun' and 'Children of the Sky.'

Guzman asked the survivors, four Spanish soldiers and a black Moorish slave named Esteban, if they knew about Cibola, the fabulous kingdom to the north. The four survivors answered that they had heard of a kingdom where metal was cast, but had not visited on their journeys. Guzman then got an expedition together and the black slave, Esteban, was to accompany the group as their guide.

The two principals of the expedition were Francisco Coronado and the priest Fray Marcos of Nizza, probably an Italian from Nice. Fray Marcos of Nizza had in fact been with Pizzaro in Peru and had witnessed the strangulation of the Inca Atahualpa after a ransom in gold had been paid to the Spanish.

Coronado led the expedition only as far as Corazones, a town in northern Mexico, where he ran out of food and had to return to Mexico City. Fray Marcos of Nizza continued on with a smaller body. Esteban went on ahead of Fray Marcos of Nizza, sending messages back to the main body. After 40 days, Esteban reached a city that was named by the Indians as Ahacus. It is believed by many historians to be the the Zuñi pueblo of Hawikuh, now 120 miles due west of Albuquerque.

Here the Indians had gold, silver, turquoise and the houses were made of stone. Unfortunately, when Esteban entered the city, the locals were not very pleased to see them, and after spending one night, the entire expedition was bludgeoned to death. One Indian escaped and made it back to Fray Marcos, where he told him what had happened.

Fray Marcos continued on to a place where he could see the pueblo. Fray Marcos later wrote that he could see the fine city where the people wore cotton clothes, used vessels of gold and silver, emeralds and turquoise studded the walls of the homes, and gold was in greater abundance than in Peru. He also said that there were mines in great abundance. He built a pile of stones, laid a cross in it and laid claim to all the seven cities of Cibola, christening the land the New Kingdom of St. Francis.

Immediately, an expedition of conquest was formed, with Coronado as the leader. He set out in 1540, crossed the Sonora desert and entered southeastern Arizona. He attacked the Zuñi pueblo of Hawikuh where a superior force of Zuñi awaited him. The mysterious fortune of the conquistadors prevailed, however, and although Coronado was twice knocked off his horse by stones, the conquistadors slaughtered hundreds of Zuñis, scattered more into the desert and lost less than half a dozen men. The city surrendered.

However, they were bitterly disappointed in this fabulous kingdom of Cibola. There was no gold, and as one of the Spanish later described it, "Cibola is built on a rock; this village is so small that in truth, there are many farms in New Spain that make a better appearance. It may contain two hundred warriors... The Seven Cities are seven little villages... Each has its own name and no single one is called Cibola, but together are called Cibola..."[161]

"So it turned out the Seven Cities of Cibola were actually the Zuñi pueblos?" asked Sarah.

"Well, there were in fact seven Zuñi pueblos. It was generally believed that Fray Marcos had fabricated much of the story. Yet, that may not be the case."

"What do you mean?" asked Sarah, finishing her spaghetti.

"Well, a Phoenix historian named Richard Petersen has written a book called *The Lost Cities of Cibola*.[161] In that book, he maintains that Cibola was not the Zuñi pueblos at all, but the huge cities of the Hohokam with their canals and ancient mines, right here in the Phoenix area. He believes that what Fray Marcos saw was the last vestiges of the Hohokam civilization and that Coronado missed these ancient cities, went too far to the east, ended up in New Mexico, and attacked the Zuñi. As Petersen points out, the Zuñis never called themselves or any of their cities 'Cibola'; they called themselves the Zuñi and continue to do so to this day. It may be that the Zuñi pueblos were the only surviving cities in the region, although Petersen believes that the Hohokam cities in the Phoenix area still existed until 1680, when they were destroyed in a comet catastrophe."

"A comet catastrophe?" It was getting late, and Sarah was ready to go. "So these lost cities of Cibola really existed but were destroyed by a comet. Is that what you think?"

"I don't know," I admitted, grabbing the check. "It seems more likely that Cibola was already in decline, starting from hundreds of years before that. It may be that a climatic change is what destroyed their civilization. I do tend to agree that Cibola was not the Zuñi pueblos, but was probably the huge civilization that existed here in central Arizona."

Sarah put her arm in mine as we walked for the door. "You and your lost cities," she said, poking me in the ribs. "At least this talk is a change from all the boring legal stuff I have to face all day. I thank you for that." As we walked to her car it suddenly occurred to me that maybe everyone wasn't interested in lost cities and ancient mysteries. Could that really be the case? Well, anything is possible, I guess.

🌹🌹🌹

The next morning I left Phoenix and headed east for Springerville, Arizona on the far border with New Mexico. Coronado and the lost cities of Cibola were still on my mind as I drove into the Superstition Mountains. Francisco Coronado (1510-1554) was unsuccessful in his lusty quest for gold and conquest. Cibola was but a ruined empire. He also searched for a great city known as Quivera, but failed in this as well. He continued on into Kansas, found no gold there, and returned to Mexico City.

The lost treasure of Cibola may have eluded Coronado, as it has many a treasure hunter over the last 400 years. Yet, it is well known that there were many mines in the "Cibola" region, and indeed, many a book on lost treasure has been filled with tales of lost gold mines, rooms full of gold, ancient artifacts and tunnel systems beneath the desert.

Several films in this vein have been made, including *McKenna's Gold,* starring Gregory Peck and a 50s Lone Ranger film based on the television series in which the Lone Ranger visits a lost Aztec city inside a mountain where an incredible vein of solid gold is found. *McKenna's Gold* is based on the true story of the Lost Adams Diggings, a fabulous vein of gold in a box canyon that "ran for miles." Apaches kept the canyon a secret and killed any prospectors who might ever enter.[253,254]

My trip took me through Globe, with some interesting ruins right in the middle of the mountain town. I continued northeast, driving farther up into the mountains up to the Apache Indian reservation. There were pine forests and wooded peaks everywhere, the desert had been left down below.

I pulled into Springerville late that afternoon to see the newest archaeological discovery in Arizona, the catacombs of Casa Malpais. Springerville is a town that can be missed if one blinks for a moment while driving through. In fact, I drove through the downtown several times before I realized that I had arrived there.

I parked my car next to movie theater at a crossroads where a bar, a hardware store, and the cinema are located. I could see a gas station down the road a bit.

"Excuse me," I asked an elderly man in jeans and cowboy hat standing near the theater, "but I'm looking for the downtown area of Springerville, can you help me find it?"

He spat on the dusty sidewalk below him and said, "Son, you're standing there. This *is* downtown Springerville."

I looked around with a bit of disappointment. "I thought there was a museum here, or something like that," I finally said.

He pointed up the street, past the hardware store, to a one story brick building with some large windows facing the road. "That's it right there. Just opened a few months ago."

In my best cowboy fashion, I moseyed down the street to the museum. There, several helpful and cheery women explained the recent archaeological discovery to me.

"It's all very exciting," said one, standing behind some empty glass counters that would eventually have some artifacts in them, or at least so I guessed. "What the archaeologists have discovered here at Springerville is unique in the entire southwest. Catacombs with mummies in them! We're all very excited, this will mean tourism. We could use some of that here in Springerville."

I signed their guest book, and read some of the newspaper clippings on the wall. One from the *Los Angeles Times-Washington Post* news service was worth quoting. It described how the archaeologist John Hohmann, now closely associated with the site, had rappelled down a rope into a fissure of basalt in July of 1990 and had discovered an intricate series of passages and rooms that had been modified by the Mogollon culture into underground tombs for the internment of the dead.

Said the article, "Hohmann had stumbled across a catacomb, an underground burial site composed of chambers and vaults. 'We don't expect to see such things in this region,' said archaeologist James Schoenwetter of Arizona State University in Tempe. 'To my knowledge, this is the only site north of Mexico that has catacombs.'

"The discovery is significant because information about how primitive cultures regard their dead sheds light on the groups' religious, social and cultural lives. In the case of the Mogollon and other prehistoric peoples of the Southwest, such information is virtually non-existant, Hohmann said.

"The fact that the Mogollon took such pains to bury their dead suggests a complex culture with a rich spiritual life, he added.

"Although Hohmann calls the burial area a catacomb, and dictionary definition support his terminology, some researchers are less comfortable with the title. 'What it conjures up in my mind is something on the order of the Christian tombs under Rome,' said archaeologist Bruce Donaldson of the U.S. Forestry Service in Springerville. The Christian catacombs required extensive excavations and feature masonry burial vaults, carved niches and elaborate stonework.

"The Mogollon burial ground is nowhere near as complex, Donaldson argued, and calling it a catacomb will evoke a distorted image.

"To a certain extent, Hohmann agrees. The Mogollon made only minor modification inside the catacombs—far less than the early Christians did. But the Mogollon invested a great deal of effort in constructing a vaulted ceiling over many of the fissures and building entryways that restrict access.

"'That's always been our focus,' Hohmann said, 'the amount of architectural work and energy that went into creating the man-made components over this fissure system, and not what was inside the chambers. Just how these chambers were created was an amazing fact to us (along with) the impressive amount of stonework and society effort that went into that creation.'

"The catacombs lie below a surface area of two to three acres. Some of the rooms are as much as 20 feet high and 30 feet long, while others are substantially smaller. Hohmann said that they contain hundreds of skeletons, but much of the contents have been removed by vandals and pot-hunters.

"Hohmann has neither photographed nor mapped the catacombs, and they are not open to the public—or for that matter, anyone else. He is doing his best to keep the locations of the entrances secret. 'We need to remember Native American religious concerns,' he said. 'We're not going to disturb those remains or anything that is in them in any way, shape or form,' he said.

"The discovery of the catacombs has brought new attention to the little-explored Casa Malpais, which now appears to have been a major trading or religious center built at the height of the Mogollon civilization. It is the largest and most recently occupied village constructed by the Mogollon, hunters and farmers who mysteriously

302

disappeared around 1400, perhaps as the result of a catastrophic drought.

"The site, at an altitude of 7,000 feet in the White Mountains near the New Mexico border, also features one of the largest kivas— a religious structure—in the Southwest and three types of American Indian architecture that are not normally found contemporaneously.

"Although Hohmann's excavations at Casa Malpais have barely scraped the surface, they are expected to provide new insight into the Mogollons' cultural sophistication and daily life.

"The Mogollon inhabited Casa Malpais for perhaps 150 years before moving on, most likely after disease and starvation had sharply reduced their numbers during a severe drought that baked the Southwest for more than a century.

"The most distinctive archaeological features are found on the upper-most terrace, which was completely walled in to restrict access. The Great Kiva is about 50 feet square and 10 feet high, constructed of closely fitted rocks and stones."

I put the article down and looked around. "Could you photocopy this for me?" I asked one of the women.

"Why certainly," she replied. I looked at more articles on the wall, and then viewed a short video tape on the discovery. The article was interesting, and the discovery of these burial catacombs was certainly of interest, even if the skeletons were only 500 years old or so.

The objections of the archaeologist Bruce Donaldson were curious. He seemed to be making a strong effort to reinforce the idea that the Mogollon were only one step removed from dwelling in the caves themselves. One can picture the familiar diorama in museums all over the Southwest, and America in fact, of stone-age men in loincloths, pounding out some deerskin with a rock clutched in one hand. What is amusing about this scene, one that can be viewed in countless museums, is that these people aren't early Neanderthal men living in caves a million years ago in Oldavai Gorge in Africa. These are "stone-age" hunters who lived in Arizona 500 years ago. We mustn't think of them as people capable of mummifying their dead, carving niches, using masonry or making elaborate stone vaults. That is something that happens in ancient Europe or Asia, not in in the American Southwest.

The fact is, and Donaldson as well as many trained archaeologists find it convenient to forget this, only a day or two walk away was the fantastic and sophisticated civilization of the Hohokam with their canals, ball courts, fine clothes made of cotton, gold and silver smithing, plus a trade in metals, feathers, turquoise and other artifacts that went well into Central America. Rubber balls found in central Arizona absolutely had to have come from the jungles of southern Mexico. These people, whom the Mogollon were no doubt associated with, were as sophisticated as any American culture. Sadly, many American archaeologists are so specialized

303

that they have never seen the huge, awesome cities in central Mexico, Guatemala or Honduras. They are also ignorant of the sophisticated mummies found in the desert of northern Chile that are dated as 11,000 years old.[57]

To these "experts," it is a sacrilege to even compare the primitive American Indian to the cultures and structures of the old world. Those who propose Old World contacts are quickly branded "racists" by the isolationists, yet these same isolationists refuse to admit that the civilizations of ancient Arizona were just as sophisticated as any in old Mexico or South America. They admit that the canals, ball courts, metallurgy and exotic trade items are there, but the people still lived in their mud and stick shacks with a loin cloth over their genitals and a piece of leather wrapped around the feet. Who wants to change the dioramas in museums across the United States?

I was taken out to the Casa Malpais site by one of the ladies who worked at the museum. It was a five minute drive from the downtown to the site, a basalt cliff near the northern edge of Springerville. There wasn't much to see, the low walls of the kiva, some large blocks of stone that had broken off the cliff. The fissures and passageways into the cliff, where the catacombs lie, could be seen, but they were unimpressive. As Hohmann had said, not even photographs exist yet of the skeletons inside the catacombs.

I would be heading the next day to the Painted Desert, the Petrified Forest and the Hopi Mesas, so I wondered where I would stay that night. I figured that I would camp out in the desert somewhere, but, since Springerville was the only town in the vicinity, I looked for a restaurant and something to do for the evening.

Walking down the mainstreet of Springerville, all of two blocks long, I checked the movie theater marquee, but I had already seen the film. Still, I might be able to bear watching it one more time... then I noticed a beer sign outside the building across the street. I peered in the window and could see a man and a woman sitting at a bar. It seemed like an odd place, I decided to go in.

It was one of the strangest places I had ever seen. Except for the bar in the center of the large room, it seemed more like a second-hand store crowded with furniture and western memorabilia for sale than a bar. A middle-aged man with a cowboy hat and his attractive, blonde, wife were sitting at the bar. Standing behind the bar was a tall, unshaven man with a wool hat pulled down over his ears. He looked more like a street person than a bartender.

All eyes were on me as I walked into the room and looked around wide-eyed. "Is this a bar?" I asked timidly, unsure of myself.

"Sure is," said the man in the wool hat behind the bar. "What'll you have?"

I took a stool next to the couple. "I'll have a beer," I replied. I looked around, there were western murals of cowboys rounding up cattle painted on the walls. Several pool-tables, juke boxes, pinball machines and various other unused gizmos scattered about the room, racks of second hand clothes, boots, hats and all sorts of junk that one might find in a Salvation Army Thrift Shop.

"This place looks more like a second-hand store than I bar," I commented in a friendly way.

"Yeah, the bar wasn't doing so good, and the town didn't have no second-hand store, so I decided to give it a try. I sold a bicycle last week." The tall, unshaven man wiped the bar as he spoke. I noticed a huge charcoal grill behind him and a sign about cooking steaks.

"Do you still serve dinner?" I asked.

"Hell no," he spat. "Stopped that years ago. Don't do much business around here anymore. I sell a few beers now and then, that's about all."

The other couple at the bar nodded and informed me that the place used to be a popular steak house and bar, but the town had slowed down a lot. There were a few other bars in town, this place had been slowly closing down over the last ten years.

"Cowboys used to come in here for steaks and drinks," lamented the bartender, who was also the owner. "Why, even John Wayne used to come in here," he said proudly, straightening up momentarily as he spoke the Duke's name. Yep, John Wayne used to own a ranch just west of town, him and his buddies used to come in here all the time. Those were the good old days."

I looked around the huge, empty bar. With a little imagination I could see all the tables full of customers, playing cards, drinking with the Duke, telling cowboy stories, eating their steaks and dancing to the twang of country music. Those days were definitely gone. Instead, a lone archaeologist and a local couple, obviously friends of the owner, sat at the bar nursing a couple of beers.

The couple suddenly got up to leave. "Thanks for the beer, Joe. We'll see you later... Probably stop in tomorrow after work."

"Right, see you," he called after them, wiping the bar in a sort of automatic reflex. We talked for a while as I sat there at the bar. I had a few more beers, and told him why I had come to Springerville.

"Yea, maybe this new archaeological find will breathe some life into this town. I want to get out, go back to Flagstaff where I'm from. I'm trying to sell this place."

He opened me another beer and I asked him how much he wanted to sell it for. Eyeing me as a potential buyer, he told me that he had it listed in some sort of national Real Estate magazine for a few hundred thousand dollars. "I'll bargain though. It's a great deal, I'll throw all this junk in with it." He motioned to the pool tables, juke boxes and things lying all over the room.

I nodded. There was something sad about this bar. It was sort of a ghost bar in a ghost town. At night I imagined that the ghosts of John Wayne and his cowboy buddies, along with some of the old cowgirls, still in their youthful prime, played cards and caroused here after midnight when the place was all locked up.

Springerville itself was something of a lost city. And deep beneath the strange town was an ancient catacomb system. Where did those ghosts play cards?

❀❀❀

I woke up the next morning with my sleeping bag covered with frost. My back ached from sleeping on the hard ground next to my truck. The sun was just starting to rise over the Mogollon Rim, a geological feature that sweeps around the northern portion of Arizona and is named after the Mogollon Indians.

I brushed off my sleeping bag and threw it in the back of the pickup. Moments later as I was cruising down the two lane blacktop towards the Petrified Forest and the Painted Desert.

I stopped at one of the gift shops at the entrance to the park and browsed around before heading into the park. According to park literature, the petrified forest was created some 180 to 200 million years ago in the so-called Triassic period. The area of the petrified forest was a great flood plain laced by many streams and swamps. Huge forests grew in the area, and various dinosaurs, massive amphibians and bizarre reptilian forms inhabited the huge swamps and forests.

Volcanoes added ash to the water, and as trees fell and were buried in the swamp, minerals in the water gradually replaced every cell in the wood until the entire log had become mineralized. What looks like a huge fallen log is a rock-hard mineralized tree with crystals of quartz and jasper coloring the ancient logs.

In later ages, these petrified logs were exposed by erosion, leaving a desert that is scattered with logs, many of them solid. So uniform are the segments of the broken logs that they often appear to have been sawed into pieces. Driving through the park, one stops at a museum, a crystal forest, an ancient house made of petrified logs, "newspaper rock" with its many petroglyphs and the stunningly beautiful Blue Mesa.

Perhaps the most interesting to me was a petroglyph etched onto a rock at the ancient Puerco Ruin site, where the foundations of an ancient city are still to be found. The petroglyph is of a gigantic "bird" biting the head off of a man. I stood on the trail at Puerco Ruin and looked at the strange petroglyph. Was it really a man? The bird had a huge beak. Was it a pterodactyl?

Later, at the museum at the far northern edge of the Painted Desert and Petrified Forest, I asked a ranger about that curious rock art.

"Oh, you mean this one?" the lady asked. She was tall and looked sharp in her Park Service Uniform. "We use that petroglyph on the papersacks that we put purchases in." She pulled out a brown paper bag, and there was the unusual petroglyph.

"What do you think that this a representation of?" I asked her.

She looked at the paper bag for a moment and then said, "Looks like a giant bird biting the head off a man, doesn't it? Those Indians

306

had quite an imagination, didn't they?"
I nodded, and bought a few books. Then, as an afterthought on my way out I stopped and asked her, "You haven't seen any pterodactyls around here, have you?"

Tunnels of the Southwest

I was later that same day at my mother's home in Sedona, a small, extremely picturesque town about 30 miles west of Flagstaff. It was good to see my mother again and have a nice home-cooked meal and a hot shower. Sedona was full of far out people with alternative ideas on everything, and I had fun visiting the many bookshops in town. I soon met a number of interesting people, and before I knew it, I was hearing strange tales of an ancient tunnel system in the Southwest.

I had heard of rumors of tunnels beneath Arizona, but I did not know much about them. However, because of my years of travel in South America, I was familiar with the legends of tunnels beneath the Andes. As I reported in my book *Lost Cities & Ancient Mysteries of South America,*[57] the gold-clad mummies of the ancient Inca Kings, and much of the treasure from the fabulous Sun Temple, are believed to still be hidden in the tunnels that run under Cuzco and the ruins of a megalithic fortress of Sacsayhuaman.

There are many stories, including one which tells of a treasure-hunter who went into the tunnels and wandered through the labyrinth for several days. One morning, about a week after the adventurer had vanished, a priest was conducting mass in the church of Santo Domingo, built on the ruins of the Incan Temple of the Sun. The priest and his congregation were suddenly amazed to hear sharp rappings from beneath the church's stone floor. Several worshipers crossed themselves and murmured about the devil. The priest quieted his congregation, then directed the removal of large stone slab from the floor. The group was astonished to see the treasure-hunter emerge with a bar of gold in each hand.[23, 43,57]

The Peruvian government got into the act of exploring these Cuzco tunnels, ostensibly for scientific purposes. The *Peruvian Seria Documental del Peru* describes an expedition undertaken by staff from Lima University in 1923. Accompanied by experienced speleologist, the party penetrated the trapezoid-shaped tunnels starting from a tunnel entrance at Cuzco.

They took measurements of the subterranean aperture and advanced in the direction of the coast. After a few days, members of the expedition at the entrance of the tunnel lost contact with the explorers inside, and no communication came for twelve days. Then a solitary, starving explorer returned to the entrance. His reports of an underground labyrinth of tunnels and deadly obstacles would make an Indiana Jones movie seem tame by comparison. His tale was so incredible that his colleagues declared him mad. To prevent further loss of life in the tunnels, the police dynamited the entrance.[60]

Stories of tunnels abound in Peru and other areas of South America. Many researchers believe that these tunnels run for hundreds of miles through the mountains, as far south as Chile, as far north as Ecuador or Columbia, as far to the east as the Amazon jungles!

As for North America, some historians believe that a similar set of tunnels exists in Arizona and New Mexico, if not Utah, Nevada and California. At the turn of the last century, while the American army was pursuing Geronimo around Arizona, he and his braves would ride into box canyons with the Calvary in hot pursuit. The Indians would literally vanish, leaving the U.S. Army totally mystified. A day or two later, it would be reported that Geronimo and his troops had suddenly turn up in Mexico, hundreds of miles distant.

This had happened not once, but several times. Is it possible that Geronimo was using a system of ancient tunnels that exist in the American southwest? Navajo Indians in New Mexico and Arizona have told me the same story—that certain members of their tribes know about these tunnels, but keep them secret.

Similarly, Christopher Columbus wrote that when he landed on the Caribbean island of Martinique, a story of tunnels was brought to his attention. The Caribe Indians told the Spaniards about the Amazon women who lived without men. Columbus and his crew were informed that these women warriors would hide in ancient subterranean tunnels if they were bothered by men. If their persistent suitors followed them into the tunnels, the Amazons cooled their passions with a flurry of arrows from their strong bows.[22, 57]

Other tunnels are said to exist in India, Tibet and other parts of Central Asia, in the Ahaggar Mountains of Algeria, and even in Europe and Britain.[16, 26, 27]

🌸🌸🌸

One day while while at my mother's house in Sedona, I was sitting at the kitchen table talking to a local resident, Richard Dannelly, a dowser and the author of a book about the vortex phenomenon around Sedona called *Sedona, Power Spot Vortex*.[164]

Richard was full of interesting information on Sedona and the rest of Arizona. "Have you ever heard about strange ruins and tunnels in the Superstition Mountains near Phoenix?" he asked me over a cup of tea.

I replied that I had heard stories of tunnels throughout the Southwest, but had not heard about ruins or tunnels in the Superstition Mountains.

"Well, it's a strange story," he began. "Some friends of mine had discovered a tunnel that goes underground for quite a distance in

308

the Superstition Mountains. Yet, every time they tried to explore the cave, a strange fear and feeling of dread would overtake the whole party, and they would always turn back. Then they went to a psychic here in Sedona, to ask him why this was happening. The psychic told them to go to a certain house here in Sedona, where they would meet a man who could take them into the tunnel without fear.

"They went straight to the house where this man was said to be, and discovered he was just that very day moving into the house. He was in fact carrying the first load of his things into the house from the driveway! They told him that a psychic had sent them to find him, whom they believed could help them explore the mysterious tunnel.

"The man agreed to help them, and after a few days they all drove down to Phoenix and to the entrance to the tunnel. With this man who had never been there before as their guide, they were able to penetrate further back into the tunnel—cave, or whatever, than ever before.

"After penetrating deep into the cave they came to cut stones and carvings in the rock. The remains of ancient structures and walls made out of well dressed rock were found. They then discovered at this place a spiral staircase built out of cut stones that descended down, down, down, into the earth.

"After some discussion, it was decided that their guide named by the psychic should descend the stairs by himself to see what was at the bottom. He did so, following the staircase into the deep bowels of the earth. After some time, he came to a large room with more cut stones. A gigantic rock-cut throne, big enough for a giant, or two people sitting together, was in the middle of the room.

"Artifacts were on the walls, though I don't know what they were. The man returned up the staircase and reported what he discovered. The others tried to convince him to return to the room and bring some of the artifacts back up, but the man refused. The team then left the tunnel, and today the entrance is still a secret."

"That's a fascinating story," I couldn't help say. "I wonder if it's true."

"I believe it," said Richard. "Though I admit that it comes to me second-hand. The man who had descended to the room has now moved away, and no one knows where he's gone. The others still live here around Sedona, I believe."

Incredible as it may seem, there is a great deal of historical evidence for such tunnels and ancient caches, both in the Superstition Mountains and in other areas of Arizona and New Mexico. In his book, *100 Tons of Gold*,[29] author David Chandler tells the long story of the huge treasure that once existed in Victorio Peak in western New Mexico, directly east of the Superstition Mountains.

Chandler's book is packed with tales of the lost cities of Cibola, lost treasure, Aztec gold, murder, sinister government involvement, and, tales of strange tunnels beneath western New Mexico.

In 1937 a half-Indian podiatrist named Doc Noss discovered a cache of Apache gold on what is now the White Sands Missile Range. It had been placed there by Apache Indians back to 1880 or earlier. Much of the gold may have been Aztec, while other portions were from the lost La Rue mine which the Spanish had worked a hundred years before. Much of the treasure was in the form of hundreds of stacked gold bars, plus other artifacts, such as swords, goblets, crowns, statues and other things.

Doc Noss was shot and killed by his partner Charlie Ryan in March of 1949. After that, the fate of the incredible treasure is unknown, although it is believed that the U.S. Military secretly took the gold in an illegal operation in 1961. Noss was known to have taken at least 88 bars of gold out of the hidden tunnels inside the mountain.

Because of an article published in the November, 1968 issue of *True Treasure* magazine there was renewed interest in the fabulous treasure, and a prospector named Harvey Snow was approached by three ranchers who lived in the area to the west of the Victorio Peak site. Snow had spent 25 years exploring the entire White Sands area, and the ranchers felt that Snow could lead them into the treasure area, by passing the Army patrols that guarded the missile range.

Snow believed that the treasure of Doc Noss was not at Victorio Peak, but on another peak, also on government property named Hard Scrabble Peak. A cowboy that Snow had met many years before had once told him of how he seen Doc Noss on Hard Scrabble Peak disappear into a secret cave on the mountain and later emerge with pack mules loaded with (presumably) gold. The cowboy had gone into the nearly invisible cave, found cut stairs going down underground and began to follow the stairs. They went deep underground, but the cowboy did not follow them to the bottom. He was very much afraid that Doc Noss would kill him, and he never returned to the cave.

Harvey Snow took the ranchers to Hard Scrabble Peak in late November of 1968. They searched the mountain for two days before running out of supplies. They then returned to the mountain with new supplies and were left there to search the southern face of the mountain. It was arranged that the ranchers would come back and get him in three days.

Snow's incredible story is then related by Chandler, "On the second day, I found the cave with the sloping steps. I went down the steps; down and down. I don't know how far. I estimated maybe thirteen hundred or fourteen hundred steps. the bottom step, the last one, was rounded at the bottom so that when you stepped on it, it would roll. It was tied to a bow and arrow with rawhide, but the rawhide had rotted away long before I got there."

Snow is describing an ingenious booby trap, apparently rigged by the Apaches, but possibly from some earlier culture. As someone stepped on the last stone of the stairway, he would trigger an arrow that was aimed at the step, thereby causing his own death. This may have been set up in 1880 at the time of the Apache chief Victorio's death.

Snow continues his story, "At the bottom you are in a big room. There is a stream of water running through. Now Noss described a cold stream, but this stream is hot. It has a copper and sulfur taste. It ran from east to west, toward the Jornada, and along what I assumed to be an old earthquake fault." The Jornada that Snow speaks of is the Jornada del Muerto, or "the dead man's route" in Spanish. The Jornada is a wide plain to the west of the White Sands Missile Range and is named after a German trader who was imprisoned by the Spanish in Sante Fe in 1670 on the charges of being a heretic and a necromancer. He escaped jail but died on the trail as he fled south, hence, "the dead man's route."[29]

Snow, now at the bottom of stairs was in a tunnel with a stream flowing through it. "I followed it, going from room to room. In many places I had to get down on my hands and knees, and in a few places on my belly. After that first room, where the steps come down, I came into another room. Here I found some things. I found small stacks — one of gold, one of copper, and one of silver.

"I figured I would come back for that and went on. I next came to a big room. Here there were a bunch of side tunnels running north and south. They were all natural, nothing man-made. Here where they intersected, they made a big W. I did not go down those north-south tunnels. I stayed with the stream, going west.

"At the far end of the main room I found some things I cannot tell you about. But I will tell you what happened next. I kept gong west, kneeling, crawling, and walking, hauling my little pack of food. I kept going through there for two days and two nights. I eventually followed that tunnel for fourteen miles.

"Where I was coming out was under the Jornada. That tunnel must not be far below the surface, because I could hear jets flying overhead, and when the train was traveling it sounded so near you thought it was in the tunnel with you.

"Finally, I felt some fresh air on my face and then I saw some light. The tunnel had been getting narrower and narrower all this time, and I figured I was about to the end of it. I came to the hole where the light was coming from and stuck my head through. I was standing in a hole covered by bushes and I was smack in the middle of the Jornada."[29]

Snow would not tell Chandler what was in the main room, whether it was bodies, or some strange artifacts. He did tell Chandler that he had subsequently made a "few trips" to the room where he found the small stacks and removed some of the metal bars.

Snow's story is fascinating and virtually unbelievable to most people. He walked for 14 miles in an underground tunnel. The 1,400 steps or so that he walked down to the subterranean river must have been a good 800 or 900 feet below the entrance. The tunnel was crossed in at least one spot by another tunnel running at a right angle to the one he was following.

The tunnel, which continued on past the spot where Snow exited the tunnel of the dry plain, the "Jornada," had an underground river flowing through it. Often, these underground rivers have beaches of gold at certain intervals in the tunnels. The subterranean river itself may have been a source for some of the gold.

And what was in the main room that Snow would not describe? Was he sworn to secrecy or was it something that was indescribable? It may have been bodies, including a recently murdered treasure hunter, or could it have been something that was from some ancient, forgotten civilization? Perhaps Harvey Snow could not tell what he had seen because he was afraid that no one would believe his story if he did mention it. His story is fantastic enough without embellishing it with further tales that would strain his credibility.

Underground rivers develop quite naturally, and they are known all over the planet. Cave exploring is fascinating, and early man at some point no doubt explored many caves and subterranean systems.

The search for precious metals, especially gold, has been happening on this planet for the past 50,000 years. Mines in southern Africa have been dated to 40,000 B.C.[58]

Some of the things that might have been in the main room, but which Snow was reluctant to describe, could have included such odd artifacts as large mummies, strange machinery, even strange light making machines.

For instance, Chandler mentions that the Hopi had a fascinating generator for making light which was made out of luminescent quartz. It consisted of a rectangular base of pure white-vein quartz with a groove in it and a bolster-shaped upper piece of the same material. Rapid friction by rubbing produced a strong glow in the dark, which was used to light the sacred kivas.

Says Chandler, The machine still worked perfectly when it was discovered by archaeologist Alfred Kidder in the Pecos ruins, as he reported in 1932. Archaeologist S.H. Ball remarked upon it, 'Here we have a perfected machine perhaps seven hundred years old; the first Indian to observe luminescence of quartz must have done so centuries earlier.'"[29]

Chandler goes on to say that similar "lightning machines" or "glow stones" have been found at several other localities in north-central New Mexico. Chandler also speaks of emeralds coming from these ancient mines that the Apache so fiercely guarded. Emeralds are not known to exist except in Colombia and Brazil.

Chandler is quoting from Stuart A. Northrop's *Minerals of New Mexico* (1959, University of New Mexico Press, Albuquerque) on both the existence of emerald mines and the quartz light machine that the ancient Indians used. These machines to generate light may still be being used by Hopi or other tribes, in secret ceremonies in their kivas.

312

Emerald mines, turquoise mines and a river of gold are a strong attraction to traders, and it is important to remember that the Gila River basin was a huge, sophisticated metropolis of artificial canals and gardens. A sophisticated buying public was near to the mines.

The emerald mines were apparently in the vicinity of Sante Fe, according to Northrop, but the location of these ancient mines remains a mystery. The ancient mines and massive gold cache at Victorio Peak and Hard Scrabble Peak, both in the Hembrillo Basin area, were constantly guarded by Apache war parties.

At one point, the Apache chief Victorio held off the American Calvary at the Hembrillo Basin spring for two days. It was unlike the Apache to stand and fight, since they used guerrilla tactics so well. The American Calvary, out of water, was fighting to get to the spring. Eventually the made it, but it was curious to them why the Apache had fought so hard over spring in the desert. The answer is that this spring, and the mountains in the immediate vicinity, was their secret headquarters.

And what a headquarters it was! Victorio Peak and Hard Scrabble Peak, as well as possibly Geronimo Peak, were all honeycombed with tunnels, caves and secret entrances. The Hard Scrabble Peak entrance led down a flight of hundreds of steps to an underground river. The last step was boobytrapped with a deadly arrow device. It is all like out of some 40s cliffhanger serial.

Just as incredibly, there was once a mural painted on a rock at Hembrillo Spring. This fascinating mural was blown up with six sticks of dynamite in 1973, probably because it was believed that the mural contained a map to the gold mine. Chandler alleges that the White Sands Military officers had something to do with it. Since the entire area of all of these peaks, and their underground tunnels lies on a special Military Reserve, the same reserve where the first Atomic Weapon was detonated at Alamagordo in July of 1945.

This mural, some 40 feet in length and 10 feet high, seemed to date from two different periods. The older, underlying mural has faded colors and shows two stick figures, wearing skirts and pointing at smaller stick figures. In association with it are a number of designs—suns, moons, snakes, and geometrical patterns usually associated with the Mogollon culture. Also depicted in this ancient painting is a mountain exploding. This may be a representative drawing of the eruption of the Black Peak volcano that has erupted periodically throughout history.

Painted on the same ledge, but not obliterating the prehistoric art, is a much more vivid, newer mural. Many colors were used—black, white, red, blue, yellow—and show quite clearly a giant figure of an Indian warrior leading smaller warriors in an attack on a wagon train. Between the warriors and the wagon train is a ghostlike object, taller than the giant warrior; a figure or object enveloped in an aura of light.

This mysterious figure could be Quetzalcoatl, though the presence of wagons seems to place this painting in the 1800s. The mysterious figure could also be the "Gray Ghost," a strange figure, tall of stature, who was seen in the mountains circa 1860. "He rode alone, and could never be approached." Eventually, while being pursued by U.S. Calvary, he was led to a secret tunnel by Apache braves, and so escaped the army and became a friend of the Apaches.[29]

The Gray Ghost stayed with the Apaches for some time, learning their language. He told the chief Victorio that he was a chief from toward the rising sun. The Apache princess Lozen fell in love with the Gray Ghost, and she never married afterwards, even after the Gray Ghost rode on to the west.

Quoting Kaywaykla, an Apache elder, "A strange wagon came through our land. Twelve men rode beside it as guards. There was also a driver, and with them an old woman. All spoke the language of old Mexico, but they were not Mexicans. Inside the wagon they carried a young woman—very beautiful. When they moved west, Gray Ghost followed."[29]

Gray Ghost was probably a Confederate Officer who had left on some mission of his own at the time of the defeat of the south. In 1868, the overthrow of Maximilian's empire in Mexico had occurred, and many French and Austrians were escaping from Mexico. The mysterious white woman in the coach was possibly a relative of Maximilian.

It seems unlikely, however, that the figured bathed in light on the Hembrillo Basin mural, now destroyed, was the Gray Ghost. Rather, he seems to be a spiritual prophet or messiah, something like a Quetzalcoatl-type messenger. Did Quetzalcoatl come here to Hembrillo Basin and the ancient gold mines at the time that he walked the Americas? Sadly, this great ancient work of art has been destroyed.

The gold that was at one time stored at Victorio Peak has been seized by the U.S. Government, particularly the Army and the C.I.A. The Army was known to have bulldozed the peak out, and even placed a steel door over the entrance to the mountain. The state of New Mexico was particularly interested in the treasure claims, because under State Law, the treasure belonged to them. The Army assured the state that there was no gold in Victorio Peak and never had been.

Never-the-less, Chandler shows that a top secret operation took place at White Sands Missile Range on August 10, 1961. On this date the Secret Service, with the help of certain Army personnel at the Range, recovered the gold, and moved it to various locations for various purposes. Former White House council John Dean told of C.I.A. operatives dealing with bars of gold in his book *Blind Ambition* (1976, Simon & Schuster, p.155): "Egil Krogh had described to me how, when he was bored with his deskwork, he had carried bars of gold bullion through Asia's 'Golden Triangle' in C.I.A. planes and bargained with drug chieftains." The gold bars used in these illegal, clandestined operations allegedly came from the tunnel system inside of Victorio Peak.[29]

🐙🐙🐙

Richard and I spent several afternoons in Sedona discussing the mysteries of Arizona. He had many a tale to tell, but I had a few of my own. I pulled out an old book to show Richard.

The book was Joseph Miller's *Arizona Cavalcade*[112] published in 1962 and an article from 1892 in the Phoenix *Herald*, is quoted under a chapter entitled *Royal Treasure?*

"This story may have to do with your strange tunnel in the Superstition Mountains," I told Richard.

The article is about a man named Andrew Pauly who claims to have discovered, while searching for some stolen horses, a "most peculiar appearance of the face of the rock in one of the remote recesses or clefts of the cliff up which I had gone looking for water, which gave me the impression of the work of some human hand. It looked like a small door cut in the rock and again skillfully closed by some dusty material. I was too thirsty to have any curiosity then, so I pulled on for the top of the range."

Andrew Pauly then returned to the place some years later, in 1892, believing that the sealed cave entrance was a door to treasure chamber, decided to return to the cave. Says the *Phoenix Herald*, "As was noted last week that he was about to go out in search of what he considered a very peculiar artificial opening in the rocks among the mountain which now prove to be not very remote from the orchard of the upper valley, Pauly started out with a prospector's outfit and succeeded in finding the object of his search, and furthermore, that it was a genuine piece of masonry in a cut opening in the solid rock and of such thickness and consistency that with a prospecting pick, hammer, and other tools, he was five days in making an opening though the cement and rock that packed the opening which is not now much larger than a man can crawl through.

"Pauly tells a wonderful story of his discovery in the chamber behind the barricade through which he has worked his way. He found a chamber apparently cut from solid rock not less than twenty by forty feet in dimensions and about ten feet in height. The floor was covered by seven immense skeletons of men who in life must have been not less than seven feet in height, and there was further evidence that they must have been warriors as the remains of what were copper shields, copper spear heads, and battle axes and other artifacts were found with the skeletons.

"A most interesting discovery was a small ornament, a crude amulet apparently, of gold, a metal that has never before been found in all the searches that have been made of the ancient Aztec mounds and ruins so plentifully distributed through this region of country. A yet more important and startling discovery was an opening at the farther end of the chamber also closed with what appears to be a sort of rude bronze door. So neatly and accurately filled into the solid rock that barring a jut of the rock over and at the sides of the door it might have grown there, so solid does it appear. It is about two by three feet in dimensions and of unknown thickness, but when struck sounds as though it either lay against solid rock or was of great thickness.

"The mystery of this second discovery now occupies Pauly's attention and he provided himself with the necessary means to remove the door or heavy bronze plate set in the side of the cave, or whatever it may be. As we have above indicated, the place may prove the treasure house of the Aztec tribes or it may prove nothing more than has been found, but at any rate the discovery is a startling and interesting one. Pauly, who works entirely alone, so far, traveled to town on foot yesterday, and guards his treasure with the greatest secrecy so far as its location is concerned, though he talked very freely with a *Herald* representative as to what he had found and what he thinks he may find which he believes to be nothing less than the treasure vault of an ancient royalty."[112]

Nothing more was ever heard about this astonishing find. This is typical, however, and when large treasures have been located, typically the finder does not wish publicity. If there is anything unusual about Pauly, it is that he is too talkative to the press, though he was a former newspaper man himself.

"At any rate," I said to Richard, "nothing more of this story was ever mentioned again. The location is apparently in the Superstition Mountains, just east of Phoenix. Is it possible that the strange cave which the psychics from Sedona had entered is the same as this ancient treasure vault guarded by the skeletons of seven foot giants?"

"Well, maybe this is the same place," Richard admitted. "It seems strange that such a story and discovery would be kept secret."

"If you think that story is wild, here is another story, one even more incredible, a story that points to an astonishing archaeological cover-up." Richard sat up straight in his chair, and with that, I began the incredible story of an Egyptian city in the Grand Canyon.

❀❀❀

The Egyptian City of the Grand Canyon

Egyptians in Arizona? An Egyptian tomb in the Grand Canyon, something similar to the Valley of Kings in Luxor, Egypt? Yet in an article published on the front page of the *Phoenix Gazette* on April 5, 1909 claimed that just such an Egyptian rock-cut cave was found!

The article in the Phoenix gazette is quoted in Joseph Miller's book *Arizona Cavalcade*[112] published in 1962 under a chapter entitled Citadel of the Grand Canyon.

The article, dated April 5, 1909, starts with four headlines, "Explorations in Grand Canyon," "Mysteries of Immense Rich

Cavern Being Brought to Light," "JORDAN IS ENTHUSED," and "Remarkable Finds Indicate Ancient People Migrated From Orient."[165] The story then continued (quoted here in full): "The latest news of the progress of the explorations of what is now regarded by scientists as not only the oldest archaeological discovery in the United States, but one of the most valuable in the world, which was mentioned some time ago in the *Gazette,* was brought to the city by G. E. Kinkaid, the explorer who found this great underground citadel of the Grand Canyon during a trip from Green River, Wyoming, down the Colorado river, in a wooden boat, to Yuma, several months ago.

"According to the story related to the *Gazette,* the archaeologists of the Smithsonian Institute, which is financing the explorations, have made discoveries which almost conclusively prove that the race which inhabited this mysterious cavern, hewn in solid rock by human hands, was of oriental origin, possibly from Egypt, tracing back to Rameses. If their theories are born out by the translation of the tablets engraved with hieroglyphics, the mystery of the prehistoric peoples of North America, their ancient arts, who they were and whence they came, will be solved. Egypt and the Nile, and Arizona and the Colorado will be linked by a historical chain running back to ages which stagger the wildest fancy of the fictionist.

"Under the direction of Professor S.A. Jordan, the Smithsonian is now pursuing the most thorough explorations, which will be continued until the last link in the chain is forged. Nearly a mile underground, about 1480 feet below the surface, the long main passage has been delved into, to find another mammoth chamber from which radiates scores of passageways, like the spokes of a wheel. Several hundred rooms have been discovered, reached by passageways running from the main passage, one of them having been explored for 854 feet and another 634 feet. The recent finds include articles which have never been known as native to this country, and doubtless they had their origin in the orient. War weapons, copper instruments, sharp-edged and hard as steel, indicate the high state of civilization reached by these strange people. So interested have the scientists become that preparations are being made to equip the camp for extensive studies, and the force will be increased to thirty or forty persons.

"Before going further into the cavern, better facilities for lighting will have to be installed, for the darkness is dense and quite impenetrable for the average flashlight. In order to avoid being lost, wires are being strung from the entrance to all passageways leading directly to large chambers. How far this cavern extends no one can guess, but it is now the belief of many that what has already been explored is merely the "barracks", to use an American term, for the soldiers, and that far into the underworld will be found the main communal dwellings of the families. The perfect ventilation of the cavern, the steady draught that blows through, indicates that it has another outlet to the surface.

317

"Kinkaid was the first white man born in Idaho and has been an explorer and hunter all his life, thirty years having been in the service of the Smithsonian. Even briefly recounted, his history sounds fabulous, almost grotesque:

"First, I would impress that the cavern is nearly inaccessible. The entrance is 1,486 feet down the sheer canyon wall. It is located on government land and no visitor will be allowed there under penalty of trespass. The scientists wish to work unmolested, without fear of the archaeological discoveries being disturbed by curio or relic hunters. A trip there would be fruitless, and the visitor would be sent on his way. The story of how I found the cavern has been related, but in a paragraph: I was journeying down the Colorado river in a boat, alone, looking for mineral. Some forty-two miles up the river from the El Tovar Crystal canyon, I saw on the east wall, stains in the sedimentary formation about 2,000 feet above the river bed. There was no trail to this point, but I finally reached it with great difficulty. Above a shelf which hid it from view from the river, was the mouth of the cave. There are steps leading from this entrance some thirty yards to what was, at the time the cavern was inhabited, the level of the river. When I saw the chisel marks on the wall inside the entrance, I became interested, securing my gun and went in. During that trip I went back several hundred feet along the main passage, till I came to the crypt in which I discovered the mummies. One of these I stood up and photographed by flashlight. I gathered a number of relics, which I carried down the Colorado to Yuma, from whence I shipped them to Washington with details of the discovery. Following this, the explorations were undertaken.

"The main passageway is about 12 feet wide, narrowing to nine feet toward the farther end. About 57 feet from the entrance, the first side-passages branch off to the right and left, along which, on both sides, are a number of rooms about the size of ordinary living rooms of today, though some are 30 by 40 feet square. These are entered by oval-shaped doors and are ventilated by round air spaces through the walls into the passages. The walls are about three feet six inches in thickness. The passages are chiseled or hewn as straight as could be laid out by an engineer. The ceilings of many of the rooms converge to a center. The side-passages near the entrance run at a sharp angle from the main hall, but toward the rear they gradually reach a right angle in direction.

"Over a hundred feet from the entrance is the cross-hall, several hundred feet long, in which are found the idol, or image, of the people's god, sitting cross-legged, with a lotus flower or lily in each hand. The cast of the face is oriental, and the carving shows a skillful hand, and the entire is remarkably well preserved, as is everything in this cavern. The idol most resembles Buddha, though the scientists are not certain as to what religious worship it represents. Taking into consideration everything found thus far, it is possible that this worship most resembles the ancient people of Thibet. Surrounding this idol are smaller images, some very beautiful in form; others crooked-necked and distorted shapes, symbolical, probably, of good and evil. There are two large cactus with protruding arms, one on each side of the dais on which the god squats. All this is carved out of hard rock resembling marble. In the opposite corner of this cross-hall were found tools of all descriptions, made of copper. These people undoubtedly knew the lost art of hardening this metal, which has been sought by chemists for centuries without result. On a bench running around the workroom was some charcoal and other material probably used in the process. There is also slag and stuff similar to matte, showing that these ancients smelted ores, but so far no trace of where or how this was done has been discovered, nor the origin of the ore.

"Among the other finds are vases or urns and cups of copper and gold, made very artistic in design. The pottery work includes enameled ware and glazed vessels. Another passageway leads to granaries such as are found in the oriental temples. They contain seeds of various kinds. One very large storehouse has not yet been entered, as it is twelve feet high and can be reached only from above. Two copper hooks extend on the edge, which indicates that some sort of ladder was attached. These granaries are rounded, as the materials of which they are constructed, I think, is a very hard cement. A gray metal is also found in this cavern, which puzzles the scientists, for its identity has not been established. It resembles platinum. Strewn promiscuously over the floor everywhere are what people call 'cats eyes,' a yellow stone of no great value. Each one is engraved with the head of the Malay type.

"On all the urns, or walls over doorways, and tablets of stone which were found by the the image are the mysterious hieroglyphics, the key to which the Smithsonian Institute hopes yet to discover. The engraving on the tablets probably has something to do with the religion of the people. Similar hieroglyphics have been found in southern Arizona. Among the pictorial writings, only two animals are found. One is of prehistoric type.

"The tomb or crypt in which the mummies were found is one of the largest of the chambers, the walls slanting back at an angle of about 35 degrees. One these are tiers of mummies, each one occupying a separate hewn shelf. At the head of each is a small bench, on which is found copper cups and pieces of broken swords. Some of the mummies are covered with clay, and all are wrapped in a bark fabric. The urns or cups on the lower tiers are crude, while as the higher shelves are reached the urns are finer in design, showing a later stage of civilization. It is worthy of note that all the mummies examined so far have proved to be male, no children or females being buried here. This leads to the belief that this exterior section was the warriors' barracks.

"Among the discoveries no bones of animals have been found, no skins, no clothing now bedding. Many of the rooms are bare but for water vessels. One room, about 40 by 700 feet, was probably the main dining hall, for cooking utensils are found here. What these

319

people lived on   is a problem, though it is presumed that they came south in the winter and farmed in the valleys, going back north in the summer. Upwards of 50,000 people could have lived in the caverns comfortably. One theory is that the present Indian tribes found in Arizona are descendants of the serfs or slaves of the people which inhabited the cave. Undoubtedly a good many thousands of years before the Christian era a people lived here which reached a high stage of civilization. The chronology of human history is full of gaps. Professor Jordan is much enthused over the discoveries and believes that the find will prove of incalculable value in archaeological work.

"One thing I have not spoken of, may be of interest. There is one chamber the passageway to which is not ventilated, and when we approached it a deadly, snaky smell struck us. Our lights would not penetrate the gloom, and until stronger ones are available we will not know what the chamber contains. Some say snakes, but others boo-hoo this idea and think it may contain a deadly gas or chemicals used by the ancients. No sounds are heard, but it smells snaky just the same. The whole underground installation gives one of shaky nerves the creeps. The gloom is like a weight on one's shoulders, and our flashlights and candles only make the darkness blacker. Imagination can revel in conjectures and ungodly day-dreams back through the ages that have elapsed till the mind reels dizzily in space.

"In connection with this story, it is notable that among the Hopi Indians the tradition is told that their ancestors once lived in an underworld in the Grand Canyon till dissension arose between the good and the bad, the people of one heart and the people of two hearts. Machetto, who was their chief, counseled them to leave the underworld, but there was no way out. The chief then caused a tree to grow up and pierce the roof of the underworld, and then the people of one heart climbed out. They tarried by Paisisvai (Red River), which is the Colorado, and grew grain and corn. They sent out a message to the Temple of the Sun, asking the blessing of peace, good will and rain for the people of one heart. That messenger never returned, but today at the Hopi villages at sundown can be seen the old men of the tribe out on the housetops gazing toward the sun, looking for the messenger. When he returns, their lands and ancient dwelling place will be restored to them. That is the tradition. Among the engravings of animals in the cave is seen the image of a heart over the spot where it is located. The legend was learned by W. E. Rollins, the artist, during a year spent with the Hopi Indians. There are two theories of the origin of the Egyptians. One is that they came from Asia; another that the racial cradle was in the upper Nile region. Heeren, an Egyptologist, believed in the Indian origin of the Egyptians. The discoveries in the Grand Canyon may throw further light on human evolution and prehistoric ages."[112,165]

"That's an amazing story," said Richard.

"How do you know that it is real. I'll bet it was fabricated by the author of that book. It sounds phony."

"We should get the actual newspaper article and check the authenticity of Miller's book," I agreed.

Richard then made the two hour trip to Phoenix and found the article on microfilm at the Phoenix Public Library. After returning to my mother's home in Sedona, we looked at it on the kitchen table.

"My God, it *is* a real article!" my mother exclaimed, lighting a cigarette and taking a puff. "Maybe the Smithsonian is covering up this find."

We gazed at the actual *Gazette* article, which most certainly did appear on the front page of the April 5, 1909 edition of the *Phoenix Gazette*. There it was in black and white. We could only ask ourselves, was it a joke or hoax? Or an actual expedition? If this had been an actual expedition, why was the discovery suppressed, with no one knowing of this discovery today?

A few choice passages from the text bear repeating: The tunnel-vault system goes for "nearly a mile underground... Several hundred rooms have been discovered, ... The recent finds include articles which have never been known as native to this country... War weapons, copper instruments, sharp-edged and hard as steel, indicate the high state of civilization reached by these strange people."

Furthermore, "the cavern is nearly inaccessible. The entrance is 1,486 feet down the sheer canyon wall. It is located on government land and no visitor will be allowed there under penalty of trespass." The vaults are located some "forty-two miles up the river from the El Tovar Crystal canyon...I saw on the east wall, stains in the sedimentary formation about 2,000 feet above the river bed. There was no trail to this point, but I finally reached it with great difficulty. Above a shelf which hid it from view from the river, was the mouth of the cave. There are steps leading from this entrance some thirty yards to what was, at the time the cavern was inhabited, the level of the river...There are steps leading from this entrance some thirty yards to what was, at the time the cavern was inhabited, the level of the river."

In other words, the explorer, G.E. Kinkaid, discovered the vaults about 2,000 feet above the present level of the river, where steps led some 30 yards to the *former* level of the river. That means that the Colorado River, by Kinkaid's testimony, has cut some 1,910 feet in the canyon since the time of the construction of the vaults. Normal geological time would place human construction on the canyon walls at this level at easily tens of thousands if not millions of years ago. Kinkaid's testimony actually is evidence that much of the Grand Canyon was cut in a very short time during some cataclysmic earth change, rather than the slow, steady millions of years claimed by Uniformitarian geologists. It is possible that a huge lake was drained down the Grand Canyon, thus causing the fast erosion.

In investigating this incredible story, any information on the two leading figures in the discovery, G.E. Kinkaid and Professor S.A.

Jordan would be invaluable. Did these two men exist? I would appreciate any information on these two men, or their alleged discoveries, that any of my readers may have.

While it cannot be discounted that the entire story is an elaborate newspaper hoax, the fact that it is on the front page, names the prestigious Smithsonian Institution, and gives a highly detailed story that goes on for several pages, lends a great deal to its credibility. What appears to be going on in this case is that the Smithsonian Institution is covering up what is an archaeological discovery of great importance, and radically changes the current views that there was no transoceanic contact in Pre-Columbian times, and that all American Indians, on both continents, are descended from ice age explorers who came across the Bering Straits.

Richard and I, faced with actual *Arizona Gazette*[165] article, decided to make a quick call to the Smithsonian in Washington D.C., though there was little chance of getting any real information. After speaking briefly to an operator, we were transferred to a Smithsonian Staff archaeologist, and a woman's voice came on the phone and identified herself.

I told her that I was investigating a story from a 1909 Phoenix newspaper article about the Smithsonian Institution's having excavated rock cut vaults in the Grand Canyon where Egyptian artifacts had been discovered, and whether the Smithsonian Institution could give me any more information on the subject.

"Well, the first thing I can tell you, before we go any further," she said, her voice polite, but a bit sharp, "is that no Egyptian artifacts of any kind have ever been found in North or South America. Therefore, since no Egyptians artifacts have ever been found in North America, I can tell you that the Smithsonian Institution has never been involved in any such excavations." She was quite helpful and polite, but in the end, knew nothing.

"Thank you for your time, madam," I said politely, and hung up.

I told Richard what she had said, and his response was, "Well, she wouldn't know about some discoveries in 1909. Since she is no doubt educated in the prevailing Isolationist dogma that no one came to America before Columbus, she probably genuinely believes that the finding of Egyptian artifacts would be ridiculous. Still, it is incredible to believe that the Smithsonian Institution, the bastion of America's scientific knowledge, would deliberately suppress such an important find."

Is the idea that ancient Egyptians came to the Arizona area in the ancient past so objectionable and preposterous that it must be covered up? Perhaps the Smithsonian Institution is more interested in maintaining the status quo then rocking the boat with astonishing new discoveries that totally overturn the previously accepted academic teachings.

Though the idea of the Smithsonian's covering up a valuable archaeological find is difficult to accept for some, there is, sadly, a great deal of evidence to suggest that the Smithsonian Institution has knowingly covered up and "lost" important archaeological relics. The *Stonewatch Newsletter* of the Gungywamp Society in Connecticut, which researches megalithic sites in New England, had a curious story in their Winter, 1992 issue (Vol.10, No.3) about some stone coffins discovered in 1892 in Alabama which were sent to the Smithsonian Institution and then "lost." According to the newsletter, the archaeologist Frederick J. Pohl wrote an intriguing letter on March 26, 1950 to the late Dr. T.C. Lethbridge, a British archaeologist.

The letter from Pohl stated, "A professor of geology sent me a reprint (of the) Smithsonian Institute *'The Crumf Burial Cave'* by Frank Burns, U.S. Geological Survey, from the report of the U.S. National Museum for 1892, pp 451-454, 1894. In the Crumf Cave, southern branch of the Warrior River, in Murphy's Valley, Blount County, Alabama [accessible from Mobile Bay by river, were coffins of wood hollowed out by fire, aided by stone or copper chisels. Eight of these coffins were taken to the Smithsonian. They were about 7 1/2' long, 14" to 18" wide, 6" to 7" deep. Lids open.

"I wrote recently to the Smithsonian, and received reply March 11th from F.M. Setzler, Head Curator of Department of Anthropology. (He said) 'We have not been able to find the specimens in our collections, though records show that they were received.'

"Thomas Wilson's comment in the *Reprint*, to the effect that Indians in North America never used coffin burials, as Europeans did, 'is all the scientific opinion that was ever offered on this material.'

"It was implied, if not stated in the *Reprint*, that burials in Crumf Cave were ancient... very old, comparable to Bronze Age... Denmark(?). This all seems to be another instance of possible pre-Columbian evidence neglected and lost."

The *Stonewatch Newsletter* than goes on to say that they had also contacted the Smithsonian for more information in December of 1991, but had so far received no reply from the Smithsonian.

Ivan T. Sanderson once related a curious story about a letter he received regarding an engineer who was stationed on the Aleutian island of Shemya during World War II. While building an airstrip, his crew bulldozed a group of hills and discovered under several sedimentary layers what appeared to be human remains. The Alaskan mound was in fact a graveyard of gigantic human remains, consisting of crania and long leg bones.

The crania measured from 22 to 24 inches from base to crown. Since an adult skull normally measures about eight inches from back to front, such a large crania would imply an immense size for a normally proportioned human. Furthermore, every skull was said to have been neatly trepanned (a process of cutting a hole in the upper portion of the skull).[50]

In fact, the habit of flattening the skull of an infant and forcing it to grow in an elongated shape was a practice used by ancient

Peruvians, the Mayas, and the Flathead Indians of Montana. Sanderson tried to gather further proof, eventually receiving a letter from another member of the unit who confirmed the report. The letters both indicated that the Smithsonian Institute had collected the remains, yet nothing else was heard. Sanderson seemed convinced that the Smithsonian Institute had received the bizarre relics, but wondered why they would not release the data. To quote him, "...is it that these people cannot face rewriting all the text books?"[50]

It is like the last scene in the popular film *Raiders of the Lost Ark* in which an important historical artifact, the Ark of the Covenant from the Temple in Jerusalem, is locked in a crate and kept in the back of some giant warehouse where no one will ever hear of it again, thus ensuring that no history books will have to be rewritten no history or anthropology professor will have to revise the lecture that he has been giving for the last 40 years! Incredibly, in the 1970s a documentary was shown on television in which a former Smithsonian security guard related how he had seen artifacts from Mount Ararat in Turkey alleged to be from a gigantic ship high on top of the mountain. The Smithsonian had undertaken the expedition in 1969 he claimed, but the artifacts were suppressed and never released to the public.

Here we see how a lost "Ark" may be truly locked away in the depths of the Smithsonian! Similarly, it is frequently claimed that the Vatican in Rome has a vast treasure trove beneath it in which fantastic artifacts and books from the past are kept—in complete secret of course!

In an effort to find out where this vault with mummies and artifacts might be located, we went down to my mom's bookstore and got a hiker's map of the Grand Canyon. Pouring over the map, I was suddenly shocked to see that much of the area on the north side of the canyon had Egyptian names. The area around Ninety-four Mile Creek and Trinity Creek had areas (rock formations, apparently) with names like Tower of Set, Tower of Ra, Horus Temple, Osiris Temple, and Isis Temple. In the Haunted Canyon area were such names as the Cheops Pyramid, the Buddha Cloister, Buddha Temple, Manu Temple and Shiva Temple. Was there any relationship between these places and the alleged Egyptian discoveries in the Grand Canyon?

We called a State archaeologist at the Grand Canyon, and were told by the female voice on the phone that the early explorers had just liked Egyptian and Hindu names, but that it was true that this area was off limits to hikers or other visitors, "because of dangerous caves."

Indeed, this entire area with the Egyptian and Hindu place names in the Grand Canyon is a forbidden zone, no one is allowed into this large area.

"That's got to be the place where these vaults are," said Richard, leaning over the map. "Why else would it have these Egyptian names?"

I looked at the map and mused, "Wouldn't it be interesting if the explorer who gave this part of the Grand Canyon these Egyptian names was named Kinkaid?" Richard nodded.

Despite the many thousands of tourists to the Grand Canyon each year, the lofty walls and spectacular buttes of this natural wonder still held many secrets which were not yet revealed to the public at large.

🐾🐾🐾

The Flagstaff area of Northern Arizona was the scene of an unusual archaeological find that ultimately culminated in the writing of the book *Psychic Archaeology*.[160] Jeffrey Goodman, a Tucson oil company executive who was interested in archaeology, decided to try and prove that mankind had been in North America for a longer period than 16,000 years, as the traditional archaeologists had always maintained. He felt that he could find evidence of human habitation in his home state of Arizona, if he only knew where to look.

Goodman consulted with the well-known psychic from Oregon, Aron Abrahamsen, who offered him his clairvoyant advice on places in Arizona where Goodman would find archaeological evidence of ancient civilization in Arizona. Abrahamsen told Goodman that a dry river bed in the San Francisco Peaks outside of Flagstaff was a place where he would find evidence of ancient human occupation.

Even though no archaeological finds had ever been found in the area, Goodman went ahead with his experiment to find a lost civilization in the area. Goodman also asked Abrahamsen to to predict that sort of geological formations that they would discover in their dig.

Goodman dug where the psychic had said, and was able to unearth artifacts beneath the dry river bed that were at least 20,000 years old. Abrahamsen correctly identified many of the geological formations that they would find, even though two local geologists had scoffed at Abrahamsen's various geological predictions. According to Goodman, in the shaft that was dug at the "Flagstaff Dig," an average of 78% of Abrahamsen's predictions were correct!

At a depth of 22 feet the team hit human artifacts that were dated at 100,000 years old, just as Abrahamsen had predicted. They discovered a number of scrapers and flaked blades that were authenticated as man-made artifacts. According to Abrahamsen, this site was an outpost of the ancient continent of Mu going back several hundred thousand years.

Goodman was not only impressed by Abrahamsen's psychic ability and the discoveries they made, but also by the similarity of the evidence that they had discovered to the mythology of the Hopi tribe just to the north of Flagstaff. Hopi tradition teaches that three worlds existed prior to the one in which we now live. Legend says that a very long time ago, in the first world, their ancestors came onto this continent from islands across the sea. The first world was destroyed by fire, the second world was destroyed by ice and the third world was destroyed by water. We are now living in the fourth world.

These four different worlds of the Hopi existed in the area of Northern Arizona Goodman's dig uncovered archaeological evidence that vindicated the Hopi mythology—or at least Goodman thought so.

An interesting legend that has been reported about the Hopi is that of a Dark Star that will appear soon in the sky. This Dark Star will herald the end of the Fourth World, or Fourth Sun. The Hopi, like the Aztecs and Toltecs, divided the periods between catastrophes by "Suns" with which they named each epoch. The was the Sun of Water, the Sun of Earth, the Sun of Wind, and our current age, the Sun of Fire.

The end of the Sun of Fire will also be indicated by an unusual blue flower that will bloom in the desert. According to tribal reports, a strange blue flower, hitherto unknown, has been found in the desert regions of New Mexico.

🐾🐾🐾

It had been fun staying in Sedona, seeing the vortex areas, and staying with my mother for a while. But I had to head east, into the Heartland of America, an area I had never explored before. I gave mom and a hug and packed my car. She gave me a special picnic bag with sandwiches, cookies, and nuts to eat on the trip, plus some passion-fruit sodas.

As I headed out of Sedona up Oak Creek Canyon toward Flagstaff, little did I know what new startling finds I was to discover. Sometimes Arizona seemed like another planet; pterodactyls, lost cities, gold treasure, weird tunnels and ancient ruins. It all seemed like a fantasy movie from the 50s with lost continents, invading armies, horrific cults, living dinosaurs and fantastic lost treasure! Maybe it was all that—and more. With the sunset in front of me I steered my old pickup down the road and into the desert ahead.

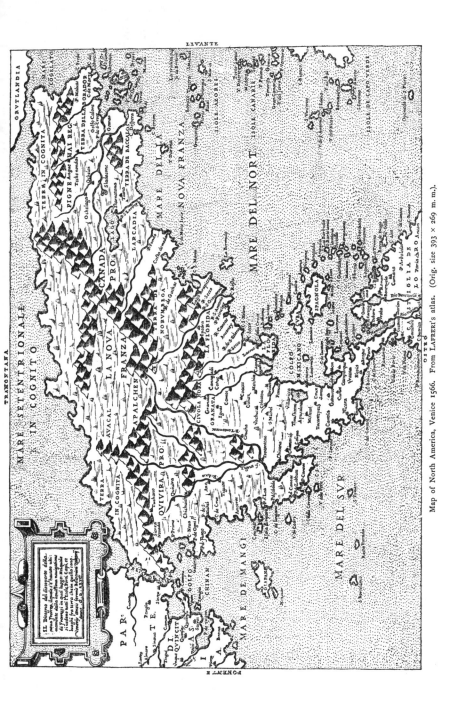

Map of North America, Venice 1566. From LAFRERI's atlas. (Orig. size 393 × 269 m.m.).

A pteradactyl-type flying lizard. Though believed to be extinct, reports of them continue to this day.

Above: The giant bird petroglyph from the Petrified Forest in Arizona. **Right:** A similar type of drawing, this one from Catal Hüyük in Turkey, showing a giant bird eating a man. American Indians had many legends of giant birds.

Above: A Navajo sand painting of a Thunderbird. **Below:** A Thunderbird depicted on a Pueblo painted dish from Kechipan, New Mexico.

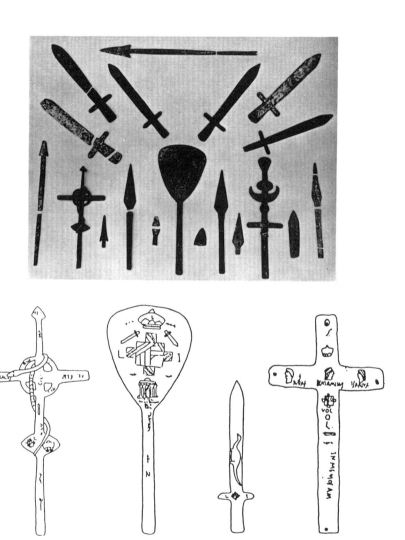

...rt of the collection of Roman artifacts that was excavated near Tucson, Arizona in ...24. The lower drawings show the detail on some of the lead and copper crosses and ...ords, showing Latin and Hebrew lettering. A dinosaur is clearly engraved on one of ...e swords.

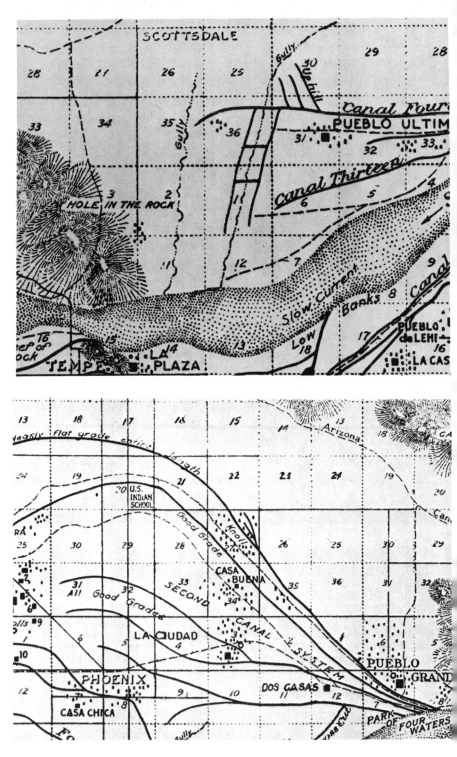

Omar Turney's 1922 map of the various canal systems around Phoenix

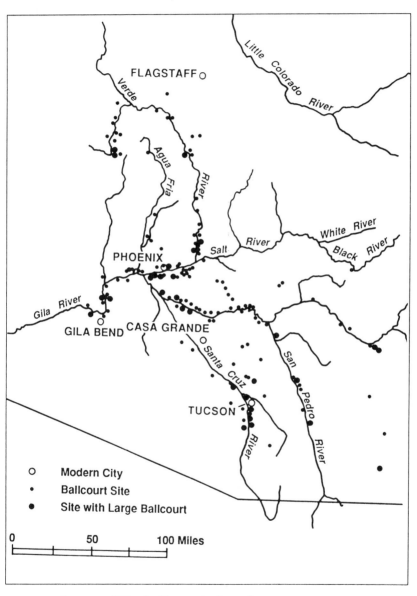

A map of the ball courts found in Arizona.

A Hohokam ball court in Arizona. Just as in Mexico and Central America, games using rubber balls were as popular in Arizona as anywhere else.

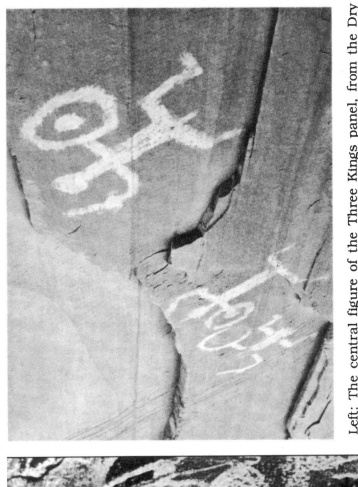

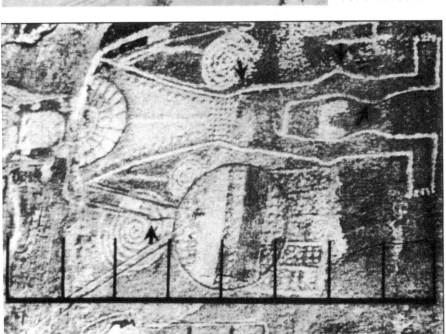

Left: The central figure of the Three Kings panel, from the Dry Fork of Ashley Creek, north of Vernal, Utah. The man, probably a Toltec-Hohokam, wears a metal collar around his neck as did Egyptians and other ancient civilizations of the Mediterranean. Right: Pictographs from the Defiance House ruins, Forgotten Canyon, Glen Canyon National Recreation Area, Utah. They show men with round shields and swords.

EXPLORATIONS IN GRAND CANYON

Mysteries of Immense Rich Cavern Being Brought to Light.

JORDAN IS ENTHUSED

Remarkable Finds Indicate Ancient People Migrated From Orient.

The latest news of the progress of the explorations of what is now regarded by scientists as not only the oldest archaeological discovery in the United States, but one of the most valuable in the world, which was mentioned some time ago in the Gazette, was brought to the city yesterday by G. E. Kinkaid, the explorer who found the great underground citadel of the Grand Canyon during a trip from Green river, Wyoming, down the Colorado, in a wooden boat, to Yuma, several months ago. According to the story related yesterday to the Gazette by Mr. Kinkaid, the archaeologists of the Smithsonian institute, which is financing the explorations, have made discoveries which almost conclusively prove that the race which inhabited this mysterious cavern, hewn in solid rock by human hands, was of oriental origin, possibly from Egypt, tracing back to Ramses. If their theories are borne out by the translation of the tablets engraved with hieroglyphics, the mystery of the prehistoric peoples of North America, their ancient arts, who they were and whence they came, will be solved. Egypt and the Nile, and Arizona and the Colorado will be linked by a historical chain running back to ages which staggers the wildest fancy of the fictionist.

A Thorough Investigation.

Under the direction of Prof. S. A. Jordan, the Smithsonian institute is now prosecuting the most thorough explorations, which will be continued until the last link in the chain is forged. Nearly a mile underground, about 1480 feet below the surface, the long main

fect ventilation of the cavern, the steady draught that blows through, indicates that it has another outlet to the surface.

Mr. Kinkaid's Report.

Mr. Kinkaid was the first white child born in Idaho and has been an explorer and hunter all his life, thirty years having been in the service of the Smithsonian institute. Even briefly recounted, his history sounds fabulous, almost grotesque.

"First, I would impress that the cavern is nearly inaccessible. The entrance is 1486 feet down the sheer canyon wall. It is located on government land and no visitor will be allowed there under penalty of trespass. The scientists wish to work unmolested, without fear of the archaeological discoveries being disturbed by curio or relic hunters. A trip there would be fruitless, and the visitor would be sent on his way. The story of how I found the cavern has been related, but in a paragraph: I was journeying down the Colorado river in a boat, alone, looking for mineral. Some forty-two miles up the river from the El Tovar Crystal canyon I saw on the east wall, stains in the sedimentary formation about 2000 feet above the river bed. There was no trail to this point, but I finally reached it with great difficulty. Above a shelf which hid it from view from the river, was the mouth of the cave. There are steps leading from this entrance some thirty yards to what was, at the time the cavern was inhabited, the level of the river. When I saw the chisel marks on the wall inside the entrance, I became interested, secured my gun and went in. During that trip I went back several hundred feet along the main passage, till I came to the crypt in which I discovered the mummies. One of these I stood up and photographed by flashlight. I gathered a number of relics, which I carried down the Colorado to Yuma, from whence I shipped them to Washington with details of the discovery. Following this, the explorations were undertaken.

The Passages.

"The main passageway is about 12 feet wide, narrowing to 9 feet toward the farther end. About 57 feet from the entrance, the first side-passages branch off to the right and left, along which, on both sides, are a number of rooms about the size of ordinary living rooms of today, though some are 30 or 40 feet square. These are entered by oval-shaped doors and are ventilated by round air spaces through the walls into the passages. The walls are about 3 feet 6 inches in thickness. The passages are chiseled or hewn as straight as could be laid out by an engineer. The ceilings of many of the rooms converge to a center. The side passages near the entrance run at a sharp angle from the main hall, but toward the rear they gradually reach a right angle in direction.

The Shrine.

"Over a hundred feet from the entrance is the cross-hall, several hundred feet long, in which was found the idol, or image, of the people's god, sitting cross-legged, with a lotus flower or lily in each hand. The cast of the

EXPLORATIONS IN GRAND CANYON

(Continued from Page One.)

which indicates that some sort of ladder was attached. These granaries are rounded, and the materials of which they are constructed, I think, is a very hard cement. A gray metal is also found in this cavern, which puzzles the scientists, for its identity has not been established. It resembles platinum. Strewn promiscuously over the floor everywhere are what people call 'cats' eyes' or 'tiger eyes,' a yellow stone of no great value. Each one is engraved with a head of the Malay type.

The Hieroglyphics.

"On all the urns, on walls over doorways, and tablets of stone which were found by the image are the mysterious hieroglyphics, the key to which the Smithsonian institute hopes yet to discover. These writings resemble those on the rocks about this valley. The engraving on the tablets probably has something to do with the religion of the people. Similar hieroglyphics have been found in the peninsula of Yucatan, but these are not the same as those found in the orient. Some believe that these cave dwellers built the old canals in the Salt River valley. Among the pictorial writings, only two animals are found. One is of prehistoric type.

The Crypt.

"The tomb or crypt in which the mummies were found is one of the contain a deadly gas or chemicals used by the ancients. No sounds are heard, but it smells snakey just the same. The whole underground institution gives one of shaky nerves the creeps. The gloom is like a weight on one's shoulders, and our flashlights and candles only make the darkness blacker. Imagination can revel in conjectures and ungodly day-dreams back through the ages that have elapsed till the mind reels dizzily in space."

An Indian Legend.

In connection with this story, it is notable that among the Hopis the tradition is told that their ancestors once lived in an underworld in the Grand Canyon till dissension arose between the good and the bad, the people of one heart and the people of two hearts. Machetto, who was their chief, counseled them to leave the underworld, but there was no way out. The chief then caused a tree to grow up and pierce the roof of the underworld, and then the people of one heart climbed out. They tarried by Paisisvai (Red river), which is the Colorado, and grew grain and corn. They sent out a message to the Temple of the Sun, asking the blessing of peace, good will and rain for the people of one heart. That messenger never returned, but today at the Hopi village at sundown can be seen the old men of the tribe out on the housetops gazing toward the sun, looking for the messenger. When he returns, their lands and ancient dwelling place will be restored to them. That is the tradition. Among the engravings of animals in the cave is seen the image of a heart over the spot where it is located. The legend was learned by W. E. Rollins, the artist, during a year spent with the Hopi Indians. There are two theories of the origin of the Egyptians. One is that they came from Asia; another that the racial cradle was in the upper Nile region. Heeren, an Egyptologist, believed in the Indian origin of the Egyptians. The discoveries in the Grand Canyon may throw further light on human evolution and prehistoric ages.

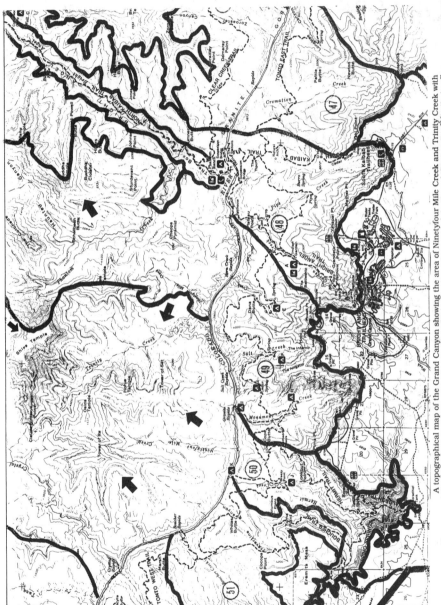

A topographical map of the Grand Canyon showing the area of Ninetyfour Mile Creek and Trinity Creek with its lower promontory with Zoroaster and Hindu passes. This area of the Grand Canyon is off-limits to all

Chapter 10

The Mississippi Valley:

Diving At the Sunken Pyramids of Aztalan

In the space of one hundred and seventy-six years the Lower Mississippi has shortened itself two hundred and forty-two miles. This is an average of a trifle over one mile and a third per year. Therefore, any calm person, who is not blind or idiotic, can see that...just a million years ago next November, the lower Mississippi River was upwards of one million three hundred thousand miles long.
— Mark Twain
Life On the Mississippi

"That way to Chaco Canyon," said the man, pointing up the road. It was getting late in the afternoon, and it would be dark soon.

"Are you sure that this old dirt road is the road to Chaco Canyon?" I asked the rancher.

He nodded his cowboy hat at me. "This is the road all right. Chaco Canyon is 64 miles north. Follow the signs. Road's pretty bad though. Are sure that pickup can make it?"

"Yeah, I'm sure," I said, and thanking the man for the directions, I put the truck in gear and headed up the bleak, dirt road. All around the winter desert landscape was barren, though there was no snow on the ground yet.

The road soon turned into one of the worst dirt roads I had ever driven in my life. In the weeks and months before, large four-wheel drive trucks had driven through the wet mud and the road had become two deep wheel tracks in mud with a high ridges on either side.

Fortunately, the mud was frozen, and with enough skill, I was able to keep the tires of my truck precariously balanced on the frozen tops of the mud ruts. For more than an hour I drove down this incredible dirt road. At parts I thought that I should turn back, but once I had gotten going, I realized that there was no place to turn around. I had to keep going forward.

It seemed incredible to me that the normal American family on vacation in their Oldsmobile could ever drive down this road. Yet, this was the main road into the largest archaeological ruins in the Western United States. My mind was boggled as to why the Gila Ruins, in southern New Mexico, had a nice paved road to the site, which was only a single small cliff dwelling, while Chaco Canyon, probably the most important site of all, had at least 30 miles of virtually impassible road to cross before one reached the site. Was there some vague effort to keep tourists from visiting Chaco Canyon? The average tourist would certainly think twice before driving this road.

The sun was setting across the plain scrub plain to the west; the sky was ablaze red, orange and purple. I suddenly screeched the truck to a stop at a bad spot in the road, a lake of melting mud, spanning several hundred yards. Unable to turn around, I decided to gun the truck and risk getting stuck. If I did, I would probably have to wait until the next morning before I would get anyone to help me move my truck.

The truck slid from side to side in the slippery mud, one wheel spinning. I raced the motor and turned the wheel wildly to the left and right. Suddenly the truck lurched forward and I got one wheel on the dry edge of the road. I had made it through the sea of mud. I drove on for a few more miles, my headlights lighting the mud ruts in front of me. I knew that I had to maintain a certain speed or I would get stuck. Then the road suddenly became paved. I breathed a sigh of relief, and saw the visitor's center to my right.

The lights were off and it was dark. I continued along the one-way paved road past several ruins, including Hungo Pavi and Chetro Ketl until I came to Pueblo Bonito, the largest of the many structures in Chaco Canyon. I parked the car and walked around the ruins with a flashlight. I seemed to be the only person in the national park.

That night I camped near my car on the edge of the ruins. As I lay in my sleeping bag, I could hear coyotes howling in the distance, and at one point, I thought I saw a figure moving through the ruins in the dim moonlight. A ghost of Chaco Canyon perhaps?

Chaco Canyon was once a great center for the mysterious Anasazi culture, a people who built great cities and roads throughout the southwest a thousand years ago, and then mysteriously vanished, leaving their cities to become ruins. Many anthropologists believe that the Anasazi are the ancestors of the Navajo, Ute and Zuñi tribes.

According to the standard archaeological history of Chaco Canyon, the Anasazi began building at Chaco Canyon in the early A.D. 900s, beginning the foundations of many of the larger structures. By the year 1000 A.D., there were more than 75 small "cities" within Chaco Canyon, most of them linked together by an extensive system of roads.

Chaco Canyon became the political and economic center of not only the entire Chaco Plateau, but of the entire Four Corners region, with other Anasazi cities in Colorado, Arizona and Utah connected to Chaco Canyon by the many roads radiating out from the site. Aerial photographs revealed more than 400 miles of connecting roads to some 75 communities around the canyon, the farthest 42 miles to the north and the ruins now called Aztec and Salmon. On the north-south road, settlements lay at travel intervals of approximately one day.

These roads were not simply trails worn by centuries of foot travel. They were the productions of relatively sophisticated engineering and required a great deal of energy and thought to plan, construct and maintain. They were laid out in long straight lines with scant regard for terrain. The roads averaged 30 feet in width, which is wide enough for ten men to walk abreast. What huge armies must have walked these wide roads?

Speaking of roads, the next morning I went to the Visitor's Center and talked to one of the rangers there. The ranger was a tall, attractive woman in her 30s. I didn't mention to her that I had just spent the night on the edge of the ruins (probably illegal), but I did mention that I thought that the road coming into the national park was so incredibly bad that I could hardly believe it.

"You drove up here from the road to the south?" she asked incredulously. "That road is pretty bad right now. It's never in too good a shape, but right now it's particularly bad."

"I was lucky that most of the mud was frozen," I told her. "But I can't understand why they don't pave the road to the park. Chaco Canyon must be one of the most important archaeological sites in America, yet I get the feeling that the Park Service doesn't really want visitors. These roads must certainly discourage tourists. I'm a pretty good driver and I'm not discouraged easily, but most people would turn around after a few miles."

"Well, I guess you're right. There's been talk about improving the roads, but the bad roads keep a lot of tourists away, and we like that, fewer tourists mean less vandalism. If they want to come to Chaco Canyon, they will just have to make that extra effort."

I walked around the ruins for the day, hiking up to the Pueblo Alto ruins on the mesa above the canyon. There were stairways cut into solid rock and huge towers that rose to the cliff top. There were many sunken, circular buildings, kivas, and other circular towers. The high walls were wonderful bits of architecture, with several different construction techniques and phases. I looked for snakes, jackrabbits and kangaroo rats. Lizards sunned themselves on the rocks. In some ways I was glad that there were few tourists, yet Chaco Canyon should be shared with everyone.

Huge discs of sandstone were found in some of the kivas, these were the bases for the large pillars that held up the ceilings in the largest kivas. One curious discovery was the remains of macaws and other parrots from Central America. They were raised at Chaco Canyon, as well as at Aztec and Salmon ruins. Feathers were important trade items, and the official tourist brochure says, "copper bells and remains of macaws or parrots... suggest contact with Mexico, perhaps with the ancient Toltecs."

It is believed that Chaco Canyon may have been a grain storage center in times of drought. The decline of the ancient city is believed to have coincided with a prolonged drought in the San Juan Basin between 1130 and 1180 A.D. Lack of rainfall combined with an overtaxed environment may have led to food shortages. People drifted away in search of better watered regions, according to this theory. Where they went, is unknown. One theory is that the Aztecs of Mexico originally inhabited this area before they migrated to the Valley of Mexico.

🐃🐃🐃

I continued my trip east, crossing New Mexico through Albuquerque and on into the panhandle of Texas. I spent the night in a small motel and was off the next morning on my way across northern Texas and into Oklahoma. My goal in Oklahoma was several unusual sites in the far eastern portion of the state, Spiro Mounds State Park and the Heavener Runestone Park.

On the bank of the Arkansas River near the present day town of Spiro, Oklahoma (only a few miles from Arkansas) lies a huge pyramid-mound complex known today as the Spiro Mounds Site. For the great Pyramid builders of the Mississippi, this was one of the farthest west sites of this sophisticated culture based on the Mississippi River System. The Arkansas River is a tributary of the lower Mississippi, and reaches far into Oklahoma and into eastern Colorado.

Like many mound sites in the Midwest, it was largely ignored by the local settlers, until one day, about 1920, when a farmer's plow exposed some artifacts from one of the mounds.

The Pocola Mining Company was soon formed to excavate the mounds of artifacts and sell them commercially. Using dynamite and road scoops, the miners dug out great quantities of pottery, pearls, masks and metal objects. The artifacts were transported by wheelbarrow to the nearby road and sold as souvenirs.

The site is generally dated from 850 A.D. to 1450 A.D. and was a group of twelve mounds, including several large pyramids, probably originally ceremonial pyramids with structures on top of them, with smaller burial pyramids around them.

The central mound at the site is called Craig Mound, and even before its excavation, it became known in the vicinity as a haunted place because an eerie blue light was often seen around the mound. Forrest Clements, commissioned as an archaeological authority to write an official history of Spiro Mounds for the Museum of the American Indian, New York's famed Heye Foundation, reported that the woman who once owned the land on which the sacred center is located was awakened one night by unusual, loud noises emanating from the structure. When she rushed to investigate what she presumed must have been drunken trespassers, she saw the mound "covered by shimmering sheets of blue flame." As she gazed in amazement at the ghostly illumination, a team of huge cats drawing a small, empty wagon appeared on the top of the mound. Without a sound, they drove around the summit several times, then vanished, as the blue haze faded away. Her vision (circa 1890) may have been of two jaguar-spirits that are associated with the mounds.[216]

When the first excavators broke into Craig Mound, they found a large tunnel that was high enough to stand in. They followed it through the very center of the structure until they came to a wall made of cedar posts. Cutting through it, they stumbled into an oval vault some 20 feet by 30 feet in dimensions, with a cedar roof arching 15 feet overhead. The whole interior of the chamber was tapestried with fabulous cloth hangings woven of fur, hair and brilliant feathers. On floor lay the full-length skeleton of a large man decked out in copper armor, polished beads, carved stone ear-spools and engraved conch shells. Near him stood an altar, on which rested a large urn filled with tens of thousands of pearls. In all, over 500 human burials were eventually recovered from the mound.[216]

The cache of pears, engraved conch shells and copper breast plates found on the skeleton was the largest pre-Columbian treasure trove discovered up to that time. Unfortunately, because of the ghastly method of excavation, solely for extracting artifacts for quick sale, this warrior in armor has now been totally lost, and few books with any information on the Spiro Mounds even mention this odd grave.

I walked around the site one winter morning. It was a gray day, and the site was deserted. At the site are a reconstructed house, two reconstructed mounds, a walking trail, and interpretive plaques. There is a museum displaying a few of the many artifacts that have come from the mounds. Some of the recovered artifacts are in the Smithsonian Museum, the Oklahoma Historical Society Museum, and the University of Arkansas Museum. The site also included a crematorium and a woodhenge (an astronomical observatory).

As I looked around the museum, and noticed a replica of the copper breastplates. I asked the director about the man in armor who was found in one of the mounds. Where were the remains of this man? The site director confirmed that such a find had been made, but had no idea where the skeleton and armor were at the moment. "Maybe at the Smithsonian," he suggested. I knew that no one would ever see it again if it had gone there.

And who might a man in armor have been? "Probably a Viking, I would guess," said the site director. "You should go on down to Heavener, a few miles away, that's where all the runestones are kept. They have a state park there."

A runestone park in Oklahoma? That sounded interesting, and in fact, that was indeed my next destination. I drove south on Highway 59 past Kerr, Oklahoma with the Kerr Museum, and on to the small town of Heavener.

In Heavener, I followed the signs to the "Runestone Park" and was led through town and up to the top of hill to the east of town. Here was a parking lot and a modern state park building manned by an employee of the state park system.

"Is this the Heavener Runestone Park?" I asked, looking over the counter at a Park Ranger in a green uniform.

"It sure is," said the ranger, getting up from his desk and coming to the counter. "Would you mind signing our visitor's register." I was signing my name when he handed me several brochures on the site. One was an eight-page brochure written by Gloria Farley, who works with the Epigraphic Society in San Diego, and was published by the Oklahoma Tourism and Recreation Department in Oklahoma City.

I read from the brochure, "the most recent research on the runic inscription of the Heavener Runestone which stands in the State Park on Poteau Mountain near Heavener, Oklahoma, indicates that it may be four hundred years older than first thought. A former translation state that it could be the date of November 11, 1012. It now appears that it is not a date, but is a boundary marker made as early as 600 A.D. and not later than 900 A.D. It says GLOME VALLEY.

"The Heavener Runestone was first discovered, according to local oral history, by a Choctaw hunting party in the 1830s. Poteau Mountain, on which it is located, was named by French trappers. It was part of the Indian Territory ceded to the Choctaw Nation when they were removed from Mississippi to present Oklahoma. The Choctaws were probably astonished if they saw the eight mysterious symbols punched into the mossy face of the huge slab of stone which stood in a lovely ravine protected by overhanging cliffs. Records tell us that there was no underbrush on the mountains then; a deer could be seen for a distance under virgin timber.

"White men began to filter into the area in the 1870's. Wilson King, with two other bear hunters, saw the carved stone before 1874, according to a statement signed by his son. However, the earliest eyewitness on record is Luther Capps, who saw it in 1898. Logging was an industry when Heavener was established in 1894. Laura Callahan remembered that in 1904, at age five, she was held up to run her hands over the mossy lettering by her father, R.L. Bailey, who owned a sawmill. In 1913, when Carl F. Kemmerer again found the stone and described it in Heavener, others already knew of the monument-like stele which was called 'Indian Rock.'

"Ten years later, Mr. Kemmerer sent a careful copy of the symbols to the Smithsonian Institution in Washington, D.C., who replied that very plainly the characters are runic, but their guess is whoever made the inscription had a Scandinavian grammar as a guide. In 1928, Mr. Kemmerer took a skinny little girl, Gloria Stewart, to the site and showed her the great stone in its setting. She was so impressed that she searched again in 1951, found the stone and renamed it 'The Heavener Runestone.'

"During the following years, many interviews were held with

oldtimers and many efforts were made to relocate other similar carved stones. It was eventually understood that although many had once existed in the area, all but two had been destroyed in the 30's and 40's by treasure hunters. It is unfortunate no one had the forethought to copy the inscriptions before destruction. On the remaining stones, one has three symbols and the other has only two, making translation very difficult.

"Although there is no test to determine the antiquity of an inscription on stone, such as the C-14 test on organic matter, the weathering of the edges of carving in relation to the hardness of the stone and exposure to the elements is viewed by this author as an acceptable guide. The site of the Heavener Runestone is in a deep ravine, protected from wind on three sides. The stone itself, twelve feet high, ten feet wide and 16 inches thick, is in a vertical position and thus is protected from erosion. Three geologists confirm that it fell eons ago into its north-south alignment. There it stood like a billboard, waiting for someone to write on the broad west face. The fine-grained Savanna sandstone is, to quote Dr. W.E. Ham, former state geologist, 'so tough that it can be broken by a geologist's hammer only with considerable difficulty.' The eight runes are in a straight line, six to nine inches in height, and still one-fourth to three-sixteenths of an inch in depth. Weathering is so slow, that a date written in lead pencil on the flat gray lichen on the stone, exposed to rain and snow, was still legible seven years later. And yet the edges of the runes are smooth and rounded by weathering."

The Heavener Runestone Park was dedicated in 1970, and attempts by various scholars to translate the runes was pursued over the years. This task was quite difficult because the runes seemed to be a mixture of two ancient runic alphabets: six from the oldest Germanic (Old Norse) Futhark which came into use about 300 A.D., and the second and last runes from a later Scandinavian Futhark used about 800 A.D. A runologist from Norway transliterated the letters as GNOMEDAL, and suggested it might be a modern name, G. Nomedal. But to do this, he had to consider that the second rune was unfinished.

In 1967, a translation was offered by Alf Monge, a former U.S. Army Cryptographer, who was born in Norway. Refusing to alter the shape of the runes, he said the correct transliteration is GAOMEDAT. He said the letters would not translate into sense because they were used as numbers, according to their places in the two alphabets. Even the numbers did not give the date directly, but had to be used in the form of a very complicated Norse Runic Cryptopuzzle, which had been invented by ancient Norse clergymen to hide a date in the puzzle. Using this method, he said the Heavener Runestone inscription is the date of November 11, 1012.

According to Farley, the authenticity of the Heavener Runestone was enhanced when in 1967, another runic inscription which was very similar to the Heavener one, was found by two 13-year-old boys on a hill in Poteau, ten miles away. In 1969, another runestone was found face down by a small stream in Shawnee, Oklahoma. Both of these runestones are now on display at the Kerr Museum near Poteau, although replicas of them may be seen at the Heavener Runestone Park.

Many other runestones were said to exist in the Heavener area, but most were destroyed by treasure hunters, according to Farley. However, two more runestones were found near Heavener, one, with the runic R and a bindrune (a combination of runes) was found on Morris Creek. The other, with three runes in triangular pattern, was found on Poteau Mountain southeast of the Heavener Runestone.

Farley relates how Dr. Richard Nielsen, who obtained his doctorate at the University of Denmark but resides in California, began working on all the runestones in America starting in 1986. He not only studied runestones in Scandinavia, some seldom seen, but also interviewed runologists at the University of Oslo. Dr. Nielsen not only authenticated the famous Kensington Runestone (in Minnesota) which he dated at 1362 A.D.

Nielsen turned his attention to the Oklahoma Runestones, and is of the opinion that the Heavener, Poteau, and Shawnee inscriptions are written, not in a mixed alphabet, but that all the runes are from the oldest Futhark. The former disagreements on whether the second Heavener rune was an A or an N, he found is actually an L. The eighth rune, which was considered as an L or a T, is also a form of L. The seventh rune in the Poteau inscription, which does not appear in this exact form in either runic alphabet, is actually a double L, or a bindrune in the form of two accepted L's. The last triangular rune at Poteau is a W, but rare.

With this new understanding of the disputed runes, Dr. Nielsen was able to offer translations for both the Heavener and Poteau Runestones. Both bear a version of the same name, one being a nickname of the other. The Heavener stone says GLOME DAL, which means "Valley owned by GLOME," a boundary marker or land claim.

The Poteau Runestone, which was part of a ledge and was broken off, say GLOI ALLW (Alu) "Magic or protection to Gloi." This word for magic was used in the language of about 600 A.D. This is part of the key to the new dating of the runes.

Farley says that there was never any dispute about the runes on the Shawnee stone, which spell the name MEDOK in the oldest Futhark. It was probably a gravestone, she says, but the site was bulldozed. Curiously, this rune, since vowels are implied, could also read as MODOK, MADOK or MADOC, as in the 12th century Welch prince, whom we will discuss in the next chapter.

Using Nielsen's translation as her guide, Farley says that a Norseman named Glome, nicknamed Gloi, owned property on Poteau Mountain as early as 600 A.D. His memorial was carved into a ledge on a foothill of Cavanal Mountain at Poteau, about ten miles away. Another possible explanation and translation for the Heavener Runestone is that it says "GNOME VALLEY" or "Valley of the Gnomes," referring to little people, rather than a Norseman named Glome. Similarly, might Gloi Allw possibly mean "the magic of gnomes"?

The ranger at the Heavener Runestone park, Eddy Herst, was quite friendly, and took me down to show me the runestone. The stone, which is huge, is located in a steep ravine, with shale cliffs and a small waterfall nearby. Carved into the massive slab were the eight runes.

"There's supposed to be another runestone farther down the creek, about half the size of this one," said Eddy, pointing out the little creek that ran by the runestone. No one can find it now, but I haven't looked for it myself."

I looked around and examined the runes, they were deeply cut and well worn. The stone slab stood perfectly upright, in a north-south position. It appeared to me to have been placed where it was, though Eddy told me that geologists felt that it had just fallen that way, by coincidence.

"That stone's too big to have been moved there," Eddy commented. Eddy than began telling me about a cave that was once said to be in the shale cliffs at the same spot as the runestone. "The old-timers around here all said that there was a cave up here at the runestone. An old-timer named Apache Jim claimed that he went inside the cave. He sent his dog inside the cave and the dog never came back. He said that there was a big room inside the cave with charcoal and animal bones, and maybe some inscriptions. The entrance was right up here by the waterfall, but no one can find it now. Must have been a cave-in."

Eddy and I climbed up by the waterfall and I looked at some cracks in the shale. There might have been a cave back there, but it was hard to tell.

Eddy then told me about a lost silver mine on Poteau Mountain somewhere. "There was this old prospector who lived around here and he also made bullets. He would come up here on the mountain to get lead and silver to make bullets with. He once told me that he had found lots of these here runestones in the area, but he pulled over all the runestones he could find. He was just an angry sort of fellow. Heck, he'd do it out of spite, he'd tie a rope to a stone with runes on it and use his mule to pull them down. Face down, so nobody could see the runes. I'll bet that he destroyed a dozen or more runestones like that. He could never pull this runestone down, though, it was too big."

That was an interesting story to me, and on our way back to the Visitor's Center, I thought about the odd tale. By all reports, this area was covered in runestones. Spiro Mound with its warrior in full copper armor probably had something to do with all this. Now there is the mystery of the lost silver mine and the missing cave that was once said to exist a few yards away from the Heavener Runestone. Might the lost silver mine and the missing cave be one and the same?

It would give the mean-old prospector and bullet maker a reason for destroying runestones, especially if he thought they would lead people to his secret silver mine. And, if his secret silver mine was located in the ravine of the Heavener Runestone, it would also give him a reason for dynamiting the entrance and blocking off the entrance to the cave.

Also, it would give a Norseman name Glome a reason to set up a property marker on Poteau Mountain. It wasn't just that he claimed some obscure valley on a mountain, but he was claiming the silver mine that came with it!

Back at the Visitors Center, Eddy told me one last thing. "A silver coin with a hole in the middle was found at the base of the mountain some years back. Gloria Farley sent the coin to the Smithsonian Institution who said that the coin was from 146 B.C. and came from North Africa. Now how about that!"

That was perhaps the icing on the cake as far the Heavener Runestone and Spiro Mounds were concerned. Had Vikings discovered an ancient mine worked by Libyans or Egyptians 100 to 200 B.C.? One thing that was for sure, the Viking explorers who came up the Arkansas River weren't just some lost Norseman who happened to come this way on an adventure. They came, they stayed, they put up boundary markers and land claims. They must have built cities, married women, and at some point or another, returned to Scandinavia with their tradegoods: silver, pearls, furs and other valuables. There's was an epic odyssey across the north Atlantic. Though current anthropologists claim that it is a racist theory to propose that any other culture other than the descendants of Siberian Ice Age hunters had anything to do with the civilizations of North America. Is it not similarly a racist argument to say that the ancient Norse were not capable of sailing down the eastern seaboard and then up the Mississippi to new worlds? Scientific logic would suggest that any seafaring civilization capable of reaching the north-east shore on North America would continue along those shore and explore up the various river systems.

🐾🐾🐾

Thoughts of a Viking colony in the Midwest were on my mind as I drove across Arkansas headed for Little Rock. I shifted gears and began passing a car on the interstate. In front of me was a large flat bed truck with bricks stacked ten feet high on it.

Suddenly, the back layer of bricks all fell off the truck and, after bouncing once on the pavement, a cloud of bricks was coming straight for me at 60 miles an hour. It was a shower of a hundred bricks coming straight for me and the windshield of the truck. It was like an instant meteor shower, how could I survive this onslaught?

My passenger, a hitchhiker, gasped for air. I looked across the highway to the car on my right. They, too, saw the cloud of bricks heading toward the car.

Fortunately, the car to my right had seen the shower of bricks coming for me, so when I suddenly swerved to the right, they had fallen back and moved to the right-hand curb. Bricks showered the pavement to the left of the pickup, and a couple of bricks hit the back of the truck, but none hit the windshield.

I turned and looked at the hitchhiker whom I had picked up a few miles back. He looked at me and said, "Wow, that was a close call. How did you avoid all those bricks?"

I looked down the road as I passed the truck. "Beats me," was all I could say.

I looked around in a daze; it had all happened in a matter of seconds. The truck continued down the highway as if nothing had happened. I kept driving as well. Within moments I had shrugged off the entire incident, just another occasion in one's life where one is clashing between two armies, unaware of the danger.

My next stop was the Toltec Mounds State Park, 15 miles southeast the state capital. Toltec Mounds is a huge pyramid site, with 18 mounds altogether, nine of which are visible. An earthen embankment six feet high and a mile long once encircled the huge site. One of the mounds at Toltec is a conical pyramid, similar to Cuicuilco in the Valley of Mexico.

Because of the many pyramids and other large mounds at the site, the early owners of the site believed that the Toltec Indians had built the complex. Modern archaeologists tell us that the Toltecs did not build the site, but "mound builders" built the mounds. Apparently, the real builders still remain a mystery.

The fact is, huge pyramids, conical mounds, effigy mounds and huge earthworks, can be found from Oklahoma to New York and from Louisiana to Minnesota.

The valleys of the Mississippi and Ohio rivers in Illinois, Wisconsin, Indiana and Iowa were once the center of activity for an obscure people called the Mound Builders. They built mounds of earth, some shaped like animals, such as the Lizard Mound and the Great Serpent Mound, which is to the east in Ohio.

Many of these sites are now state, national or private parks. The many sites include the Hopewell Mound Group in Ohio, recently saved from being turned into a subdivision by the *Archaeological Conservancy;* Savage Cave in Kentucky, a site of one of the longest occupations in the U.S.; the Cahokia site in Illinois; Powers Fort in Missouri, a large Mound Builder complex; Stackhouse Mound in Ohio, one of the only well preserved Adena ceremonial centers left; the Portsmouth, Ohio complex; the pyramids of the Sun and the Moon at Aztalan in Wisconsin; the effigy mounds of Iowa, and the Toltec mounds of Arkansas and Oklahoma. It was a vast world out there of pyramids, huge river forts, weird burials and even sunken cities.

🐾🐾🐾

It was getting late when I reached St. Louis. I called an old friend,

Alex, and told him I was in town.

"David, it's good to hear from you. Do you have a place to stay?" asked Alex.

"Well, no, not really..." I answered hesitantly.

"You can stay here. I have a comfortable couch here in my apartment. I'll give you directions on how to get here." Half an hour later I was at Alex's apartment and he was pouring me a beer. We talked about lost cities, travel, strange phenomena, various conspiracy theories, UFO technology and other unorthodox topics. Alex was an amazing guy, in his 40s now. He had been a radio disc jockey, a Naval officer, a martial arts instructor, a UFO investigator, and a zillion jobs in between. Currently he was selling lawn care products for a major company.

"It pays the bills," said Alex, "at least for now. But tell me about your journeys. You've probably been all over the world since I last saw you."

I hadn't been all over the world on this last trip, but I had traveled quite a bit in South and Central America. I told him of some of my adventures, and then mentioned what appeared to be a Smithsonian cover-up of the Grand Canyon finds, as well as other important archaeological discoveries.

"That doesn't surprise me one bit," said Alex. "They've been keeping all the important discoveries in America a secret for the past hundred years. You know, the largest pyramid in North America is right here in the Midwest. But you'd never hear about that from the Smithsonian. The park service here won't even call them pyramids. They call them mounds, instead. But they're pyramids, absolutely. I'll take you there tomorrow."

The next day, we drove out to the Cahokia Pyramid site in Alex's car.

The Cahokia site is sometimes called Monks' Mound, after trappist monks who farmed the terraces in the early 1800s. It is a stepped pyramid that covers some 16 acres — more than the area covered by the Great Pyramid of Egypt. Study of the mound has indicated that it was rebuilt several times; the last rebuilding dates from around AD 1100. At its summit are the buried remains of the foundations of a temple 104 by 48 feet, which could have dominated the region.

Other mounds may have been used as burial places or had a military function. Perhaps there was some Mexican influence. Why did the Mound Builders abandon their sites? Pollution and overcrowding, some experts now suggest, pointing to accumulations of garbage, could have fouled the region's water supply.[39]

During the middle-ages, Cahokia was a larger city than London. Yet today it is an abandoned site, about which we know almost nothing. Yet, it may be the largest pyramid in North America (contending with the giant pyramid at Cholula near Mexico City)!

Originally there were over 120 pyramids and mounds at the Cahokia site, though the locations of only 106 have been recorded.

Many were altered or destroyed by modern farming and urban construction. About 68 are preserved in the historic site boundaries.

The mounds are all entirely made of earth, though some mounds in the Midwest have stone structures within them. It is estimated that over 50 million cubic feet of earth was moved by the builders for the pyramid construction. There were essentially three types of structures, the most common of which is the stepped pyramid or platform mound. The other two types of mounds are conical and ridgetop. Ridgetop mounds are generally thought to have been used for burials, though only certain special people, kings and aristocrats were buried in mounds. While tourist literature at Cahokia says that "Most Cahokians were probably buried in cemeteries, not in mounds," the actual truth seems to be that most people were not buried at all, but cremated. Crematoriums have been found at many mound sites, including Spiro Mound and Aztalan in Wisconsin.

It is generally believed that some 20,000 people once occupied the Cahokia site, living inside a 15-foot-high wooden stockade that surrounded the various pyramids. The site is named after a tribe of Illini Indians, the Cahokia, who lived in the area when the French arrived in the late 1600s. What the actual name of the city was in ancient times is unknown. The site is generally said to have existed from 700 A.D. until its decline about 1300 and by 1500, it is believed to have been totally abandoned. As with many ancient sites, it may well be much older than 700 A.D.

Cahokia is only one of hundreds, even thousands of pyramids throughout the central U.S. Modern scholars, in their tenacious belief that American Indians were primitive, tribal and relatively disorganized, see the various sites in Wisconsin, Illinois, Iowa, Ohio, Tennessee, Arkansas, Oklahoma, Georgia, Mississippi, and Alabama as unrelated. However, the evidence seems to indicate that the entire Midwest region was all one cohesive nation with a lively and sophisticated trade network using the extensive river system.

At Cahokia, sheets of copper, plates of mica, shells and turquoise have all been found at burials. These various materials all originate from vastly separated areas of the Midwest.

Furthermore, some rather interesting skeletons and artifacts have been discovered in many mounds throughout the Midwest:

•In his book, *The Natural and Aboriginal History of Tennessee*, author John Haywood describes "very large" bones in stone graves found in Williamson County, Tennessee, in 1821. In White County, an "ancient fortification" contained skeletons of gigantic stature averaging at least 7 feet in length.[157,158]

•Giant skeletons were found in the mid-1800s near Rutland and Rodman, New York. J.N. DeHart, M.D., found vertebrae "larger than those of the present type" in Wisconsin mounds in 1876. W.H.R. Lykins uncovered skull bones "of great size and thickness" in mounds of the Kansas City area in 1877.[158]

•George W. Hill, M.D., dug out a skeleton "of unusual size" in a

351

mound of Ashland County, Ohio. In 1879, a nine-foot, eight-inch skeleton was excavated from a mound near Brewersville, Indiana. (*Indianapolis News*, Nov. 10, 1975)[158]

•A six-foot, six-inch skeleton was found in a Utah mound. This was at least a foot taller than the average Indian height in the area, and these natives—what few there were of them—were not mound builders.[158]

•"A skeleton which is reported to have been of enormous dimensions" was found in a clay coffin, with a sandstone slab containing hieroglyphics, during mound explorations by a Dr. Everhart near Zanesville, Ohio. (*American Antiquarian*, v.3, 1880, page 61)[158]

•Ten skeletons "of both sexes and of gigantic size" were taken from a mound at Warren, Minnesota, in 1883. (St. Paul *Pioneer Press*, May 23, 1883)[158]

•A skeleton "seven feet six inches long, and nineteen inches across the chest" was removed from a massive stone structure that was likened to a temple chamber within a mound in Kanawha County, West Virginia, in 1884. (American Antiquarian, v. 6, 1884, 133f. Cyrus Thomas, *Report on Mound Explorations of the Bureau of Ethnology*, 12th Annual Report, Smithsonian Bureau of Ethnology, 1890-91)[158]

•A large mound near Gastersville, Pennsylvania, contained "a kind of vault... in which was discovered the skeleton of a giant measuring seven feet two inches ... On the stones which covered the vault were carved inscriptions..." (*American Antiquarian*, v. 7, 1885, 52f)

•In Minnesota, 1888, were discovered remains of seven skeletons "seven to eight feet tall." (St. Paul *Pioneer Press*, June 29, 1888)

•A mound near Toledo, Ohio, held 20 skeletons, seated and facing east, with jaws and teeth "twice as large as those of present day people," and beside each was a large bowl with "curiously wrought hieroglyphical figures." (Chicago *Record*, Oct. 24, 1895; cited by Ron G. Dobbins, *NEARA Journal*, v. 13, fall 1978)

•The skeleton of "a huge man" was uncovered at the Beckley farm, Lake Koronis, Minnesota; while at Moose Island and Pine City, bones of other giants came to light. (St. Paul *Globe*, Aug. 12, 1896)[158]

🐾🐾🐾

What ever happened to the Mound Builders? It is believed by many archaeologists that the last survivors of the Mound Builders were the Natchez Indians of the lower Mississippi River Valley. Not surprisingly, they were centered around present day Natchez, Mississippi. According to Peter Farb in his opus, *Man's Rise To Civilization as Shown by the Indians of North America from Primeval Times to the Coming of the Industrial State,*[114] the Natchez were "devout worshipers of the sun."

The chief of the Natchez was known as the Great Sun. The most important nobles were known simply as Suns. The ancestors of the

Natchez built the gigantic pyramids up and down the Mississippi as temples to worship the sun in. To them God was manifested them as the the solar disk. It was a monotheistic religion that goes back through history to the Toltecs, Quetzalcoatl, Incas, early Christians, Shintoists and ultimately to the great Aton religion of ancient Egypt.

The ancient Atonists and early Christians, known today as Nestorians, Coptics, or Gnostics, not only believed that the sun was the source of life on earth, but that higher intelligence resided within the sun. It is the belief of Nestorian Christians that Archangels reside on the sun.

Furthermore, it was the belief of early Christians that Jesus of Nazareth was an Essene adept who had studied in India, and his body was used the Archangel Melchizedek for the important and prophesied advent of Christ on earth. Early Nestorian Christians believed that the six year ministry of Christ was as an archangel on earth, and since archangels live on the sun, it was natural to identify Christ with our Solar disk. Therefore, Christ, by their cosmology, was both the *Son* and the *Sun* of God.

It was this very schism in the early church that led to the Nicene Creed in 431 A.D. and the formation of the Catholic Church which suppressed this theology under pain of the death. The Patriarch of Constantinople at the time, Saint Nestorus, was banished to the Libyan Desert and his church forced into Eastern Anatolia.

It is from St. Nestorus that the term Nestorian Christians come from. They are found all through Asia, and Marco Polo discovered them in Mongolia. Coptic Christians were forced out of northern Egypt, especially the Alexandria area. This is the same period in which the great library at Alexandria was destroyed by rioting religious mobs. Coptics were able to remain in Southern Egypt, Sudan and Ethiopia, however. Later the Moslem invasion forced all Christians to convert to Islam, and today Coptic Christians remain only in Ethiopia and in small pockets in Egypt.

It is a fascinating thought to relate the ancient Mississippi Pyramid builders with the ancient Sun Worshiping Atonist of Egypt and later with early Nestorian Christians.

According to Professor Barry Fell, a former Harvard professor and the president of the Epigraphic Society, the Micmac Indians of Maine and Eastern Canada used a hieroglyphic writing derived from ancient Egyptian. Similarly, he reports that the Zuñi language is taken from ancient Libyan. He devotes an entire chapter of one of his books, *America B.C.*,[8] to the *Egyptian Presence* and also discusses such curiosities as Aton worship in Oklahoma and Iowa, both part of the Mississippi River System. He also discusses a bilingual Egypto-Libyan inscribed tablet now housed in the Museum of the American, New York that was originally discovered in 1888 in a shell mound at Eagle Neck, on the eastern tip of Long Island.

In an article in the Baton Rouge, *Post and Courier* of Sunday, December 22, 1991 Barry Fell is quoted as saying that there's reason to believe that Egyptians sailed to the lower Mississippi delta, set up outposts and married with local Indians. According to Fell, most scholars believe the languages of the Atakapa, Tunica and Chitimacha tribes "have no known relationship to any other language and they have been classified therefore as a unique category."

Fell theorized that an expedition of Egyptians sailed to the New World, paddled up the Mississippi and set up shop. "The speech that I found in the Atakapa and the other two tribes of the lower Mississippi seemed to me to be just what might be expected if an Egyptian expedition had established a trading outpost in the lower Mississippi in ancient times, and if the members of it, or some of them, had either been abandoned or had of their own volition remained behind in America."

Such a colony "could have survived only by merging with local Indians to produce a mestizo population, speaking a tongue derived from the several different contributory dialects."

In typical fashion, the "experts" of academia take a dim view of Dr. Fell's claims of ancient Egyptian contact. In the above mentioned article, a Louisiana State anthropologist named Lyle Campbell says that Fell's scholarship "leaves something to be desired."

"You can always find accidental similarities" between languages, Campbell said. "You see these accidental similarities all the time— like between Aztec and ancient Greek. Some people see these accidental similarities and just go ape over them. They look for specific things and say specific things about them and its very entertaining, but they don't use any professional criteria at all."

Fell defends himself in the article by saying that he used very exacting standards in proving his theory, and he criticized the scholarly establishment for clinging to a narrow, provincial view of history. Fell has found similarities between Egyptian and Atakapa words for such as "to cure," "to flow," "to fear," "to be first," "to barter," "to sink," "to float," and "to journey."

Campbell is apparently just plain ignorant of the wealth of evidence that has been built up to support the conclusion that in ancient times various seafarers from many nations were traveling all over the world. Sadly, most of this evidence is suppressed and never finds its way into the University text books and "experts" such as Campbell are educated with the bizarre mind-set that only seafarers like the the Polynesians could have ventured out into unknown oceans, while all other ancient navigators were bound by some undefinable law to never sail beyond the sight of land. It is perfectly logical to the pundits of knowledge, and all other views are simply too fantastic to be true.

❀❀❀

As I stared up at the huge pyramid of Cahokia, I wondered how many ancient ceremonies to the sun had taken place on top of the grand structure. The ancient pyramid had a base larger than the Great Pyramid of Egypt and stood more than ten stories high. At one point at least 20,000 people resided in the six-square-mile city. The massive complex sits at the juncture of the Missouri River and the Mississippi River. The rivers of North America, as all over the world, were the transportation highways in which the people and goods of the civilization traveled.

The fantastic size of the Mound Builders civilization makes it seem unlikely that it was sparked by a few lost Egyptian sailors. Many voyages and ships must have made the journey. The travel between the ancient Mediterranean and North America must have begun in an early historical period, more than 3,000 years ago, and continued uninterrupted for thousands of years.

Eventually, however, it was interrupted. The Punic Wars and the ultimate razing of Carthage were the first interruption. Shortly thereafter was the rise of the Toltecs in Central America. Chinese and Hindu-Indonesians continued the transpacific trade routes. Romans, Jews and Celts eventually resumed the transatlantic trade and continued this until the fall of Rome and the creation of the Catholic Church in 431 A.D., which plunged Europe into a thousand years of dark ages. Just the mention of transatlantic contact was grounds for excommunication or possible torture.

Until Columbus made his voyages to the Caribbean, only Vikings and Irish Monks made the journey, though there is evidence that Welsh, Basque and Portuguese journeys to North America also took place in the Middle Ages. It is well to point out that Iceland was at its political and cultural zenith during this "Dark Age" on the continent of Europe.

By the time the first Colonial explorers reached the Mississippi, the Natchez Indians were already severely in decline. The French explorer Du Pratz made a sketch of the Great Sun being carried on his traditional litter carried by eight litter-bearers. At Cahokia as well, the Great Sun lived on the summit of the pyramid as a god-like leader; a Priest King.

Soon afterward, however, the Natchez were completely wiped out and absorbed by the French in a series of Indian Wars along the Mississippi.

According to legend, the bearded, robed Quetzalcoatl visited the Pyramid Builders and inspired them to love one another, live in harmony with the land, and build great works. But later, like most North American Sun Kingdoms, they degenerated back to human sacrifice and ceremonial warfare. A statue showing the beheading of a captured prisoner was discovered in the Natchez area.[114]

Like the Incas or Aztecs, the Natchez chiefdom "was a theocracy, pure and simple, and both secular and sacerdotal authority were embodied in the Great Sun. His large cabin was built atop a mound; nearby stood a similar mound, crowned by the temple."[114]

While the Natchez were described by the French as "the most civilized of the native tribes," it was later reported that in 1725 the

355

death of the chief's brother, Tattooed Serpent, touched off a sacrificial orgy. To keep him company, several aides and servants plus his two wives joyously agreed to be strangled. Human sacrifice had been forbidden by Quetzalcoatl, but was still practiced to varying degrees by the many residual sun kingdoms in the Americas.[166]

Still, the Incas, the Toltecs and other Sun Worshipers of the Americas attempted to stop human sacrifice, and live more humanely. In this same context, the Mississippi River system was once the center of a great and advanced civilization. The very word *illi* is the root word for all that is cultured and advanced. In his study of the root origins of thousands of words, Henry Brinkley Stein in his 1940 book *Thirty Thousand Gods Before Jehovah*, points out that "For some unknown reason there exists within the midst of our languages a very significant word, the meaning of which has been lost for many generations...This is the world *Illi* or *Illium*, the name of Troy, and the name of one of the oldest epics in the world. From it is derived the word civilization, for the Illi were the city builders and the Illi who lived in cities were the *civilli*. The word capitol originally means the head Illi from the chief hill in Rome which was originally possessed by the Illi."

According to Stein's book, the ancient Illini Indians of Illinois were part of the sacred Illi who had originally ruled at Troy some three or four thousand years ago. Illinois was the land of the Civilli; a land of pyramids, forts, huge trading vessels destined for copper mines in the north, and a land of vast vision and teaming wilderness.

🌸🌸🌸

Late that afternoon, as the sun was setting, Alex and I stood on the summit of the Cahokia Pyramid. At my feet was a gum wrapper. Unlike the copper and clay objects found the mounds, this gum wrapper would decay in a few days. Barry Fell of the Epigraphic Society once commented that it is sad that we feel we can know so much about an ancient civilization just by looking at their discarded dishes and bowls. If someone 500 years from now found some of my broken kitchenware in a garbage pit, what would it tell them about me? Not much.

Other discoveries of note at Cahokia are the Woodhenge and the Birdman. Archaeological excavations have partially uncovered remains of four, and possibly five, circular sun calendars that once consisted of large, evenly spaced log posts. Those calendars, called woodhenges because of their similarity to Stonehenge in England, were probably used to determine the changing seasons and other astronomical calculations.

Here we see how the pyramids of Illinois and the Midwest functioned in exactly the same way as pyramids in Central America and Mexico functioned: they were sometimes astronomical observatories, sometimes burial crypts, and sometimes ceremonial buildings where the Priest-King would officiate.

The "Birdman of Cahokia," now the official emblem of Cahokia, was a sandstone image found atop the mound in 1971. The rock carving shows a hybrid monster with a human head and torso, beaklike nose, and wings that are formed of serpents and falcon feathers. Other birdman-type depictions have been found at Spiro Mounds in Oklahoma and Etowah Mounds in Georgia.

Who is this birdman of Cahokia? Birdman motifs are found in remote Pacific Islands (Easter Island has a famous Birdman cult) to ancient India (the flying god Garuda).

Near Cahokia, on a cliff by Alton, Illinois, is a strange rock painting that may hold a key to the "Birdman" of the ancient city. The rock painting is of a gigantic "bird" that the Illini Indians called a *Piasa,* the "bird which devours men."

The rock painting has been there for hundreds of years, and was first described by the French missionary-explorer Jacques Marquette in 1673. He described the rockpainting and the Piasa at that time in these words, "On the flat face of a high rock were painted, in red, black and green, a pair of monsters, each as large as a calf, with horns like a deer, red eyes, a beard like a tiger, and a frightful expression of countenance. The face is something like that of a man, the body covered with scales, and the tail so long that it passes entirely round the body, over the head, and between the legs, ending like that of a fish."

According to local Indian legend, the giant bird had its home high in a cave in the bluff over the Mississippi River. In the beginning, it was able to coexist with the Illini, but during a battle between two tribes, the Piasa carried away two warriors, feasted on them and then acquired a taste for human flesh. Soon children and adults were being carried away in the talons of the bird and eaten. All the Illini now lived in fear of the great bird.

A plan was devised by a brave name Massatoga. He would stand and chant, acting as bait for the Piasa, while twenty of the bravest warriors hid in ambush. As the dreaded Piasa came to devour Massatoga, the other warriors sprang from their hiding places and attacked the huge creature, killing it. They then painted a huge depiction of the Piasa on the cliff at Alton so that the memory of the terrifying beast would be preserved for generations.[171]

The rock painting still exists to this day, though it was been repainted several times over, so the original rock painting has been long gone. Was there some connection between the Birdman of Cahokia and the Piasa? Was the Piasa what the American Indians from British Columbia to Georgia called a "Thunderbird"?

In southern Illinois, near Cahokia and the Piasa petroglyph, occurred a strange incident at 8:10 P.M. on July 25, 1977. Ten-year-old Marlon Lowe of Lawndale, Illinois, was snatched off the ground and carried through the air by an immense bird.

Another Lawndale resident named Cox noticed two large "birds" descending out of the southwest while Marlon was jogging with some friends while the birds swooped down behind the boy, who was unaware of their presence. Marlon was still running when one of the birds snatched him with its claws and carried him into the air.

Marlon's mother Ruth saw the attack and ran screaming after the bird and boy. After carrying him for about 35 feet, the giant creature dropped Marlon, who fell unharmed to the ground. The two birds flew off to the north-east. In all, six persons witnessed the event.

Mrs. Lowe later described the birds as looking like giant condors with six inch beaks and necks one-and-a-half feet long with a white ring in the middle. Except for the ring, the birds were black. The wing spans of the birds were estimated as being from eight to ten feet.

The incident attracted national attention, though the "experts" declared it an impossible occurrence. Mrs. Lowe was branded a liar by the local game warden (even though six people witnessed the event) and pranksters began leaving dead birds on the doorstep of the Lowe residence. The stress from the attack turned Marlon's hair from red to gray over a period of time, and for more than a year afterwards he refused to go out after dark.

Cryptozoological researchers Loren Coleman and Mark Hall believe that the Thunderbirds seen in Illinois, Pennsylvania, Tennessee and other areas may be Teratorns, a supposedly extinct bird that once roamed both North and South America. Many fossils of Teratorns, the largest birds known to have existed, have been found at the La Brea tar pits in Los Angeles. Some Teratorn fossils indicate a wingspan of 17 feet, and the largest of known Teratorn fossil, one from Argentina, had a wingspan of 24 feet. Andean condors, the largest of known birds, has a wingspan of about ten feet.[171,172,173]

If these giant birds were still alive today, as Coleman and Hall believe they are, they certainly could account for the strange tales of gargantuan birds actually attacking people, even to the point of lifting them off the ground.

But what of pterodactyls? The Piasa of Alton, Illinois, seems like a combination of both a Teratorn and a pterodactyl. The Piasa's long tail and horns make it seem like a pterodactyl, though descriptions of giant birds in Illinois are clearly of an avian, rather than reptilian nemesis. Coleman is of the opinion that the pterodactyl stories from Texas and Arizona are encounters with what he thinks is a species of giant bat, coming from the jungles of Central America.

As the sun set over the ancient city of Cahokia, I looked at the Birdman that was used on all the official park brochures. Birdman, Batman or Piasa...why had he been found on top of North America's largest pyramid?

۞۞۞

From St. Louis I headed north into Illinois. In southern Illinois is the famous Koster Site, named after the farmer on whose land it was found. Whenever he plowed his land near the foot of a limestone bluff, he found potsherds. In 1969, a test excavation was begun and by the time the excavation was finished, 13 layers of habitation had been found going back at least 9,500 years. One of their conclusions was that a stable society had existed on the spot as early as 6400 B.C., almost 4000 years earlier than scientists had previously thought that sedentary people had lived in the area. They ate highly nutritious foods, and once again, the age of civilization had been pushed back a few more thousand years, despite what the "experts" had said earlier.

I continued north, passing Springfield, the capital of Illinois, and headed for an unusual community in northern Illinois. Some friends were now living at the intentional community of Stelle, a "utopian" community, that was started in the early 1970s as an alternative to the hustle and bustle of modern life.

Stelle is located in the corn and soybean fields south of Chicago, and though the Windy City is only 60 or 70 miles away, one would think that it was a 1,000 miles away when at Stelle. Stelle itself was something of a lost city, I sometimes thought when walking through the many parks.

Pulling into Stelle from one of the farm roads of rural Ford county, it seemed oddly commonplace and middle class. Sort of like a modern suburb that had been suddenly transported into the prairie wilderness of North Dakota.

Stelle is more than a suburb of families in the cornfields, however. The city is designed to be self-sufficient and has its own telephone company, reverse osmosis water treatment plant, a sewage treatment plant (one of the smallest towns in the world with sewage treatment), a modern factory, telephone company, many small "entrepreneur" businesses, a gasohol plant, a hydroponic greenhouse, its own schools, community center and orchards.

It was good to see some of my old friends again, including Bill, Harry, Carl and many others. I met Carl of the World Explorers Club, and saw the Adventures Unlimited downtown warehouse. They were busy developing an archaeology adventure program, and I was happy to give them my advice. Sharing the same building was George Blackman, a well-known artist whose ceramic vessels were in art galleries around the world.

I learned from a number of residents that the small, intentional city has had its ups and downs. The founder of the community, Richard Kieninger, had started a group in Chicago in the 1960s that ultimately built the city, but he had now moved to Texas and was largely disassociated with the city. Economics had been an on going problem, with many of the residents having to commute daily to Chicago or some other nearby city to find work.

Typically low-key, Stelle has gone out of its way to seem normal and not create too much publicity. Still, the city continued to survive, and many enterprising people had managed to start their own business' and thrive in the quiet, away-from-it-all environment.

I stayed with some of my friends at Stelle; Morrey, Harry (also of the Artstone Collective in Tucson), Carl, Carole and others. They had a communal house with lots of rooms, and it was refreshing to have a bed to sleep in, instead of the usual couch. Eventually the huge old farm house became known as the World Explorers Club, and I became a founding member of the erstwhile organization of travelers, vagabonds, explorers and adventurers. My stay at Stelle and the World Explorers Club was to last for quite sometime, and I found it to be an excellent base for exploring the U.S.A. and over a period of time, I came and went from its hallowed walls of travel books, archaeology volumes and other tomes of history, philosophy and religious studies.

Chicago was close by, and after a half hour of driving through the cornfields, one was soon on the interstate being sucked into the metropolis of Chicago, the third largest city in the U.S.

One afternoon in Chicago, while Harry and I were sitting at one of sidewalk cafes on Rush Street, near the shores of Lake Michigan, I read aloud from the *Reader,* a free weekly newspaper in Chicago—"It says here that Lake Michigan was used for aircraft carrier landing practice. In fact, the aircraft carrier that they landed on was a freshwater, coal fired, paddle-wheel aircraft carrier. Because of the many flight accidents, the bottom of Lake Michigan is littered with vintage Navy aircraft!"

"It's not only littered with vintage Navy aircraft," Harry said, "It's got sunken cities!"

I put down the paper and picked up my cup of tea. Taking a sip I said, "You're joking. So what lost city is at the bottom of Lake Michigan?"

"Beats me," he replied. "But it's there." He then pulled out the daily paper for Jan. 3, 1990 and said, "It's right here in today's paper." Harry then read parts of the story, a fascinating article that was also widely reported on television at the time.

"Divers have discovered a field of ancient wood stumps 80 feet below the surface of Lake Michigan, and geologists believe the find may possibly be the oldest record of human culture in the area. The discovery could be the remains of an ancient forest, or human dwellings that could be as old as 8,000 years, scientists said.

"Divers Alan Olson, Keith Pierson and Taras Lyssenko discovered the field of wood stumps about the size of a city block while searching for old shipwrecks in June somewhere off Calumet Harbor. The stumps measure about one foot in diameter and stand upright one to three feet off the bottom of the lake, the divers said."

Frank Pranschke of the Illinois Geological Survey said, "A piece of wood doesn't mean anything, but when you say 80 feet of water, that is exciting. If it proves to be a forest, then we know there was land there, and that the lake receded 80 feet. If it turns out to be some ancient structures, then it's an archaeological find, and there may be artifacts or remnants of human life down there."

Dr. Charles Shabica, Professor of Earth Science at Northeastern Illinois University in Chicago had the wood carbon dated and was given a date of 6,000 B.C. He further confirmed that via underwater video and side scan sonar, they had mapped the posts and found them to stand uniformly along the bottom in rows, and could be either the roof posts of wooden dwellings or perhaps part of an ancient harbor, the posts appearing to be "moorings."

"So there is a lost city in Lake Michigan," I laughed. "I thought you were joking."

Harry put down his newspaper and smiled through his thick beard. "Would I kid you about *lost cities?* No way!"

🦬🦬🦬

Chicago does have megalithic remains of a mysterious nature. Historical researcher Frank Joseph revealed in issue number two of *World Explorer* magazine,[129] that in the heart of Chicago's Loop on the south bank of the mouth of the Chicago River, once stood a large and curious stone. On one side was expertly fashioned the face of a man, his eyes closed and mouth open, with a chin-beard. At the top of the stone was a depression like a small trough. Three interconnecting holes linked to the trough appeared on either side of the stone and through the parted lips of the face. The relief sculpture measured a foot wide and 17 1/2 inches high, incised to a depth of 1 1/2 inches. Its top hollowed to 4 1/2 inches deep, 18 inches long by 9 inches wide, the 3,000 pound granite block originally stood on an eight by ten foot sand dune overlooking Lake Michigan.

Geologists believe the stone was either deposited by a glacier (which would date it to only 10,000 years ago) or was part of the Canadian Shield, an area of rock at least 570 million years old. It stood outside the stockade of Fort Dearborn, the early settlement that would eventually grow to become the Windy City. Daniel Webster stood on the stone while he harangued the fort's inhabitants in 1837.

When the military outpost was torn down near the close of the nineteenth century, the stone was moved from its original location at what is now Whacker Drive and Michigan Avenue to the Sanitary District's headquarters. A few years later it found its permanent home on display at the Chicago Historical Society, where it may be seen today on the first floor behind the main lobby.

Joseph believes that the one and half ton monolith is a Phoenician mooring stone from 1200 B.C. Says Joseph, "An integral part of the Phoenicians' religion was infant sacrifice to appease the gods and win their favor. The child was taken to a Tophet, a sacred site often out in the open, featuring a rude stone altar, usually not very large, with a depression at the top very much like a baptismal font. There the baby's throat was then cut and the sacrificial blood allowed to run through a hole in the altar.

"A possible scenario suggested by the Waubansee Stone includes a Phoenician sailing vessel, loaded with a cargo of raw copper, skirting the western shore of Lake Michigan heading south from the

361

mines of the upper Peninsula. The ship turns into the mouth of the Chicago River, where hawsers are thrown from bow and stern to hands waiting ashore. The lines, passed through holes in the granite mooring stones on the southern bank, secure her fore—and—aft. At a proper moment, an infant, possibly purchased in trade with local Native American Indians, is placed in the hollow at the top of the Waubansee Stone. There its throat is cut. Sacrificial blood courses through the stone and out the open mouth of the sculpted face, into the river. It is a most important ritual dedicated to the water-gods for safe passage home during the long, perilous voyage to the Mississippi, down to the Gulf of Mexico and out across the Atlantic Ocean."

🐸🐸🐸

One day, Frank told me about the Wisconsin pyramid site known as Aztalan, and how it was believed that several submerged pyramids were in a lake nearby known as Rock Lake. Tales of lost cities have always made my blood flow with a heightened vigor, and the possibility of a sunken city in the Midwest, especially one with pyramids, piqued my interest.

I immediately made plans with Carl, managing director of the World Explorers Club, to drive up to Aztalan. The archaeological site, Wisconsin's largest, lies in southern Wisconsin, near the Illinois border, between Milwaukee and Madison. The nearest town is Lake Mills, a pleasant community that was started as a lumber town and is now a popular summer recreation spot, largely because of the adjacent lake, Rock Lake.

Frank met us at a restaurant in downtown Lake Mills and from there the three of us drove out to the Aztalan pyramid site. I was immediately impressed by the two main pyramids facing each other across a broad plaza. It was like a miniature version of Teotihuacan in Mexican, a Pyramid of the Sun facing a Pyramid of the Moon.

Aztalan was first discovered in 1835 by a local settler named Timothy Johnson. In 1837 Nathaniel Hyer took up the cause of saving Aztalan, and it was he who gave the ancient pyramid site its name. The truncated pyramids on the banks of the Crawfish River seemed to Hyer to be the site described in Aztec legend. The great German naturalist Alexander von Humboldt had written of the Aztec legend that they had come from a land by flowing waters far to the north of their Mexican home. Hyer believed that Aztalan was the place, here were pyramids as in the Valley of Mexico, and it was certainly a place of flowing streams far to the north.

Even though most archaeologists laugh at the idea of Wisconsin as the original homeland of the Aztecs, the name has stuck. Attempts to save the mounds in the 1800s were a failure, and the site remained as private property. Pot hunters picked up countless artifacts, the mounds were partly leveled and plowed, and "Aztalan brick" was hauled away to fill in the local roads. The land was finally purchased in 1921 and Aztalan Mound Park was presented to the Wisconsin Archaeological Society.

A huge stockade, like that of Cahokia and other sites, once surrounded the entire city. Archaeologists have determined through carbon dating that the stockade was burned circa 1300 A.D. and apparently most of the inhabitants killed. Gruesome evidence of cannibalism was found associated with this attack on Aztalan. Apparently, the occupants of Aztalan fought off invaders (or maybe they *were* the invaders), were defeated, their city destroyed, and the dead were eaten. Captives were probably executed, while women typically are forced to assimilate into the conquering tribe.

The ancient Aztalan people themselves, however, do not seem to have been cannibals at all. Evidence of a crematorium at the site has been found, and it appears that the dead were ceremonially cremated, though burials of uncannibalized bodies have been found. Two cultures for which cremation was the main technique of disposing of the dead are the Hindus and Buddhists of the Orient as well as the ancient Atonists of Egypt. Both cremated the dead because they believed that the soul could not reincarnate until the former body had completely ceased to exist.

Another theory on Aztalan is that the original inhabitants themselves practiced cannibalism, and it was for this reason that Aztalan was eventually attacked by other tribes who were tired of being captured and eaten. While this is the theory expounded in several books[160] these same books take the narrow view that Aztalan was only barely connected to the rest of the pyramids and mounds found all over the Ohio and Mississippi River system. Why had the people from Illinois moved up to Wisconsin? "No one knows," says Folsom in *America's Ancient Treasures*.[160] The fact is that the sophisticated pyramid building civilization of the Midwest colonized and traveled over a vast area, and Aztalan was the nearest major site to the all important copper mines in Michigan north of Wisconsin. Aztalan lies at the border of the deep snow line, where winter life north of this area is severely hindered by three to five months of deep snow.

Carl, Frank and I returned to Lake Mills where Frank had chartered a boat for us to dive with. As I was putting on my scuba gear, Frank was talking excitedly about the various structures in Rock Lake. His 1989 article in *FATE*[176] had chronicled some of his explorations, and he told us how there were at least nine different structures in the lake, including two large tent-like pyramids and a conical pyramid. The most important structure he named the "Limnatis Pyramid" after the Roman goddess Diana in her manifestation of as Protectoress of sacred lakes.

The first modern settlers in Lake Mills, during the 1830s, heard tales of "stone teepees" under the water from local Winnebago Indians. As time passed, during periods of extended drought, when the lake level was low, fishermen sometimes glimpsed what appeared to be large, rectangular structures beneath the surface.

During one such period, the mayor of Lake Mills himself caught sight of a pointed, submerged structure and a search for the structures was on. Aerial photos were made, and occasionally a structure was discovered, only to be lost again. The pyramids of Rock Lake were elusive, and by the late 1960s, most professional archaeologists were skeptical that any structures existed in the lake.

In 1988, Frank and Craig Scott of Muskegon, Michigan, had used a side-scan sonar to locate some of the pyramids, and afterward they dove on an enormous structure off the north-east shore in nearly 60 feet of water. We had no side-scan sonar on this trip, but Frank and the boat operator knew where to dive.

Carl helped from the boat as Frank and I got our dive ready for the descent. It was spring time, the time when the water in the lake was clearest. One of the problems that has hindered identification of structures in the lake is that Rock Lake is generally quite murky, having a visibility of only a few feet most of the time because of algae and the loose silt on the bottom of the lake which is easily disturbed.

"Now is a good time to dive," said Frank, pulling the hood of his wet suit over his head. "This is the time of year when the lake starts to warm up and it is especially clear. The algae isn't in full bloom yet, and even though the water is cold, we should have good visibility."

"I can't see anything down there," said Carl, looking down into the dark, cold water.

"We should be over one of the pyramids now," said our boat captain.

"Are you ready for the descent?" Frank asked as he checked his regulator.

I looked down into the deep, murky water. I'm a good swimmer, and love to snorkle and scuba dive, but I've never liked cold, dark water. I checked my regulator and amount of air in my tank. "I guess I'm ready," I said hesitantly.

"Frank, isn't there some legend of a monster in the lake?" asked Carl as he looked over the lake.

Frank nodded. "Rocky, the monster of Rock Lake. He's probably down there somewhere."

"Rocky?" I asked. "Rocky the monster of Rock Lake?" I looked around half expecting some large animal to surface near the boat. "You mean there's supposed to be a monster down there?"

"Probably just a legend," said Frank nonchalantly. "People claim to have seen him, but there aren't any photographs that I know of." With that, Frank flipped over backward into the water and was gone.

Carl looked at me mischievously. "I'll make sure that they put a memorial to you by the lake if the monster gets you," he said.

I nodded and smiled as I edged on to the edge of the boat. "Thanks, Carl, that's thoughtful of you," I said, putting my regulator in my mouth and taking a deep breath. I gave Carl and the boat captain the thumbs up signal and flipped over backward into the lake.

The cold water hit me like an arctic wind. Shivers ran through my body as the bubbles around me danced in the lake. I looked around for Frank, and saw him hovering in the water beneath the boat. He looked at me and we gave each other the okay sign of making a circle with the thumb and forefinger of a hand. Frank then pointed down into the murky depths of the lake and we each pulled on our buoyancy control vests to release air so that we would start our descent to the bottom of the lake, some 60 feet away.

We followed the nylon anchor line down, down, down. At 20 feet we passed a thermocline, a layer of icy cold water. So intently was I staring at the anchor line disappearing into the dark green depths of the lake, I hardly noticed the sudden shivering of my body.

At the bottom, the anchor rested on a sloping bed of mud. Frank motioned to me to follow him along the bottom, and with a strong kick of my flippers, I was propelled along the bottom in the direction of the Limnatis Pyramid. A dark shape now loomed in front of us, Frank reaching it first.

Just as Frank had described it, we were on the edge of a sloping wall of loose rocks. It was like the corner of a tent-shaped structure made of stone. Keeping our depth, we moved along one wall, which was about 100 feet long. The pyramid itself rose only about 18 feet from the mud of the lake floor, though it is believed that about 12 feet of it are now below the mud and silt.

After traversing the pyramid, we ascended to the summit and swam along it. Many of the stones appeared to have been squared, and one large stone on the top, referred to by Frank as the "altar stone," seemed particularly man-made. Frank later pointed out several L-shaped stones, that Frank believed to be alignment stones for astronomical purposes.

Following Frank's lead, we took off into the murky gloom again to look for more structures. Below us the lake dropped off into greater depths, and I turned my head from side to side, looking for structures, or possibly, some large creature that might be following us in the water.

In the darkness of the lake, I thought I saw a shape and made a turn. I saw nothing, but upon looking back, I could not find Frank. The gloomy darkness of the lake had swallowed him, and he was nowhere to be seen.

I gave a few extra kicks in the direction he had been traveling, my heart pounding at the thought of being alone in the darkness of the lake. I kept calm, taking deep breathes of air from my tank. Then I saw Frank's flippers ahead of me. I reached out and touched him on the leg.

He jerked suddenly and turned to look at me. I gave him the OK signal, and he signaled me back.

Checking my airsupply, I saw that my time was running out. Frank had conserved his air better than I, but we agreed to ascend. We came back to the choppy waves of the surface and inflated our buoyancy vests. The boat was several hundred feet from us.

I waved at Carl and the captain, who started the motor to come over and pick us up.

"Did you find anything?" asked Carl.

"There's something down there," I said pulling the regulator out of my mouth. Carl helped me get back in the boat. Moments later I was flopping like a fish on the bottom of the craft, trying to get my flippers and tank off.

"So the monster of Rock Lake didn't get you," said Carl with a smile.

"Not this time," I replied, "but its spooky down there. Pretty spooky."

❀❀❀

Later, at a restaurant that night in Lake Mills, Carl, Frank and I sat around talking about Rock Lake, Aztalan, and the mysteries of Wisconsin.

Frank told us how other divers had retrieved fragments of a plaster-like substance coating a section of the western wall of the Limnatis Pyramid. Analyzed at the University of Wisconsin in Madison, these samples proved to be "unnaturally formed," and, as Frank pointed out, the stockade walls of Aztalan were originally covered with a similar plaster.

So, what were pyramids doing at the bottom of Rock Lake? One theory was that the builders of Aztalan, or someone before them, had purposely damned the local river, thereby flooding the valley where the structures had been built. It was like making your own sunken city. Other theories suggest that an earthquake created a natural dam, thereby flooding the valley. When this flooding occurred, no one can say. It may have happened around 1300 A.D., or it may have occurred hundreds of years earlier, possibly even thousands.

And what of the destruction of Aztalan? Who had built the city, and who had destroyed it?

According to Kingsley Craig, a historical researcher and an epigrapher working with the Epigraphic Society, Aztalan was destroyed about 1250 A.D. by a roving army of 20,000 Mongol men and women, who, in 1233 A.D., had escaped from Genghis Khan in Mongolia and traveled in a mass migration into Canada and down into the Midwest. According to Craig, these Mongols, because the men had long hair, and because their women fought with them became known historically in North America as *Amazons.* His belief is that many of the legends of Amazons in Europe and Asia are referrals to the fierce Mongols.

According to Craig, these marauding Mongols, in much the same manner as the Mongol invasion of western Asia and Europe, laid siege to Aztalan, and destroyed it. They then moved down the Mississippi valley destroying the cities and temple areas as they went. According to Craig, this was the destruction of Aztalan.

Craig's theory is that the Mongols eventually settled in the Gallina River area of northern New Mexico, near the small town of Cuba, northwest of Santa Fe. Here at the Gallina River Valley are 500 towers down a steep gulch.

In 1933, the archaeologist Frank C. Hibben uncovered a 700 year-old archaeological mystery that has yet to be solved. His little-known discovery of series of "medieval-looking fortifications" in the remote Gallina River valley were published in the *Saturday Evening Post* for December 9, 1944 under the title of "The Mystery of the Stone Towers." Except for Hibben's article, published 10 years after his expedition, almost nothing is known about this strange and remote valley.

The towers had first been discovered by a rancher searching for gold. He found no gold, but instead he found evidence of a mass slaughter in the valley from a fierce battle. Inside the stone towers were the skeletal remains of the defenders, many with arrow heads still embedded in their chests and skulls.

Hibben described the towers as generally square and from 25 to 35 feet high. Each tower had a parapet at the top for men to stand on and fight. There were no doors or windows in the towers, they could only be entered or exited from the top. Massive slabs of sandstone were perfectly fitted into the floor.

Inside the first tower, where a few defenders had died and had fallen back inside when the roof collapsed, were the well preserved remains of women-warriors. Says Hibben, "The remarkable dryness of the

Southwestern climate, together with the charring action of the fire, had perfectly preserved the bodies and the evidence with them. They were better preserved than many Egyptian mummies. Here was the body of a woman sprawled backward over one the storage bins. She had been crushed by falling stones from the top of the wall, but her body was remarkably preserved even to a look of intense agony on her somewhat flattened face Studded in her breast and stomach were the charred ends of 16 arrows of cane with flint heads. She still clutched in her left hand a bow, even with a part of the string still on one end. It was a short bow, powerful looking, of oak wood, and yet the body was undoubtedly that of a woman."

Hibben calls the attack on the Gallina towers, "vengefulness without any quarter." Through tree-ring dating, Hibben said the dates for the construction of the towers from the year 1143 A.D. to the year 1248 A.D. Apparently, in one century, the towers were built and "equally apparent is the fact that some people swept through the country and destroyed them all."

Hibben says, "It seems obvious that the Gallina people were not ordinary Pueblo Indians. The physical make-up of the skeletons in the towers was slightly different. Many of the their utensils and weapons were radically different. For instance, their typical cooking pots with the pointed bottoms are absolutely un-Pueblo-like. The fact that they used elk antlers for axes and adzes is unlike the Pueblos. The very fact that they built stone towers in itself distinguishes them from any of the pueblo peoples that we now know. In one of the towers we found a handful of pieces of pottery of a type which is not indigenous to the Southwest at all. This is a variety of pottery known in Nebraska, and even farther to the east in the Mississippi Valley." Concludes Hibben, "They came from the plains, possibly as far east as the Mississippi Valley itself, and brought with them a number of their characteristics." Hibben, after analyzing the arrows that killed these people, decides that the Pueblo Indians were responsible for the total decimation of these mysterious people.

So the questions that remain are who were these Gallina River Valley people and where did they come from? Why had they moved to the Gallina River area and built their towers? Why had the Pueblo Indians made such a gigantic effort to eradicate these powerful warriors? According to Hibben, they had migrated to New Mexico from the Mississippi Valley.

According to Kingsley Craig, one of the few historical researchers to be aware of the Gallina River Valley people and their strange history, the Gallina people were the very same Mongol marauders who are the ancestors of the Dene. They came down through Canada, warring and slaughtering as they came. After destroying Aztalan, they moved on down the Mississippi valley, crossed the Great Plains and finally settled in the Gallina Valley.

Craig maintains that the Pueblo Indians, in a remarkable mobilization of all the various tribes, finally sieged them in Gallina, and killed the Mongolian warriors to the last man and woman, leaving not even one alive. Typically, in the wars of the American Indians on each other, the men of a defeated tribe were all killed, and the women absorbed into the victorious tribe. However, because the Gallina River Mongols had such fierce women warriors, "Amazons," fighting with them, the Pueblo Indians had little desire to take these women captive. It probably would have been impossible anyway.

"Mongols coming to Wisconsin to destroy Aztalan?" asked Carl. "That's a pretty wild theory."

"Yet, there is other evidence," I suggested. I pulled out an unusual book published by the Institute for the Study of American Cultures (ISAC) in Columbus, Georgia. The book was *The Dene and Na-Dene Indian Migration 1233 A.D.—Escape from Genghis Khan to America* by Ethel G. Stewart.[177] The book is a thick hardback that is authoritatively researched and presents a strong case that the Dene and Na-Dene Indian tribes, known commonly as Athapaskan Indians, came into America as late as the 13th century.

Who were the Dene and Na-Dene? Na-Dene was the Asiatic-Alaskan language spoke by Athapaskan Indians who migrated into North America from Siberia. Says the *Smithsonian Book of North American Indians*,[178]: "...about A.D. 750, some Athapaskan dispersed to settle the coasts of Alaska, British Columbia and California, giving rise to the ancestors of Pacific Northwest tribes such as the Haida, Tlingit and Hupa. Others moved east across central Canada north of the Great Plains. About the fifteenth century A.D., some Na-Dene appeared in the Southwest...their arrival caused some disruption among well-established south-western cultures about the time of the first European contact." And, "The bow and arrow probably came to the Plains dwellers via the Na-Dene, Athapaskan speakers who migrated south out of the Asia-Alaska region into western Canada and the Plains. The people of Wyoming's High Plains adopted the bow quickly, because it has important advantages over the atlatl and spear."[178]

"It is interesting," said Carl, "that the charge of racism among archaeologists about any suggested pre-Columbian contacts in North America must now include the very same people that allegedly made the first voyage across the Bering Straits in the first place. Is it a racist suggestion to suggest that the same people made the same trip many times over, the last in 1233 A.D.? The whole thing makes me laugh!"

Frank and I nodded in agreement. The history of North America was one of continued invasion, a history much more interesting than a few ice age hunters following game into Alaska and eventually populating two huge continents.

1200 A.D. was an eventful time in east Asia as well as in North America. Aztalan was destroyed about this time. 1250 A.D. is when the Hopwell people came to an end. The Gallina culture in New Mexico also came to an end at this time. The Toltec Empire of Mexico and Arizona came to end in the thirteenth century and it was this century that the Aztecs migrated into the Valley of Mexico. Perhaps the Aztecs did originally come from Aztalan as the early namers of the ancient city suspected.

I finished the last of a plate of spaghetti and looked at Frank and Carl. The memories of the dive in the lake were still fresh in mind. The green plaza and large pyramids of Aztalan were just down the road. Maybe Rocky, the monster of Rock Lake was just the collective spirit of the many who had fought and died defending the ancient city. Like the truth about North America, when would it be set free?

🐉🐉🐉

A few nights later I attended a meeting of the Wisconsin Mounds Society in Madison. There I met with Dr. Scherz of the University of Wisconsin and a number of people who were keenly interested in the prehistory of the Midwest, and were not shackled by the dogmatic views presented by the "experts." It was refreshing to be with a group of intelligent and intellectual people who shared my own views on varied origins of American cultures and a fascination with intriguing puzzles in history.

There was an interesting report on Sanskrit words in American Indian languages and Dr. Scherz produced a curious book called *Hindu America* [93] and showed it to the group.

Then, an older man, large and clean shaven, stood in front of the group and told about a cave that he had discovered in southern Illinois and about the various artifacts he had discovered inside it. His story was as fascinating and exciting as any Indiana Jones film, and, curiously, he resided in Indiana, just near the Illinois border.

The man was Russell Burrows and his story was about the discovery of *Burrows Cave* in a remote valley that he has so far kept a secret.

In April of 1982 Burrows was engaged in his "get away from it all" hobby of metal detecting the old homesteads in Southern Illinois for the purpose of finding relics such as axes, wedges, etc., as well as the personal items of our early settlers. On this particular day, he was in search of one of these early sites and was into the second week of the search without luck. He had taken a seat on the bluff which overlooks a small valley to rest and give the situation some thought when he decided that he was on a wild goose chase. He stood up and had turned to begin the long walk out, when suddenly he found himself falling into a pit which had been secreted beneath a large oval stone which, as he later discovered, was fitted into the pit opening and designed to flip or turn over when stepped on and trap anyone who might have the misfortune to step on. Fortunately, the stone, instead of turning over, slid off to one side and left the pit open.

At the bottom he found himself staring at a very large face cut into the wall of the pit. There were many other figures cut into the wall of that pit as well as "strange" symbols. He also noticed that the face was done in such a way that it was watching a sealed up portal or doorway.

At this point he took a good hard look at the valley and began, for the first time, to realize that it was a strange sort of place. He decided to forget the homestead he was searching for and have a good look around. Thus, he told the group, began the search of the valley which has resulted in the controversy–is Burrows Cave genuine, or is it a hoax?

According to Burrows' description, the valley lies on a south-east to north-west heading and is about 500 or so yards in length with a width of about 75 feet to about 300 feet and has a depth at the cliff walls ranging from 20 feet to about 40 feet. The walls of these cliffs are water worn and undercut to some degree and there are several very large blocks of limestone/sandstone lying at the base of the wall on the west side. The floor of the valley is rather flat with a small creek running through the valley from the south to the north. He began his search at the south and soon located the entrance to the fabulous cave now called Burrows Cave.

He crawled under a ledge and was in the process of looking for petroglyphs when he noticed that the back side of the overhang he was under had a hollow sound to it. He began to dig along the back wall of the overhang. At about two feet depth, he uncovered the top of a portal and further digging revealed that the portal was sealed with cut and fitted stone blocks. In the center of the portal was a carved head which had the appearance of a wild boar and a careful study indicated that the head was a key stone. He was five days in figuring how to get that head out and finally accomplished that task by sliding a long slender piece of steel into the crack. In so doing, he pushed another stone out of what later proved to be a notch in the stem on the back of the head. Once this was done, the head slipped out and the rest of the seal was removable. He had the presence of mind to number those blocks in the order that they were removed and, as it was now clear that a cave was on the other side, he stored those blocks inside for future replacement.

He told the group that he had been into caving for the better part of his life and so had no fear of going into this one. The cave was rather tight top to bottom, but the width was a good size. The average distance from the top or ceiling to the top of what has proven to be silt ranged from 18 to 24 inches and the width at the widest point is close to 55 feet with a narrow point of just under three feet. It was obvious from the smoke blackened ceiling that fire light had been used at some point in the past and so the depth of 18 to 24 inches was most likely not the true measurement. He found that, by the use of shotgun cleaning rods, a measurement of nine to 12 feet was the true depth from the floor to the ceiling. One question was, "Where did all of the silt come from?" He was to find the answer to that question later.

So began the exploration of this cave and the discovery of the many artifacts confined therein. The first thing he noticed were wall lamps which were cut out of a projection of solid stone. These lamps were two-headed, that is, having a head on both ends. One seems to be looking at the entrance of the cave while the other seems to be looking into the reaches of the cave. They all have blackened rims and the area above each is blackened with soot. He found these lamps about 20 to 25 feet apart and on both sides of the cave. Also he noticed that the ceiling is blackened with soot which indicated that torches had been used to light the cave.

For several days after his first entry, he continued to explore the cave. He came into an area of the cave which was very large where he discovered another figure, this one was black and very well executed. There were four more in a half circle. The statues, he claimed, looked Egyptian.

It is at this point of the exploration that he began to dig. Because of the close quarters, he was unable to dig these statues out, but was able to clear the silt down to hip level. He found that each one of the statues was standing with its left foot forward and its left arm extended. In each of the left hands, which was doubled into a fist, a hole could be seen and it is clear that each of these statues held a staff or something like a staff which by measurement was just under three quarters of an inch in diameter. Each statue was wearing a pointed hat with well done etching and all were bare chested except for crossed belts on three of them. They were belted at the waist but he could not state whether or not they are wearing trousers or a

371

skirt, though his impression is that they were wearing a skirt. Their other furnishings were arm bands, wrist bracelets and a very wide, well-done necklace. By using the shotgun cleaning rods, he determined that the statues are in excess of eight feet tall.

Looking closely along the walls of the cave he located 12 portals which are also sealed with cut and fitted blocks of stone. He has found 12 of these to date. After removing the stones of one of the portals and shining a light into the area behind the seals, he found himself looking at a full skeleton. As the blocks of stone were large, he had no trouble getting through the opening.

The skeleton was laid out upon a solid stone block large enough to hold not only the remains but artifacts as well. These artifacts included axe heads of marble and other stone material, an axe head of what appears to be bronze, a short sword of what also appears to be bronze as well as other artifacts which could be considered as personal weapons. Also to be seen are bronze spears in a set of three, the longest being at or about six feet in length and the shortest being about three feet. There were also several jars of what appeared to be clay standing about the crypt. Also in the crypt were the remains of arm bands, head bands and other such items. He could observe no wounds to the bones.

In another crypt, he found that three persons had been entombed—a female and two children. The female had a point lodged in her chest and it had punctured a rib and gone into the area of the heart. The children each had a large puncture of the head about two inches in width and about three to four inches in length. These wounds were in the forehead. Various items were found around the skeletons.

It was a fascinating tale that Russel Burrows was telling the group. He then walked to a slide projector and began to show some slides of the artifacts found in the cave. While various photos of metal plates and coins were shown, Burrows told us about his efforts to have the site and the artifacts authenticated.

"I knew that I had better contact someone with training in archaeology and try to get some answers. So I contacted an anthropologist at Eastern Illinois University, located at Charleston, Illinois and he said that he would make an attempt to help figure out what I had found. I gathered up several artifacts and went to see this scholar. He had no idea what I had and he said so. He did however, say that he would try to find someone who could assist in figuring out the puzzle.

"I returned home and later that afternoon, I received a call from this fellow. He told me that he had called the state archaeologist and after describing to her what he had seen, he was told, and I quote word for word what he said she told him: 'Oh, I know what those things are. They were made by a cult in Southern Illinois about one hundred years ago and hidden in caves or buried.' I could not believe what I was hearing. Here is a fellow who is a scholar, or rather, supposed to be a scholar and he is accepting this statement from another scholar as fact when the artifacts have not been seen or studied. That state archaeologist is so good at her field that she can make a determination from a telephone description."

Burrows continued to flash slides for the audience. Many of the artifacts that he showed were plainly Egyptian. Some were a dull yellow color.

"Is that item made out of gold?" I asked as a slide of metallic plate came on the screen.

Burrows looked at me and hesitated. "Yes, it is gold," he said.

"And did you discover the reason for the cave being filled with silt?" I asked.

"Yes," Burrows answered me. "I began to realized that the artifacts being recovered were being found in a straight line from the entrance to the next obstruction and that indicated to me that these things had been moved by water—water with a lot of force behind it to move some of the slabs of stone. Some of them are quite heavy, so it was no little trickle that had gone through this cave.

"Then I remembered something that I had seen in the north and of this valley—a hole filled with water. I eventually came up with the theory that the 1811-1812 earthquake that made the Ohio and the Mississippi Rivers had run backwards for three days and had also opened a seam in the stone bed of a long forgotten river or lake. In so doing, that body of water came rushing into the cave and after filling the cave, just sat there until it finally seeped and drained away, leaving all of the mud, sand and goodness knows what else built up in the cave and after drying out, it became the silt that was in the cave.

"A study of topo maps did reveal that the area has the look of a waterway and so it is possible that a river or lake could have gone underground at some time in the past. I have to believe that this is the case because there is no other explanation. Time will tell the whole story."

"How many artifacts have you recovered from the cave?" asked one person at the meeting.

"So far, I've recovered in excess of two thousand artifacts from the cave," Burrows replied.

"So what's your theory on the origin of the objects?" asked someone else.

"Apparently, they're Egyptian objects deposited there about 2,700 years ago," he replied matter-of-factly.

It was starting to get late, and the meeting officially was closed. People drifted away and the slide projector was shut off. I was quite amazed at the revelations revealed that evening, some eight or nine years since the actual discovery of the cave. As several people had pointed out, it was either a fantastic and elaborate hoax, or it was all quite genuine.

In the Epigraphic Society's *Occasional Publications,* vol. 17, 1988, a quick review of the some of the Burrows Cave artifacts was given, and it was decided that they were not actual Egyptian artifacts, but crude fakes. According to the Epigraphic Society, in 1976 Barry Fell inadvertently placed an incorrect copy of the famous Cuenca Elephant tablet (from Ecuador) on the cover of one of their *Occasional Publications.* It contained a misshapen "ya" symbol, that had been incorrectly copied by Fell. Later, Fell corrected the mistake, but Fell claims that one of the relics from Burrows Cave is a crude copy of the incorrect Cuenca Tablet first published in 1976.

I asked Joseph Mahan, the director of the *Institute for the Study of American Cultures,* a Yuchi Indian, and the respected author of *The Secret: America in World History Before Columbus,*[181] whether he thought that the discovery at Burrows Cave was authentic. Mahan replied that he was convinced that it was authentic, and that Barry Fell's objection was not valid because the "ya" symbol is used in various ways, including Fell's "misshapen ya" and the Burrow's Cave artifact. He pointed out that there were a number of "elephant tablets" around, including the Cuenca tablet and the Davenport Stele. "I'm completely convinced that the find is authentic," he told me over the phone. "There are gold coins, statues and 2,000 other artifacts which would be very difficult to fake. I respect Barry Fell a great deal, but in this case I believe that his criticism is invalid."

So a controversy most definitely exists around the Burrows Cave artifacts. The cave is still being kept a secret, though several people have now been inside it, and it would be more difficult to fake large stone statues buried in silt, cut-stone crypts and ancient skeletons. In the case of the Burrows Cave artifacts, only time will tell what the truth is.

🐗🐗🐗

Farther north in the upper part of Wisconsin, as well as in the Upper Peninsula of Michigan, north of Wisconsin, are ancient copper mines that go back to 5000 B.C. or more. On Isle Royale, an island in Lake Superior, now a National Park near Thunder Bay, Ontario, hundreds of ancient, open-pit copper mines are to be found. Much of the ground is pure copper—in 1874 one solid mass of copper was found on Isle Royal which weighed 5,720 pounds. On it were clear marks that showed where prehistoric hammerstones had battered off chunks of copper. Obviously, the huge boulder of copper had once been even larger.

Along the south shores of Lake Superior are more than 5,000 open pit copper mines, extending for 100 miles. Every copper mine now functioning in the area has been found to have been worked in prehistoric times. However, as yet, "no indications of settlement, no human or animal bones, and no burials have been found here. There are no indications that the Indians knew or cared anything about the place."[94]

At Oconto, Wisconsin, just north of Green Bay, can be found Copper Culture State Park. Here, in 1948, a young boy found some bones in a gravel pit. His first thought was that there had been a murder, and he reported his discovery to the sheriff. It was an archaeologist, however, who solved the mystery, as the bones belonged to an Indian who had been buried for a very long time. In the same gravel pit were other burials, many of them, and made in three different ways: some of the bodies had been cremated; some of the bodies had been buried with the flesh removed; and about half had been buried while the flesh was still intact. Most interesting of all were the many copper tools discovered with them.

Carbon 14 tests then showed that these people, now called the Old Copper culture, had lived about 5,000 years ago. This date shows that copper was being mined in North America at the same time the copper age in Asia and Middle East was also happening.

One curious aspect of the Wisconsin and Michigan copper miners is that from 5000 to 3000 B.C. (possibly even at older dates than this) copper was mined in the area, yet, at a later time copper was not being mined or used at all by Wisconsin Indians, certainly not when the first European settlers arrived in the area in the early 1800s. It has often been said that one reason that the Europeans were able to conquer and colonize Canada and the United States so easily was that the Indians residing in these areas at the time were essentially a stone-age culture with few, if any, metal tools. While this may have been true in the 1600s and 1700s, it certainly was not true in 3000 B.C. Some sort of technological reversion had most definitely occurred.

Many books on North American Indians do their best to play down the entire copper mining episode, suggesting that a few remote tribes happened to stumble on a boulder of copper, hammer out a spearhead or two, then decide that copper is inferior to stone arrowheads (which are harder) and continue to use stone.[160] The Smithsonian has a display of a few Indians in loin clothes breaking up copper chunks with some rocks, the whole diorama looking suitably primitive.

Instead, the facts are quite different. According to an article in the prestigious *American Antiquities Magazine* entitled *Metallurgical Characteristics of North American Prehistoric Copper Work*,[179] "The use of native copper in some prehistoric cultures of North America was both extensive and technically skillful. The remains of pits sunk into every major native copper lode in the Lake Superior region show that the material was mined in quantity. Float copper, found on the surface, was also used. The Indians appreciated some of the properties of copper and made use of these in shaping tools, weapons, and ornaments of high-quality workmanship."

Other fascinating revelations in the article include the following statements, "The shapes of the objects suggest that they were formed by a considerable amount of hammering. Local etching differences due to segregation in the native metal are absent in most of them; this indicates an annealing temperature above 600°C, which is sufficient to homogenize the copper....One of the objects, #52230C, is unusual in that it has a cast microstructure, but it is probably spurious (The tin, lead, and nickel contents are far too high for native copper, but could be matched in smelted and fire-refined copper from Europe). The microstructure is typical of a casting with no twins. The grain boundaries intercept the surface perpendicularly, indicating that the present surface is the original, undistorted surface of the casting. This suggest that the ax was not shaped by hammering, nor even ever used, although it is patterned after a worn wrought implement."[179]

The article went on to state that "The grain size in most of the objects corresponds to annealing temperatures of 700° to 800°C — far higher than is necessary simply to soften the metal for further working. The question arises whether the prehistoric Indian ever took his annealing temperature high enough to cause partial or complete melting of the native copper during working...a partially worked lump of copper from the Turner Mound, a site of the Hopewell couture prior to A.D. 300 (artifact #29875) ...The particles of oxide along the grain boundaries and within the grains, as well as the obvious diffusion gradients revealed by etching, are indications of an unusual treatment and may have been caused by heating to a temperature at which the copper was hot-short (above 1000°C).[179]

Who were these ancient copper miners, and where did their copper go? It has been suggested that the estimated 100 million to 500 million tons of copper that came out of Wisconsin and Michigan circa 3000 B.C. went to the Mediterranean to fuel the blossoming Copper Age that was happening there at the time. Even the lower figure of 100 million tons of copper represents a far greater quantity than primitive America could in all probability absorbed. There are only a few instances of copper artifacts found in the United States and Canada. Copper scrolls have been found in some mounds, and some skeletons found in mounds were wearing copper armor, such as the skeletons found in Spiro Mounds, Oklahoma, Walkerton, Indiana, and Fall River, Massachusetts. [94]

Dr. Eiler L. Henrickson of Carleton College in Minnesota has expressed the belief that most of the copper from these ancient mines was removed to the ancient Near East circa 3,000 B.C. These ancient copper miners were likely to have been Egyptians and Phoenicians. During a later copper age, the mines were used by other cultures, including Norse, Celts, and perhaps the Toltecs.

Whoever the miners were, the fact is that no one knows what happened to the vast amount of mined copper that came out of these ancient mines, and it has never been explained why the mines ceased to have been worked.

❀❀❀

Back in Stelle, I was busy digesting the many diverse clues to ancient civilizations in the Midwest. There were the fascinating effigy mounds in southwest Wisconsin on Iowa, not to mention the famous Serpent Mound in Ohio of a gigantic snake swallowing an egg. For whom were these gigantic figures meant? Much like the gigantic figures on the Nazca Plain in Peru, they meant little to ground observers, but seen from the air took on whole new meanings, namely whatever animal design that may be. While it might be said that these were magical hunting totems meant to help in the hunt, this could hardly be said of the Serpent Mound of a snake swallowing an egg.

Ohio has quite a few mysteries, aside from the many mounds, pyramids and forts. On March 17, 1992, the New York Times reported a story of a prehistoric building found in Ohio that was carbon dated to 10,200 B.C.

Said the article, "Archeologists say carbon-dating shows that post holes and pits uncovered at a construction site in Medina, Ohio, are 12,000 years old, making them the oldest evidence of structures in North America.

"The site is about five miles west of Akron in northeast Ohio. It was uncovered in 1990. Carbon-dating by the University of Arizona put the structure at about 10,200 B.C., said David Brose, chief curator of archeology at the Cleveland Museum of Natural History.

"Until the discovery, the oldest known structure in North America dated back 6,200 years. Those post holes were found in the Illinois River Valley in the 1960's, he said.

"John E. Blank, a professor of anthropology at Cleveland State University, said the discovery ranked among the most important archaeological finds in the Eastern United States in 20 years.

"Mr. Brose designated the discovery as the Paleo Crossing Site. The site includes three post holes and two pits in an area of about 150 square feet.

"Archeologists compared the site to a corner of a burned-out house. The find shows evidence of a structure but no indication of its size or style, they said.

"Sharp stones, known as Clovis points, also were found at the site. Similar specimens, first discovered in Clovis, N.M., date back 12,000 years. The points found are two inches long and were probably attached to shafts and used as weapons, Mr. Brose said."[180]

I leaned back in my chair at the World Explorers Club that evening and closed my eyes. It was only a few years ago that archaeologists were arguing whether man had even existed in North America 12,000 years ago, and now they were wondering what style of houses the contractors built in the fashionable suburbs of the time.

Whether it was sunken cities in Wisconsin, Runestones in Oklahoma, birdmen in Illinois, 7,000 year-old copper mines in Michigan, or this new discovery in Ohio, North America never ceased to fascinate me. My travels around the world had taken me across the Sahara, down the Amazon, over the Himalayas and through many adventures. Who would have thought that there would be just as much excitement here in the "boring" Midwest?

The excavation of Craig's Mound at Spiro Mounds in Oklahoma, 1936-1941.

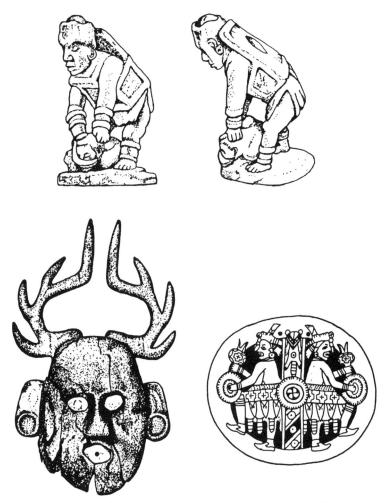

Top: A ceramic pipe believed to show a human sacrifice. Note the unusual costume of the man. From Spiro Mound. Below left: A deer mask from Spiro Mound, similar to Celtic Masks. Below right: Design on a carved shell. Note the Swastika symbol of ancient India.

Heavener Runestone

Poteau Runestone

Shawnee Runestone

Top: The Runic inscriptions from the Heavener, Poteau and Shawnee Runestones. Below: The Germanic (Old Norse) Futhark of 24 runes. Bottom: The Scandinavian Futhork of 16 runes.

Birds-eye view of Cahokia Mound.

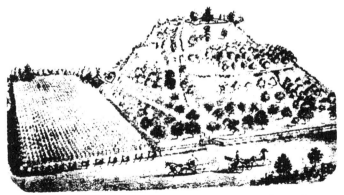

The Cahokia pyramid from an 1873 atlas of Madison County, Illinois.

The winged bird-man of Cahokia,
now the symbol of the site.

The Piasa rock painting at Alton, Illinois as shown in *The Valley of the Mississippi* by Henry Lewis published in 1854.

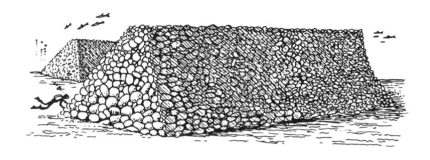

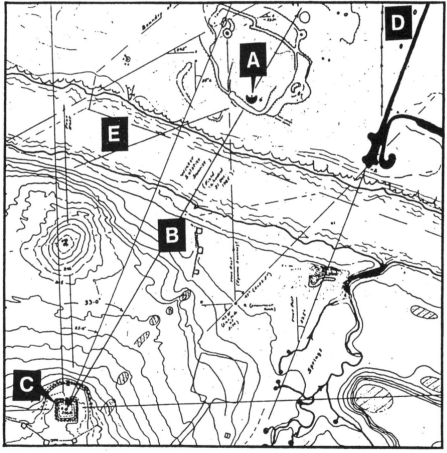

Above: An artists conception of the underwater pyramids at Rock Lake in Wisconsin. **Below:** Dr. Scherz's map of the alignments at Aztalan. A-Cresent Moon Mound. B-Stone monolith's original position. C-Aztalan's Pyramid of the Sun. D-Turtle Effigy Mound aligned to Winter solstice. E-Summer solstice sunrise alignment of Pyramid of the Sun.

Pl. I.

ANCIENT WORKS   Sec. 36. Town 20. Range 18. – East side of   L. WINNEBAGO.

Surveyed in 1853, by I. A. Lapham. – 200 ft to an in.

200 Yds.

330 Yds.

"Perpendicular"—Cliff of Limestone.   200 feet high

LAKE WINNEBAGO

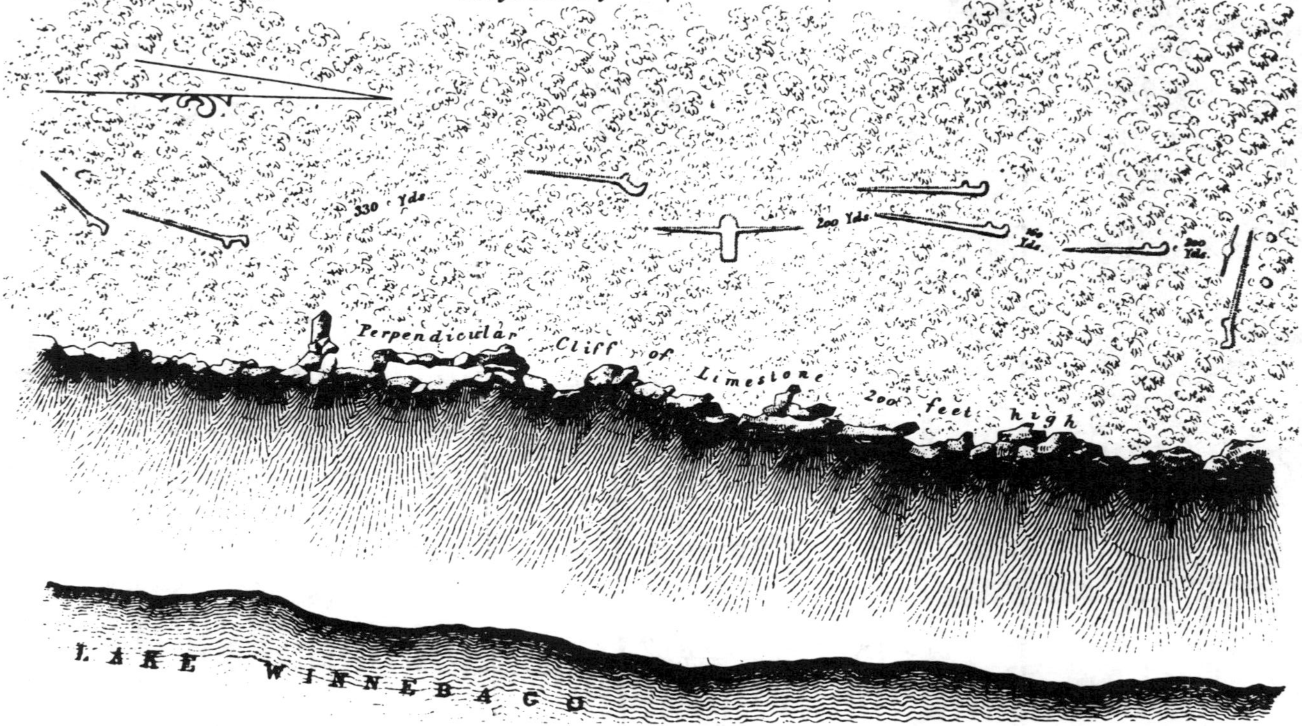

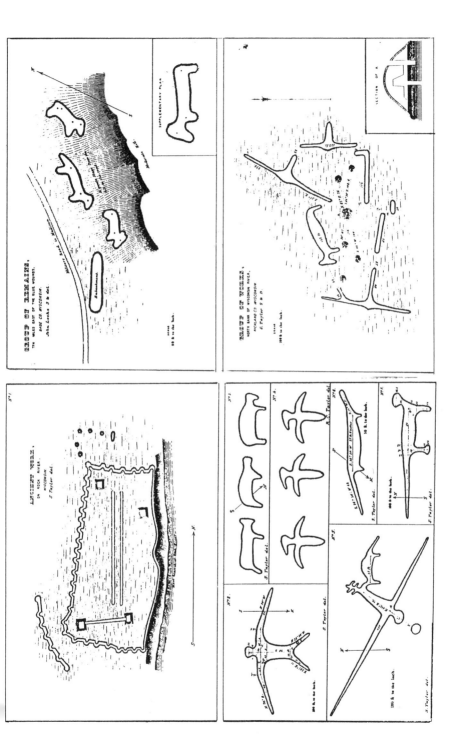

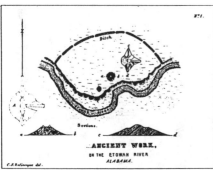

ANCIENT WORK,

ON THE ETOWAH RIVER
ALABAMA.

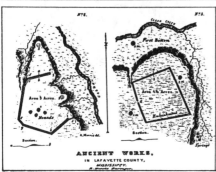

ANCIENT WORKS,

IN LAFAYETTE COUNTY,
MISSISSIPPY.

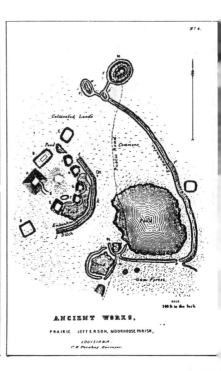

ANCIENT WORKS,

PRAIRIE JEFFERSON, MOORHOUSE PARISH,

LOUISIANA

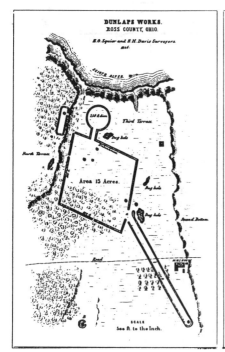

DUNLAPS WORKS.
ROSS COUNTY, OHIO.

E.G. Squier and E.H. Davis Surveyors.
1846.

Area 13 Acres.

SCALE
See ft. to the Inch.

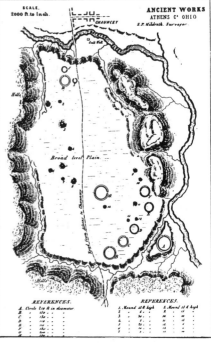

SCALE.
2000 ft. to Inch.

ANCIENT WORKS
ATHENS Cº OHIO
S.P. Hildreth, Surveyor.

Broad level Plain.

REFERENCES.

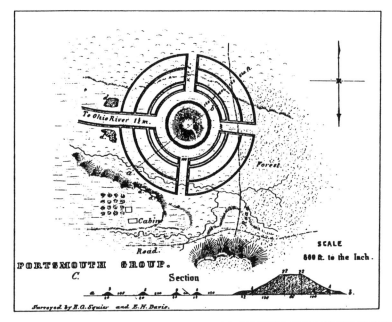

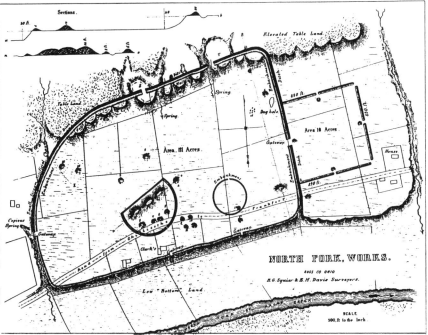

This page and opposite: Illustrations of pyramids, effigy mounds and other gigantic earthworks from the 1848 Smithsonian work on the Ancient Monuments of the Mississippi Valley. **Above:** Particularly interesting are the huge earthworks at Portsmouth, Ohio, where concentric canals and fortification are like a miniture version of Atlantis.

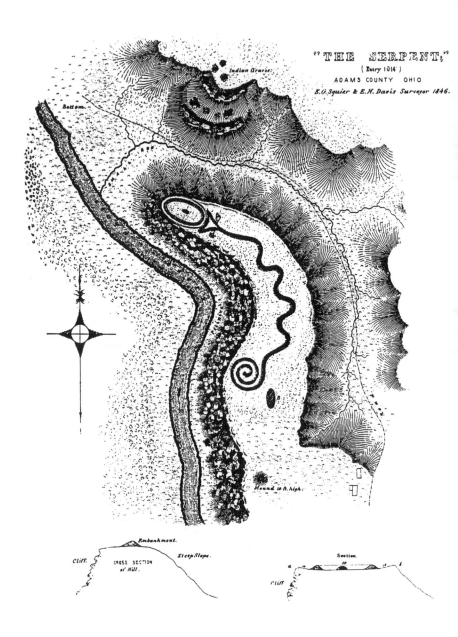

"THE SERPENT;"
(Entry 1014)
ADAMS COUNTY   OHIO
E. G. Squier & E. H. Davis Surveyor 1846.

Indian Graves.

Bottom.

Mound 10 ft. high.

Embankment.

Cliff.   CROSS SECTION of Hill.   Steep Slope.

Section.

Cliff

Chapter 11

Florida and the Caribbean:

The Search For Atlantis

*Travel is fatal to prejudice, bigotry
and narrowmindedness*
—Mark Twain

One bright, spring morning, I left the World Explorers Club and headed south for Florida and the Caribbean. Carl, Morrey and I had breakfast and discussed my trip.

"Be sure to stop in Key Largo and see our old buddy Steve Mallet," said Morrey. "You can probably stay on his yacht while you're down there."

"Check out Coral Castle near Miami, and try and get some good photos of the Bimini Wall. Those giant underwater stones seem to be just like the massive walls in Peru," said Carl, finishing his cup of coffee.

"OK, you guys, I'd better head out, I want to get as far down the road as possible today," I said, grabbing my coat. The truck was all tuned up and ready to go. I had camping equipment and books to sell for Adventures Unlimited in the back.

I dropped in downtown at Adventures Unlimited's offices and George Blackman's art studio nearby to say goodbye to everyone there. With that I was pulling out of town and heading down the country roads toward southern Indiana and Tennessee.

It was good to be on the road again. I enjoy being snowed in for a few months in the winter. It gives me time to read, work on my books, and just relax and organize my life. But after a while, I'm ready to hit the road, have some wind in my face, and an unknown destination in front of me. Once again I was living for the moment. My mind raced at the many adventures that were yet to come. As the great Zen commentator Alan Watts once said, "The joy of travel is not nearly so much in getting to where one wants to go as in the unsought surprises which occur on the journey."

The farms and fields of America were spread before me. I intended to drive the back highways and rural roads as much as possible. This was the real America, I thought, leaning on my window, the Heartland of this great country. People were honest, friendly and hardworking. Rural America is what this country is all about.

Indiana and Tennessee have their share of lost cities and ancient mysteries. As all over the Midwest, there are remains of many ancient pyramids, mounds and habitation. At Brewersville Indiana, on the banks of the Sand River, a stone pyramid was excavated in 1879 that was 71 feet in diameter and between three and five feet high. It was found to contain a number of skeletons, one of which was nine feet eight inches long. It wore a necklace of mica and at its feet stood a rough human image made of burned clay with pieces of flint embedded in it. Weapons nearby were unlike those used by the Indians.

The digging was made under supervision of the Indiana state archaeologist and included guest scientists from Ohio and New York, as well as the neighborhood physician, Dr. Charles Green and the owner of the property, a man named Robinson. The bones and artifacts were preserved by the Robinson family in a basket at a grain mill near the site, until a flood swept the mill away in 1937.[94]

At Walkerton, Indiana, 20 miles from South Bend, a group of amateur archaeologists opened a mound in 1925 and unearthed the skeletons of eight giants ranging from eight to nine feet long. All were wearing heavy copper armor. Through the bungling of these diggers and the complete disinterest of the archaeological establishment, these discoveries have now been scattered and lost. One wonders if they might have ended up in the Smithsonian's secret vaults?

🐘🐘🐘

By late afternoon I was in the back country of Kentucky heading for Tennessee. Kentucky, too, has its share of mysteries. According to Charles Berlitz, a mastodon's skeleton was discovered at Blue Lick Springs in Kentucky at a dig that had reached twelve feet below the surface. Incredibly, as the excavating team dug deeper, looking for more bones, they came across a set-stone pavement, *three feet under* the mastodon.[174]

Jim Brandon, author of *Weird America*,[94] says that a sizable complex of tunnels is supposed to lie somewhere beneath Lexington, Kentucky. According to Brandon, "G.W. Ranck relates in his 1872 *History of Lexington* that hunters from the pioneer settlement of Boonesborough in 1776 discovered rocks of 'peculiar workmanship' with a tunnel behind them. Small at first, this portal eventually expanded to a sort of gallery, four feet wide and seven high, that inclined sharply down into the rock. The ramp led after a few hundred feet to a chamber 300 feet long, 100 feet wide, and 18 feet high. Inside this lay idols, altars, and about 2,000 human mummies.

"According to the legend, these catacombs were subsequently explored a number of times. In 1806, they were visited by Thomas Ashe, the Irish travel writer. Eventually, the story goes, the entrance was lost as the city grew overhead... W.D. Funkhouser and W.S. Webb conceded in their authoritative Archaeological Survey of Kentucky that 'limestone caves and spring water passages in the rock are present beneath and in the vicinity of Lexington,' but as for the mummy chamber: 'the tale is probably nothing more than the figment of a well-developed imagination and there are absolutely no facts to support it.' Apparently Funkhouser and Webb had not actually investigated the admitted caverns, however, but formed their opinion on the negative evidence of a lack of received facts."[94]

The story of the tunnel and the mummies is quite possibly fact. At Mammoth Cave National Park just north of Bowling Green, were found a number of different mummies. There have been strange reports since 1809 of unusual preserved cadavers in and around the huge cave network. One of these mummies was found in 1920 on a ledge deep in the cavern; it was red-haired and less than three feet tall, so naturally it is now labeled a "child." Many of the remains were fragile and have not survived, but one mummy can presently be seen at the state Museum of Anthropology in Lexington.

Mammoth Cave is believed to be the world's largest cave system. It has been determined that the Mammoth Cave connects with the Flint Ridge system. Mammoth Cave has still not been entirely explored, and probably never will be.

The Mammoth Caves are believed by some to be part of a vast subterranean system that exists all over the world. Whatever the case, Mammoth Caves have some strange mysteries. Besides red haired midget mummies, there are found in Mammoth Caves a series of human footprints found molded here and there in the rock floor of the cave. Dr. Lathel F. Duffield, director of the Kentucky Museum of Anthropology at Lexington (in 1978) told Jim Brandon in *Weird America* that the footprints had been accidentally stamped in when the rock was liquid mud. Dr. Duffield did not say what sort of time period he was talking about, but one would think a rather uncomfortably long time for conservative scholars.[94]

Other humanoid footprints in solid stone have been found in Kentucky. In January of 1938, geologist Wilbur G. Burroughs announced that he had found a series of 10 humanoid footprints molded in sandstone. They were located in the north end of Rockcastle County, on the farm of O. Finnell, in an "Upper Carboniferous rock formation." Burroughs believed that the tracks were "so human in appearance that they might have been made by one of the earliest ancestors of man." He found that left and right feet were distinctly imprinted and that arch structures were clearly visible. Sadly, vandals destroyed these prints in 1960s.[94]

In 1925 Burroughs explored a "fort" that he said was of Stone Age vintage, covering 320 acres atop a mountain near Berea, Kentucky.

he described the remnants of walls 1,200 feet long, observing that they would have resisted any but the most modern artillery.[94]

❀❀❀

A Louisville historian named Reuben F. Durrett, has attempted to explain the many legends of white Indians in Kentucky by explaining that they are the descendants of the Welshman, prince Madoc. Durret lists reports of skeletons dug up in the of present-day Sand Island around the year 1900 that wore brass-plated armor bearing symbols of the mermaid and the harp, elements of the Welsh coat of arms. He also mentions a tombstone fragment that bore the date 1186. He believes Sand Island to have been part of a Welsh colony. So far Sand Island has not been archaeologically excavated.[94]

The story of Prince Madoc is a fascinating bit of Americana. More than three centuries before Columbus, an obscure Welsh prince named Madoc is believed to have landed in Mobile Bay. The Welsh prince was Madoc ab Oain Gwynedd, and according to Welsh history and various American historians, he sailed into Mobile bay in 1170, was delighted in "this pleasante and fruitful lande," returned to Wales to collect some of his fellow countrymen, and returned to found a new nation.

Centuries later came reports from European travelers in the New World of a mysterious tribe of "Welsh Indians" believed to be the descendants of Madoc, and who actually spoke Welsh. Several books recount the adventure of Prince Madoc including *Madoc & the Discovery of America*[144] by Richard Deacon and *Brave His Soul*[145] by Ellen Pugh.

A number of curious stories are told of these "Welsh Indians" including a story of how shortly after the American Revolution, when the lands west of the Mississippi were still claimed by Spain or England, an English surveying party visited a camp of Mandan Indians in what is now Missouri. When the officer in charge spoke to his orderly in Welsh (as they were both Welshmen), they were suddenly astonished when a nearby Indian suddenly joined in the conversation. Apparently the three all spoke the same language. They started to compare words and found that the Mandan language was about 50 percent Welsh.

Mandan Indians often had blue eyes and their skin was much lighter than most other Indians. Mandan women were especially attractive to the English explorers and said to be "exceedingly fair." The English/Welsh officer then remembered the story of Prince Madoc and how he had escaped Wales in 1170 A.D.

In 1792 a Welshman named John Evans was hired by his countrymen to find the "Welsh Indians" of North America. He journeyed to New Orleans and then up the Mississippi in search of them. Unfortunately, he was captured by the Spanish, and in order to save his own life, he became a spy for them. Even though he apparently made contact with the Mandans, and was satisfied that they were originally Welsh, he was paid by the Spanish to deny the fact, as it was politically unsuitable for Welsh Indians (theoretically British subjects) to be living in Spanish held New World territory.

Later, the famous American painter George Catlin lived with the Mandan Indians in 1833. He agreed with others that the Mandans had a Welsh origin. They had dark brown hair instead of black, he said, and some of them even had fair hair. Their eyes were many different colors: brown, gray, blue, and hazel. Catlin painted many portraits of the Mandans, paintings which are well known and widely circulated in books on Native American tribes.

Sadly, only a short time later, most of the Mandan Indians, including the elderly "storytellers" and "rememberers" were wiped out by a plague brought by European explorers. The few Mandans who survived were absorbed by other tribes. Pure-blooded Mandans ceased to exist, as did their own orally recorded history.

🐾🐾🐾

I spent the night camping in a rural area of Kentucky, and continued on the next day through Tennessee toward Florida. Tennessee is full of ancient pyramids, mounds and strange inscriptions. The Smithsonian Institution devoted an entire volume on ancient earthworks in Tennessee in 1880.[168]

Similarly, sometime in the late 1880s, a farmer named J.H. Hooper of rural Bradley County, near Cleveland, Tennessee, found a stone with peculiar markings on a wooded hillside of his farm. Digging around a bit, he exposed a wall of red sandstone that was inscribed with unknown characters and drawings for about 16 feet of its length. A total of 872 symbols were discovered, arranged in wavy parallel and diagonal lines. Among these were depictions of strange animals, such as a two-legged, bearded kangaroo-like animal (see illustration at the end of this chapter).

A number of archaeologists of the day showed up to inspect the inscriptions, but the only known report was published in 1891 by one A.L. Rawson in the *Transactions* of the New York Academy of Sciences. Rawson noted the peculiar fact that there seemed to have been a deliberate effort by the long-ago inscribers of the glyphs to conceal what they had so laboriously chiseled out.

Apparently the letters had first been carved into the rock, after which "a dark red cement... was worked in and raised above the surface, and a cement placed over the whole, against which the outer course of stones was placed, fitting closely." Archaeologist J. Hampden Porter remarked, "As a rule inscriptions are intended to be read... I do not remember any instance of a designed concealment like this."

Rawson makes the rather absurd statement that, "Accidental imitations of Oriental alphabets are numerous." One can only wonder how one "accidentally" imitates something like stone

393

inscriptions. Yet, despite its patent absurdity, archaeologists make statements like this continuously, simply because genuine inscriptions "just can't exist." Rawson's final comment is at least a bit more enlightened, "Some of these forms recall those on the Dighton Rock [in Massachusetts], and may belong to the same age. How many other hidden inscriptions there may be in this, the geologically oldest continent, it is impossible to say but delightful to conjecture." Apparently the inscriptions of Bradley County, Tennessee are in a Phoenician-type script.[94]

About 35 miles to the northeast of Bradley County is Monroe County, where along the banks of Bat Creek the famous Bat Creek inscription was found under Burial Mound #3. The well-known and respected historian, Professor Cyrus H. Gordon, has championed the Bat Creek Inscription as evidence of ancient Mediterranean explorers in several books, including *Before Columbus*,[158] and *Riddles in History*.[6]

The small slab of stone covered with ciphers, nine letters and one partial letter, to be exact, was found in 1885 by Smithsonian Institution archaeologists. The stone was discovered inside of an unrifled burial mound 28 feet in diameter and five feet high. Cyrus Thomas of the Smithsonian describes the find as follows: "Nothing of interest was discovered until the bottom was reached, where nine skeletons were found lying on the original surface of the ground surrounded by dark colored earth. These were disposed as shown on p.166. No. 1 lying at full length with the head south, and close by, parallel with it, but with the head north, was No. 2. On the same level were seven others, all lying close side by side, with heads north and in a line. All were badly decayed.

"No relics were found with any but No. 1, immediately under the skull and jaw bones of which were two copper bracelets, an engraved stone, a small drilled fossil, a copper bead, a bone implement, and some small pieces of polished wood. The earth about the skeletons was wet and pieces of wood soft and colored green by contact with the copper bracelets. The bracelets had been rolled in something, probably bark, which crumbled away when they were taken out. The engraved stone lay partially under the back part of the skull and was struck by the steel prod used in probing."[158]

This was the description published, with illustrations in the *Twelfth Annual Report of the Bureau of Ethnology to the Secretary of the Smithsonian Institution 1890-91* (published in 1894), pages 392-394 and figures 272, 273. Thomas, without understanding the nature of the writing, published the text upside-down on page 394 and erroneously surmised it to be in Cherokee script.

Here at last was an inscription in ancient Mediterranean writing which could not be branded a forgery by the Smithsonian Institution, because *they themselves had found it!* Fortunately, they did not realize the importance of the stone, as their apparent policy from 1895 on was to suppress such evidence when they could.

Still, modern scholars were having trouble in deciphering the inscription. Henriette Mertz in 1960 was the first to recognize that the stone was upside-down and contained ancient Mediterranean writing. She believed the stone inscription to be Phoenician and published her version of it on page 130 of her book, *The Wine Dark Sea*.[185]

But it was Joseph Mahan, the Director of Education and research at the Columbus, Georgia, Museum of Arts and Crafts and author of *The Secret*,[181] who realized that the script was Canaanite. Mertz was partially correct, because Phoenician writing contains some Hebrew letters. The inscription is sometimes referred to as Canaanite-Phoenician. Professor Cyrus Gordon spends an entire chapter of his book *Before Columbus* translating the stone. Without going into details, I will only say that he translates a portion of the stone as QS-LYHWD(M) or "for the Judeans" or, using the entire inscription and extrapolating on the partial letter, "The Golden Age for the Jews." Gordon also relates the inscription to the Bar Kokhba coins with Hebrew inscriptions with a date of A.D.135 that were found in Kentucky.[158]

As far as Tennessee and lost cities goes, Memphis, named after the ancient Egyptian city of the Nile Delta, could not be more aptly named. Immediately across the Mississippi from Memphis, in St. Francis County, Arkansas, is a complex of ancient pyramids, canals, artificial lakes with paved bottoms, huge mound complexes and evidence of extensive human occupation at a city that was probably as large as Cahokia in Illinois. In 1881, *American Antiquarian* published a series of excellent articles detailing these ancient remains which are the apparent reason that Memphis was given the name that it has today. It was believed by the early settlers that an ancient Egyptian city had once existed there, and they may have been right.

The city of Memphis itself has a mysterious and bizarre tunnel system beneath it with walled and arched masonry structures that lead deep underground. Jim Brandon relates that an entrance to this tunnel system, explained as a military construction during the Civil War, can be found at the east end of the Harahan Bridge, near the Holiday Inn, though a locked iron grate now covers this entrance to a larger tunnel that runs parallel to the Mississippi, and which apparently heads into the city center.[94]

In northern Georgia can be found Fort Mountain, six miles east of Chatsworth, where a step-like path leads to a giant wall running 885 feet along the mountainside. The structure ranges from two to seven feet high, with an abundance of loose rock alongside that suggests it could have been higher once. Dotting the ground by its sides, at fairly regular intervals, are 29 pits, about large enough to hold a squatting man.

The local Cherokee Indians have a legend that the wall was built by a race of white people who worshiped the sun, which is one reason why the wall is aligned from east to west. Otherwise, this "Great Wall of Georgia" has yielded no weapons, other artifacts or skeletal remains. Other theories range from its being a Cherokee game trap (despite the Cherokee's own theories), or a construction by Prince Madoc and his Welch settlers.

The South has its share of mysteries, lost forts, pyramids, Egyptian, Phoenician, Hebrew remains, along with the giants in armor that tend to come with all that. As the late afternoon sun glowed dimly in the sky, I reached the border of Florida, a sun worshiper's promised land. What promises did it hold for me?

🌣🌣🌣

According to popular belief, Florida was discovered by the Spanish explorer Ponce de León 1513 on his quest for the Fountain of Youth, which according to legend could miraculously cure sexual debility. Whether de León was inflicted with this problem, history does not know, but we do know that he took an expedition from Puerto Rico to a land that he called Pascua Florida. Though he found no fountain while he cruised the coast, his expedition did discover the Gulf Stream, and on his way back to Puerto Rico, his expedition discovered the Yucatán peninsula.

As I headed across the flat, swampy ground in the north of the state, it seemed that Florida was still a fountain of youth, although it was no longer lost. Thousands of young people head for the beaches of Florida each spring, and retirees from the north head for Florida in search of their lost youth as well.

In many ways, I was no different from them. What did I hope to find on my trip to Florida? While it may be a land of beaches, sunshine and Disney World, was it an area of lost cities and ancient mysteries? It was indeed.

I was curious about the tales of sunken ruins in the Caribbean and was determined to see some of them. Florida itself had ancient structures, mounds and canals.

Along the southern bays and Rivers of the south, strange artifacts have been found. The *Stonewatch Newsletter* of the Gungywamp Society in Connecticut, published a story in their Winter, 1992 issue (Vol.10, No.3) about some large wood coffins discovered in 1892 at the Crumf Cave in Alabama. According to the newsletter, the archaeologist Frederick J. Pohl wrote an intriguing letter on March 26, 1950 to the late Dr. T.C. Lethbridge, a British archaeologist.

The letter from Pohl stated, "A professor of geology sent me a reprint (of the) Smithsonian Institute 'The Crumf Burial Cave' by Frank Burns, U.S. Geological Survey, from the report of the U.S. National Museum for 1892, pp 451-454, 1894. In the Crumf Cave, southern branch of the Warrior River, in Murphy's Valley, Blount County, Alabama [accessible from Mobile Bay by river, were coffins of wood hollowed out by fire, aided by stone or copper chisels. Eight of these coffins were taken to the Smithsonian. They were about 7 1/2' long, 14" to 18" wide, 6" to 7" deep. Lids open.

"I wrote recently to the Smithsonian, and received reply March

11th from F.M. Setzler, Head Curator of Department of Anthropology. (He said) 'We have not been able to find the specimens in our collections, though records show that they were received.'

"Thomas Wilson's comment in the *Reprint*, to the effect that Indians in North America never used coffin burials, as Europeans did, 'is all the scientific opinion that was ever offered on this material.'

"It was implied, if not stated in the *Reprint*, that burials in Crumf Cave were ancient...very old, comparable to Bronze Age... Denmark (?). This all seems to be another instance of possible pre-Columbian evidence neglected and lost."

The *Stonewatch Newsletter* then goes on to say that they had also contacted the Smithsonian for more information in December of 1991, but had so far received no reply. As was discussed in earlier chapters, the Smithsonian seems to have in its possession a number of highly intriguing artifacts, though they have either lost them, or they refuse to reveal them at this time.

Many of the artifacts in Florida cannot be removed, however, as they are large mounds and canals. *Science News* (138:6, 1990) had an article on mysterious Florida canals in which it described circular canals up to 1,450 feet in diameter and six feet deep that have been discovered all over central Florida. Dug in the savannas and flood plains around Lake Okeechobee, the man-made circles include gaps where drainage canals extend outwards. forty of these circular earthworks have been located by R.S. Carr. Some are as old as 450 B.C.; others as recent as the 16th century. Mounds and large plazas are also part of this impressive example of pre-Columbian engineering.

Carr supposes that the circular canals were fish traps, but no fish bones or other supporting evidence for this theory have appeared. Another thought is that the earthworks drained agricultural land, but no maize pollen has been found. Could they have been ceremonial sites? Perhaps like the Mayas, the canals were for many purposes, irrigation, water supply, transportation and a food source of fish, turtles and other aquatic life. Perhaps the reason that corn pollen has been found is that none has survived the centuries since this civilization vanished. No one really knows.

An article in *American Antiqurian*, No. 7, 1885,[17] by Andrew Douglass discusses several ancient canals in Florida. Douglass begins the article by saying, "While exploring the South-west coast of Florida, I was much interested in two ancient canals which I examined, and whose object seemed quite inexplicable. The first occurs about three miles north of Gordon's Pass, an inlet thirty-three miles south of Punta Rasa, and twenty miles north of Cape Roman...It was apparent...that erosion of the coast had here occurred to a great extent, for stumps of dead palms could be seen a hundred yards or so to sea, and suggested the probability of a great change in the contour of the land during not remote years. One of our party followed the line of embankment or sand-dune while the other two kept along the beach. At a distance of three and a-half miles from the inlet the former announced the Canal, and we soon joined him and saw the object of our search before us. Where we stood it was buried in the sand embankment, but from that it was plainly visible straight as an arrow, crossing the low intervening morass and penetrating the sandy pine ridge, half a mile, or nearly so, away. The bottom was moist and full of tall grass; the sides and summit of the embankment covered with a dense chaparral of oak scrub and scrub palmetto. Its direction from our stand-point was about one point South of East...The width from the summit ridge upon each bank was 55 feet, and the depth from that summit level to centre of the excavation 12 feet. At the bottom the width was 12 feet, the banks being almost perpendicular for some 5 feet, and then receding on an easier angle at the summit. This summit was about eight feet above the level of the meadow, through which for nearly half a mile it was excavated, till it reached the higher level of the sandy pine land beyond.

"The whole canal is about one mile and half in length, reaching from the Lagoon to the Sea. With the exception of the curve at the Eastern terminus it is perfectly straight. In passing through the pine woods it intersects sand ridges, in which it is excavated to depth of forty feet. The bottom is everywhere the same width I have described, but at points where he has crossed it in hunting, he finds a trench about four feet in breadth, and at present, two feet deep running along the center, leaving a breadth of about four feet on each side. Mr. Weeks [the local rancher, who is their guide] was of the impression that this supplementary trench was designed to accommodate the keel of a boat as it ran along the conduit."

Douglass concludes his description of this first canal by saying, "It is a work of enormous labor indeed...My own idea is that by whomsoever constructed, it was designed to relieve the lowlands to the eastward of great accumulations of fresh water in the rainy season, at some remote period when there was no Gordon's Pass, and when the exterior conformation of the coast was far different from what it is at present...Who were the constructors, is a question, even more difficult to settle. There is no record of such a work in any local tradition, or in any history that we now possess. Indeed, there is nothing more obscure than the history whether ancient or modern, or the Southwest Coast of Florida."[17]

Of the second canal that was discovered on the Southwest coast, Douglass says, "The other canal I visited is quite as inexplicable, and even more surprising for its extent and dimensions than this...The sheet of water on the coast north of Caloosahtchee river known as Charlotte Harbor, Charlotte Sound and Carlos Bay, has on its eastern border a long island known as Pine Island. It is about 18 miles long, and from there to five miles broad, extending in a direction nearly north and south...One of the largest of [these] shell mounds that I have ever seen is found on the west coast of Pine Island, some four miles from its northern end. The heaps cover a space of several acres and rise in steep ridges to the height of, in some instances, 25 feet."

After Douglass describes how he stumbled onto the remains of the canal, he describes the canal from the summit of a huge mound of shells, "Looking eastward from its summit, we could discern about 460 yards distant, the sand mound, as I afterward ascertained, 20 feet in perpendicular height, with depression of 8 feet between the two summits, and the longest diameter of its base 300 feet. While these two mounds lay on a line due east and west, the canal passed between them angularly, coming from the south-east. The dimensions of the latter were at this point 30 feet in width from the bottom of the opposite banks, and seven to eight feet in height to the summit of the banks, which was also at an elevation of some three or four feet above the level of the adjacent sand of the Island surface.

"Far as the eye could reach, we could trace this canal in a direct line through the sparse pine woods; its course being especially marked by the tall fronds of the cabbage palms...I was assured by an old settler that it crosses the entire Island in a direct line on the course which I observed. At this point, the direct width of Pine Island is three and a half miles. The canal however, crossing at the angle indicated must exceed five miles in length."[17]

Apparently, ancient canals, shell mounds and even pyramids can be found all over Florida. It is surprising to historians that a sophisticated civilization once lived in Florida, and though they have disappeared, they left clear traces of their advanced civilization.

Whoever built the canals in Florida, probably also built the pyramids that have been found in the Everglades. A brief article on the Florida pyramids appeared in *Science*, May 22 of 1931 and was reprinted in William Corliss' *Ancient Man: A Handbook of Puzzling Artifacts*.[17] Said the article, "On the very edge of the Everglades, near Lake Okechobee, Mr. Stirling encountered a great plan of earthworks, elaborately laid out in embankments and mounds, and covering an area a mile square. So large and conspicuous are these earthworks, Mr. Stirling said, that it is surprising that no previous explorer has ever reported their existence or their significance. The nearest approach to anything like them are the famous Fort Ancient earthworks in Ohio, which were also made by prehistoric mound-building Indian tribes.

"The most prominent feature of the Everglades site is a flat-topped rectangle of earth built 30 feet high and 250 feet long. This was apparently the focusing point of attention for whatever ceremonies were held at the site. earthen embankments enclose a court in front of this high place. Back of it a semi-circular bank of earth was raised.

"This is only a small portion of the earthworks. A curious formation consisting of a large semi-circular bank extends in front of the high palace and its court. And out from the semi-circle start a number of parallel lines of banks with circular mounds at the ends.

Within the great semi-circle is a platform of earth six feet high and a quarter of a mile long."[17]

How long has man been in Florida? It wasn't long ago that the "experts" were telling us that man could not have entered North America before 3,500 B.C. This date has been pushed back a number of years, and is still hotly disputed, but no one was ready for Dr. Carl Clausen's discovery of a 12,000 year old skull in a Florida sinkhole that *still had living brain matter preserved inside it.*

In the north part of the town of Port Charlotte is the Little Salt Springs archaeological site. This hourglass-shaped, 200-foot-wide sinkhole set the scientific world agog in 1972 when Dr. Clausen, then Florida's chief marine archaeologist, found a human skull with a portion of the brain intact. "It's extraordinary—almost unbelievable. I was really shaken," Clausen recalled. He thought at first that the brain was a mineral formation or else some foreign growth inside the skull.[182]

In 1959, a skull also containing an intact brain was found by a Colonel William Royal not far from Little Salt Springs. This skull was determined to be over 10,000 years old. There have been similar finds of humans and elephants in caverns in central Florida. Dr. J. Manson Valentine, Florida's famous maverick archaeologist, believes that these skeletal remains with intact brains must have been caught in a catastrophic flood of hot, mineralized water.[182]

The various caves deep within the spring had a bizarre assortment of stalactites, indicating that the sink had once been dry; also wood, human brains and two hand-sized prehistoric shark's teeth were found. Just above the narrow hour-glass portion of the sink hole, at 90 feet below the surface, the archaeologists were surprised to find the bones of prehistoric bison, mastodon, mammoth, giant ground sloth and giant land tortoise. Higher up on the sloping walls of the underwater cavern they found long, shaped wood pins driven into the limestone. Had these served some purpose for helping early man descend to the ledge below when the spring's water level was much lower? The carved tips had been sharpened by man, Dr. Clausen concluded. Carbon-dating of a section of the stake later revealed it to be 9,572 years old.

Perhaps the most interesting of the many finds that came from Little Salt Spring was an oak boomerang. It has a right-angle top with one side almost twice as long, giving it an elongated L-shape. The boomerang was carbon dated to 9,080 years old and is the oldest boomerang ever found in the world. Clausen learned that it is a style similar to the nonreturning killing boomerangs used in Australia.[182] Boomerangs are not just an Australian device, but have been found all over the world. King Tutankhamen's tomb was found to contain a chest of boomerangs, and these are now on display at the Egyptian Museum in Cairo.

❁❁❁

I pulled into the driveway of the small marina on Key Largo where Steve's yacht was docked. A young boy in rubber sandals and swimming trunks came running up to me.

"David, you're here!" he cried. His blonde hair was bleached by the sun and his wiry body was, like his father's, long and skinny.

"Sage Mallet, good to see you," I said, giving him a hug as he ran up to me. "Where's your father?"

"He's on the yacht, getting things ready for tonight's dinner. Come on, I'll help you get your things." I grabbed a bag of clothes and toiletries, plus a few books as presents, locked up the truck, and followed Sage down to the marina. Steve was tying up some lines on the deck.

"Hey, you're here," he called from the deck of the yacht.

"Nice yacht," I said, handing him my bag before hauling myself over the railing and on to the bow of the ship. It was good to see Steve again, I had known him for some years, before his divorce, and he had met me once at Miami airport on my way to South America.

After showing me around the ship, Steve started up the inboard motor and we motored out of the marina to anchor off shore by a small island off the keys. We then drank beer and barbecued shrimp on the back of the boat. Sage, Steve's only child, was the first (and only) mate, scampering back and forth around the boat and into the cabin like a monkey on espresso looking for his missing organ grinder.

Naturally, as the moon appeared above the water and the pile of empty beer cans started to rise, the conversation drifted to the topic of the ever popular Bermuda Triangle.

Countless books have been written on the Bermuda Triangle, sometimes called the Devil's Triangle, and it's a fascinating subject. Most books claim that some sort of vortex, or time warp, is responsible for missing ships, vanished airplanes, instruments that go haywire and weird magnetic and atmospheric phenomena. Other researchers, such as Lawrence Kusche in his book, *The Bermuda Triangle Mystery—Solved,* [191] maintain that there is little mystery to the disappearance of the planes and ships. According to Kusche, the Bermuda Triangle area just happens to be in a shipping lane that gets a lot of traffic, and therefore, has a proportionally high number of accidents and missing ships. Kusche claims that the disappearances are nothing more than would be expected of an area with frequent storms and a high amount of traffic.

Yet, there is good evidence that an energy vortex, or "gravitational anomaly" as they are sometimes called, is operating in the heavily trafficked waters off of Florida. In this area between Miami, Bermuda and Puerto Rico, literally hundreds of ships and planes have vanished. In a few odd cases, ships have been found derelict without crews. Very little wreckage has been found.

In 1990 it was announced that the five Navy torpedo bombers that had vanished in the Bermuda Triangle on Dec. 54, 1945 had been discovered off the waters of Fort Lauderdale. Later it was announced that these were not the missing planes, but a different set of crashed airplanes, with two of the craft having the same identification number.

According to Charles Berlitz, the grandson of the founder of the Berlitz Language schools, and the author of the world-wide bestseller, *The Bermuda Triangle,* plus other books on Atlantis and mysteries of the world, there are quite a few strange instances that have been recorded concerning the bizarre and life-threatening effects that happen in the Bermuda Triangle.

According to Berlitz:

•An oceanic investigative party on the yacht New Freedom, in July 1975, passed through an intense but rainless electromagnetic storm. During one tremendous burst of energy, Dr. Jim Thorpe photographed the exploding sky. The photograph when developed showed the burst in the sky, but it showed, too, a square-rigged ship on the sea about one hundred feet away from the New Freedom, although a moment before the sea had been empty.

•John Sander, a steward on the Queen Elizabeth-I saw a small plane silently flying alongside his ship at deck level. He alerted another steward and the officer of the watch while the plane silently splashed into the ocean only seventy-five yards from the ship. The QE-I turned around and sent a boat over, but no indication of anything was found.

•Another "phantom plane" silently crashed into the ocean at Daytona Beach on February 17, 1935, in front of hundreds of witnesses, but an immediate search revealed nothing at all in the shallow water by the beach.

•A Cessna 172, piloted by Helen Cascio, took off for Turks Island, Bahamas, with a single passenger. About the time she should have arrived, a Cessna 172 was seen by the tower circling the island but not landing. Voices from the plane could be heard by the tower, but landing instructions from the tower evidently could not be heard by the pilot. A woman's voice was heard saying, "I must have made a wrong turn. That should be Turks, but there's nothing down there. No airport. No houses.

In the meantime, the tower attempted to give landing to the unresponsive Cessna. Finally the woman's voice said, "Is there no way out of this?" and the Cessna, watched by hundreds of people, flew away from Turks into a cloud bank from which it apparently never exited, since the plane, the pilot, and the passenger were never found.[193]

As Berlitz points out, the plane had been visible to the people on Turks, but when the pilot looked down, apparently she saw only an undeveloped island. Had she been seeing the island at a point in time before the airport and the houses were built? Where did this plane finally land? Did it land on the beach of some past or future world?

Various theories have been put forth to explain the Bermuda Triangle mystery. Sudden giant waves or eruptions of underwater volcanoes, whirlpools and "holes in the ocean" have all been used as possible causes. Most researchers are willing to admit, though, that some sort of electromagnetic disturbance that causes instruments to malfunction is operating in the area.

There are local stories of strange dense compact fogs on the surface of the water or in the sky. According to local belief, ships or aircraft that enter these odd clouds do not emerge.

Tom Gary, author of *Adventures of an Amateur Psychic,* claims that the Bermuda Triangle's destructive force comes from energy emanating from beneath the sea. "There is speculation that a power structure is still underwater in the Bermuda area," wrote Gary. According to him, the structure sits atop a large core that extends down through the crust of the earth. "When conditions are right the power structure works intermittently, causing ship and plane captains to lose control of their craft."

According to Gary, streaming ions form an electric current that produces a magnetic field and this causes instrument failure in craft in the vicinity. Magnetic compasses, fuel gauges, altitude indicators, and all electrically operated instruments are affected. Pilots who have survived such activity have reported battery drainage as well.

An incredible story is told by Ray Brown of Mesa, Arizona that concerns an ancient pyramid off the Berry Islands in the Bahamas. In 1970, Brown claims to have been in a big storm while on the Berry Islands, having been looking for sunken galleons. In the morning after the storm, he says their compasses were spinning and their magnometers were not giving any readings. "We took off north-east from the island. It was murky but suddenly we could see outlines of buildings under the water. It seemed to be a large exposed area of an underwater city. We were five divers and we all jumped in and dove down, looking for anything we could find," said Brown in an interview with Charles Berlitz.

"As we swam on, the water became clearer. I was close to the bottom at 135 feet and was trying to keep up with the diver ahead of me. I turned to look toward the sun through the murky water and saw a pyramid shape shining like a mirror. About thirty-five to forty feet from the top was an opening. I was reluctant to go inside... but I swam in anyway. The opening was like a shaft debouching into an inner room. I saw something shining. It was a crystal, held by two metallic hands. I had on my gloves and I tried to loosen it. It became loose. As soon as I grabbed it I felt this was the time to get out and not come back.

"I'm not the only person who has seen these ruins—others have seen them from the air and say they are five miles wide and more than that in length."[192]

Berlitz reports that three of the other divers have since died in accidents in the Bermuda Triangle and that Brown occasionally shows the crystal that he allegedly took from the sunken pyramid to lecture audiences. Berlitz has seen the crystal himself, though it is not necessarily from a pyramid in the Caribbean. Brown will not reveal the exact site of the city, but he believes that the pyramid and other buildings extend far below the ocean floor. He was only lucky that the storm the day before had cleared the ruins of sand and silt.

"What a bullshit story," bellowed Steve, taking a shot of rum, then chasing it with the last of his beer. "There might be something to this Bermuda Triangle stuff, but that story sounds fishy to me."

I had to agree with him. Somehow, swimming into an ancient pyramid after a storm and grabbing a crystal ball seemed to strain credulity too much, though I had to admit that I'd heard stranger things before. After a few beers and a bottle of Steve's rum, tales of lost cities in the Bermuda Triangle tended to get wilder and wilder.

🍄🍄🍄

I left my truck parked at the marina in Key Largo, and Steve drove me up to the airport in Miami so that I could catch a flight to Puerto Rico. My plan was to be in Puerto Rico for a few days, then go to Jamaica and return to Miami.

I landed in Puerto Rico and found a cheap hotel in downtown San Juan, the capital of this U.S. Territory. Puerto Rico was sort of a cross between Latin American countries and the U.S.A. I was interested in the Caribbean as a spot for lost cities, and Puerto Rico seemed like a good place to start.

According to Rene Noorbergen in his book *Secrets of the Lost Races*,[92] the Caribbean was the location of a highly developed civilization which was destroyed in the cataclysms at the close of the last ice age, about 10.000 B.C. "Since 1968, strange finds have been made in coastal waters around the Caribbean, notably in the Bahama Banks. At depths ranging from 6 to 100 feet there are numerous giant stone constructions—walls, great squares, crosses and other geometric shapes, even archways and pyramids—all encrusted with fossilized shells and petrified mangrove roots, indicating their great age. Among the first finds made were stretches of a wall composed of blocks measuring as much as 18 by 20 by 10 feet and weighing approximately 25 tons each. The wall appears to have encircled the islands of North and South Bimini to form a dike. Along with the sea wall, 3- to 5-foot sections of fluted columns were also discovered, some still fixed in their original positions, while others were found lying in a jumble on the sea floor, covered with sand. Since the pillars appear at regular intervals along the sunken wall, it is believed they may have formed one continuous portico. Both the wall and pillars reveal a high level of engineering skill in their construction.

"Not far from the Bimini sea wall, divers have uncovered a stone archway at a depth of 12 feet, a pyramid with a flattened top and a base 140 by 180 feet, plus a huge circular stone construction, made of 20-foot blocks, that appears to have been a well-designed water reservoir when it existed above sea level."[92]

According to Noorbergen, there are other sunken structures in the

404

Caribbean besides those found at Bimini: "Andros Island, near Pine Key, possesses its share of submarine structures as well. In 1969 airline pilots photographed a 60-by 100-foot rectangular shape, clearly visible through the calm waters. The eastern side and the western corners were partitioned off. What is amazing is that this submerged rectangle is an almost exact copy in size and design of the Temple of Turtles, an ancient Mayan sanctuary found at Uxmal in Yucatan, indicating that the survivors of this Caribbean civilization center may have influenced the development of the early Central American cultures and the culture of the Mound Builders."

Noorbergen further states, "Other sunken ruins in the Caribbean area include a sea wall 30 feet high, running in a straight line for miles off Venezuela, near the mouth of the Orinoco River; an acropolitan complex, complete with streets, covering 5 acres in 6 feet of water off the Cuban coast; remains of sunken buildings off Hispaniola, one measuring 240 by 80 feet; several stone causeways, 30 to 100 feet below the surface, which leave the shores of Quintana Roo, Mexico, and Belize, British Honduras, and continue out to sea for miles toward an unknown destination; a sea wall running along a submarine cliff near Cay Lobos; and huge stone squares, rectangles and crosses, clearly of human design, off the windward and leeward sides of all the keys down to Orange Key.

"These Caribbean ruins are perplexing to archaeologists and to orthodox historians, for the architecture is far beyond the capabilities of either the Amerinds or the Spanish conquistadors. It is even more disturbing that the most recent period, when the present Caribbean sea floor was above sea level and the mystery walls, pyramids and temples therefore could have been built, was during the Ice Age. Apparently the Caribbean civilization evolved during the time the ocean levels were at their lowest, and it eventually was submerged when the Bahama shelf was inundated by the rising of the sea caused by the melting of the northern glaciers. The flooding in all probability was very gradual, for many of the gargantuan submerged walls appear to have been dikes built in an attempt to protect certain areas from the rising sea. But the walls were not enough. The ocean waters eventually rolled over the land, and the Caribbean civilization disappeared."[92]

Many of the islands of the Caribbean were uninhabited when Columbus first discovered them, though there are many signs of habitation. The vague, official history of the Caribbean is that the first inhabitants were the Arcaicos or Archaics (old-people), who were then displaced by the Igneri, a sub-group of the Arawaks who cultivated tobacco and corn. Later the Tainos arrived, and eventually the Caribe Indians, who were to have a fierce reputation as warriors and cannibals.

Puerto Rico was inhabited by Tainos at the time of the European invasion. They called the island Boriquen, "Land of the Noble Lord," after the creator Yukiyu who was believed to reside in the heart of the present-day Caribbean National Forest in the heart of the island.[197]

Many of the Caribbean tribes had women as chieftains, and were therefore thought of as Amazons by some of the early explorers. It is curious that St. Croix in the Virgin Islands was uninhabited when the first Spanish came to colonized the island, because St. Croix had at least 40 Indian village sites and is rich in artifacts. Archaeologists have uncovered a row of flat stone slabs on St. Croix standing on edge at Salt River, with petroglyphs and pictographs on them. Hundreds of "three pointer" religious stones were found there, and are still picked up along the shore and inland.[198]

In Puerto Rico is what is considered the most important archaeological site in the Caribbean, the Caguana Indian Ceremonial Park and Museum near Utuado. It was originally excavated by the the archaeologist J.A. Mason in 1915 and consists of ten ball courts, called *bateyes,* situated on a small spur of land surrounded by deep ravines on three sides, a natural amphitheater. The largest ball court measures 60 by 120 feet and has huge granite slabs weighing up to 2,000 pounds along the western wall. Some are carved in strange animal-humanoid glyphs.[197]

This ball game was played throughout the Caribbean, and was virtually identical to the ball games played by the Maya and other Mesoamerican cultures. Two teams of players with thick wooden belts lashed to their waists, would hit a heavy, elastic ball, probably rubber from the jungles of the Yucatán, keeping it in the air without the aid of their hands or feet. These ball courts are evidence that the entire Caribbean was once traveled widely by the Maya and other Central Americans, and that the Caribbean was intricately connected, at least at one time, with the rest of Mesoamerica.

The geology of the Caribbean is unusual, and J. Manson Valentine believes that Venezuela was once connected to Florida via a land-bridge that spanned the entire Caribbean. On nearby Cuba and Hispaniola, there is a very curious animal. This animal is called the *solenodon,* and it is a small rodent-like animal that is a relative of the *tenrec* of Madagascar. It is a brown, ratlike mammal with a rather strange way of walking called "unglitude." It places only the edge of its foot on the ground. Asleep by day, it prowls at night, preying on insects, worms, mollusks, and small vertebrates. Standing on hind legs and tail, it tears its quarry apart with its claws before dining.[197] Just how this strange animal came to be found only in Cuba, Hispaniola and Madagascar is a puzzle that zoologists have a difficult time in figuring out. Theories must of course include land bridges from the mainland of North America to Cuba and Hispaniola, as well as some sort of migration from Madagascar or Africa.

Another odd discovery made in Haiti (Hispaniola) was of a stone sphere on the Ile á Vache just off the coast by the archaeologist Godfrey J. Olsen. This large stone sphere was covered in swastikas, the ancient Hindu design, which is used by various cultures around the world. The stone is estimated to be about 2,000 years old, but may be much older.[111]

I went to Utuado and visited the ball courts of the Caguana Indian Ceremonial Park. It was an impressive sight with the steep sides of the natural amphitheater. Huge granite slabs lined the western wall, and the strange inscriptions of man-animals were interesting.

Back at my hotel, I decided it was time to move on. My stay in Puerto Rico had been pleasant, but I wanted something a bit more removed from the familiar American look that San Juan has. I booked a flight to Jamaica and was soon staying in a small bungalow on Negril Beach, on the western side of the island.

Jamaica was quite different from Puerto Rico, I felt that I was more in Africa than the Caribbean. My small bungalow on the beach in Negril was quiet, but as soon as I got on the beach, I was assaulted by various vendors and wandering man or women with their massage oils, wanting to give me a massage. They were difficult to shrug off, a persistent lot, so one was generally obliged to buy to a beer, a banana or some pineapple juice every hour or so.

I was happy to relax in the sun, watch the waves hit the sandy beach and listen to the drifting melodies of reggae music from one of the hotels. As my mind drifted off, I thought of perhaps the most famous explorers of all time, a mysterious man, who, almost single-handedly, changed the course of history.

🐾🐾🐾

THE MYSTERIOUS IDENTITY OF COLUMBUS

The Christopher Columbus that we all learned about in school may have been an entirely different sort of person than we are taught. Is it possible that Columbus knew perfectly well that he would reach a New World, rather than China, as he told the Spanish Royalty?

Columbus was a fascinating person, and the more one studies this incredible man, the more fascinating he becomes. The man who sailed in 1492 for the New World was a mystic, an adventurer, a utopian idealist and man of great courage and vision.

Despite the popular grade school depiction, there is a great deal of evidence that Columbus was not actually Italian, but a Spaniard who had assumed the identity of a young Italian wool merchant whom he had once met and who had died at sea. By coincidence, the young Italian wool merchant from Genoa had the same name as himself (at least in translation).

Christobal Colón, known to us as Columbus, was by some evidence a Spanish Jew. For this reason he decided to conceal his identity. Also, he was in possession of several maps that showed the coasts and islands of North and South America.

The real Columbus was a far more interesting and incredible person than our grade school teachers ever told us. According to William Anderson [96] and many other Columbus researchers, we must

407

examine two parallel lives—one of Cristoforo Colombo, born in the latter half of 1451 to Dominick and Susana Colombo in Genoa (Italian "Genova") in the Liguria section of Italy, and the other of Cristobal Colón, born in mid-1460 to Prince Carlos (Charles IV) of Viana, and Margarita Colón in the Jewish ghetto of Majorca, near the village of Genova which is now a district of Palma, the principal city.

After meeting the younger Italian wool merchant at sea, Cristobal Colón the Spanish-Jewish sea captain decided to use the Italian identity to be able to deal with the Spanish Court, which was persecuting Jews at the time. It should be remembered that Spain had only been liberated from the Moors in early 1492. Because of the close collaboration between Jews and Moslems in Spain (and in Morocco and all over North Africa), all Jews were officially expelled from Spain. In fact, the day that all Jews were to have left Spain under penalty of law, was the very day that Columbus set sail for the "New World."

Contrary to our popular school education, the various details of Cristobal Colón/Columbus' life are not at all well detailed, and very little in the way of facts has come down to us through history. Generally speaking, the modern authority on Columbus is Samuel Eliot Morison's *Admiral of the Ocean Sea* [97](1942). Morison was a Pulitzer Prize winner, Book-of-the-month Club author, an admiral in the U.S. Navy, and a Harvard professor. Morison's is the traditional Columbus as an Italian weaver who believed the world is round, convinces the queen of Spain to fund an expedition, and discovered America after thousands of years of isolation—Just as we learned in our sixth grade history class.

In the book *Sails of Hope*,[98] the famed researcher who has sent hundreds of Nazi World War II criminals to their just desserts, Simon Wiesenthal gives evidence, as do other authors, that the origin of the Columbus so famous in American history is the one who grew up in Spain.

In his book, Anderson shows how many of the so-called facts in Columbus' life just don't add up. He starts with the place and date of birth of the navigator:

Says Samuel Eliot Morison: "There is no mystery about the birth, family and race of Christopher Columbus. He was born in the ancient city of Genoa sometime between August 25 and the end of October, 1451."[97]

However, says Wiesenthal: "He is one of history's most controversial and shadowy figures, with mystery surrounding his birth, his character, his career and his achievement."[98]

According to the Universal Jewish Encyclopedia: "His place and date of birth, generally described as Genoa, in 1446 or 1451, are sharply disputed... Local Genoese records referring to the Colombo family are assumed to be identical with the family of the later Spanish admiral."[100]

One of the inconsistencies in Columbus' life is that he took part in the bombardment of Genoa, his supposed native city! Says Morison: "There is no more reason to doubt that Christopher Columbus was a Genoese-born Catholic Christian, steadfast in his faith and proud of his native city, than to doubt that George Washington was a Virginian-born Anglican of English race, proud of his being an American."[97]

Says the Encyclopedia Britannica: "The fact that in the battle (i.e. of August 13,1476) he fought on the Portuguese side, against Genoa, shows him to be no Genoese patriot... One explanation...is that Columbus came from a Spanish-Jewish family settled in Genoa."[99]

Anderson points out that the family of the Italian Columbus was quite poor, yet says Morison: "Domenico Colombo was not a journeyman weaver dependent on wages, but a master clothier (to use the old English term), who owned one or more looms."[97]

Says Wiesenthal: "His father, Domenico Colombo, is supposed to have been a tower sentinel in Genoa and later a weaver in Savona. The family just managed to sustain itself by manual labor."[98]

The Italian Columbus was poorly educated. Says Morison: "One thing is certain, he had little if any schooling."[97]

Conversely, says Wiesenthal: "(He) had an excellent command of Latin and Spanish...was well informed in history, geography, geometry, religion, and religious writings...Columbus's whole bearing as a mature man belies the notion that he came from people of small means and had no more than an elementary education behind him."[98]

The references cited provide other contradictions but do not suggest the obvious answer: there *must* have been two men. For that we go to two obscure publications of Brother Nectario Maria of the Venezuelan Embassy in Madrid: *Juan Colón the Spaniard* published by the Chedney Press of New York (now defunct) in 1971, and *Cristobal Colón Era Espanol y Judio,* (Christobal Columbus was Spanish and Jewish) privately printed in Madrid in 1978. Morison was aware of the alleged duality but "those who insist that Colón the discoverer was a different person from Colombo the Genoese" were rejected along with "others with even wilder theories."[97]

Nectario presents evidence that Colón was the illegitimate son of Prince Carlos (Charles IV) of Viana, Spain, and Margarita Colón, of a prominent Jewish family in the ghetto of Majorca. The author found a letter from the prince to the governor of Majorca, dated October 28, 1459, describing the meeting with Margarita, from which can be deduced the birth of Cristobal in the summer of 1460.

This premise provides logical answers to "mysteries" concerning his education and marriage, and reconciles with generally-accepted facts:

1472-73— He was in the crew of the pirate Rene d'Anjou on the Mediterranean Sea.[99] It would not be unusual for a boy to run away to sea at 12, especially from a fatherless home. Prince Carlos Colón died in 1461 under suspicious circumstances; some scholars believe he was poisoned on orders from his step-mother.

1473-74— He sailed to the Greek island of Chios. The Britannica asserts: "Columbus must be believed when he says he began to navigate at 14."[99] A capable boy of that age with two years of experience would likely be given an occasional turn at the wheel.

1476— He fought with Casenova-Coullon (possibly a relative) against Genoese ships. When his ship caught fire, he swam to the southwest tip of Portugal, near the seamanship academy of Prince Henry, the Navigator,[99] who is believed by some historians to have reached America around 1395.[106]

1477— He sailed to England, Ireland and Iceland.[99]

1478— Married in Portugal to Filipa Moniz Perestrello of a prominent Portuguese family.

1478-83— He and his wife lived with her brother, Bartholomew Perestrello II, who had inherited the captaincy of the island of Porto Santo in the Madeiras. From this base, Colón made several voyages to the Gold Coast of Africa.[99] He acquired the papers of Bartholomew I as well as documents from another visitor to the island, Alonso Sanchez de Huelva, who will be discussed later. Colón gained much of his navigational skill during this time, as well as broadening his self-education—the earliest notation in his voluminous library is dated 1481. Morison concedes that "Columbus's exact movements during the eight or nine years that he spent under the Portuguese flag can never be cleared up.[97] Records of Colón are sketchy; records of Colombo end abruptly with his death in 1480.

1484— Colón went to Portugal, where his petition was rejected by the king, probably because there is evidence of a voyage to America in 1472 by the Portuguese mariner Jaoa Vaz Cortereal (known also as Telles) who had a Norse pilot, Pothorst (Jan Skolp).[107] Colón's wife had died during this period, so he left his young son Diego at the monastery at La Rabinds, near Palos, Spain, and went to live with Luis de la Cerda, Count of Medina Celi, at Puerto Santa Maria, for the next two years.[99]

1486— Met Ferdinand and Isabella, with the help of the Jewish bishop and professor of theology at Salamanca, Diego de Deza.[100] At about this time, he became involved with Beatriz Enriquez, to who was born their son Fernando on August 15, 1488.

1488— Colón wrote to their majesties on July 7, 1503: "I came to serve you at the age of 28." [97] The U.J.E. gives the date as 1487. [100]

1489— He was granted the privileges of being lodged and fed at public expense.[99] The next two years are "conjectural" according to Morison. They may have been spent with Beatriz, with his son Diego at La Rabida, or with the Count of Medina Celi.

1491— He appears at Cordoba, where his petition to Ferdinand and Isabella is successful, largely through the efforts of Luis de Santangel, financial minister to the king.

Some of the records of the Italian Colombo are in direct conflict with those of Colón as shown above; other records show the probability that the two men met in Portugal or in Porto Santo—or both. Of the "fifteen or twenty notarial records and municipal records" found by Morison, these are a few:

October 31, 1470— Genoa, a wine purchase is recorded by Domenico Colombo and his son Cristoforo, "over age 19."

March 20, 1472— Colombo witnessed a will in Savona.

August 26,1472— He purchased wool in Savona.

August 7, 1473— Sale of House in Genoa.

1474— Lease of land in Savona, occupation of lessee shown as "wool buyer."[97]

"After that, no trace of the family for nine years," according to Morison.

But Nectario was able to find records of several wool-buying trips to Portugal by Colombo, during the years 1475-78. In 1479, he went to the Madeiras to buy sugar (which was also noted by Morison). Nearest to Portugal in the Madeiras is the island of Porto Santo, where Colón was living at the time. Colombo would certainly have reported to the captain of the island, Bartholomew Perestrello, Colón's brother-in-law. Nectario reports that Manuel Lopez Flores records the death of Colombo at sea the following year, 1480. There is no evidence that Colombo was pushed overboard by Colón.

Acceptance of this origin of Colón provides logical answers to two major mysteries that have puzzled historians for centuries:

(1) How had he managed to marry a woman of such prominence? Difficult for a penniless Italian weaver and wool merchant, it would have been no problem for the son of a Spanish prince, legitimate or not;

(2) Where did he obtain funds for his broad education, then available only to the wealthy who employed tutors? Such funds would have come from the royal treasury—actually, there are records of such payments from 1487 to 1489, as previously noted.

A Spanish-Jewish origin is supported by several well-known facts. He invariably wrote in Spanish, and in some letters he referred to Spanish as his "mother tongue." He spoke fluent Spanish, apparently without foreign accent. He was able to meet and obtain vital aid from several prominent Jews: Diego de Deza, who arranged for his introduction to their Spanish majesties; Abraham Senior and Isaac Abravanel, who had considerable influence at the court; Gabriel Sanchez, royal treasurer; Juan Cabrero, royal chamberlain; and Luis de Santangel, mentioned above.

Several crew members were Jewish, including Bernal, the ship's doctor, and Marco, the surgeon. Abraham Zacuto provided astronomical tables which saved the lives of Colón and his crew on the fourth voyage. By the use of the tables, he was able to predict the eclipse of the moon on February 29, 1504, which so awed their Indian captors that they released Colón and his men unharmed. Aboard also on the first voyage, was a Hebrew interpreter, Luis de Torres, who was probably the first man ashore, and who initially reported the use of tobacco by the Indians. [97]

Colón signed his name with the Spanish form "Cristobal Colón" and in his will insisted that his descendants not vary the signature. He often employed the cryptic form:

S
SAS
XMY
Xpo ferens

This was interpreted by Maurice David in *Who Was Columbus?* as Hebrew for "The Lord, full of compassion, forgiving iniquity, transgression and sin." In letters to his son Diego, in the upper left corner, regularly appear the Hebrew letters *beth he,* for "be'ezrath hashem" (with the help of God) which pious Jews employ to this day. [97]

Colón assigned Spanish names to islands he found, such as San Salvador, Punta Lazada and Punta de la Galera: there is no record of his assigning Italian names to any islands. He is known to have been an accomplished map-maker, primarily a Jewish talent where the activity was centered in Majorca...

Anderson points out that there are three men of limited fame who played critical roles in Colón's voyage and its historical account:

ALONSO SANCHEZ de HUELVA:

Nectario found a letter to the Spanish rulers indicating that Alonso Sanchez left the port of Huelva on May 15, 1481, in the ship "Atlante" with a crew of sixteen. It stated that the vessel reached the island of Santo Domingo (called "Quisqueya" by its inhabitants) and on its return stopped at Porto Santo in the Madeiras, where its captain lived for a time. After his sudden death, the ship's papers were given to Colón, who was helping in the business of his brother-in-law, captain of the island. It is difficult to believe that such a sensational document is authentic and has been kept a secret for 500 years. It would, however, provide an important clue—it states that Alonso Sanchez's first mate was—

MARTIN ALONZO PINZON:

A wealthy shipowner of Palos, Pinzon was responsible for Colón's acquisition of the Niña and the Pinta, and for hiring the crew for the expedition. Garcia Fernandez, steward of the Pinta, stated that "Martin Alonzo...knows that without his giving the two ships to the Admiral he would not have been where he was, nor would he have found people, because nobody knew that said Admiral, and that by reason of the said Martin Alonzo and through his said ships the said Admiral made the said voyage."[97] Some historians suggest that Pinzon was the actual leader of the expedition to the New World and that Colón was merely a "front" because of his favor with the Spanish monarchs. As later captain of the Pinta, Pinzon was second in command to Colón.

The steward's letter reconciles with accepted facts:

(1) Pinzon's descendants tried for half a century to obtain some of the honors and wealth which had gone to Colón. In the series of lawsuits recorded it was disclosed that Colón had access to the Vatican Archives, which contained records of Viking voyages over a period of several centuries, probably including the original of the famed "Vinland Map" of which Yale University has a 20th century copy. It also indicated that Pinzon had obtained from Rome information about lands to the west of the Atlantic.[97]

Pinzon was able to get Colón to alter his course on October 6th.[97] What better reason would the Admiral have had for accepting the urging of a subordinate than the fact that Pinzon had been there before?

PETER MARTYR:
Also known as Father de Angliera (or Angheria), Martyr wrote the first biography of Colón and is credited with coining the term "New World." Born in 1457 near Lake Maggiore in northwestern Italy, 100 miles north of Genoa, he interviewed Colón extensively after the first voyage.[97] He would have quickly determined that Colón was *not* a native of northern Italy, but would naturally be reluctant to deprive an alleged countryman of his honors by publicizing the fact. He did, however, reveal it in a letter to a close friend, Count Giovanni de Borromeo, who in 1494 left the deposition found in the binding of a book purchased a few years ago from a street vendor in Milan. (A copy is said to be in the library of Barcelona University—the original is held by the family of the count.) The letter reads in part:

I, Giovanni de Borromeo, being forbidden to tell the truth that I have learned as a secret from Senor Pedro de Angheria, Treasurer of the Catholic King of Spain, must preserve for history the fact that Christobal Colón was a native of Majorca and not of Liguria... He had been advised to pretend, for political and religious reasons, in order to request the help of ships from the King of Spain. Colón, after all, is the equivalent of Colombo, and there has been found living in Genoa one such Cristoforo Colombo Canajosa, son of Domingo and Susana Fontanarossa, who should not be confused with the West Indies navigator.[98]

There is, of course, a possibility that the letter was forged. However, until a battery of experts has submitted it to the necessary scientific tests, the letter fits neatly into the jigsaw puzzle that has baffled historians for centuries.

Says Anderson, "Studies by the Norse author Kare Prytz and by such American scholars as James Enterline and Paul Chapman indicate that Colón had access to a number of maps reflecting trans-Atlantic voyages over a period of several centuries. The existence of the American continents was known throughout Europe, certainly as early as 1070, from the writings of historian Adam of Bremen. Commerce continued with Norway and Iceland, and with Bristol in England, and America. By the end of the 15th century, Europe was ready to develop the lands that lay beyond the

413

Atlantic. If Colón and his almost-namesake, Colombo, had never been born, the final re-discovery, and the development, of the New World would have been postponed only a few years."[96]

That Columbus was a Spanish Jew also gives new interpretation to his reasons for wanting to sail across the Atlantic. Columbus (Colón) sailed from Spain on August 3, 1492, the very day that Jews had been banished from Spain. To beat the deadline, he had his crew report on board at 11:00 P.M. on the 2nd, contrary to custom which permitted sailors on long voyages to spend the last hours with their families. Coincidentally, the expulsion date was the anniversary of the second destruction of the Temple of Jerusalem. An estimated 300,000 Jews were banished from Spain in advance of the August 3, 1492, deadline.

Was Columbus looking for a new homeland for exiled Spanish Jews, or perhaps searching for a lost Jewish city or Kingdom on the other side of the Atlantic?

In the twelve volume set, *Life of Christopher Columbus*, it says that Columbus' son wrote of his father: "Their progenitors were of the Royal Blood of Jerusalem." (Vol. 12, page 2) This statement makes one think that Colón/Columbus was deeply concerned with ancient Jewish history.

It seems highly likely that Jewish merchants, in league with Phoenicians of Tyre, explored and exploited mineral wealth in both North and South America. King Solomon's mines have been claimed by some to be located in New Mexico or at the mouth of the Amazon.

Inscriptions in archaic Hebrew near Las Lunas, New Mexico, supposedly tell of their voyage and establishment of their city. However, there is a great deal of debate about what the inscription actually says, even by those who believe it genuine.

> King Solomon made a fleet of ships in Ezion-Geber, which is beside Eilat on the shore of the Red Sea in the land of Edom. And Hiram sent in the navy of his servants, shipmen that had knowledge of the sea, with the servants of Solomon. And they came to Ophir, and fetched from thence gold, four hundred and twenty talents, and brought it to King Solomon...Once in three years the fleet came in bringing gold, silver, ivory, apes, peacocks...a very great amount of red sandalwood and precious stones.
> —*I Kings 9:26-28, 10:22, 11.*

King Solomon (circa 1000 B.C.) and his father-in-law, the Phoenician King Hiram of Tyre, built refineries and a port on the Red Sea, and with Phoenician naval expertise, made the dangerous voyages to Ophir. Ships apparently left from the Mediterranean ports as well. The Phoenicians and their "ships of Tarshish," so-called after the Phoenician port in Spain called Tartessos, were well suited to the venture of going after the gold of Ophir, having sailed throughout the Atlantic.

The land of Ophir, however, remains a mystery.

It has been suggested that Tartessos in Spain itself was Ophir, after all, they were "ships of Tarshish". Others felt that Ophir was in Somalia, or maybe Sofala, on the Mozambique coast near Zimbabwe.

The German scholars Hermann and Georg Schreiber say in their book *Vanished Cities:* "At one time the idea arose that the Ophir of the Bible may have been in what is now called Peru. But that is out of the question; no merchant fleet sailed so far in the tenth century B.C. The Solomon Islands, north of Australia, have also been suggested. But that is pure nonsense; all these have in common with King Solomon is the name, by which they were first called in 1568. Moreover, there is no gold in the Solomon Islands. It is also impossible to equate Ophir with the Spanish port of Tartessus, as a modern church lexicon does; no one who wanted to sail from Palestine to Spain would build his ships on the Red Sea!

"Flavius Josephus, the great Jewish historian of the first century A.D., guessed that Ophir was located in Farther India. But India was more interested in importing than in exporting gold.

"The search for the famous land of gold has therefore been restricted fundamentally to southern Arabia and the African coast. Arabia, however, is also out of the question. If Ophir had been situated there, as some scholars still maintain, Solomon would not have needed the assistance of the King of Tyre; he would simply have used the ancient caravan routes of the Arabian peninsula."[108]

Orville Hope, in his book *6000 Years of Seafaring,*[7] asserts that King Solomon's Ophir was actually in New Mexico, where Hebrew inscriptions, refineries, and fortifications have been found near Albuquerque.

Apparently, the Jews had a two or three thousand year history of sailing to the Americas. The historic voyage of Columbus in 1492 was merely the most well publicized.

Even as late as 734 A.D., Jews seeking refuge from persecution sailed from Rome "...to Calalus, an unknown land." This land is now believed to be Las Lunas.[7,8]

Just a few years earlier, seven bishops and a reported 5,000 followers fleeing from the Moors in Spain sailed from Porto Cale, Portugal, for the island of Antillia. They landed on the west coast of Florida, according to some historians, and made their way inland to found the new city of Cale, which later may have become modern Ocala.

The Jews from Rome could have learned of this Portuguese exodus, gone to Porto Cale, hoping for exact sailing directions. Once in America, they called the new land Calalus, a sort of latinized Cale. The Portuguese voyage was certainly known to Columbus, who thought he would find their descendants on an island. Perhaps he thought that the European wreck he found on his second voyage was from this expedition.[7]

Peter Martyr wrote in 1511 that after Columbus discovered abandoned gold mines on the island of Haiti, or Hispanola, he believed it to be the land of Ophir. Columbus himself wrote that he had taken into possession for their Spanish Majesties "Mount Soporo (Mt. Ophir) which it took King Solomon's ships three years to reach." Here we see that it was Columbus' belief that the gold mines on Haiti were believed to have been worked by ancient Jewish and Phoenician seafarers, and Columbus named the mountain after the Biblical Ophir.

In his excellent book on forgotten places and old maps, *No Longer On the Map*,[194] the historian Raymond H. Ramsay says that Columbus' son Bartolomé confirms the identification of Hispaniola and that his father believed himself to have found the land of Ophir, from which King Solomon's ships had fetched gold for the holy Temple in Jerusalem.

Ramsay quips that this conjecture of ancient Jewish and Phoenician seafarers to the Caribbean circa 1000 B.C. by Columbus is of special interest to all students of American history—Columbus' own conjecture *is the first post-Columbian theory of a pre-Columbian discovery of America.*

✿✿✿

Columbus was in possession of several maps which showed large portions of North and South America, even parts of Antarctica. The famous Piri Reis map states in the legend that it is redrawn from other charts, including maps once used by Columbus. This map is now at the Topkapi Museum in Istanbul and it testifies that the Atlantic was being navigated long before the European Dark Ages. Dating from 1513, the Piri Reis map shows the entirety of the west coast of North and South America, plus a good portion of Antarctica, just a few years after Columbus made his first voyage to the New World. This map's strangest aspect is that it accurately shows details of Antarctica's land mass which are today covered with ice, which we have only known were accurate for the last few years!

Says the Turkish Admiral Piri Reis in a handbook for sailors called the *Kitab i Bahriye*, Columbus was inspired by a book containing information about these lands, which were claimed to be rich in all sorts of minerals and gems. "This man Columbus tried with the book in his hand to convince the Portuguese and Genoese that an expedition would be very worthwhile. His ideas were rejected and so he turned to the Spanish *bey*. Here to his first request was not granted, but was later on accepted after the matter had been pressed."[111]

And what was the book which Columbus was in possession of? Admiral Piri Reis tells us that the book was *Imago Mundi* by the French cardinal Pierre d'Ailly (also known as Aliaco, or Petrus Alliacus), a philosopher, astrologist and cosmographer at the

416

University of Paris. It is known that he had put forward the suggestion that there was land beyond the Atlantic, which he based on his belief that the world was round.[111]

Armed with the *Imago Mundi* and several maps of the Atlantic, Columbus was able to convince the Spanish leaders of the usefulness of an expedition to "India." Columbus was indeed a fascinating and great man, far more interesting than an Italian wool merchant. Columbus was truly a great sailor—but he was not the discoverer of America!

Columbus was to have a curious encounter on his second voyage across the Atlantic. As related by Washington Irving in his book *Life and Voyages of Christopher Columbus*, in the summer of 1494, while exploring the West Indies, Columbus anchored his ships off the coast of Cuba near a beautiful palm grove and sent a landing party to shore to get a fresh supply of wood and water.

As the others in the group cut wood and filled their water casks, an archer strayed into the forest with his cross-bow in search of game, only to return a few minutes later to relate a baffling and frightening experience. The man, clearly shaken, reported that just a few moments before he had suddenly come upon a band of about 30 well-armed Indians, which was unsettling enough, but nothing compared to the sight of three white men who were in the company of the natives.

The white men, who wore white tunics that reached to their knees, immediately spotted the intruder, and, as the Indians watched impassively one of the three stepped toward the hunter and started to speak when the hunter took to his heels and ran.

Upon hearing the story, Columbus' men got to their boats and made with all haste back to the fleet. The next day Columbus dispatched another party to search for the strangers and the following day still another, but no trace of them was ever found, much to the explorer's frustration.[110]

Were these strange white men in simple robes Irish monks, still wandering North and South America for the past thousand years in the wake of St. Brendan and those before him?

🌺🌺🌺

I sat back on the beach at Negril, a quiet beach resort on the west side of Jamaica. The sun was going down over the Caribbean Sea and I was drinking a Red Stripe beer on the beach. I lay back and looked out over the burnt-orange clouds dotting the sky at sunset.

The story of Columbus and the early exploration of the Caribbean was a fascinating one. The real Columbus was an incredible personality, a man with knowledge, courage and a mystical zeal who pursued lofty goals based on high ideals. Sadly, he died in prison, a victim of Spanish political intrigue.

Not far to the north of Jamaica is Cuba and to the east is Hispanola and then, sweeping in a southern arc toward Venezuela, are the Antilles, an ancient name applied to the West Indies. These Antilles, and the name itself, have everything to do with lost cities and the exploration of North America.

Associated with the Antilles is the legend of Seven Cities of Gold, similar to the legend that was to develop in Arizona and New Mexico about Seven Gold Cities of Cibola. Dr. Cyclone Covey, a history professor at Wake Forest University in North Carolina, writes about a Roman Jewish colony in Arizona and a Portuguese community in Florida in his book *Calalus*.[109] Various Jews had sailed from the Portuguese port of Porto Cale and founded a city in Florida, naming it Cale. This city is now modern day Ocala in north-central Florida.

Covey believes that other Jews escaped Rome and also left Porto Cale, Portugal for the New World. The Latin form of Porto Cale was Calalus, which became a Jewish-Roman outpost in 775 A.D. The city, situated where modern Tucson lies today was then named Rhoda. One of the leaders, or captain of one of the ships, Covey believes, was born on the island of Rhodes.[109]

The story of the Seven Cities of Gold goes back to 8th-century Spain and the year 711 when the Moorish forces under their general Tariq descended on the Visigoth, or "West Goth," kingdom which had once dominated the western area of the late Roman Empire, but which, since its defeat by Clovis the Frank in 507, had been reduced to a feeble remnant of its former glory. King Roderick (Rodrigo in Spanish) rode to battle at the head of his troops, but he was killed and his forces defeated in the battle of Guadalete. The next decade-and-a-half were a horror. The Moorish forces overran all of present-day Spain and Portugal up to the Pyranees. Christian refugees escaped in every available direction, often by ship. There is every reason to believe that some Christian refugees left by sea to the Canary Islands, the Madeiras and even to the Caribbean and Florida.

There arose a legend, which persisted throughout the Middle Ages, of seven Portuguese bishops who managed to escape by ship, with a considerable number of the people of their dioceses, and to reach an island somewhere in the Atlantic where they established seven cities. Part of the legend was that the people of the Seven Cities would one day return in force to help their Spanish compatriots defeat the Moors.[195, 194]

The legend of the Isle of Seven Cities was kept alive in Spain, and apparently became known elsewhere. In the 12th century the Arab geographer Idrisi spoke of an Atlantic island of Sahelia which once contained seven cities until the inhabitants killed each other off in civil wars.[194]

By the late 14th century, theoretical locations of the Seven Cities were beginning to show up via Spanish and Italian maps on various "imaginary" islands in the North Atlantic. Sometimes the Seven Cities were shown in Brazil but more usually on Antillia, a large island depicted on the maps as opposite Spain and Portugal. According to the map historian Raymond Ramsay, a French map of

1546 appears to be the first to have placed a specific island of *Sete Cidades* in the Atlantic, where it remained on many maps for centuries.[194]

The legends of cities probably spurred a certain amount of Atlantic exploration, and there were rumors during the 1430s and 1440s of a couple of Portuguese expeditions which were blown off course in the Atlantic to end up at the Isle of the Seven Cities, where the people still spoke Portuguese and asked if the Moors were still in control of their ancestral land. In each case, the rumor had it that some sand from the beaches of the isle was brought home and proved to be rich in gold.[194,195]

There is a more authentic record of a Fleming whose name is given as "Ferdinand Dulmo," who in 1486 requested the permission of King João II of Portugal to take possession of the Seven Cites, but there is no record that anything was done about it.[194,195]

Was there a specific island in Caribbean that was the legendary island of Christian refugees? If so, which island was it? The word Antilles is a Latin derivative which means merely "Opposite Island" (Although Alexander von Humboldt, for no apparent reason, suggested an alternative derivation, from the Arabic *al-tin*, "the dragon"). [194,195]

Ramsay believes that the first time the word was used was the Pizigani brother's map of 1367, where an island labeled "Atilae" appeared in the approximate position of the Azores, which at the time had not been officially discovered. The word appears again as "Attiaela" on an anonymous Catalan map of about 1425 and then on Battista Beccario's map of 1435 where it is spelled Antilia or Antillia from then on.[194]

European geographers apparently took it for granted that a large island was out there on the far side of the Atlantic and the Martin Behaim globe of 1492 showed Antillia with a notation that in 1414 a Spanish ship "got closest to it without danger." This would seem to imply that the island was known, and regarded as a sailing hazard even earlier than that. There are also references to a Portuguese voyage of the 1440s as having reached Antillia, but this is most likely the same one which was supposed to have visited the Seven Cities.[194,195]

Columbus himself, while in Lisbon in about the year 1480, wrote a letter to King Alfonso V in which he mentioned "the island of Antillia, which is known to you."[194] Columbus also had a letter from the well-known Italian geographer and physician Paolo Toscanelli, dated 1474, recommending Antillia as a good stopping-point to break his voyage to the East Indies and take on supplies.

Columbus felt that the Biblical Ophir and the legendary island of Antilla were one and the same. Columbus' friend and first biographer, Peter Martyr, said in 1511 that Columbus believed himself to have found the land of Ophir "but, the descriptions of the cosmographers well considered, it seemeth that both these and the other islands adjoining are the island of Antilla."[194,195]

419

It has even been suggested that American Indians have journeyed by boat to Europe. According to a number of authors, including Charles Berlitz,[193] during the reign of Augustus Caesar, 2,000 years ago, when the Romans were ruling much of Europe, a, long, narrow, hollow seafaring vessel washed ashore from the North Sea. Speaking a strange language, the copper-colored travelers it carried frequently pointed to the craft and then to the west. Unable to understand the barbarians, Roman soldiers took them hostage and escorted them to the Roman proconsul, Publius Metellus Cellar, who enslaved them.

According to Berlitz, "The travelers would have disappeared into the shadows of history except for a carved likeness of one of them, a bust resembling a Native American. Apparently, the Indians became lost off the North American coast, and the canoe was carried by the upper, easterly Atlantic current—all the way to Europe."

Says Berlitz, "Columbus, who also used the Atlantic current—the lower, westerly stream—during his voyages to the New World, may have been aware of Publius's slaves. A dedicated student of earlier Atlantic crossings, he once described the story of two dead men, dark in color and perhaps Chinese, found floating in a long, narrow boat washed up on the western shore of Ireland, near Galway."[193]

🐾🐾🐾

I had enough of the beaches of Jamaica, so I returned to Miami and once again found myself on Steve's yacht. Over some shrimp and a cold beer, Steve informed me that he had to go to Bimini to look at a yacht and do some welding.

"Bimini?" I asked. "That's great, I've always wanted to go to Bimini. That is where the huge underwater walls are located. When do we go?"

"Tomorrow," he said, "early, so we had better get some sleep. Sage is in Michigan with his mom, I need a first mate on this trip."

"You're on," I said, crushing a beer can and tossing it into the trash. That night I dreamed of the lost continent of Atlantis, and the next morning we pulled up anchor and began the 50 mile trip to the Bahamas.

Naturally, I was as curious as could be about these sunken ruins in the Caribbean and was determined to see some of them. Sitting around on the deck of Steve's yacht in Key Largo, we plotted a trip to Bimini.

Bimini Island is a small member of the Bahamas, located about fifty miles east of Miami. Besides having sandy beaches, coral reefs, a variety of sunken ships, and some excellent fishing areas, Bimini is also the site for a series of very unusual underwater stone formations. This assemblage of huge blocks, many existing in straight patterns, are submerged under only 20 or 30 feet of water.

The Bimini Wall was first discovered in 1968 by Dr. J. Manson

Valentine, Florida's maverick archaeologist. Valentine first saw the wall from the surface of the water when the sea was especially clear. He was with three other divers at the time, Jacques Mayol, Harold Climo, and Robert Angove. Said Valentine in an interview, "An extensive pavement of rectangular and polygonal flat stones of varying size and thickness, obviously shaped and accurately aligned to form a convincingly artifactual arrangement. These stones had evidently lain submerged over a long span of time, for the edges of the biggest ones had become rounded off, giving the blocks the domed appearance of giant loaves of bread or pillows. Some were absolutely rectangular, sometimes approaching perfect squares. (One remembers that absolutely straight lines are never present in natural formations.) The larger pieces, at least ten to fifteen feet in length, often ran the width of parallel-sided avenues, while the small ones formed mosaic-like pavements covering broader sections... The avenues of apparently fitted stones are straight-sided and parallel; the long one is a clear-cut double series interrupted by two expanses containing very large, flat stones propped up at the corners by vertical members (like the ancient dolmens of Europe); and the southeast end of this great roadway terminates in a beautifully curved corner; the three short causeways of accurately aligned large stones are of uniform width and end in *corner stones*..."

Another team of divers claim to have discovered the underwater wall as well. Three divers, Robert Ferro, Michael Grumley and Count Pino Turolla went to Bimini in 1968 to dive at the underwater ruins. They dove and photographed the wall, and discovered sections of pillars, all in 30 feet or so of water. They chronicle their adventures in the book, *Atlantis: Autobiography of a Search.* [200]

Dr. David Zink of the U.S. Air Force Academy in Colorado began doing research around Bimini that continues to this day. His book, *The Stones of Atlantis*,[40] chronicles his many adventures, with many good photographs, in the waters around Bimini. Dr. Zink firmly believes that the Bimini Road is a man-made structure, but he has debunked a few of the other structures in the area, including a rectangular structure off Andros Island that was once believed to have been a temple site, but is now believed to be a sponge pen built in the 1930s. In 1974 they even photographed an unusual stone column standing upright that was believed to be the point of an obelisk that stood 40 to 50 feet tall, though most of it was buried in the ocean floor mud.

Many believers in Atlantis have been very excited by these finds just opposite Miami. The noted American psychic, Edgar Cayce, had predicted that the first portion of the lost continent to be discovered would be located in this general area. Cayce, who died in 1945, had predicted that the first portion of Atlantis to rise would be found in 1968 or 1969. Aerial reconnaissance of this region in 1968, and subsequent dives, did indeed reveal these stone structures breaking the surface of the ocean floor.

Another possibility is that these massive blocks are more likely the product of an early indigenous Indian civilization. Such a development could have served as the mother culture of the Olmecs and Mayan in nearby Mesoamerica, as well as influenced the high centers of South America. At present, however, the weight of evidence is that these rocks, may just be unique natural formations. Geologists and archaeologist have not found enough evidence to convince them to change their point of view. They contend that the area is simply composed of a rather unusual type of fractured beach rock.

If these rocks were actually placed here by an ancient civilization, then they should have been moved into position prior to the great rise in sea level near the end of the Pleistocene Epoch. Jacques Cousteau's exploration of certain submerged Caribbean caves disclosed stalactites and other calcium carbonate structures which could only have been formed above water. It is estimated that 18,000 years ago the sea level was some 500 or 600 feet below its present position. The Cousteau team also noted that the stalactites in a "blue hole" near British Honduras had an incline of some 15°. This degree of inclination certainly suggests some type of major geological movement.

Evidence of worked stone has definitely been located in the Bimini area. Dr. David Zink's expedition recovered a large stylized marble head as well as a dressed stone slab whit a tongue-and-groove pattern on the sides.

Steve and I rented a small boat and some dive gear from a local shop on Bimini. Our guide, Tony, took us out in the motor boat to the area off the Bimini Road. We left Alice Town and headed northeast past Bailey Town and Paradise Point until we came to the dive site.

"This is it," said Tony, shutting off the engine. Tony helped Steve and I get our tanks on. I checked my regulator and tank pressure. Within moments we were ready to go.

"Are you as excited as I am?" I asked Steve.

Steve looked at me coolly. "Yea, yea, sure. Lost cities, Atlantis and all that stuff. I just hope there aren't any sharks or hungry barracuda down there." Then he smiled and said sarcastically, "I hope one of your Bermuda Vortex things doesn't happen. I don't want to get sucked up into space or tossed into some time-warp. I've got to get back to Alice Town and finish that welding job!"

I laughed and sucked hard on my regulator. With that, I gave Steve and Tony the thumbs up signal and flipped over backward into the warm, clear water. Moments later Steve joined me in the tepid Atlantic. Below us I could see the geometric formation of the massive blocks of stone.

Steve and I began our descent to the ocean floor. My eyes were wide, as I viewed the massive stone blocks. I touched down gently on top of a large, rounded block, placing both my hands on it. I was astonished at how similar it looked to the massive, rounded blocks at Sacsayhuaman, the megalithic fortress above Cuzco in Peru.

Steve was on my left, and we both examined the blocks and the line that separated them. After a few minutes on the bottom, we began moving northeast along the bottom, following the "road." It was a fascinating and exciting dive. My mind raced as I viewed each block in turn, often stopping to examine details, and occasionally looking back at where we had just been.

Eventually, we reached the far side, and began to retrace our steps, when Steve signaled to me that his air was almost out. We agreed to surface, ascending slowly. We broke the water about a 100 yards from Tony and the boat. He saw us immediately and started the motor. Soon, he was helping us get back in the boat.

"How was it down there guys?" he asked. "Did you find Atlantis?"

We laughed. I pulled off mask and said, "Those look like man-made blocks to me. Maybe that is part of Atlantis."

"That's what everybody says," nodded Tony. "Now that you've seen the Bimini wall, will you continue your search for Atlantis?"

The waves of the the outboard motor made a white foam over the blue waters covering the last of Atlantis. I looked at Steve, who was grinning wildly. The search would have to continue. We both knew that.

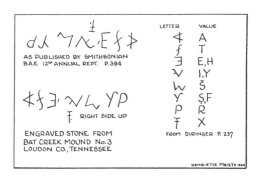

Poverty Point, northern Louisiana: six enormous concentric banks of earth-works. They once formed an octagon, part of which has been washed away by an arm of the Mississippi. *Photo by Dr. Junius Bird, courtesy American Museum of Natural History, New York*

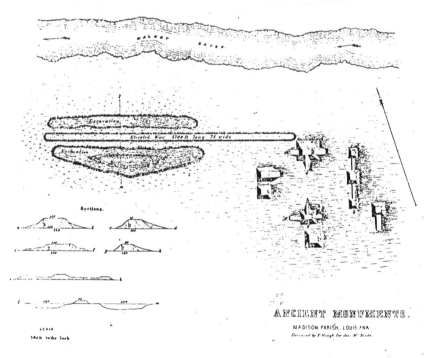

Ancient pyramids of Madison Parish, Louisiana.

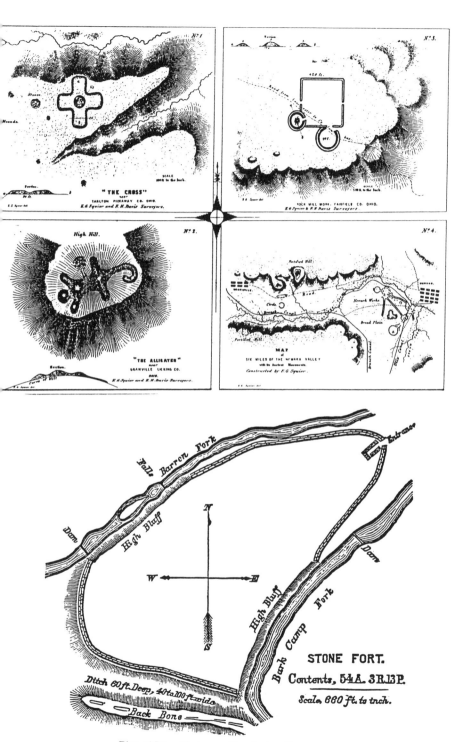

Plan of Stone Fort, near Manchester, Tennessee.

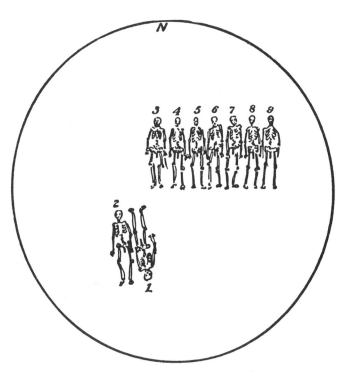

Above: The Bat Creek stone. **Below:** A diagram of the positions [of the] skeletons in the mound. The stone was found beneath the head [of] skeleton number one.

The Micmac hieroglyphic script, here in an 1865 translation of Psalm 115.

Bull-Roarers
A, Australia; B, western Texas. (length of B~16 inches)

Curved Throwing Sticks
A, Australia; B, western Texas. (length of A~ 26 inches)

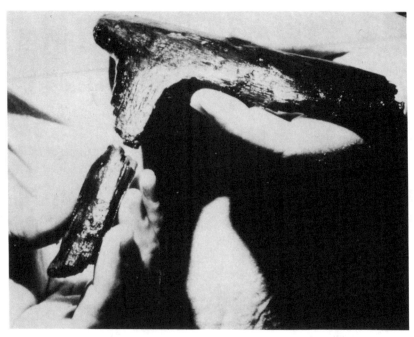

Shaped wood hunting boomerang recovered from Little Salt Spring excavation carbon-dated to 9,080 years, making it the oldest boomerang ever found in the Western Hemisphere and, possibly, the world.

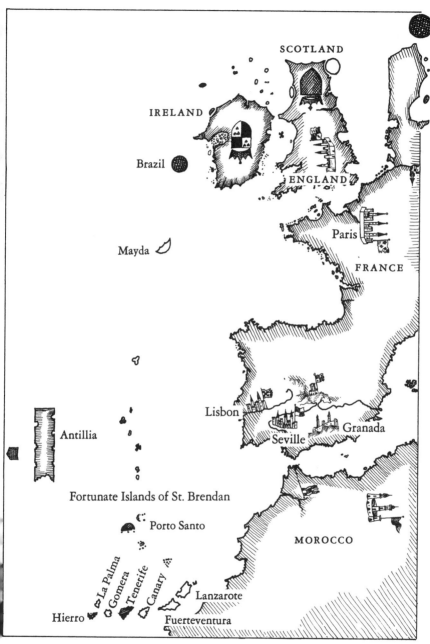

The Pareto Map of 1455 redrawn. It includes such legendary islands as Antillia, the Fortunate Isles of St. Brendan, and Brazil—which was already in the vocabulary of sailors and mapmakers of 1455. It is beleived that this is one of the maps that Columbus carried with him on his first voyage.

Divers, Count Turolla and Carter Lord, provide a point of reference for the size of the 'sea-wall' rocks.

Note the many right angles and the way the stones are fitted together into a pattern. The large stone in the bottom of the photograph is approximately twelve feet across.

Sections of a pillar, discovered and photographed by Count Pino Turolla, November 29, 1969, off Bimini, in 15 feet of water.

Different sized pillars are clearly seen. Large pillar showing grooves is five feet in circumference. *(Photo by Count Turolla)*

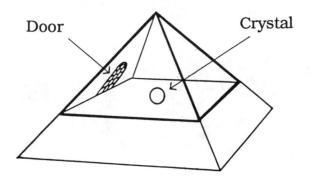

Door   Crystal

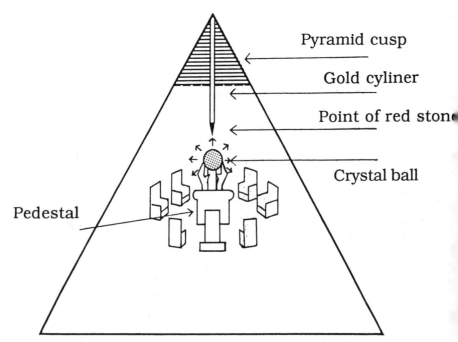

Pyramid cusp

Gold cyliner

Point of red stone

Crystal ball

Pedestal

Diagram of the underwater pyramid alledgedly
containing a crystal in the Bermuda Triangle.

Chapter 12

New England and Eastern Canada:

The Megaliths of Norombega

*I have yet to see any problem,
however complicated,
which when you looked at it in the right way,
did not become still more complicated.*
—Poul Anderson

Fully recovered from the dive at Bimini with Steve, we were back at the marina in Key Largo docking his yacht. It had been good seeing Steve again, but now I had to head north to New England. Friends in New York and Boston were waiting for me, and I knew that I had to get back on the road.

I said goodbye to Steve and, with a full tank of gas, headed north out of the Keys. I stopped briefly at the strange modern "megalithic" site of Coral Castle in Homestead, Florida, just south of Miami, for a quick visit. It is estimated that the strange Latvian immigrant, named Edward Leedskalnin, quarried and built his mini-city with 1,100 tons of coral blocks that make up the 20 foot surrounding walls and megalithic structures that are contained within.

Leedskalnin came here in the 1920s, began his modern megalithic structures in nearby Florida City, but then moved the structures to Homestead in 1936. He moved the many tons of blocks by himself, never allowed anyone to ever see him working or learn the secret of how he lifted the blocks, and claimed to know the secrets of the builders of the pyramids.

I walked through the bizarre compound with its astronomical alignments, gigantic rocking chairs, an obelisk and other strange stone objects. I was most impressed by the gigantic swinging door weighing nine tons which could be moved by child. Leedskalnin allegedly built the whole complex for a lost love back in Latvia, but how he did so remains a mystery. He may have done it all with a simple pulley with block and tackle, though the enormity of doing everything himself would impress even the most skeptical visitor.

With the swamps, beaches and condominiums fading behind me, I was heading up the Atlantic Coast for North Carolina. I spent a night camping along the shore and was up early, passing through Savanah and Charleston, heading for Virginia.

With my radio playing *Last Train to Clarksville,* I pulled into this small town and stopped for gas. It was just near Clarksville, Virginia, by the Roanoke River near Jeffries that the farmer James V. Howe found ancient ironworkings in the 1940s and 1950s. Eventually, he discovered other such sites as far away as Brunswick County, 50 miles to the east. he found swords and other weapons, chisels, nails, and even threaded nuts. Along with these iron pieces, he uncovered a broken bronze cup, a bronze spindle whorl, and two other bronze fragments.

The bronze artifacts, Howe concluded, must have been brought in from somewhere else, since he found no traces of copper or tin at any of the ironworking sites. For that matter, even the workers of the iron must have been from somewhere else, since the Indians have no such traditions. The Brunswick County part of the riddle was made more mysterious by the discovery, in 1950, of two inscribed rocks about a mile apart just outside the village of Dolphin. Some epigraphers think the marks indicate a Roman origin of the stones.

Howe was just as baffled by the attitude of the traditional archaeologists as he was by his discoveries. When the damming of the river was announced, the Smithsonian undertook a very quick dig in 1951 but then refused to run carbon 14 tests on any of the materials that had been dug up. A number of universities and labs that Howe applied to for carbon dating also refused to date them.[201.94]

Today, the original sites found by Howe are now underwater. The bronze cup and some of the iron artifacts are said to be at the Smithsonian, though no one seems to know where. Charles M. Boland, who wrote, *They All Discovered America,*[201] observed that the bronze cup is practically identical with Roman Pompeian cups displayed in the Museum of Naples, Italy.

Another "Roman" artifact was brought up from the ground while men were boring a water well opposite Elizabeth, Virginia, in September of 1833. It was a coin, brought up from a depth of 30 feet, about the size of an English shilling of the period. It was oval in shape, and unlike anything ever seen there before by even the oldest inhabitant. According to historian W.S. Forrest, the figures on the coin were distinct, representing a warrior or hunter and other characters apparently of Roman origin.[94]

❀❀❀

I stopped and saw some relatives in Washington D.C. and marveled for a few days at the various monuments, buildings and naturally, the Smithsonian Institution. I have always admired the founding fathers of the United States, and it brought back pleasant memories of history to see the grand monuments in marble that are built to them. Here was something lasting, something worthy of the classical civilizations of Greece and Rome, and, in our capital, there is even a hint of the ancient Egyptian architecture.

I spent one full day walking around the Smithsonian, and I made a few fruitless enquiries as the whereabouts of a few of the lost artifacts that have been sent there and never seen again. Enquiries as to the Egyptian vault allegedly excavated by Professor Jordon of the Smithsonian in the Grand Canyon drew snorts of derision from the archaeologists that I talked to, as if they had never heard anything so ridiculous in their lives.

Well, at least they weren't trying to cover anything up, I decided. They were obviously not only unaware of that episode of American history, but were blissfully unaware of any unusual artifacts that had been discovered anywhere in America, including the Bat Creek stone tablet with Canaanite-Phoenician written on it which was excavated by the Smithsonian itself in 1885. It was comforting to know that America's history was resting firmly in the capable hands of these scholars who had so well learned their history from those before them, a history that was neatly selected so as to present as complete and solid a picture of American prehistory as possible. Never mind the facts, however. These merely confuse those with wild imaginations.

🦬🦬🦬

From Washington D.C., I drove up to Boston. I was glad to be at my old friend, Greg Deyermenjian's house in Boston one late spring afternoon. I had not seen Greg since we had lived with an uncontacted tribe of Machiguenga Indians in the remote jungles of eastern Peru some years before.

Greg was of Armenian heritage, a tall, skinny guy with gold wireframe glasses and short black curly hair. He worked as a psychologist at a mental hospital to earn money, but also had a degree in anthropology. Every year he would go to the jungles of eastern Peru to live with certain native tribes there.

Greg and I had lived with them for a month on one of our expeditions searching for Paititi, the lost city of the Incas, and we had much to talk about and catch up on (see my book, *Lost Cities & Ancient Mysteries of South America*,[57]).

I felt right at home with Greg; his apartment was packed with history and archaeology books. I instantly looked over his bookshelf and picked out a few select volumes.

"Hey great, you've got *Maps of the Ancient Sea Kings* by Charles

435

Hapgood," I exclaimed, snatching the book off one of his bookshelves.

I had always admired Greg. He was honest and courageous. While moving through the remote mountains and jungles of Peru, often with an armed guard, I had always trusted his common sense and leadership. Our quest for the lost city of Paititi, one that, according to legend, contained the gold-clad mummies of the ancient Inca kings, was a goal that even most Peruvians would shy away from. One of our friends had died recently in Peru on a similar quest for Paititi. However, Greg, like myself, relished the hardships and diversity of such a search.

Greg showed me around Boston for a few days and I went by myself to Cambridge where Harvard College and the Peabody Museum are located, enjoying the bookstores and atmosphere of the university area.

After a few days of seeing the sights of Boston, Greg and I took a day trip up to *America's Stonehenge* in New Hampshire, a modern megalithic site. *America's Stonehenge*, formerly called *Mystery Hill*, is a sprawling complex of megaliths that covers over an acre (the entire complex, including surrounding stone walls covers over 30 acres) on the top of Pattee's Hill, a 245-foot eminence about 25 miles from the Atlantic in a now increasingly urbanized area. It is only an hours drive or so from Boston.

There is evidence that the complex has been built over a natural cave system, much as the many Mayan pyramids, and other cultures did in Central America. However, the site is clearly not Mesoamerican. The stones in the complex are huge stones, some of them 20-ton monoliths.

The huge complex was first discovered in the 1820s by a farmer named Jonathan Pattee who lived on the hill. Archaeological "officialdom" has since satisfied itself that the whole complex was built by Pattee and his five sons in some eccentric plan to spend their Sunday afternoons and maybe fool the archaeologists.

William B. Goodwin, an amateur archaeologist of Hartford, Connecticut, was the main advocate of the idea that the site was the remnant of Irland-it-Mikla, or Great Ireland, of Norse exploration sagas. He thought it had been built by Irish Culdee monks, who possibly fled the Norse across the Atlantic after the ninth century. Subsequent research has undermined this research, proving that the site is far older than the ninth century. In the 1950s, amateur archaeologist Frank Glynn discovered pottery shards that seem unrelated to any known Amerind ceramics. He further called attention to a white pine tree growing through one of the walls that was found to have a tree-ring age of at least 30 years prior to the birth of farmer Pattee in 1796.

This is quite important in view of the fact that the academics (who refuse to visit the place, much as they refused to carbon date the articles found at Clarksville, Virginia) insist that the complex was built by Pattee and "his five sons" as a weekend project over the years. This hypothesis was further undermined when it was revealed that Pattee did not have five sons, but one son and four daughters.

The professional archaeologists lost further ground when carbon-dating proved that the site had been in existence by at least 1690, or about 10 years before the first European settlers in the area. Further carbon-dating was done after enough charcoal was found at an excavation for analysis in 1969. Conducted by the Geochron Laboratories of Cambridge, Massachusetts, the result was an age determination of 3,000 years. In 1970, an additional radiocarbon dating showed that America's Stonehenge was at least 4,000 years old. This, of course did not change the academics opinion on the site, not wanting to be confused by the facts.

The site was opened to the public in 1957 by Robert E. Stone of Derry, New Hampshire, for the purposes of research and preservation. During the following years, research was conducted on many fronts, the most exciting being the carbon-14 tests and the recognition of the many astronomical alignments. According to Robert Stone, like Stonehenge in England, America's Stonehenge was built be an ancient people well versed in astronomy and stone construction. Through several independent surveys by qualified researchers, it has been determined that the site is a very accurate astronomically aligned calendar. It was and still can be used in determining specific solar and lunar events of the year. These events include the annual summer and winter solstices (June 21 and Dec. 21) and equinoxes (March 22 and Sept. 22). These can be viewed by making special arrangements with the management.

Greg and I met with Robert Stone at the visitors center, and he showed us around the complex. We walked up to the top of the hill where the central part of the massive complex was located. Here, the centerpiece is a T-shaped cavern. This has internal structures that have been compared with a hearth and chimney, and "couch," all sculpted from rock. From the couch, a pipe-like orifice ascends to open below a great, grooved stone table in the air above. The table weighs about four and a half tons, and the top surface easily holds an adult human fully stretched out.

Around its edges runs a deep channel, and naturally this has led to conjecture that the platter may have been used for human sacrifice, with the grooves set up to catch the blood. The tube from the crypt below is often called a "speaking tube" because voices coming from inside the chamber sound rather spooky, and could be used as some sort of bogus oracle. The human sacrifice concept is only a theory, but certainly there were historical cults who practiced human sacrifice, including the Phoenicians. The skeptical archaeologists who subscribe to the "eccentric farmer" theory and refuse to examine the site, believe that the table was used by Pattee as a cider press or for making soap.

Another intriguing feature near the east end of the complex is a shaft, about 18 feet deep, with walls cut into solid stone that are curved on three sides and flat on the fourth. From the bottom of this pit, remarkable clusters of quartz crystals have been recovered that supposedly do not occur naturally anywhere within 100 miles of here. Possibly these quartz clusters are what are known as "Power Crystals," though everything is speculation at this point. Robert Stone however believes that this rock-cut pit may have been a crystal mine, and was dug for the specific purpose of mining the crystals. No one knows for sure.

There are many other constructs spread over the 30 acres on the hilltop, including dolmens, standing stones, and "beehive" shaped houses that are also found commonly in Irish and Scottish megalithic sites. There are some inscriptions at the site, possibly Phoenician and ogam, as well as depictions of the double-bladed ax heads used by the Norse as well as the ancient Minoans from Crete.

The whole site was fascinating and unquestionably of megalithic proportions. Greg and I were amazed. Robert Stone patiently answered our many questions and pointed out small details to us.

"Over here is the Summer Solstice Sunrise Monolith," said Stone, as we walked over to a gigantic, upright slab of granite. "The sun rises directly over this standing stone on June 21st of each year. The top of the stone is shaped to match the slope of the notch in the distant horizon from which the sun rises. To view this, one must stand over here in the middle of this stone circle."

"This is amazing," said Greg. "I've lived in Boston all my life and this is the first time that I've ever been here. I saw the megaliths of Peru before I visited the ones in my own back yard."

"There are dolmens, standing stones and megalithic chambers all over New England," said Stone. "Over here is the North Pole Star Stone. It was determined in 1975 that this stone lined up with the pole star Thuban around 2,000 B.C. and is on the main central axis from which the other alignments were determined."

"What does that Harvard say about this place?" I asked as we walked back to the main complex.

"Harvard?" said Stone. "They say that it was all built by an eccentric farmer and don't want to waste their time looking into it carefully. Barry Fell, a former Harvard professor and the president of the Epigraphic Society has been here several times, and he says that it is an authentic ancient megalithic site that is astronomically aligned. However, the college of Harvard refuses to do any studies at the site. They ignore the carbon-14 tests and other evidence."

"Maybe that's because they have to tow the official line, no matter what," I suggested. "There is evidence that the Smithsonian and other research institutions are well aware of the great deal of evidence for pre-Columbian contact, but official policy which began at the the turn of the century was to totally deny any such evidence, and cover it up when ever possible."

"That may well be the case," admitted Stone. "I was told once by a former employee of the Smithsonian that they had taken a boat load of unusual artifacts out into the Atlantic and dumped them in the ocean. Later, when she defended controversial sites such as this one at a meeting, she was fired. When I have talked with the universities, they insist that this must be a modern construction, yet they refuse to examine the site or look at any evidence to the contrary. Either they are blind idiots who care nothing for real scientific investigation, or they are trying to cover up America's real history. I find their attitude rather unscientific."

Greg and I bought some books at the bookstore in the visitor's center, and headed back to the car.

"Thanks for bringing me out here, Greg," I said.

"I'm glad we came too," he said. "I just can't see why Harvard or some other university won't look at this site, its incredible."

"Sometimes people won't look at things because they are afraid it will change them," I said. "By refusing to come here, they can continue to maintain that megaliths in New England don't exist. If they actually came to this spot, they might be forced to change their opinion, and that would mean that the history books would have to be rewritten. Maybe they don't want that."

Greg paused for a moment as he unlocked his car. "Maybe you're right," he said. "Maybe you're right."

🐾🐾🐾

There are plenty of other similar megalithic sites in New England, although America's Stonehenge is apparently the largest. The three books by Barry Fell, *America B.C.*, *Saga America*, and *Bronze Age America*, [8,202,187] are full of examples. Other well researched books on megaliths, "ogam" inscriptions, astronomical alignments and ancient explorers include *The Search For the Lost America*,[203] *Ancient Celtic America*,[204] and *The Norse Discovery of America*.[206]

Back at Greg's place in Boston, we talked about the evidence for ancient seafarers, pre-Columbian visitors, megaliths and the like. Greg is an anthropologist, and generally speaking, a scientific person.

"America's Stonehenge is an interesting place, but don't you think that some of these researchers are jumping to conclusions," said Greg over a brown rice and tofu dinner.

"Well, I must admit," I said, "that some people want to believe strange things, and the weirder and wilder these things are, the more such people will believe them. But, Barry Fell and the Epigraphic Society are doing their research methodically. I mean, are all these inscriptions just plow scratches? Are these dolmens and standing stones just freaks of nature? That to me is certainly as incredible as Irish, Viking and Mediterranean sailors."

"What about these books?" asked Greg, pulling out a couple of new titles that attempt to debunk Barry Fell and others. The books were *Frauds, Myths and Mysteries: Science & Pseudoscience in Archaeology*,[207] and *Fantastic Archaeology: The Wild Side of North American Prehistory*.[208]

Both books were an entertaining, and highly critical look at the various "odd-ball" theories of "Africans, Atlanteans, Celts of various types, Chinese, Iberians, Israelites, Vikings and vanished races that, in various theories, had "discovered" the New World. Both

439

authors seemed to think such wild theories showed more about the theorists and their unscientific approaches, rather than any real evidence of such a contact. Even Viking remains, such as Runes in Minnesota or Oklahoma were discounted as not evidence of anything, and those who somehow believed in such things were people who lacked critical thinking habits. Any similarity between Old World cultures and New World cultures was purely because of a common biological heritage, as "minds work in similar ways."

Both books take a close look at Barry Fell and his claims of finding numerous inscriptions all over North America "everywhere there is a scratch on a rock." America's Stonehenge in New Hampshire is "obviously of colonial origin" as are all the other dolmens, standing stones and megalithic vaults. Barry Fell and the others (myself included, of course) constitute the "lunatic fringe" of pseudoscientific nuts who could use a good dose of scientific logic to temper their various arguments.

"It seems to me," I said to Greg, "that the ones who need to examine the logic of scientific reasoning are these isolationists who cling to their antiquated ideas. Is it logical to assume that Vikings and Irish would sail to Greenland and Newfoundland, but would not continue down the coast of North America once they are already on this continent? Is it logical to assume that Asians would cross from Siberia to Alaska when gigantic ice sheets covered North America, but would not make the same journey at a later date when the ice was gone and the journey would be much easier? These authors conveniently ignore any real evidence, the Bat Creek stone discovered by the Smithsonian, the huge skeletons in copper armor found in mounds, the copper mines of Lake Superior, the Iron smelters of Ohio, the undeniable fact that many Mesoamericans are depicted with full beards and mustaches when American Indians are supposed to be beardless. Its like some sort of Orwellian doublespeak in which the real logic is twisted, and only sailors like the Polynesians can sail thousands of miles through vast ocean expanses, while sophisticated navies can never leave the sight of land for fear of falling off the edge of the world. These so-called authorities are the lunatic fringe, while Barry Fell and his companions are using the real scientific deductive reasoning."

Greg finished his brown rice and took a bite of seaweed. He was obviously thinking carefully. "Well, I guess you have a point," he finally said. "Perhaps with the five-hundredth anniversary of Columbus coming up, the academic powers that be are mustering up their guns for one last salvo at the diffusionists before the war is finally lost. It is disturbing to think that there may be some sort of planned suppression of the evidence happening."

I finished the last of my brown rice and tofu and nodded.

"More seaweed?" asked Greg. He was washing down a handful of vitamins with soymilk, as was his after dinner practice.

"No thanks," I said. "But I could go for a beer."

Greg laughed and headed for the refrigerator. "Okay," he said, "with that last speech, you deserve one."

"Thanks," I said. "At least there is some reward for being on the lunatic fringe."

With that, we both laughed.

🦬🦬🦬

I left Boston the next day and headed for Newport, Rhode Island to investigate the controversial tower there. On the way I thought about some of the evidence for a Celtic kingdom in New England. In 1831, the skeleton of a male wearing heavy metal plates was dug up at the corner of what is now Fifth and Hartley streets in downtown Fall River, Massachusetts. The metal appeared to be copper or bronze, and after some debate, the skeleton was taken to be that of a Viking. Henry Wadsworth Longfellow wrote his poem, The Skeleton in Armor, on the basis of this discovery, recounting the story of a Viking building a tower for his lady fair. This tower is the Newport, Rhode Island tower, believed by many to have been built by Vikings.

In 1843 the skeleton was destroyed, with other artifacts, in the great fire that swept through Fall River, burning most of the city. In the 1880s, experts at Harvard's Peabody Museum decided that the metal objects were not copper, but brass and this allegedly made the armor of recent English manufacture. Later, in 1938, the anthropologist C.C. Willoughby decided that the burial had been of a Wampanoag Indian, which is an odd deduction, since, according to the Peabody Museum, he was wearing British brass armor. Both deductions are particularly alarming when viewed in light of the fact that the artifacts and skeleton under discussion had been destroyed many years earlier! The experts make their convoluted deductions, ignoring facts, making final decrees that are illogical and narrow-minded, without even seeing the evidence, and no one seems to notice. The hallowed halls of learning have spoken, and let's not have any arguments.

Despite these bizarre deductions, it is most probable that the Fall River Man in Armor was indeed a Viking or perhaps some other warrior, possibly a Toltec, and was indeed probably wearing copper armor, rather than brass. The copper for the armor might even have come from the Lake Superior copper mines and manufactured somewhere in America. Other skeletons in armor have been found at Spiro Mounds, Oklahoma, and Walkerton, Indiana.[94]

About ten miles from Fall River is Dighton Rock on the east side of Assonet Bay, near the mouth of the Taunton River. Dighton Rock has a jumble of weird symbols inscribed on the 7-by-11-foot face of this waist-high, reddish-brown rock (not plough scratches, I hope). Cotton Mather, the famous theologian and witch-hunter, described the rock in 1690 and made a drawing of the figures, so if it is a hoax, it is quite an old one. The general opinion is that the rock is authentic, though no one has so far come up with an accepted decipherment of the rock. Theories abound, however, and the inscriptions are variously thought to be Egyptian, Phoenician,

Persian, Roman, Japanese, Chinese, Norse, Portuguese and the work of the Devil.[94] Perhaps with Dighton Rock, we really do have a case for a "lunatic fringe." Barry Fell, America's master epigrapher, has not attempted to decipher Dighton Rock, as far as I know.

At Goshen, Massachusetts, just north of Northampton, is a strange tunnel system with sophisticated masonry installed in a hill west of town. It is known locally as Counterfeiters' Den from an old tale that counterfeiters were apprehended a few miles southwest of the spot.

The complex was discovered during a hunt for a rabbit that had dived into a burrow near the top of the shaft. At that time, the top of the vertical tunnel was completely disguised with bushes, several inches of sod, and a covering of flat stones. This shaft is about 15 feet deep and three and a half feet in diameter. There are branching horizontal tunnels, one of which is level with the main tunnel and the other is three feet higher.

The bottom tunnel leads eastward, is about two feet wide by two and a half feet high, and has stone sidewalls with flat flagstones spanning the top. The same tunnel runs west for about 75 feet until the tunnel is caved in. The upper tunnel is caved-in about 15 feet from the vertical shaft. Engineers have marveled at the enormous efforts of labor that must have gone into its construction, especially the laying of stone lintels from within the shaft.

Its purpose or builders remain unknown, although it is generally accepted that it was not made by the counterfeiters. It has been suggested that it was once a well, a shelter from Indian attacks or part of the Underground Railroad. No one knew anything about it until it was discovered in the late 1800s and the various theories make little sense. Wells generally do not have lateral tunnels, plus, it would have been nearly impossible to build if ground water were nearby; no Indian attacks ever occurred in the area, and it does not seem to be connected to any nearby houses. It remains a mystery.[94]

At Pelham, Massachusetts is one of New England's many "beehive caves," which are caverns that look like a mere hole in the ground though the interior is shaped like a conical igloo, built with mortarless stones. There is a flat lintel stone across the entrance.

Another beehive structure is located about 12 miles north of Pelham, while a free standing beehive structure is located at Upton, Massachusetts, 12 miles southeast of Worcester. It is larger than the others and has a 14-foot entryway of megalithic stones to an entrance only four feet high.[94]

Archaeologists generally ascribe these strange structures to "colonial rootcellars." However, it is frequently pointed out that it would be extremely difficult to move produce in and out of these odd structures. Others point out that these structures are very similar to the beehive caves and domes built by Culdee monks of Ireland and Scotland many centuries ago. Others point out that the structures are best suited for a race of people not more than three feet tall.

I arrived in the early afternoon at Newport and headed straight for Touro Park where the controversial Newport Tower stands in a city park. I found a parking place in the busy yacht harbor area of the city and walked up to the park where the tower was centrally located.

The circular tower is three stories high, with the third story partially blown off. The solid upper stories are perched on eight stone pillars with neatly executed arches between each pillar. Official archaeological opinion is that the tower was built in 1675 by Governor Benedict Arnold when it supposedly replaced an earlier wooden structure that blew down earlier in that year. Supposedly, Arnold patterned the mill after one he had seen in Chesterton, England.

The problems with this theory are manifold. For one thing, windmills have a strong torquing force and a large stone mass on top of eight pillars is a poor engineering solution, as well as more difficult to build than a tower with solid walls. Also, there are no millstones in evidence, nor a record of any. The open bottom area would be impractical for working with flour on a wet or windy day, of which Newport has many. Furthermore, the tower in Chesterton, England was built as an observatory, not a windmill. Historian Philip Ainsworth Means observed that if Benedict Arnold had designed the tower as a windmill, it would have been unique in the history of the world.[94,206,212]

The general assumption by the "lunatic fringe" is that the tower is Norse, built probably in the 12th century. Viking historians such as Holand,[212] Boland,[201] and Chapman,[206] point out that the tower is built using the Rhineland foot (12.35 modern inches), a unit of measure used in the low countries of Germany and Scandinavia during the period of Norse exploration of America.

Chapman points out in his book, *The Norse Discovery of America*,[206] that a civil engineer named Edward Richardson used schematic drawings to show that the place for a fireplace on the second floor, along with a window opposite it, carried the beam of light from the fireplace directly down the channel entrance of the harbor. The fireplace, which uses one of the columns as a flue had to have been precisely placed for this purpose. The same is true of the opposite window.

Says Chapman, a navigation expert, who first charted Columbus' voyage correctly across the Atlantic (featured in *National Geographic*'s Nov. 1986 issue): "The building also has a window on the second floor which is south facing. This serves as a lookout over the Atlantic which is visible out to 11.4 nautical miles and could alert people in the tower to approaching ships who would then have to come around Newport Neck in order to enter the harbor. The design of the structure leaves little room for doubt that it was constructed for navigational purposes."[206]

Hjalmar Holand in his book, *Explorations in America Before Columbus*,[212] shows several examples of identical towers in Norway and Sweden, including the seal of the medieval city of Konghelle which features a round tower that is identical to the Newport Tower. These towers were at the same time used as churches, defensive forts, and often lighthouses. The Newport Tower apparently served the same function.

Chapman goes one step further by reprinting the famous Mercator map of 1569 that shows a tower at Narragansett Bay some 67 years before the English settled in Rhode Island in 1636. Mercator's map is credited as being the first map to show the Appalachians as a continuous mountain range stretching parallel to the east coast. It shows a land called "Norombega" with a medieval tower at the mouth of a bay. Chapman identifies this spot as Newport, and the medieval tower as the Newport Tower. A blow-up of this curious structure on Mercator's map shows an adjoining structure to the tower, now gone, and of course, a roof, which has now been blown off.[206]

🕱🕱🕱

I headed north again, back into New Hampshire and then to Maine. My goal was Halifax in Nova Scotia, a city on the extreme eastern end of the Trans-Canadian Highway. In many ways it was like the end of the continent, a sort of Ultima Thule, a land on the far reaches of the earth.

I spent the night in Bar Harbor with relatives and continued along Highway One into the remote areas of northern Maine along the Canadian border. This is a land of lakes, moose, and forest.

The land of Norombega on Mercator's 1569 map, the most detailed of North America at the time, was the entire New England area, including Maine, New Brunswick, Nova Scotia, Quebec and Newfoundland. The ancient Norse presence in America was far more extensive than a few isolated forts, and apparently, they were only the last of many ancient voyagers to the New World.

Of course, if Norombega was an ancient kingdom worthy of its Norse heritage, one would think that there would be evidence for its existence. If the various megalithic chambers and standing stones throughout New England were not proof enough (many are probably too old to be evidence for Norse settlements) then there must be other artifacts and most importantly, inscriptions.

At Monhegan Island, 15 miles from Port Clyde by ferry, off the coast of Maine, can be found runic inscriptions. The runes are on Manana, a rocky outcropping adjacent to Monhegan, on the side where the two islands approach to form a harbor. Both islands are jagged, storm-lashed islets that are reached only by sea going vessels, and have a number of strange inscriptions.

The main runic markings are over a spring, and above the inscription, on a horizontal rock platform, are three holes bored a foot apart into the rock in triangular pattern. Each hole is about three inches in diameter and an inch dep. The inscription is about six inches tall and two feet long, with the line slanting downward.

Early historians who viewed the inscriptions felt them unimportant. G.H. Stone wrote in 1885 that the inscription was merely "a freak of surface erosion." The figures were discovered in 1808, and so far do not seem to have changed much, and runic scholars are convinced that a genuine inscription is there.

Runic scholar Olaf Strandwold puzzled over the inscription for years, and came up with various decipherments. Runic inscriptions, like Hebrew, Phoenician, Libyan, some forms of ogam and other scripts are difficult to decipher because they have no vowels. Therefore, a cryptogram is created with a sentence full of consonants, but no vowels. The problem is further complicated by the inscription itself, where the break between words must often be guessed at, and often, the rune, or "letter" itself, is meant to stand for a number, rather than a letter.

Several translations of the strange markings have been forwarded, though no agreement has been reached. There are more runes at Popham Beach State Park, about 22 west of Monhegan Island, though unfortunately some of them were stolen in the early 1970s. Runologist Alf Monge, who also worked on other rune stones, such as in Heavener, Oklahoma and the famous Kensington Runestone in Minnesota, translated one of the runic inscriptions at Popham as: "Henrikus sailed 34 days, 6 October 1123." Henrikus was a Norse bishop whom Viking partisans widely believe to have sailed to Norombega between 1114 and 1123.[94]

Ancient Norombega must hold many surprises, I thought, pulling off the road for the night in northern Maine to spend the night camping near one of Maine's many lakes. There were some bizarre things in Maine, reports of Big Foot and other critters, plus a weird staircase cut into solid rock on a cliff near South Windham, seven miles northwest of Portland on U.S. 202. The staircase is cut into a rocky bluff on private land, about 25 feet off the ground, beginning and ending nowhere.[94]

I crossed into Canada around noon the next day at Houlton, getting checked briefly by Canada Immigration, and then heading for Woodstock, New Brunswick. It was exciting to be in Canada. I always like foreign countries, and Canada, while certainly the most similar country to the United States, still has its own special flavor.

I headed down Canadian Highway Two to Fredericton, the capital of New Brunswick, with the sun shinning brightly and the road stretched out before me. I stopped and picked up two hitchhikers, a couple of young guys from Toronto that were heading for Halifax. We tossed their backpacks in the back and they sat up front with me.

Soon, we had passed Fredericton and were pulling into Moncton in eastern New Brunswick. Moncton is the site of one of the best known "Magnetic Hills" in North America, a spot where cars, balls and other objects appear to roll uphill. A large tourist sign led us to the spot, where we stopped the car at the bottom of a hill, turned off the engine, and then watched in amazement as the car appeared to roll uphill.

"We're rolling uphill!" said Tom, one of the hitchhikers.

"There must be some large meteorite underneath us pulling the car forward," said Carey, the other hitchhiker.

445

It certainly seemed like we were rolling uphill, though, apparently non-magnetic objects, such as rubber or plastic balls roll uphill as well. According to most information, it is merely an optical illusion, and because of the hilly terrain, we only seem to be going uphill, when in reality we are rolling downhill. I wasn't so convinced myself, and felt there may actually be a gravity anomaly here.

Some writers, such as Jacques Bergier in *Secret Doors of the Earth*, (1975), claim that gravity is inverted here, and tells of an entire Indian village that vanished not far from here. He gives no other references or information, but atleast there is evidence of a vortex in the area. Certainly, Magnetic Hill is an amusing attraction.

We then crossed a narrow strait between New Brunswick and Nova Scotia. Nova Scotia was originally named *Acadia* by the explorer Giovanni da Verrazzano in 1524. He was more educated than most of the early explorers, so it is reasonable to assume that he gave the name *Acadie* or *Acadia* to the lands he was claiming, equating them with the *Arcadia* of ancient Greece. Verrazzano's region grew to include all of Nova Scotia, southeastern Quebec and the eastern part of Maine. One theory is that Verrazzano was told by the Micmac Indians of the area that this country was called cady or quoddy, which means "land" or "territory" in the Micmac language. Hence Verrazzano used a sort of pun in the name of Acadia. It is also from the word Acadia that we get our word *cajun* to refer to French-American people and things related to them, such as cuisine.

There is an interesting parallel between Verrazzano's Acadia, ancient Greece and the ancient Egyptians, who were controlled by the Greeks after Alexander the Great's invasion. According to Barry Fell in *America B.C.*,[8] the Micmacs are the descendants of Egyptian explorers and settlers who came to North America. Fell came to this theory when he was shown the Lord's Prayer written in Micmac hieroglyphics printed in 1866. The Micmac hieroglyphic system was supposedly "invented" by a French priest, but Fell recognized that the Micmac hieroglyphic system was virtually identical to the ancient Egyptian hieroglyphic system, with many, or most, of the hieroglyphs having the same meaning in both languages.

Fell devotes several pages in his book to comparing Micmac hieroglyphs to ancient Egyptian and relates that Micmac hieroglyphs were already in use in 1738 when Abbé Maillard adopted them for his *Manuel Hieroglyphique Micmac*. Fell points out that Egyptian hieroglyphs were not deciphered until 1823, when Champollion published his first paper on the Rosetta Stone. After a good deal of research, Fell was convinced that the Micmac Indians, and other Algonquian Indians had been using a system of Egyptian hieroglyphs for at least 2,000 years. He quotes Father Eugene Vetromile who said in 1866, "When the French first arrived in Acadia, the Indians used to write on bark, trees, and stones, engraving signs with arrows, sharp stones, or other instruments. They were accustomed to send pieces of bark, marked with these signs, to other Indians of other tribes, and to receive back answers written in the same manner, just as we do with letters and notes. Their chiefs used to send circulars, made in the same manner, to all their men in time of war to ask their advice, and to give directions."[8]

🐟🐟🐟

We camped that night by an old shack on the Bay of Fundy, Tom and Carey, the two hitchhikers, making a fire while I gathered some driftwood. Later we ate a road-kill guinea hen that Tom suddenly produced, roasting it slowly over the fire and putting butter on it to baste it.

They were off on a summer adventure, taking a few weeks to explore eastern Canada, maybe going up to Prince Edward Island. They questioned me about my adventures, and were amazed that I had traveled for many years across Asia, Africa and South America.

"How did you do it?" Tom asked. "Were you born a millionaire or something?"

I laughed. "Hell no," I said. "You don't have to be a millionaire to travel around the world. I used to live on a few dollars a day. I hitchhiked quite a bit as well, especially in Africa and the Middle East. If I had a few thousand dollars on me, I could go for a year, depending on where I was. I would stop and look for work from time to time as well. It wasn't so hard once I got going. It's getting started that is the hard part. Cutting yourself off from your job, friends, family and responsibilities is the hard part as like the great Chinese philosopher Lao Tzu once said, 'the journey of a thousand miles begins with a single step'."

Tom and Carey looked into the campfire in silence. In their minds they were resolving to travel the world as I had done, or so I guessed. Canadians, like Australians and New Zealanders, have a greater sense of wanderlust than many Americans, I believe. These two appeared ready to begin a world-wide adventure at any time. I tried to encourage them as much as I could. I firmly believe that travel is the best education one can get, though I must admit that having traveled around the world and seen many sights doesn't impress very many employers, unless you want to be a travel writer.

Looking out over the Bay of Fundy, I thought of Henriette Mertz's book, *The Wine Dark Sea.*[185] This scholarly and interesting book takes the voyage of Odysseus, (Ulysses to the Romans) from Homer's ancient Greek epic, *The Odyssey* and tracks the voyage of the legendary sailor through the North Atlantic. According to Mertz's detailed itinerary, Odysseus sails out through the straits of Gibraltar and into the North Atlantic, eventually arriving at the Bay of Fundy, which she identifies as the "monsters" of Scylla and Charybdis. Homer has Odysseus attacked by Charybdis; being "sucked down the salty sea—we could see within the swirling cataclysm of the great vortex and at the bottom the earth appeared black with sand while round about the rock roared terribly...," he is in reality (according to Mertz) caught in the deadly tidal bore of the

Bay of Fundy.

As I drifted off to sleep in sleeping bag, the great exploits of the ancient seafarers of epic legend came to my mind; those of Jason and the Argonauts, Odysseus, Hercules, Sinbad and others. These brave adventurers weren't afraid of the ocean, they were hardly afraid of anything, though certain supernatural forces did give them a fright. Still, a cry and an oath to their gods usually gave them the strength to carry on...

🐃🐃🐃

It was about noon the next day when I left Tom and Carey off in Halifax. Since this was my destination on the far east coast, I wanted to spend a day or two here, so I walked around, went to the port and some of the tourist shops. In the evening I had dinner in one of the seafood restaurants and hung out in one of the bars for part of the evening. In some ways, Halifax was a bit of a let down, not quite the Mecca for lost cities that I had somehow imagined, but it was a pleasant enough place.

South of Halifax is Mahone Bay, and on an island in that bay is one of the most famous, and mysterious treasures in the world. Oak Island allegedly has a lost treasure deep within a bizarre shaft that has befuddled treasure-seekers for two centuries. In 1795, three youths rowed over from the mainland for a day of exploration. They found an oak tree with a sawed-off limb projecting over a large circular depression in the ground and came back the next day with picks and shovels.

Their digging revealed a circular shaft about 13 feet wide. They discovered a platform of logs at the ten-foot level, and again at the 20 and 30 foot levels. As the continued the excavation over a period of many years, they discovered a platform of logs every ten feet to a depth of 80 feet. At 90 feet they discovered a round flat stone with markings that they could not decipher. The stone was later "deciphered" and allegedly read, "ten feet below two million pounds are buried." The whereabouts of this stone has not been known since 1935.

At 98 feet, confident that the treasure was near, they stopped digging for the weekend. When they returned to the shaft they were dismayed to find that the pit was now half full of seawater. They pumped out the water, reached the 110-foot level, but finding nothing, they reluctantly abandoned the island and their search.

Subsequent searches in the 1800s created side tunnels and various dams to keep the pit from flooding. Allegedly at the 154-foot level, two chests were discovered in 1897. A depth of 170 feet was attained in 1935, and two years later, a depth of 180 feet. A second tunnel to the sea was discovered in 1942 and in 1971 a consortium out of Montreal purchased the island and reached a water-filled cavity at the 212-foot level. According to news reports of the day, a submarine television camera that was lowered into the cavity sent

448

back images of three chests and a severed hand. Divers were lowered into the cavity but arrived too late, for in the meantime it had been eroded by seawater. The quest for this treasure, one of the world's costliest, continues to this day.[213]

The treasure has been variously thought to have been laid by pirates such as William Kidd, Henry Morgan or Blackbeard, or by Norsemen, or, more likely, it was a British or Spanish payroll that was secreted in the shaft during one of the many wars of the Spanish Main, or even the American Revolution, waiting for the fighting to cease. If the treasure had been Blackbeard's, the secret doubtlessly went to the grave with him. In 1718 Lt. Robert Maynard of the Royal Navy was sent by Gov. Spotswood of Virginia in the sloop *Ranger* to capture Blackbeard. Maynard caught Blackbeard at Ocracoke, North Carolina and Blackbeard was killed in the battle. Perhaps, he had just finished creating the Oak Island pit.

Other more far-out theories are that the pit was made by the Incas, hiding their treasure from the conquistadors and that it was an Atlantean tomb. In a small, privately published book, Canadian Atlantis researcher, Alexander Stang Fraser theorizes that the Grand Banks to the east of Labrador and Nova Scotia was the site of fabled Atlantis, now submerged. Fraser maintains that a flood tunnel security system, apparently designed to drown excavators at the pit site, would seem to have precluded withdrawal of the presumed treasure of the depositors. "This contradiction indicates that this was not originally a well protected buried treasure situation, but a unique type of tomb. The protection of a tomb by the sea is consistent with the maritime activity of the Atlanteans, and Mahone is in the general area of the proposed location of the former Atlantis."

Fraser calls the Grand Banks the Elysian Plain of Plato's account of Atlantis, and it is an interesting theory that this large area, just beneath the surface of the Atlantic, was at one time above water, and may have contained a civilization. It seems unlikely, however, that the Oak Island Money Pit has anything to do with this "sunken land."

🏵🏵🏵

Maps of Iceland, Greenland and the coasts of Labrador, Newfoundland and New England from the middle ages are of particular interest. Curiously, just as the Piri Reis map shows parts of Antarctica ice free, the Zeno brothers map of 1380 shows Greenland ice free!

This map was the result of a voyage made by the two Zeno brothers from Venice in the early fourteenth century. Their explorations supposedly took them to Iceland, Greenland and perhaps as far as Nova Scotia. They drew a map of the North Atlantic which was subsequently lost for two centuries before it was rediscovered by a descendant of the Zenos.

According to Rene Noorbergen, a study of the chart reveals that the Zeno brothers could not have been the original map makers. The brothers supposedly touched land in Iceland and Greenland, yet their chart very accurately shows longitude and latitude not only for these locations, but also for Norway, Sweden, Denmark, the German Baltic coast, Scotland, and even such little-known landfalls as the Shetland and Faroe islands. The map also shows evidence of having been based on a polar projection, which was beyond the abilities of the fourteenth-century geographers. The original map makers likewise knew the correct lengths of degrees of longitude for the entire North Atlantic; thus, it is very possible that the map, instead of being a product after the fact, was drawn up by the Zeno brothers before their voyage and was used to guide them in their exploration of the northern lands.[92]

Just how ancient the original source maps may have been is indicated by the fact that the Zeno map shows Greenland completely free of ice. Mountains in the interior are depicted, and rivers are drawn flowing to the sea, where in many cases glaciers are found today. Captain Mallery, whose initial work on the Piri Reis map led him to study other Renaissance charts such as the Zeno brothers', took special note of the flat plain shown stretching the length of the Greenland interior on this map, intersected midway by mountains. The Paul-Emile victor French Polar Expedition of 1947-49 found precisely such topography from seismic profiles.[92]

As with the revelation that Antarctica at one time was free of ice and perhaps inhabited, we find similar legends of a civilized people who once lived in northern lands which are now buried under thousands of feet of ice: the legends of Thule, Numinor and the Hyperboreans. Egerton Sykes, in his *Dictionary of Nonclassical Mythology*, page 20, states his belief that the Norse legend of Fimbelvetr, the "terrible winter" that launched the epic disasters of Ragnarok and destruction of the gods of Valhalla, may reflect a historical fact: the obliteration of a prehistoric civilization in the boreal regions by the Ice Age catastrophe.[92]

This catastrophe was probably a shifting of the poles, or in other words, a slippage of the earth's crust ten or twenty degrees. During such a slippage, woolly mammoths and other animals happily grazing in temperate pastures suddenly found themselves freezing to death in the Arctic, and formerly temperate areas, such as Greenland, began to accumulate ice. Conversely, the former glaciers, such as were in Manitoba and Wisconsin began to melt.

It is interesting that perhaps the Zeno brothers map shows what may have been the lost land of Thule, a legendary northern land mentioned by such Greek and Roman historians as Diodorus Siculus (*The Library of History*, 1st century BC), Strabo (*Geography*, 1st century BC) and Procopius (*The Gothic War*, 4th century AD).

Essentially, Thule was an island in the North Atlantic, some six-days sail from the Orkney Islands and was ten times the size of Great Britain. The early historians declared that there were giant forests there, many wild animals and several races of men, some of whom were very primitive while others were more civilized, though they practiced human sacrifice. It was also noted that the sun did not shine for 40 days and nights in the winter, and did not set for a similar time during the summer. Curiously, a huge forest of trees, now petrified, exists on Baffin Island, further confusing any ideas about the last ice age, where, strangely, huge herds of woolly mammoths and rhinos were wandering central Alaska and huge forests existed on Baffin Island in the arctic, yet giant glacial ice sheets were in Michigan and Wisconsin. And now, even more strangely, it appears that Greenland may have been free of ice at the same time!

The lost land of Thule was important in Norse mythology, to the Teutonic Knights of the Middle Ages, and eventually to inner occult groups in Nazi Germany. The Thule Society, of which Adolf Hitler and other high ranking Nazis were members, met in Berlin and formed an occult core to the Nazi movement.

It was believed that Thule (generally identified as Greenland) had been an island to the north of Atlantis, to which many Atlanteans had fled just prior to the destruction of Atlantis. Did the Zeno brothers map come from such a time, after the sinking of Atlantis, but before the ice had completely covered Greenland, the world's largest island?

❦❦❦

After a few days of camping around Halifax, I headed back west to New Brunswick and onto Quebec and Ontario. I would have liked to have visited Newfoundland, but this remote island state can only be reached by ferry and my time and money were running dangerously low.

The Zeno brothers in the relation of their 1380 voyage, published in 1558, spoke of a lost island called Estotiland. Estotiland was an island smaller than Iceland in the North Atlantic, apparently above Labrador. It was crossed by four rivers and had a mountain in the center. It lay north of the island of Drogio, where men eat each other in splendid temples. According to the Zeno brothers, the people of Estotiland possess every single art in the world, except that of using a mariner's compass.[214]

Estotiland would seem to be a good example of the medieval imagination and the desire of early explorers to embellish their accounts with details that made sense to the European minds at the time, but seem totally ridiculous to us today. Will many of the cherished dogmas of current science be equally ridiculous to the scientists and historians of a future epoch?

Labrador has its share of strange inscriptions, including curious inscriptions at Grates Cove on the northern most tip of the Avalon Peninsula, known since at least 1822 and there is an ogam stone at St. Lunaire-Griquet, which is near to L'Anse aux Meadows, the first authenticated Norse settlement in North America.

It was in 1960 that the Norwegian explorer Helge Ingstad found a

451

group of mounds which he theorized as a Norse Viking site. The next year he returned with his archaeologist wife, Anne and for seven summers, they and archaeologists from all over the world uncovered what are now the admitted remains of a Norse settlement. Besides the remains of curve-walled Norse houses, they excavated what appeared to be a sauna and the remains of a blacksmith shop, where iron from a nearby bog had been smelted and made into tools. Charcoal from the site revealed a date of about 1000 A.D.[160]

For years, the stuffy archaeologists in their ivory towers had maintained that Columbus had been the original "discoverer" of America, and that Vikings, for reasons unknown (falling off the edge of the earth?), had never ventured beyond Iceland and Greenland. With the discoveries at L'Anse aux Meadows, for the first time, some admission of Viking exploration of North America had to be made.

Far more important are the discoveries of an extremely ancient culture that inhabited northern New England, Nova Scotia and Labrador, known as the Red Paint People. This archaic civilization is called the Red Paint people because they used the mineral red ocher in burial ceremonies, sprinkling quantities of it on the dead and over all the gifts they placed in the graves.

A fascinating television documentary aired on PBS titled "The Red Paint People" related some extremely interesting facts about the Red Paint People, facts which are apparently being ignored by the scientific establishment. The documentary spoke about the 16th century legend of the Lost City of Norombega, a "magnificent city of magic." As already discussed earlier, many of the early mapmakers had a country called Norombega in the New England, Nova Scotia area, including the famous Mercator map of 1569.

The PBS documentary went on to mention that the Red Paint People built megalithic chambers, apparently used metals and were a seafaring race who used harpoons, often made of swordfish parts. They were later named the "Maritime Archaic" culture, and given a date of at least 4,000 B.P. (or 2,000 B.C.).

According to the documentary, many of the stone alignments along the shores of Nova Scotia, Quebec and Labrador were thought to be navigational aids. Even such conservative writers as Folsom in *America's Ancient Treasures*,[160] have said about the Maritime Archaic: "The fact that they were able to venture out to sea in boats of sort is obvious, for Newfoundland is an island, and at its nearest point the mainland is ten miles away."

Said the narrator of the PBS documentary, "An advanced sea culture of North America is very surprising." The solution to the mystery of the Red Paint People, or Maritime Archaic, came from Norwegian scientists who pointed out that the Red Paint People are found throughout the arctic, from central Siberia, across Scandinavia and into North America.

A 7,000-year-old burial mound in Denmark at Ledveg had a skeleton of a woman and a child, both covered in red ocher, the tell tale sign of the Red Paint people. The documentary further named an American site in Quebec, formerly known as L'Anse Mort, and now known as L'Anse Amour, in which a Red Paint People burial mound was excavated and remains were carbon dated as 7,500 B.P. (5,500 B.C.), which caused the narrator to comment, "did the traditions of the Red Paint People come from North America to Europe," rather than the other way around?

A 1981 newspaper article from the Boston *Globe* and carried by United Press International had a headline of "Europeans in N.E. 7,000 years ago?" and reported that a number of skeletons were unearthed in an unidentified location north of Boston, that were at least 7,000 years old. The skeletal remains and artifacts found with them were covered in red ocher. James P. Whittall II, director of archaeology for the Early Sites Research Society said, "this is one of the most significant archaeological sites ever found in New England." Said the newspaper article, "One skeleton—found to be about 7,200 years old—was of a man who was 5 foot 8 and about 54 years old when buried. The age of the bones—dubbed the "old man"—was established by Dr. Jeffrey L. Bada of the Scripps Institution, University of California, San Diego, using a method known as amino acid racemization.

"Whittal said this date was compatible with radiocarbon 14 testing of cremational pit burials from the same site dating to 7,245."

The article went on to say, "More surprising, Whittal said, were tests results which indicated the "Old Man" may have originated in Ireland.

"Dr. Albert E. Casey of the Medical Center of the University of Alabama, an expert in craniometry—the scientific measurements of the skull—studied the "Old Man's" skull. Casey believes certain common racial characteristics can be determined by such measurements. Based on the examination, he reported to Whittal that the skull's measurements were most compatible to the Irish race. ... Their conclusion was it was of European origin. In addition, the studies determined the "Old Man" had suffered from a congenital deformity, had highly developed legs as if he were a heavy runner and squatter, was left handed and apparently ate well.

"Among other things determined was that the "Old Man" had suffered from otosclerosis, an ear disease rarely seen in non-caucasians but most often found in white skinned, blue eyed types."

The Red Paint People are a well established fact in New England and Eastern Canada. Folsom devotes a number of pages to them in his authoritative *America's Ancient Treasures*,[160] however, since his book is heavily flavored with the traditional "Isolationist" viewpoint, he makes no mention of Red Paint People burials in Scandinavia or Russia, and even devotes a small mini-article in the book on page 88 to "Fanciful Archaeology" in which he says, "At one time or another the Celts, the Welsh, the Irish, Phoenicians, Egyptians, the Africans were all put forward as originators of great achievements in the New World...For none of these theories is there any evidence that withstands scientific scrutiny." Perhaps Folsom should watch PBS sometime!

ΦΦΦ

At Fort Chimo on Ungava Bay (750 miles north of Quebec City) are rock walls dating from A.D. 500, which intrigue many archaeologists. There are also piled-up blocks of stone which look like statues, though no chippings of stone have been found in the vicinity. Thus, the blocks may have been transported to the spot, but by whom?

The culture of the Eskimos who now inhabit the region appears to have nothing in common with that of the people who raised these stones. Eskimo legends tell of these stones having been erected by a race of giants whose language differed greatly from their own.

Some scholars believe that these mysterious giants could have been the Vikings who came from Norway. Others speculate that the Indians who were members of the Dorset culture might have established themselves at Ungava Bay. As yet there is no proof supporting either of these two assertions.[39]

Paul Chapman in his book, *The Norse Discovery of America*,[206] makes an interesting comment about the Beothuck Indians of Newfoundland, a tribe now extinct. He describes the capture of an Indian woman who was later given the Christian name of Mary March. In 1819, the Governor of Newfoundland sent an expedition to capture a Beothuck Indian alive so the native could learn English and be returned to the tribe to act as a translator. At Red Indian Lake the expedition encountered three wigwams and the Beothuck inhabitants immediately fled.

The woman was captured, and later a tall Beothuck, the woman's husband, approached the Canadians when he saw that his wife was unable to escape. The explorers described the man as approximately 6 feet 7 inches tall and had a full beard. He stood about 10 yards from his wife and her captors and delivered a long oration in the Beothuck language lasting for about 10 minutes. As it was, neither side in the confrontation spoke the other's language and neither party could explain its actions. The English Canadians were unable to explain that they came in peace and would return the woman once she learned English, and the expedition's behavior was sufficient to prove to the Beothucks that their motives were unfriendly.

When the tall, bearded, Norse-looking Beothuck's oration had no effect on the captors of his wife, he attempted to remove their hands from her, at which time a struggle ensued, and he was shot and killed. She was taken to St. John's, learned English, but died of tuberculosis before she could be reunited with her tribe. The Beothucks vanished forever from history, presumably becoming extinct. This sad story indicates the often tragic nature of contact between two cultures, neither of whom really mean harm to the other, but unable to communicate, a great tragedy results. Chapman asks, "Were the Beothucks the descendants of Norse settlers?"

454

🐾🐾🐾

It took me several days to drive through Quebec, stopping in Quebec City and Montreal to see the sites. I continued on to Ottawa and Toronto. I tried to contact an old friend in Toronto, but his parents told me that he had moved to Calgary, so I slept in the back of my truck in downtown Toronto for a night.

A day later, I was crossing from Ontario into Michigan at Port Huron. I proceeded onto Lansing, Michigan, where I stayed for a few nights with an old friend, Syd Mitchell. Syd and I had met in Peru some years before. He had been in the Air Force and was now a draftsman for an engineering company. I enjoyed the comforts of a guest room, a shower, and a cold beer with Syd.

Like me, he appreciated archaeological mysteries, and he informed me that central Michigan was the site of one of the great archaeological scandals of the 1800s. As Henriette Mertz relates in her book, *The Mystic Symbol*,[186] in the 1870s and the following 50 years, thousands of slate, copper and clay tablets bearing an undecipherable mixture of cuneiform, hieroglyphic, Greek and Phoenician writing were dug up from Michigan mounds by farmers and others. The academic world quickly pronounced them as fraudulent and thousands of the tablets were destroyed.

Mertz believes that the tablets were authentic, and were the work of 4th century A.D. Nestorian Christians who had fled from the Middle East and Mediterranean area at the time of the signing of the Nicene Creed, in order to escape religious persecution and conflict.

The first of the more than 3,000 artifacts unearthed in Michigan was unearthed on a spring morning in 1874 by a farmer who was clearing timber nearby the village of Crystal, in central Michigan northwest of Detroit. It was a beautifully worked slate loom shuttle that had curious markings carved next to the face of man with curious Egyptian-like headgear. Within the course of the next few months, additional unexplainable pieces came to light in an area between the villages of Crystal, St. Louis and Edmore, including large slate tablets, a small clay box, and a copper measurement compass, some of them with strange looking inscriptions.

Other pieces had been found as early as the 1850s and were kept in a museum owned by a Professor Edwin Worth in Springport, Indiana. This museum was quite popular for many years, but unfortunately, it burned down in 1916. Some of the artifacts were recovered from the burned remains. In the fall of 1890, a young man hired to dig post holes on the Davis farm near Wyman, Michigan, began to find various artifacts such as a clay jar, tablets and other artifacts that contained the various cryptic symbols. An archaeological society was formed and photographs of the various artifacts were sent to universities. The articles were unanimously denounced as frauds, and it was decided that they were the work of an "unbalanced religious fanatic."

Despite the fact that thousands of tablets were destroyed, in a zealous effort to protect an unsuspecting public of a fraud, many of the tablets were saved, and Mertz published a number of them in her book. Many are have highly detailed inscriptions, some in what appears to be "Demotic," the transitional Egypto-Greek language that is found on the Rosetta Stone. Other tablets have Egyptian hieroglyphs and cuneiform.

One tablet shows a volcano erupting, another apparently shows copper being smelted, and another shows the crucifixion of Christ. Several tablets have elephants and inscriptions on them.

Says Mertz of the accusations of forgery, "Why was it that one man alone had been charged with fabrication of more than 3,000 artifacts? Why would he have buried them in seventeen counties in Michigan— many far removed from any habitation? Why, if only one mound in eight or ten yielded a specimen, would he have gone to the extra labor of constructing mounds with nothing inside: How long would it take for one man to manufacture 3,000 articles in four different substances—slate, clay, stone and copper—transport them to isolated areas where no roads existed, bury each one in a mound and then construct additional mounds in which he put nothing? These are questions that the academic community failed to answer but must be answered."[186]

Another overlooked find just south of Michigan is the abundant iron-smelting furnaces discovered in Ohio. Arlington Mallery in his book, *Lost America*,[215] gives details on the discovery of several iron furnaces from southern Ohio that were used in prehistoric times. One furnace that Mallery uncovered in the Allyn Mound near Frankfort, Ohio was of a beehive type with charcoal and iron ore found inside. The mound was about 60 feet in diameter and seven feet high. Mallery compared the furnace to the primitive Agaria iron smelters still used in India.

Mallery's book had an introduction by Matthew W. Sterling, then Director of the Bureau of American Ethnology of the Smithsonian Institution. Sterling said in the introduction, "It will be difficult to convince American archeologists that there was a pre-Columbian iron age in America. This startling item, however, is one that should not long remain in doubt. The detailed studies of metallurgists and the new carbon-14 dating method should be sufficient to give a definite answer on this point."[215]

Curiously, this was basically all that was ever heard again about the iron smelting furnaces in Ohio. The Smithsonian has never once mentioned them, either as "forgery forges" or authentic iron smelters. Both Mallery and Sterling are dead. Lost America's iron smelters, like so many other discoveries have been conveniently ignored. Meanwhile, those who dare to challenge the status quo and demand the release of suppressed evidence, are branded "racists" and members of "lunatic fringe."

wo of the megalithic structures at America's Stonehenge, North Salem, NH.

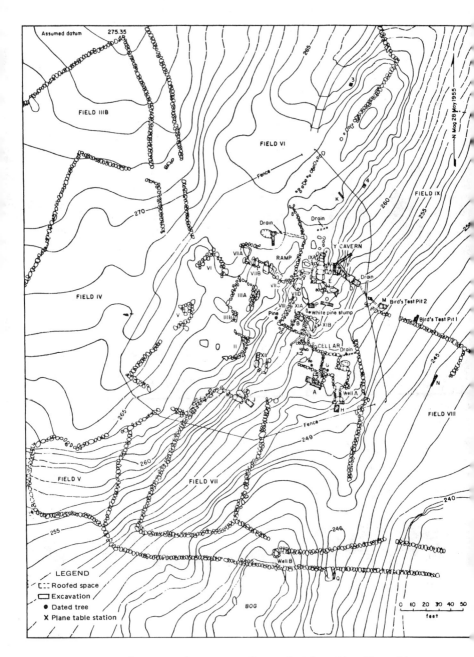

Topographic Map of Mystery Hill, North Salem, New Hampshire.
(After *North Salem, N.H., Site Excavations* Report, 1955 by
G.S. Vescelius.)

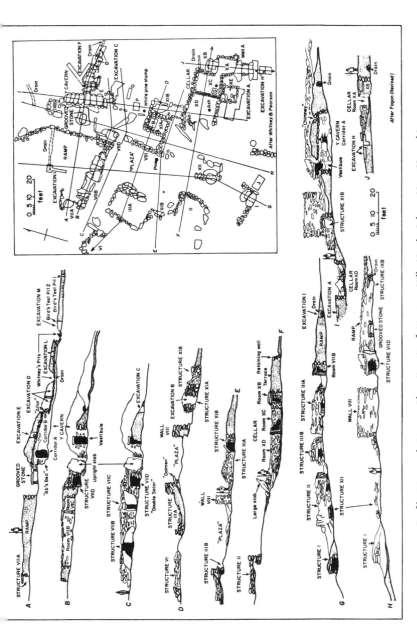

Profile Map and Layout Plan (inset) of Mystery Hill, North Salem, New Hampshire. (After *North Salem, N.H., Site Excavations Report*, 1955, by G.S. Vescelius.)

A section of Mercator's 1569 map
New England showing the country
Norombega. A blow-up of the tow
is on the left.

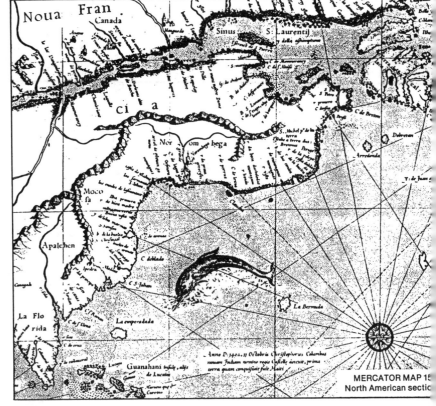

MERCATOR MAP 15
North American sectio

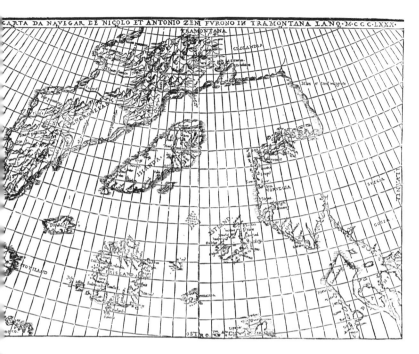

The Zeno brothers map of 1380 showing Greenland ice-free with mountain ranges and rivers in the interior of the island, now covered with glaciers.

The strange tunnel system at Goshen, Massachusetts.

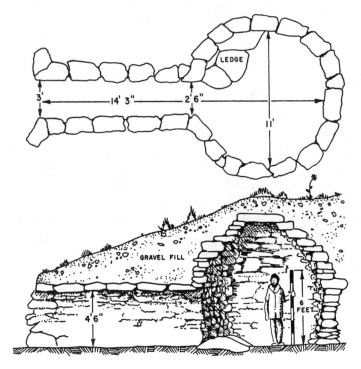

The dry masonry underground chamber at Upton, Massachusetts

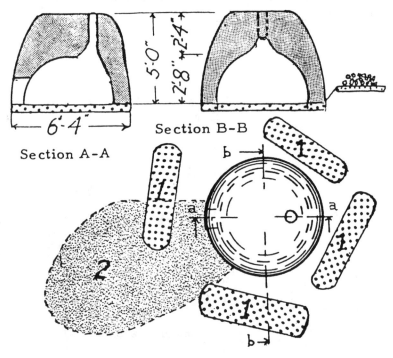

Plan of the ancient Allyn Mound Iron Furnaces.

A giant dolmen, the "Balanced Rock" of North Salem, New York. Photo by Bruce Scofield.

A sample of carvings found on a rock wall of Bradley County, Tennessee. Adapted from *Transactions of the New York Academy of Sciences*, 1891.

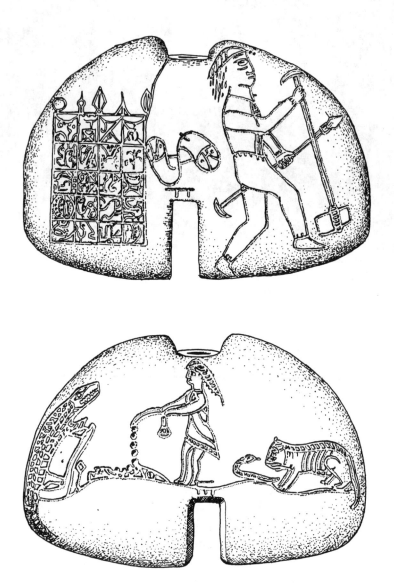

Two of the Wilmington, Ohio tablets, no. 3 and 4. The man in the top tablet appears to have mining tools with him. The designs o inscriptions to his left are unrecognized. The woman in the table below is feeding (?) several animals, including an aligator.

Chapter 13

The Rocky Mountains:

Exploring Ancient Nevada Seas

*The most beautiful thing we
can experience is the mysterious.*
—Albert Einstein

Back at the World Explorers Club in Kempton, I was greeted by Carl with a serious look on his face.

"I was just visited by the FBI," he said, helping me bring my backpack in from the truck.

"Really?" I said. "What did they want?"

"They wanted to know if we were trying to steal the lost treasure of Paititi and the 14 gold-clad mummies of the Inca kings and smuggle them into the United States."

I laughed out loud. "You're joking. You must be."

"I'm not joking, and it's not funny. That crazy Peruvian in Cuzco, Fernando, filed a false FBI report claiming that we're trying to steal the lost treasure of the Incas and smuggle it into this country. That jerk! Who does he think he is?"

"I'm flattered in a way that the FBI thinks that I'm trying to steal El Dorado, only a vast legendary treasure worth billions. I might as well go out and find Noah's Ark. That would probably be easier." I could hard believe what he was saying. "I'm surprised that the FBI took it seriously," I said.

"They were very serious," said Carl. "I explained to them that the accusation was pretty farfetched. Paititi is still just a myth to most people; archaeologists don't believe in it." Carl opened each of us a beer and we sat down at the dining room table, where we discussed the visit of stern-faced G-men.

"You know, David," said Carl, taking a sip of beer, "one of the problems with being the 'real-life Indiana Jones' is that it is illegal."

"I'm illegal?" I asked, puzzled. "How can I be illegal by just being me?"

"Well," said Carl, "if you're the real-life Indiana Jones going around taking gold statues out of lost temples in the jungle and all that stuff, then you're illegal. The FBI warned me about that. The last thing they said when they left was to warn me that it was illegal to bring Peruvian artifacts into the country."

"But I'm not bringing any artifacts into the country. I don't care about that stuff. I just take photographs and memories. I don't even take pottery shards. I'm a collector of books, not artifacts."

"I know it," said Carl, "but the FBI doesn't know it. According to that crazy Peruvian asshole, you're stealing the lost treasure of the Incas, and that's illegal. After I filled them in on the *Paititi* legend, they realized how ridiculous the story was. But they still warned me about bringing artifacts into the United States."

"Well, I'm sorry that you had to be grilled by the FBI," I said to Carl. "Since we're not smuggling the lost treasure of the Incas into the country, I suppose that everything is okay. Did you tell Greg Deyermenjian about this?"

"Yeah, I called Greg," said Carl. "He laughed. I don't think that he was named in the FBI report, just you and me."

"Well," I said finally, "it's flattering to know that I'm supposed to have discovered the lost city of Paititi and am in possession of the ancient treasure of the Incas—tons of gold that the conquistadors didn't get. If that were true, I should just go to Hollywood and have them make a movie of my life. I could make millions that way, without getting into trouble with the FBI!"

With that Carl also laughed. Indeed, sometimes lost cities and ancient artifacts are a very serious matter.

There was a lot to do around the *World Explorers Club* and for the next month or two I was busy helping with orders, fixing the roof on one of the buildings, and generally just puttering around the office.

After a while, I was ready to get on the road again, and I began packing up the truck for a trip out west. My father and stepmother were back from an extended vacation in Alaska, and it was a good time to go out to Colorado and visit them. One afternoon, I started up the rusty old pickup, and pulled out of the driveway of the clubhouse, pointing the hood ornament west.

Once again the road stretched out ahead of me, and I was ready for an adventure. Unknown America lay before me, a land of backyards, farms, and freight trains, ancient forts, pyramids, caves and lost treasure. A land that was ancient; a land that had gone through many earth changes.

I passed a sign on the road that said, "40,000 Used Hubcaps!" I supposed they were all for sale, and you could buy them one-at-a-time, or all 40,000, if you preferred. That was America and its free enterprise system. All the hubcaps any man had a right to want. I hit the wheel with my fist, "This is really the land of plenty!"

Somehow that hubcap sign made me remember reading once about some guy who had hitchhiked across America with a couch. He could only get rides in pickup trucks, but he could sit on his couch, and even sleep on it while he was waiting for rides. Carrying a couch with you wherever you go is a bit of an awkward gimmick, though, I thought to myself as I crossed the Mississippi River into Iowa.

I stopped to get some gas in Davenport, Iowa's easterly city on the mighty Mississippi. In 1874, the Reverend M. Gass excavated the

Davenport Mound and discovered a number of stone tablets which apparently had an odd assortment of Phoenician and other languages. Barry Fell of the Epigraphic Society deciphered the famous calendar stone and reported that there were three different languages to be found on the stone: Egyptian, Iberian Punic (a form of Phoenician), and Libyan. Fell believes the stone to depict a seasonal Djed Festival of Osiris which he dates as occurring about 700 B.C.[8]

Here once again we have evidence for an ancient Sun Kingdom with roots in Atonist Egypt. The ancient rulers of the Midwest were a river culture that built large pyramid sites and worshiped the sun, just as in the Nile Valley. Many of the tablets, branded forgeries by the academic community, have disappeared. The Davenport Calendar Stone can be seen at the Putnam Museum in Davenport, however.

Another inscribed stone, this one with runic characters, was found to the north of Davenport near Alexandria, Minnesota. It is the famous Kensington Rune Stone which was found by a farmer named Olaf Ohman in the tangled roots of a 40-year-old aspen tree on November 8, 1898. Since the area was only then being cleared for settlement, clearly the stone had been made long before the current European settlement of Minnesota.

The first complete translation of the stone came from Hjalmar Holand, a student at the University of Wisconsin, in 1907. According to Holand, who later wrote about the Kensington Rune Stone and other Viking evidence in North America in his book, *Explorations In America Before Columbus*,[212] the stone has the longest runic inscription in the world. He translates it as follows:

> 8 Goths and 22 Norwegians on
> exploration journey from
> Vineland round about the west   We
> had camp by [a lake with] 2 skerries — 1
> day's journey north from this stone
> We were [out] and fished one day   After
> we came home [found] 10 red
> with blood and dead   AV[e]   M[aria]
> Save [us] from evil

Along the edge of the stone is the following:

> Have 10 of [our party] by the sea to look
> after our ships 14-days-journey
> from this island—year—1362

When Holand approached farmer Ohman, who is often accused of forging the stone, to buy it, Ohman wanted only ten dollars for it. Holand could only afford five, so Ohman gave him the stone. Certainly, for a forger, eager to gain from his fakery, Ohman was pretty inept. He may have been an expert on the use of ancient runes, but he was a poor businessman. Like most of the accusations of forgery on the many stone tablets discovered throughout

America, there is little evidence, if any, that the persons named actually did any faking of inscriptions. That mattered little to the "experts" who made the accusations; since stone tablets with inscriptions, whether runic or Iberian Punic, could not exist in North America, they simply had to be forgeries, probably made by the discoverer of the tablets. It is all logical in a bizarre, pseudo-scientific way.

In the 1880s, a number of strange discoveries in Minnesota mounds was published in the *Minnesota Geological Survey,* the St. Paul *Pioneer* and the St. Paul *Globe.* At Chatfield, Minnesota, a half-dozen skeletons of enormous size were discovered. Similarly, at Clearwater, Minnesota, seven gigantic skeletons were uncovered in mounds. They were reported to be buried head down, and their skulls had receding foreheads and complete double dentition (two rows of teeth in the mouth).[94]

At LaCrescent, in the LaCrosse, Wisconsin, vicinity, mounds yielded giant skillets and huge bones. Near Dresbach, five miles north, mounds dug up in the expansion of a brickyard contained the bones of people who must have been more than eight feet tall. Similar remains were turned up at Moose Lake, Pine City, and Warren. According to the St. Paul *Pioneer,* the Warren mound yielded not only 10 gigantic human skeletons, but skeletons of dogs and horses.[94]

It is officially said that horses were extinct in North America at the time of the European colonization, though some scholars believe that the wild mustangs of the west and the small horses on outer bank islands of South Carolina were already here by 1500. It is a fact that horses at one time roamed North America, and it is also a fact that ancient seafarers often traveled with several horses held in a sling in the center of the boat. The ill-fated DeSoto expedition of 1543 had quite a few horses with them. As they took to boats to escape pursuing warriors, the last thing the survivors of the expedition saw was Indians killing the five horses that they abandoned. Horses were food to native Americans, like deer or buffalo. They did not begin riding them until well after the Spanish colonization.

Evidence of Vikings in even remoter areas of the great plains than Minnesota was found when aerial infrared photography was used on an alleged Viking fort in Lyman County, South Dakota, 22 miles south of Pierre. The photo was taken in 1967 and a report of it was published in *Photogrammetric Engineering* (issue no. 33, 1967) and later in a Kodak publication on the uses of infrared photography in archaeology.[17]

In Ottawa County, Kansas, in the north-central part of the state, is found the curious Rock City. This is a group of about 200 unusual sandstones in two roughly curved rows about a quarter-mile in length, standing in the middle of a vacant prairie. Although all are severely weathered, it is quite clear that the rocks are much more uniformly spheroidal than could be expected in a random natural formation. Called "concretions" by geologists, these rocks, ranging in size from 8 to 27 feet across, are supposed to have been shaped by water-borne calcium carbonate deposited between grains of sand, cementing them together. Then along comes a marvelous geological process called "selective erosion" and somehow, these round balls are formed.

Rather, they may be ancient man-made balls, and are highly similar, though more eroded, to the strange stone balls found in Costa Rica. These stone spheres are admitted by scientists to have been man-made, though what their purpose was has never been figured out. Was Rock City in Kansas made for the same enigmatic purpose many thousands of years ago?

Nebraska was the site of other giant bones. In the 1879 autobiography of William Cody, *Buffalo Bill*,[219] Buffalo Bill Cody and companions are five miles above Ogallala on the South Platte when a Pawnee Indian comes to the camp with the bones of a giant. The surgeon of the group pronounces one of the giant bones to be a human thighbone, and the Pawnee then tells a curious legend.

According to Buffalo Bill's own account, "The Indians claimed that the bones they had found were those of a person belonging to a race of people who a long time ago lived in this country. That there was once a race of men on the earth whose size was about three times that of an ordinary man, and they were so swift and powerful that they could run along-side of a buffalo, and taking the animal in one arm could tear off a leg and eat the meat as they walked.

"These giants denied the existence of a Great Spirit so he caused a great rain-storm to come, and the water kept rising higher and higher so that it drove those proud and conceited giants from the low grounds to the hills, and thence to the mountains, but at last even the mountain tops were submerged, and then those mammoth men were all drowned. After the flood had subsided, the Great Spirit came to the conclusion that he had made man too large and powerful, and that he would therefore correct the mistake by creating a race of men of smaller size and less strength. This is the reason, say the Indians, that modern men are small and not like the giants of old, and they claim that this story is a matter of Indian history, which has been handed down among them from time immemorial."[219]

I had been driving all night across Nebraska on my way to Colorado and many of the mysteries of North America kept playing back through my mind. It was like a shaman in Madison, named Trickster, had told me: I had roamed the seven seas and the four corners of the earth in search of the astonishing past, and was finding amazing lost cities and ancient mysteries right in my own back yard!

I blinked my headlights at a truck, and then wondered about the mysteries of Nebraska. It seemed flat and dotted with quiet farms. What strange artifacts or buried cities were out there?

In the summer of 1889, farmer J. R. Mote of Phelps County, near Kearney, Nebraska, was excavating a cave when he came across a "large brown stone weighing over twenty pounds. When the clay was removed from it" according to an article in the August 7, 1889 issue of the San Francisco *Examiner*,[174] "a large fossil, representing a clenched human hand, was revealed. The specimen had been broken from the arm just above the wrist, and the imprint of a coarse cloth or some woven material was plainly outlined on the back of the hand. At the time of the discovery nothing was said of it," the article continued, since "Mr. Mote does not belong to the curious class of people."

The article continued, "A small boy in the family, whose faculty for smashing things was just beginning to develop, conceived the idea of opening the hand. When broken, to his astonishment, there rolled out eleven transparent stones."

Mr. Mote had enough curiosity to consult a jeweler who proclaimed them to be genuine first water diamonds, without a flaw. Said the article, "The jewels are nearly all uniform in shape and are about the shape of lima beans. They have the appearance of being water worn, but are still beautiful stones."

It was stories of mummified hands clutching diamonds that intrigued me the most about the Rocky Mountains and western states. Were there more stories like this one?

In esoteric lore, there is often talk of different *Halls of Records,* vaults and repositories in the earth, often cut out of solid rock. Incredible as these may seem, exactly such a vault has already been constructed. It is part of the Mount Rushmore complex, and was built by the famous sculptor Gutzon Borglum. Borglum began his Hall of Records in the 1930s, cutting into solid rock about two-thirds of the way up the mountain in a small gorge to the right of the gigantic heads of Washington, Jefferson, Lincoln and Roosevelt. The granite was excavated to a depth of 30 feet before work was halted.

Borglum wrote in his book, *Mt. Rushmore, National Memorial,* which I purchased at the tourist center there, "The facade to the Hall's entrance is the mountain wall 140 feet high; supporting pylons cut into the mountain, flank the entrance. The entrance door itself is 12 feet wide and 20 feet high; the walls are plain, dressed granite and of a fine color.

"The floor of the Hall will be 100 by 80 by 32 feet to an arched ceiling. At the height of fifteen feet an historic frieze, four feet wide, will encircle the entire room. Recesses will be cut into these walls to be filled with bronze and glass cabinets, which will hold the records stamped on aluminum sheets, rolled separately and placed in tubes. Busts of our leaders in all human activities will occupy the recesses between the cabinets." Borglum died in 1941, and so the Hall of Records was never completed as planned, though a rock tunnel was cut 70 feet into the mountain, just as with vaults in Egypt.

Edgar Cayce and others have spoken of different Halls of Records beneath the Sphinx in Giza, beneath Chichén Itzá or some other lost city in the Yucatán, or somewhere in Tibet or the Gobi Desert. Here in South Dakota, Borglum has created a modern mystery. Said Borglum, "Without some record that will last as long as the heads themselves, it can easily become another puzzle to future civilizations, as witness the unexplained monuments in Central and South America, Easter Island, Egypt and the Mid and Far East."

Indeed, perhaps a lesson on how we view the past might be taken from Borglum's vault, cut deep into a mountain. Will future archaeologists see it as the robbed tomb of a great king, or the time capsule of some alien visitor? Maybe they will try and suppress the knowledge, denying that the bizarre rock-cut tunnel exists. South Dakota, if not now, at least in the future, is a weird place.

🐃🐃🐃

I was heading for my father's house in Durango, in the Four Corners area of Colorado, when I thought I would stop in at Boulder and visit my cousin. Rick was getting his masters degree in Electrical Engineering at the University of Colorado, and he offered to put me up for a couple of nights in his dorm room. I thankfully accepted his offer, and parked my trusty pickup truck in the student parking area and took my sleeping bag inside.

While in Boulder for a few days, I attended a conference on the Gaia concept of the earth, Gaia being the ancient Greek goddess of the earth, and the conference was an interesting mix of ecology, far-out science and technology, earth-grid points and other things.

I attended one rather interesting program, which included a slide show entitled *Colorado Stonehenges* by an engineer associated with the International Tesla Society. His name was Toby Grotz, and he spoke about everything from time warps, the earth grid, and the Pleiades star cluster to petroglyphs west of Grand Junction, Colorado, near the Utah border.

Eventually he came to the Colorado Stonehenge part, which was an odd collection of basalt columns and stacked stones in a gully near Limon, which is in southeast Colorado, near the Kansas border. They are near the Kapeshapaw River, and are apparently the remains of a circle of standing stones. He alleged that he had had some sort of UFO encounter here, and that the stones represented the center of a great civilization that had existed even before Atlantis and Lemuria.

I was interested in the site, to say the least. The stones were long logs of basalt or granite, obviously weighing many tons each, and quite apparently stacked in a pattern by intelligent beings, rather than just being a strange geological formation. I had seen similar ruins or "stonehenges" in my travels around the world. One that was nearly identical was to be found at the Marilinga Atomic Test Site in South Australia, north of Adelaide (see my book *Lost Cities of Ancient Lemuria & the Pacific*[59] for more information on this site). Other similar sites could be found at Sillustani on the Peruvian shores of Lake Titicaca, and among Olmec ruins at La Venta.

While the ruins were interesting, and doubtlessly of archaeological value, I was skeptical of his claims that this Colorado Stonehenge was of such antiquity that it was from the times of Atlantis or Lemuria (not to mention before these civilizations, as Grotz had said). The time frame seemed too distant, ten to twenty thousand years, nor were the ruins so substantial that they could have withstood the tremendous forces generated in the sort of pole shifts that would have sunken entire continents. The gigantic waves and earthquakes would have toppled far greater constructions (and did) than this. These were not massive, perfectly cut and fitted stones the size of freight cars, but smaller logs, perhaps eight to twelve feet long weighing several thousand pounds.

471

Impressive, but not beyond the work of a dozen people with even the crudest building techniques.

I surmised that the site may well have marked an important astronomical observatory, and quite possibly an earth-grid vortex spot, but it was hardly some relic from Atlantis or Lemuria.

When I asked Grotz about this after his fascinating talk and slide show, he suddenly admitted to me that it was probably built by Cherokee Indians, and the Lemurian ruins were beneath it, far underground. I nodded and smiled to myself, wondering why he hadn't said that in his talk. Perhaps it didn't have the sensational sound that he had wanted, and he omitted mentioning that the slides he was showing were Cherokee Indian constructions, rather than "pre-Lemurian." These sorts of sensational statements tend to crop up quite a bit when it comes to lost cities, especially when involved with "psychic" impressions, and it behooves the genuine researcher to be discriminating about the stories of lost cities and ancient ruins.

🐾🐾🐾

After the conference, I headed for Durango by way of Aspen and Leadville, Colorado.

There is a strange story of a lost ship discovered near Leadville. In early 1880, the editor of the Leadville Chronicle, Orth Stein, published a bizarre story that many modern writers believe he fabricated. This may be so, but the story is a fascinating tale anyway, and fits well into any discussion of lost cities and ancient mysteries.

According to the newspaper report, which was later picked up and published as far away as New York, two prospectors, Jacob Cahee and Louis Adams, grubstaked by Denver and Leadville speculators, were prospecting in an area near Red Cliff, an area that they believed had not been previously explored by others. They decided to sink a shaft in what looked like good dirt. After digging through about 30 feet of wash, they were about to give up when they struck a lime formation stained with iron.

Thus encouraged, they continued digging with new vigor. About 15 feet further they hit a hollow sound. Believing they were nearing a subterranean passage or gallery, they secured themselves to the top of the shaft by ropes and continued cautiously.

After a few more feet the earth gave way and the two men fell downward. The ropes held and they found themselves suspended in a large, irregular cave, some 240 feet long and about 180 feet wide at its broadest point.

They had fallen into one end of the cave so they had little difficulty in swinging themselves against a natural stairway of granite boulders to one side. With miners' lamps they explored the sanded floor, and here and there they found huge crystals of quartz. Enormous stalactites hung from the ceiling 50 feet above; catching the feeble rays of light, the crystals threw back myriads of rainbow hues.

The cave at first appeared to be empty, but finally they saw a huge

472

dark object at one end. As they approached they saw, to their amazement, the outline of some sort of sailing craft. Close inspection proved that it was indeed a ship, though quite a different ship than any that they had ever seen or known of before.

It was about 60 feet long and about 30 feet wide. It lay tilted forward at an angle of about 15 degrees over a rough pile of stones. The body of the craft was built of short lengths of some dark and very porous wood, resembling black walnut. Both ends of the ship curled up and back toward the ship, and it appeared as if the vessel was intended to sail both ways.

The planking was apparently double-riveted on with nails of extremely hard copper, only slightly rust-eaten, and with heads cut or filed in an octagonal shape, while along the upper edge of the ship, eleven large rings of the same metal were found, evidently for the security of the rigging.

At the bottom edges of the craft, and running its entire length, were two keels some four-and-a-half feet deep and six inches thick, hung on metallic hinges. They were fastened at the ends with rough copper rods, extending upward and bent over so as to attach to two masts rising from the upper edges.

The description of the outside of the ship was given in great detail. The whole ship was intact, but the wood crumbled to the touch, so the two men did not venture inside.

However, lying on the ground nearby, they found a gold instrument that bore a rude resemblance to a sextant. The only writing found was at one end of the ship about midway on the bow and enclosed in a metal ring. Here they found 26 copper characters riveted to the wood and bearing much resemblance to Chinese hieroglyphics.

No human remains were found, but the men did not preclude the possibility that some might be inside. Clearly, they were amazed and dumbfounded at their incredible discovery that defied all logic.

The men finally climbed up through their artificial opening to the dark night outside. They built a campfire and were very silent, as men are wont to be when something of a supernatural nature has just occurred.

The next morning they lowered themselves into the cave once again, fully expecting it to be empty and to find that they had dreamed or imagined the sights of the day before...but the ship was still there!

After another inspection, they climbed back up again and eventually arrived at the cabin of a well-to-do miner, who owned 30 properties down the gulch. Cahee and Adams showed the cave to the mine owner and another expert from the city, to let them verify what they had seen.

As is often the case with a cave of some fantastic lost treasure, the four men tried to hide the opening of the cavern as much as possible, and vowed secrecy until such time as they could present their tremendous discovery to the world.

This was the last that was ever heard of the strange ship that was entombed in the Colorado mountains, although Orth Stein had an interesting comment to make on the discovery. He said that the only possible explanation was that "ages and eons, perhaps, ago, a vessel bearing a crew of bold adventurers tossed by the waves, then receding, left it stranded there. The awful upheaval and convulsions of nature, which we know so little of and can only be speculated on, pressed the face of the earth together and sealed it in a living grave. And this is but a groping guess, yet in what strange old seas the vessel sailed, what unknown, ancient waters pressed against its peaked prow, under what prehistoric skies it pitched, what man can tell?"[138]

It is an amazing story, and easily discounted as fabricated, yet, if it is a hoax, it is a clever one. The "Chinese hieroglyphics" as inlaid copper is especially interesting. While it would be foolish to accept this story as fact, it is amusing to speculate on such a story on a "what if..." basis.

Let us imagine for a moment that this newspaper article from the early days of Colorado history were true; what does it indicate? The ancient ship with bizarre hieroglyphic writing would obviously be many thousands of years old. It would be an artifact from an antediluvian time, trapped in a cataclysmic upheaval that created at least a portion of the Rocky Mountains.

Could this ancient ship, so eloquently described, be something from the lost continents of Atlantis or Mu? Present geological dating would put the upheaval of the Rockies as millions of years ago, yet such a cataclysmic event may be much closer in time to us, even within only tens of thousands of years.

That ancient ships were sailing seas in ancient Arizona, California, Nevada, and even Colorado is not such a fantastic concept. As we shall see, there is a great deal of evidence to show that many portions of the western United States were inland seas and navigable waterways until fairly recent times. According to various psychics, such as Edgar Cayce and the Native American shaman Sun Bear, these areas will soon be part of our planet's seas and oceans again within the next decade or so. To uniformitarian geologists who maintain that geological change is incredibly slow, taking place slowly over millions of years, this would be impossible. Yet to cataclysmic geologists, devastating earth changes and mountain uplifting can take place in a matter of days when the conditions are right.

Yet, this is hardly proof that the above story is true. What is curious is that back in 1880, a bunch of miners or a bored newspaper editor would have the historical and educational background to concoct a story that actually could be true with our new understanding of geological change and the incredible antiquity of human civilization.

While a ship at a high altitude in the Colorado Rockies is mind-boggling to most people, including me, there is concrete evidence of equally incredible artifacts being found in similar circumstances. The various reports of out-of-place-artifacts (called *ooparts* by Fortean researchers) are verification of some ancient civilization destroyed in a cataclysm of awesome proportions. Each also shows that the current geological dating is arbitrary at best, and wildly inaccurate at worst.

ΩΩΩ

I drove down from the mountains around Leadville heading south toward the Great Sand Dunes National Monument. This strange sand dune beach against the Rocky Mountains has been one of the strangest deserts in the world. The park is a stretch of sand dunes encompassing 57 square miles at an elevation of 9,000 feet. Geologists are in complete variance as to what they are doing here in a mere 10-mile-square area that is not found in other areas of the Rockies.

The sand dunes are said to have been created by wind, but they look more like an ancient beach. Two rivers disappear into the dunes, the Medano and the San Luis. The dunes are beautiful natural wonders, and geologically anomalistic. Is it possible that these dunes are part of the shoreline of an ancient lake that washed the shores of the Rocky Mountains, now 9,000 feet above sea level?

Colorado is full of strange reports of unaccountable objects. I mused over a report from the *The American Antiquarian* published in 1883 which said that in about 1880, a Colorado rancher went on a journey to fetch coal from a seam driven into a hillside. The particular load that he collected was mined about 150 feet (45 meters) from the mouth of the seam, and about 300 feet (90 meters) below the surface.

When he returned home, the rancher found the coal lumps were too big to burn on his stove. He split some of them— and out of one of the lumps fell an iron thimble!

At least, it looked like a thimble—and "Eve's thimble" was the name given to the object in the locality, where it became well known. It had the indentations that modern thimbles have, and a slight raised "shoulder" at the base. The metal crumbled easily, and flaked away with repeated handling by curious neighbors. Eventually it was lost.

In 1883 it was not thought that tribes of American Indians had ever used thimbles, nor metallic objects at all. Besides, this seam of coal was dated as between the Cretaceous and Tertiary periods, which are generally dated at about 70 million years ago.

It was an impossible artifact, yet, it fit snugly into a cavity in the coal. Like similar out-of-place-artifacts (the great scientist Ivan T. Sanderson called them *ooparts*) it appears to be quite genuine, yet totally impossible by today's geological dating and accepted history of the planet.[81]

Similarly, in 1967 human bones were reported to have been discovered in a vein of silver in a Colorado mine. A copper arrowhead four inches (ten centimeters) long accompanied them. The silver deposit was, of course, several million years old and much more ancient than humanity, according to generally accepted ideas.[81]

A similar bizarre object is the *Coso Artifact,* found in the Coso Mountains of California. More on that strange object in the next chapter.

Just north of Leadville, in Casper, Wyoming, a similar tale nearly as bizarre happened in 1932 that is absolutely true and still

475

mystifies researchers to this day. In October of that year, a couple of gold prospectors were working a gulch at the base of the Pedro Mountains about 60 miles west of Casper when they spotted some "color" in the rock wall of the gulch and used an extra heavy charge of dynamite to rip a section of the rock out in their search for mineral wealth.

The powerful blast exposed a small natural cave in solid granite, a cave not more than four feet wide, four feet high and about 15 feet deep. When the smoke had cleared, the miners got down and peered into the opening. What they saw was shocking, for peering back at them was a tiny mummy of a man-like creature!

He was on a tiny ledge, legs crossed, sitting on his feet, arms folded in his lap. He was dark brown, deeply wrinkled with a face that was almost monkey-like in some respects. One eye had a definite droop as though this strange little fellow might be winking at his discoverers. The ancient mummy was astonishingly small, only about 14 inches high!

The prospectors carefully picked him up, wrapped him in a blanket and headed back for Casper, where the news of their discovery attracted considerable attention. Scientists were skeptical, but interested; for according to conventional archaeology it would be impossible for a living being to be entombed in solid granite. Yet, the creature was real!

The mummy was examined and X-rayed by scientists. It was only 14 inches tall, weighing only about 12 ounces. The X-rays showed unmistakably that the tiny mummy had been an adult. Biologists who examined it declared it to be about 65 years old at the time of death. The X-rays showed a full set of teeth, a tiny skull, a full backbone and ribs and completely formed arms and legs. The mummy was not a clever hoax but a genuine biological entity with normal, though miniature, features.

The features had had an overall bronze-like hue. The forehead was very low, the nose flat with widespread nostrils, the mouth very wide with thin twisted lips in a sardonic smile.

According to the popular science writer Frank Edwards, the Anthropology Department of Harvard said that there was no doubt about the the genuineness of the mummy. Dr. Henry Shapiro, head of the Anthropology Department of the American Museum of Natural History, said that the X-rays revealed a very small skeletal structure covered by dried skin, obviously of extremely great age, historically speaking, and of unknown type and origin. The mystery mummy, said Dr. Shapiro, is much smaller than any human types now known to man.[52]

Common speculation was that the mummy was a deformed, diseased infant, though anthropologists who examined the mummy were of the opinion that, whatever it was, it was fully grown at the time of death. Edwards says that the curator of the Boston Museum Egyptian department examined the creature and declared that it had the appearance of Egyptian mummies which had not been wrapped to prevent exposure to the air. Still another expert, Dr. Henry Fairfield, ventured the supposition that the mystery mummy of the Pedro Mountains might be a form of anthropoid which roamed the North American continent about the middle of the Pliocene Age.[52]

The cave was examined as well, but no traces of human residence, no artifacts, no carvings, or writings—nothing but the tiny stone ledge on which this mummy had been sitting for countless ages. How had it come to be entombed in the solid granite wall anyway? To my knowledge, no carbon dating was ever done on the mummy.

While the mummy was on display in Casper for many years, it has since disappeared, and its current whereabouts are today unknown.

Edwards also mentions that a three-foot-tall red-haired "midget" mummy was discovered on a ledge in Mammoth Cave, Kentucky, in the 1920s. Even though it was in a state of mummification, unlike the Wyoming mummy, it seemed to be only a few hundred years old. A Viking midget buried in Kentucky?[52]

Coral E. Lorenzen, who recorded the details in her 1970 book *The Shadow of the Unknown*, also gives several examples of Native American legends of tribes of little people, including Wyoming legends of the Shoshoni and Arapaho Indians of these little men who hunted with poison arrows. One story she relates is the account of twelve Shoshoni braves who had just killed a number of buffalo and were skinning the carcasses when they suddenly found themselves surrounded by a band of little men who screamed and threatened them. One of the buffalo that the Indians had killed was a rare white buffalo and as the party decided to beat a retreat from the screaming horde, a brave grabbed this particular skin and threw it round his shoulders. Immediately the little men backed off, screaming with fear. The braves stopped, puzzled, and then realized it was the white skin that had changed the mood of the little men: the pelt obviously had some significance for them, and, armed with it, the Indians obviously had nothing to fear from their adversaries. Perhaps the lesson here is that when attacked by little people, grab a white buffalo pelt!

Miss Lorenzen also says that there is a legend that the Pueblo tribe of the Stone Lions in New Mexico were attacked by pygmies who slaughtered many of their number and drove the rest away. She adds, further, that in 1950 she saw the mummified remains of a number of little people in glass cases in the Carlsbad Caverns in New Mexico.

While discussing these strange stories of little people, I am reminded of the stories of the miniature tunnels at the ancient city of Monte Alban (see chapter 7).

In light of these stories, the story of a lost ship discovered inside a Colorado mountain may not seem quite so fantastic. The tale is probably a combination of several old miner's tales from the campfires of the west. Yet, who is to say that there may not be some truth to the tale of the discovery of an ancient Chinese ship in a desert canyon somewhere in Colorado?

I continued on my drive to Durango, the town in southwestern Colorado where I had grown up, going to grade school and junior high, before my parents had divorced when I was 15. The high pass of Wolf Creek still had snow on it, and as I rounded one dangerous curve and hit a patch of black ice, the truck started to skid off the road.

I braked and started to fishtail toward an unguarded shoulder of the road. Beyond that was a near-vertical drop of several hundred feet. I let off on the brake for a moment to stop my sideways movement and slammed on the brakes again, praying that the truck would stop in time. The truck spun sideways and I plowed into a snow bank on the edge of the dropoff.

Looking down from my driver's door, it was a sheer drop of several hundred feet. I felt like I was in some cartoon with the truck tottering uneasily on a precipice. Slowly I moved to the passenger door and exited the truck onto the road.

I scratched my head and looked around; another few feet and the truck would have been tumbling down the mountainside, with me in it. What was I to do now?

Just then a large American pickup truck came along the opposite direction and saw me standing on the edge of the road with my own truck on the edge of the precipice. It pulled up alongside of me and the driver rolled down his window. He was an older gentleman in a green jacket and a plaid hunter's cap.

"Having some trouble, son?" he asked casually.

"Yeah, my truck nearly went off the road. Do you have a tow rope?"

"I sure do," he said calmly. "We'll have you out in jiffy." And with that he pulled his truck around and brought out a strong nylon strap with hooks on each end. We attached one end to the front of my car and the other to the front end of his. He first pulled my front end back around toward the road, and then back up so I was on hard ground again and would be able to continue my journey. The whole episode lasted less than ten minutes.

"Thank you, sir, for your help," I said, helping him roll up his tow strap.

"Think nothing of it, son," he said in a kindly way, putting his truck into gear. With that he continued his journey and I did likewise.

Colorado has a number of enigmatic ruins. Along the Apishapa River Canyon in southeast Colorado is a scattered network of stone structures, often perched high atop certain cliffs and promontories. These structures are apparently towers, watching the river below. These ruins are largely circles, made with large granite slabs from eight to ten inches thick, and most are severely weathered. The largest of the stone circles, most probably used as astronomical circles, is at Big Horn Medicine Wheel in Wyoming, though some may be the remains of towers. At one site in Apishapa Canyon, four stone circles have a tall menhir, or stone pillar standing in their center.

Similar ruins, made of large slabs of granite, lie on Monarch Pass, which is the headwaters of the South Arkansas River. On the top of the pass, controlling traffic to the west coast, are several megalithic stone buildings, where slabs of granite are leaned against each other. Other similar stone structures are in the Pueblo, Walsenburg and Saguache area. Probably, these structures were constructed along the rivers and high passes to control the various trade traffic.

The area of eastern Colorado was particularly important in ancient times because many of the rivers had their origin here. Northern New Mexico was the source for the major river systems of the Rio Grande, Pecos, Brazos, and Red. The Arkansas River, and the South Platte extension of the Mississippi, coming south from Nebraska, both began at high passes such as Monarch Pass. On the other side of these passes was the Colorado River system, stretching deep into Colorado through Grand Junction to an area only a few miles from Boulder. In the vicinity of Denver, no less than four major river systems come together. It seems likely that the east-west trade across the Great Plains typically centered around the area. Where the Rio Grande comes close to the Salt River in southwestern New Mexico is another area where forts and cities were built to facilitate the east-west river trading.

It was another couple of hours into Durango, and as I rounded a bend I could see the familiar valley nestled in the San Juan mountains of the Rockies. Driving down the main street, the town was at once familiar and drastically changed. Old landmarks from when I was younger were now gone, and a great deal of new development had occurred in the many years that I had been away.

Still, Durango was a pleasant town, with a great deal of appeal, and the spectacular scenery hadn't changed at all. I stopped in at my grandmother's house on Fifth Street. It was comforting to see that not everything had changed in Durango since I had been gone. Her front porch and yard were exactly as I had remembered it from the 60s.

I burst in the front door to find her sitting at her spot on the dining room table, reading letters from relatives as she often spent her time. "Grandmother!" I cried. "How are you?"

She looked up at me with a puzzled face, peering through her bifocals at the strange figure who stood in her living room. "Who is that?" she asked.

I walked toward her. Her gray hair was almost purple in the afternoon sun. Sun shown through prisms hanging on the window casting rainbows on her dress.

"It's me, David, your grandson," I said, walking up to her.

"David! My, you've been gone a long time. How are you?" She pushed herself up from her chair to be standing as I reached her. Tears welled up in my eyes as we hugged. There had been times in my travels around the world when I thought I might never see my family again. Now, it was the greatest joy in the world to see my only living grandparent again, and she was in her 80s.

I called my father at his office a few blocks away and he joined us at her house. That night we all went out to dinner, including my stepmother, and had a good meal at one of the local Mexican restaurants on Main Street.

I rested for nearly a week in Durango, visiting some old friends and taking side trips to various towns in western Colorado and northern New Mexico.

One day I drove up into the mountains to the north of Durango to the old mining town of Silverton. The narrow gauge railroad, the only one left in the United States, still takes tourists from Durango to Silverton, passing through the San Juan Wilderness along the way.

Silverton is still a small mining and tourist town with a frontier look to it. I parked on Main Street and went into the local drugstore to sit at the soda fountain and have something to drink. I settled on an old-fashioned snow cone and looked out the window.

Silverton has a curious history, and one strange incident changed the town forever. On July 3, 1875, a wealthy Scotsman by the name of Edward Ennis stepped off the overland stage and began his obsessive quest to find a lake of gold.

Within a few days of arriving in town, he announced at a meeting in a local saloon that he wanted to buy all of the claims in the Cunningham Gulch area. He offered to pay double what any man thought his claim was worth. He told them that a psychic in New York had given him a map to a "Lake of Gold" inside the mountain, and that he intended to dig a tunnel to it.

He spread a map on the table in front of the astonished miners, who figured that the crazy foreigner was mad, and told the crowd, "This is her map. The arrow shows where she says we should tunnel. I'll need hundreds of you miners, and I'll pay top dollar to every man jack of you. Gentlemen, it is my opinion that all of us here, every man in this saloon, will become rich beyond his wildest dreams. A psychic has made it clear that the gold is there in plenty, a lake of gold, and she has never guided me wrong in the past."

Within three days, work started on the tunnel to the lake of gold. Meanwhile, city officials hired a private detective to investigate Ennis and determine if the Scotsman was as wealthy as he claimed. The detective reported back that the man was indeed a millionaire many times over with large bank accounts in New York and Denver.

However, the nameless psychic never said that tunneling to the lake of gold would be easy, and months of digging turned into years. Edward Ennis poured millions into the venture, with the mountain becoming honeycombed with tunnels. Ennis scrambled around in the dangerous tunnels, insisting that the miners bypass valuable veins of silver and direct their energies towards finding the lake of gold that the psychic assured was not far away.

Occasionally the psychic would send urgent letters from New York, advising Ennis to "dig higher," "dig lower," "dig to the right," "dig to the left." "Study the map...study the map..."

One letter warned, "Beware of a flood, be sure the men can escape. Edward Ennis—be prepared."

A few days later the miners dug into a huge wall of rock and suddenly tons of water crashed into the tunnel, and a wave of deadly water began to surge through the mine. In a scene like that in the film *Indiana Jones and the Temple of Doom*, Ennis had ore carts on rails ready for just such an emergency and the miners were able to get into the ore carts and escape down the tracks while a tidal wave of water threatened to engulf them. Because of the warning, not a single life was lost.

The miners had new respect for Ennis and his psychic directions and work continued for ten years altogether on the ambitious project to find the lake of gold. In 1885 the twisting maze of tunnels extended more than a mile into the earth below Cunningham Gulch.

Sadly, the bank in New York where Ennis kept most of his millions collapsed overnight, plunging many wealthy New Yorkers into poverty, among them Edward Ennis. The tunneling stopped, and Edward Ennis, a broken man, returned to New York by train. He never made it to New York, however, dying while on the trip.

The years passed, and the crazy Scotsman was all but forgotten in Silverton. Then, in 1901, a Scotswoman named Mary Murrel came to Silverton. She brought with her a large and wealthy syndicate of Eastern investors who together bought the Ennis claim and once again began the tunneling.

Highland Mary, the miners called her, and she told the townspeople that she was unrelated to Edward Ennis, but that she had his treasure map and believed in it. She, too, was convinced that she would find the legendary lake of gold. Mary's syndicate brought in dynamite experts from England and Wales, and they began to blow the heart out of the giant mountain.

The blasting worked. Just 1,200 feet from where the work had stopped upon Edward Ennis' death, in the area where the map had predicted, the miners found the famed "Lake of Gold." There were rich veins of gold that yielded millions of dollars worth of high-grade ore, along with a fortune in silver, zinc and copper. Everyone connected with the mine, called the Highland Mary Mine, became extremely wealthy, just as Edward Ennis had said they would.

And Mary Murrel, Highland Mary, became one of the wealthiest women in the world, yet, no one knew who she was. Was she the psychic who had been behind Edward Ennis the entire time? After all the gold had been removed from the mountain, Highland Mary vanished from the west, and from history. Where she went and what happened to her wealth remains a mystery to this day, yet the Highland Mary Mine still exists as testimony to a psychic's map to a subterranean "Lake of Gold."

Finishing my blueberry-flavored snow cone at the drugstore in Silverton, I thought about the miles of tunnels in the mountain. If our civilization were to be wiped out, as many have been before us, and these strange tunnels were to be discovered inside a mountain in a remote mountain range, what might we think of them? Would archaeologists create some bizarre story of a subterranean cult or would occultists with vivid imaginations believe that some tunneling dwarves from a hollow earth had found their way to the surface of our earth? Perhaps the story of the Highland Mary Mine is stranger than both.

❀❀❀

Montezuma's Lost Treasure

One of the great lost treasures of the world is said to be located in the Four Corners area of New Mexico, Arizona, Utah and Colorado. This incredible treasure, actually seven treasures, is enough wealth to topple governments, change the course of history, and cause enough gold-crazed murder and mayhem to make any Indiana

481

Jones movie seem tame by comparison. It is a story involving lost cities, conquistadors, ancient kingdoms, and the mystical lure of the world's most sought-after mineral: gold.

The story of Montezuma's lost treasure begins in 1519, when Spanish troops led by Hernando Cortez marched on the Aztec capital of Tenochtitlán. Without a battle, Cortez took Montezuma captive, and began to rule Mexico through the king.

However, Cortez had renounced allegiance to Governor Velázquez of Cuba and in 1520 the conquistador had to return to the Mexican coast to defeat a Spanish army sent by Velázquez under Panfilo de Narváez which had been sent to remove Cortez from power and establish Velázquez's "legitimate" government.

While Cortez and Narváez battled for control of Mexico on the coast, Tenochtitlán was under the control of Cortez's general, Pedro de Alvarado. The Aztecs rallied against the Spanish invaders and drove Alvarado and the Spanish forces out of the city. It wasn't until 1521 that Cortez was able to retake the city, and with that battle the destruction of the Aztec Empire was complete.

It was during this brief period of independence in 1520 that Montezuma ordered his buildings stripped of their gold, silver, and jewels. Gold ingots were taken from the treasury and seven caravans of one hundred porters, each carrying approximately 60 pounds of gold, was sent to the north. When the plague of the Spaniards had passed, the gold would return to Tenochtitlán.

The mystery of this vast gold treasure, seven caravans with approximately 50 million dollars in treasure apiece, has never been solved. Even the area in which the treasure was deposited is disputed. One account says that the caravans went approximately 275 leagues north from Tenochtitlán, and then turned west into high mountains, where the gold was hidden in various caves in canyons.

The length of a league is disputed and variable (a vague term at best in such a legend as this), and the area in which the treasure may be hidden may be in the Sierra Madre of Mexico (interesting to think of the Humphrey Bogart film *Treasure of the Sierra Madre* in this connection) or even farther north.

There are many legends that the seven caravans of Montezuma's treasure went into the area of the Four Corners of New Mexico, Arizona, Colorado and Utah. In fact, this area was apparently the ancestral home of the Aztecs.

The Pueblos of the American Southwest had a long connection with the Aztecs of Mexico, and many of the cliff dwellings and other structures had such names as "Montezuma's Castle." In the Four Corners area are such common names as "Aztec" (as in the name of the town Aztec, New Mexico, and the ruins there by the same name), "Montezuma" (as in Montezuma County, Colorado, or Montezuma's Castle State Park in Arizona), "Cortez" (as in Cortez, Colorado), and other place names.

In the July 14, 1876, issue of the Taos, New Mexico *Weekly New Mexican*, there's a report of a young Mexican who arrived in town to look for one of the seven caravans of treasure. He claimed to have some special knowledge of where one of the treasure troves was hidden, probably from a distant relative, and soon had others from the town helping him search for the treasure.

With a group of people from town, they searched among the rocks in the mountains outside of town. The young Mexican suddenly scrambled up a cliff ahead of the rest of the party. After a long silence he called out that he'd found a cave "filled with gold and lit into the blaze of day with precious stones." At that moment, according to the newspaper account, a powerful wind blew him off the cliff. He was dashed against the rocks below, and didn't live to tell the location of the cave. No one else has been able to find this cave. Or at least no one has found this cave and told the press and the Internal Revenue Service about it.

Kanab, Utah, is said to be in the vicinity of another of the treasures. In 1914 a prospector named Freddie Crystal rode into town. He told a wealthy rancher named Oscar Robinson that he'd done a lot of research into the Montezuma legend while in Mexico, and he'd found an old book that gave him a solid clue. It seems that the book had drawings of symbols which Montezuma's men had supposedly inscribed on the rocks in a canyon near Kanab. Freddie figured he could find the treasure, if he could just come up with a grubstake.

It wasn't unusual for a businessman to outfit a prospector under an agreement to share any wealth discovered, and Robinson agreed to do just that. Crystal and his string of packhorses trailed off into the mountains, and weren't seen again for eight years.

By 1922 the town had almost forgotten about the prospector and his tales of buried Aztec gold. It was pretty exciting when he came ambling back out of the mountains. He told the townspeople of Kanab that he had found the treasure, but he needed their help to get it out.

Kanab just about closed up shop and migrated en masse into the mountains with Crystal. There, in a canyon on White Mountain, they found strange symbols carved into the cliffs that exactly matched those Freddie said he'd found in the old book in Mexico. Nearby was a giant tunnel which had very carefully been sealed a long time ago.

The townspeople attacked that with a zeal that matched the original conquistadors, but day after day they found nothing but more rock. After three months everyone but Freddie had given up. Eventually he did too. He said he was going back to Mexico to get more clues, and he was never seen again.

I stopped for a cold drink at the cafe in Kanab and asked the waitress where White Mountain was. She pointed out the window into the desert, and poured me another glass of water while we looked out at the mountains.

"Are there really symbols carved in the rocks of a canyon out there?" I asked her. She assured me there were.

I dug into another piece of apple pie, and thought, "Did the lost treasure of Montezuma lie just outside the window?"

❀❀❀

The Church of the Latter-day Saints, better known as the Mormon Church, has a curious history, and one that in fact is of great interest to those of us who deal with the subject of lost cities and ancient artifacts. The church was founded by a young man named Joseph Smith who grew up on a farm in Palmyra, upstate New York, allegedly under the direction of angelic beings.

The first supposed meeting with angels took place in 1820, when Smith was only fourteen. These visions and meetings with angels continued for several years, Smith claimed, and ultimately led to the historic discovery in 1827 of golden tablets inside an artificial mound in Palmyra. On these tablets Smith was told by the angels that the "true history" of the former inhabitants of North and South America was written.

Smith then translated these tablets, he claimed, with the help of the angels and some crystal balls that were also discovered within the mound. The result is the present day *Book of Mormon*, which is the basis for the church. The golden tablets then disappeared, but not before eleven witnesses testified that they had seen them, including Joseph Smith's father and two brothers.

Skeptics have tried to prove that Smith's document was a reworking of a 19th century romance by a writer named Solomon Spaulding, though it seems unlikely that a poorly educated youth such as Smith could have concocted such a document. Indeed, no matter what one may think of the *Book of Mormon* and the Church of Jesus Christ of Latter-day Saints, the creation of the *Book of Mormon* is a remarkable achievement by any person, and adds more to the mystery as the book is an incredible story which reflects, at the very least, the current theories, totally independent of the Mormon Church, of ancient Jews in America, and of wandering Christian missionaries in pre-Columbian times.

The *Book of Mormon* claims to be the record of the first inhabitants of the Western Hemisphere and covers a period from 600 B.C. to 400 A.D. It is made up of 14 books and is over 500 pages long. The first two books, I and II Nephi, trace the flight of Lehi, a descendant of Joseph who was sold into Egypt by his brothers, and his family and followers from Jerusalem to a land of promise across the sea. Once there, two of the sons, Laman and Lemuel, led a rebellion against their father and were punished by being cursed with dark skin. From this offshoot of the original Jewish settlers came the Lamanites, from whom the American Indians are descended, so claims the *Book of Mormon*.

Another son, Nephi, remained faithful, however, and the later chapters are largely the story of the fortunes of the Nephites up to and beyond the coming of Christ to the Americas following the crucifixion and resurrection. The chronicle concludes with a final battle between the Lamanites and the Nephites, and the decimation of the Nephites by the Lamanites. It is during this apocalyptic battle in upstate New York that the golden tablets which Joseph Smith was to discover (with the aid of angels) were buried at the site of the battle by the prophet Moroni, Mormon's son.

Joseph Smith's translation of the *Book of Mormon* was published in 1830 and his new "church" grew rapidly. In 1831 he and his brother Hyrum established themselves at Kirtland, Ohio. Problems with neighbors caused the ever-growing group to relocate in

Missouri and then to a new Zion at Nauvoo, Illinois, on the Mississippi River. Hostility against the group again occurred, culminating with a murderous mob lynching both Joseph and his brother Hyrum on June 27, 1846. Joseph Smith was only 39 at the time.

Under the new leadership of Brigham Young, the main group of the Mormons continued to move west. Brigham Young had had a vision of a promised land in a valley and in 1847 the Mormons settled in the valley of the Great Salt Lake in Utah.

Originally the Mormons had wanted to create a nation in the west called Deseret. Deseret was to encompass all of Utah and much of the American Southwest. The Mormons, under a cooperative theocracy, thrived in Utah, with Brigham Young as their leader. Under cooperation with the U.S. government, Young became the territorial governor. However, because of the Mormon practice of polygamy (Brigham Young had 27 wives) Utah was denied statehood until 1896. Brigham Young died in 1877 and in 1890 the head of the Mormon Church, Wilford Woodruff, agreed to outlaw polygamy, which led the way to statehood. The Mormon nation of Deseret was never realized, and many polygamous Mormons fled to Mexico and Canada.

There are many interesting aspects about Mormonism and its doctrines. The golden tablets allegedly discovered by Joseph Smith draw an interesting parallel with the golden books of the Maya and similar early Christian tablets found by the thousands in Michigan, Ohio and other areas in the mid-1800s. That Christ may have walked the Americas is a fascinating subject and one that is popular with many historians, not just Mormons. However, it can probably be said that in 1830 this was by no means a common idea, and most people had never heard of the Aztec, Mayan, Toltec and Inca stories of Quetzalcoatl, Kukulkan, Viracocha and other wandering Saints whose lives so closely parallel those of Christ and his apostles.

While I am not a Mormon, nor was I raised a Mormon, there seems to me to be a certain amount of truth to the version of ancient American history as portrayed in Smith's book.

For instance, it is likely that Jewish colonists did come to the Americas, especially Mexico, Florida and the Eastern seaboard, including the Palmyra, New York, area. The Americas have been inhabited for tens of thousands of years, if not hundreds of thousands, and by civilizations far more ancient and advanced than Jewish colonists of 600 B.C. Most Mormons point out that the Jews referred to in the *Book of Mormon* were just one group of many colonists to the Americas in ancient times, and they encountered many ancient and well-established civilizations already in existence such as the Mayas and other groups.

That Christ or some of his disciples, whether early Christians or actual apostles, journeyed through the Americas preaching brotherly love, cooperation and harmless living would also seem to be almost certainly true. Native American legends from both North and South America confirm this over and over. The very conquest of Mexico and Peru was realized because of prophesies foretold by these same wandering prophets.

485

Perhaps the most mysterious part of the saga of the Mormon Church is not what was revealed to Joseph Smith and Brigham Young, but what was *not* revealed. For instance, Joseph Smith was given several powerful, ancient, and no doubt very valuable crystal balls that allegedly also came out of the mound in upstate New York. These "talking stones" as they are called in the *Book of Mormon* were used by Smith to get answers to various questions he had, including the meanings of the gold tablets.

The British writer on antiquities, John Ivimy, makes a stirring suggestion at the end of his popular book on Stonehenge, *The Sphinx and the Megaliths*.[217] He spends the bulk of the book trying to prove his thesis that Stonehenge was built by a group of adventurous Egyptians who are sent to the British Isles to establish a series of astronomical sites at higher latitudes in order to accurately predict solar eclipses, which the observatories in Egypt could not do, because they were too close to the equator.

Ivimy gives such evidence as the megalithic construction, keystone cuts in the gigantic blocks of stone, the obvious astronomical purpose, and most of all, the use of a numbering system that is based on the number six, rather than the number ten, as we use today. Ivimy shows that the Egyptians used a numbering system based on the number six, and that Stonehenge was built using the same system. Ivimy then suggests that the Mormons used a number system based on six when building their temples, especially the great temple in Salt Lake City.

Ivimy quotes Brigham Young in describing six towers for the temple, and how the temple is built with six-foot walls using huge blocks of stone quarried from a mountain twelve miles away. He mentions how a canal was originally planned to move the blocks, much as the blocks at Stonehenge are believed to have been moved.

In the end, Ivimy's thesis is quite controversial: he believes that Brigham Young and the original Mormon settlers to Utah are the reincarnation of the same Egyptian group of settlers who were sent to Britain to build Stonehenge. Says Ivimy, "Reference has already been made to the vast wooden dome, built entirely without metal, that roofs the Mormon Tabernacle. Could its construction have been inspired by a dim recollection of how the same people, in another incarnation some centuries later, had built a dome over what had then become the Temple of Hyperborean Apollo?"[217]

Perhaps this is part of the revelation that Joseph Smith did not, or could not reveal in 1830, the ancient cosmic truths of reincarnation and karma, as taught by all the great religious leaders before him, Krishna, Zoroaster, Buddha, Mahavira, Lao Tzu and Christ. Perhaps Ivimy is right that the early Mormons were reliving an earlier group incarnation in which they must undertake a dangerous mission to unknown lands and establish a special "temple." What will be the next exciting mission that this group of ancient Egyptian adventurers will undertake? Is it time for the next migration to another "promised land"?

🐾🐾🐾

After stopping for a day in Salt Lake City to visit the Mormon Tabernacle, I made a detour up into Wyoming to visit the Grand Tetons and the Red Desert. Shortly thereafter, I was camped in the shadow of the towering mountains of the Tetons. Curiously, the Grand Tetons are said to have their own lost city.

In 1899 an unusual book was published entitled *A Dweller On Two Planets.*[127] It was first dictated in 1884 by "Phylos the Thibetan" to a young Californian named Frederick Spencer Oliver who wrote the dictations down in manuscript form in 1886. The book was not published until 1899, when it was finally released as a book.

The book is a long and complicated history of a number of persons and the karma created by each of them during their many lives, especially the karmic relationships and events of the "amanuensis" Frederick Spencer Oliver and his different lives as Rexdahl, Aisa and Mainin with the many lives of "Phylos" as Ouardl, Zo Lahm, Zailm and Walter Pierson.

A Dweller On Two Planets has remained a popular occult book for nearly a century largely because it contains detailed descriptions of life in Atlantis plus devices and technology which were unquestionably well in advance of the time in which it was written. As the cover of one of the book editions states, "One of the greatest wonders of our times is the uncanny way in which *A Dweller On Two Planets* predicted inventions which modern technology fulfilled after the writing of the book."

Among the inventions and devices mentioned in the book are air conditioners, to overcome deadly and noxious vapors; airless cylinder lamps, tubes of crystal illuminated by the "night side forces"; electric rifles, guns employing electricity as a propulsive force (rail-guns are a similar, and very new invention); monorail transportation; water generators, an instrument for condensing water from the atmosphere; and the *vailx,* an aerial ship governed by forces of levitation and repulsion.

Much of the wording and terms are identical to the Edgar Cayce readings, such as "night side forces" and the term "Poseid" for Atlantis. While verification of any of the information in both books is impossible, the material is fascinating and of definite interest to any student of the Vimanas of ancient India. In *A Dweller On Two Planets,* the hero, Zailm (an earlier incarnation of Phylos and Walter Pierson), visits Caiphul, the capital of Atlantis, and views many wonderful electronic devices and the monorail system.

Later, the electromagnetic airships of Atlantis are introduced along with radio and television (don't forget, this book was written in 1886). It is explained that the airships, similar to zeppelins, but more like a cigar-shaped airship, are electro-magnetic-gravitational in nature. They move through the air using a form of anti-gravity and are capable of entering the water as a submarine or traveling through the air.

The book also contains a fascinating trip by one of these airships to visit a building on the summit of the Tetons. The main subject of the book, Zailm, visits "Umaur", a colony of Poseid. The description may be a rare psychic look at the ancient North American continent of 11,000 years ago.

Zailm first travels to South America and then, according to the text, "we came to the Isthmus of Panama, then over 400 miles in breadth; to Mexico (South Incalia) and to the immense plains of the Mississippi. These latter formed the great cattle-lands whence Poseid drew most of its supplies of flesh-foods, and where, when the modern world discovered it, enormous herds of wild progeny of our ancient stock roamed at will.

"...Still farther north than this, in the present 'Lake Region,' were large copper mines, whence we obtained much of our copper, and some silver and other metals. A cold region was this, far colder than it is today, for it lay in the edge of the retreating forces of the glacial epoch, an epoch not over until much more recently than geologists have hitherto thought, and even still think.

"To the west lay what in early American days were called the 'great plains.' But in the days of Poseid they had a far different appearance from that which they bear today. Not then arid, nor very sparsely inhabited, though vastly colder in winter, owing to the nearness of the vast glaciers of the north. The Nevada lakes were not then mere dried up beds of borax and soda, nor the 'Great Salt Lake' of Utah a bitter, brackish body of the water of its present comparatively small size. All lakes were large bodies of fresh water and the 'Great Salt Lake' was an inland sea of fresh floods, bearing icebergs from the glaciers on its northern shores. Arizona, that treasure house of the geologist, had its now marvelous desert covered with the waters of 'Miti,' as we called the great inland sea of the region. Verdure (green vegetation) was on all the slopes of all the hundreds of square miles not covered with lovely bodies of water. On the shores of Miti was a considerable population, and one city of no small size—colonists all, from Atl.

"...From the city of Tolta, on the shore of Miti, our vailx arose and sped away north, across the lake Ui (Great Salt Lake) to its northwestern shore, hundreds of miles distant. On this far shore arose three lofty peaks, covered with snow, the Pitachi Ui, from which the lake at their feet took its name. On the tallest of these had stood, perhaps for five centuries, a building made of heavy slabs of granite. It had originally been erected for the double purpose of worship of Incal (the Sun, or God), and astronomical calculations, but was used in my day as a monastery. There was no path up the peak, and the sole means of access was by vailx."[127]

Then, in a break in the story, Frederick Spencer Oliver alleges that such massive, granite slab-walls were discovered in 1866 by a Professor Hayden, allegedly the first person to climb Grand Teton. Says the text, "In the neighborhood of twenty years ago, more or less, counting from 1886, an intrepid American explorer...went as far west as the Three Tetons. These mountain triplets were the Pitachi Ui, of Atl. Professor Hayden, having arrived at the base of these lofty peaks, succeeded, after indefatigable toil, in reaching the top of the greater peak, and made the first ascent known to modern times. On its top he found a roofless structure of granite slabs, within which, he said, that 'the granite detritus was of a depth indicating that for eleven thousand years it had been undisturbed.' His inference was that this period had elapsed since the construction of the granite walls. Well, the professor was right, as I happen to know. He was examining a structure made by Poseid hands one hundred and twenty-seven and a half thousand years ago, and it was because Professor Hayden was once a Poseida and held a position under the Atlan Government, as an attache of the government body of scientists stationed at Pitachi Ui, that he was karmically attracted to return to the scene of his labors long ago. Perhaps knowledge of this fact would have increased the interest he felt in the Three Tetons."

The narrative then resumes the journey: "Our vailx alighted upon the ledge without the temple Ui just as nightfall came on. It was very cold there, so far north, and at such an altitude...The primary cause of our visit was our desire to pay devotion to Incal as He arose next morning... Next morning after sunrise our vessel lifted and departed for the east, that we might visit our copper mines in the present Lake Superior region. We were conducted in electric trams through the labyrinths of galleries and tunnels. When we were about to leave, the government overseer of the mines presented each of our company with various articles of tempered copper."[127] The group then returns to Poseid, making part of the journey underwater.

The book is curious and the statements quite interesting, to say the least. Do massive granite slabs in the form of walls exist on the top of Grand Teton? If they did they would certainly be in poor condition and if they exist, they might be thought to be natural.

The ancient copper mines of the Lake Superior region do indeed exist and are a mysterious archaeological fact.

I leaned back against my pack and looked into the campfire I had prepared. The flames licked the wood and glowed in the dark. Was there a lost city on Grand Teton? I would like to see a photo of this one! Who was this Professor Hayden? Surely some records must exist? Oliver quotes from Hayden, but does not give us the source. Perhaps from a newspaper report?

We are also given the names of some fascinating places: Tolta for the city on the shores of an inland sea named Miti. This is apparently the ancient sea that once covered most of Arizona and New Mexico. Was the city of Tolta in the Rocky Mountains or in the Sedona-Flagstaff-Hopi Indian area of Northern Arizona? Did the Toltecs take their name from the ancient glory of Tolta?

What of the underground tunnels and galleries in northern Michigan and Wisconsin? Could ancient mining from Atlantis account for some of the bizarre and semi-mythical tunnels in the Rocky Mountains, California and the Southwest? Were more ancient tunnels to be found in Northern Michigan, Minnesota and Wisconsin? Curiously the Hopi have a myth that they emerged from subterranean tunnels after the destruction of the third world to repopulate the fourth world. Atlantean mining works, ancient electric trains, a megalithic fortress on top of Grand Teton—perhaps truth genuinely is stranger than fiction.

With the coals of my campfire in the Tetons still warm, I drove west into Utah again and then past the Great Salt Lake, much smaller than it was in the time of Poseid, according to Oliver, and drove into Nevada.

To the south was the glitzy city of Las Vegas with its gambling casinos, huge resorts and and the constant live shows of popular entertainers and dancing girls. It is interesting to note that a bizarre "Lost City" of a modern kind is located only a hundred miles or so from Las Vegas, a lost city both strange, and at the same time rather frightening.

The Nellis Air Force Bombing and Gunnery Range located to the northwest of Las Vegas is a vast area of ultra-top-security government land larger than many New England states. A portion of the Nellis Air Force Range is known as the "Dreamland" complex. Part of the "Dreamland" complex is known as "Area 51." Area 51 is where the United States' most advanced weaponry systems are believed to be under development. The Area 51 portion of the vast desert facility is where it is claimed that the U.S. government is both building its own flying saucers with so-called "anti-gravity" propulsion systems as well as examining all UFOs that have either crash landed or been captured by a supposed elite unit of the military. These spacecraft, and their occupants, are now said to be undergoing examination by top specialists in the medical, metallurgical, and propulsion fields.

The entire Dreamland complex is mainly underground to prevent any unauthorized observation from satellites, overflights, or individuals hiking in the surrounding mountains. It should be mentioned that this facility is guarded by a small army of current military and intelligence services personnel, as well as a reputed hand-picked force of ex-servicemen who served in the Navy's Seals, Army's Airborne or Special Forces, and the Air Force's Air Commandos. It is known that these guards have at their disposal armored vehicles, helicopters, mobile radar units, highly sensitive detectors on the ground, and more. There is also a strong working relationship with the Lincoln County Sheriff's Department, for any kind of assistance when called.

All U.S. government vehicles that are authorized to enter this restricted area have on their front license plate a "CSC" tag. It has been speculated that "CSC" stands for "Central Space Center" but nobody who knows is talking about what that logo means.

Area 51 was first coded "Operation Snowbird" and it is believed by a number of UFO researchers that its main mission was to test fly captured UFOs. Area 51 was decided to be an ideal location because it is located between two concealing mountain ranges in the dry lake bed area of Groom Lake. The only road into the area was upgraded to a two-lane one suitable for heavy-duty trucks.

The Area 51 facility at Dreamland is similar to another American installation on the other side of the world. This is the Pine Gap facility in central Australia, near to the town of Alice Springs and the tourist destination of Ayers Rock.

Pine Gap is supposed to be a satellite tracking station, but all that one can see above ground is a small shack and a dome. No Australian has ever been inside Pine Gap, but rumor has it that the facility goes twelve stories underground, has two giant ELF (Extremely Low Frequency) towers inside it, and a huge factory for manufacturing flying saucers. Every day, two Hercules C-147 Starlifters fly into the base, possibly from the Area 51 Dreamland facility. Each plane can carry about one hundred thousand pounds of freight. What could they be carrying for a satellite tracking station? Rumor says that it is material for the manufacture of the flying saucers, using some sort of anti-gravity drive.

In the December, 1991, issue of *Popular Mechanics* magazine, the cover story was about the Stealth Bomber, which is built and tested at the Dreamland site in Nellis Air Force Range, among other areas. The article, which was about the new supertechnology being utilized in the new generation of aircraft, had this to say about a super-secret aircraft being tested by the U.S. government; "According to reports over the past two years, a vast black flying wing, estimated at between 600 and 800 feet in width, has passed silently over city streets, empty desert and rural freeways. The craft moved so slowly one observer said that he could jog along with it. A pattern of seemingly random white lights on the vehicle's underside provided 'constellation camouflage' against the starry sky. Observers who followed the craft long enough detailed unlikely maneuvers in which the vehicle stopped, rotated in place and hovered vertically, presenting a thin trailing edge to the ground."

Such a craft is obviously using some sort of technology that utilizes artificial gravity fields, allowing it to hover and fly without the conventional airfoil of normal craft. This is apparently the sort of craft being developed in the super-secret underground cities of Dreamland's Area 51 and Australia's Pine Gap (for more information on the underground city of Pine Gap, see my book *Lost Cities of Ancient Lemuria & the Pacific* 59).

🐲🐲🐲

South of Las Vegas, near Searchlight, Nevada, is Grapevine Canyon, where on a cliff, a short distance from the Colorado River, can be found a rock that is covered with petroglyphs bearing a strong similarity to ancient Chinese.

Orientalist Jonathan Endicott Gardner examined the inscriptions in the 1930s and affirmed that, whatever their origin, the marks had a stronger resemblance to ancient Chinese characters found in China than do modern-day pictographs now in use there. The suspicion that they may have been a modern day fake is nullified by the covering of "desert varnish" which occurs extremely slowly, being a coating of iron and manganese oxides.

A number of authors, including Henriette Mertz in her classic *Pale Ink*,[183] believe that ancient Chinese manuscripts describe Chinese exploratory expeditions into California, Arizona and Nevada. Mertz's book details two Chinese manuscripts, the *Shan Hai Kang* or *Classic of Mountains and Seas,* written by a certain Yu in about 2250 B.C., which has been called the world's oldest geography book. Yu was an emperor-presumptive of China who claimed to have had a sort of grand tour across "the great Eastern

Sea" to a fabulous land that is quite apparently North America. Mertz and Gardner believe that Yu's expedition may have made the inscription at Grapevine Canyon.

Another Chinese expedition to North America allegedly occurred in the fifth century A.D., when a Buddhist monk named Fu Sang wrote a similar book about his journey to North America. According to Mertz, the Chinese called the Grand Canyon the "Great Luminous Canyon."

In this same area is the strange and ancient Salt Mine of St. Thomas, four miles south of that town, and now covered by Lake Mead at high water. It was an ancient salt mine that had apparently been worked for thousands of years, using stone tools. It was evident that the miner would grasp a heavy hammer with grooves cut for his fingers, and pounding away, would cut a full circle around a column of salt and then undercut the top and bottom, being left with a solid column of salt weighing as much as a ton. These solid columns of salt were then loaded onto ships and sailed down the Colorado as part of the river traffic trading in the ancient Southwest. Perhaps it was meant to supply the huge cities of Cibola, those of the Hohokam around present-day Phoenix.[17]

$$\maltese\maltese\maltese$$

I leaned on the sunburned elbow of my left arm and squinted through the windshield at the dusty wasteland around me. A green road sign pocked with bullet holes said that Winnemucca was only 21 miles ahead. My bizarre destination on my quest for giants and ancient seas in Nevada was getting closer.

Geologists agree that in ancient times, most of Nevada was an inland sea, known geologically as the Lahontan Sea or Lake. This lake has been drying up for thousands of years, and such lakes as Tahoe, Walker and Pyramid are the last remains of the Lahontan Sea. Nevada was a different place back then, a lush lake district with plenty of animals, including huge ground sloths, mastodons, and rhinos. Man lived here too. In 1930, the remains of a giant ground sloth were found in Gypsum Cave, Nevada, by the archaeologist Mark Harrington working for the Southwest Museum of Los Angeles.[120]

Arrow shafts and other objects, plus many feet of sloth dung were found in the cave. Several complete ground sloth skulls were recovered, including the well-preserved shreds of hide and bunches of coarse hair. The animal was well preserved. Harrington declined to estimate the time frame, saying only that sloths were supposed to be extinct by 10,000 B.C.[120] Considering that the animal hadn't even completely decomposed, a much more recent date seems more appropriate, perhaps about 3,000 B.C. Sometime around this time, the lakes began to dry up, the large animals became extinct, and Nevada started becoming a desert. There is even an indication, as with a similar giant ground sloth cave in Chile, that the sloths were domesticated, or held captive, in the cave. What but a giant man could domesticate a twelve-foot-tall ground sloth?

The Piute Indians, living on the desert floor of this now dry lake, had a difficult and primitive existence at the time of the European invasion of the 1800s. In response to the sudden impact of the new civilization on Nevada, and the loss of hunting lands, was the fascinating phenomena of the Ghost Dance ceremonies and the Piute prophet Tavibo. In the 1860s, a Piute Indian living near Walker Lake began to have visions and announced himself as the Piute Prophet who would bring back the game and lush hunting lands of the past (as I said, Nevada had been, and still is, drying up and becoming a desert), but he would put the Indians on the same friendly level with the Europeans as their equals.

Not only this, but Tavibo, who would go into long trances, "astral traveling" to the spirit world, claimed that with the Great Spirit's help, all of the dead ancestors of the Piutes (as well as the Shoshoni and Bannock tribes) would come back to life. In an eyewitness account of the time, Tavibo lay in a trance and then sat up. He described his journey to the Great Spirit, and how all the souls of their ancestors were already on their way back to earth to turn Nevada into a terrestrial paradise. The Prophet taught his followers the "Ghost Dance" or "Spirit Dance," which was performed in a circle, at night, but without a fire. Tavibo became known as Wovoka, or Messiah, to thousands of Indians in Nevada and the Great Plains.

Wovoka's mysticism was very similar to that of the Taoists of the Boxer Rebellion. Wovoka stressed that the warriors "must not hurt anybody, the white men would be punished for their injustices to the Indians, the dead would be restored to life, and that bullets could not hurt them."[178]

The Taoists of the Boxer rebellion also believed that bullets could not harm them because of their "mystical warrior powers." Modern technology prevailed, however, and some disillusion in the prophetic powers of Tavibo/Wovoka surfaced when Sitting Bull was killed at the Battle of Wounded Knee on December 15, 1890. As a follower of Wovoka, the Indian Prophet, he had believed himself bulletproof.[178] Even with the death of Tavibo in the 1890s, the Ghost Dance was continued for twenty years, and has achieved a legendary status.

One of the strange stories that I had wanted to investigate in Nevada was one of red-haired giants found in a cave that had been studied by the University of California at Berkeley. In 1911 miners began to work the rich guano deposits in Lovelock Cave, 22 miles southwest of the Nevada town of Lovelock. They had removed several carloads of guano when they came upon some Indian relics. Soon afterward a mummy was also found; reportedly it was that of a six-and-a-half-foot-tall person with "distinctly red" hair.

According to legends of the local Piute Indians, a tribe of red-haired giants called the Si-te-cahs were once the mortal enemies of the Indians in the area, who had joined forces to drive the giants out. Legend relates that a race of giant "freckle-faced redheads" once roamed the Humboldt Sink area of northern Nevada. Piute legend indicates that the feared red-haired giants were cannibals.

It was also said that the red-haired giants came in boats to the Lovelock-Winnemucca area and were then chased into a cave where the red-haired giants had their camp. The Piutes stacked huge piles of wood at the entrance to the cave and suffocated the giants.

The strange legends of red-haired giants with boats in Nevada is even told in the first book ever written by a Native American woman. The author was Sarah Winnemucca, the daughter of Chief Winnemucca, and the book was *Life Among the Paiutes*, published in 1882. This was thirty years before the astonishing discoveries were to be made in Lovelock.

The discovery of the vast remains at Lovelock are well told in an article from the Humboldt Star, on May 13, 1929. "In 1911, James H. Hart of Nevada, learning from David Pugh, a resident of Lovelock, that there was an Indian cave filled with bat guano which might be of commercial value, filed claim on the cave in partnership with Pugh, and started excavating. A large opening was blasted through the cave wall, a tram-car line constructed, and fifty carloads of the guano taken out. The work had not progressed far when relics of prehistoric Indian occupants began to crop up. Hart, realizing the value of these relics to archaeologists, notified J.C. Merriam, then on the faculty of the University of California, who took up the matter with the University of Nevada and the Nevada historical society."

The article then goes on to mention the curious fate of one of the red-haired skeletons under the heading *Mummy Used by Lodge:* "But money was temporarily lacking, and before an expedition could be sent much valuable material was destroyed. The best specimen of the adult mummies found, reported to be six feet six inches in height, went to a fraternal lodge for initiation purposes.

"Finally, in 1912, finances having been arranged, the University of California sent Llewellyn L. Loud of the museum of anthropology to the scene. In spite of the work that had been done on the guano, Loud managed to accumulate 10,000 specimens singlehanded. An outstanding feature of this collection was the profuse textile material, including over 1500 fragments of basketry and 1400 of matting. The climatic conditions are so fine for preservation of even delicate material that Professors A.L. Kroeber and R.W. Lowie, in a preface to the report just published by the University Press, state that the situation recalls those in Egypt and Peru and is rivaled by few other archaeological sites in North America. The cave was not very large, but during the successive occupancies by humans and bats, debris and guano had piled up to a depth of from a foot or so to fourteen feet five inches.

"Some of the human material was found buried in pits, as if left by the former inhabitants for safe-keeping. The guano diggers reported that they had uncovered thirteen buried bodies, and Loud found 32 more. Some of these were represented by fragments of bones, some by complete skeletons, and some by remarkably preserved mummies. In addition to human and animal remains, and the basketry and matting mentioned above, Loud found a great variety of artifacts of bone, stone, horn and leather. There were fishhooks, fish nets, sandals, moccasins, bird skins, feathers tied together, stuffed birds' heads, blankets of fur and feathers, articles of clothing, and many other objects."[220, 221, 222]

University of California archaeologist Llewellyn Loud gave an account of his return to Lovelock Cave at the end of 1924, this time with Mark Harrington, and they published their definitive work on the cave in 1929, entitled simply *The Lovelock Cave*.[220]

In systematic excavations, the cave was found to contain the remains of 12 more bodies, making the total of bodies recovered from the cave almost 60. Harrington estimates the age of the cave as 4,000 years old or so, occupied by 1,000 B.C. at least. Says the Humboldt Star of May 13, 1929, "In the pits or caches which dotted the various floor levels of the cave, Loud and Harrington found the best-preserved artifacts. These caches were dug by the Indians as receptacles for storing seeds, pine nuts, dried fish or other food, or for storage of such valuables as fur robes, ceremonial plumes. Decoys found, in one case eleven in one pit, were remarkable in workmanship. The bases of the decoys were constructed of carefully coiled and woven rushes in the form of a float, and the tops were made into replicas of ducks by the use of actual skins, feathers and paint. The finished decoys were works of art."[222]

Today some of the bones, including a giant skull and some femurs, can be seen at the museums in Winnemucca and Lovelock. I stopped in at the Lovelock museum to look at the bones and other artifacts. The ladies who ran the museum were friendly and helpful, and very familiar with the stories of the red-haired mummies.

"I remember this photo," said Wanda, the director of the Chamber of Commerce, "of a man holding a skeleton by the hair and standing on a big crate. He was holding this skeleton over his head and this skeleton was tall. At least seven feet tall if not more. And it had long red hair. That is the story, and the photo is real. I think that Wilbur Green has that photo."

"Yes, the Greens were cousins of the Reids', who dug up most of the cave," said another lady who ran the museum. "They had a tram line and ore carts going into that cave back then. You wouldn't believe it now if you saw the cave."

"We don't have much of that stuff around here anymore," said Wanda. "Some of the duck decoys and a few skulls. We don't know where the red-haired mummies are. Maybe in Carson City with some of the other things. Many of the artifacts are there. We are trying to get some of it back here for our museum."

"One of the skeletons was used by some secret society," commented the other gal.

"So the red-haired mummies are real?" I asked the two charming ladies of the Lovelock Museum.

"Oh, yes, it's established scientific fact," said the director, with Wanda nodding behind her. "The University of California at Berkeley came and verified everything. You must go see it yourself."

I took their advice and drove out the ten miles through a dirt track over the dry lake bed to the Lovelock Caves. I scrambled up the rock cliffs of the former river bed, following the trail by the many before me. It was a small but interesting cave. There were no red-haired mummies, or even any trace of them, in sight. There was a plaque from the National Park Service stating that this was Lovelock Cave and that it had been excavated in 1924. It was an offense to remove anything from the cave because it was a National Park. That is all it said. It did not say anything about red-haired mummies, Piute legends, thousands of artifacts, fifteen cartloads of guano or the skeletal remains of 60 people.

I squatted in the cave and explored small passageways. It was all kind of disappointing, but in view of the startling finds, it was one of the archaeological discoveries of the west. Yet, today, it is largely unknown. With whom could I discuss this riddle of ancient lakes, red-haired seafarers, and other mysteries?

My quest for answers to the ancient seabeds and giants of central Nevada now led me to the Winnemucca BLM office where I spoke with the resident archaeologist, a woman named Peggy. Peggy was young, and had earned a masters degree in geology and archaeology. She now worked for the Bureau of Land Management (BLM) as the district archaeologist.

She was helpful but cautious. I asked her if she was familiar with the stories and she said she had heard many of them, but had never seen the skeletons. What about the red hair, I asked?

"Well, the red hair was probably bleached out by the bat guano," she said. "They were probably the mummies of Piutes."

"What about the legends?" I asked, "and the huge stature?"

"Indian legends are just legends," she said. "Some of the people may have been as tall as six and a half feet. The skeletons have disappeared anyway."

"You know, that Viking explorers may have penetrated into Nevada isn't so fantastic," I said, smiling and warming up to her a little bit. She was reserved, and was on her guard in case I was some "Gods From Outer Space" nut.

"There is a good deal of evidence that Vikings explored many areas in the Midwest and even along the Pacific coast," I went on. "What is amazing to me is the story of these red-haired giants arriving here in this desert wasteland via ship! That would certainly be impossible today!"

"That is for sure," she smiled. "Maybe that's why I have trouble believing it. How could it be possible?" For the first time, perhaps, she was taking the ancient Indian legends seriously. "They did find a lot of fishing equipment in the cave, including duck decoys and fish traps. At one time there was a large lake here. But I don't think that it was as big as you think. Most of the artifacts are now at the Carson City Museum. I don't know where the skeletons are."

I thanked her for her information, and walked out to the parking lot.

Just as I was leaving, though, she suddenly came up to the truck door and said, "You know, one thing that is strange about the artifacts at the Carson City Museum is the fiber sandals. They are in fact huge. You look at them and think, wow, these are for giants!"

Other bones and artifacts of "giants" have turned up in the Lovelock-Winnemucca area. In February and June of 1931, skeletons were found in the Humboldt lake bed near the cave. The first of these was eight and one-half feet long and appeared to have been wrapped in a gum-covered fabric somewhat after the Egyptian manner. The second was almost 10 feet long according to the *Lovelock Review-Miner*'s article of June 19, 1931. On September 29, 1939, the *Review-Miner* reported the discovery of a seven-foot-seven-inch skeleton on the Friedman Ranch near that town.[94]

Some Indians told the rancher, Reid, who decided to collect as much information as he could, on mummies, giants and whatnot in the Lovelock area, that they had encountered, but hadn't disturbed, petrified bodies of the peculiar giants lying in the open in a wilderness area south of Lovelock Cave. One of the most fascinating objects attributed by the Indians to these people is a stone pyramid in New York Canyon near Job's Peak on the east side of the East Humboldt Range, 215 miles southeast of Lovelock in Churchill County. Unfortunately, this has been somewhat disarranged by earthquakes in recent decades.[94]

Sadly, I was informed that many odd relics, including skeletons, were destroyed when some years back, a shed containing many of the artifacts caught fire and burned to the ground. The shed had also contained carvings on marine shells and articles laboriously made of colored feathers.

🐚🐚🐚

Another strange story of Nevada giants occurred in July of 1877. Four prospectors moved along the hills of Spring Valley near Eureka, Nevada, in search of precious metals when one spotted something sticking out of a ledge of rock. What he found wasn't gold, but evidence of an ancient giant.

Using their picks, the prospectors soon chipped out human leg and foot bones that had been encased in solid quartzite. The black bones, which had been broken off just above the knee, included the knee joint, knee cap, lower leg bones, and a complete set of foot bones. The man who had once walked on this leg was obviously huge—from knee to heel, the bone was 39 inches long.

The men quickly took their find to Eureka, where it was examined by local physicians. The doctors ruled that the bones were human, and extremely old. After the Eureka newspaper wrote articles about the giant leg bone, several museums sent archaeologists to look for the rest of the remarkable man's skeleton—but no further traces were discovered.[193]

There are many strange fossils and fossilized footprints in the United States and around the world. According to a U.S. Department of the Interior booklet, The Story of the Great White Sands, "In the fall of 1932 Ellis Wright, a government trapper, reported that he had found human tracks of unbelievable size imprinted in the gypsum rock on the west side of White Sands [New Mexico]. At his suggestion a party was made up to investigate. Mr. Wright served as guide, O. Fred Arthur, Supervisor of the Lincoln National Forest, Edgar Cadwalader and one of his sons from Mountain Park, and the writer made up the party. As Mr. Wright had reported, there were 13 human tracks crossing a narrow swag... Each track was approximately 22 inches long and from 8 to 10 inches wide. It was the consensus that the tracks were made by a human being, for the print was perfect and even the instep plainly marked..."

ꞗꞗꞗ

I continued on my way to California, turning north into Nevada's Black Rock Desert and stopping to see Pyramid Lake, on the Piute Indian Reservation. The lake is named after a huge, natural rock formation sticking out of the lake which is pyramidical in formation.

The area was once the lake bed of a huge sea called by geologists Lake Lahontan. Terraces can be seen on the slopes of mountains, and Lake Pyramid is that last that remains of this huge lake.[224,225]

There are walls of large blocks of stones in various places near the shore of Lake Pyramid. It is believed that some of the piles of rocks are ancient breakwaters and docks from which to launch boats. They are currently quite a distance from the lake however.[225]

Piutes on the reservation maintain that there are caves (kept secret by them), about 55 miles west of Pyramid Lake on the reservation, that still contain bodies and articles. The bodies are said to be red-haired giants. Local Indians also maintain that the footprints of some sort of lake monster can be seen on the bottom of the lake in clear weather.[94]

There is a legend of giants that the Washoe Indians had a battle with before the coming of the Piutes. The Washoe Indians, upon first coming to the lake, discovered a dozen camps where many giants lived. The Indians attacked and the giants threw huge boulders at them. After a fierce battle, many giants were killed, and the others fled. With the giants gone, the Piutes then moved north to Pyramid Lake from Walker Lake. The Washoe and Piutes then lived in peace along the lake. Sometimes large piles of rocks are claimed to have been made by the giants before the coming of the Washoe.[223]

The California border was up ahead of me. Soon I would cross a pass over the Sierra Nevadas. Behind me the large basin that is Nevada faded into the distance of my rear view mirror. The ancient seas of Nevada were dry and barren: would they one day have their basins refilled with the rolling waters of teeming fish? Perhaps the healing waters of Mother Earth were destined to cleanse the radioactive domes created during the atomic tests of the last half a century.

As I looked at the green forests of Northern California ahead of me, I realized that it was time for me, as well, to come in from the wasteland.

An aerial infrared photo made in 1965 of a prehistoric fortress along the Missouri River, 22 Miles south of Pierre, South Dakota. The presence of bastions, their 200-foot spacing, and other evidence indicate that the fortifications may have been built by Norse settlers about 1362 A.D. (courtesy of carl H. Strandberg, Staff Engineer, Itek Data Analysis Center, Alexandria, Virginia.)

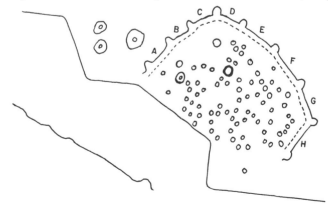

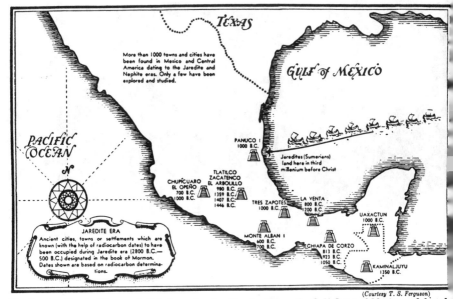

(Courtesy T. S. Ferguson)

The Jaredite Era in Mormon belief. Sumerian Jaredites landed on the Gulf Coast of Mexico and found the centers which are now ancient ruins.

(Courtesy T. S. Ferguson)

The Nephite Era in Mormon belief. Israelites came to America about 600 B.C., one group of them, th Nephites, occupying the ancient cities shown on the map.

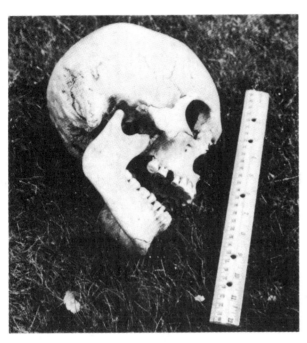

Two skulls from the Lovelock, Nevada caves now in museums in Lovelock and Winnemucca.

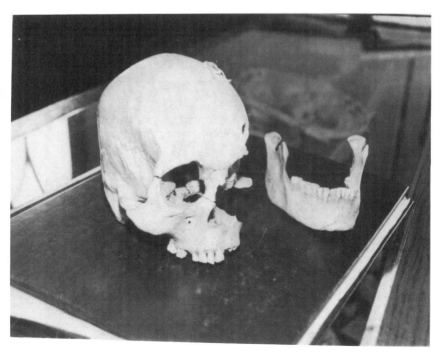

Discovering some of the skeletons at Lovelock, Nevada.

The Courthouse Wash panel, Utah.

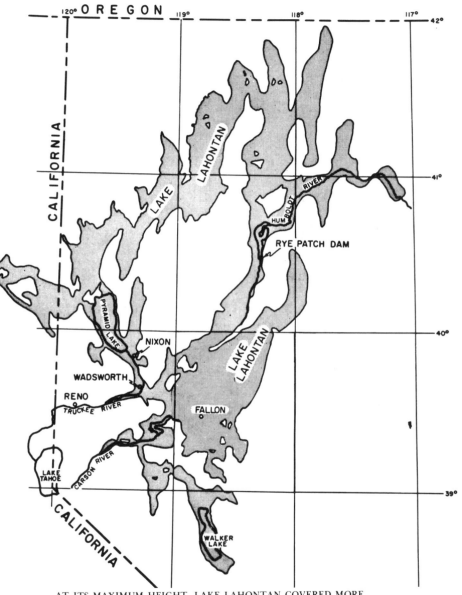

AT ITS MAXIMUM HEIGHT, LAKE LAHONTAN COVERED MORE
THAN 8,000 SQUARE MILES.

A stone wall near Pyramid Lake, Nevada. It may have been a dock when the lake was larger.

An old print of the "Pyramid" of Pyramid Lake.

rrace form by the ancient Lake Lahontan can be seen high above the
y lake bed of Pyramid Lake.

Two photos from the Horseshoe Canyon Annex, Canyonlands National Park, Utah

Chapter 14

California:

The Mysteries of Mount Shasta

Go forth into the world, my son,
and learn that which is written by nature.
Nature is the great schoolhouse
provided for man in which to learn.
Nature does not theorize.
Nature does not lie.
Nature is truth personified.
...Every rock has a tale written on
its wrinkled and weathered face,
and the tales are true.
Every blade of grass,
every leaf on tree and shrub
has a whisper for listening ears. . .

*—The departing words to young James Churchward
from the old Rishi who told him to search for "Mu"*

Vitrified cities, Indian riddles, tunnel systems, underground rivers of gold, and lost continents were what I was thinking about as I crossed over into the California state line. The strange mysteries of California now lay ahead of me and I was determined to explore as much as I could.

Looking out at the desert landscape, I thought about how ancient this land was and about who might have lived here. It's possible that Death Valley may be an area where an advanced civilization lived, but like the Dead Sea in Israel, it is now gone. Death Valley, however, is not a sea, but one of the most terrible deserts of North America.

Secrets of the Lost Races[92] author Rene Noorbergen discusses the evidence for a cataclysmic war in the remote past that included the use of airships and weapons that vitrified stone cities. "The most numerous vitrified remains in the New World are located in the Western United States. In 1850 the American explorer Captain Ives

William Walker was the first to view some of these ruins, situated in Death Valley. He discovered a city about a mile long, with the lines of the streets and the positions of the buildings still visible. At the center he found a huge rock, between 20 to 30 feet high, with the remains of an enormous structure atop it. The southern side of both the rock and the building was melted and vitrified. Walker assumed that a volcano had been responsible for this phenomenon, but there is no volcano in the area. In addition, tectonic heat could not have caused such a liquefication of the rock surface.

"An associate of Captain Walker who followed up his initial exploration commented, 'The whole region between the rivers Gila and San Juan is covered with remains. The ruins of cities are to be found there which must be most extensive, and they are burnt out and vitrified in part, full of fused stones and craters caused by fires which were hot enough to liquefy rock or metal. There are paving stones and houses torn with monstrous cracks...[as though they had] been attacked by a giant's fire-plough.'

"Other vitrified ruins have been found in parts of Southern California, Arizona and Colorado. The Mojave Desert is reported to contain several circular patches of fused glass."[92]

These vitrified ruins in Death Valley sounded fascinating—but did they really exist?

In Titus Canyon, petroglyphs and inscriptions have been scratched in to the walls by unknown prehistoric hands. Some experts think the graffiti might have been made by people who lived here long before the Indians we know of, because extant Indians know nothing of the glyphs and indeed regard them with superstitious awe.

Says Jim Brandon in *Weird America,*[94] "Piute legends tell of a city beneath Death Valley that they call *Shin-au-av*. Tom Wilson, an Indian guide in the 1920s, claimed that his grandfather had rediscovered the place by wandering into a miles-long labyrinth of caves beneath the valley floor.

"Eventually the Indian came to an underworld city where the people spoke an incomprehensible language and wore clothing made of leather. Wilson told this story after a prospector named White claimed he had fallen through the floor of an abandoned mine at Wingate Pass and into an unknown tunnel. White followed this into a series of rooms, where he found hundreds of leather-clad humanoid mummies. Gold bars were stacked like bricks and piled in bins.

"White claimed he had explored the caverns on three occasions. On one his wife accompanied him and on another his partner, Fred Thomason. However, none of them were able to relocate the opening to the cavern when they tried to take a group of archaeologists on a tour of the place. Wilson did, however find a shaft into the stone that no one had seen before. It ended blindly.

"During his lifetime, there was endless speculation on the source of wealth enjoyed by Walter Scott, an eccentric local character who built the "castle" and racetrack still located at the far north end of the valley. Those who knew him claimed that, when funds were running low, "Death Valley Scotty" would check out for a few days of wandering in the nearby Grapevine Mountains bringing back suspiciously refined-looking gold that he claimed he had prospected. Many believe that Death Valley Scotty, who spent millions on a huge castle-estate, got his gold from the stacked gold bars in the tunnel system beneath Death Valley."[94]

❀❀❀

Death Valley has its mysterious race track of moving stones, and other tales of bigfoot, UFOs, lost mines and weird giant skeletons There are even a number of tales of lost ships in the desert.

The Race Track Playa (beach) is a spot in Death Valley where large rocks mysteriously move across the desert. This is evidenced by the trails in the mud of the dry lake bed on which these rocks lie. Because tracks of the moving stones can clearly be seen in the dried lake floor, scientists have wondered just how it is these stones move for hundreds of yards across the desert?

The answer is that in certain conditions, a light rain wets the dry lake surface. Then strong winds suddenly blow in, sailing the rocks over the now slippery lake surface. Curiously, this is one method that the Egyptians used to move their megalithic statues, on a sled with someone pouring water in front of the runners to turn the earth into a slippery surface.

Giants have been occasionally discovered in California. In 1833, soldiers digging a pit for a powder magazine at Lompock Rancho, California, hacked their way through a layer of cemented gravel and came up with the skeleton of a man about twelve feet tall. The skeleton was surrounded by carved shells, huge stone axes, and blocks of porphyry covered with unintelligible symbols. The giant was noteworthy in still another respect: he had a double row of teeth, both upper and lower.[52] When local Indians began to attach a religious significance to the skeleton and artifacts, the authorities ordered it secretly buried, so it is lost to science.

Another giant man was found off the California coast on Santa Rosa Island in the 1800s. He also had a double row of teeth.[52]

Even more bizarre is a report of caves and mummies in Death Valley from the *Hot Citizen*, a Nevada paper, on August 5, 1947. The brief story had a headline: EXPEDITION REPORTS NINE-FOOT SKELETONS. The story is here reprinted in full:

> A band of amateur archaeologists announced today they have discovered a lost civilization of men nine feet tall in Californian caverns. Howard E. Hill, spokesman for the expedition said the civilization may be "the fabled lost continent of Atlantis."
>
> The caves contain mummies of men and animals and implements of a culture 80,000 years old but "in some

509

respects more advanced than ours," Hill said. He said the 32 caves covered an 180-square-mile area in California's Death Valley and Southern Nevada.

ARCHAEOLOGISTS SKEPTICAL

"This discovery may be more important than the unveiling of King Tut's tomb," he said.

Professional archaeologists were skeptical of Hill's story. Los Angeles County Museum scientists pointed out that dinosaurs and tigers which Hill said lay side by side in the caves appeared on earth 10,000,000 to 13,000,000 years apart.

Hill said the caves were discovered in 1931 by Dr. F. Bruce Russell, Beverly Hills physician, who literally fell in while sinking a shaft for a mining claim.

"He tried for years to interest people in them," Hill said, "but nobody believed him."

Russell and several hobbyists incorporated after the war as Amazing Explorations, Inc. and started digging. Several caverns contained mummified remains of "a race of men eight to nine feet tall," Hill said, "they apparently wore a prehistoric zoot suit—a hair garment of medium length, jacket and knee length trousers."

CAVERN TEMPLE FOUND

Another cavern contained their ritual hall with devices and markings similar to the Masonic order, he said.

"A long tunnel from this temple took the party into a room where," Hill said, "well-preserved remains of dinosaurs, saber-toothed tigers, imperial elephants and other extinct beasts were paired off in niches as if on display.

"Some catastrophe apparently drove the people into the caves," he said. "All of the implements of their civilization were found," he said, "including household utensils and stoves which apparently cooked by radio waves."

"I know," he said, "that you won't believe that."

This is an amazing story indeed! Nine foot mummies in zoot suits were hardly typical news stories back in 1947! One has to wonder, if this story were true, what ever happened to these caves, artifacts, and mummies? The extinct animals on display in the caves sound particularly fascinating, and it was this portion of the tale that caused the Los Angeles County Museum officials to lose interest in the story, as it too incredible to be believed. While of doubtful authenticity, this is certainly an interesting story, to say the least. The last comment about cooking food with radio waves being unbelievable is ironic. That is the one thing that modern readers of the story could believe was true—considering the widespread use of microwave ovens today (who had heard of them in 1947?).

Plenty of oddities exist in this area.

In 1961, Wally Lane, Mike Mikesell, and Virginia Maxey, co-owners of the LM&V Rockhounds Gem and Gift Shop in Olancha, California, went into the Coso Mountains in the Inyo National Forest to look for unusual rocks. Near the top of a 4,300 ft. peak overlooking the dry bed of Owens Lake they found a fossil-encrusted geode. When they opened the geode, as they are generally hollow with crystals inside them, they found something that resembled a spark plug. Photos, including X-rays of the object can be found at the end of this chapter.

In the middle of the geode was a metal core, about .08 inch (2 millimeters) in diameter. Enclosing this was what appeared to be a ceramic collar that was itself encased in a hexagonal sleeve carved out of wood that had become petrified, presumably at a later date. Around this was the outer layer of the geode, consisting of hardened clay, pebbles, bits of fossil shell, and "two nonmagnetic metallic objects resembling a nail and a washer." A fragment of copper still remaining between the ceramic and petrified wood suggests that the two may once have been separated by a now-decomposed copper sleeve. Based on the fossils contained in the geode, the object was estimated to be at least 500,000 years old! [39,63]

A book by Frank Edwards entitled *Strangest of All* [228] recounts the discovery of several similar out-of-place objects: "Somewhere in the dusty storage room of a museum there lies a chunk of feldspar which was taken from the Abbey mine near Treasure City, Nevada, in November of 1869. This fist-sized piece of stone was unusual because firmly embedded in it was a metal screw about two inches long. Its taper was as clearly visible as was the regular pitch of the threads. Having originally been of iron, it had oxidized, but the hard stone which held its crumbling remains had faithfully preserved its delicate contours. Trouble with this exhibit was that the feldspar in which the screw was embedded was millions of years older than man himself (as estimated by science), so the annoying exhibit was sent off to a San Francisco academy and quietly forgotten.

"That object was as unanswerable in its way as the challenging discovery of Tom Kenny of Plateau Valley, in the western slope of the Rockies in Colorado. In 1936 Tom was digging a cellar in which to store vegetables for the winter. At a depth of ten feet he found his digging blocked by a smooth, level pavement. Further work revealed that the pavement was made of tiles, each five inches square and handmade. They had been laid in a mortar which was subjected to chemical analysis; it showed that the mortar was of a different composition from anything found in that valley. The perplexing pavement is there today. Scientists can only agree that it is very old, at least twenty to eighty thousand years. But there remains the chilling fact that the pavement lies in the same geological layer as the fossils of the three-toed Miocene horse, which roamed that part of the world from six to thirty million years ago!

"The strange pavement on Tom Kenny's farm has a counterpart in Kentucky, where workmen at Blue Lick Springs unearthed the bones of a mastodon at a depth of twelve feet. Three feet deeper they found a broad stone pavement made of well-cut and neatly-fitted stone slabs—another incredibly ancient work of man that remains unsolved.

"Nor does the record end there. In 1851, in Whiteside County, Illinois, the twisting bit of a well driller brought up two artifacts from sand at one hundred twenty feet. One was a copper device shaped like a boat hook; the other a copper ring of unknown purpose. And in 1971, near Chillicothe, Illinois, drillers brought up a bronze coin from one hundred fourteen feet—another bit of evidence that man had been there. But when, no man can say."[228]

In another anomalous instance, Edwards recounts the tale of the discovery of the Nampa Image:

"In the drilling of wells, considerable debris is brought up from the layers of earth and stone through which the drills grind their way. So it was that on the afternoon of a blazing August day in 1889, on the farm of M. A. Kurtz near Nampa, Idaho, the drill brought up a tiny baked-clay figurine from a depth of three hundred feet. Kurtz noticed the inch-long object in the mixture of sand and clay. He washed it off and discovered to his amazement that it was an unmistakable image of a man with one leg broken off at the knee, presumably as the result of contact with the drill bit. If genuine, this inch-long oddity might constitute evidence of human existence long prior to the accepted dates. If it were a hoax, how did it get down in that deep layer of sand, three hundred feet below the surface? Word of the discovery brought considerable publicity to Nampa and considerable derision from its contentious neighboring cities of Boise and Caldwell. Newspapers carried the report and the pictures of the tiny image and thus it was that Charles Francis Adams of Boston, an official of the new railroad that ran through Boise, became interested. He acquired the controversial little image and had it placed on display in a Boston museum. Its very existence resulted in the customary scientific squabbling. To admit that it might be genuine would mean jeopardizing the long-held scientific opinions on the antiquity of man in this hemisphere, so the stand-patters denounced the image as a fraud. But there were many eminent men of science who came and saw and went away convinced that the Nampa Image was a genuine relic, an artifact tens of thousands of years old, lost ages ago by some Dawn Man in the sandy bed of a stream and brought up in fair condition by an astounding freak of chance. Unfortunately, the argument as to its age cannot be resolved by the carbon-dating technique, which is applicable only to organic materials. Experts at the Smithsonian Institute who have examined the Nampa Image can only say that it is of unusual design, primitive in concept and material. As to its age, they declined to venture a guess. If it is a hoax, Mr. Kurtz certainly never made any effort to gain either money or publicity from its finding. Today it rests in a glass case at Boise's Davis Park Museum. Scientists cannot agree whether it is antique or merely unique."[228]

It was reported in *Scientific American* in 1852 (No. 7, page 298) that during blasting work at Dorchester, Massachusetts, in 1851, the broken halves of a bell-shaped vessel were thrown by the force of an explosion from the vessel's resting place within a bed of formerly solid rock. The vase, just under five inches high, was made of an unknown metal and embellished with floral inlays of silver—the "art of some cunning workman," according to the local newspaper report.

The editor of *Scientific American* gave as his opinion that the vase had been made by Tubal Cain, the biblical father of metallurgy. In response, Charles Fort, who collected such oddities in his four books, said, "Though I fear that this is a little arbitrary, I am not disposed to fly rabidly at every scientific opinion."[39]

In 1891, Mrs. S. W. Culp of Morrisonville, Illinois, was breaking a lump of coal for her stove and noticed a gold chain firmly embedded in the now-split chunk. In 1851 Hiram de Witt, of Springfield, Massachusetts, accidentally dropped a fist-sized piece of gold-bearing quartz that he had previously brought back from California. The rock was broken apart in the fall, and inside it de Witt found a two-inch cut-iron nail, slightly corroded. "It was entirely straight and had a perfect head," reported the *Times of London*.[39]

There are probably hundreds of reports of anomalistic items like these, reports of artifacts that are unquestionably man-made, yet, according to uniformitarian geology, must be hundreds of thousands, if not millions of years old! As I have pointed out earlier, geological dating of coal, fossils, geodes, etc., is done on a scale of geological strata. Lower strata is, of course older than strata above it. On the assumption that geological change is slow and uniform, then strata, such as a coal deposit, will be thrown into the "five million years old" category, or the "fifty million years old category," or whatever.

On the distinct possibility that uniformitarian geology and dating are completely erroneous, dating for such objects that would initially appear to have a startlingly ancient date, say hundreds of thousands or millions of years, can actually be of a much more recent manufacture. I suggest that this is the case with most of these artifacts. While it seems that most of them are authentic, they are probably closer to tens of thousands of years old, rather than millions of years old.

The other interesting thing to note here is the mechanism for burying artifacts in coal, stone and geodes—this is the same mechanism that creates fossils—not slow geological change, but sudden geological cataclysms, like the one that supposedly sank the ancient Pacific continent. It also appears that such cataclysms are not isolated, rare events, but occur with alarming regularity!

Much of Central California was a great inland sea at one time. Now most of this sea has dried up. Maps drawn from 1600 to 1700 by the Spanish showed California as a separate island from the mainland. They did not yet realize that the Sea of Cortez and the Salton Sea did not connect with Tulare Lake Basin in Central California.

The Henry Briggs map of 1625 shows California as an island. The early tales of a huge inland sea in central California and confusion over the Salton Sea and the Colorado River delta area contributed to the false concept that California was an island. *Insula California* was then shown on several maps.

Later, more detailed Spanish maps showed a huge inland sea which started at the San Francisco Bay and went inland. Even as late as 1753, a map published by the famous French cartographer Philippe Buache shows a large inland sea, which he named on the maps Mer de l'Ouest.

Bauche even has his Mer de l'Ouest washing the shores of the fabled kingdom of Quivera. Quivera lies on the southeastern shore of this sea, approximately in the area of the extensive ruins at Chaco Canyon, New Mexico. The kingdom of Cibola can be found in the Casa Grande area, the site of the present day metropolis of Phoenix, a city which has truly risen from the ashes.

Bauche's map also demonstrates quite nicely how the Arizona-New Mexico Cibola area was the ideal meeting place on the navigable rivers of the Colorado/Gila and the Rio Grande. Bauche's Mer de l'Ouest seems to be a confusion of the Great Salt Lake in Utah, which was probably larger in the 17th century and may have included some of the dried up lakes in Nevada, with the Tulare Sea.

A map published in 1830 by Jose Maria Narvaez entitled *Plano del Territorio de la Alta California* showed the remains of an inland sea, and labeled it a huge marsh-lake. Central California is labeled *Cienegas de Tulares*, or the Marshes of Tulares. Apparently the sea disappeared quite rapidly, and featured prominently in the the Tulare Indian mythology.

Sometime in the mid-1800s the entire tribe left the Tulare area. The local newspaper editor ran out to ask the Indians where they were going. "To Yosemite," he was told. "Ocean coming back."

But the ocean didn't come back. Instead, what little remained of the Tulare Lake and Marsh system, dried up and vanished in a sudden event. Only a last little bit of Tulare Lake was left in the area. Today the lake basin is crisscrossed with freeways and housing developments.

Today, there is evidence that there is a great subterranean lake beneath California, similar to the large underground river beneath the Nile discovered by ultrasound in the 1960s. The great inland sea of Tulare was gone, literally sucked into the ground over a period of several months until only a small lake remained by 1840. Even this continued to dry up until only a tiny lake remains in the Tulare Lake Basin.

The Indians had left because the ocean was "coming back." Curiously, instead of the ocean coming back what was left of the lake dried up and virtually nothing remains. Yet, perhaps the ocean will still come back to Central California, and the time may be soon.

According to Jim Brandon in *Weird America*,[94] "Early in February of 1952, well-drillers found artesian water on a ranch near Fresno at a depth of 580 feet. But at the same time, fish two and one-half inches long with small spikes on their backs began gushing up with the water and fell flopping to the ground. A biologist at California State Polytechnic College knew of no underground streams in the area. The fish were identified as sticklebacks by Dr. Earl S. Herald, curator of the aquatic biology at San Francisco's Steinhart Aquarium, who said there had been similar incidents earlier in California: 1870—unidentified fish from a well in San Jose; 1874—thousands of young freshwater trout from a 143-foot well at Port Hueneme, near Ventura; 1884—sticklebacks from 191-foot well at San Bernardino; 1951—five squawfish from a 543-foot well in Lincoln. Other well-drilling surprises have happened in Boise, Idaho; Peoria County, Illinois; and Norfolk, Virginia."[94]

I couldn't help wondering where are all these fish were coming from. The disappearance of the huge inland sea of California probably had something to do with it, I figured. Most of the water probably drained out into the Pacific through the San Francisco Bay and the "Golden Gate." Here we see how the Pillars of Hercules and the legend of the lost land of Atlantis has its counterpart in California. A legend exists with such themes as the loss of a paradisal country similar in climate and geography as the Mediterranean associated with a narrow sea gate into the ocean, in this instance the modern designation "Golden Gates."

Perhaps in the future some dedicated Atlantis researcher will suggest California as the actual site of Atlantis. The eastern United States has already been suggested by Henrietta Mertz in her book *Atlantis: Dwelling Place of the Gods.*[147]

As I headed south out of Fresno, I couldn't help thinking that one day the ocean will come back, just like the Tulare Indians said...

🐾🐾🐾

I stopped in Blythe and the Joshua Tree area to camp in the desert for a few days. Near the south boundary of Joshua Tree National Monument is perhaps the oldest abandoned mine in North America. It is believed to be a jade mine that, in the absence of other contenders, was worked by Toltecs or Mayas. The mineral of the mine is said to compare closely with the jade tribute ornaments found in ancient Central American temples. The latest workings of the mine are estimated to have been around 1500 B.C. The mine is located east of the Interstate 10 entrance road in the park, along Black Eagle Mine Road. It is privately owned and normally closed.[94]

This would be the only other known source of jade in the Americas besides the Motagua jade source in Guatemala. Jade was the most valuable of all things to the Mayas, as well as the Chinese. The Toltecs, known to us as the Hohokam Indians, probably worked the ancient mines for a time.

A fantastic underground river of gold is fabled to exist at the Kokoweef Mine 60 miles south of Las Vegas, near Death Valley. One of the great lost mine stories of the west, the river of gold is an underground river with beaches, and the sand of these beaches has a very high percentage of gold.

The story begins in 1927 when a prospector, one Earl P. Dorr, was given a map by two Pah-Ute (Piute) Indian brothers. They said the map marked the entrance to some caverns and at the bottom of these caverns was gold. He would be very rich. Dorr was skeptical but arranged to search for the entrance. He struck out with his partner, Morton, who was a mining engineer and geologist, to the supposed site of the entrance close to the top of Kokoweef Peak. It was a desolate and wild country that Dorr and his friend ventured into, and they came well supplied because they didn't know what to expect.

The first part of the Indians' claim proved to be correct. There was indeed a cleverly concealed aperture in the limestone. After a cursory examination past the narrow opening, they gathered their carbide lanterns, food, water, and other equipment and began their descent.

What began as just a downward-sloping passageway opened up to form a cavern network. Their lights flickered against the chamber walls producing strange shadows which combined with grotesque natural wonders created by nature. They looked at each other in amazement. Then, lured by the unknown, they continued.

At some junctures where the chambers became chimneys, they thought they would be unable to pass. But they were always able to squeeze through, just barely. After many hours of descent their world beneath the mountain opened up into a gigantic cavern. They estimated that it had to be over 2,000 feet deep. Still the men continued, past a waterfall some 1,000 feet high, cascading to a point far below them. They were startled by the rushing of air and the hint of light. Perhaps a more accessible entrance, Dorr and Morton thought.

They reached the bottom of the cavern and there found an underground river that was 300 feet wide. For a distance of many miles they followed the course of the river. Its banks were laden with black sand. They could see the gold in it and picked up samples periodically, stuffing them in their pockets. Then, as they watched, the river began to shrink. Slowly the water receded until the river was only about 10 feet wide. The black sand sparkled in their lights, but Dorr and Morton were now low on food and had been traveling for two days. It was time for the long hike back. They stopped frequently, for Morton was actually in poor physical shape. They realized that the water volume of the river was increasing. The river was rising. This prompted Morton to comment that it must be somehow connected with the ocean tides.

Several days later, two prospectors who had set up a small camp in the valley below Kokoweef Peak heard an anguished cry for help. Earl Dorr, wild-eyed and disheveled, rushed into their camp and beseeched them to help him. His partner had wearied from exhaustion, he said, and was lying helpless some 300 feet down in some caverns. The men, following Dorr, hurried to attempt to rescue Morton.

Some time later, Morton was brought out. But he was in very bad condition and medical attention was needed quickly. As the men hastened to carry him down the mountain, the black sand which he had stuffed into his pockets spilled on the ground. Dorr became extremely agitated. His secret was out. The rescuers were prospectors and they curiously eyed the glint of gold in the sand. They then looked back to the top of Kokoweef Mountain in deep speculation.

Dorr now had a problem. He had no claim to the caverns. His river of gold would be found and others would profit, not him. In his very poor state of mind, he devised a plan that he would later regret. While the prospectors made Morton comfortable, Dorr returned to the caverns. But first, he got some dynamite where they had cached their supplies. With lengths of fuse wound around his neck and dynamite tied to his belt, Dorr entered the caverns.

About 300 feet down, the caverns became very tight. There was barely enough room for a man to pass through. He strategically placed the dynamite and lit the fuse.

The prospectors in the camp with Morton heard the explosion. Later, Dorr walked into camp muttering that his gold was safe. Unfortunately, in his greed to keep the gold for himself, he had totally blocked the mine, with excavation of the caved-in area impossible at that time.

Dorr purchased property next to the mountain and placed a mining claim on the underground beach with sands of gold. His partner Morton died of natural causes and for more than seven years, Dorr searched for the other entrance to the cavern which he was sure existed. Finally he was forced to tell his story and look for investors to finance a major tunneling operation. Dorr believed that a 350-foot long tunnel could be sunk in the mountain that would reach the vast cavern beneath the mountain.

According to Jim Webb in a *Sun* Magazine article published in Las Vegas on Sunday, April 27,1980, Earl Dorr filed an affidavit with California authorities in 1934 which stated that he had found the underground river with beaches of gold. This affidavit was later published in the *California Mining Journal* in 1940.

In the affidavit, Dorr certified that the caverns existed 250 miles east of Los Angeles, and that he had explored them for eight days in May of 1927. Dorr says that "we found the caverns to be divided into many chambers, filled and embellished with usual stalagmites and stalactites, besides many grotesque and fantastic wonders that make the caverns one of the marvels of the world." Dorr described the subterranean river and the sand along its banks rich in gold.

Before Dorr died in 1957, he made many attempts to make a tunnel back to the cavern and the underground river. In the late fifties he went on secret forays by himself into the Mescal range nearby, because he was sure that the caverns passed in that direction. Dorr believed the caverns could be entered that way, and it is possible that he eventually reached the fantastic treasure he had once possessed. But he seems to have died a pauper in search of lost dream.

Was Dorr's affidavit to the state of California a hoax? It does not seem so. Dorr spent his life trying to return to the cavern beneath Kokoweef Mountain. Dorr's story not only checks out, but a modern company continues to tunnel in the Kokoweef Mine attempting to make a tunnel to the fantastic river of gold or to some connecting tunnel. The Legendary Kokoweef Caverns, Inc. have a concession on the mine, and are continuing to tunnel through the mountain. They have fixed ladders, walkways and stairs that go for hundreds of feet through the ancient passageways and shafts in the mountain. Like any modern mine, the shafts are lighted with electric lights strung along the tunnel, and the operators hope to eventually connect with the trail leading down to the river.

The entire tale is fascinating. Underground rivers such as this are known for a fact to exist, and that gold would exist in the sand on beaches along the river is also natural occurrence. Since gold is indestructible and quite heavy metal, it tends to wash down streams and rivers and collect in pools and other areas. Placer mining is then the sifting of this gold-rich sand by swishing the sand around in the pan. Almost all sand contains a little gold, but it is sand with a high percentage of gold that makes processing of the sand worthwhile. An underground river with beaches could have thousands, even millions, of years for gold sand to collect.

Therefore, the story is credible. One wonders what else may have been in these caverns that Dorr did not tell? There are things that he saw that he may have never told, because he didn't think that anyone else would believe him. For instance, to go down more than 3,000 feet into a huge cavern meant that there must have been some sort of trail, probably stairs, cut into the walls of the cavern, winding down a tortuous path to the canyon floor. Were there strange artifacts, cut stone work, or mummies in various spots in the bizarre tunnel system? Very possibly, especially if one considers the many other strange reports about the Death Valley area.

It is interesting to compare this story with Harvey Snow's account of the 1,300 to 1,400 steps that went down from a secret entrance on Hard Scrabble Peak in New Mexico to an underground river. Snow then traveled in westerly direction for two days along the banks of this underground river before he came out the tunnel.[29] Was this underground river the same as the one discovered by Dorr? (See chapter 9 for more on this strange tunnel.)

Camping for the night around the Mescal mountains, I threw another bit of wood on my campfire and wondered about the truth of these various stories. Were the remains of an ancient civilization still to be found out in the scorching deserts of eastern California? What little left above ground was literally fused rock, while strange tales of tunnels with rivers of gold and nine-foot mummies. Weird extinct animals in various forms of preservation were enough of a bizarre twist to strain the credulity of any person. Fortunately, California has its share of odd-balls, and even the most unbelievable will find some sort of willing listener. In this case, though the tales are unbelievable tales or stories to most people, there is evidence to show that at least portions are true.

❀❀❀

Near to Blythe are gigantic figures etched in the desert that are similar to the enigmatic figures in the Nazca Desert of southern Peru. According to a *Literary Digest* article on November 12, 1932, Army Air Corps flyers in California photographed shapes of giant human and animal figures ranging from 50 to 167 feet in length. Just like the Nazca figures, they were made by removing the topsoil and exposing the lighter soil underneath. George Palmer, who spotted the figures while flying from Hoover Dam to Los Angeles, wrote, "Near two of the human shapes are figures of serpents and four-legged animals with long tails. One giant, or god, appears just to have stepped out of a large dance ring."[17]

Arthur Woodward, ethnologist of the Los Angeles Museum, made "...efforts to find out who made the figures, but to no avail. The Mojave and Chemehuevi Indians who once frequented this area said they had no knowledge of them. But he found new hope upon learning that there was another similar figure near Sacton, Arizona, on the north branch of the Gila River, which the Pima call *Haakvaak*, or 'Hawk-Lying-Down.' "[17]

What is particularly amazing about these "pictographs" scraped into the desert floor is that it is generally agreed that the animal in several of the pictographs is none other than a horse. Says Richard Pourade of the San Diego Museum of Man in the book, *Ancient Hunters of the Far West*,[231] "In the desert near Blythe, California, are raked gravel 'pictographs' of the Mojave Indians. One of them is a crude representation of a man; the other of a horse. The horse clearly places these gravel arrangements in the historic Indian period, as the original Western horse vanished from the continent many thousands of years ago and only was reintroduced by the Spaniards arriving from Europe."

However, the well-known "Western History" writers Choral Pepper and Brad Williams comment in their book, *The Mysterious West*, [232] that "a covering of 'desert varnish' on rocks scraped aside to outline the figures suggests a date preceding that of the arrival of the

519

Spanish conquistadors, who introduced the horse to North America. However, the animal figure...appears to be a horse."

As far as local Indians making them since the Spanish arrived, Arthur Woodward, ethnologist of the Los Angeles Museum, has already said that "...The Mojave and Chemehuevi Indians who once frequented this area said they had no knowledge of them."

Orville Hope, a horse expert, claims in his book, *6000 Years of Seafaring,*[7] that horses already existed in North America when Europeans arrived. Small "dwarfish" horses left by Vikings were on the outer banks of the Carolinas, and Bashkir horses could be found in wild herds in the remote regions of the west, especially the deserts of Nevada, California and Utah.

Says Hope, "Peter Damele was the owner of a ranch in central Nevada near Austin. Before the end of the 19th century, he rounded up a herd of wild mustangs, in which were several horses of a different breed. They were of medium size with calm eyes and large powerful shoulders. Their bodies were covered with long curly hair, their manes and tails were short and shaggy." The Dameles discovered that any of the wild horses could have a curly-haired colt as offspring, as long as those genes were present. The mystery of the curly-haired horses remained for some time until they discovered that the curly-haired horses were Bashkir horses from the steppes of Central Asia, the same horses that the Mongols rode. Hope claims that Bashkir horses have been in North America since long before the Spanish arrived. Indian hunters, however, only killed horses for food, and did not attempt to domesticate them until after the arrival of the Spanish with their "horse technology."

> *Long ago a great flood came to the desert and everyone was forced to move up into the hills to await the leaving of the water. Almost every year in the time of the spring there was a flood, but this was the greatest flood of all and it lasted the longest time. One day, after the third dance had been held, there appeared a great bird with white wings that moved slowly across the top of the water. It came to rest on the top of a hill that the water barely covered, and never was it able to free itself. Soon the waters went away and the great bird fell over on its side and died. The wind blew away its white wings and the body of the great bird slowly slid down the hill where soon the wind threw sand over it to bury it. Sometimes the wind blows away the sand and the body of the great gird can be seen again, but the bird is an omen of evil and harm will come to whoever draws near.*
> —Old Indian Legend[232]

The story of a lost ship in the desert of southern California is intriguing, and has a good deal of support. Indian legend speaks of such a ship coming into the Salton Sea during a storm when there was great flood, and not being able to get back out. Ancient ships have been reported in the desert for the last several hundred years. In the *Los Angeles News* of September, 1870 was a story entitled "Interesting Discovery." It went on to say, "By many it has been held as a theory that the Yuma desert was once an ocean bed. At the intervals, pools of salt water have stood for a while in the midst of the surrounding waste of sand, disappearing only to rise again in the same, or other localities. A short time since, one of these saline lakes disappeared and a party of Indian reported the discovery of 'big ship' left by receding waters. A party of Americans at once proceeded to the spot and found embedded in the sands the wreck of a large vessel. Nearly one-third of the forward part of the ship, or barque, is plainly visible. The stump of the bowsprit remains and portions of the timbers of teak are perfect. The wreck is located 40 miles north of the San Bernardino and Ft. Yuma road, and 30 miles west of Dos Palmos, a well known watering place in the desert..."[233]

A similar tale is told of one Jesus Almanerez, a young Santa Rosa Indian from the Juarez Mountains of Lower California, who chanced upon a ship in the desert in 1898. He was working for the Yuha Oil Well Company, gathering wood with a mule train when his lead mule stopped abruptly. "The animal's ears pointed sharply. The Indian raised his eyes and almost lost his breath in surprise. A huge canoe lay half buried in the side of a sand hill. It had a long neck which rose into the features of some kind of beast. Along the sides of the vessel hung round copper plates."[233]

Since this was an evil omen to the local Indians, Jesus Almanerez could not be persuaded to return to the site, and he in fact quit his job and returned to his tribe. Another similar story is told by the librarian of Julian, California, a small town near San Diego. Myrtle Botts, the former librarian of Julian, and her husband, Louis, liked to go out into the Yuma Desert to camp on weekends. One spring in 1933, near Agua Caliente Springs, they met an old prospector who told them that there was a ship to be seen in a nearby canyon.

The next morning, the Bottses hiked into the canyon. As the grade got steeper, they took a rest. Then, they saw, jutting out of the canyon wall, almost immediately overhead, the forward portion of a large and very ancient vessel. A curved stem head swept up from its prow. Along both sides of the vessel were clearly discernible, circular marks in the wood, quite possibly left by shields which at one time had been attached to the vessel. Near the bow, on one side of the ship, were four deep furrows in the wood. The craft was high enough to hide its interior from the Bottses' view and the side of the canyon was so steep that it could be scaled only by an expert mountain climber.

For a long time, the Bottes studied the curious sight, then slowly retraced their steps to their camp, taking careful note of the landmarks in order to experience no difficulty in returning to the ship. Suddenly, the big earthquake of 1933 struck southern

521

California just as they were returning to their camp. Both were thrown to the ground and their car was bounced along the desert in front of them. The canyon they had just exited became a disaster of landslides. If they had lingered for any longer, they would have been buried in tons of earth. Later they looked again for the ship, but it was buried.[232]

Mrs. Botts researched the ship they had seen in the desert, and concluded that it could have been Phoenician, Roman or Viking. *The Mysterious West* gives several curious accounts of ships in the desert and Indian or Spanish legends concerning them. The Seri Indians, who live on Tiburon Island in the Gulf of Mexico, sing a song of the arrival by ship of "Came From Afar Man" who many, many years ago appeared at Tiburon Island in a huge boat with many men with yellow and orange hair. Also with them was a woman with red hair. They stayed at the island to hunt and fish for many days and then left.[232]

There is the tale of a rancher named Nels Jacobsen, in California's Imperial Valley, who reportedly found a skeleton of an ancient boat near his house some six miles east of the Imperial Valley in 1907 and salvaged the lumber from it to build a pig pen.[232]

There are also records of a Spanish expedition led by a Captain Juan de Iturbe in 1615 to command a pearling station off of La Paz in the Gulf of California. Iturbe sailed through a wide channel at high tide and found himself in another sea, the Salton Sea, but was unable to get his ship back out afterwards. Iturbe then was forced to abandon his ship, with its valuable cargo of pearls and walk back to Mexico, where he filed his report on what had happened.[232]

Southern California has been going through dramatic climatic changes over the last 500 years or so, gradually turning more and more into a desert. Former rivers such as the Los Angeles River and the Rio Hondo are just dry beds. Maps show lakes that no longer exist. One of these was Owens Lake in Inyo County, a deep body of water more than 20 miles long and 10 miles wide. At one end the lake bordered the small town of Cartago, on what is now Highway 395, west of Death Valley. At the other end was the now defunct community of Keeler, a mining town for the once abundant Cerro Gordo silver mines.

Between the two towns plied a steamer some 90 feet long with the name of *Mollie Stevens*. The *Mollie Stevens* carried lumber on her decks, passengers in her cabins, and silver bullion from the Cerro Gordo mines in her hold. At Cartago, the silver was unloaded for transportation by mule train into Los Angeles.

In 1878, the *Mollie Stevens* picked up an exceptionally heavy load of bullion at Keeler and set forth for Cartago. The load was reputed to be worth more than a half million dollars. In addition to the five-man crew, there were also aboard six passengers. In the middle of the lake, the steamer ran head-on into a heavy squall. The waves broke over the bow, and in a matter of a few moments, the overladen ship plunged to the bottom of the lake. So quickly did the mishap occur that the crew had no time to launch the lifeboat. One miner managed to survive by floating through the storm with the aid of a hatch cover.

The story of the tragedy was forgotten over the years, and like the other great lakes formerly in eastern California, Owens Lake grew smaller and smaller, eventually becoming a meadow and then merely parched desert. In December of 1961, Bob White, a pilot from Lone Pine, California, was flying with two friends over the former lake bed, unaware of the story of the lost ship, when he thought he saw a rock that looked like a ship's propeller. They landed the small plane on the lake bed and investigated the unusual rocks. Indeed, it was the remains of a ship, and they salvaged the propeller and some oar locks from the lifeboat that was so fragile, it fell apart when they touched it.

A week passed before they learned the story of the *Mollie Stevens* and its valuable cargo. They attempted to return to the site of the ship to recover the silver bullion, but as of 1967, had been unsuccessful in discovering the site again.[232]

Southern California has a strange and unusual history. Rock alignments and rock circles, typically called "sleeping circles," abound throughout the area. In 1969, the Calico Hills site, near Yermo, became the site of great controversy. Crude flints, reported to be human artifacts, were found in alluvial-fan gravels of the Pleistocene age. Geologists began estimating the age of gravel and therefore the artifacts found within it, as from 30,000 to 120,000 years of age, with an upper limit of age at 500,000 years old. This caused a great deal of controversy among the traditional academics whose history books being used in the universities claimed that man did not enter North America until about the time of the last Ice Age, circa 10,000 B.C.

Clovis points from New Mexico that were dated at 10,000 B.C. or so fit neatly into their official history of North America, but not flints that were 50,000 to 100,000 years old or more. No less of a scientist as Dr. Louis S.B. Leakey of Oldavai Gorge fame in East Africa stepped into the fray and pronounced the site authentic, and said that the flint objects were indeed human-made tools with an age of 50,000 to 100,000 years old![17]

❀❀❀

I stayed with some friends in Los Angeles for a week, visiting the La Brea Tar Pits, site of various prehistoric animals caught in the tar some 10,000 to 15,000 years ago. I called back to the World Explorers Club and discovered that someone in Los Angeles wanted to meet me and show me something quite interesting.

I called the fellow up, (his name was Robert Stanley) and we met one afternoon at his apartment in Santa Monica. He was a young L.A. guy who had grown up in the city. He told me that he had been hiking in the mountains around Los Angeles for many years.

"I think I have found the ruins of a lost civilization," he told me, as we got in my truck to drive into the mountains above Malibu. "I call them the ruins of Kalimu because I believe that they are the remnants of an ancient civilization that existed at the same time as the lost continent of Mu in the Pacific and the great Rama Empire of India that you have written about in some of your books."

"It sounds interesting to me," I confessed. "I have always wanted to see some megalithic ruins here in California."

We first stopped at a huge wall of fused rock that was on private land as we drove into the mountains high above Los Angeles. It was quite an amazing wall, a large, rock-fused wall running vertically across the hills. The owner of the land, on which a portion of this weird wall runs by his garage, happened to be outside in his yard, and I walked over him to ask some questions after I had looked at the wall.

"Did you build this wall?" I asked him.

He laughed. "Hell, no," he answered. "That wall is a natural geological formation. It's unusual, I know. It seems just like a rock wall, don't it?" That was all he could tell me, and I was quite amazed. The "wall" was vertical, consisted of about ten feet of fused rock, and was certainly a curious natural formation, and ancient beyond any doubt.

"Weird, eh?" said Robert, when I got back to the truck. "But that's nothing. Keep driving up this road, I'll show you the important stuff."

We parked the truck along the side of the road near the top of one of the mountains, and then began a half-hour hike into a remote valley that was hidden in the mountain tops. There was a trail, and it was obvious that hikers frequently came into the area, but it was still secluded and remote.

As we turned a corner, suddenly we could see huge carved rocks that looked like faces. Carved into the steep rock face were what looked like an Egyptian pharaoh's head, a Buddha, a Hindu king with a tall helmet, a camel, and other animals. At the top of the trail was an enormous sphinx that was over 200 feet tall.

I gasped at the site, as it was not only surprising, but quite incredible. "You are right," I said to Robert, "these stones are impressive. They appear to have been carved, just as you said." I got out a small camera and took some photographs.

"According to the local Chumash Indian creation legends," said Robert, "modern man was created after the flood. They say that there was once a large beautiful, lush, and fertile coastal valley which they still refer to as Mu. It was located between what is now the Channel Islands and the Southern California coast. I believe that these people of Kalimu were the descendants of the ancient Dravidians, the same people who built the Rama Empire of India."

As we walked back to the truck, I asked Robert how he had discovered the unusual rocks.

"I discovered the ruins of Kalimu in the fall of 1985, accidentally, while looking for traditional artifacts," he said. "It really surprised me when I began seeing all the faces carved out of the rock, because I had dreamed of this place for about 25 years before physically finding it."

"What about the rocks just being naturally weather-worn rocks?" I asked.

"Well, that is what some people say, but I feel that it is beyond coincidence that so many are obviously humans and animals. There are also ruins underwater near here," he said. "This area was destroyed in the pole-shift that caused world-wide floods. I am convinced of that."

I dropped Robert off at his apartment and thanked him for showing me the strange rocks above Malibu. He told me that he could be reached in care of UNICUS magazine, 1142 Manhattan Ave. #3, Manhattan Beach, California, 90266, if anyone else would care to see the unusual rock forms. As I drove away, my mind reeled from what I had seen. Did a lost city really exist above Los Angeles? It was an incredible thought!

🐾🐾🐾

Like the old song says, "L.A. is a great big freeway," and after a week in town, I was ready to get on that great big freeway and head out of town. On my drive up from Los Angeles to Santa Barbara, I thought of the strange roasted mammoths on the nearby Channel Islands. These twelve or so islands are about nineteen miles off the coast of California, opposite Los Angeles, Ventura and Santa Barbara.

The islands are part of the Pacific tectonic plate, while most of California and the rest of the United States sits on the North American plate. Both sedimentary and igneous rock are found on the islands. All the islands have fascinating and unique forms of flora and fauna.

All of the islands share natural similarities and possess large plant communities of the unique plant *coreopsis,* also called the sea dahlia, and the sunflower tree. The weird, almost grotesque plants average two feet in height but can grow to ten feet. In the summer it is a twisted, woody stem with a stubby green growth with some yellow flowers shooting out. In the fall, the clustered plants, bare of blossom or leaf, look like a dwarfed, misshapen, mysterious forest, all black and brown with knobby branches.[151]

Other unusual plants include the unique Island Cherry, the California poppy and a stand of Torrey pine trees which, along with the Santa Cruz Island pine, are remnants of an archaic Pleistocene forest that has survived up to this day.

The unique Island Fox inhabits six of the larger Channel Islands, but is not found on the mainland of California. The animal is related to the Gray Fox but is said to be more feline. It is a mystery to biologists and geologists how this fox came to the mainland because current geological thinking maintains that the islands were not connected to the mainland in the last million years or so, although earlier geological theories supported the idea that the islands were once connected to the mainland. Curiously, Chicki Mallan in her excellent book *Guide To Catalina*,[235] says that there is a mystery concerning the arrival of the fox. "One possibility is rafting on a tree trunk washed out to sea from the Mainland during a heavy rainstorm; another is he could have been brought to the islands by Indians traveling from the Mainland."[235]

The obvious explanation is that the Channel Islands were most definitely connected to other parts of California, though it may well be that the islands, like the entire area of Southern California that is west of the San Andreas Fault, was part of a Pacific continent that is now largely submerged.

Chicki says in the history section of her guidebook, "Catalina has a mysterious and complex history. For the last 30,000 years, no less than five aboriginal cultures have occupied the Santa Barbara Channel Islands, but the history of man is clouded; there are few definite answers to long-asked questions. For a brief period, there was wild speculation that Catalina's first inhabitants may have been a cultured race of white giants, survivors from a sunken continent. Old ships' logs and other written accounts refer to the 'white-skinned' Indian communities on Catalina Island, but no evidence exists that whites inhabited the islands."[235]

While the scholars of today argue about their theories of foxes getting to the islands on drifting logs, they ignore the electrifying discovery of the remains of a "dwarf mammoth" that were found in a depression called "the Fire Pit." According to California State archaeologists, several "mini-mammoths," baby elephants, or whatever they were, were roasted in a charcoal pit that radio-carbon tests indicate is 29,700 years old![235]

These "dwarf mammoths" were only six feet tall and were apparently feasted on by ancient men of large stature who had *double rows of teeth,* if the skeletons dug up at Lompoc Rancho across the channel are any indication.[52] It would seem that the mammoths and the giant men of 30,000 B.C. who feasted on them are all connected to a prehistoric era of not so long ago that is clearly evidenced in the nearby La Brea Tar Pits; a world of woolly rhinos, camels, mammoths, cave bears and sabertooth tigers. Included are giant armadillos as big as a truck named *glyptodons*, twenty-foot-tall ground sloths, and horses of every size and shape.

In more recent times, the islands were inhabited by the Gabrielino Indians as the Spanish missionaries called them. They called themselves the *Pimugnans*. The Friar Torquemada for the Vizcaino expedition of 1602 described the natives as warm, friendly people who were physically hardy.

The Channel Island Indians are believed to have been great traders. Archaeologists have found Catalina obsidian carvings in Indian sites as far away as Nevada and New Mexico. Many artifacts were removed from the island in the early 1900s, and are now exhibited at the Heye Foundation's Museum of the American Indian in New York.[235]

The islanders are said to have been fierce wizards by the mainland tribes. There were legends of a mysterious temple complex where the Indians from all the Channel Islands gathered once a year to worship *Chingichnich*, their Sun god.[235]

Their highly formalized and ritualized religion involved temples called *yuva'r*, sacred open-air enclosures with elaborate poles and banners decorated with feathers. An image of *Chingichnich* was placed in the *yuva'r* and only old men possessing great power could enter. Long and involved ceremonies were performed for every important event in life: birth, puberty, marriage, and death. Offerings of food and goods were presented not only to *Chingichnich*, but also to totems of the owl, raven, crow, and eagle.[235]

These ancient Sun Worshipers, similar to the Natchez Pyramid builders, the Toltecs, and the Incas, also used a jimson weed drink in some of their religious ceremonies. In ceremonies that involved initiations into manhood, a drink was made from the leaves and given to the young men following a three-day fast. Afterwards, they would dance until they passed out in stupor. Their dreams during this time were thought to be prophetic and held great significance for the rest of their lives. This ceremony is referred to as the "Toloache Cult." Old-timers described the *yerba santa* as having the power to induce a "gentle sleep," but it is found only rarely on the island today.

The islanders were decimated by disease and battles with marauding whalers which started in 1806. By 1832 the last few natives sought refuge at missions on the mainland. From this point on the islands were virtually deserted. Starting in 1846 the entire island of Catalina was sold to various individual owners and corporations, sometimes for as little as $1,000, and today the islands are popular vacation spots.

There is reason to believe that somewhere in the interior of Catalina Island are the remains of a temple complex, probably underground passages, and a huge gold treasure that was once associated with the Sun Temple. In fact, it was this gold treasure, openly housed at the Sun Temple, for which the early whalers were so eager to battle the islanders for.

In 1824, the Yankee brig *Danube* was wrecked on the rocks near San Pedro, along the southern California coast. Samuel Prentiss and other survivors of the wreck made their way to the nearby San Gabriel Mission. At the mission Prentiss met an old Catalina Island Indian named Turie who took a strong liking to Prentiss. The old man, in his seventies, was dying, and told Prentiss that he was a chieftain on Catalina and that there was a great treasure buried there. He sketched a crude map and told Prentiss that it was near or beneath a tree.

Prentiss returned to the wreck of the Danube, built a small vessel and attempted to reach Catalina. A storm hit him during the voyage and he was almost drowned. The map and everything he owned were lost. Still, for thirty years he continued to look for the treasure, now without the map.

He finally died in 1854, reputably the first European to expire on Catalina. However, he passed on his knowledge of the treasure to Santos Louis Bouchette, the son of one of the survivors of the ship wreck. Bouchette eventually found an ancient gold mine on the island with which he got instantly rich. With new-found wealth, he was able to acquire heavy outside financial backing. He married a flamboyant French dancehall girl, continued to look for the lost treasure of the Sun Temple, and built a mansion on the island.

Some say that he eventually found the treasure, though this is doubtful. He was last seen loading his personal sailing boat with silver ore and some provisions, and he was never seen again.

I stopped in San Francisco for a week or two, staying with relatives in the east Bay area. I looked up a number of old friends, including Peter, whom I had been with in Mexico City for a few days. Peter took me on drives around Marin County and the east Bay in search of weird rock walls.

He showed me an article from the San Francisco *Chronicle*, (Dec. 31, 1984) that discussed some of the strange and ancient walls found around San Francisco. According to the article, along the hills east San Francisco Bay are long stretches of walls constructed from closely-fitted basalt boulders. Some of these boulders weigh more than a ton. In some places, the walls reach five feet in height and three feet in width. They extend for miles along the hill crests from Berkeley to Milpitas and beyond.

The article quoted an archaeologist named Russell Swanson, who estimated that the walls, if strung together, would run for 20 miles. Much of the walls has been destroyed over time, but what remains is impressive. The searches of property records going back to the Gold Rush and the studies of Spanish mission records give no hints of who built the walls or why. Evidently they are centuries old, probably prehistoric.

The question that arises, of course, is who would want to build walls around the San Francisco Bay from ponderous boulders for miles along ridge crests? The walls are believed to stretch all the way to San José, with more mysterious walls being found in Marin County to the north of the bay.

Peter and I drove out to weird granite blocks that also appeared to be squared and cut, typically standing by themselves in some field north of San Francisco.

"Don't these rocks seem like they are man-made?" asked Peter as we stopped at one of the megaliths.

"I guess," I said. In some of the rocks, holes had been apparently drilled for some unknown purpose. Mooring stones are known to have such holes, but these stones were far from the ocean. It was a mystery.

Looking out over the bay with Peter one night, I wondered about the strange walls, weird rocks, roasted baby mammoths, and the strange carved heads of "Kalimu." Was it all just some strange fancy of the imagination, or were there really the remains of some ancient civilization in California that were being ignored by the traditional archaeologists? Perhaps the answer to the mysteries of the past in California was so astonishing that it was better to just ignore them.

As I headed north out of San Francisco, my quest for answers to the riddles of lost cities and ancient mysteries in North America now led me to that famous mystical mountain in northern California: Mount Shasta.

Mount Shasta has long been a source of mystery to those involved in studies of the paranormal. It has been called the North American Mecca for mystical phenomena. Stories about Mount Shasta range from ancient Masters who live inside the mountain to frequent UFO sightings.

While many of these tales are fantastic and perhaps far-fetched, others are based on real occurrences which defy explanation. Among the legends surrounding Mount Shasta is one which states that the mountain was a last refuge for a group of survivors of the cataclysm that sank the lost continent of the Pacific, called variously Mu or Lemuria.

Located on the northern extremity of the Sierra Nevada range, Mount Shasta is the cone of what scientists believe to be a dormant volcano. Today it extends to a height of 14,380 feet above sea level, though scientists believe that at one time the land in this region was actually higher and that Mount Shasta may well have been the highest mountain in California. To the east of the mountain is the Shasta Forest, the heart of which lies less than 30 miles from the base of the mountain. Most of the phenomena reported concerning the mountain have occurred in the area between the center of the forest and the base of the mountain.

Mount Shasta has always been regarded as a mysterious place, even by the local Siskiyou Indians that traditionally lived around the mountain. According to one Indian legend, Mount Shasta was made by the Great Spirit whose home lies inside the mountain. Even today the Indians will not ascend the mountain out of respect for the Great Spirit. Indian stories regarding the mountain add to its sense of uniqueness and mystery. The Indians have always believed that California was inhabited by a super-race whose colonies isolated themselves, preserving their strange culture intact and separate from others. One location occupied by this mysterious race of "invisible people" according to tradition has been Mount Shasta; one Wintun Indian, Grant Towendolly, recalls a story his father had told him in which he once heard the laughter of children coming from the mountain.[236]

Elements of the Indian legends lend credence to the belief that

California and Mount Shasta may have been part of an advanced and ancient civilization and that its legacy is a race of people who at one time (and perhaps still today?) occupied the area.

The very name of California is a mystery, the actual source of the name being unknown. In tracing the roots of the word, the California Historical Society has only been able to discover that it is first mentioned in a Spanish book *Las Sergas de Esplandián* by the conquistador García Ordóñez de Montalvo circa the year 1500. It has not been traced to either Indian or European sources.

According to Chaman Lal, a University of Bombay archaeologist and author of *Hindu America?*,[93] the name California comes from ancient Hindu and is named so because of the profusion of Kali Temples built by early Hindu explorers. Kali Temples have been found as far into the Pacific as Hawaii (see my book *Lost Cities of Ancient Lemuria & the Pacific*[59] for more information on Kali Temples throughout the Pacific).

Chaman Lal's whole thesis that ancient Hindu sailors and settlers are the basis for many current Native American tribes is one shared by Thor Heyerdahl, Barry Fell, the *Epigraphic Society*, and many other practicing archaeologists. Ancient Hindu exploration and trading well into the Pacific is evidenced by the existence of Bali and many other parts of Indonesia that are still Hindu in their culture and religion. The rest of Indonesia was forcibly converted to Islam by the Moslem expansion a thousand years ago.

The constant use of beetle nut and Indian Pepper Root (*Kava* in Fiji, *Sakau* in Pohnpei and Yap) throughout Micronesia shows the ancient Hindu influence into the western Pacific. Curiously, the strange and undeciphered Rongo Rongo writing at Easter Island has been shown to be similar to ancient Indus Valley writing of three thousand B.C.!

Biting into my turkey sandwich at a take-out stand along the highway, I looked out at the snow-covered mountain. It was clean and bright in the sun. It made me think of the indomitable human spirit and the adventurous determination of mankind. I too have this thirst for knowledge and adventure. I yearn to know what lies beyond the horizon, beyond the shore, over the mountain. Ancient man was no different, and his quest for precious metals and spices took him across oceans to new worlds even in the most ancient of times.

Mount Shasta twinkled in the sunlight, standing calm against the deep blue sky. Circular lenticular clouds looking like UFOs dotted the horizon. I took another bite of my turkey sandwich and looked around. Suddenly I noticed that the manager of the snack shop was from either India or Pakistan. I laughed. Maybe the ancient Indians had finally returned to "Hindu America"!

An interesting Native American legend in the Mount Shasta area states that before the advent of man, the earth was populated by a race of animal people. Because of his great wisdom and shrewdness, the Coyote was the leader of the animals. In the Indians' own version of the Great Flood legend, the Coyote is said to have angered the Evil Spirit. The Evil Spirit responded by making the waters rise until all the land was covered except for the top of Mount Shasta. On the summit of the mountain the animals sought refuge, and they remained there until the waters had receded. Then they returned to the valleys below and became progenitors to the species of today.[236]

The Rosicrucians (AMORC) also have a tradition regarding the ancient history of California and Mount Shasta through information derived from ancient manuscripts brought from China and Tibet. From this source much information has been gained concerning the connection between California and the lost Lemurian continent.

Harvey Spencer Lewis, writing under the pen name Wishar S. Cerve, published a book though his AMORC organization in San Jose, California entitled *Lemuria, The Lost Continent of the Pacific,*[229] which discusses the emigration of Lemurians to California. According to the ancient manuscripts allegedly in his possession, before the catastrophe the mountains in the northeastern part of Lemuria (now northern California) were higher than they presently are today, and were perhaps the highest mountains in the world. This made the Mount Shasta region an ideal place of refuge for those seeking to escape the great deluge which occurred with the supposed sinking of the continent. He says, "The fact that only a few thousands succeeded in reaching the mountains would indicate that the last great catastrophe of Lemuria was more or less sudden and decidedly complete in its submergence of the land."[229]

His records state that some of the people from that civilization had apparently anticipated the possibility of the catastrophe and had established a base of supplies in the mountains, in a technical anticipation to present-day Cheyenne Mountain outside Colorado Springs (a hollowed-out mountain with an Military command base inside). These they protected in well-built structures made of very hard stone and marble in "typically Lemurian fashion." Lewis (Cerve) claims these structures exist today in a state of only partial ruin, and are examples of the architecture of a people who lived millennia back in time.[229]

As I started up the ramp of Interstate 5 north of Sacramento heading north up to Red Bluff and Redding, I saw a young woman hitchhiking. She had a small backpack at her feet and was holding her thumb out in a bored sort of way. I stopped and asked her where she was going. She said she was going up to Eugene, Oregon.

"Can you give me a ride?" she asked hopefully.

"Well, I don't know if I'm going all the way to Eugene," I said. "But I can give you a ride part of the way at least. Hop in." She tossed her pack in the back of the pick-up, and we got underway. She was in her early twenties and was an American Indian. She was a Modoc Indian, had grown up on their reservation in Washington State, and had been living in San Francisco for awhile. Now she was off to see friends in Eugene and look for a job. I was happy to have a rider for a while. She leaned back, her long black hair draped on the seat.

"You're a Modoc Indian?" I asked her, a bit surprised.

"Yes, we live in southern Washington state, near to the Klamath Indian Reservation. Have you heard of it?"

"No, I haven't," I replied. "Have you ever heard of the Welsh Prince Madoc who supposedly sailed to America in the 12th century?"

"No, I haven't. Curious name, though. Prince Madoc, you say?" She looked out the window a bit distracted. She had taken a bus out of San Francisco, but didn't have enough money to get all the way to Eugene.

"Beautiful day, isn't it?" I said. "I've been watching Mount Shasta all day."

"It's a beautiful mountain, and mysterious as well," she said. We talked about Mount Shasta and the legends. I looked out the window at the mountain. Were there any ancient structures, like the rock walls of the Bay area on Mount Shasta?

One reported sighting, possibly a hoax, of what is said to be Lemurian architecture was made by Professor Edgar Lucin Larkin, Director of the Mount Lowe Observatory in Southern California. Larkin, who has been safely dead since 1924, was involved in a test of one of the new features of a long-distance, portable telescope used for auxiliary purposes in an unnamed California observatory high in the mountains near Mount Shasta in the early 1920s. Larkin found himself scanning the top of the California mountain range on which the observatory was located.

Sighting nearby mountains as a means to develop a scale for gauging the distances between the telescope and the objects viewed, he focused the mechanism upon Mount Shasta, an object whose snow-capped peak stood out clearly against the deep blue sky. He moved the telescope so that the sections viewed ranged from the peak of the mountain to its base. Referencing a map which accurately showed the distances between the base and peak of the mountain and his point of observation, Larkin began noting measurements.

In the middle of his study, Larkin was surprised to discover a glimmering curved surface located in the forest covering the side of the mountain. Although he had been aware of legends of mysterious lights on the mountain, he had never come across any evidence conclusive in his own mind regarding the mysteries of Mount Shasta. At first sight it appeared to him as though he were looking at the gold-tinted dome of some Oriental building. At twenty minute intervals, given that the sun's movement changed how the light hit the structure and therefore, what he was able to observe about it, Larkin made notes of what he saw through the telescope. All together, he saw two domes rising above the trees on Shasta and a part of a third one some several hundred feet distant from that spot. He also observed between the trees the corner of another structure apparently made of marble.

He waited for the sun to set to see if he could make any new observations given the change in lighting. He was surprised to find that as night fell, the dome became partly illuminated by great white lights which surrounded it. It made the dome observable in spite of the fact that there was no moon out that night.

He then waited for sunrise to make further observations. He made out the face of still another structure as well as puffs of smoke rising from between the trees. Before he was through, Larkin had spent an entire week studying the face of Mount Shasta.

His observations led to further investigations into the area. However, according to the Rosicrucian information, expeditions to this area have met with various obstacles. Reports of such attempts to do so have told of meetings with strangers who have physically picked up the explorers and turned them around setting them back on the trail from where they had come, or stranger yet, the presence of some mysterious force field which prevented people from proceeding beyond a certain point. Supposedly, vehicles would not operate within the bounds of a certain area near the mountain and strange-looking cattle had been seen emerging from that area only to turn around and run back to the mountain as if responding to some signal.[229]

While this is an amusing story, and one which should be seen with a certain amount of skepticism, it does illustrate the basic modern legends concerning Mount Shasta. In the appendix to *Lemuria— The Lost Continent of the Pacific*, [229] Spence (Cervé) says, "In regard to the story attributed to Professor Larkin, it has been argued that it would have been impossible for him to have seen any part of Mt. Shasta through a telescope from any mountain peak in California, unless he were within a few hundred miles of Mt. Shasta at the time. We do not know where Mr. Larkin was located when he made the discovery attributed to him, and therefore cannot argue that point. Mr. Larkin did publish, however, in his featured newspaper and syndicated articles various comments about this mysterious tribe which he believed he discovered accidentally. Even some time before this discovery, Mr. Larkin showed considerable interest in the study of the remnants of ancient Lemuria." This hardly settles the story, and if anything, it seems as if Larkin was so absorbed in the mystery of Lemuria, that he may well have made up the story, attempting to lend credence to his own beliefs.

One of the most famous incidents of a possible discovery of Lemurian architecture involved a man named J. C. Brown and occurred near the turn of the century. In 1904, Brown, who at the time was a prospector, claimed to have made an intriguing discovery somewhere in the Cascade mountain range (Mount Shasta is located in the Cascades). Brown had been hired by the Lord Cowdray Mining Company of England to prospect for gold in this area. While on his second trip to the region, Brown found a man-made tunnel carved into a solid rock wall. Apparently, a landslide had destroyed a wall which had hidden the tunnel.

He followed the tunnel until he came to a large man-made cavern. The room was lined with sheets of tempered copper. Strange shields hammered from gold were hung on the walls. In various niches within the cavern, Brown saw unusual artifacts and statues. In addition, strange drawings and undecipherable hieroglyphics were found in rooms lying off of the main cavern as well as the bones of people who had apparently belonged to some sort of giant race.

Brown did not immediately report his discovery of the treasure for fear that his employers would usurp the rights to it. Instead, he waited 30 years, until after his retirement. In 1934 he finally told his tale. In a short time, eighty people from Stockton California were ready to assist him in the rediscovery of the cavern.

On June 19, 1934 they set out on their journey into the Cascade mountains. The night before Brown was to have shown the party the entrance to the cavern, they camped out beside a stream. Some time during the night, he mysteriously disappeared. The disappearance was investigated by the Stockton police who were stymied by the incident. Apparently, Brown had not led them all there as a hoax for any attempted personal gain, for not a cent had been stolen from any person in the party. They theorized that Brown had been abducted, but by whom or for what reason, no one ever learned. He was never seen again.[230]

According to the Rosicrucians (AMORC), stories were quite common in northern California many years ago of strange-looking persons who would emerge from the forests from time to time. These people would run back into hiding if seen or discovered by anyone. Occasionally they might come into one of the smaller towns and trade for modern commodities using gold nuggets or dust as payment. They refused to accept change for the items they purchased leading some to theorize that the gold was not of value to them, nor did they really need money of any kind. Garbed in an unusual costume not recognized as being either American Indian or European, these people are described as being distinctive in features and complexion; tall, graceful, and agile, having the appearance of being quite old and exceedingly virile.

Perhaps a little more fantastic than this are the accounts of people being spotted unexpectedly on the highways dressed in pure white robes and sandals and disappearing into thin air at any attempt to approach them or photograph them. Spence (Cerve) claims that these people have been observed holding midnight ceremonies attended by four or five hundred figures. They would group around a fire having some unknown nature and origin. The light emanating from it was different in appearance from wood, oil or gas burning, being brilliantly white and bordering on almost a violet hue. Apparently, on nights when such lights could be observed from a distance, sounds of beautiful music, singing and chanting could be heard at towns nearby.

Two people who have claimed actual contact with "Mystery People of Mount Shasta" are Abraham Mansfield and a friend of his who related a story similar to Mansfield's own experiences. Mansfield claimed he was approached by a group of Indians who said that they were direct descendants of Lemurian colonists. He was led through a remote area near Mount Shasta to a sacred place which held an ancient Etruscian gold mine and a set of records which the Indians called the "Plates of Time" on which were written in strange characters, the ancient knowledge of the Lemurians. Supposedly the Indians were responsible for locating in each generation "Keepers" of the ancient Lemurian treasures. Mansfield had somehow become chosen for the task.

Mansfield wrote two small books detailing his experiences with the Indians and the history behind the mines entitled *The King of the Lemurians* and *The Young Chief and the Old Chief of the Secret Indian Mine.* His third book was entitled *The Golden Goddess of the Lemurians* (1970). All his books were privately printed by his group, The Lemuria Foundation, in Redding, California. In *The Golden Goddess of the Lemurians,* he relates the story of his friend's meeting with the Lemurians as it had been told to him. In 1931 on the northeast side of Mount Shasta, this man had gotten lost while searching for a deer he had wounded. He wandered around until he became totally exhausted and considerably frightened. He was approached by a stranger who was about seven feet tall and who introduced himself as a Lemurian. The man offered to take him to his cave lined with gold saying that he would die of cold if he stayed on the side of the mountain.

During his stay inside the mountain, which, according to the Lemurian, was about a mile beneath the surface, Mansfield's friend saw rooms lined with gold and furniture suggesting the presence of a society of people. He saw a network of gold-lined tunnels or "flues" in the mountain which the Lemurian said extended for miles and connected with other faraway places like underground highways. He didn't see any other people and the Lemurian said that everyone now lived deeper within the mountain. He was shown gardens which grew vegetables of an unusually large size. He was shown Etruscan jewelry just as Mansfield himself had claimed to have seen and was also told by the Lemurian about the Plates of Time.

The Lemurian told him that this was the location of the same Etruscan mines of which Mansfield supposedly became the keeper. The Lemurian claimed to belong to a race whose ancient civilization was highly advanced and had been hidden beneath the earth for a long time now.

Mansfield's friend was brought back to the surface after some recuperation time. Because there were so many similarities between Mansfield's claims and this man's experiences, he approached Mansfield and shared his story with him after becoming aware of Mansfield's work. Mansfield story is typical of the tales told about the mountain. Something may indeed be happening.

🐾🐾🐾

I looked in the rearview mirror of the truck that I was driving and then down at the speedometer. A highway patrolman with his lights flashing was behind me, and I had been speeding. It hardly seemed possible in the old truck, but it was true. I pulled over and got out of the truck.

I got about halfway to the patrol car behind me, when the officer told me to stop. "Hold it right there! Don't move!" he yelled, pulling out his pistol.

I stopped in my tracks, and the patrolman stepped out of his car pistol in his hand. "Was I speeding officer?" I asked innocently.

"That's right, son," said the officer. "Now reach into your wallet for your driver's license—real slow..."

I produced my license and stood next to the truck. The police officer relaxed and put his gun in his holster.

"Are the California highways so dangerous?" I asked him, never having had a police officer pull a gun on me before for a speeding ticket.

"You'd better believe it, son," he said. "Haven't you heard about the riots in Los Angeles? Thirty people dead. They're calling in the Marines to patrol the streets."

"Really?" I exclaimed. I hadn't been listening to the radio, so I had not heard the news. I then tried to argue my way out of the ticket. told him that I was an archaeological researcher on my way to Mount Shasta and wrote books about lost cities and ancien mysteries. "Please don't give me a ticket, officer," I begged.

He smiled as he wrote out the ticket. The hitchhiking Modoc Indian lass was sitting in the cab, and I chatted amiably with the officer on the highway.

"If you're interested in lost cities and ancient mysteries," he said "then you should stop in at the bookstores in Mount Shasta, they'l tell you all about those Lemurians."

"Lemurians?" I said in surprise. "How do you know abou Lemurians?"

"Everyone knows about Lemurians around here, son," he replied "Why, Mount Shasta is their secret home, or something like that. I've never seen one myself, but there's plenty of strange stuff that goes on around that mountain. Not scary or anything, just kind o inexplicable. Ask the folks in Mount Shasta or Weed, they can tel you all about it." With that he tore off his ticket and handed it to me "Next time, son, watch your speed." And with that he got back into his patrol car and drove off.

I was left standing there with the ticket in my hand. I looked at it To my surprise, it was only a warning. I breathed a sigh of relief. guess it was my lucky day.

An interesting documented case of a UFO sighting over Shasta occurred on October 12, 1956. David S. Williamson, a resident o Shasta, left his sister's cottage to walk home to his apartment. As he rounded the corner of the cottage, an unusually brilliant star just above the summit of the mountain peak attracted his attention. He wondered what star it could be as it shone brighter than any star or planet he had ever seen. Then it began to move. Williamson yelled to his sister to come outside and see the strange light. After a few moments, he retreated to the warmth of his apartment and continued his observation from there using a set of binoculars. With the magnified view he was able to observe that the light was actually being caused by a set of four lights arranged in a diamond shape and connected to one another by lines of light "something like a neon tube." Two nights later he observed the same group of lights just before 8 PM and in the presence of four other people. Seven nights later yet, at almost the same time he again observed lights in the sky, this time 14 lights in all grouped in two rows and having the appearance of "looking at a lighted room through windows." Over the next several minutes, he noticed that the formation of the lights in these rows changed a total of four times. A few minutes after this observation, Williamson saw a UFO descend from the sky, come below the top of the Shasta peak and hover there.[230]

Indians in the Shasta area report the existence of UFOs over the mountain. In 1930 shortly before his death, Chief Potentio, member of the old Cahuilla Tribe and 108 years old told of the silver ships that came and went from the highest point of the mountain. He said, "Sky ships come from the morning star," pointing to the planet Venus.

The *Rosicrucians* also report that "boats" exist which have flown out of the Shasta region high in the air over the hills of California as well as other nearby areas. They say such boats have been spotted at sea and as far north as the Aleutian Islands. The airships were unusual in that they made absolutely no sound, giving no indication of having been powered by a motor of any kind.

In the strange book, *A Dweller On Two Planets*,[127] originally published in 1899 (though written in 1886), there are several incidents which relate directly to the mysteries of Mount Shasta. One is the use of *vailxi* by Atlanteans, a submersible, cigar shaped airship. These airships are the Atlantean equivalent of an Indian-Rama empire *vimana*. At one point in the book, the author, in an Atlantean incarnation (named Zailm) goes from Atlantis to Rama in a vailx, and at one point stops at a "vimana port" and monastery on top of Grand Teton in Wyoming. The ruins of this ancient structure are said to be on Grand Teton today (see chapter 13).

In another part of the book, in a different incarnation in the early 1800s as a prospector named Walter Pierson, the author is in the vicinity of Mount Shasta and meets a strange oriental-looking person named Quong who instructs Pierson for some days, tames wild animals, tells him he has watched him for many years, gives him fatherly advice, and then takes him inside Mount Shasta by means of a secret tunnel. Quong shows him several rooms, cut into solid rock with gold bearing quartz crystals on the walls, and an oriental-looking carpet on the floor. After talking for awhile, Quong plays an odd pan flute as played in Peru or Greece, and then Pierson falls asleep.

The next day, Pierson meets with some other persons with Quong, including American Indians, Europeans, some "Hindu-looking" gentlemen, and an Egyptian. They tell him that Mount Shasta is the headquarters for their age-old brotherhood, which they call the Lothinian Brotherhood.

It is a strange book, and according to some sources, such as the *Lemurian Fellowship*, it is a mixture of fact and fiction. Perhaps, in an effort to sort out the "esoteric truth" about Mount Shasta, the Lemurian Fellowship of Ramona, California can help us. Founded in 1936, the Lemurian Fellowship, under the direction of Dr. Robert Stelle, claims to be the mundane school of the *Lemurian Brotherhood*, whose real name is the *Lothinian Brotherhood*, as Phylos claimed.

The *Lemurian Fellowship* further claimed that, as Phylos had said, Mount Shasta had been, indeed, the secret headquarters for the *Lemurian Brotherhood*, of which the Master Quong was the chief officer. With the use of left over Atlantean *vailxi* stored in the depths of the dormant crater, members of the *Brotherhood* could go anywhere they wanted, including any of the other secret *Brotherhood* retreats around the world.

According to the Lemurian Fellowship, the so-called Thirteenth School of "Mu" relocated somewhere on the Tibetan Plateau just prior to the pole shift and sinking of the Pacific continent about 24,000 years ago. It is this Thirteenth School of Lemuria that became the nucleus of what was later to be called *The Great White Brotherhood*. This site is allegedly in the Kun Lun Mountains of western Tibet, known in ancient Chinese tradition as the *Land of Kwan Yin*, or the *Land of Hsi Wang Mu* (see my book *Lost Cities of China, Central Asia & India*[16] for more information on this topic).

Later, after the devastating geographical changes had turned a small group of islands in the Atlantic into a small continent known as Poseid (Atlantis) and the cataclysmic uplifting of the South American continent had occurred, the first of the seven secret Brotherhoods was started by Quong in Mount Shasta. Six more Brotherhoods around the world were started in various places, each with an esoteric school where students could study. The head of each of the seven Brotherhoods supposedly meets in a council known as the *Council of Seven*.

Nestorian Christianity plays an interesting part in the story here, because the Archangel Melchizedek is said to be the eighth member of the Council of Seven, meeting with the Council at Mount Shasta or other places. According to the Nestorian Heresy, the Archangel Melchizedek was the Christ of Biblical prophesy and testimony, but Nestorian Theology was outlawed within the Holy Roman Empire in 431 A.D.

According to the *Lemurian Fellowship*, after the destructive war between Atlantis and the rest of the world circa 8,000 B.C., it was the Archangel Melchizedek's plan through the *Great White Brotherhood* to uplift mankind through the gradual rise of civilization. The plan, a "Divine Conspiracy" known as the "Great Plan" was embodied in the construction of the Great Pyramid of Egypt.

This plan includes the creation of a new Golden Age, "The Kingdom of God," the "New Jerusalem," the "New Renaissance," etc. in the years following a cataclysmic pole shift in the year 2000. This "Great Plan" was devised to coincide with a natural cataclysm, supposedly occurring on May 5, 2000. This date was chosen because of a planetary alignment which would have a gravitational effect similar to the "Jupiter Effect" combined with the increasingly lop-sided rotation of the earth due to the massive accumulation of ice at the south pole.

According to this theory, when the Earth's crust slips forward, rotating to equilibrium on the slippery inner core, Europe will be at the north pole, and North America will slide south. The geography of the planet will be radically changed.

Much of the Earth and the entrenched power structures of political and economic control will be destroyed. However, new countries and nations will rise, and a new Golden Age, based on Cosmic Law, cooperation and harmless living will arise on our planet. According to the Lemurian Fellowship and many other groups, this will be a literal Kingdom of God on earth, as Melchizedek had taught his students in the Lord's Prayer: "Thy Kingdom come, Thy will be done, on Earth, as it is in Heaven."

ॐॐॐ

It didn't sound like too bad an idea to me, I thought, as the shining white dome of Mount Shasta faded into the distance behind me. The world seemed pretty screwed up, and the powers that be weren't making it any better. With Los Angeles burning while the troops patrolled it behind me, pointing my truck into the forests of Canada seemed like a good idea.

In May 1936, *The Rosicrucian Digest,* a publication of AMORC and Harvey Spencer Lewis, announced that because of all the attention that Shasta was attracting, the Lemurians were abandoning their site on Shasta in favor of a more secret location. According to the *Digest,* a delegation of them had come to Lewis' office in San Jose where the Grand Lodge of the Rosicrucian order (AMORC, there are at least three Rosicrucian orders operating currently in the USA, AMORC is one of them) is located to tell him this and to ask that he not divulge their new location.

The *Lemurian Fellowship* claims that the "Lemurian Brotherhood" began moving their headquarters from Mount Shasta into a remote mountain area of the Yukon sometime in the late 1800s. Apparently, the members of the Brotherhood had their own airships, which they used during their move (Allied Van Lines not being sufficient) to their supposed new base of operations in the Yukon. In theory, many of the UFOs seen around Mt. Shasta are airships of the Lemuria Brotherhood, left over from those ancient days of yore.

The whole subject of Mount Shasta, particularly when combined with the Melchizedek lore, which goes back to the Old Testament, can come up with some pretty strange material, much of quite unbelievable. To add to the fantastic stories concerning Mount Shasta, are several people who are giving conferences around the U.S. claiming that they are from Telos, the city beneath Mount Shasta. At a bookstore at Mount Shasta I had picked up a flyer that was for a metaphysical workshop.

"Secrets of the Subterranean Cities," was the headline. It then went on to offer an "Advanced Melchizedek Workshop" with "Sharula," a "Melchizedek Priestess born 266 years ago in the Lemurian city of Telos, located beneath Mt. Shasta. One of only a handful of Subterraneans currently working on the surface, she shares her knowledge of the true history of Atlantis and Lemuria her personal experiences with the Confederation of Space Fleets and the mysteries of the Melchizedek temple teachings." "Sharula channels Adama, a 600-year-old Ascended Master, and High Priest of Telos."

Sharula further claimed that more than one million people lived in the subterranean city beneath Telos. She claimed that Telos was active in space duty with the Ashtar Command and also that "vector fields of energy called stargates have been opening and will continue to open around this planet..." Sharula also claims that part of her mission is bring technology from Telos to the surface of Earth for the benefit of mankind.

Well, Earth could probably use those technologies, but I wondered what the NORAD Defense Command at their hollowed-out Cheyenne Mountain in Colorado Springs would think of an underground city of a million people beneath California? Perhaps all those underground atomic bombs they have been testing in Nevada are part of their war on Telos, the Lemurian City.

It all seemed kind of silly when people like Sharula suddenly came on the scene, but like many before her, she seemed eager to help others and spread the word of the mysteries of Mount Shasta. Perhaps she had gone a bit too far, claiming that she was 266 years old and all that. No one had gone so far as to make a claim like that before. Sharula is most certainly a hoaxer, but at least she has done her homework and gotten the lingo right.

The claim of a large city beneath Mount Shasta is interesting in light of the fact that the Cascade Range of mountains, of which Mount Shasta is a part, is an active volcanic range. It has been predicted by many Native American Shamans, such as Sun Bear in Spokane, Washington, that the Cascade volcanos are going to all erupt. This could include Mount Shasta and nearby Mount Lassen.

With all that magma moving up from the earth's core, the million people in Sharula's underground city might have some enviromental problems. Maybe that's why she lives in Sante Fe, New Mexico.

With all of the modern activity going on around Mount Shasta, it made sense, as the Rosicrucians had claimed, that the secret Masters of Mount Shasta had moved their base to the Yukon where they exist with more peace and quiet, much like Superman in his Fortress of Solitude near the North Pole. Like the Masters of Mount Shasta, he had crystals for keeping information as well.

It seems quite possible that some sort of ancient, high tech place might have existed at Mount Shasta, though it seems doubtful that a million people, or even any number even remotely near that figure, ever lived inside the mountain. Generally, it is said that the few who maintain such ancient repositories as those that allegedly exist at Mount Shasta, Tibet and other places, do not make contact with the outside world or the unitiated.

As the sky turned to oranges and reds at the sunset, I wondered, were these tales of the *Masters of Mount Shasta* really true? Possibly, but then, there seemed to be a large smattering of fiction mixed in with the fact. Yet, were fragments of the story true? California was a place where anything could be true. This was not just a state of weird cults, flower children and martial law, with tales ancient mummified giants in zoot suits, roasted mammoth barbeques, and subterranean tunnel systems. What was really true? As Shakespeare had said, "There are more things in heaven and earth than dreamed of in your philosophy, Horatio."

Two photographs of the strange rock formations above Malibu, called Kalimu by the discoverer.

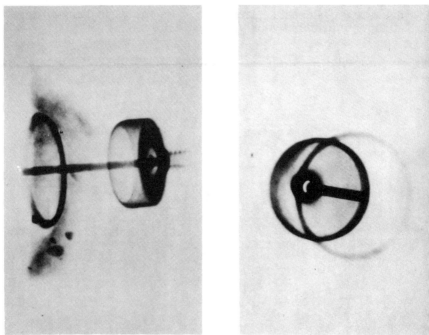

Above: The Coso Artifact, found inside a geode from the Coso Mountains California. Below: X-rays of the artifact.

Another old print of California, showing it as an entirely seperate land mass to the rest of North America.

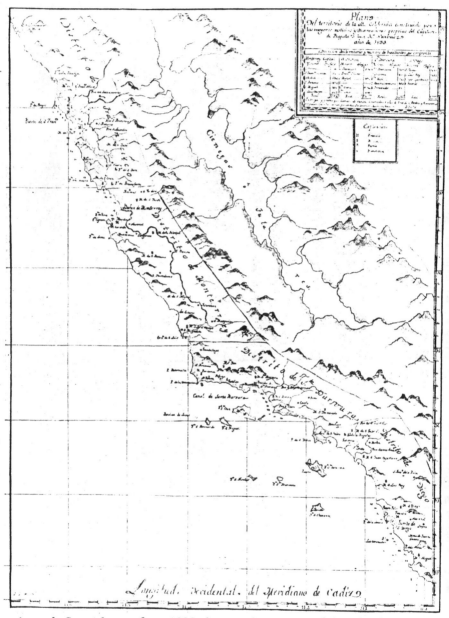

An early Spanish map from 1830 showing the remains of the inland sea
in California's central valley.

Essai d'une Carte que Mr Guillaume Delisle 1er Géographe du Roy et de l'Académie des Sciences avoit joint à son Mémoire presenté à la Cour en 1717 Sur la

MER DE L'OUEST   BAYE D'HUDSON

La gravure de l'Original n'est que d'un simple trait, et la Mer est lavée en couleur d'eau.

Assinipoils

CANADA

Sioux   Lac   Superieur
Pointe du St
Esprit   Nipissiriniens
Outaouacs

MER DE L'OUEST

Aouia
le Missouri   Hurons
Neu
tres

C. Blanc
C. Mendocin

Quivera   Panis
Rivre de l'ouest   Ilinois

CIBOLA
Nouveau
Mexique

Mississipi

Virginie

CALIFORNIE
Mer Vermeille
Choumans   L O U I S I A N E

Caroline

MER

DU

SUD   Floride
Embouchure
du Mississipi

GOLFE DU MEXIQUE

MEXIQUE

"Cette MER DE L'OUEST (disoit Mr Delisle dans un Mémoire imprimé en
1706. au sujet d'un Procès de contrefaction) est une de mes Découvertes. Mais
comme il n'est pas toujours à propos de publier ce que l'on sçait ou ce que l'on
croit sçavoir, je n'ai pas fait graver cette Mer de l'Ouest dans les ouvrages que j'ai
rendu publics, ne voulant pas que les Etrangers profitassent de cette Découverte,
quelle qu'elle pût être, avant que l'on eut reconnu dans ce Royaume si l'on en pour-
roit tirer quelque avantage. Mais je l'avois mis sur le Globe Manuscrit que j'eus
l'honneur de présenter (en 1697.) à M. le Chancelier Boucherat, et j'ai donné
(en 1700.) à M. le Comte de Pontchartrain les preuves de l'existence de cette Mer."

e French cartographer Philippe Buache's 1753 map showing a huge
and sea, Mer de l'Ouest with the city of Quivera on its shores.

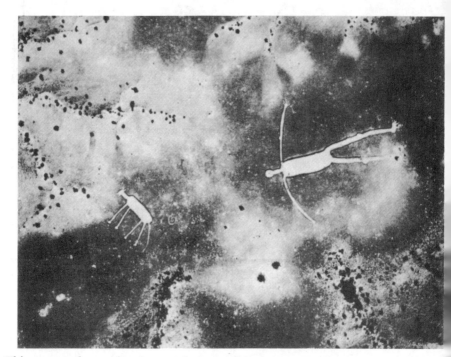

This page and opposite: An aerial photo of the giant-sized figures scraped onto t
desert floor near Blythe, California. Both figures are different, and the anim
near to each one seems to be a horse. A covering of "desert varnish" on roc
scraped aside to outline the figures suggests a date preceding that of the Span
conquistadors, who are said to have introduced the horse to North America.

Redwoods

Grand Teton

Mount Shasta

Great Salt Lake

Lovelock

The Golden Gates

Central Nevada Seas

The Central
California Sea

Malibu

Grand Can

Channel Islands

Cibola

Salton Sea

A hypothetical map of the former seas of Nevada, Utah and California.

Chapter 15

Western Canada & the Pacific Northwest:

Lost Cities of the Evergreens

When you have eliminated the impossible,
Then you have the solution, no matter
how improbable it may seem.
—Sherlock Holmes

We camped that night in the forests on the Oregon-California border. Mount Shasta was silhouetted in the twilight. Snow hung on the mountains tops and stood out against the darkening blue sky.

I gave Susan my sleeping bag, because she didn't have one. "I thought I could make it in one day to Eugene," she said.

I put some wood on the campfire. "It's a nice night. I don't think it should rain," I said. "I love camping out in the woods."

"I grew up in the woods," she said. "They are like home to me."

I lay down by the fire. There was so much to do. So many places to see. One never knew what new friends one would meet on the road. I put my head on Susan's lap, and zipped up my coat. In the sky the stars twinkled above the pine trees.

In southern Oregon, at the basin of the Klamath Falls, are a set of mysterious hieroglyphics of incredible antiquity which extend for hundreds of feet along a solid rock wall. No one has yet explained the origin of these symbols, whose uniformity suggest that they belong to a language of some sort. When American Indians were first discovered in this part of California and Oregon as well as the writings, the Indians disclaimed any knowledge of their origins or interpretation. Students of various forms of Indian writing say that the ancient writing is totally unlike anything any of the American Indian tribes have ever produced.

However, one amazing fact is that among the symbols to be found in this writing is the ancient mystic emblem of the Druidic lamp, used only by the Druids and found nowhere else among sacred and mystical symbolism until now.

Other surprising pieces of evidence connect this area to other civilizations of the world, yet how they became connected is not known. Part of the lake valley of the Klamath Falls region was known to the Modoc Indians who lived there as "Walla-Was-Skeeny." They said that this term meant "The Valley of Knowledge" yet these words were unlike any other words in their language or dialect. It was later found that the Indians had inherited this name from the descendants of the early tribes who were still living there when the Indians came. It was called the Valley of Knowledge because it was the seat of learning for some ancient tribes of people. "Walla-Was-Skeeny" was really an attempt to pronounce the Latin words, Vallis Scientia, meaning "valley of knowledge." The Modoc Indians had also inherited the word "wocus" which they use for Lilly, while in Latin the word for Lilly is "lotus." The Modoc Indians called the ruins of a walled-in preserve on the top of a mountain in Klamath County "moynia." In Latin, any walled in place is called "moenia." Some of the hills in the region are called "collil" and the Latin word for hills of this nature is "collis." Finally, there is a mountain point which the Indians claim has the name "Mu-Pi." Both of these symbols are letters of the Greek alphabet.

The fact that these words, along with the Druidic Lamp, are to be found in Northern California suggests only two possibilities. Either people had somehow managed to travel to this distant place to establish elements of their culture here or the similarities were due to the fact that the people inhabiting these various distant places had evolved from one common origin.

Bruce Walton in his anthology, *Mount Shasta, Home of the Ancients*,[230] says that a strange stone monolith at the outskirts of the Shasta forest was found bearing hieroglyphic writing as well as a corresponding English translation. It read "Ceremony of Adoration to Guatama." Guatama was a term which the ancients used to refer to the continent of North America.[230]

Walton says that the Mayans are descended from a colony of Lemurians who colonized Central America after the destruction of their homeland. "Notice that one of the major centers of Mayan civilization, Guatemala, takes its name from the term that the ancients used to refer to North America, 'Guatama.' This is also the name given to the Siddhartha, also known as Guatama Buddha, who is worshiped by millions of people in the Far East. Here again we have the influence of ancient Hindu explorers and the Buddhist missionaries that followed them."[230]

Says Walton, "One similarity existing between cultures spread throughout the world are the Central American god-men Kukulkan and Quetzalcoatl which also have their counterpart in Buddhistic and Chinese tradition. Other similarities include identities in ancient calendars, hieroglyphics, the art of tattooing, the mummification of bodies, pyramids, and the practice of flattening the heads of infants by binding."

Walton believes that a lost land, "Mu," is the solution to the similarities in the many diverse American cultures. While "Mu" may not be the solution to many American Indian practices, there is evidence in tribal myths for such a lost land. In Joseph H. Wherry's book, *Indian Masks and Myths of the West*,[238] he says that the many migration myths prevalent among the Indians of the Northwest and California "suggests an intriguing land somewhere in the Pacific Ocean where the 'first people' worshiped a high being named Mu." Two Indian tribes name the place where they came from as having been an island or continent, the name of which was Elam-Mu. One of these tribes, the Hokan-Siouan, begin the legend of their origin in this way:

"In the dim and distant past the forebears of many California Indians lived on an island somewhere in the Western Ocean. This island was Elam and they worshiped the powerful god named Mu.

"Bear Mother was the mother of fifty daughters and the head of the people and she had large fields on other nearby islands where crops were tilled. It was the habit of the daughters and the people to go in their canoes to the island where they tilled their crops during the day. Every evening they returned to their village on Elam where Bear Mother watched over the fires in all of the dwellings while her clan was working..."[238]

🐾🐾🐾

The next morning, Susan and I stopped to get some coffee and breakfast rolls at a gas station and get back on the road to Eugene.

We made a quick stop at an unusual tourist spot called the Oregon Vortex. I had just crossed the California-Oregon border when I started to notice the signs. "Can you believe your eyes?" asked one billboard along the road. I decided to check it out for myself.

The Oregon Vortex is in the Grants Pass area, at Gold Hill. The site is on a hillside overlooking Sardine Creek and near the abandoned working of the Gray Eagle Mine, where 30 million dollars in gold was dug in the late 1800s. Although this remote forest clearing was regarded as cursed by the Indians and avoided by them, the first recorded disturbances seem to have occurred around 1890, when the scales in the mine's assay office began to act up.

The shed was abandoned and then slid partway down the mountain in a storm to its present spot in the center of the "vortex." The vortex, now a tourist attraction, is said by the present owners to be spherical field of force, half above the ground with a diameter of exactly 165 feet four and one-half inches.

I paid so that Susan and I could go inside. The guided tour through the vortex started with a demonstration of strange phenomena within the ramshackle cabin. Perceptual distortions and optical illusions are part of this part of the tour, as the cabin is at angle on the hill, and balls appear to roll uphill.

There is some kind of gravitational anomaly going on here, for it can be demonstrated independently of the leaning shack that plum bobs hang at an angle toward the center of the circle, and their weights can more easily be pushed toward the center than toward the outer rim. Cigarette smoke or confetti thrown over the area can, on a calm day, demonstrate an eddy pattern, moving in spiral vortex pattern as if stirred by an invisible hand.

"Horseback riders have to beware when approaching the vortex," said our guide, "because their mounts often shy or spook when coming to the vortex. Birds avoid flying overhead and do not nest in adjacent trees."

I was most impressed when I was asked two men of equal height, one of them me, were asked. I was asked to be involved in a demonstration with another man of equal height. I stood inside the vortex, while the other man, stood a few feet away, but outside of the delineated vortex area.

"Who is taller?" asked our guide. Everyone responded that the man outside the vortex was taller, and that I was noticeably shorter. Both of us were standing next to yard-sticks that showed our height in inches.

"Now, the two of you switch places," said the guide. We did, and then everyone said that I was the taller one, and the other man, inside the vortex, had shrunk. Yet the yardsticks that we stood against showed that each of us were the same height.

"When a person steps inside the vortex, his molecular structure shrinks," said the guide. "The yardstick shrinks as well, so you are still six feet tall, according to the yardstick, though you have shrunk."

As at the Sedona Vortices in Arizona, I could feel a strange tingling sensation while in the vortex. It was all rather strange, and the Oregon Vortex is only one of many all over the world. At Santa Cruz, south of San Francisco is another similar vortex, now also a tourist attraction. Several artificial vortex tourist attractions have been created, utilizing optical illusions rather than a real vortex phenomena. One of these is located at Knott's Berry Farm in southern California.

Back at the Visitor's Center I bought a couple of books. "Thanks for the tour," I told the lady who had sold us our tickets. "It was all very interesting."

I turned to Susan, "I'm not shrunk anymore, am I?"

She laughed. "Maybe just your head is shrunk. The rest of you looks normal." With that, we all laughed.

❄❄❄

My Modoc Indian navigator, Susan, directed me to her friend's house in Eugene, where I was invited to a shower and a hot meal. After a day's rest, I continued my drive through the vast forest and wave-swept coast that is Oregon.

Oregon has quite a few odd-ball structures lying about. According to Jim Brandon in *Weird America*,[94] about two miles southwest of Galice, near to Grants Pass and the Oregon Vortex, is a group of ancient "beehive" stone structures of the kind conventionally dubbed as "kilns," whether for charcoal or limestone depending upon which expert one talks to. "The are others in Oregon south of Bend, near the Arnold Ice Cave. Some authorities believe that the Spanish built these; others aren't so sure. Similar structures exist near Florence, Arizona."

Throughout Oregon and Washington can be found enigmatic granite boulders, including stone circles, that are called by geologists "glacial erratics." Glacial erratics are stones that are unrelated to surrounding rocks and are said in traditional geology to have been rafted to their present positions around Washington and Oregon on icebergs far from their source up the Columbia River at a time when both the river and the various valleys around the Columbia River were flooded during the close of the last ice age.

Some glacial erratics are absolutely huge blocks of stone. In the Willamette Valley of Oregon there is the Belleview erratic, which once weighed about 160 tons, though it has been slowly chipped away at by tourists and now only weighs about 90 tons. One so-called glacial erratic near to Pendleton, Oregon, is a virtual circle of standing stones. It appears to be a genuine megalithic site, rather than ice-borne rocks.

In their book, *Cataclysms On the Columbia*,[240] the authors contend the various erratic rocks are the cause of awesome ice-age floods which swept across the face of eastern Washington, down the Columbia River Gorge and up the Willamette and Tualatin Valleys—catastrophically altering thousands of square miles of the Pacific Northwest.

The cause of this cataclysm was a huge lake backed up behind a glacial tongue over the present town of Missoula, Montana, to a depth of 4,000 feet. The ice dam was repeatedly breached by hundreds of cubic miles of backed-up ice melt waters. These waters swept across eastern Washington at speeds of up to 95 miles per hour, carving out hundreds of cubic miles of the deep loam soils and leaving in their wake the scarred land and deeply-cut valleys which are such a striking feature of the Washington badlands.

The waters converged in the Columbia Gorge, tearing and ripping it to the shape it is today, spilling over into the Willamette and Tualatin valleys, leaving such landmarks as Rocky Butte, the Tualatin badlands, Lake Oswego, and the erratic boulders strewn throughout the Valley. A similar flood-cataclysm may have carved out some of the lower portions of the Grand Canyon in Arizona.

The cause of such a cataclysm may have been a poleshift, a slippage of the earth's crust, causing the ice at the north pole to shift forward. Lake Missoula was a huge lake that covered much of western Montana and Idaho 10,000 years ago. To the north of the lake were the great ice-sheets of the "Ice Age." To the south of Lake Missoula was an ice-free area that teamed with huge animals, mammoths, rhinos, camels, ground sloths, huge prehistoric bison, horses, sabre-toothed cats, and man.

Who were these men? All legends in the world called these ancient men *giants*. Indeed, the prehistoric American was, by the contents of many mounds in the Midwest and caves in the West, a man of great stature. Tall enough to combat the gigantic species around him.

Giants are actually a pretty common topic in Oregon and Washington, because of the high incidence of encounters with giant hairy humanoids known generally as Sasquatch or Big Foot. These shy giants who live in the most remote parts of the Pacific Northwest are sometimes said to be ten or eleven feet tall. The reports of these giant creatures come from all over the world. They are thought be the survivors of Neanderthal man by some researchers. To others, they are the "missing link." These reports include photos of the giants themselves, casts of their footprints, and hundreds of stories and legends about encounters with them.

My last stop in the U.S. before I hit Canada on my trip up north was Seattle, a great city where my brother is currently living. I enjoyed staying at his house and relaxing, going on day trips around the Seattle area. One night with some friends at a country dinner, I was told by a university student that students from the University of Washington go out frequently to the Cobb Seamount, a flat-topped mountain 120 feet below the surface of the Pacific, just off-shore of the Washington coast.

"There is a sunken city on the Cobb Seamount where they have found pottery dated at 18,000 years before today," said Tom, the university student.

"That is amazing," I said, taking a sip of hot, herbal tea.

"Yea, back then the sea levels were different," Tom said. "There was an article all about it in the *Seattle Times* on Sept. 10, 1987. I remember that date. I always talk about this stuff. These people made mummies of porpoises and whales, kind of like the Egyptians used to mummify animals. They were some kind of maritime culture, like the Haida Indians of British Columbia. They supposedly mummified their dead."

Indeed, it is no secret that pottery and evidence of human habitation on Cobb Seamount has been found. This has been a star program of the University of Washington for years. It is amazing to think, though, that if there really is a lost city on Cobb Seamount, maybe this has something to do with the lost land of Elam-Mu, as talked about in the Modoc Indian legends.

There are ancient remains in Washington that may be related to the lost city on the Cobb Seamount. Near the southern tip of Puget Sound, just outside of Seattle, are hundreds of acres of strange mounds which have so far defied conventional explanation. Because the largest of these earthen mounds are found on the Mima Prairie they have earned the name "The Mima Mounds."

Scientists have proposed a number of explanations for the estimated 100,000 mounds scattered among the area:

1. The mounds were built by ancient men.
2. The mounds were made by giant fish during a period when the

prairie was under water during the last glaciation.
  3. The mounds are giant anthills.
  4. The mounds were made by gophers.
  5. The mounds were made by the freezing and thawing of mud as glaciers retreated, creating polygonal shapes which were eventually worn down into mounds by erosion.

From a good vantage point at the edge of one of the prairies, you can see thousands of mounds, all beautifully symmetrical, rising up from the ground like huge globes partially buried in the earth. There are as many as 10,000 in a square mile. The biggest ones are seven or eight feet high while the smaller mounds are barely discernible bumps. The mounds can be anywhere from six feet to seventy feet in diameter. The bigger the mounds, the more symmetrical they seem to be. Generally, the mounds in any one area are about the same height.
In 1841 the United States Exploring Expedition under the command of Commander Charles Wilkes excavated several of the mounds, believing them to be burial sites. However, not one single bone or artifact was found. Since then, hundreds of the mounds have been opened, but no bones or artifacts of any type have been found.
Curiously, the word Mima is from Chinook language and its meaning is related to death and burial. However, there is no known Indian legends to explain the mounds. The mounds are set close together, but there is apparently no pattern to their arrangement.
The same sort of pebbly gravel and black silt mixture that makes up the mounds also covers the prairies between the mounds. However, between the mounds, the mixture is only a few inches deep; in the mounds, it reaches from top to bottom. Boulders are scattered around some of the mound prairies.
Because a large number of big stones, some the size of a football, have been found inside the mounds, the theories that ants or gophers built the mounds has been discarded. The fish nest theory has never been accepted as credible, as it was part of the theory that a species of freshwater sucker had created the mounds. Subsequently, it has been pointed out that when the area was underwater, it would have been part of the Pacific Ocean, rather then freshwater lake.
The freezing and thawing theory of the mounds is hardly popular because critics argue that the climate after the glaciers retreated was much the same then as it is today, and no evidence of this bizarre freezing and thawing has ever been shown to create mounds as found on the Mima Prairie.
Therefore, we are left with the most probable explanation, the same one as early explorers came up with: that the mounds were created by men. Is the Mima Prairie the remains of some ancient lost city?
If so, what was the purpose of the mounds? Apparently they were not burial mounds, as has been shown. As I stood looking out at the

hundreds of mounds, I wondered where I had seen something like this before.

Two examples came to my mind. One was the ancient field of mounds on the Island of Bahrain in the Persian Gulf. This island is covered with thousands of similar mounds from a prehistoric time. They are universally acknowledged as having been made by man.

The other example of a society that built a large number of mounds is the ancient Maya of Central America. In the Petén jungles of Guatemala, literally thousands of mounds can be found scattered through the jungle. Most are still sitting in the jungle, unexcavated.

We know what the Mayan mounds were used for: they were the base for houses. Actually, the mounds were originally small pyramids used to elevate the wooden dwellings of the common people in the Mayan civilization. Over time the small earthen pyramids became weathered so that the original pyramid shape had been lost.

Could this also be the solution to the Mima Mounds? Were the once small earthen pyramids used to elevate homes? If that is the case, then they are so ancient that only the heavily eroded mound remain. Was the Mima Prairie than covered with thousands of small earthen pyramids 10,000 years ago? It seems like the best explanation.

This train of reasoning leads us to a startling conclusion, however one that incorporates one of the alternative explanations for the mounds, and that theory is that the mounds were once under water!

Apparently, the mounds were originally part of a city that must have included houses, artifacts, stone temples, streets and other normal aspects of city life. Then the civilization was destroyed and the area was under water. Erosion, both underwater and above water eventually weathered the pyramids, leaving some large mounds while nearly obliterating others.

When did the Mima Prairie rise up from the sea again? Perhaps only about six thousand years ago, or less. We might guess that the city had existed some ten thousand years ago, was then underwater for four thousand years, and then has been part of the wind- and rain-swept prairie for the past six thousand years.

As the sun was setting over Puget Sound, I started the old truck and headed north to Seattle. The lost city of the Mima Prairie faded away in my rearview mirror. What ancient stories did it hold that would never be told?

🐾🐾🐾

While at my brother's house one day, I was reading the newspaper and happened to come upon a curious article about the bizarre enigma of a multi-ton block of earth that had been picked up and placed 73 feet from the hole from which it came. In a mystery that is of both a technological and geological nature, in mid-October of 1984 on remote plateau in eastern Washington, scientists flocked to this gigantic, 10-by-7-by-2-foot chunk of earth that had been somehow bitten out of a wheatfield, rotated counterclockwise 20 degrees and then set down intact 73 feet away.

Whether this is a coincidence or not, the strange, literally inexplainable, occurrence happened on the 30,000-acre Colville Indian Reservation, though the exact site of the slice of earth removed from the ground was the Timm Brothers Ranch. Though there are really no explanations for this weird oddity, it is an unquestionable fact. Hundreds of scientists have examined the site, and it stands to this day: a hole in the ground and the gigantic plug of earth that once filled it, 73 feet away.

There have been a number of UFO reports in the vicinity, and the general belief is that some sort of UFO is responsible for lifting out a slice of Washington real estate. It is made even more interesting when one learns that the UFOs are allegedly coming from the nearby Air Force bases of McChord and Fairchild. This area of Washington state seems to be similar to the Dreamland Site of Area 51 outside of Las Vegas.

As I headed out of my brother's place one Seattle morning, I wondered about the weird Chinook Indians and the Flatheads of Montana, where I had gone to high school. The Chinooks and Flatheads practiced the curious custom of using boards that apply pressure on the soft skulls of very young children to force them to grow in an elongated shape. This was a practice in the Pacific Northwest that continued until the 1800s.

In this strange practice of head-shaping, some connection with the identical practice of the Mayas and certain ancient South American civilizations, as those around Nazca and Pisco, must be recognized. However, orthodox archaeology recognizes no connection between the Indians of the Pacific Northwest and Central and South America. Mayan nobility, as shown earlier in this book, shaped their heads in this same way. It is even more alarming to note that the ancient Egyptians also used this same bizarre technique.

❦❦❦

Crossing over the border into Canada was quite simple. I showed them my driver's license, and then proceeded on to Vancouver. Within an hour, I was knocking on the door of Norman and Shelly's apartment, two friends from my travels in the Pacific.

I slung my pack down in Norman's apartment while he scrounged up a beer out of his fridge.

"So, how's the search for lost cities and ancient mysteries going?" he asked.

I told him about some of my recent experiences, including my hunt for the red-haired mummies of Lovelock, my trip to "Kalimu" and Mount Shasta, and other adventures.

"Canada's got its lost cities, too," he said. "Here, look at this book." He tossed a book at me. The title was *A Death Feast At Gimlahamid*,[244] by Terry Glavin, a reporter for the Vancouver *Sun*.

"What's this book all about?" I asked, flipping through it.

"It's about a lost city somewhere up in central B.C." said Norman "The lost city of Dimlahamid. The Wet'suwet'en and Gitksan people claim that they have been living for tens of thousands of years along the Bulkley and Skeena Rivers. They say that their ancient capita was called Dimlahamid, a great city that spread for miles along the rivers. According to local traditions, the metropolis had to be abandoned after a series of wars and ecological upheavals. Yet, so far, no trace of the great city has been found."

"It sounds very interesting," I replied, taking a sip of beer and flipping through the book. It was largely about the contemporary legal problems of the Wet'suwet'en and Gitksan tribes and their struggle for their land in the Queen's courts of British Columbia Part of the strategy on the Indians' part was showing their great and extremely ancient heritage which centered around their once-great capital, Dimlahamid, now a lost city.

Says Glavin, "In 1898, at Hagwilget... Chief Johnny Muldoe was digging a posthole for his house when he found a hollow, clay-lined pit, at a depth of four or five feet, capped by a large stone. Under the stone he found 35 intricately carved stone batons, some of which showed traces of ochre. They were cylindrical, some almost two feet in length. They were sculpted to depict fish and birds, and evidently they were not meant for use as weapons of war.... he had been told an old story accounting for the stone batons in which a woman, one of the few survivors of a devastating attack on the nearby village of Gianmaax, had buried the weapons and insignia of her people in cache at about the site of Chief Muldoe's posthole. She was said to have died in a repeat attack, taking the location of the cache about the site of Chief Muldoe's posthole. She was said to have died in a repeat attack, taking the location of the cache with her to the grave. The story is noticeably similar to an origin saga of the Gitksan fireweed clan that takes place thousands of years ago at the advent of the time of Dimlahamid. In this account the woman' daughter marries the son of the Chief of the Sky, and she returns to earth with four children and with the crests the fireweed clan carr among its possessions to this day—the sun, the rainbow and the stars—and a magic stone baton, an earthquake charm. It is pointed at the enemy village, causing it to turn over, killing the inhabitant in revenge. The baton was lost, and sky people moved to Dimlahamid. As it turns out, all but three of the stone batons Chief Muldoe discovered that day in 1898 have also been lost."[244]

Glavin explains in his book the importance of red ochre to the natives, and there is an interesting conjecture as to whether the Wet'suwet'en and Gitksan clans are descendants of the so-called "Red-Paint People" of the entire arctic region, including Canada Scandinavia and Siberia.

The search for the lost city of Dimlahamid (also called Dzilke) very real, and continues to this day. Says Glavin, "As early as 191 anthropologist Edward Sapir had concluded that whatever Dimlahamid was, and wherever it was, it was clear that the cla system, so deeply rooted in the cultures of the North Pacific coast, originated in distinct, animal-named hunting bands that gathered at Dimlahamid, or Dzilke, or whatever it was, and later established themselves over hundreds of thousands of square-miles of coastal forests, mountains and river valleys. The extent and elaboration of the Gitksan 'myth' of Dimlahamid was recorded for the outside world as early as 1923, when a local amateur anthropologist, Constance Cox, learned of it from Kam Ya'en, a fireweed chief from Gitsegukla. Archeologist Harlin Smith searched for it in the 1920s, and so did the pioneer anthropologists Marius Barbeau and Diamond Jenness. They found no evidence of this metropolis on the Skeena, no evidence of any city on the Bulkley. The National Museum of Man sent a survey crew through the area in 1966 and no remains of any city were found. Through the 1970s, more researchers combed the hills and valley bottoms from Gitsegukla to Moricetown and came back empty."[244]

Like many ancient civilizations before them, Dimlahamid is destroyed in a great catastrophe. "The last great catastrophe, before the final snowfall, occurs in the saga of the Medeek, a ferocious spirit sometimes associated with the grizzly bear and sometimes with the mountain lion. It is a story of a great ecological upheaval that occurred in the vicinity of Dimlahamid about 3,500 years ago....Trees are uprooted and thrown skyward as some supernatural force makes its way down the creek towards the riverbank. The Medeek appears on the opposite shore, gazes out upon Dimlahamid and crosses the river. An epic battle ensues. River levels rise and fall, mountainsides crumble, and the battle continues along the Street of Chiefs. The Medeek destroys everything in his path, and is eventually driven back into the Skeena River."[244] The Medeek seems to be the personification of an earthquake, a huge earthquake that no doubt shook the entire western coast of Alaska, Canada and the Pacific Northwest. California may have been affected as well.

I had never been to Vancouver before, and I was quite impressed at the beauty and ethnic diversity of the city. I slept on the couch of their apartment, and in the mornings Shelly was off to her family's shoestore, which she managed.

One day, Norman took me to the University of British Columbia's Museum of Anthropology. It was a modern museum on the grounds of the university, and had exhibits from all over the world, although it was Canadian history that I was particularly interested in. There was a collection of old totem poles with deep relief carvings and a deep range of colors. According to the museum, most poles usually do not tell a story; rather, they display a variety of figures from the histories of the families who raised them. Ravens, bears, beavers, and frogs are often represented as clan or family insignias. Some poles once stood as part of house structures either in the interior or forming the entrance. Other freestanding carvings were raised in honor of deceased high-ranking officials.

As we walked through the museum, I commented to Norman that since most artifacts in British Columbia were made of wood, there being an incredible abundance of trees in the state, most artifacts would decay after a few years. In a civilization where houses, tools, ceremonial objects and just about everything was made of wood, there would be few truly ancient artifacts to examine.

Our guide through the museum was a young lady of Haida Indian ancestry. She was from the Queen Charlotte Islands, like all Haida, and was aware of their stories of maritime adventures. She told us of how at the famous potlatch ceremonies, where a chief would make lavish gifts to his guests, thereby indebting them to him, the greatest gift that they could give was a piece of copper armor plating. The Haidas' most prized possessions were the ancient breastplates of copper handed down through the centuries. At important potlatch feasts, they would break off a piece of copper from one of the breast plates and offer it to an important guest.

"Where did these copper plates come from?" I asked her.

She looked at me with her dark eyes. "I don't know where it came from," she said. "I guess they got it while trading. The Haida traded and raided all down the west coast of North America, you know."

Indeed, according to the textbooks, the Haida were the "greatest of the coast-dwellers, arrogant seafarers who lorded it in long raids to Vancouver Island or the mainland and who exulted in their mastery of island fortresses out in the Pacific in the center of the halibut fisheries. Their precise, fluent stone-carving in argillite challenges comparison today."[246]

"Since the Haida were such excellent seafarers, there must be many stories of their voyages," I said to the charming museum guide.

"Oh, yes," she assured me. "The Haida still talk about the yearly voyages that they made to Hawaii. They would go as a large fleet to Hawaii from the Queen Charlottes catching fish and whales. They would trade with the Hawaiians and return to their own villages."

I turned to Norman. "There's an interesting story. I don't most anthropologists would like to admit that there was contact between British Columbia and the Hawaiian Islands in ancient times."

"The Haida were like the Vikings of the West Coast," said Norman. "They had huge ocean-going ships like the Polynesians. They could have gone all over the planet. Maybe they did. Certainly Thor Heyerdahl, with all of his voyages trying to simulate ancient ocean migrations, would not be surprised."

In fact, in full Thor Heyerdahl enthusiasm, three non-Haida Canadians set sail on May 14, 1978 in a forty-foot dugout canoe, cut from cedar according to native instructions, set sail for Hawaii to prove that the Haida were indeed an ocean-going civilization similar to the Polynesians. They arrived 76 days later in Honolulu on July 28, proving, at least in theory, what the Haida had been saying all along: contact between Hawaii and British Columbia had been going on for hundreds, if not thousands of years.

There is plenty of evidence of ancient seafarers in British Columbia. In 1882 in the Cassier Mountains in the northwest part the province, miners uncovered a cache of coins which had their origin in Ancient China. An account of the discovery was written by

James Dean and published in the *American Naturalist*, 18:98-99, 1884, under the title "Chinese Coins in British Columbia": "In the summer of 1882 a miner found on DeFoe (Deorse?) creek, Casiar district, Br. Columbia, thirty Chinese coins in the auiferous sand, twenty-five feet below the surface. They appeared to have been strung, but on bringing them up the miner let them drop apart. The earth above and around them was as compact as any in the neighborhood. One of these I examined at the store of Chu Chong in Victoria. Neither in metal nor makings did it resemble the modern coins, but in its figures looked more like an Aztec calendar. So far as I can make out the markings, this is a Chinese chronological cycle of sixty years, invented by the Emperor Huungti, 2637 B.C., and circulated in this form to make his people remember it."[17,213]

John Colombo, the author of *Mysterious Canada*,[213] comments on the article about the Chinese coins, "The present whereabouts of the cache of coins is unknown. Coins were used by the ancient Chinese but not as early as the year 2637 B.C." Actually, what Colombo doesn't realize is that the date is obviously a typographical error. The story is referring to Emperor Chi-Huang-ti (Huungti in the article), the same emperor who built the Great Wall, had every book in China destroyed by royal command, and left an army of full-sized clay warriors in a pyramid near Xian, China. The period of his life was the Ch'in dynasty, which is typically dated as from 221 to 207 B.C. Therefore, the date of 263 B.C. for the "chronological cycle of sixty years" would be more correct. Emperor Chi-Huang-ti is also known to have sent a huge expedition of thousands of men and women in an armada of huge junks to the "Golden Land" in search of the "magic fungus of immortality." The expedition failed to return, and lacking the "magic fungus," the emperor died circa 207 B.C. One wonders if this expedition ended up in British Columbia.

Colombo goes on to mention another discovery of Chinese coins. The find was made in the Chilcotin River area in the days when the province was still a colony. The account titled "An Indian Antiquity," appeared in the *Niagara Herald* on July 25, 1801: "a piece of copper coin has lately been discovered in opening a spring in the village of Chillicothe, in the North Western territory. Impressions upon paper of both sides of this coin have been sent by John S. Willis, Esq., to a gentleman in Philadelphia. They appear to be Chinese characters. Upon presenting them to Mr. Peale, for his museum, he produced four pieces of copper coin procured at different times from China, which are exactly similar to the one found in the spring at Chillicothe, as far as a judgment can be formed from comparing them with the impressions of the latter upon paper.—The Chillicothe coin is now in possession of governor St. Clair."[213]

One day, while looking out over the ocean at Vancouver Island from Norman and Shelly's apartment, I though of the strange tunnel that was said to exist in the Jordon Meadows-Leechtown region, which is located in the vicinity of the Sooke River west of Victoria on Vancouver Island. According to *Mysterious Canada*, "The story goes that veteran prospector named Ed Mullard, working his way through the bush, was astonished to find carved rock stairs which led him down to an archway carved into the face of a bluff and down again into a subterranean cellar. The Mystery Tunnel continued farther down into the darkness, but Mullard had only matches with him for illumination and had to turn back. In later years he described the tunnel as neither a natural cave nor a mine, and tried to relocate it but never with success.

"Mullard died in May 1959, and on the Remembrance Day weekend the Victoria *Daily Colonist* sponsored an expedition in search of the Mystery Tunnel. Members of the expedition explored the most likely candidate, Survey Mountain, but found no rocky stairway. As noted by T.W. Paterson in *Mystery Tunnel of Leechtown* in *Canadian Treasure Trails* (1976), there are tales that the Mystery Tunnel was the work of Spanish explorers and conquistadors who before they withdrew from the West Coast in 1795 constructed a stronghold for their golden treasure, booty from the empire in Central and South America. Mullard maintained he had recovered a bar of Spanish gold from the site but never produced it."[213] There are tales in this same area of a Spanish cannon lost in Jordan Meadows; of a bronze tablet in the fork of a tree; of mystic symbols and ancient dates carved in tree trunks on the island's west coast; of a Spanish monastery and massacre at Sooke's Boneyard Lake, of a beautiful Madonna carved into stone beside the Leech River and of two ancient swords, one shaped like a cutlass, found near the Sooke Potholes which is also in the same area of Vancouver Island.

❦❦❦

I left Vancouver one morning, heading east into the interior of British Columbia, passing Chilliwack and heading north into the Kamloops. My goal was the Rocky Mountains and the National Parks of Jasper and Banff.

Canada was beautiful, but it was by no means a cheap holiday. Everything was quite a bit more expensive than I was used to paying in United States. Well, no matter, with a full tank of gas and some groceries to make a campfire meal with, I was happy. And with the many mysteries of western Canada and Alaska to contemplate, I was intellectually occupied for some time to come.

In the 1920s, the distinguished folklorist Marius Barbeau first noted the melodic resemblance between traditional funerary songs sung by Buddhists in Asia and those sung by Indians on the reserves along the banks of the Nass and Skeena Rivers in northern British Columbia. Barbeau noted that the tune scaled a high curve touched a top note, then dropped over wide intervals to the bottom where it droned leisurely. He reasoned that the songs came from "a common Asiatic source"—India, China, Japan, Mongolia—through Siberia, across the Bering Strait, and into Alaska and the northwest coast of Canada—the route taken by the Asian migrants themselves

In addition to their songs, they brought with them their clan structure, totemic system, and characteristic, one-sided drum.[213]

Barbeau, in 1927, also collected several "Monkey masks" used in feasts by the Niska and Tsimshian Indians of the same area. John Colombo in *Mysterious Canada*,[213] asks whether these masks might not represent Sasquatch or Big Foot? It is an interesting question, as there are no monkeys in British Columbia, or in the United States. If the masks are not meant to be Sasquatch, then what do they represent? If they are monkeys, where did the Indians of coastal British Columbia ever see these monkeys? Perhaps on a raiding trip into the jungles of Central America, although the closest monkeys to ocean-going natives of British Columbia would be found in Japan. Since modern "experts" do not concede that ancient North Americans ever traveled outside of the continent, nor concede that Sasquatch exist, they have a double problem with the origin of "Monkey Masks."

Another curious discovery was made in the Queen Charlotte Islands and reported by a Mr. F.W. True in *Science* (4:34, 1884): In August of 1883 a pair of tusks from a Babirussa, a type of wild boar that only lives on the Indonesian Island of Celebes and adjacent islands, was discovered in the grave of an old medicine-man near the northwest end of Graham Island. Therefore the question arises, How did the tusks of a rare Indonesian boar come into the possession of the Indian medicine-man? Mr. True suggests that the tusks were trade goods found on a wreck of a Japanese junk that had made its was across the Pacific to the Queen Charlotte Islands some time before the turn of the nineteenth century.[17]

It may well be that the Haida made trips to Indonesia, as well as Hawaii, or just as likely, that the Indonesians, great seafarers themselves, made the trips across the Pacific. The Polynesians and Micronesians, through whose territory one would pass on a ship between Indonesia to Hawaii and British Columbia, are said to have been the ancestors of the Polynesians, anyway. Despite the admonition of the conservative "experts" who claim that ancient man did not cross oceans in boats, it is an indisputable fact that the Polynesians colonized far-flung islands thousands of miles away from other land areas. While there seems to be no question to any scholars that this was done, the fact is conveniently forgotten when discussing other seafaring races.

One amusing suggestion concerning the Haida is that they are the descendants of Chinese Jews. John Colombo in *Mysterious Canada* quotes from Eric Downton's book, *Pacific Challenge: Canada's Future in the New Asia* (1986): "Perhaps the most fascinating speculation concerning early Asian migration to the territory now known as British Columbia is the possibility that Jews from China accidentally landed there at the close of the thirteenth century. The existence of a flourishing and influential Jewish community in China almost a thousand years ago is a confirmed fact. The late Father Jean Marie Le Jeune, who pioneered linguistic studies among the Indians of British Columbia, recorded that he found Hebraic words in native languages west of the Rockies, and that some Coast Indian ceremonial rites are strongly suggestive of Hebraic ceremonies and usages. To account for the possible appearance of Chinese Jews in North America, a theory has been developed about the unsuccessful attempt by the powerful Mongol ruler, Kublai Khan, to invade Japan from ports in China and Korea in A.D. 1281. A typhoon scattered the Mongols' armada. Speculation suggests that junks carrying a Jewish contingent in Kublai Khan's army were blown by the typhoon out across the Pacific to finally make landfall off the North American coast, perhaps in the area of the Queen Charlotte Islands.[213]

I camped for the night in the forest around Kamloops and continued east on Canadian Highway One to the Canadian Rockies. I entered the park from west side and was soon standing beside the magnificent Lake Louise with the majestic Rockies all around me. Snow-covered rocky pinnacles towered around me, and the deep blue air was crisp and clean.

According to certain esoteric groups such as the Theosophical Society, the Rosicrucians (AMORC) and the Lemurian Fellowship, a secret sanctuary, inside some rocky fortress, exists somewhere in the Canadian Rockies. Says John Colombo, "It is said that Madame H.P. Blavatsky claimed that hidden in the vastness of the Rocky Mountains lies a secret sanctuary where ancient adepts and sages live to this day, preserving the Secret Doctrine, and guiding the destiny of the planet."[213]

It has been said that this secret center is near Banff, though others, such as the Lemurian Fellowship, maintain that this secret headquarters is farther north in the Yukon. Essentially, the secret Brotherhood inside Mount Shasta, according to AMORC and the Lemurian Fellowship, moved to a new headquarters somewhere in the Canadian Rockies, starting in the late 1800s.

In 1937, the popular western writer Max Brand wrote a novelette that was largely based on just such a belief in a secret sanctuary cut into a steep granite mountain in a remote part of the Yukon or Alaska. Originally published in *Argosy* magazine, and reprinted as a book in 1980, the novel was entitled *The Smoking Land,* and it included such scenes as anti-gravity airships similar to the vimanas or vailxi of Mount Shasta that vanished into the secret recesses of an hollow mountain. Whether Brand (whose real name was Frederick Faust) had heard such tales from prospectors up north, or was somehow familiar with some of the Mount Shasta material, we have no way of knowing. His book, however, is certainly fiction.

Camped for the night at a campground outside of Banff, I made some soup over the campfire, and looked up at the stars. Alberta and the Canadian Rockies had their share of mysteries. For hundreds of years (no one knows how long) the Blackfoot and Cree Indians worshiped a meteorite in southern Alberta known as the Manitou Stone. According to tradition, in the distant past it came blazing out of the sky and crashed into the bank of Battle River, north of present-day Lacombe, Alberta. The shiny iron stone was a mass of metal that has the look of a profile of a man. The stone was kept in a special sanctuary on top of a hill until Methodist Missionaries seized the stone in 1866. Today it is in the Provincial Museum of Alberta in Edmonton where its weight is listed as 320 pounds. It is interesting to note here that the center of the Islamic faith is also a meteorite, the famous Black Stone in the Kaba at Mecca, in Saudi Arabia. How many other meteorites have been worshiped throughout history?

In southern Alberta is the Milk River, which begins in Montana and flows through the southeast corner of Alberta, and is the sole river in Canada to flow southward into the Gulf of Mexico. The river has cut an impressive canyon with steep walls and imposing sandstone columns, called *Hoodoos,* through Alberta's Dry Belt region. According to *Ancient Celtic America,*[204] Barry Fell and the Epigraphic Society believe that "inscriptions" on the Hoodoo rock columns, known as the Hoodoo Petroglyphs, are ancient Celtic Ogam writing. They claim that in 1855 James Doty, the first white visitor to the area to record seeing the petroglyphs, learned from the Indians that the rocks had been inscribed many years earlier by white men.

The petroglyphs were allegedly made by early Celtic explorers coming up the vast river system from the Mississippi. Barry Fell's reading of the inscriptions indicates that the ogam concerns divination: "Diseases. Times of flood. Omens of disaster. Death in Battle. Withering of corn cobs and prairie." Another inscription reads, "Birds bring good luck. Eastern quarter. Here is good luck. The secret writings interpret the auguries of the geese, from the gabble, its when, its whence, and its whither."[204]

Other ancient inscriptions on the Milk River include the Writing-on-Stone Provincial Park carvings south of Lethbridge. Here can be found all kinds of "writing" though no one may ever decipher these strange glyphs. Henriette Mertz in her book *Pale Ink,*[183] about two Chinese voyages to the Americas, mentions the Milk River inscriptions by name, and claims that they are Chinese glyphs made by one of the exploration parties. The book "Fu-Sang," traditionally said to have been written in 499 A.D. is said to mean "Fir Tree" when translated from Chinese. Asks Mertz, Did the ancient Chinese know British Columbia as the land of the fir tree?

The largest Medicine Wheel in North America is on a hill in the vicinity of Majorville, a small prairie community southeast of Calgary. Suzanne Zwarun, a Canadian Medicine Wheel researcher who believes that all Medicine Wheels are astronomically oriented, believes that the Majorville Medicine Wheel is 1,000 years older than Stonehenge in England. Zwarun said in the article, entitled "Medicine Wheels Decoded," published in the Canadian *Weekend Magazine* for July 25, 1977, that there was evidence that the Majorville Medicine Wheel was in continuous use from 2500 B.C. to perhaps 1500 A.D.

The wheel is formed of boulders and has 28 spokes radiating from the hub. There are small cairns outside the wheel marking important astronomical alignments, and the wheel itself is an impressive 30 feet in diameter. At the hub is a pile of boulders weighing some 50 tons.[204] Other Medicine Wheels are found in Pincher Creek and Ellis, Alberta. The Ellis site is now, curiously, on the Suffield Military Reserve and is off-limits to tourists. Many other Medicine Wheels are in the U.S.A., principally on the Great Plains. The Big Horn Medicine Wheel in Wyoming is particularly famous.

As John Ivimy points out in his book, *The Sphinx and the Megaliths*,[217] the farther north one's astronomical observatory goes, the more accurately one can predict solar eclipses. Ivimy puts forth the theory that Stonehenge was built by the Egyptians in order to have a high-latitude observatory. Similarly, the Majorville Medicine Wheel is located at a high latitude, in fact the same latitude as Stonehenge: 50° North. Ivimy would contend that this latitude was an ideal latitude for astronomical observatory, as would Gerald S. Hawkins of *Stonehenge Decoded*,[247] and *Beyond Stonehenge*.[248]

Since the Majorville Medicine Wheel, the largest so far discovered, wasn't found until 1960, it seems likely that other Medicine Wheels have yet to be found. Perhaps the largest Medicine Wheel is yet to be discovered.

❁❁❁

The next day I drove up to Jasper, crossing the Sunwapta Pass, to camp in the shadow of Mount Robson, the highest peak in the Canadian Rockies. The highest peak in Canada is Mount Logan at 19,520 in the St. Elias Range near Glacier Bay and the Alaskan border. Mount McKinley in Alaska is the highest peak in North America at 20,320 feet high.

I had always loved mountain climbing, and my early fascination with mountains is largely what got me traveling around the world in the first place.

As I looked up at the stars that night, I thought about my life. I thought about my own adventures around the world, leaving for the Far East and the Himalayas at 19, and then traveling through the Middle East and Africa for five years. My subsequent travels had taken me throughout the Pacific to South America, where I had had spent several years. Now I had returned to North America, where I had grown up, and found it not to be the country that I left behind, or even ever thought had existed. It was a country of legendary proportion; a country that was ancient, incredible, and as fascinating as any area of the world. Why was I surprised?

On January 7, 1811, the Canadian explorer and geographer David Thompson was in the vicinity of present-day Jasper when he came upon an extraordinary set of footprints. They were said to be the tracks of a mammoth in the January snow.

Says Thompson's journal as quoted in *Mysterious Canada*,[213] "Continuing our journey in the afternoon we came on the track of a large animal, the snow about six inches deep on the ice; I measured it; four large toes each of four inches in length to each a short claw;

the ball of the foot sunk three inches lower than the toes, the hinder part of the foot did no mark well, the length fourteen inches, by eight inches in breadth, walking from north to south, and having passed about six hours. We were in no humour to follow him: the Men and Indians would have it to be a young mammoth and I held it to be the track of a large old grizzled bear; yet the shortness of the nails, the ball of the foot, and its great size was not that of Bear, otherwise that of a very large old Bear, his claws worn away; this the Indians would not allow. Saw several tracks of Moose Deer."

Incredibly, Thompson, a well-known early explorer in Canada, actually saw a mammoth when he returned to the same area in October of that same year. His journal for October 5 read: "I now recur to what I have already noticed in the early part of last winter, when proceeding up the Athabasca River to cross the Mountains, in company with... men and four hunters. On one of the channels of the River we came to the track of a large animal, which measured fourteen inches in length by eight inches in breadth by a tape line. As the snow was about six inches in depth the track was well defined, and we could see it for a full one hundred yards from us, this animal was proceeding from north to south. We did not attempt to follow it, we had no time for it and the Hunters, eager as they are to follow and shoot every animal made no attempt to follow this beast, for what could the balls of our fowling guns do against such an animal? Report from old times had made the head branches of this River, and the Mountains in the vicinity, the abode of one, or more, very large animals, to which I never appeared to give credence; for these reports appeared to arise from that fondness for the marvellous so common to mankind; but the sight of the track of that large beast staggered me, and I often thought of it, yet never could bring myself to believe such an animal existed, but though it might be track of some monster bear."[213]

The thought of a few mammoths that had once roamed North America in huge numbers, somehow surviving the cataclysmic change that wiped them out, was a romantic image. The gigantic graveyards of mammoth and woolly rhino bones in Alaska, Canada and Siberia, were the very enigma that spawned the current theory of crustal slippage, or "pole shifts."

The famous 19th-century French naturalist George Cuvier, associated with the Museum of Natural History in Paris and widely acknowledged as the founder of vertebrate paleontology, once said, "Life on earth has often been disturbed by terrific events. Numberless living beings have been the victims of these catastrophes, such violent sweeps that entire races of living beings have been extinguished forever and have left no other memorial of their existence than some fragments which the naturalist can scarcely recognize."

Cuvier once described a disaster that had apparently occurred in far northern part of the Pacific Ocean in an area off Siberia today known as the Laptev Sea. The earliest scientific exploration of these areas in 1805 and 1806 surprisingly uncovered evidence of a cataclysm.

At a site on the Liahknov Islands, a deposit was discovered: a layer of broken trees 200 feet deep. It appeared that millions of trees had been wrenched out by the roots in one violent blow of nature. Encased in the mud beneath the splintered wood were found the broken and frozen bodies of millions of animals. Some belonged to extinct species, like the woolly mammoth, and some were of contemporary species, such as bison. Ivan Liahknov, discoverer of the islands, reported, "Such was the enormous quantity of mammoths' remains that it seemed that the island itself was actually composed of the bones and tusks."

Greed and avarice turned these paleontological finds for the most part into billiard balls and piano keys. Indeed, for a time, the area supplied half the world's ivory.

Scientists agreed that vegetable-eating creatures such as bison could not have existed in the polar climate present today on the Liahknov Islands. In the stomachs of frozen animals they found undigested food currently not grown anywhere in the area for hundreds of miles away. Fractured bones and other microscopic evidence pointed toward simultaneous death.

Cuvier surmised that at some time in the remote past, a huge wave had swept these creatures up from some distant spot and dragged them through the forest, tearing them apart and burying them.

What incredible geological event could create such massive destruction? Whatever it might have been, it is the event generally credited as being the cause of extinction of the woolly mammoths and other Ice Age mammals. Evidence of cataclysmic events in geology are responsible for the division of the science of geology into two opposing schools.

These two schools are known as Uniformitarianism and Catastrophism. Uniformitarianism, currently the prevailing school of thought, holds that earth changes are gradual in nature happening slowly over thousands if not millions of years. Nearly all dating of fossils and geological strata is done according to this theory. It is through this "theory" that the dates of so-many millions of years for this age and so-many million years for that age are arrived at.

While Uniformitarianists will admit that volcanoes occasionally erupt suddenly and earthquakes do happen, they maintain that the general workings of nature are gradual and easily observable. Mountain ranges inch their way up or down over millions of years, continents inch their way around the globe over millions of years and occasionally glaciers creep down from the poles and cause mass extinction. Most people will recognize this school as being in alignment with the geology that they were taught in high school or typically on television documentaries.

The other school, catastrophism, holds that major earth change can happen very suddenly, much like Cuvier's destructive wave. In a violent wrenching of the earth's crust or a sudden slamming of two continental plates, mountain ranges can be created in a few days oceans can spill out of their basins, large lakes can be created and continents can sink!

Though different from what is taught in schools today, this explanation of earth changes is more in line with ancient myths, legends, and traditions. One well-known example of this is the legend of a great flood. Interestingly, prevailing geological thought is slowly moving more in the direction of catastrophism. For instance, catastrophism fits perfectly into the presently accepted plate tectonic theory.

Why is there resistance to catastrophism in academic fields? There are several reasons. It is not a very pleasant thought that everything we hold as stable today could be destroyed overnight when Mother Earth has the hiccoughs! The very notion itself could send Wall Street into a spin. Furthermore, when our current scientific dogma was being formulated in the late 1800s, their chief enemy were the Christian Churches that used the *Bible* as history. Any evidence found scientifically that tended to give credence to such Biblical stories as a cataclysmic flood or that some ancient people were literal giants, was suppressed or denied. It was further decided that since the treatment and treaties with the various indigenous tribes by the conquering Europeans had been so abysmal, it was better to justify this by saying that the former inhabitants of the United States and Canada had been primitive stone-age hunters for the past 10,000 years.

🐾🐾🐾

If the Alaska and Canadian Arctic once had huge herds of woolly mammoths, rhinos, elk and other mammals roaming around it, can we suppose that there were ancient cities once among the fertile plains?

While most evidence of ancient habitation would probably have been obliterated by the weight of millions of tons of moving ice, and water in either a poleshift or the slow creep of glaciers, incredibly, some evidence of these cities survives! According to Rene Noorbergen there are extensive ruins of a sophisticated prehistoric culture that once existed in the Arctic region.

"At Ipiutak on Point Hope, northern Alaska, there are the ruins of a large settlement of 800 structures laid out in carefully planned blocks and avenues—a community large enough to have supported several thousand individuals. Unfortunately there are very few artifacts that can tell us anything about the Ipiutak settlement. What we do know is that the ancient settlement was far from being a simple hunting community. There are indication that these people had a knowledge of mathematics and astronomy comparable to that of the ancient Mayas. Archaeologists are astonished that a community the size of Ipiutak could have existed at all, for it is situated on the permafrost, far north of the Arctic Circle, where today small bands of Eskimo hunters scratch out a meager livelihood. Ipiutak could have supported so large and sophisticated a population only if the climate of Alaska was decidedly different from the present, and the only time when this region was considerably warmer was before and at the beginning of the last Ice Age.[92]

"Ipiutak was very probably settled by these people of the Arctic high civilization center who escaped the first onslaught of the polar glaciation but were overwhelmed as the freezing conditions advanced farther south. The Ipiutak cemetery reveals that the inhabitants were tall, blond individuals, similar to the Cro-Magnons of Europe.[92]

"Not long ago Russian archaeologists discovered the remains of a number of prehistoric settlements very similar to Ipiutak in the midst of the frozen taiga in northeastern Siberia. Here too, the climate is very hostile to all forms of life, yet the archaeologists found evidence of large Paleolithic, neolithic and even Bronze Age populations that appear to have lived simultaneously in the same area. In Yakutia, Paleolithic rock drawings have been discovered that are much like cave paintings of Magdalenian France and Spain. Between Yakutia and western Europe, the land and the prehistoric cultures it supported are completely devoid of evidence of any similar artistic development. The only possible link between Siberia and the European Cro-Magnon civilization is through the north, in the direction of a common homeland and origin in the Arctic. Historian Will Durant, in his *Story of Civilization,* made a statement which may contain more truth than previously realized: 'Immense volumes have been written to expound our knowledge, and conceal our ignorance, of primitive man....Primitive cultures were not necessarily the ancestors of our own; for all we know they may be the degenerate remnants of higher cultures that decayed when human leadership moved in the wake of the ice.' "[92]

It seems quite probable that the mystery of the Red Paint people who existed throughout Siberia and the American Arctic is related to the ancient cities of the north.

A carbon date of 30,000 B.C. was released by the University of Toronto in May of 1975 for the Old Crow archaeological site which is in the Arctic Circle 750 miles east of the Bering Sea. The site had been discovered in 1966 by two archaeologist, Peter Lord and C.R. Harrington. After nine years of work, a team of archaeologists from the University of Toronto headed by William Irving let it be known that they had carbon-dated bone implements, artifacts, scrappers and man-modified tools as from 25,000 to 30,000 years old. There were more than 120 sites over a 150-mile area around Old Crow. Some 20,000 specimens were taken from the site, and Irving "expressed the belief that the area, which is 750 miles east of the Bering Sea and was ice-free during the last glaciation 10,000 years ago."[213]

These people of Old Crow, living along the shore of an ocean, or a great wall of ice, or what? This amazing ice-free corridor down into the Great Plains, where glaciers are carving out Wisconsin and Illinois, but in the Yukon and Alaska, huge herds of mammoths, woolly rhinos, prehistoric moose, elk, camels, and other animals were all grazing in the luxuriant vegetation of the Arctic Circle. Baffin Island, now Arctic tundra, had a huge forest on it at the same time as glaciers were carving out Wisconsin. It all makes sense, doesn't it? However, it is difficult to see how a large ice cap from an ice age would leave a huge swathe of semi-tropical land extending into the unaccountably ice-free Arctic areas adjacent to the pole. Add to this the large population now said to be encamped on these shores over 10,000 years ago, and we now have a historical puzzle that would make any geologist, archaeologist or historian clench his teeth. Never mind, its all neatly glossed over and no one mentions it if they can help it.

When I counted my money the next morning, I realized that I had only a few dollars. Somehow, I thought that my money would hold out until I got to Alaska, but I only had enough money for about two more tanks of gas. I didn't have any credit cards. Should I turn back? Where was I going anyway?

Again, I asked myself, what was my search for? It was an America Lost and Found. Maybe a self, an identity that was lost and found. I had found an America wholly different from the one my school teachers had taught me. An America of awesome antiquity and high civilization. A civilization once wiped out in a great catastrophe. Was this same catastrophe going to happen again? According to modern Native American Shamans, it is about to occur in the very near future.

Which way would I point the old truck? I decided to toss a coin. I could get a job somewhere. Maybe I could pick apples back in Banff if I had to.

As I tossed the Canadian dollar coin into the air, I suddenly thought of the famous quotation from Herman Melville: "America has been settled by people of all nations. All nations may claim her for their own. We are not a narrow tribe of men...No, our blood is as the flood of the Amazon, made up of a thousand noble currents all pouring into one...We are not a Nation so much as a World."

GIANT
HUMAN
FOOT
PRINT

FOUND:
PULUXY
RIVER
BED
GLEN
ROSE
TEXAS

A Chinook Indian woman and child. Her own head has been elongated
the Maya and other cultures of Central America did. Her child is
cradle that will deform his head to appear the same as hers. Note
writing-like tatoos on her skin.

OREGON GEOLOGY
GLACIAL ERRATICS

THE ROCK VISIBLE ON THE HORIZON TO THE NORTH IS A FINE-GRAINED ROCK OF SEDIMENTARY ORIGIN, A GLACIAL ERRATIC WHICH WAS RAFTED BY AN ICEBERG FROM A SOURCE FAR UP THE COLUMBIA RIVER TO THIS LOCALITY AT A TIME WHEN BOTH THE RIVER AND THE WILLAMETTE VALLEY WERE FLOODED NEAR THE CLOSE OF THE ICE AGE. ERRATICS, OF WHICH THIS IS ONE OF THE LARGEST OF MANY FOUND IN THE WILLAMETTE VALLEY, ARE SO CALLED BECAUSE THEY WERE TRANSPORTED FROM THEIR ORIGINAL RESTING PLACE AND ARE UNRELATED TO ANY LOCAL ROCKS.

Roadside sign on Highway 18 describing the Belleview erratic, located on the crest of a ridge about 1500 feet to the north (Ore. Dept. of Transp. photo).

A circle of boulders, probably a megalithic stone circle, but called glacial erratics by geologists, near to Pendleton, Oregon.

Aerial photo of the Mima Mounds in Washington State.

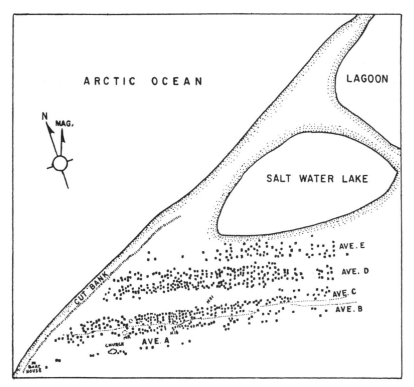

Plan of the buried Arctic city of Ipiutak, aproximately one mile long.

A mass of jumbled bones, ivory and wood from the cataclysmic tidal wave that destroyed the huge herds of mammoths, rhinos, and other animals that were grazing in the temperate plains of Alaska some 10,000 years or so ago. Photograph taken near Cripple Creek, Alaska.

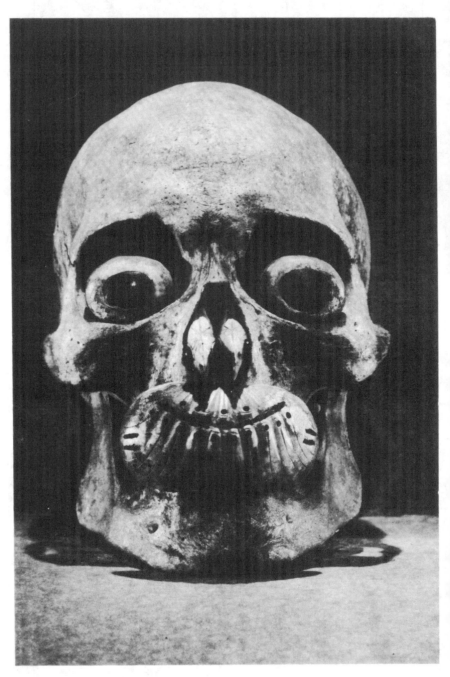

Skull with ivory eyes with inlaid pupils, ivory nose plugs and ivory mouth cover from the buried Arctic city of Ipiutak, northwest Alaska.

BIBLIOGRAPHY & FOOTNOTES

1. **History's Timeline**, Fay Franklin, 1981, Crescent Books, NYC.
2. **American Genesis**, Jeffrey Goodman, 1981, Summit Books, NYC.
3. **The First American**, C.W. Ceram, 1971, New American Library, NYC.
4. **Ancient Roman Shipwreck Found In Brazil**, Robert Marx, *Fate* , Sept. 1983.
5. **Voyagers to the New World**, Nigel Davies, 1979, William Morrow, NYC.
6. **Riddles in History**, Cyrus H. Gordon, 1974, Crown Publishers, NYC.
7. **6000 Years of Seafaring**, Orville L. Hope, 1983, Hope Press, Gastonia, NC.
8. **America BC**, Barry Fell, 1976, Demeter Press, NYC.
9. **Mysteries of Forgotten Worlds**, Charles Berlitz, 1972, Doubleday, NYC.
10. **Lost Worlds**, Robert Charroux, 1973, Collins, Glasgow, Great Britain.
11. **Chariots of the Gods**, Erich Von Daniken, 1969, Putnam, NYC.
12. **Pathways to the Gods**, Tony Morrison,1978, Granada Books, London.
13. **The View Over Atlantis**, John Mitchell, 1969, Ballantine Books, NYC.
14. **The Bridge to Infinity**, Bruce Cathie, 1983, Adventures Unlimited Press.
15. **Investigating the Unexplained,** Ivan T. Sanderson, 1972, Prentice-Hall, Englewood Cliffs, NJ.
16. **Lost Cities of China, Central Asia & India**, David Hatcher Childress, 1991, Adventures Unlimited Press, Stelle, Illinois.
17. **Ancient Man: A Handbook of Puzzling Artifacts**, William Corliss, 1978, Sourcebook Project, Glen Arm, MD.
18. **The Anti-Gravity Handbook**, ed. by D.H. Childress, 1985, AUP, Stelle, IL.
19. **Ice, The Ultimate Disaster**, R. Noone, 1982, Crown Publishers, NYC.
20. **It's Still A Mystery**, Lee Gebhart & Walter Wagner, 1970, SBS, NYC.
21. **The Incas**, Garcilaso de la Vega, (first published 1608), 1961, Orion Press, NYC.
22. **The Ancient Kingdoms of Mexico**, Nigel Davies, 1982, Penguin Books, Middlesex, England.
23. **Lost Cities of the Ancients–Uncovered!** , Warren Smith, 1976, ZebraBooks, NYC.
24. **He Walked the Americas**, L. Taylor Hansen, 1963, Amherst Press, Amherst, WI
25. **They Found Gold**, A. Hyatt Verrill, 1936, G.P. Putnam's Sons, New York.
26. **The Subterranean Kingdom**, Nigel Pennick, 1981, Turnstone Press, Wellingborough, Northamptonshire, UK.
27. **The Ancient Atlantic**, L. Taylor Hansen, 1969, Amherst Press, Amherst, WI.
28. **Legends of the Lost**, Peter Brookesmith, ed., 1984, Orbis, London.
29. **100 Tons of Gold**, David Chandler, 1978, Doubleday, Garden City, NY.
30. **In Search of Lost Civilizations**, Alan Landsburg, 1976, Bantam, NYC.
31. **The Maya World**, Elizabeth P. Benson, 1967, Thomas Crowell Co. NYC.
32. **The Maya**, Michael D. Coe, 1966, Praeger Publishers, New York.
33. **Secret of the Forest**, Wolfgang Cordan, 1963, Victor Gollancz Ltd. London.
34. **Fascinating Facts**, David Louis, 1977, Crown Publishers, New York.
35. **Cataclysms of the Earth**, Hugh A. Brown, 1967, Twayne Pubs., NYC.
36. **The Path of the Pole**, Charles Hapgood, 1970, Chilton, Philadelphia.
37. **Pole Shift**, John White, 1980, Doubleday, NYC.
38. **Strange Artifacts**, William Corliss, 1974, The Sourcebook Project, Glen Arm, MD.
39. **The World's Last Mysteries**, Reader's Digest, 1976, Reader's Digest Association, Inc., Pleasantville, NY.
40. **The Stones Of Atlantis**, David Zink, 1978, Prentice-Hall, Englewood Cliffs, NJ.
41. **The Lost Continent of Mu**, James Churchward, 1931, Ives Washburn, NY.
42. **The Children of Mu**, James Churchward, 1931, Ives Washburn, NY.
43. **Secret Cities of Old South America**, Harold Wilkins, 1952, Library Publications, Inc., NYC.
44. **A History of Mexican Archaeology**, Ignacio Bernal, 1980, Ignacio Bernal, Thames & Hudson Ltd., London.
45. **Strange Life**, Richard Corliss, 1976, Sourcebook Project, Glen Arm, MD.
46. **Alien Animals**, Janet Bord, 1981, Stackpole Books, Harrisburg, PA.
47. **The Mysterious Past**, Robert Charroux,1973, Robert Laffont, NYC.
48. **Living Wonders**, John Mitchell & Robert Rickard, 1982, Thames & Hudson, NYC.
49. **Enigmas**, Rupert Gould,1945, University Books, NYC.
50. **More "Things"**, Ivan T. Sanderson, 1969, Pyramid Books, NYC.
51. **Strange World**, Frank Edwards, 1964, Bantam Books, NYC.
52. **Stranger Than Science**, Frank Edwards, 1959, Bantam Books, NYC.
53. **On the Track of Unknown Animals**, Bernard Heuvelmans, 1958, MIT Press, Cambridge, MA.
54. **Maya**, Charles Gallenkamp, 1960, Frederick Muller Ltd. London.
55. **Nicaraguan Antiquities**, Carl Bovallius, 1886, Swedish Society of Anthropology & Geography, Stockholm.

56. **Nicaragua**; Its People, Scenery, Monuments, Resources, Condition, and Porposed Canal, E.G. Squire, 1860, Harper, NY.
57. **Lost Cities & Ancient Mysteries of South America**, David Hatcher Childress, 1987, AUP, Stelle, Illinois.
58. **Lost Cities & Ancient Mysteries of Africa & Arabia**, David Hatcher Childress, 1990, AUP, Stelle, Illinois.
59. **Lost Cities of Ancient Lemuria & the Pacific**, David Hatcher Childress, 1988, AUP, Stelle, Illinois.
60. **The Chronicle of Akakor**, Karl Brugger, 1977, Delacorte Press, NYC.
61. **Atlantis, The Lost Continent Revealed**, Charles Berlitz, 1984, Macmillan,London.
62. **Timeless Earth**, Peter Kolosimo, 1974, University Press Seacaucus, NJ.
63. **Mysteries of Time & Space**, Brad Steiger, 1974, Prentice Hall, Englewood Cliffs, NJ.
65. **Sacred Mysteries Among the Mayas & the Quiches**, Augustus LePlongeon, 1886, Kegan Paul (Agent), London & NY.
66. **Queen Moo & the Egyptian Sphinx**, Augustus LePlongeon, 1900, Kegan Paul (Agent), London & NY.
67. **The Mayan Factor**, José Argüelles, 1987, Bear & Co., Sante Fe.
68. **Time & Reality in the Thought of the Maya**, Miguel León-Portilla, 1988, University of Oklahoma Press, Norman,OK.
69. **Mysteries of the Ancient World**, National Geographic Society, 1979, Washington D.C.
70. **Atlas of Ancient Archaeology**, Jacquetta Hawkes,1974, McGraw Hill, NYC.
71. **Atlas of Ancient History**, Michael Grant, 1971, Macmillan, London.
72. **Antisuyo, The Search For the Lost Cities of the Amazon**, Gene Savoy, 1970, Simon and Shuster, NYC.
73. **Project X: The Search For Immortality**, Gene Savoy, 1981, Jamillian Unversity.
74. **Popul Vuh**, Translated by Dennis Tedlock, 1985, Simon & Schuster, NYC.
75. **The Ancient Maya**, Sylvanus Morley, 1946, Stanford University Press, Palo Alto, CA.
76. **In Quest of the White God**, Pierre Honoré, 1963, Hutchinson & Co. London.
77. **Maya Cities**, Paul Rivet, 1960, G.P. Putnam's & Sons, NYC.
78. **Central America; Archaeological Mundi**, Claude F. Baudez, 1970, Nagel Publishers, Geneva, Switzerlan
79. **Fair Gods & Stone Faces**, Constance Irwin, 1963, W.H. Allen, London.
80. **Megalithomania**, John Michell, 1982, Thames & Hudson, London.
81. **Legends of the Lost**, Peter Brookesmith, ed, 1984, Orbis Publishing, London.
82. **Quest For the Lost City**, Dana & Ginger Lamb, 1951, Santa Barbara Press, Santa Barbara, CA.
83. **Relación de las Cosas de Yucatan**, Friar Diego de Landa, 1579, (published as **Yucatan Before & After the Conquest**, 1937, The Maya Society, Baltimore, reissued 1978, Dover Publications, NYC).
84. **Incidents of Travel in Central America, Chiapas and Yucatan**, John L. Stevens, 1841, Harper & Bros. N (reprinted by Dover, 1969, NYC).
85. **Mexico**, Michael D. Coe, 1962, Thames & Hudson, London.
86. **Maya Explorer**, Victor Von Hagen, 1947, University of Oklahoma Press, Norman, OK.
87. **Mexican Cities of the Gods**, Hans Helfritz, 1968, Praeger Publishers, NYC.
88. **The Lost World of Quintana Roo**, Michel Peissel, 1963, E.P. Dutton Co. NYC.
89. **The Great Temple and the Aztec Gods**, Doris Heyden & L.F. Villaseñor, 1984, Editorial Minutiae Mexica Mexico City.
90. **Oaxaca: The Archaeological Record**, Marcus Winter, 1989, Editorial Minutiae Mexicana, Mexico City.
91. **The Oaxaca Valley**, 1973, Instituto Nacional de Antropología e Historia, Mexico City.
92. **Secrets of the Lost Races**, Rene Noorbergen, 1977, Barnes & Noble Publishers, NYC.
93. **Hindu America?**, Chaman Lal, 1960, Bharatiya Vidya Bhavan, Bombay.
94. **Before Columbus**, Cyrus Gordon, 1971, Crown Publishers, New York.
95. **The Rebirth of Pan**, Jim Brandon, 1983, Firebird Press, Dunlap, IL.
96. **Viking Explorers & the Columbus Fraud**, William Anderson, 1981, Valhalla Press, Chicago.
97. **Admiral of the Ocean Sea**, Samuel Eliot Morison, 1942, Little, Brown, NYC.
98. **Sails of Hope**, Simon Wiesenthal, 1973, Macmillan, NYC.
99. **Encyclopedia Brittanica**, 1973 edition, Volume 6.
100. **Universal Jewish Encyclopedia**, 1969 edition, Volume 3.
101. **Megalithic Man in America?**, George F. Carter, 1991, The Diffusion Issue, Stonehenge Viewpoint, Santa Barbara, California, USA.
102. **Arizona Cavalcade**, Edited by Joseph Miller, 1962, Hastings House Publishers, NYC.
103. **Nicaragua**, E.G. Squier, 1860, Harper, NYC.
104. **Aboriginal Monuments of the State of New York**, E.G. Squier, 1850, Smithsonian Institution, Washington D
105. **Ancient Monuments of the Mississippi Valley**, E.G. Squier & E.H. Davis, 1848, Bartlett & Welford, NYC (originally a Smithsonian Publication).
106. **Atlantic Crossings Before Columbus**, Frederick Pohl, 1961, Norton, NYC.
107. **They All Discovered America**, Boland, 1961, Doubleday, NYC.
108. **Vanished Cities**, Hermann & Georg Schreiber, 1957, Alfred Knopf, NYC.

109. **Calalus**, Cyclone Covey, 1975, Vantage Press, NYC.
110. **Mysterious America**, Loren Coleman, 1983, Faber & Faber, Boston.
111. **Hidden Worlds**, Van der Veer & Moerman, 1974, Souvenir Press, London,
112. **Arizona Cavalcade**, edited by J. Miller, 1962, Hastings House, NYC.
113. **Men Out of Asia**, Harold Gladwin, 1947, McGraw-Hill, NYC.
114. **Man's Rise To Civilization As Shown by the Indians of North America from Primeval Times to the Coming of the Industrial State,** Peter Farb, 1968, E.P. Dutton & Co., NYC.
115. **The Ancient Stones Speak**, Dr. David Zink, 1979, E.P. Dutton, NYC.
116. **Danger My Ally**, F.A. Mitchel-Hedges, 1954, Elek Books, London.
117. **The Crystal Skull**, Richard Garvin, 1973, Doubleday, NYC.
118. **The Atlas of Archaeology**, K. Branigan, consulting editor, 1982, St. Martin's Press, NYC.
119. **Nu Sun, Asian American Voyages 500 B.C.**, Gunnar Thompson, 1989, Pioneer Press, Fresno, California.
120. **Conquistadors Without Swords**, Leo Deuel, 1967, St. Martin's Press, NY.
121. **Nicaraguan Antiquity**, Carl Bovallius, 1886, Swedish Society of Anthropology & Geography, Stockholm.
122. **A Forest of Kings**, Linda Schele & David Freidel, 1990, Morrow & Co. NYC.
123. **Extraterrestrial Intervention: The Evidence**, Jacques Bergier, 1974, Henry Regnery, Chicago.
124. **In Witch-Bound Africa**, Frank H. Mellard, 1923, Lippencott, Philadelphia.
125. **Searching For Hidden Animals**, Roy Mackal, 1980, Doubleday, Garden City, NY.
126. **Dig Here**, Thomas Penfield, 1962, Treasure Chest Publications, Tucson.
127. **A Dweller On Two Planets**, Frederick Spencer Oliver, 1884, Borden Publishing, Alhambra, California.
128. **The Lost Reams**, Zechariah Sitchin, 1990, Avon Books, NYC.
129. **World Explorer**, Vol. 1, No. 2, 1992, World Explorers Club, Kempton, IL.
130. **Mystery of the Crystal Skulls Revealed**, Bowen, Nocerino & Shapiro, 1988, J & S Aquarian Networking, Pacifica, California.
131. **Warlords & Maizemen**, A guide to the Maya Sites of Belize, Edited by Byron Foster, 1989, Cubola Productions, Belize.
132. **Mystery Cities**, Thomas Gann, 1925, Duckworth, London.
133. **Secrets of Mayan Science/Religion**, Hunbatz Men, 1990, Bear & Co. Sante Fe, New Mexico.
134. **A Guide to Ancient Maya Ruins**, Bruce Hunter, 1986, University of Oklahoma Press, Norman, Oklahoma
135. **Cobá, a Classic Maya Metropolis**, Folan, Kintz & Fletcher, 1983, NY
136. **Facts & Artifacts of Ancient Middle America**, Curt Muser, 1978, E.P. Dutton, NYC.
137. **Preliminary Catalogue of the Comalcalco Bricks**, Neil Steede, 1984, Centro de Investigacion Precolombina, Tabasco, Mexico.
138. **Vimana Aircraft of Ancient India & Atlantis**, Childress, Sanderson, Josyer, 1991, AUP, Kempton, Illinois.
139. **Incidents of Travel in Yucatan**, John L. Stevens, 1843, Harper & Bros. NY.
140. **Mysteries of Ancient South America**, Harold Wilkins, 1946, Citadel, NY.
141. **Mysteries of the Mexican Pyramids**, Peter Tompkins, 1976, Harper & Row, NYC.
142. **The Unexplained**, William Corliss, 1976, Bantam Books, New York.
143. **Cortés and Montezuma**, Maurice Collis, 1954, Harcourt Brace Jovanovich, New York.
144. **The Maldive Mystery**, Thor Heyerdahl, 1986, Adler-Adler, Bethesda, MD.
145. **Mu Revealled**, Tony Earll, 1970, Paperback Library, New York.
146. **Quetzalcoatl**, Joes Lopez Portillo, 1965 (English Translation ©1977), James Clark & Co., Cambridge, UK.
147. **The Cities of Ancient Mexico**, Jeremy Sabloff, 1989, Thames & Hudson, New York.
148. **Conquest of Mexico**, William Prescott, 1843, London & New York.
149. **The Conquest of New Spain**, Bernal Díaz, (1492-1580), 1963, Penguin Books, London.
150. **African Presence in Early America**, Ivan Van Sertima, 1987, Rutgers State University, New Brunswick, NJ.
151. **The Lost Realms**, Zecharia Sitchin, 1990, Avon Books, New York.
152. **The 12th Planet**, Zecharia Sitchin, 1976, Avon Books, New York.
153. **Zone of Silence**, Gerry Hunt, 1986, Avon Books, New York.
154. **Mystery In Acambaro**, Charles Hapgood, 1973, New Hampshire.
155. **Host With The Big Hat**, Erle Stanely Gardner, 1969, William Morrow & Company, NYC.
156. **Unknown Mexico**, Carl Lumholtz, 1902, Charles Scribner's Sons, NYC.
157. **The Natural and Aboriginal History of Tennessee**, John Haywood, 1959, McCowat-Mercer, Jackson, TN.
159. **The Mothman Prophesies**, John Keel, 1975, Signet, New York.
160. **America's Ancient Treasures**, Franklin & Mary Folsom, 1971, University of New Mexico Press, Albuquerque.
161. **The Lost Cities of Cibola**, Richard Petersen, 1985, G & H Books, Phoenix.
162. **The Hohokam**, Edited by David Noble, 1991, School of the American Research Press, Sante Fe, NM
163. **Psychic Archaeology**, Jeffrey Goodman, 1977, Berkley Books, NYC.
164. **Sedona, Power Spot Vortex**, Richard Dannelley, 1989, The Vortex Society, Sedona, Arizona.

579

165. **Explorations In Grand Canyon**, *Arizona Gazette,* April 5, 1909, Phoenix, Arizona.
166. **The Ancient Sun Kingdoms of the Americas**, Victor von Hagen, 1957, World Publishing Co. Cleveland, OH.
167. **Mexico Mystique**, Frank Waters, 1975, Swallow Press, Chicago.
168. **Explorations of the Aboriginal Remains of Tennessee**, Joseph Jones, 1880, Smithsonian Institution, Washington, D.C.
169. **Madoc & the Discovery of America**, Richard Deacon, 1966, George Braziller Co. New York.
170. **Brave His Soul**, Ellen Pugh, 1970, Dodd, Mead & Co., New York.
171. **Curious Encounters**, Loren Coleman, 1985, Faber & Faber, Boston.
172. **Thunderbirds! The Living Legend of Giant Birds**, Mark A. Hall, 1988, Hall Publications & Research, Bloomington, Minnesota.
173. **Natural Mysteries**, Mark A. Hall, 1989, Hall Publications & Research, Bloomington, Minnesota.
174. **World of Strange Phenomena**, Charles Berlitz, 1988, Fawcett, NYC.
175. **The Ancient Aztalan Story**, Helen Schultz, Ed., 1969, Aztalan Historical Society, Lake Mills, Wisconsin.
176. **The Lost Pyramids of Rock Lake**, Frank Joseph, FATE, Oct. 1989.
177. **The Dene and Na-Dene Indian Migration 1233 A.D.**, Ethel G. Stewart, 1991, ISAC Press, Columbus, Georgia.
178. **The Smithsonian Book of North American Indians**, Philip Kopper, 1986, Smithsonian Books, Washington.
179. **Metallurgical Characteristics of North American Prehistoric Copper Work**, David Schroeder and Katharine Ruhl, American Antiquity, Vol. 33, No.2, 1967.
180. **New York Times**, March 17, 1992.
181. **The Secret: America In World History Before Columbus**, Joseph Mahan, 1983, ISAC Press, Columbus, Georgia.
182. **Man: 12,000 Years Under the Sea**, Robert F. Burgess, 1980, Dodd, Mead & Company, New York.
183. **Pale Ink**, Henriette Mertz, 1953 (1972, revised, 2nd edition), Swallow Press, Chicago.
184. **Atlantis, Dwelling Place of the Gods**, Henriette Mertz, 1976, Swallow Press, Chicago.
185. **The Wine Dark Sea**, Henriette Mertz, 1964, Swallow Press, Chicago.
186. **The Mystic Symbol**, Henriette Mertz, 1986, Global Books, Chicago.
187. **Bronze Age America**, Barry Fell, 1982, Little, Brown & Co., Boston.
188. **Ancient America**, John Baldwin, 1872, Harper & Brothers, New York.
189. **Archaeology and the Book of Mormon**, Milton Huntcr, 1956, Deseret Book Company, Salt Lake City.
190. **Book of Mormon Evidences in Ancient America**, Dewey Farnsworth, 1967, Deseret Book Company, Salt Lake City.
191. **The Berumuda Triangle Mystery—Solved**, Lawrence Kusche, 1975, Warner Books, New York.
192. **Atlantis, The Eighth Continent**, Charles Berlitz, 1984, G.P. Putnam's Sons, New York.
193. **World of the Odd & Awesome**, Charles Berlitz, 1991, Fawcett, NYC.
194. **No Longer On the Map**, Raymond H. Ramsay, 1972, Viking Press, NYC.
195. **Legendary Islands of the Atlantic**, William Babcock, 1922, New York.
196. **Across the Ocean Sea**, George Sanderlin, 1966, Harper & Row, NYC.
197. **Guide to Puerto Rico & the Virgin Islands**, Harry Pariser, 1986, Moon Publications, Chico, California.
198. **The Romantic History of St. Croix**, Florence Lewisohn, 1964, St. Croix Landmarks Society, Christiansted.
199. **The Bermuda Triangle**, Charles Berlitz, 1974, Doubleday, New York.
200. **Atlantis: The Autobiography of a Search**, Robert Ferro & Michael Grumley, 1970, Doubleday & Co. Garden City, New York.
201. **They All Discovered America**, Charles Boland, 1961, Doubleday, Garden City, New York.
202. **Saga America**, Barry Fell, 1980, New York Times Books, New York.
203. **The Search For Lost America**, Salvatore Trento, 1978, Contemporary Books, Chicago.
204. **Ancient Celtic America**, William McGlone & Phillip Leonard,1986, Panorama West Books, Fresno, CA.
205. **Ogam Consaine & Tifinag Alphabets**, Warren Dexter, 1984, Academy Books, Rutland, Vermont.
206. **The Norse Discovery of America**, Paul Chapman, 1981, One Candle Press, Atlanta, Georgia.
207. **Frauds, Myths, and Mysteries: Science & Pseudoscience in Archaeology**, Kenneth Feder, 1990, Mayfield Publishing Co., Mountain View, California.
208. **Fantastic Archaeology: The Wild Side of North American Prehistory**, Stephen Williams, 1991, University of Pennsylvania Press, Philadelphia.
209. **Men of the Earth**, Brian Fagan, 1974, Little, Brown & Co. Boston.
210. **Elusive Treasure**, Brian Fagan, 1977, Charles Scribner's Sons, New York.
211. **America In 1492**, Alvin Josephy, Jr., Ed., 1991, Alfred Knopf, New York.
212. **Exploration In America Before Columbus**, Hjalmar Holand, 1956, Twayne Publishers, New York.
213. **Mysterious Canada**, John Robert Colombo, 1988, Doubleday, Toronto.
214. **The Dictionary of Imaginary Places**, Alberto Manguel & Gianni Guadalupi, 1980, Macmillan Publishing Co., New York.
215. **Lost America**, Arlington Mallery, 1951, Overlook Co., Washington, D.C.
216. **Historical Sketch of the Spiro Mound**, Forrest Clements, 1945, Museum of the American Indian, Heye

Foundation, Volume XIV, New York.

217. **The Sphinx and the Megaliths**, John Ivimy, 1974, Abacus, London.
218. **Joseph Smith, The First Mormon**, Donna Hill, 1977, Doubleday & Co., Garden City, New York.
219. **Buffalo Bill** (Autobiography), William Cody, 1879, Frank Bliss Co., Hartford, Connecticut, reprinted 1978, University of Nebraska Press.
220. **The Lovelock Cave**, Llewellyn Loud & Mark Harrington, 1929, University of California Press, Berkeley.
221. **Lovelock Cave**, Nevada Historical Review, Vol. 1, No. 4, Spring 1974, Sparks, Nevada.
222. **Early Nevada History Is Traced in Lovelock Cave**, Humbolt Star, May 13, 1929. From the U. of California Dept. of Anthropology report, 1929.
223. **Nevada's Cannibal Problem**, Pioneer Nevada, Vol. 1, 1951, Reno, Nevada.
224. **Nevada's Black Rock Desert**, Sessions Wheeler, 1978, Caxton Printers, Caldwell, Idaho.
225. **The Desert Lake: The Story of Nevada's Pyramid Lake**, Sessions Wheeler, 1967, Caxton Printers, Caldwell, Idaho.
226. **Exploring Death Valley**, Ruth Kirk, 1956, Stanford University Press.
227. **Exploring the Fremont**, David Madsen, 1989, Utah Museum of Natural History, University of Utah.
228. **Strangest Of All**, Frank Edwards, 1956, Ace Books, New York.
229. **Lemuria—The Lost Continent of the Pacific & The Mystery People of Mount Shasta**, Wishar Cervé, 1931, The Rosicrucian Press, San Jose, CA.
230. **Mount Shasta, Home of the Ancients**, Bruce Walton, 1985, Health Research, Mokelumne Hill, California.
231. **Ancient Hunters of the Far West**, Richard Pourade, editor, 1966, Union-Tribune Publishing Co., San Diego, California.
232. **The Mysterious West**, Brad Williams & Choral Pepper, 1967, World Publishing Company, Cleveland, Ohio.
233. **Triangle of Terror**, Adi-Kent Jeffrey, 1975, Warner Books, New York.
234. **Subterranean Worlds**, Walter Kafton-Minkel, 1989, Loompanics Unlimited, Port Townsend, WA.
235. **Guide To Catalina**, Chicki Mallan, 1988, Moon Publications, Chico, CA.
236. **The Mount Shasta Story**, Arthur Eichorn, 1957, Forbes & Co. Chicago.
237. **Secrets From Mount Shasta**, Earlyne Chaney, 1953, Astara, Upland, CA.
238. **Indian Masks & Myths of the West**, Joseph H. Wherry, 1969, Funk & Wagnalls, New York.
239. **Indian Mounds of the Middle Ohio Valley**, Susan Woodward & Jerry McDonald, 1986, M & W Publishing Company, Newark, Ohio.
240. **Cataclysms On the Columbia**, Allen, Burns & Sargent, 1986, Timber Press, Portland, Oregon.
241. **Northern California, Oregon, and the Sandwich Islands**, Charles Nordhoff, 1874, reprinted by Ten Speed Press, Berkeley, CA.
241. **Captain Cook and the Spanish Explorers on the Coast**, Edited by Efrat & Langlois, 1978, Province of British Columbia Press, Victoria, B.C.
242. **British Columbia Prehistory**, Knut R. Fladmark, 1986, National Museums of Canada, Ottawa.
243. **Exploring Rock Art**, Donald Cyr, 1989, Stonehenge Viewpoint, CA.
244. **A Death Feast in Dimlahamid**, Terry Glavin, 1990, New Star Books, Vancouver, B.C.
245. **Enviroment of Violence**, C. Warren Hunt, 1990, Polar Publishing, Calgary.
246. **Canada**, J. B. Brebner, 1960, University of Michigan Press, Ann Arbor.
247. **Stonehenge Decoded**, Gerald S. Hawkins, 1965, Doubleday, Garden City, New York.
248. **Beyond Stonehenge**, Gerald S. Hawkins, 1973, Dorset Press, NY.
249. **Digging Up America**, Frank C. Hibben, 1960, Hill & Wang, New York.
250. **The First Americans**, G.H. Bushnell, 1968, Thames & Hudson, London.
251. **Lost Tribes & Promised Lands**, Ronald Sanders, 1978, Harper, New York.
252. **A Pilgrim's Guide to Planet Earth**, 1981, Spiritual Community Publications, Berkeley, California.
253. **Lost Mines of the Great Southwest**, John D. Mitchell, 1933, Rio Grande Press, Glorieta, New Mexico.
254. **Coronado's Children**, J. Frank Dobie, 1930, Literary Guild, New York.
255. **Prince Henry Sinclair**, Frederick Pohl, 1974, Clarkson Potter Publisher, New York.
156. **The Lost Discovery**, Frederick Pohl, 1952, Norton & Co., New York.
157. **Vatican Manuscripts Concerning America as Early as the 10th Century**, reproductions by the Royal Danish Sanction and the Papal Secretary of State, 1906, Norrœna Society, Copenhagen.
158. **In Quest of the Great White Gods**, Robert Marx, 1992, Crown, New York.
159. **How the Ancients Discovered America Long Before Columbus**, Hans Holzer, 1992, Bear & Co., Santa Fe, New Mexico.

INDEX

583

588

LOST CITIES

LOST CITIES OF ATLANTIS, ANCIENT EUROPE & THE MEDITERRANEAN
by David Hatcher Childress
Atlantis! The legendary lost continent comes under the close scrutiny of maverick archaeologist David Hatcher Childress in this sixth book in the internationally popular Lost Cities series. Childress takes the reader in search of sunken cities in the Mediterranean; across the Atlas Mountains in search of Atlantean ruins; to remote islands in search of megalithic ruins; to meet living legends and secret societies. From Ireland to Turkey, Morocco to Eastern Europe, and around the remote islands of the Mediterranean and Atlantic, Childress takes the reader on an astonishing quest for mankind's past. Ancient technology, cataclysms, megalithic construction, lost civilizations and devastating wars of the past are all explored in this book. Childress challenges the skeptics and proves that great civilizations not only existed in the past, but the modern world and its problems are reflections of the ancient world of Atlantis.
524 PAGES. 6x9 PAPERBACK. ILLUSTRATED. BIBLIOGRAPHY & INDEX. $16.95. CODE: MED

LOST CITIES OF CHINA, CENTRAL INDIA & ASIA
by David Hatcher Childress
Like a real life "Indiana Jones," maverick archaeologist David Childress takes the reader on an incredible adventure across some of the world's oldest and most remote countries in search of lost cities and ancient mysteries. Discover ancient cities in the Gobi Desert; hear fantastic tales of lost continents, vanished civilizations and secret societies bent on ruling the world; visit forgotten monasteries in forbidding snow-capped mountains with strange tunnels to mysterious subterranean cities! A unique combination of far-out exploration and practical travel advice, it will astound and delight the experienced traveler or the armchair voyager.
429 PAGES. 6x9 PAPERBACK. ILLUSTRATED. FOOTNOTES & BIBL. $14.95. CODE: CHI

LOST CITIES OF ANCIENT LEMURIA & THE PACIFIC
by David Hatcher Childress
Was there once a continent in the Pacific? Called Lemuria or Pacifica by geologists, Mu or Pan by the mystics, there is now ample mythological, geological and archaeological evidence to "prove" that an advanced and ancient civilization once lived in the central Pacific. Maverick archaeologist and explorer David Hatcher Childress combs the Indian Ocean, Australia and the Pacific in search of the surprising truth about mankind's past. Contains photos of the underwater city on Pohnpei; explanations on how the statues were levitated around Easter Island in a clockwise vortex movement; tales of disappearing islands; Egyptians in Australia; and more.
379 PAGES. 6x9 PAPERBACK. ILLUSTRATED. FOOTNOTES & BIB. $14.95. CODE: LEM

LOST CITIES OF NORTH & CENTRAL AMERICA
by David Hatcher Childress
Down the back roads from coast to coast, maverick archaeologist and adventurer David Hatcher Childress goes deep into unknown America. With this incredible book, you will search for lost Mayan cities and books of gold, discover an ancient canal system in Arizona, climb gigantic pyramids in the Midwest, explore megalithic monuments in New England, and join the astonishing quest for lost cities throughout North America. From the war-torn jungles of Guatemala, Nicaragua and Honduras to the deserts, mountains and fields of Mexico, Canada, and the U.S.A., Childress takes the reader in search of sunken ruins, Viking forts, strange tunnel systems, living dinosaurs, early Chinese explorers, and fantastic lost treasure. Packed with both early and current maps, photos and illustrations.
590 PAGES. 6x9 PAPERBACK. ILLUSTRATED. FOOTNOTES & BIB. $16.95. CODE: NCA

LOST CITIES & ANCIENT MYSTERIES OF SOUTH AMERICA
by David Hatcher Childress
Rogue adventurer and maverick archaeologist David Hatcher Childress takes the reader on unforgettable journeys deep into deadly jungles, high up on windswept mountains and across scorching deserts in search of lost civilizations and ancient mysteries. Travel with David and explore stone cities high in mountain forests and hear fantastic tales of Inca treasure, living dinosaurs, and a mysterious tunnel system. Whether he is hopping freight trains, searching for secret cities, or just dealing with the daily problems of food, money, and romance, the author keeps the reader spellbound. Includes both early and current maps, photos, and illustrations, and plenty of advice for the explorer planning his or her own journey of discovery.
381 PAGES. 6x9 PAPERBACK. ILLUSTRATED. FOOTNOTES. BIBLIOGRAPHY. $14.95. CODE: SAM

RIDDLE OF THE PACIFIC
by John Macmillan Brown
Oxford scholar Brown's classic work on lost civilizations of the Pacific is now back in print! John Macmillan Brown was historian and New Zealand's premier scientist when he wrote about the origins of the Maoris. After many years of travel throughout the Pacific studying the people and customs of the south seas islands, he wrote Riddle of the Pacific in 1924. The book is packed with rare turn-of-the-century illustrations. Don't miss Brown's classic study of Easter Island, ancient scripts, megalithic roads and cities, more. Brown was an early believer in a lost continent in the Pacific.
460 PAGES. 6x9 PAPERBACK. ILLUSTRATED. $16.95. CODE: ROP

LOST CITIES & ANCIENT MYSTERIES OF AFRICA & ARABIA
by David Hatcher Childress
Across ancient deserts, dusty plains and steaming jungles, maverick archaeologist David Childress continues his world-wide quest for lost cities and ancient mysteries. Join him as he discovers forbidden cities in the Empty Quarter of Arabia; "Atlantean" ruins in Egypt and the Kalahari desert; a mysterious, ancient empire in the Sahara; and more. This is the tale of an extraordinary life on the road: across war-torn countries, Childress searches for King Solomon's Mines, living dinosaurs, the Ark of the Covenant and the solutions to some of the fantastic mysteries of the past.
423 PAGES. 6x9 PAPERBACK. ILLUSTRATED. FOOTNOTES & BIBLIOGRAPHY. $14.95. CODE: AFA

24 hour credit card orders—call: 815-253-6390 fax: 815-253-6300
email: auphq@frontiernet.net   www.adventuresunlimitedpress.com   www.wexclub.com

LOST CITIES

TECHNOLOGY OF THE GODS
The Incredible Sciences of the Ancients
by David Hatcher Childress

Popular *Lost Cities* author David Hatcher Childress takes us into the amazing world of ancient technology, from computers in antiquity to the "flying machines of the gods." Childress looks at the technology that was allegedly used in Atlantis and the theory that the Great Pyramid of Egypt was originally a gigantic power station. He examines tales of ancient flight and the technology that it involved; how the ancients used electricity; megalithic building techniques; the use of crystal lenses and the fire from the gods; evidence of various high tech weapons in the past, including atomic weapons; ancient metallurgy and heavy machinery; the role of modern inventors such as Nikola Tesla in bringing ancient technology back into modern use; impossible artifacts; and more.
356 PAGES. 6x9 PAPERBACK. ILLUSTRATED. BIBLIOGRAPHY. $16.95. CODE: TGOD

VIMANA AIRCRAFT OF ANCIENT INDIA & ATLANTIS
by David Hatcher Childress, introduction by Ivan T. Sanderson

Did the ancients have the technology of flight? In this incredible volume on ancient India, authentic Indian texts such as the *Ramayana* and the *Mahabharata* are used to prove that ancient aircraft were in use more than four thousand years ago. Included in this book is the entire Fourth Century BC manuscript *Vimaanika Shastra* by the ancient author Maharishi Bharadwaaja, translated into English by the Mysore Sanskrit professor G.R. Josyer. Also included are chapters on Atlantean technology, the incredible Rama Empire of India and the devastating wars that destroyed it. Also an entire chapter on mercury vortex propulsion and mercury gyros, the power source described in the ancient Indian texts. Not to be missed by those interested in ancient civilizations or the UFO enigma.
334 PAGES. 6x9 PAPERBACK. ILLUSTRATED. $15.95. CODE: VAA

LOST CONTINENTS & THE HOLLOW EARTH
I Remember Lemuria and the Shaver Mystery
by David Hatcher Childress & Richard Shaver

Shaver's rare 1948 book *I Remember Lemuria* is reprinted in its entirety, and the book is packed with illustrations from Ray Palmer's *Amazing Stories* magazine of the 1940s. Palmer and Shaver told of tunnels running through the earth—tunnels inhabited by the Deros and Teros, humanoids from an ancient spacefaring race that had inhabited the earth, eventually going underground, hundreds of thousands of years ago. Childress discusses the famous hollow earth books and delves deep into whatever reality may be behind the stories of tunnels in the earth. Operation High Jump to Antarctica in 1947 and Admiral Byrd's bizarre statements, tunnel systems in South America and Tibet, the underground world of Agartha, the belief of UFOs coming from the South Pole, more.
344 PAGES. 6x9 PAPERBACK. ILLUSTRATED. $16.95. CODE: LCHE

ATLANTIS: MOTHER OF EMPIRES
Atlantis Reprint Series
by Robert Stacy-Judd

Robert Stacy-Judd's classic 1939 book on Atlantis is back in print in this large-format paperback edition. Stacy-Judd was a California architect and an expert on the Mayas and their relationship to Atlantis. He was an excellent artist and his work is lavishly illustrated. The eighteen comprehensive chapters in the book are: The Mayas and the Lost Atlantis; Conjectures and Opinions; The Atlantean Theory; Cro-Magnon Man; East is West; And West is East; The Mormons and the Mayas; Astrology in Two Hemispheres; The Language of Architecture; The American Indian; Pre-Panamanians and Pre-Incas; Columns and City Planning; Comparisons and Mayan Art; The Iberian Link; The Maya Tongue; Quetzalcoatl; Summing Up the Evidence; The Mayas in Yucatan.
340 PAGES. 8x11 PAPERBACK. ILLUSTRATED. INDEX. $19.95. CODE: AMOE

MYSTERIES OF ANCIENT SOUTH AMERICA
Atlantis Reprint Series
by Harold T. Wilkins

The reprint of Wilkins' classic book on the megaliths and mysteries of South America. This book predates Wilkins' book *Secret Cities of Old South America* published in 1952. *Mysteries of Ancient South America* was first published in 1947 and is considered a classic book of its kind. With diagrams, photos and maps, Wilkins digs into old manuscripts and books to bring us some truly amazing stories of South America: a bizarre subterranean tunnel system; lost cities in the remote border jungles of Brazil; legends of Atlantis in South America; cataclysmic changes that shaped South America; and other strange stories from one of the world's great researchers. Chapters include: Our Earth's Greatest Disaster, Dead Cities of Ancient Brazil, The Jungle Light that Shines by Itself, The Missionary Men in Black: Forerunners of the Great Catastrophe, The Sign of the Sun: The World's Oldest Alphabet, Sign-Posts to the Shadow of Atlantis, The Atlanean "Subterraneans" of the Incas, Tiahuanacu and the Giants, more.
236 PAGES. 6x9 PAPERBACK. ILLUSTRATED. INDEX. $14.95. CODE: MASA

MAPS OF THE ANCIENT SEA KINGS
Evidence of Advanced Civilization in the Ice Age
by Charles H. Hapgood

Charles Hapgood's classic 1966 book on ancient maps produces concrete evidence of an advanced world-wide civilization existing many thousands of years before ancient Egypt. He has found the evidence in the Piri Reis Map that shows Antarctica, the Hadji Ahmed map, the Oronteus Finaeus and other amazing maps. Hapgood concluded that these maps were made from more ancient maps from the various ancient archives around the world, now lost. Not only were these unknown people more advanced in mapmaking than any people prior to the 18th century, it appears they mapped all the continents. The Americas were mapped thousands of years before Columbus. Antarctica was mapped when its coasts were free of ice.
316 PAGES. 7x10 PAPERBACK. ILLUSTRATED. BIB. & INDEX. $19.95. CODE: MASK

One Adventure Place
P.O. Box 74
Kempton, Illinois 60946
United States of America
Tel.: 815-253-6390 • Fax: 815-253-6300
Email: auphq@frontiernet.net
http://www.adventuresunlimitedpress.co
or www.wexclub.com/aup

ORDERING INSTRUCTIONS

✓ Remit by USD$ Check, Money Order or Credit Card
✓ Visa, Master Card, Discover & AmEx Accepted
✓ Prices May Change Without Notice
✓ 10% Discount for 3 or more Items

SHIPPING CHARGES

United States

✓ Postal Book Rate { $3.00 First Item
50¢ Each Additional Item

✓ Priority Mail { $4.00 First Item
$2.00 Each Additional Item

✓ UPS { $5.00 First Item
$1.50 Each Additional Item

NOTE: UPS Delivery Available to Mainland USA Only

Canada

✓ Postal Book Rate { $6.00 First Item
$2.00 Each Additional Item

✓ Postal Air Mail { $8.00 First Item
$2.50 Each Additional Item

✓ Personal Checks or Bank Drafts MUST BE
USD$ and Drawn on a US Bank
✓ Canadian Postal Money Orders OK
✓ Payment MUST BE USD$

All Other Countries

✓ Surface Delivery { $10.00 First Item
$4.00 Each Additional Item

✓ Postal Air Mail { $14.00 First Item
$5.00 Each Additional Item

✓ Payment MUST BE USD$
✓ Checks and Money Orders MUST BE USD$
and Drawn on a US Bank or branch.
✓ Add $5.00 for Air Mail Subscription to
Future *Adventures Unlimited* Catalogs

SPECIAL NOTES

✓ RETAILERS: Standard Discounts Available
✓ BACKORDERS: We Backorder all Out-of-
Stock Items Unless Otherwise Requested
✓ PRO FORMA INVOICES: Available on Request
✓ VIDEOS: NTSC Mode Only. Replacement only.
✓ For PAL mode videos contact our other offices:

European Office:
Adventures Unlimited, Pannewal 22,
Enkhuizen, 1602 KS, The Netherlands
http: www.adventuresunlimited.nl
Check Us Out Online at:
www.adventuresunlimitedpress.com

Please check: ☑

☐ This is my first order   ☐ I have ordered before   ☐ This is a new ad

Name	
Address	
City	
State/Province	Postal Code
Country	
Phone day	Evening
Fax	

Item Code	Item Description	Price	Qty	Tota

Please check: ☑

☐ Postal-Surface
☐ Postal-Air Mail (Priority in USA)
☐ UPS (Mainland USA only)

Subtotal ➠	
Less Discount-10% for 3 or more items ➠	
Balance ➠	
Illinois Residents 6.25% Sales Tax ➠	
Previous Credit ➠	
Shipping ➠	
Total (check/MO in USD$ only)➠	

☐ Visa/MasterCard/Discover/Amex

Card Number

Expiration Date

10% Discount When You Order 3 or More Items!

Comments & Suggestions	Share Our Catalog with a Fr